American Social Science Series

GENERAL EDITOR
HOWARD W. ODUM

*Kenan Professor of Sociology and Director of the School of
Public Welfare in the University of North Carolina*

THE NEGRO IN AMERICAN CIVILIZATION

A STUDY OF NEGRO LIFE AND RACE RELATIONS IN THE LIGHT OF SOCIAL RESEARCH

BY

CHARLES S. JOHNSON

FISK UNIVERSITY

NEW YORK

HENRY HOLT AND COMPANY

FOREWORD

To construct a reasonably faithful contemporary picture of Negro life and relationships with the white race in the United States, was the purpose of the long process which has culminated in this book. The initiative was taken by sixteen national organizations engaged for the most part in day-to-day tasks of social work for the Negro and the improvement of relationships between white and colored in this country. They came together and formed a central Executive Committee in the autumn of 1926. They differed in activities and in their ideas of the best methods of solving what has come to be known as "the race problem," but they were united in believing that they and all others actively at work on this subject needed to know more about it. They were aware of numerous studies which had been made in their own organizations and in others like them and in universities and research organizations, but for the most part the results of these studies had not been assembled or reflected upon as a whole to see what light might come out of them. Nor had they been integrated into the thought and action of the workers in these organizations. Moreover, the public was not aware of the facts nor their significance.

With this need and this common objective in view, it was decided to hold a Conference, but to make the Conference itself merely the occasion for a long preparatory period in which the results of social studies and the meaning of official statistics would be analyzed and formulated for discussion.

For the Conference and the preparation for it, each organization was to contribute experience. No new staff was to be organized. The Executive Committee chose as its executive secretary Dr. George E. Haynes, and part of his time was made available for this very great service by the Commission on the Church and Race Relations of the Federal Council of Churches, of which Commission Dr. Haynes is secretary. His office was also contributed as headquarters for the executive work for the Conference.

For the vital task of analyzing social data and forming it into a synthesis for the Conference, the Committee chose Dr. Charles S. Johnson to serve as research secretary. Dr. Johnson was then editor of *Opportunity* and director of research for the National Urban League. The League generously released part of his time and in addition gave office space for his work. Three months before the holding of the Conference, at a time when a large part of the task of formulating the data must be completed, Dr. Johnson was transferred to head the Department of Social Science at Fisk University; and the University, with generosity and understanding of the importance of the undertaking, followed the lead of these other organizations and made his continued service available. He was assisted by other members of the faculty and research students at Fisk. In addition, the work of mimeographing the 244 pages of memoranda which became known as The Data Book for the Conference was carried on in what might be called a data factory organized at the University.

A Research Committee was appointed as adviser to the research secretary and the Conference. Its members were Graham R. Taylor, Chairman, formerly executive secretary of the Chicago Commission on Race Relations and now of the Commonwealth Fund; Mrs. Gertrude E. McDougald Ayer, vocational guidance director, Harlem public schools, New York; Glenn A. Bowers, Industrial Relations Counselors, Inc.; Dr. Louis I. Dublin, statistician, Metropolitan Life Insurance Company; Dr. Joseph A. Hill, United States Census Bureau; Dr. George W. Kirchwey, lawyer, criminologist, New York School of Social Work; Professor Broadus Mitchell, historian, Johns Hopkins University; Professor Howard W. Odum, sociologist, University of North Carolina; Leonard Outhwaite, Laura Spelman Rockefeller Memorial; Professor Robert E. Park, sociologist, University of Chicago; Forrester B. Washington, director, Atlanta School of Social Work; Dr. Leo Wolman, economist, Amalgamated Clothing Workers of America; Monroe N. Work, editor, Negro Year Book, Tuskegee Institute.

The research secretary, with the advice of the Committee, prepared an outline of a wide survey of the present state of knowledge on problems of the Negro race in America, including an analysis of investigations already made, a cross-section view of those in progress, and observation of the individuals and organizations capable of carrying forward further investigation on these subjects. The review included investigations made by voluntary agencies and by individuals and also analysis of governmental records and reports, including data obtained from the United States Census Bureau and municipal and state records of health, education, housing, crime and other major divisions of the subject. These major divisions, as they finally worked out for the Conference, were: Population, including the facts about migration; Health, including vital statistics and special studies of racial susceptibility and immunity; Education; Industry and Agriculture; Recreation; Housing, including the facts about residential segregation; Law Observance and Administration, including data on crime, the methods of administering laws, and juvenile delinquency; Citizenship, in connection with which the facts about lynching were considered as involving denial of the right of trial and conviction through orderly procedure of courts; Race Relations and programs looking toward active interracial cooperation.

The significance of such a plan of approach was voiced at the Conference itself by Dr. Wesley C. Mitchell, chairman of the Social Science Research Council, in a letter expressing the interest of the Council:

There seems to be no group of social problems in which men's attitudes have been characterized by a larger measure of emotion and a smaller measure of science than the problems with which the National Interracial Conference is dealing. Whatever the Conference can contribute toward raising the discussion from the level of feeling to the level of knowledge will be a gain. The surest way to promote social progress is to seek clearer insight into human behavior. Nor is the scientific method slow in the long run. In economic matters, we have learned that the "roundabout" method of production is the quickest, when we are looking for large results. In moving freight, we save time by building railways. While the social sciences are still in a relatively early stage of their development, they offer mankind the best prospect of gaining that self-mastery for which our sages have longed.

The Social Science Research Council had indeed expressed its interest earlier in concrete form. The plan for research presented to the Council's Advisory Committee on Race Relations had been endorsed with a recommendation that an appropriation be sought by the Social Science Research Council for this work. The Advisory Committee believed that in its own task of formulating projects for research such a survey as that contemplated by the National Interracial Conference was a necessary foundation. Without some such review of the field as a whole, it is not possible to be sure that the relatively more important questions regarding research will have first consideration. It was felt, moreover, that in developing research on such problems the task cannot be completed by a presentation of projects intellectually conceived, however well formulated. If research is to give real illumination in social relationships, it must grow out of present vital needs. When the relationships to be studied are between racial groups, it is obvious that representatives of both races should take part in carrying it forward and in interpreting its results. The Executive Committee of the National Interracial Conference was just such a representative group, embodying practical experience and including representatives of both the white and Negro races.[1]

Through the Social Science Research Council, acting on this recommendation of its advisory committee, a modest appropriation of $5,000 was provided to pay the salaries of a research assistant and stenographers and to provide for traveling ex-

[1] The organizations whose representatives constituted the Executive Committee were American Friends Service Committee, Interracial Section; American Social Hygiene Association; Commission on Interracial Cooperation; Council of Women for Home Missions; Federal Council of Churches, Commission on the Church and Race Relations; Fellowship of Reconciliation; Home Missions Council; The Inquiry; National Association for the Advancement of Colored People; National Board Y.W.C.A.; National Catholic Welfare Conference; National Council Y.M.C.A.; National Federation of Settlements; National Urban League; Phelps-Stokes Fund; Protestant Episcopal Church, Department of Christian Social Service. The Federal Council of Churches, Commission on the Church and Race Relations, began the movement which culminated in the National Interracial Conference. This beginning was in a national conference organized by the Commission in conjunction with the Commission on Interracial Cooperation and held in Cincinnati, Ohio, in March, 1925. The proceedings were published by the Commission on the Church and Race Relations of the Federal Council of Churches in a volume entitled *Toward Interracial Cooperation*.

penses of a small research staff. Only the contribution of
services, especially those of the research secretary, made possible the completion of such a study with so moderate an expenditure. More important even than the financial support,
though that was indispensable, was this recognition by the Social Science Research Council of the significance of the task
undertaken by these organizations.

The Conference itself ceased to exist with its closing meeting. A Committee on Findings was appointed to gather up
suggestions for the programs of the participating organizations. The research secretary assumed the responsibility of
formulating the problems on which further research was needed
and submitting a report on this subject to the Advisory Committee on Race Relations of the Social Science Research Council. Finally, Dr. Charles S. Johnson, research secretary, was
charged with the task of gathering all this material together in
a book. This volume is the result. It is neither the proceedings of the conference nor the report of an investigation. It
is a synthesis of many studies put through the process of a conference which hammered it into coherence and reality. In it
may be said to be merged not only the results of social research
but the work and the life experience of many individuals, some
born in slavery, others descendants of slaves but now young
men equipped through courses in colleges or universities to take
their part in a new day, pioneers among the white race who
could remember the Civil War, and side by side with them
young people with new enthusiasm and a feeling for the coming of a new era in American life. It stands under its title,
The Negro in American Civilization, as the result of the efforts
of one group of organizations "to construct a reasonably
faithful contemporary picture of Negro life and the status of
race relations."

As to the findings and their significance, this book will speak
for itself. One result only need be emphasized here. The synthesis of available data revealed a sound basis for planning programs of improvement. That the Negro is racially susceptible
to disease, racially incapable of education or racially apt to vio-
late laws, is a case not proved. In many instances the data have
been inconclusive or misinterpreted, notably in statistics of

crime. Change in conditions which produce ill health and crime and improvement in opportunities for education have demonstrated the capacity of the Negro to profit by these changes. Experience has actually shown the possibility of improvement in health and progress in education and in law observance. The causes of many of the unfortunate conditions which prevailed several years ago and still exist in some parts of the country, at least, are actually removable causes. In other words, there is here a task of planning and engineering. A fatalistic attitude which is skeptical of the possibility of action is not supported either by experience or by sound facts.

What of the status of the Negro in American civilization? First of all, his is a changing position, set against a background of shifting economic and social conditions. Is he receiving justice, which all Americans would agree is the heritage of their nation? What is justice? Socrates and his fellow inquirers tried to answer the question, and finally, after many fruitless attempts, Socrates suggested that justice was to be found in the good society. In the process of picturing the good society it was agreed that justice is the final outcome of a wisely functioning scheme of relationships. "In a state which is ordered with a view to the good of the whole, we should be most likely to find justice, and in the ill-ordered state injustice." After long and searching discussion of the essential elements in the good society, this definition was accepted: "Justice will be admitted to be the having and doing what is a man's own and belongs to him," or, in other words, "the power of each individual in the state to do his own work."

The power of the Negro in the United States to do his own work is still hindered at many points. Economic opportunities are limited and restricted. Educational facilities in the sections of the country where the largest number of Negroes live are quite inadequate for either race, and more so for the children of Negroes. Hence conditions are below the standard which should prevail. In a number of states the Negro is deprived of his vote and is unable to help himself to secure an equal measure of justice from the state. Disfranchised citizens cannot share either in the responsibilities or the privileges of citizenship. All these are limiting factors in American civilization. Their limitation is not only upon the doing of justice to the

Negro, but also upon the quality of justice in the nation. That this quality of justice in the nation may be achieved through interracial cooperation is a hope for which the findings of social research as revealed in this book give substantial support.

MARY VAN KLEECK,
Chairman, Executive Committee,
National Interracial Conference.

New York, March 6, 1930.

CONTENTS

PART ONE

THE PROBLEM

PART ONE
THE PROBLEM

CHAPTER I

THE SEVEN LABORS IN THE NEW WORLD

The Conquistadors under Nicholas de Ovando who followed promptly the trail of Columbus to the New World, brought with them the young priest Bartolomé de las Casas, celebrated for his piety and judgment. His father had accompanied Columbus on his second voyage and both had been charged by the Court of Spain to deal lovingly with the Indians in the hope of bringing them to a knowledge of the sacred Catholic faith. In the name of God slavery came to the Indians and under the lash of their conquerors and the relentless labor in the mines and in the fields they sickened and died. Las Casas in Haiti witnessed this incredible destruction and with the Jeronomite priests engaged himself passionately to the end of his life in preserving the pitiable remnants of the Caribbeans.[1] A gentle, unoffending and hospitable race, they numbered no less than 1,000,000 persons when Columbus found them, formed into kingdoms and ruled peacefully by their Caciques. Under the unmitigated cruelty of Dovadillo, and the fresh adventurers who stamped into the Islands after the withdrawal of Columbus, these numbers were reduced to a bare 60,000. It is recorded that entire villages committed suicide inviting others to join them in their final and mournful resistance.[2] Las Casas was witness to many of the scenes of this stupendous tragedy. In vain he protested and phrased his stinging polemics in righteous anger. The clearing of the forest, the tilling of the soil and work in the gold mines in this "Paradise of God" had to go on. Las Casas then petitioned the King in mercy to allow the free importation of Negroes who alone could withstand these severities. Six hundred he would send to each of the Islands. Vasco Nuñez had testified to the sturdiness of these laborers, for when

[1] Helps, Sir Arthur, *Life of Las Casas.*
[2] Las Casas, Bartolomé, *Brevisime Relacion de le Destruycion de las Indias Occidentales.*

3

he prepared his timbers for the four brigantines that passed through the Isthmus from the Atlantic to the waters which flowed into the Pacific, he had used several hundred Indians and thirty Negroes. And of this experiment Herrera records that 500 Indians perished in executing the terrible labor. The thirty Negroes survived! They not only survived but "prospered so much that it was the opinion, unless a Negro should happen to be hanged, he would never die; for, as yet, none had been known to perish from infirmity." And so it happened that the Spanish Court in 1511 decreed that a large number of Negroes should be transported to the New World "because one Negro does more work than four Indians." [3]

The market in men opened by the Portuguese on the west coast of Africa began to show its first profits and the trade was on. Santo Domingo received annually 20,000 Negroes, each with the name and owner of his destined plantation branded with a hot iron upon his shoulder. The commerce and untold wealth of the New World, founded upon this black labor, and the market in black slaves opened vast areas for economic exploitation. The search for a new route to the Orient, which began it all, was abandoned, and the future of Europe turned abruptly from the Mediterranean to the Atlantic. A papal Bull of demarcation had created for Spain and Portugal a monopoly on the wealth flowing in from the New World. The English and the Dutch feared there was danger to all Europe in this monopoly of American resources, and together set about to crush it. [4]

With no pretense at religious motives, 24 Negroes in 1553 were brought from the Coast of Africa and quietly sold in the English market. Under Elizabeth the intrepid John Hawkins, who later became the most heartless of man stealers, sailed forth in the good ship *Jesus* to get Africans whom he sold into the Spanish colonies. He returned to England laden with rich tropical productions. Swiftly in his wake came Sir Francis Drake, bent upon breaking the grip of Spain, and there resulted the first circumnavigation of the globe. International disputes over the pirating of these sea dogs brought the contention that these were "no private but public actions" and a

[3] Herrera, de Antonis, *Historia Generale.*
[4] Beer, G. L., *The Origins of the British Colonial System, 1578-1660.*

culmination was the clash and destruction of the Spanish Armada. The Cavalier favorite of Elizabeth, Sir Walter Raleigh, moved first in the direction of the fabled El Dorado and landed in Guiana, but later came to North America.

Almost simultaneously with the landing of the Pilgrim fathers on Plymouth Rock in the famed *Mayflower,* and just thirteen years after the founding of the first successful English colony in America, a barnacled and sea-worn brig sailed up the James River in Virginia and landed at Jamestown. It was under Dutch command and for the gentlemen-adventurers in the colony, helpless against the vast unexplored and untilled forest and in the very presence of limitless wealth, it brought twenty *Negars.* One year later the cotton plant was first cultivated in the new province, foreshadowing a destiny to which these Negroes have been linked for these three centuries.

"The people," says Weston, "who could subdue and cultivate the New World, existed only in Africa." [5] The population of Europe was small, reduced further by its long wars and just emerging itself from a backward culture. In a sense not to be dismissed too lightly, America, including its islands, was settled chiefly from Africa and by Negroes. Before 1800 the number of Negroes brought here was more than twenty times that of all Europeans combined. Benjamin Franklin in 1751 computed the emigration from England to North America to be only about 80,000. The Virginians wanted gold, silver, copper, pearls and precious stones, but it was not long before they were disillusioned in this romantic quest.[6] The colony dragged out a pitiful existence until John Rolfe introduced the cultivation of tobacco and the use of it became a protested habit in England. So began the industrial history of North America to which the natives of Guinea were so completely essential. Tobacco soon became the staple export crop.

Plantation and colony meant the same thing when Virginia was founded. The system of land grants made the plantation system inevitable. The twenty *Negars* brought by the Dutch were not immediately recognized in the Colony as slaves but accepted on much the same basis as the indentured servants, the redemptioners, the convicts and the beggars kidnapped from the

[5] Weston, George Melville, *The Progress of Slavery,* 1851, pp. 153-156.
[6] Hakluyt, Richard, *Discourses,* Vol. I, pp. 86, 105.

chop houses around the English wharves. The muster rolls of the settlement of Virginia in 1624 and 1625 found 23 Africans all of whom were listed as "servants" as were the whites of this class.[7] Thirty-four years after the Negroes came, Anthony Johnson, a Negro and undoubtedly one of the first twenty arrivals,[8] got a court judgment sustaining his claim to the perpetual service of John Castor, another Negro.[9] The status of slavery was not crystallized for fifty years. Then an Act was passed to determine who should be slaves. It decided that servants brought in by ships after 1670 be applied the test of Christianity to determine who should be servants for a limited time or slaves for life.

The plentifulness and cheapness of land, the impossibility of keeping hired or even indentured labor fixed the logic of slavery. By no other means could the staples be produced that Europe wanted and which were the chief motives for colonization. Neither the slaveholding colonies nor the New England and middle colonies could have prospered without the markets kept alive by this slave labor. But tobacco could exhaust the soil in a few years; and as the colonies spread interest centered around rice cultivation introduced from Madagascar.[10] Only the Negro could survive the hot, wet fields and the miasma of the swamps which proved so promptly fatal to the white laborers. When Sir John Yeamans came to South Carolina from Barbados in 1671 he brought Negroes and the Barbadian slave code with him. Charleston became the point of export of a great rice area. An English army officer's daughter, Eliza Lucas, introduced indigo in 1741 which these Negroes developed. In 1775 the value of the export of this staple exceeded a million pounds. Into the old French settlement in Louisiana the Spaniard, Silis, came with some knowledge of sugar making. Etienne de Bore, a Creole planter, whose estate lay to the south of New Orleans, bought a supply of seed from him in 1795, and with his Negroes from Barbados trained in the making of sugar developed

[7] Ballagh, James Curtis, *A History of Slavery in Virginia.*
[8] *The Journal of Negro History,* Vol. I, No. 3, pp. 234-241.
[9] Hening, William Walter, *Statutes at Large of Virginia,* Vol. II, p. 283, Richmond, 1821.
[10] Phillips, U. B., *Documentary History of American Industrial Society—* Plantation and Frontier Documents, Vol. II.
——, *American Negro Slavery.*

a $12,000 crop the next year.[11] Sugar plantations sprang up like a wild growth. In 1849 there were counted 1,536 plantations with 100,000 Negroes.

Before a new cycle could begin the tobacco culture fell into decline. Thomas Jefferson marked its failure from the commencement of the Revolutionary War. Rice and indigo followed the fate of tobacco. Slave hands were needlessly plentiful. Enforced labor was losing a bit of its purpose. The colonies were rather lukewarm on the matter, and, as Patrick Henry remarked to Lafayette, held on more from a habit of dependence than any other motive.[12] The line between slaves and mere laborers was not rigid. Lafayette himself had observed that white and black seamen and soldiers had fought and messed together in the Revolution without bitter differences. Down in Granville County, North Carolina, a full-blooded Negro, John Chavis, educated in Princeton University, was conducting a private school for white students and was a licentiate under the local Presbytery, preaching to white congregations in the state. One of his pupils became Governor of North Carolina, another the state's most prominent Whig Senator. Two of his pupils were sons of the Chief Justice of North Carolina. The father of the founder of the greatest military academy of the state attended his school and boarded in his home.[13] Pennsylvania gave proof of the weakening of slavery by passing an Act in 1780 for the gradual abolishment of slavery and there followed an epidemic of laws in the upper Southern states, prohibiting further importation.[14] In 1794 George Washington was advising a friend to convert his slaves into other forms of property, and was importing cotton from England for the clothes-making establishment which he conducted as a side line. A little cotton was being grown and a feeble home industry had developed, but it had not as yet even threatened to become a staple. The green seed, short-staple variety which alone thrived, except in a strip of about forty miles along the coast of South Carolina and Georgia, was impracticable for any important commercial development. The fibres clung to the seed and had

[11] Gayarre, C., *History of Louisiana.*
——, *The Journal of Negro History*, Vol. I, No. 4, p. 374.
[12] Helper, H. R., *The Impending Crisis*, p. 200.
[13] See New York *Times Magazine*, May 18, 1924.
[14] Turner, Edward Raymond, *The Negro in Pennsylvania*, p. 74.

to be cut or torn away through a process which proved tedious and expensive. Every step save the first one of a vast new industry had been developed in a rapid succession of inventions.[15] James Lees had improved the carding machine; Sir Richard Arkwright, in Lancashire, England, had invented the spinning frame; Edward Cartwright had invented the power loom and Samuel Compton had bred a field work animal par excellence in the mule.

The clever Yankee, Eli Whitney, after graduating from Yale in 1793, left Massachusetts to teach school in the South, at a time when necessity was urging some immediate mechanical solution of the cotton farmers' plight. He heard the perplexed discussions of planters and, stimulated by his friend, devised a model which met all the essential requirements. A mad clamor for this invention followed. After unsuccessful attempts to corner the market he sold his rights to the state of South Carolina for $50,000, and the benefits were opened freely to all the planters. From this point the history of the South and of the Negro changed. Cotton culture spread over most of the fertile stretches of South Carolina, Georgia, Alabama, Mississippi, North Tennessee and Lower Texas. Slave-holders moved from Virginia, Maryland, Delaware and New Jersey into the rich delta stretches of the South, which facilitated the development of plantations. To buy slaves became a crowning ambition. In the Piedmont region of South Carolina where in 1790 there were 15,000 slaves, the number increased 70 per cent the first decade after and 90 per cent the next until it overtook the white population. In 1800 there were 3,489 Negro slaves in Mississippi and in 1840 there were 136,621. In 1791 the first important exportation of raw cotton to England was made. This amounted to 189,316 pounds.[16] In 1794, the year after Whitney's invention, it was 1,601,760 pounds and in 1837 it reached the prodigious quantity of 444,211,573 pounds, of which 438,000,000 pounds were of the once unmerchantable upland variety. The price of slaves increased, being a limited commodity. South Carolina imported from Africa down to the

15 Phillips, U. B., American Negro Slavery.
16 McCulloch, Commercial Directory, Vol. I, pp. 519-522.
Vance, Rupert, Human Factors in Cotton Culture.

last moment and later proposed to reopen the trade. Slavery was profitable! Cotton was king!

The first struggle developed between the capitalist planter, frequently backed by funds from the North, and the independent farmer of the South.[17] The novel new economic system of land control showed its superiority over the independent owner and they were either bought out or driven back to the poorer land. There was movement westward, but always to be followed by the slaveholders who controlled the destinies of the poor whites as well as the blacks. It is pointed out that the perfection of the plantation system meant the ruthless destruction and expulsion of white farmers; for ideally it had little need of whites. Only a proprietor, an overseer, a physician and their families were essential and the fewer the whites the greater the profits.

From feeble interest in slavery with occasional flares of abolitionist sentiment; from the concern over some employment for the large numbers of Negroes in the country, there developed a passionate defense of the institution and a rationalization of the use of Negroes as slaves. Scholars began to provide arguments of a native and inescapable mental, moral and cultural inferiority.[18] The Bible was brought into service in defense of the institution. It is as much the order of nature, it was contended, that men of superior facilities and power, should enslave other men, as that some animals should prey upon others. The Creator did not intend that every individual human being should be highly cultivated, morally and intellectually, for, as one can see, in the Negro he has imposed conditions on society which would render this impossible. Since Providence has decreed that there can be but a certain portion of intellectual excellence in a community, it is better that it should be unequally divided; it is better that a part should be fully and highly cultivated and the rest utterly ignorant. The doctrine of racial inferiority was enunciated with a bitter finality and fury. "Although meta-

[17] Weston, George Melville, *The Progress of Slavery.*
Helper, H. R., *The Impending Crisis.*
[18] Elliott, E. N. (Ed.), *Cotton Is King,* and Pro-slavery Arguments. See essays by Dr. Cartwright.
Dew, Thomas Roderick, *Review of the Debate in the Virginia Assembly of 1831-32,* Madison Pamphlets, Vol. XIV.
Van Evrie, John N., *Negroes and Negro Slavery.*

physicians may dispute about causes which have debased the intellects of Negroes and precluded their expansion," argued the learned Dr. J. C. Nott of Mobile, and his associate Dr. Glidden, America's first outstanding ethnologists, "it cannot be denied that the dark races are in respect to intellect and virtue greatly inferior to the whites of fairer complexion." [19] President Dew of William and Mary College wrote, "It is the order of nature that the beings of superior faculties and knowledge, and therefore of superior power, should dispose of those who are inferior. The exclusive owners of property ever have been, ever will and perhaps ever ought to be the virtual rulers of mankind." [20] The reverend clergy contributed to this literature and orthodoxy of defense. Noah's curse and the endorsement of his curse in the law of Moses gave the right and privilege to the races of Shem and Japheth to enslave the race of Ham. Man was made in the image of God, and since God, as everyone knows was not a Negro, it follows that the Negro is not a man. "Servant obey your master." The Greek word "doulos" usually translated *servant,* the learned divines argued, properly and commonly means a person held to service for life—a slave. The glory of God is promoted by the cheerful obedience and faithful conduct of Christian slaves. The philosophy, which was as much a defense against the growing Abolitionist propaganda as it was a defense of their economic system, built up a passionate solidarity among the planter group and taught the poor whites the degradation of labor,—the poor whites backed off into the niggardly hill countries. These black slaves were a form of organized labor controlled by the masters. Two-thirds of the white population had no connection with slavery and reaped but a fraction of the vast returns from it. One thousand families received $50,000,000 a year while the remaining 600,000 got about $60,000,000. Slave labor was used for all kinds of work and the more intelligent of the Negro slaves were trained as artisans to be used and leased. Slave artisans would bring twice as much as an ordinary field hand in the market. Master craftsmen owned their staff. Some masters,

[19] Nott, Josiah Clark, and Glidden, C. R., *Types of Mankind;* or Ethnological Researches, etc.
[20] DuBois, W. E. B., *Suppression of the African Slave Trade to the United States.*

as the system became more involved, hired slaves to their slave artisans. Many slave artisans purchased their freedom by the savings allowed them above the normal labor expected.

The advertisements for runaways and sales are an index to this skill. They received the same or better wages than the poor white labor and with the influence of the master got the best jobs. The contractors for masons' and carpenters' work in Athens, Georgia, in 1838 were petitioned to stop showing preference to Negro laborers. "The white man is the only real, legal, moral and civil proprietor of this country and state. The right of his proprietorship reaches from the date of the studies of those white men, Copernicus and Galileo, who indicated the sphericity of the earth; which sphericity hinted to another white man, Columbus, the possibility by a westerly course of sailing, of finding land. Hence by white men alone was this continent discovered; . . . the white men alone, aye, those to whom you decline to give money for bread and clothes, for their famishing families, in the logic manner of withholding work from them . . . defending Negroes too in the bargain." [21] In Atlanta in 1858 a petition signed by 200 white mechanics and laborers sought protection against the black slave artisans of masters who resided in other sections. The very next year sundry white citizens were aggrieved that the City Council tolerated a Negro dentist to remain and operate in their midst. "In justice to ourselves and the community it ought to be abated. We, the residents of Atlanta, appeal to you for justice." A census of free Negroes in Richmond County, Georgia, in 1819 showed carpenters, barbers, boat corkers, saddlers, rafters, waggoners, blacksmiths, spinners, millwrights, hostlers, weavers, harness makers, seamstresses, sawmill attendants and steamboat pilots. A Negro shoemaker made by hand the boots in which President Monroe was inaugurated. Harriet Martineau marvelled at the slave workmanship in the delicately tiled floors of Thomas Jefferson's home at Monticello. There still stands in the big house of the old plantation, heavy marks of the hands of these Negro craftsmen; strong mansions built of timbers hewn from the original oak, mortised and pinned together by wooden pins. Negro women skilled in spinning and

[21] Phillips, U. B., *Documentary History of American Industrial Society.* Plantation and Frontier, Vol. II.

weaving worked in the mills. Buckingham in 1839 found them
in Athens, Georgia, working alongside white girls without apparent repugnance or objection.

Negro craftsmen in the South, slave and free, fared better
than their brothers in the North. In 1856, in Philadelphia, of
1,637 Negro craftsmen recorded, less than two-thirds could use
their trades, "because of hostile prejudice." The Irish, who
were pouring into America from the very beginning of the
nineteenth century, were being used in the North on approximately the same motives of preference which governed Negro
slavery. "An Irish Catholic," it was argued in their favor,
"seldom attempts to rise to a higher condition than that in
which he is placed, while the Negro often makes the attempt
with success." Had not the old Puritan, Oliver Cromwell,
while the traffic in black slaves was on, sold all the Irish not
killed in the Drogheda Massacre, into Barbados?[22] Free and
fugitive Negroes in New York and Pennsylvania were in constant conflict with this group and the bitter hostility showed
itself most violently in the draft riots of New York. These
Hibernians controlled the hod carrying and common labor jobs,
opposing every approach of the Negro as a menace to their
slight hold upon America and upon a means of livelihood. The
Germans absorbed many of the domestic and catering positions
at the same time that they were creating new standards of skill
in trades.

Came the Civil War and the dark days of Reconstruction.
The plantation system, although archaic and disastrous to the
fullest development of society was not utterly destroyed. Some
of its old features showed even above the financial crash. But
pressure was released for the first time from the independent
white farmers, and the poor whites. They entered the cotton
system. They took over lands of the now impracticable large
plantations. They moved into Texas and Oklahoma and even
to the wire grass in Georgia.[23] From a relatively small share in
the cultivation of cotton, a few years after the war found them
making 40 per cent of it, and in 1910 they were, according to
Rupert Vance's computation, producing 67 per cent of this

[22] Beard, Charles and Mary, *The Rise of American Civilization*, Vol. I,
p. 105.
[23] Vance, Rupert B., *Human Factors in Cotton Culture*.

crop. They came into power and in states like South Carolina and Mississippi, under the leadership of violent spokesmen enunciated a racial policy. No period had been quite so full of sharp hatreds. Unavoidable, perhaps, but the course of race relations in America since has been a living down of these scenes. Then were born the ogres: "Would you want your daughter to marry a Nigger?", "white supremacy," the orthodoxy: "blood will tell," "the solid South," the religion of conscious "white domination." Slowly, implacably, the "poor whites" came to life again, seeing in the Negro one who had carried the sting of his competition to the point of having defiled hard work for all respectable white people by having been a slave to it. They came into power, and becoming articulate, through their leaders, reduced to cold, brutal ritual a position which could not be reached by counter-argument.[24] Judge Benjamin Tillman, of Quitman, Georgia, summed up this philosophy in a burst of feeling which stands as the keynote of a period not so remote: "The Negro bears about him a birthright of inferiority that is as unalterable as eternity. He who, in the morning of Creation, set the shifting sands as a barrier to the mad waves of the mighty deep and said thus far, has also set his seal upon the Negro forever in his black skin, kinky hair, thick lips, flat nose, double layer of skull, different anatomy, as well as analogy, from white men. His stupid intellect is fulfilled in prophecy, uttered thousands of years ago, but no less true today, "A servant of servants shalt thou be." [25]

Between 1881 and 1907 all the Southern states enacted laws separating the races on railroad cars, street cars and schools, laws excluding Negroes from jury service and the primaries, while the Northern states were enacting Civil Rights Bills.[26] On the wild wave of the poor white's coming to power, few voices dared to be raised in protest. Coming to power meant coming into political office and the redoubling of the fear of losing this power through colored adherents to the opposing party. There were evasions of the amendments, intimidations, circumventing procedure, and movement toward a codification of the new common law, a fixing of those complaints of

[24] Simpkins, Francis B., *The Tillman Movement in South Carolina.*
[25] See the Compendium of Facts of the Plant System of Railways and Steamship Lines for speech of Judge Tillman.
[26] *Negro Year Book.*

Negroes which are heard to the very present. Legislation was enacted which aimed at securing for themselves an economic advantage which the old system had denied them. The law regulating association of the races in the textile industries of South Carolina had the effect of barring Negroes entirely from this fast-growing industry. In 1879, 600 Negroes migrated in mass under "Pap" Singleton to Kansas to escape the severities of this new struggle and to seek new economic opportunities.[27] Ten years later, 35,000 went to Arkansas. What happened in this situation could not be wholly unexpected. Cotton is an uneconomical crop. Its nurture requires seven times as many hands as any ordinary crop and only for certain periods of the year. It is one crop which has yielded very slowly to labor-saving devices and can be profitably grown only with cheap and abundant labor. The foremost cotton-producing countries, which include India, China, and Africa, depend upon masses of cheap labor for its development. The concentration on the single crop system, the increasing congestion of Negroes in the cotton areas, the actual pressure against the yield of 'a soil unnaturally restricted by the boll weevil which had destroyed hundreds of millions' worth of cotton since it crossed the Mexican border, placed another serious pressure against Negroes, whose status brought down this pressure upon them with greatest severity. Instead of a normal development in these sections into independent farmers, after a period, the proportion of Negro owners began to dwindle. Land became more difficult to buy. These lands, worn out through constant and unvaried yields of cotton, gave back less and less in return for the labor invested, and the margin of new lands narrowed beyond their grasp. Carl Kelsey pointed out several years ago this unnatural obstacle to land ownership by the Negro farmer. Only those with sufficient wealth to put the remaining new land through a long period of development, or give the worn-out lands the required rest, could profitably invest. Exhaustion of the soil and the enormous risks of cotton cultivation under the present system have been behind the agitation of the new South for crop rotation. Faced with these uncompromising barriers and the involved credit system which grew up around cotton,

---

[27] "Pap Singleton, Moses of the Colored Exodus," by W. L. Fleming in the *American Journal of Sociology*, July, 1909.

the Negroes were churning about in the South, seeking a vent. Steadily, this mass moved southward and westward; the old belts in the black delta land began losing by degrees their Negroes. The center of the Negro population had moved southward and westward without a break for 130 years. Nor did it turn again until the coming of the World War over fifty years later, when hope dawned for them in the industries of the North. They face now, in the cities, in industry and in the new agricultural economy, a new period. Like quiet shadows, a bit agitated and grotesque, they have followed the course of American industrial expansion. Within a decade, more than 1,000,000 of these workers suddenly moved north. "The dust will fly," the celebrated Frederick Douglass observed of a similar phenomenon forty years ago, "but the earth remains." It is yet true. For four-fifths of the population remained in the section to which they were carried, when the cotton industry was born.

CHAPTER II

MIGRATION

In 1910 there were in the Northern states 1,025,674 Negroes. Increase was slow; migration from the South in a tiny, restrained stream added only about 10,000 a year to these numbers. Then came the war with its sudden and widespread economic unsettlement. With immigration immediately checked, the established industries expanded, and specialized war industries added, a labor void was created sufficient to upset long-established customs. During the period of 1916 to 1920 more than a half million Negroes moved North, and during the later period, 1921 to 1925, a number equally large. The census for 1920 shows an increase of 447,551 over 1910. The bulk of these, together with the half million or more who have migrated since 1920, have moved to a few cities, and for the most part, those cities with basic industries requiring large numbers of unskilled laborers. Of 1,272 Northern counties in 1920 there were 671 with less than 100 Negroes, and 83 with no Negroes at all. Over 60 per cent of the Negro population of Illinois lived in Chicago and over two-thirds of Michigan's Negro population in Detroit. Eight cities—Chicago, Detroit, New York, Newark, St. Louis, Pittsburgh, Philadelphia, and Cleveland—had in 1920 a combined Negro population of 526,145, or 34 per cent of the entire population of the North and West. If industrial districts centering around large cities are considered, about three-fourths of the Negro population of the North could in 1920 be accounted for in the following ten: Indianapolis, Detroit-Toledo, Cleveland-Youngstown, Kansas City, Pittsburgh, Columbus-Cincinnati, St. Louis, Chicago, Philadelphia, New York. Professor Monroe N. Work of Tuskegee, who is responsible for this classification, placed the figure at 1,139,505. The increase in some of these Northern cities in 1920 had been quite startling, as a brief listing will show:

City	Negro Population 1910	Negro Population 1920	Increase 1910-1920
Chicago, Illinois	44,103	109,458	148.2
Cleveland, Ohio	8,448	34,451	307.8
New York, N. Y.	91,709	152,467	66.3
Detroit, Michigan	5,741	40,838	611.3
Philadelphia, Pa.	84,459	134,339	58.9
St. Louis, Missouri	43,960	69,854	58.9

There are no such uniformly exact figures for the period since 1920. It is, however, known in a few cities, and in others may be estimated with reasonable accuracy. The Detroit school census taken in 1925 shows 81,831 Negroes, an increase of over 100 per cent since 1920. No less than 50,000 have moved to New York City during the same period, and test counts in three New Jersey cities and Buffalo, New York, where in local surveys by the Department of Research and Investigation of the National Urban League, it was possible to secure the exact date of arrival of Negro newcomers, indicate that the volume of increase for the first five years of the present decade was two-thirds as large as the increase for the full decade of 1910-1920.

The route northward followed roughly the path of the Underground railroad. Cities of the West: Chicago, Detroit, Indianapolis, St. Louis, and Cleveland, received a black population from the Southern states along the great Mississippi Valley, and more particularly, along the route of the Illinois Central Railroad. The states feeding this section are: Louisiana, Mississippi, Tennessee, and Texas. The cities of the Northern section have drawn principally from Florida, Georgia, the Carolinas, Alabama and Virginia. Each state represents a fairly distinct background of social and economic life with fixed customs, traditions and habits of work and life. In Louisiana these Negroes worked in cane as well as cotton; in Virginia and the Carolinas they worked in tobacco, lumber and turpentine; in Georgia, Mississippi, Alabama and Texas they raised cotton. In the cities of the North, these different backgrounds were thrown into a single pattern, the migrants faced with totally new problems and living modes.

Historically the Southern Negroes are a rural type. There are, in fact, few large cities in the South. Their *metier* is agriculture. Through the years their bodily and mental habits have been adjusted to the simple routine of nurturing the soil. The wave which separated them from the soil to place them suddenly in the midst of a complex industrial structure is important enough to warrant the more careful examination which is possible now that the hysteria which accompanied the movement has subsided.

Long before the trumpet blast of war the roots of the exodus were planted. Whether due to the plantation system which had given to the South its pre-eminence in cotton, or to backward farming methods, or to an inadequate distribution of land or to the failure to reclaim lands, the concentration of Negroes in the cotton areas began in time to show curious results in the pressure against the available means of subsistence. The condition of the Negro tenant farmer before 1914 suggests the force of this pressure.

In the state of Georgia, a survey made by the state university in 1913 revealed that the average annual cash income of the Negro rural family was $290. The average size of the rural Southern Negro family was 4.3. A truck farmer is able to reduce his cash expenditures by raising his own food and it is estimated that about 60 per cent of his food is thus obtained. Cotton growers cannot eat their product and must buy what they need, and the difference between cost and credit prices for these workers ranged as high as 70 per cent. The South imported from the North and West practically all of its breadstuffs and meats. A pertinent recommendation to the farmers of the South by one of its own prominent agricultural experts was that they raise more cows and fewer dogs. The shortage in milk supply for children was an exceptionally dangerous item and without doubt registered in the serious infant mortality. A striking example of the difference which population makes is evident in a comparison of Iowa, an agricultural state, with Alabama, also agricultural. The average Alabama farm had 38 acres, using but 1.5 work animals and depending upon cheap labor. The average Iowa farmer had 138 acres and an average of 8 work animals and the gross income of Iowa farmers was five times that of Alabama farmers. Added to the disproportionate relation between this population growth and the yield of the soil, there had been the boll weevil moving up from the Mexican border leaving a blight upon some 400,000 acres; floods and financial depression; for it is a strange fact that the more cotton produced even after the hazards of production are passed, the lower will be the price and, as follows, the lower the converted yield of the soil to the tenants.

A most natural result followed this situation. Long before industries beckoned, there was profound restlessness in the South. This shifting and movement took three distinct directions and these have not been confined to Negroes. The first was urbanization; the second, the quest for more productive lands; the third, a movement to the industrial centers.

During the 30-year period, 1890-1920, there was an increase in the rural population of 896,124 Negroes as compared with 2,078,331 for cities. The urban increase has been just about 100 per cent more rapid than the rural. In 1890, 19.8 per cent of the Negro population lived in cities; in 1920, this proportion grew to about 40 per cent. In the Southern states, between 1890-1900; the rural population increased 13.6 per cent, and between 1910-1920, it actually decreased 3.3 per cent. The Negro population increase in Southern cities, considered as a whole, had been as late as 1920 greater than the increase in the North, considered as a whole, despite the half-million added during the last decade. Here, of course, is the economic factor at work, hand in hand with greater mobility, increased transportation, restlessness, and the monotony and uncertainty of agricultural life over against the allurements of the city.

There is a natural parallel in Negro migrations with the immigration of Jews from Russia. Prior to 1880, immigration from Russia was negligible. It increased from 5,000 in 1881 to 17,000 in 1882. There were prosperous conditions in the United States and persecution in Russia. But although persecution continued, this migration slumped after 1882, and continued low for several years, then with the return of prosperity in the United States rose to 81,511 in 1892. Despite the fact that the Jews were expelled in 1891 from Great Russia by Imperial Edict, in 1893 the numbers arriving in the United States began to decline, due to depression in this country. With the later industrial development occurring along with depression and pogroms in Russia this immigration began to take on vast proportions and in 1906 there were 263,000 arrivals.

Professor Harry Jerome's valuable study of Migrations and Business Cycles for the National Bureau of Economic Re-

search, proves useful in making certain comparisons between
European and Negro labor, and in pointing the way to significant interpretations.   A value of these figures also lies im-
portantly in the fact that what is true of general migrations
is true of Negro migrations:

(1) Emigration tends to be large in depression years and
low in boom years.   The peaks of Negro migration have been
reached in 1878 and 1879, 1916-1918 and 1923.   In these
years there were floods and crop failures coincidental with boom
periods outside the South, and with aggravated demands for
workers.

(2) Unskilled labor shows the greatest fluctuations. There
is a vast difference in the fluctuations between skilled and unskilled, skilled and professional workers throughout these
periods and throughout the year.   Similarly, there is a vast
fluctuation in the migration between North and South Europeans, the latter contributing the unskilled workers in greatest proportions.   Negroes, the American Migrants, are used
first and generally as unskilled laborers and workers.

(3) There is with unrestricted immigration a rough approximation to seasonal demand and to periods of increased
business activity.   A significant difference appears between
long and short distance migration.   With the first, adjustment
is more difficult; with the second, a reduction in immigration
more quickly follows a reduction in actual demand for workers.

(4) The high periods of immigration occur during March,
April, and May, and the low periods in the fall.   This is precisely the case with Negro migration, except that we have
been accustomed to saying that they were waiting for spring
and warm weather before moving North, and that they went
home in the late fall because they feared the rigors of Northern
winters.

(5) Immigration tends to increase the intensity of boom
periods by making possible an "intensified expansion" of industry and, at the same time, checking the regularization of
industry.

(6) Finally, the easy availability of reserve labor leads to
reduction in wages through competition; it leads to large turnover, to employers' changed attitudes toward workers of a class
or race, and to workers' attitudes toward new workers.

On this last it is necessary only to refer to the fairly common practice during the first period of the recent Negro migrations, of the carrying of a double wage scale for white and Negro workers, and the frequent practice now of carrying a double wage scale for Negroes and Mexicans; to the extraordinary charges against Negro turnover in industry, which in itself is very little different, if at all, from the turnover of unskilled workers generally; to the vast and frequent contradictions in employers' judgments about the abilities of Negro workers which follow the swift changes of demand; to the welcome of new workers by labor when these accessions are for the less desirable unskilled work, which automatically lifts the older labor into a higher grade and the fierce objections, sometimes outbreaks, when the entrenchments of white labor are endangered.

The causes of the Negro migration northward have been variously catalogued and may be grouped under two heads: "Economic Causes" and "Sentimental Causes." The migration of 1916-19 was distinguishably different in character, though not seriously different in volume, from the migration of 1921-1924. With the restlessness, which was economic at bottom, were other forces.

Along with the rest of the section the Negroes of the South had felt some measure of the moving times: literacy had increased, and, slowly but gradually, standards had developed. The hundreds of small and obscure schools of the South sending out yearly their graduates had not been without effect; the development of good roads, and increased mobility, the newspaper—particularly when it could bring such vivid flashes of the outside world as the *Chicago Defender, The New York Age* and other Negro newspapers, all aided in producing a dissatisfaction with the monotony and drudgery of farm life which no mere argument or proposed measures of reform could still.

What happened in this situation could not be wholly unexpected. The pressure of poor crops in 1914 and 1915 fell first upon owners and then with full severity upon the tenants and laborers. Moving to the cities, their excess numbers glutted the labor markets, bringing down wages in the face of rising living costs. In the poorer rural sections the Negroes and whites were thrown into more acute competition and abuses against which the Negroes had no redress added to their unfortunate plight.

The migration of 1916-1918 was a leaderless mass-movement. They were ready for the spark of suggestion which touched them off and sped them blindly northward. In 1915 the experiment of employing Negro boys from the Southern colleges was tried in the Connecticut tobacco fields. Some of the tobacco growers even went a step further on the strength of this success and imported a few Negro families during the same year to insure workers the year around. News of the advantages of the North spread. Quite unwittingly the United States Department of Labor, through its practice of assisting in the movement of labor to acute points of demand, was giving the first impetus to the Negro migration. The practice was quietly discontinued on the protest of Southern Congressmen, who disapproved the drawing off of the South's labor supply. The bottom structure of industry was the first to feel the demand for new laborers. With jobs more plentiful and wages forced upward, such necessary work as road maintenance and construction and the heavy unskilled steel processes suffered the loss of men lured by higher wages. In the spring of 1916 and 1917 the Pennsylvania Railroad brought thousands for work on the roadbeds. These soon moved on to the better paying jobs in near-by cities. All wrote home glowing tales of success. The North was painted as a land of freedom and of plenty. These letters provided an enormous immediate urge to migration. As an aid to understanding the psychological aspects of the almost hysterical behavior of this large group, hundreds of these letters were collected. The two letters which follow were written early during the migration and sent back to friends in the South. This is a letter from an early migrant to his friends in Hattiesburg, Mississippi.

DEAR M——

I got my things alright the other day and they were in good condition. I am all fixed now and living well. I certainly appreciate what you done for us and I will remember you in the near future.

M——, old boy, I was promoted on the first of the month. I was made first assistant to the head carpenter when he is out of the place I take everything in charge, and was raised to $95 a month. You know I know my stuff.

What's the news generally around H'burg? I should have been here 20 years ago. I just begin to feel like a man. It's a great deal of pleasure in knowing that you got some privilege. My children are going to the same school with the whites and I don't have to umble to no one. I have registered—will vote the next election and there ain't any "yes sir"—it's all yes and no and Sam and Bill.

Florine says hello and would like very much to see you.

All joins me in sending love to you and family. How is times there now? Answer soon, from your friend and brother.

The lure and excitement of the city are pictured in this letter from a migrant in East Chicago, Indiana, to his friend in Union Springs, Alabama.

DEAR OLD FRIEND:

These moments I thought I would write you a few true facts of the present condition of the North. Certainly I am trying to take a close observation—now it is true the (col) are making good. Never pay less than $3.00 per day or (10) hours—this is not promise. I do not see how they pay such wages the way they work labors. They do not hurry or drive you. Remember this is the very lowest wages. Piece work they can make from $6 to $8 per day. They receive their pay every two weeks. This city I am living in, the population 30 thousand (20) miles from Big Chicago, Illinois. Doctor, I am somewhat impressed. My family also. They are doing nicely. I have no right to complain whatever. I rec. the papers you mail me some few days ago and you no I enjoyed them reading about the news down in Dixie. I often think of so much of the conversation we engage in concerning this part of the world, I wish many time that you could see our People up here as they are entirely in different light. I witness Decoration Day on May 30th, the line of march was 4 miles. (8) brass band. All business houses was close. I tell you the people here are patriotic. I enclose you the cut of the white press. The chief of police drop dead Friday. Burried him today. The procession about (3) miles long. Over (400) auto in the parade—fire dept—police force, Mayor and alderman and secret societies. We are having some cold weather—we are still wearing overcoats. Let me know what is my little city doing. People are coming here every day and are find employment. Nothing here but money and it is not hard to get. Remember me to your dear Family. Oh, I have children in school every day with the white children. I will write you more next time. How is the lodge?

Your friend,

Excitement grew, labor agents were busy, rumors circulated, the Negro papers urged, a religious significance was given to it. A party of sixty-eight from a town in Mississippi, when they crossed the Ohio River held religious services, praying and singing, "I done come out a de land of Egypt, ain't that good news."

These parties were a favorite method of leaving; there was a saving in transportation, the group was kept intact and together they were able to give aid to one another until all were comfortably established in their new homes.

The letters are useful, too, in illustrating the particular "causes" of the movement. A brief selection is given which covers a variety of these causes, besides throwing some light upon the character of the migrants. These letters were written to individuals, Negro newspapers, to the various Urban Leagues and social agencies in the North.

Houston, Tex.
2/25/17.

Dear Sir:

Would you please to be so kind to advise us on what condition to get in touch with some club on migration movement. We have 1000 of idle people here and good working people would be trully glad to except of that good opportunity of coming North and work. Now please give us the full details of the movingment so we can get together now please advise right away of the main headquarters of the club for we are ready for business just as soon as we can get a understanding from the main club for we have lots of people in Texas want to no direct about it and want to go. We take your paper in this citey and your papper was all we had to go by so we are depending on you for farther advise. Dear editor you muss excuse our bad letter for we rote it in a hurry.

Yours truly,

Charleston, S. C.
April 29, 1917.

Kind Sir:

I would like very much to have you take me in consideration. I am strong and ambitious. Would work under any conditions to get away from this place, for I am working and throwing away my valuable time for nothing.

Kindly let me hear from you at your earliest.

Respectfully,

Jacksonville, Fla.,
May 25, 1917.

DEAR SIR:

Kindly inform me by return mail are there any factories or concerns employing colored laborers, skilled or unskilled? The south is ringing with news telling of the wonderful openings for colored people, and I am asking you to find the correct information whether I could get employment there or not. Please find postage enclosed, for immediate reply.

Yours respectfully,

Brookhaven, Mississippi,
April 24, 1917.

GENTS:

The cane growers of Loisiana have stopped the exodus from New Orleans claiming shortage of labor which will result in a sugar famine.

Now these laborers thus employed receive only 65 cents a day and the high cost of living makes it a serious question to live. There is a great many race people around here who desires to come north but have waited rather late to avoid car fare, which they have not got. Isn't there some way to get the concerns who wants labor, to send passes here or elsewhere so they can come even if they have to pay out of the first month's wages? Please don't publish this letter but do what you can towards helping them to get away. If the R. R. Co would run a low rate excursion they could leave that way. Please answer.

Very respectfully,

Florida,
Dec. 12, 1916.

DEAR SIR:

I can't tell that my family is safe. I do not know when trouble might start in this town and in the excitement some of my family be murdered.

Yours,

Augusta, Ga.,
April 27, 1917.

SIR:

I'm desirous of leaving the South but before so doing I want to be sure of a job before pulling out. I'm a member of the race, a normal school graduate, a man of a family and can give reference. Confidentially this communication between you and me is to be kept a secret.

My children I wish to be educated in a different community than here, where the school facilities are better and less prejudice shown and in fact where advantages are better for our people in all respect. At present I have a good position but I desire to leave the south. A good position even though its a laborer's job paying $4.50 to $5.00 a day will suit me till I can do better. Let it be a job there or anywhere else in the country. I'm quite sure you can put me in touch with some one. I'm a letter carrier now. I must say that I have nothing against Detroit Michigan.

I shall expect an early reply. Remember keep this a secret please until I can perfect some arrangements.

Yours respectfully,

The second migration beginning in the fall of 1921 and continuing at great pace through 1924 proceeded without excitement. There were communities of Southern Negroes in the North to absorb these drafts and soften the first contacts of newcomers with the new environment. It was the sudden introduction of these large numbers that, through a series of distinct problems in housing, politics, industry and public contacts, provoked the riot in Chicago in 1919 and the riot in 1917 in East St. Louis, each taking a toll of thirty-eight lives.

The effect of the migration of Negroes upon the South is recorded most authentically in reports of the Commissioners of Commerce and Labor for the states of Georgia and Louisiana.

"That labor conditions in Georgia have reached a very acute state is apparent to everyone who has investigated the matter. The shortage has been brought about by several causes, which have affected every line of endeavor. The war has called to the colors many engaged in industrial pursuits and the selective conscription act will take many more, making it extremely difficult for manufacturing plants to operate to full capacity with a certainty of losing so many more badly needed operators. While all large employers of labor have suffered, the exodus of the Negro to points in other states has precipitated a crisis in farming operation that is more or less alarming." [1]

[1] Fifth Annual Report of the Commissioner of Commerce and Labor, State of Georgia, year ending December 31, 1916, pp. 5-6.

The Commissioner of Labor for Louisiana in his report for 1922 revealed some of the motives and measures back of the upward trend in Negro wages in the South following the migration.

In our efforts to conserve labor in the state and reduce to a minimum the exodus of Negro labor to other points throughout the country, the Commissioner appealed to the employing interests to be fair and human by their workers and advised the workers by talk and public appeals through the press not to be carried away by glowing promises of high wages, short hours of service, reduced rentals and cheaper rates of living, as well as other assurances often given which were a delusion and a snare. While our efforts may not have been the dominating factor in preventing a general exodus of labor, governmental records and the most authentic statistics compiled through other recognized agencies, show conclusively that fewer Negroes left Louisiana than other Southern states, and in justice to the average employer, the commissioner must say the number of complaints filed with this department have been materially reduced and hearty cooperation has been given, thus reducing the exodus of labor.

It is true several thousand went to the Central-northwestern and Eastern sections of the Country, the vast majority going to accept employment in industrial occupations, while some of the carriers also shipped large numbers out of the state to be used in construction work, but before the latter condition assumed any large proportion a conference was held with proper representation which not only materially reduced, but practically eliminated further shipments.[2]

In 1917 the Southern Sociological Congress met to consider means of checking the migration. The measures solemnly adopted are an explanation of motives and forces more eloquent than the words of the migrants themselves. They set down these as immediately necessary: A general and substantial increase in wages; movement on the part of the farmers to deal more fairly in business matters with the Negro tenants by making clear at the outset the terms of all contracts, and by keeping strict accounts and making prompt settlements with them; the correcting of certain former abuses such as short weighing of coal, discounting of store checks, and unfair

[2] Twelfth Biennial Report of the Department Commissioner of Labor and Industrial Statistics of the State of Louisiana, 1923-1924, pp. 13-14.

prices in the commissaries; instituting a crop diversification in order to keep the laborers supplied with work the year round; better housing; better school conditions; the drawing together of the two races through the medium of county meetings for the study of problems growing out of racial relations.

CHAPTER III

THE INTERPLAY OF NEGRO AND IMMIGRANT LABOR

Negro and immigrant labor have taken curious courses in relation to each other. Attention has been drawn to this in two studies,[1] one of which was concerned for the most part with the immigrant, the other with the native white. In both cases it appears that the Negro population has acted as a barrier to immigrant labor. Commenting upon the effectiveness of the Negro population in limiting immigrant settlement to the north and west, Dr. Carpenter points out that Negroes have been sufficiently numerous in the South to occupy most of the agricultural land, leaving scant opportunity for the land-seeking immigrant; that he has been sufficiently numerous to satisfy, in part at least, the sectional need for unskilled labor; and that wage scales, involved in the complex of the tradition of Negro labor in the South, have little attraction for the newcomer. Whatever the cause, it is quite clear that the South is differentiated from the rest of the country not merely in having a large Negro population, but in not having any considerable foreign population A further speculation attributes the industrial backwardness to the absence of these foreign workers and the increased buying power of this influx of cheap labor which they carried to the North and West.

Dr. Gillette, through a method largely statistical, attempted to discover whether or not and to what degree immigration into the United States had retarded the natural increase of the native stock. Applying the method of correlation to population figures for native whites, foreign born and Negroes, he finds that "the rate of increase of native whites is in inverse

[1] Carpenter, Niles, 1928, *Immigrants and Their Children*, Department of Commerce Publication, Census Monograph VII; Gillette, J. M., "The Effect of Immigration upon the Increase of Population in the United States," in *The Urban Community*, edited by E. W. Burgess, University of Chicago Press.

29

proportion to the percentage of foreigners in the population."
"The presence of Negroes," he concludes, "exerts an influence
directly contrary to that of the presence of foreign whites. The
highest rates of increase among the native whites is greatest
where the percentage of Negroes in the population is greatest.
Since the position of the Negro is one of status, he does not
compete with whites for wealth or position. Hence he is an
advantageous factor and stimulates, or at least does not restrict, increase of population."

The discussions leading up to the recent immigration legislation have stressed two general types of immigration described
as the old and the new. With the first, which included the
English, Germans, Irish, Norwegians and Scandinavians, there
is but small relationship to the question of Negro labor. For
these racial groups came first as pioneers and farmers, or as
skilled and professional workers. Figures compiled by the
Immigration Commission make very clear this occupational
division. For the period 1890-1900 there is indicated the increase or decrease of various racial groups according to occupations. In the case of the Germans there was a notable decrease
in farmers, workers in the building trade and laborers, a similar
decrease for the Irish and English and corresponding increase
in manufacturers, salesmen, and professional men. The only
other increases noted among these three was a German increase
in machinists. On the other hand, with Hungarians, Bohe-
mians and Italians, there were small increases all along the line
but huge ones in unskilled labor. Whereas the Germans showed
a decrease of 25.3 per cent in the field of unskilled work, the
Italians showed an increase of 52.8.[2]

For the period 1900 to 1910 there are similar differences
between these two groups. The total persons of the old immigration coming in during these ten years was 2,273,782 and for
the new 4,949,070. Of the skilled workers the old constituted
19.5 per cent with just half that proportion represented by the
new. In common labor (including farm labor) the old immigration showed a proportion of 23.8 per cent while that of the
new was 59.8 per cent.

This has an important bearing upon the present situation of
Negro labor since it is the unskilled fields of work that make

[2] Report of the United States Immigration Commission, 1911.

the most insistent demands for new recruits; it has been in these fields that the competition of foreign and Negro labor has been keenest; and it is around the immigrant workers in these fields and Negro workers that the question of replacement, in the North especially, revolved.

In the ten years 1900 to 1910 there were admitted from all countries a total of 8,795,386 immigrant aliens. Of this number 5,788,449, or more than 65 per cent, came from the four countries: Austria, Hungary, Italy and Russia, the countries supplying the greatest abundance of recruits for unskilled processes of industry. If, therefore, we have the geographical distribution of these four groups for the decade of this immigration, we may get a sufficient gauge on the sections making largest demands for cheap labor, and at the same time, the sections affected by the shortage, which would be expected to make the most insistent demands for substitute labor.

	Italy	Poland	Hungary	Russia
New York	545,173	247,519	78,374	529,243
Illinois	94,407	162,405	34,437	117,899
Michigan	30,216	103,926	33,607	45,313
Connecticut	80,322	46,623	13,233	38,719
New Jersey	157,285	90,419	40,370	73,527
Pennsylvania	222,764	177,770	71,380	161,124
Ohio	80,658	67,579	73,181	43,690
Total	1,210,825	896,241	344,582	1,009,515

Of the four groups, in 1920, Italy, Poland, Hungary and Russia, New York had 1,400,309; New Jersey had 361,601 and Pennsylvania had 633,038. The Italians, a rural people like the Negroes, have provided common laborers for construction, railroad building and maintenance, the mines, and for unskilled work connected with large factories. In some instances they have gone back to the land as in the scattered colonies in the South and in rural parts of Connecticut, Massachusetts and New Hampshire. The fact remains, that although 85 per cent of them were farmers at home, the proportion is exactly changed in their present status in this country. The Hungarians and Poles went into the great steel mills of Pennsylvania, into the stockyards, iron and steel plants of Illinois, and into the similar industries in New York state, particularly in Buffalo, which is reputed to be the third largest Polish city in the world.

These groups, with others in somewhat smaller proportions,

manned the lower branches of the industry when the war and the rigid immigration restriction checked the numbers. In 1914 there were 1,218,480 aliens admitted, with 303,338 leaving; but in 1918 only 110,617 came and 94,585 left. The total increase from immigration for that year was only 16,032. It was scarcely an accident, therefore, that the first migration of Negroes from the South reached its peak during this year.

In 1921 the Immigration Act on a 3 per cent quota became effective. For the twelve months ending June, 1922, the Department of Labor figures showed a net immigration of 88,520. But in this number there was an actual loss of more than 10,000 men, the surplus of immigration over emigration being in women and children. The 3 per cent law contemplated an annual entry of about 360,000 persons. When emigration is deducted it appears that instead of admitting 45 per cent of the normal population influx of other years it actually admitted only about 11 per cent. The further restriction in 1924 to 2 per cent of the racial population in this country in 1890 instead of 1910 accomplished two things: it reduced immigration enormously and it reduced it most drastically among those groups that had been supplying the unskilled recruits. The present quotas for the four countries, Italy, Austria, Hungary and Russia, which in the last decade were averaging about 600,000 persons each year, even adding to the number the New Poland, with 5,982 eligibles, is only 11,333.

On the other hand, Great Britain and Ireland together could send 62,572 and Germany alone 51,227. This introduces the very vital question of man-power in relation to the continued industrial expansion in America. As pointed out most effectively by Mr. Stuart Chase, machinery has made large scale compensations for the correctable wastes of man-power. The American Engineering Society and other organizations, as well as individual initiative in insistence upon new methods of labor conservation, have had considerable effect and eventually will have even more. However, the adjustment to machinery could not be quite so complete and sudden. General Richard C. Marshall, Jr., former chief of the Construction Division of the Army, and later General Manager of the Associated General Contractors of America, i.e., the head of the construction industry in America, made rather significant comments on this situation. In construction alone he estimated that there were needed annually 35,000 new skilled workers and 12,000 additional common laborers merely to replace those lost by death, promotion and retirement. Construction employs about 22 per cent of the skilled and common laborers of all the mechanical and manufacturing industries, and incidentally offers the largest single industrial opportunity for Negro workers. If all of the manufacturing industries are taken into account, 214,000 new manufacturing and mechanical workers would be needed annually to replace losses caused by death and retirement. The population is increasing at the rate of 1,400,-000 annually, about 14 per 1,000. To keep pace with the growth of the population and its increasing requirement for goods, and consequently for labor, there is required at least an addition of 14 actual laborers annually per 1,000. If to the 214,000 workers needed annually for replacement there are added these actual laborers per 1,000 (calculated by applying 14 per 1,000 new workers needed as a result of population growth to the 11,000,000 men now engaged in manufacturing and mechanical industries) there would be a total of 368,000 new workers needed annually to man the industries. In response to this situation three developments have been noted: (1) Negro workers have moved into positions once pre-empted by alien immigrants; (2) There has been an increase in Mexican labor from the South; and (3) there has been a most astounding reduction in actual man-power required in industry.

The Bureau of Conciliation of the United States Department of Labor in 1923 canvassed 273 firms for figures on the distribution and assimilation of the migrants, and found 60,421 new Negro workers of whom 14,951 were doing skilled work and 45,470 unskilled work. During the single year September 1, 1922, to August 31, 1923, 18,050 new workers had been added to the payrolls, of which number 4,157 were skilled. The general increase in Negro skilled workers was 38.5 per cent; of the unskilled 44.0. Some states showed an increase in skilled Negroes as high as 186.8 per cent. In the stockyards of Chicago there were 5,300 Negroes in 1920 as compared with 39 in 1910, and 3,201 in the iron and steel industries in 1920 as compared with 17 in 1910.

A picture of this labor substitution with the old and new

immigration factors, the first and second generation differences, and the numerical disproportion between the foreign and Negro stock is possible from the detailed examination of one fairly representative city. Buffalo, New York, is selected because it has been affected by both types of immigration, and has certain basic industries. In 1910 the bottom structure of the city's work was supported by the foreign-born population. Of the total male workers in the manufacturing industries, 55,283 were foreign-born, 49,040 native-born of foreign or mixed parentage, 34,321 native white and 738 Negroes. In specific occupations the racial factor was conspicuous. The foreign-born made up 52 per cent of the tailors, 74 per cent of the general (manufacturing) laborers, 83 per cent of the railroad laborers, and 57 per cent of the janitors and sextons. The mixed parentage group stood first as machinists, commanding 43 per cent of the jobs, while the foreign-born stood next with 30 per cent; they also commanded 51 per cent of the plumbing and steam-fitting work, while the rest was divided about equally between foreign-born and native-born; they had the largest number of brakemen, teamsters, and clerks. The native whites held a slight margin of excess in all such occupations as managers and superintendents, conductors, salesmen in stores, real estate agents, physicians and surgeons, bookkeepers and accountants.

Here we find what seems to be a rough division of society; a suggestion of occupational stratification related to race and length of residence. The large supply of crude immigrant labor made possible a higher grade of work for those who had been in the country and in the work longer, and for the native-born. The second generation of foreign-born usually had superior work. The positions held by the native whites were, as a rule, further advanced, and from the standpoint of both work and pay, more desirable. The position of the Negro workers in this hierarchy was unimportant. Domestic service positions, in which division they had the greatest numbers (641 Negroes) were the largest. They were too insufficient to exercise any important influence.

Between 1911 and 1915 there were 15,582 alien arrivals in Buffalo, and between 1906 and 1910 there were 16,736. Negro labor was not needed. In the mechanical and manufacturing industries in 1910 there were only 107 Negroes employed, and 59 of these were ordinary laborers. Immigration to Buffalo after 1914 was reduced to about 1,500 males, for the five years 1915 to 1920. The deficit had to be supplied and the number of Negroes in the industries increased from 107 in 1910 to 1,186 in 1920, and the population from 1,773 in 1910 to a present population of nearly 10,000.

In the present structure the native whites still lead in the advanced occupations, which include architects, chemists, civil engineers, dentists, electrical engineers, lawyers and judges, physicians, teachers, manufacturing officials, bankers, brokers, etc. The mixed parentage group leads in the number of manufacturers, builders and contractors, foremen, city and county officials and inspectors, mail carriers, detectives, policemen, electricians, stationary engineers, jewelers, mechanics, millwrights, varnishers, paperhangers, structural ironworkers, tinsmiths, toolmakers, switchmen, semi-skilled workers in glass, iron, furniture, lumber, metal (other than iron and steel), rubbers, clerks and collectors. These, it will be noted, are the highest paid skilled and the petty official positions.

The foreign-born lead in number of blacksmiths, brickmasons, cabinetmakers, carpenters, metal grinders, iron molders, plumbers, tailors, shoemakers, semi-skilled workers in house building, slaughter houses, railroad shops, beverage industries, automobile factories, textile industries, and laborers in practically all lines providing unskilled work.

The Negro workers show a fluctuating importance among the industries, coming with greatest numbers into places most difficult to fill. Their largest proportion is in blast furnaces and rolling mills, where they constitute 19.7 per cent of all the workers. The next highest proportion, 8.01 per cent, is in the semi-skilled positions in steam-rolling mills; the next, 5.2 per cent, is in the slaughtering and packing houses; and the next, 4.6 per cent, in brass mills. As crane-men and derrick-men they provide 4.5 per cent of all the workers. This latter is a skilled process. The largest proportions among all the occupations are in personal and domestic service, where they contribute 29.6 per cent of all the porters (not in stores), 13.5 per cent of all the servants, 20.8 per cent of all the waiters, and 9.05 per cent of the janitors.

If they do not count seriously in numbers as compared with the groups of larger total population in the city, they are significantly massed in certain lines, thus rendering their comparatively small numbers important. They exceed their proportion in the population (0.9) in more than forty fairly important occupations. For example, the Negro proportion of stationary firemen, furnace-men and chauffeurs is over twice as large as their population proportion; the proportion of crane-men, four times as large; semi-skilled workers in rolling mills and janitors, eight times as large; domestic servants and rolling mill

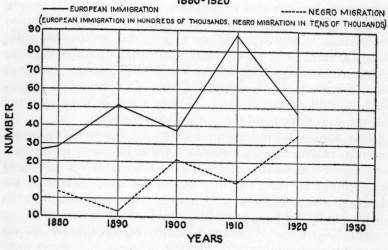

Figure 1

laborers, more than twenty times as large as their population proportion.

For those who are puzzled to know why, after sixty years of freedom, four-fifths of the Negroes have remained in the South, there is explanation in the following graph which pictures coldly the interplay of foreign and Negro migration to the industrial North. Reading European immigration in hundreds of thousands and Negro migration in tens of thousands the trends become strikingly apparent. For the decade 1870 to 1880, European immigration totalled 2,812,191 and Negro migration 42,473. A period of prosperity followed in the decade 1880 to 1890, new immigrations were spurred and a high point of 5,246,613 was reached. The effect upon Negro labor is unmistakable. The North not only failed to draw Negro migrants during that decade, but suffered an actual loss of 57,403 Negroes, who were pushed, by the fierce competition, back into the South. The decade ending in 1900 showed a decline in European immigration; the numbers fell to 3,678,567. In this decade, Negro migration took a sharp upward turn and a deposit of 200,000 was left with the North. During the next decade, 1900-1910, European immigration reached its highest point with 8,795,386 and again the Negro numbers were forced down to 79,791. The war decade, with its gross reduction in immigration, is reflected in the sharp upward turn of the Negro trend mounting higher than any preceding period.

The new factor of important bearing is Mexican immigration. Mexico is not on a quota basis, and although the only requirement for admission is payment of a visa fee and small head tax, there are thousands of illegal entries. They have gone for the most part into farming sections abandoned by whites and Negroes in Texas and California and into the industrial centers on the work which Negroes were first engaged upon in 1916 and 1917. As yet there is but little actual competition, the Mexicans taking the least desirable jobs, pushing up Negroes one grade as the Negroes in turn pushed up the foreign-born, who in turn pushed up the native whites. In many places Negro workers are given a better scale of wages than Mexicans, as whites are in many instances given a better scale than Negroes.

CHAPTER IV

THE NEGRO WORKING POPULATION

Sixty per cent of the Negro population over 10 years of age, male and female, are working: 81 per cent of the men and 39 per cent of the women. Over 2,000,000 of these workers are farmers and more than 1,000,000 are domestic servants. Together these two occupations account for more than 67 per cent of the occupations of Negroes compared with 34 per cent, which is the normal distribution. Of the Negro farm population 57.5 per cent are laborers, 32.4 are tenants and 10.1 are owners. There has been a decrease both in the number of Negro owners and renters.

Between the census years 1910-1920 the percentage of the Negro population 10 years of age and over engaged in gainful occupations decreased from 5,192,535, or 71 per cent of the total population, to 4,824,151, or 59.9 per cent of the population. This decrease was more marked among the female workers than among the males.[1] The Federal census statistics for 1920 show that 54.7 per cent of the female population were gainfully employed in 1910; only 38.9 per cent of that group were employed in 1920; while among the males the decrease was from 87.4 per cent of the total population to 81.1 per cent. Since the decrease in gainfully employed among all male workers was only 3.1 per cent, and 2.3 per cent among all female workers between the years 1910 and 1920, it is reasonable to conclude that the effect of diminished employment was far more pronounced upon Negro workers than upon other racial groups.

Lauck and Sydenstricker compiled, from United States Immigration Commission statistics in 1911, data covering the distribution of Negroes in 21 basic industries employing 507,256

[1] It is quite probable that this was due to a change in census methods, particularly in the data of enumeration which reduced the count of agricultural workers in 1920.

wage earners.[2]   The Negroes were an essential part of the
labor supply in bituminous coal mining and in construction
work, principally in the South; iron ore mining, cigars and
tobacco, slaughtering and meat packing.   Of 16 basic industries employing women, manufacturing carpets, electrical supplies, foundry and machine shop products, paper and wood
pulp, rope, twine, and hemp, sewing machines and typewriters,
Negro women were important in none.   The highest per cent,
0.1, was in rope, twine and hemp manufacturing.

The largest industrial groups of Negroes in 1920 were in the
following divisions of employment:

Laborers

Building trades	135,000
Lumber (saw mills)	106,200
Iron and steel	105,600
Miscellaneous Industries	86,200
Food	27,700
Tobacco	21,200
Textiles	18,800
Chemical works	17,500
Clay and Brick yards	8,800
General Metal Industries	4,000
Paper and Pulp Mills	2,900
Tanneries	2,500
Clothing	1,400
Printing	1,200
Total	535,000

These unskilled laborers constitute 60.3 per cent of all Negroes
in manufacturing industries.

Semi-skilled Workers

Iron and Steel Industries	23,600
Cigar and Tobacco Industries	19,800
Food Industries	15,800
Clothing Industries	13,900
Lumber and Furniture Industries	9,600
Textile Industries	9,300
Chemical plants (principally fertilizer works)	2,300
Miscellaneous industries	23,000
Total	117,300

These constitute 13.2 per cent of all Negroes in manufacturing
industries.

[2] Lauck, W. Jett and Sydenstricker, Edgar, *Conditions of Labor in American Industries.*

Skilled Workers

Carpenters	34,200
Brick and Stone Masons	10,600
Mechanics	9,000
Molders	6,000
Painters	9,300
Plasterers	7,000
Tailors	6,900
Engineers (Stationary) crane-men, etc.	6,300
Plumbers (gas and steam fitters)	3,500
Blacksmiths, forgemen and hammermen	8,900
Total	102,300

These constitute about 10 per cent of the Negroes in manufacturing industries. The remainder are scattered through a hundred or more different occupations among which are toolmaking, coppersmithing, electrotyping and lithographing, engraving, glass blowing and watchmaking. Other important occupations not classed as manufacturing include coal mining, which employs 54,000 Negro operatives, longshore work, engaging 27,200, and various divisions of railroad work, in which 136,-065 find employment. The distribution is of especial interest in this last group of occupations for its comparatively large proportion of skilled and semi-skilled workers.

Baggage men and freight agents	111
Boiler washers	2,577
Brakemen	4,485
Conductors	38
Engineers	111
Firemen	6,478
Foremen and Overseers	1,195
Inspectors	202
Laborers	95,713
Porters, Train and Pullman	20,224
Superintendents	2
Switchmen and Flagmen	2,874
Telegraphers	97
Telegraph and Telephone Linesmen	202
Miscellaneous	1,961

Most of these workers are in Southern states; indeed, thirteen Southern states, led by Georgia with 10,865, account for 87 per cent of them. Eighty per cent of the carpenters and 68 per cent of the bricklayers are in the Southern states. The best chances for work in iron and steel plants are in the North, but for lumber, the building trades, tobacco and textiles, the majority of the work is in the South.

Selecting carpenters as a skilled class which would reflect

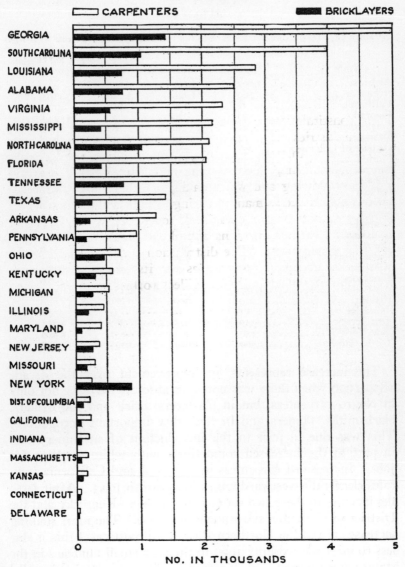

NUMBER OF NEGRO CARPENTERS AND BRICKLAYERS BY STATES

Figure 2

recent changes, the figures are given of trends in 25 states, between 1900 and 1920.

TABLE I

Number of Negro Carpenters by States for the Census Years 1900-1920

State	1900	1910	1920	Per Cent Increase 1900-1920
Alabama	1,807	2,601	2,552	41.2
Arkansas	569	1,120	1,250	119.6
California	41	137	210	412.1
Colorado	29	29	22	(−24.1)
Connecticut	41	59	82	100.0
Delaware	24	37	47	95.8
District of Columbia	256	286	217	(−15.2)
Florida	1,150	2,181	2,052	78.4
Georgia	3,385	4,537	4,952	46.2
Illinois	170	259	443	160.5
Indiana	107	158	201	87.8
Iowa	25	26	38	52.0
Kansas	102	145	169	61.7
Kentucky	701	813	599	(−14.5)
Louisiana	1,711	2,811	2,843	66.1
Maryland	290	383	438	51.0
Massachusetts	107	140	175	63.5
Michigan	68	90	502	638.2
Minnesota	4	9	22	450.0
Mississippi	1,497	2,258	2,173	45.1
Missouri	219	309	289	31.0
Nebraska	11	22	41	272.7
New Jersey	110	215	362	138.1
New York	136	402	857	530.0
North Carolina	1,500	1,979	2,127	41.8

The increase represents an improvement over the decade 1890-1900 when there was noted an absolute decrease not only in Negro carpenters, but in plasterers, brick and tile makers, blacksmiths, tanners and in ten other important occupations. This was due in part to the introduction of machinery and in part to the increased competition with white workers for jobs. Increase of carpenters in Arkansas and California indicates clearly the westward migration prior to 1915. After 1910 the increase in these two states is negligible. Kentucky and the District of Columbia show actual decrease. The most striking increases are in the Northern states. In most cases this is due less to migratory volume than to the very small numbers in the states prior to 1910. Such increases, however, tend to parallel the percentages of increase in population in these same Northern centers.

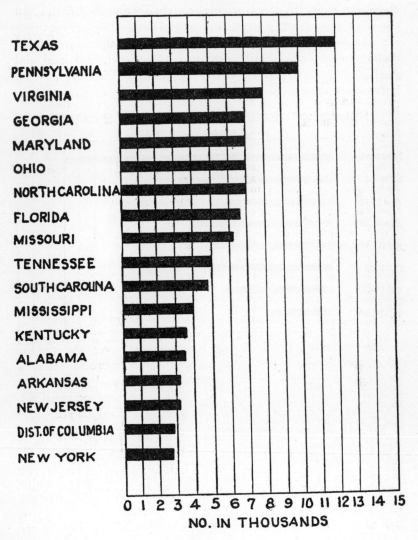

NUMBER OF NEGRO BUILDING LABORERS
BY STATES

TEXAS
PENNSYLVANIA
VIRGINIA
GEORGIA
MARYLAND
OHIO
NORTH CAROLINA
FLORIDA
MISSOURI
TENNESSEE
SOUTH CAROLINA
MISSISSIPPI
KENTUCKY
ALABAMA
ARKANSAS
NEW JERSEY
DIST. OF COLUMBIA
NEW YORK

0 1 2 3 4 5 6 7 8 9 10 11 12 13 14 15
NO. IN THOUSANDS

Figure 3

A distribution of mass employment of Negroes by states is obtained by selecting the four occupations providing the largest amount of work of all grades, in the manufacturing field.

When distributed according to leading Negro occupations by states these trends of mass employment appear as follows: In the Northern states, general building provides the largest number of jobs in Ohio, Illinois, New York, New Jersey and Indiana; automobile manufacturing, in Michigan, and iron and steel work in Connecticut, Pennsylvania and Wisconsin. This latter work stands second in importance in five of these states,

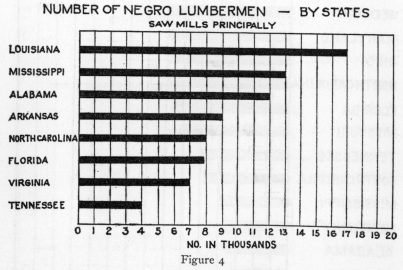

NUMBER OF NEGRO LUMBERMEN — BY STATES
SAW MILLS PRINCIPALLY

NO. IN THOUSANDS

Figure 4

with brass mills in Connecticut, tanneries in Wisconsin, ship-building in Pennsylvania and meat packing in Indiana providing a considerable measure of work. In the "Border" states, general building takes first place, with steel mills following in Maryland, tobacco in Kentucky and meat packing in Missouri. Of twelve Southern states, general building provides the largest number of jobs in North Carolina, Georgia, Virginia, Oklahoma, and Texas, while saw and planing mills lead in Alabama, South Carolina, Mississippi, Arkansas and Louisiana. Next in importance are steel mills in Alabama, and general industrial labor in Mississippi, Oklahoma and Texas. The tobacco industry in North Carolina and Virginia, turpentine distilleries in Louisiana, petroleum refineries in Texas and the skilled trade of carpentry in South Carolina, Tennessee, Georgia and Mississippi have important numbers.

Ratio of Negro Workers Among the Industries. The general distribution of Negro workers throughout the United States gives an index both to the amount of work performed and to their importance in the structure of American industries. They provide 21.0 per cent of the building laborers, 24 per cent of the chemical laborers, 60 per cent of the tobacco workers, 14 per cent of the iron and steel laborers, 89.5 per cent of the saw and planing mill unskilled hands, 16 per cent of the blast fur-

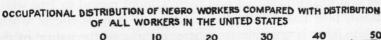

OCCUPATIONAL DISTRIBUTION OF NEGRO WORKERS COMPARED WITH DISTRIBUTION OF ALL WORKERS IN THE UNITED STATES

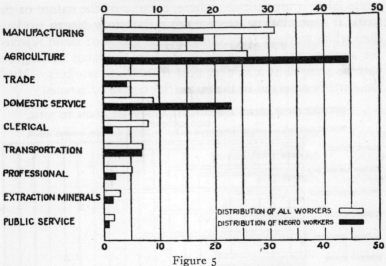

Figure 5

nace and rolling mill unskilled hands. In work requiring some measure of skill they are 29 per cent of the glass workers, 42 per cent of the fish packing and curing hands, and 31.7 per cent of the longshoremen. On the other hand, they have fewer than their population proportion of carpenters (3.8 per cent of all carpenters), iron molders (5.5), cotton mill workers (1.2), coal miners (7.7) and petroleum workers (3.0). This relationship can be suggested graphically. If we regard the present distribution of all workers in terms of work units in each of the main occupational divisions, and compare these with the actual distribution of Negroes, their economic position and relation to industry become apparent.

If they were "normally" distributed they would have twice their present number of workers in the mines, nearly half their present number of farmers, about three times as many more persons in trade, almost twice their present number in manufacturing, about a third of their present numbers in domestic and personal service and five times as many more in clerical positions.

The peculiar relationship of Negroes to the economic structure has carried other serious implications both for the Negroes and the general course of industry and agriculture. This labor, at first institutionalized, and used without regard to free white labor, now has divided importance. It is most useful where white labor is unavailable; where, because of the nature of the work, it is possible to secure more satisfactory Negro workers than white workers from the available group of those rejected for superior grades of work, and where the labor of Negroes may be secured at a smaller cost than white workers. Much the same is observed in the industrial course of women.

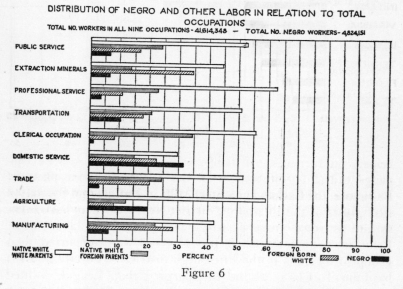

DISTRIBUTION OF NEGRO AND OTHER LABOR IN RELATION TO TOTAL OCCUPATIONS

TOTAL NO. WORKERS IN ALL NINE OCCUPATIONS – 41,614,348 — TOTAL NO. NEGRO WORKERS – 4,824,151

Figure 6

NEGRO WORKERS IN SPECIAL INDUSTRIES

Iron and Steel. The belief, whether or not well-founded, that Negroes are not as easily affected by heat as other workers, has been revealed on numerous occasions as responsible for opportunities in iron and steel mills, which they have improved. In thirteen states, this work ranked among the four industries with largest numbers of Negro workers. The Tennessee Coal and Iron Company in Birmingham not only employs large numbers of Negroes but has developed model housing and community projects which seem to insure their tenure. In the open hearth department of the Duquesne plant of the Bethlehem Steel Corporation 20 per cent of the workers were Negroes, and this number represents about half of all Negroes employed in the plant. Eighty per cent of the Negroes in this department were semi-skilled or skilled, serving as gas makers,

NUMBER OF NEGRO IRON AND STEEL WORKERS – BY STATES

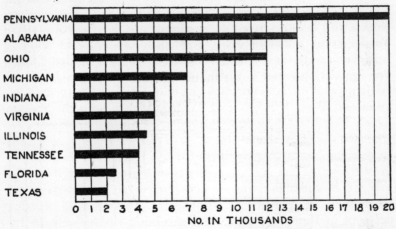

Figure 7

helpers on furnaces, ash hoppermen, ladle liners, and narrow gauge railroad switchmen. In the Sparrows Point plant in Baltimore, the Lackawanna Steel Mills in Buffalo and the major steel plants of the Pittsburgh district Negro workers have been, as late as 1925, from 15 to 21 per cent of the labor force. Prior to 1913 fewer than 100 Negroes were employed in a group of 23 mills in the Pittsburgh district. A study in 1923 by John T. Clark, of the Pittsburgh Urban League, located 16,300. The depression of 1924 forced a general reduction in workers and in 1925 the mills were again visited to observe how these workers fared. Nine of the largest plants at 82 per cent of normal strength and a total force of 29,500 retained Negro workers in a proportion of 22 per cent.

The steel strike of 1919 has not been without its effect in keeping the quota of Negro steel workers higher than their population proportion. It was largely through the availability of these workers, fresh from the South, as strike breakers, that the strike failed. The Interchurch World Movement's Report [3] on the strike observes that Negro workers were imported into Gary, Youngstown and Pittsburgh and were shifted from plant to plant. In Gary they were marched ostentatiously through the streets; in Youngstown and near Pittsburgh they were smuggled in at night. Many of them were conscious of strike breaking. For this attitude, the report holds, the steel strikers rightly blamed American organized labor, because in the past the majority of A. F. of L. unions have been in fact white unions only. The disinclination of a sufficiently large number of the Negroes to ally with labor organizations, at least for several years afterwards, strengthened materially their positions in the industry.

Mining. Of the six major coal areas in the United States, the Appalachian region which stretches from Pennsylvania to Alabama and includes portions of Ohio, Eastern Kentucky, Virginia and West Virginia and Tennessee, has been the area in which Negro workers have played their most important rôle. The two states, Alabama and West Virginia, have provided the largest number of Negro miners. Their relation to the industry in other states has not, however, been entirely negligible. Of 310,719 bituminous mine workers they were 52.7 per cent of all workers in Alabama; 19.9 per cent in West Virginia; 2.4 per cent in Illinois; 1.9 per cent in Ohio; 1.6 per cent in Indiana; 1.4 per cent in Pennsylvania and 10.9 per cent of the combined force in 11 other states. Foreign workers formed a large proportion of workers in all the states except Alabama, where the Negro numbers were highest. On the other hand, in Pennsylvania, where the foreign group was largest (55.4 per cent) the Negro workers showed their lowest numbers, 1.4 per cent. Before 1900 Negroes were 50 per cent of the force of the largest mines in the central Appalachian system. When G. T. Surface [4] studied this area in 1909 he could report that "at every operation visited it was found that the maximum

[3] *The Interchurch World Movement Report on The Steel Strike of 1919,* Chapter VI, Organizing for Conference, pp. 177-178.
[4] Surface, G. T., "Negro Mine Laborers, Central Appalachian Coal Field." *Annals of the American Academy of Political and Social Science,* March, 1909.

producing Negro miners were on a par with the maximum producing miners of all other classes." The strike of 1902, in which they participated, proved destructive to their position, and they suffered serious depletion in numbers. Most competent in pick mining, the introduction of the machine and of foreign workers, particularly the experienced miners from Britain, brought further displacement. The numbers, despite these drafts, continued fairly high and in 1910 they were 7.6 per cent of the coal employees and 29.6 per cent of the iron ore miners, and in 1920 they were doing 7.7 per cent of the coal mining. During the coal strike in West Virginia in 1922 the numbers already there were supplemented by hundreds from Virginia, North Carolina and Alabama, many of these entering the mines for the first time. They have been arrayed on both sides of the long and bitter controversy between operators and miners in the northern and southern portions of the state.

In 1923 the Bureau of Negro Welfare and Statistics of West Virginia announced that its records showed 22,421 Negro miners in the state. Five southern counties contained 17,543 Negro miners, or 73 per cent of all Negro miners in the state. These counties have been the scene of several attempts of the United Mine Workers to gain a foothold. At one time two counties were more than half organized and most of the miners were Negroes.[5] They had been advanced to important positions in the industry and held many offices in the labor organizations, until the sudden discontinuance of union activities.

A survey by this Bureau in Northern West Virginia, in 1925, to determine the extent of participation of Negroes in the strike which had developed over the proposed cut in wages, revealed that there had been a 350 per cent increase in Negro miners there; that where they were not employed it was due to a deliberate effort to keep them out; that Negro strike breakers were not being imported; that the Negro and foreign workers were the main support of the union; and that more Negroes were employed under non-union conditions than otherwise.[6]

In the Pennsylvania fields anthracite mining, which requires a different skill, has not until recently employed many Negroes.

[5] Harris, A. L., "The Negro in the Coal-mining Industry," *Opportunity,* February, 1926.
[6] Report of the West Virginia Bureau of Negro Welfare and Statistics, 1923.

According to the United States Coal Commission's Report,[7] of the 147,456 men in the anthracite mines only 46 were Negroes. They have important numbers, however, in the other fields of the state. Gerald E. Allen,[8] in 1927 located 4,390 in the 112 mines of seven operators. Eighteen mines of the Pittsburgh Coal Company had an average of 45 per cent Negro employees.

The Federal Council of Churches, following the strike in the coal fields of Western Pennsylvania,[9] conducted a survey of the area and found that whereas in 1924 there were 586 Negroes in a total of 11,563 miners, in 1927 there were 3,704 Negroes in a total of 9,076. The per cent thus had increased from 5.0 to 40.0.

The condition of the coal industry is being felt by the Negro workers along with the rest. With the introduction of machinery there is on the whole less disposition to use Negroes. The larger number of excess miners, as a result of over production and an actual curtailed use of coal, diminishes further the chances for employment except in such unfortunate emergencies as strikes.

Cotton Mills. The movement of cotton mills south has been concurrent with the movement of Negroes north. Quite as important as proximity to sources of raw material are the Southern 54-hour week as against the 48-hour week legislation of the New England mill states; the unrestricted night work for women; and native-born cheap white labor. The mill owners have discovered the mountaineer whites who have, "probably since the time of the American Revolution led an existence in a little world of their own." In the new impetus to industrialization of the South this industry leads. The importance of the Negro is small although the mills are virtually at his door. South Carolina, several years ago by legislation requiring minute separation of the races in all operations of the textile industry, plant structure and individual relations, forced the alternative of complete separation, and thus dual plants, or no Negroes in the industry. The latter obtained legally in

---

[7] Report of the United States Coal Commission, Part III.
[8] Allen, Gerald E., *The Negro Coal Miner in the Pittsburgh District.* Unpublished thesis, University of Pittsburgh, 1927.
[9] *The Coal Strike in Western Pennsylvania.* Federal Council of Churches, Report for May, 1928.

South Carolina as it did by common consent and practice in the other states. Except for a few scattered mills manufacturing rough cotton socks, there are no mills operated by Negroes. One probable reason for the exclusion is the number of women employed and the fear of too close contact between the races at work. Professor Broadus Mitchell, of Johns Hopkins University, holds that the reason Negroes are not in the one characteristic industry of the South is that it is the *one* characteristic industry. Nevertheless, 17,477 Negro men and 7,257 women are reported in the textile mills. Excluding the workers in New York, the others appear to be working almost exclusively in the opening, packing, and shipping departments, or in such general work as trucking, yard work, sweeping and cleaning in the mills. For example, the Labor Commission of Georgia reports 4,758 Negro men and women in the textile mills. These were entirely draymen, porters, scrubbers and floor cleaners.

Tobacco. In Kentucky, Virginia and North Carolina Negro workers are freely used in tobacco re-handling. The industry is important in these states by reason of proximity to the producing areas. In the cigarette factories of Petersburg, Virginia, for example, of 1,200 women workers, 500, or about 42 per cent are Negroes; 100 Negro men and boys and 500 Negro women and girls are employed in the smoking, plug, twist and leaf tobacco factories. The Women's Bureau studies found this to be a field engaging the largest number of Negro women. A notable distinction in the industry is in the types of work done. Negroes do practically all of the re-handling; white women are exclusively used in manufacturing the tobacco after the sorting and preparation. The former do mostly handwork; the latter use machines.

Automobile Manufacturing. This is one of the comparatively new industries and it centers heavily in Michigan. There were, in 1929, according to figures provided by the Detroit Urban League, about 40,000 Negroes engaged in the manufacture of automobiles and automobile accessories. The Ford plant employs the largest number. More than 10,000 were on the pay roll in 1926, before the reorganization of the plant, and there is a number equally large at present. The range of work is from unskilled, which holds the great bulk, to skilled work and foremanship. One concern has Negro draftsmen, tool makers and machinists. Few of the earlier charges against Negro efficiency survive. The complaints against irregularity, sickness, and "pay day lay-off" are seldom heard. However, there have been occasional minor disturbances among individual workers which, in one instance at least, brought the threat of wholesale discharge.

Slaughtering and Meat Packing. In 1880 one lone Negro was employed in Armour's killing gang in Chicago. During the strike of 1894 Negro labor entered the meat industry in numbers for the first time. After its termination few were retained. When the strike of 1904 was called there were 500 in the yards, some of whom belonged to the unions. Additional strike breakers were brought in. They did not become a permanently large factor until after 1916 when the numbers were increased by thousands. Many of the old workers had been moved into the better paying, even though temporary, war industries and a general labor shortage, as a result of war demands and the drafts, was felt. There are at present about 8,000 in the yards in Chicago, engaged in all grades of work. Some are elected to serve as members of the employee representation boards.

Other plants in East St. Louis, Indianapolis, and Los Angeles employ them freely and attribute to them a special fitness for this work.

Garment Making. It has been observed that the second generation of those foreign-born workers who had provided most of the labor, for the making of women's and children's garments, tended away from the industry. This has been particularly true of the cheaper goods which require continued pressure for profitable production, and yield small returns for the workers. Employers after 1915 turned to Negro women. The number of such workers increased from less than 100 in 1910 to over 3,000 in 1920, and since 1920 the increase has been steady. The industry accounts for the third largest single group of workers in New York City.

In Philadelphia a survey of 126 garment shops employing 5,822 women in 1927,[10] located 842 Negroes, or 14 per cent of

[10] Colored Women as Industrial Workers in Philadelphia, p. 113. Armstrong Association, 1927.

the garment workers. Four shops used Negro women exclusively and 9 others used more Negro than white women. In both Chicago and Baltimore, shops employ considerable numbers of Negro women. The rates of pay are smaller than for white and they are limited to the coarser fabrics. The saving in wage rates not infrequently accounts for the employment of this labor. A long history of competence as dressmakers and seamstresses has aided in placing Negro women in this field, but the difference both in the operation and speed of the power machines makes necessary essentially new adjustments.

Longshoring. The work of loading and unloading ships demands the peculiar combination of strength and agility, and Negroes are given preference in this work in practically every important port. It is one of the oldest occupations in which Negroes hold an unbroken prestige. It is, in New York City, the largest single male occupation for Negro men. Over 7,000 were so engaged in 1920. Buffalo, Norfolk, Baltimore, New Orleans, Savannah and Galveston show large Negro percentages, and the locals of the International Longshoremen's Union, which freely admit Negroes, have more Negro members and local and national officers than any other labor organization in the United States.

A study of Negro longshoremen of the New York deep-water docks,[11] as to occupational history, nativity, marital status, relations with unions, domestic conditions, and leisure time activities was made by E. Franklin Frazier in 1921. The seasonal character of the work was an outstanding feature. Thirty per cent of the men worked only 6 months during the year; 65 per cent worked 6 months or less; while only 30 per cent of the men were employed for 8 months or more. The wages varied from $250 to $1,400 per year with 70 per cent of the number earning less than $900 yearly. The study was undertaken during a period of industrial depression and offers a clear picture of the effect of such depressions on the Negro worker.

In a study of the conditions of the longshoring industry of the Chicago port [12] in 1915 by Charles B. Barnes, 100 work-

11 Frazier, E. Franklin, *Negro Longshoremen,* Russell Sage Foundation, 1921.
12 Barnes, Charles B., *The Longshoreman,* Russell Sage Foundation, New York, 1915.

men were interviewed, of whom 17 were American Negroes. The study tends to confirm the observation that contrary to practice in many fields race is not a handicap to Negroes in the selection of workmen. It is not, however, customary to hire Negroes and whites in the same group. A company will hire all Negroes or all whites.

Other Special Industries. Manufacturers of lamp shades, artificial flowers, mattress covers, and the packing industry engage important numbers of Negro women in Chicago; plate glass works in Pittsburgh used shortly after the war 29.8 per cent Negroes. The per cent in 1927, however, had declined to 4.0. Knitting of sweaters and hosiery in Pennsylvania, oyster and shrimp canning on the gulf coast, peanut factories, fireworks plants, in Virginia, and certain retanning processes of leather work for the New England shoe industry find Negro labor profitable. The Pullman car shops, located in Buffalo, Chicago and other cities use large groups of Negroes, and, fortunately for the Negro industrial schools, every trade taught, including blacksmithing, cabinetmaking, plumbing, saddle making, has a place in the shop. As a consequence the graduates of these schools are eagerly sought. Cement and asphalt work in road construction, the light, power and gas-making plants in both Northern and Southern cities freely used this labor. The report of the Commissioner of Labor of Georgia for the year 1923 shows 5,315 Negro workers in electric power and light companies. Brick and tile manufacturing and cotton oil mills, particularly in the South, require this labor. The most considerable though scattered employment, however, is that provided by railroad shops and round houses for Negro men, and laundries for Negro women.

The Trend in Negro Wages. The market rate is about the only standard for wages. Where the unions insist upon a higher scale, supported by arguments of increased living costs, the result is simply a dual wage scale, one for union workers, the other for those who take what employers feel that they are able to pay. When labor is plentiful wages go down; when scarce wages go up. The marginal character of Negro workers exposes them to the extreme fluctuations in the prices paid for labor. "The simplest economic discrimination," says Scott Nearing, "is in the rate of pay."

At least these observations may be made of the wages for Negro workers:

1. For unskilled work in the North, there is little difference between wages paid to Negroes and wages paid to non-union whites.
2. In most sections of the South, for unskilled work, the wages for Negroes are less than the wages paid to whites.
3. For skilled work in the North the scale of wages for whites and Negroes is practically the same, but Negroes do not get free access to the work.
4. For skilled work in the South Negroes have greater access but in most sections there is a dual wage scale.
5. The *entrance* rates of pay whether as a result of recent admission to industry, or of deliberate design are, in general, the *Negro* rates of pay.
6. On piece rates in the North there is the same scale, but Negroes are not freely allowed the piece work bringing highest weekly pay.
7. On piece work in the South there are occasional differences in scales as well as limitations to work bringing the lowest weekly returns.

Two exceptions to these tendencies appear. In certain plants, as a compensation for failure to advance Negro workers (where they have been long in the employ of a company) small increases in rates of pay are granted instead; and in a few lines of work where Negro labor has been especially favored because of the exceptionally poor grade of white workers available, Negroes have received slightly higher rates. For example, in Virginia Negro laborers and bricklayers' helpers have held a slight margin of excess over whites for a period of 23 years.

Sources of wage data are notoriously faulty, and although scattered wage rates are available for different years and occupations and localities, the serious gaps in information make impossible the construction of any dependable indices of the Negro rates.

Negro Wages in the South. In 1900 wages for Negro unskilled workers in mills and shops ranged from $5.50 to $8.25 weekly, varying with the locality. In Georgia and Virginia general laborers earned $4.75 weekly and railroad workers

$5.00. Railroad firemen earned $14.72. Carpenters could earn $10.00 in Virginia and $13.75 in Georgia. The average pay to Negroes in the South for skilled work appears to have been $10.50 and about $6.60 for unskilled work. Dr. W. E. B. DuBois while at Atlanta University cooperated with *The Tradesman* of Chattanooga in an inquiry in 344 plants employing Negroes in the South in 1902. Some 16,000 Negroes were employed, of whom about 20 per cent were skilled workers, receiving on an average of $2.00 a day while unskilled labor received about $1.00 per day. Farm labor received $2.00 to $2.75 per week in Georgia, usually with board; $2.70 in South Carolina and $1.50 to $2.50 in Virginia. Domestic servants received from $2.00 to $3.75 weekly, depending upon the nature of the work. The rate for tobacco strippers was $3.50, for stemmers $4.09 and packers $6.53 weekly.

Just prior to the migration from the South in 1916 these rates for Negroes were current in the South: In Virginia, general laborers $9.00, bricklayers' helpers $13.32, carpenters $10.38, plasterers $16.20; in Georgia, laborers $7.50 to $9.00, semi-skilled workers $9.00 to $12.00; skilled workers in plants $10.00 to $14.00. After the war and the general increase in wage rates, laborers in Georgia received $6.87 to $11.00, and in Virginia from $7.00 to $10.00. Farm laborers' rates had improved also to $3.50 and $4.00 weekly. T. R. Snavely [13] found in a study of the migration in 1917 that saw mills and turpentine distilleries were willing to pay $1.50 to $2.00, shipbuilding from $1.75 to $2.00 per day, and during September to December cotton planters would give $1.00 to $1.75 per 100 pounds for picking cotton. These were pressure prices which followed the large emigration of Negro workers.

The reports of the Industrial Commissioner of Virginia provide wage rates for Negro bricklayers and bricklayers' helpers which are fairly complete. The period covered is from 1904 to 1925. During this period bricklayers' wage rates increased from $2.10 to $8.71 and bricklayers' helpers from $1.91 to $4.18. Dr. Pinchbeck's Study of Negro artisans in Virginia [14] shows an increase in rates of pay for day laborers from

[13] Snavely, T. R., *Negro Migration in 1916-1917.* Report of United States Department of Labor, pp. 70-3.
[14] Pinchbeck, Raymond, *The Virginia Negro Artisan and Tradesman,* pp. 105-6.

$1.13 in 1900 to $3.11 in 1923. The peak was reached in 1919 when the rate was $3.56.

Negro Wages in the North. In 1917 Negro common labor received from 32 to 40 cents per hour in Illinois, Pennsylvania and Indiana. The rates varied slightly by states as well as by industries, but these represented, generally, a considerable increase over the rates obtaining at the same period in the South. The increases, however, were not the highest rates paid in the Northern industries.

Data assembled by Ira de A. Reid on Negro rates in Pittsburgh, in relation to the union scale reveal that these Negro rates consistently scaled downward from the prevailing union rates 35 per cent and more, and where the rates were fixed the Negroes were from 8 to 10 per cent less. Negro plumbers received from .60 to $1.44 per hour; union plumbers, all white, receive $1.60 per hour. Negro moulders received .60 and union moulders .75 per hour.

Detroit, the automobile center, paid generally highest rates of wages to Negroes as well as other workers. The Mayor's Interracial Committee in 1926, in its investigation of Negro industrial status,[15] offers data on rates of pay for that year based both upon employers' schedules and upon earnings of heads of families.

AVERAGE WAGE RATES: EMPLOYERS' SCHEDULES

Average Rate Per Hour	Firms	Employing
80 to 90 cents and over (note)	5	43 men
70 to 79 "	4	384 "
60 to 69 "	17	1,111 "
50 to 59 "	52	7,207 "
40 to 49 "	15	1,045 "
Under 40 cents	1	3 "
Other than by the hour	16	699 "
Not given	9	1,079 "
Total	119	11,571 men

NOTE: The average rate per hour at Ford's at this time (July 7, 1926) was 85 cents per hour. They employed about 10,000 Negroes in all parts of the plant, but their average wage rate could not be determined.

Differential Rates of Pay for White and Negro Workers. The pay of Negroes is usually less than that received by white workers and this occurs most frequently in the Southern states.

[15] Mayor's Interracial Committee, *The Negro in Detroit, 1926.* Study conducted by Forrester B. Washington and Robert Lansdale.

Ordinarily this is deliberate, and may be traced, in part, to the disposition of employers to compensate in larger pay to the white worker for the temporary social disadvantage in accepting work with which Negroes have been traditionally associated; in part to the belief that Negroes can "live on less" than the white worker; and in part to the desire to attract white workers of good quality. However, non-racial factors occasionally enter to produce the same result. For example, entrance rates of pay are less and where Negroes are newcomers to work they must accept these entrance rates. Labor organ-

SHOWING THE COMPARATIVE AVERAGE DAILY WAGE OF NEGROES AND WHITES IN CERTAIN TRADES LISTED UNDER GENERAL CONTRACTORS IN VIRGINIA

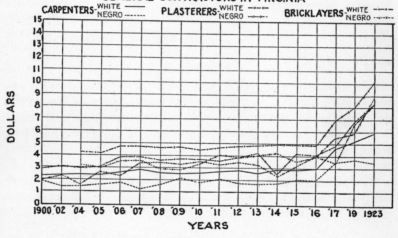

Figure 8

izations frequently determine rates for union and non-union men, and until recently organization has not troubled Negro workers seriously.

One circumstance has been important, however, in a large number of the new industrial positions of Negroes: the condition of employment for them, just as in the case of women, whether peacefully or as strike breakers, is smaller pay.

The course of wages for the two racial groups of workers is carefully traced by Dr. Pinchbeck [16] in Virginia. He found

[16] Pinchbeck, Raymond B., *The Virginia Negro Artisan and Tradesman*, pp. 105-6.

that the average daily wage of white plasterers over a period of 23 years was 20 per cent greater than the Negro average; for white lathers the average was 18 per cent greater; and for white bricklayers over the recorded period of 19 years the average was 29 per cent greater.

Summarizing these trends he says:

In those classes of work in the building trades involving primarily manual labor the wages of Negroes tend to closely approximate those of whites doing the same work. In the case of bricklayers' help the average wages of Negroes for the period exceed those of whites, by nine cents. However, in this instance the wages of white and Negro laborers is particularly significant in proving the strong tendency toward the coincidence of the wages received by the two races in unskilled labor. In two instances, 1906 and 1923, the average wages of Negro laborers in the building trades have exceeded those of whites. As the more skilled trades are considered the differences in the wages of Negroes and whites grow larger.

The reason for the difference in wage rates has some explanation in the fairly general exclusion of Negro skilled workers from trades unions in Virginia, the insufficiency of numbers of these workers in any given locality to permit effective separate organization, and the marginal nature of their position in the state's industries.

The Chamber of Commerce of Petersburg, Virginia, advertises its dual wage scale and a New York garment-making concern in 1927 posted this pay rate:

"White workers $24.00; Colored workers $20.00."

In one city in the South in which Negro and white iron workers are organized their union rates actually vary.

The deliberate double wage scale, while common enough, is yet less prevalent than the other forms of discrimination which effect the same result. In Baltimore the Negro women garment workers may not touch "white goods" which bring higher rates. Dr. T. J. Woofter, in his *Basis of Racial Adjustment,* observes that Negroes on piece work in certain plants are often assigned the most difficult patterns making production smaller, and where rates differ as in rough and smooth stone masonry they get only those which pay less. The laying off of Negro workers first in periods of depression, the method of classifying approximately the same work as skilled and unskilled, with different rates of pay, and limitation of Negro workers to "flat rates" instead of piece work when more can be earned on the latter, are additional factors in the lower pay of Negroes. For all of these differences there are explanations. In general these reduce to the blunt fact that employers tend to pay only what they must, and the Negro workers, recognizing their lower cost as a requisite of selection, where there is serious competition with white workers, accept what they can get.

Negro Wages and Living Costs. The National Industrial Conference Board's estimate of average minimum cost of maintaining a fair American standard of living for the family of an industrial worker in 1928 was as follows for the twelve selected cities:[17]   For New York City the weekly cost was set at $31.92; in Dayton, Ohio, a medium-sized city, it was $28.91; in Butler, Pennsylvania, selected apparently as one of the small cities, it was $27.87.

Assuming no unemployment, the most recent studies of Negroes available indicate that not many heads of families are able to meet such a standard unaided.   In New York City in 1927 a study of some 2,400 Negro families revealed that 87.2 per cent received less than $125.00 monthly, that is, less than $31.25 weekly.   Negro families in Fort Wayne, Indiana, a typical small city, received from $900.00 to $1,100.00 a year, or from $18.75 to $23.00 weekly.

A study of the incomes of 343 white unskilled workers and 80 Negroes from payrolls of employers in Chicago by Dr. Leila Houghteling in 1927 reveals that of the Negro families 50.0 per cent received less than $1,200.00 yearly as compared with 19.5 per cent of the whites.[18]   Those receiving less than $1,300.00 were 68.7 and 33.5 per cent, respectively.   The Department of Public Welfare in Chicago, under Mary McDowell, made an analysis of 1,244 families by specified earnings of the heads of families.   Five hundred and ninety of these families were Negroes.   Thirty per cent of them earned less than $80.00 per month; 44 per cent earned less than $100.00 per month; 75 per

---

[17] *The Wage Earner in New York and Other States,* National Industrial Conference Board, Inc., 1928.
[18] Houghteling, Leila, *The Income and Standard of Living of Unskilled Laborers in Chicago,* pp. 24-5.

cent earned less than $125.00 per month; 3 per cent earned more than $250.00 per month. The percentage of Negro workers in each group, except the $250.00 or more class, was smaller than in either the Mexican or foreign-born groups. In the southern section an index of present earnings may be found in 400 Negro families studied in January, 1929, in Nashville, Tennessee. The median weekly wage was $18.50.

These differences between earnings and an adequate maintenance budget appear to be distinctly reflected in other social problems discussed elsewhere in this volume.

The Detroit study [19] makes possible a direct comparison of wages received in Detroit with those received in the former homes of migrants. Of 1,000 families investigated it appears that in Detroit 15 per cent were receiving less than $25.00 weekly, whereas 71 per cent had received less than $25.00 in their former homes.

[19] Adapted from figures in Study of Mayor's Interracial Committee, Detroit, 1926.

CHAPTER V

NEGRO WOMEN AND CHILDREN
IN INDUSTRY

Range of Women's Work. Negro women came to industry
on the concurrent tides of the industrialization of women generally and of Negro men. The labor shortage following the
war was responsible for the speeded industrialization of both
groups. In the case of Negro women there has been not only
the handicap of race but of sex in industrial employment. In
1920 the Women's Bureau, cooperating with the Division
of Negro Economics of the Department of Labor, made an investigation in 17 localities of 9 states to gather urgently needed
data regarding these newcomers to industry. They found [1]
11,812 Negro women in 150 selected plants, or about 16.8 per
cent of all the workers. The prevailing occupations were found
to be in munitions, textiles, paper products, tobacco products,
candy, glass and clothing. The fever of war was abating and
some 20 additional plants which had employed Negro women
had discharged them before the inquiry began. It was made
clear in these instances that they had been used only because
white men and girls were temporarily not available. One-third
were working 10 hours and more per day, most of them were
on the less skilled processes of the work, and in some instances,
notably tobacco and glass, the unfavorable surroundings were
so serious as to prompt severe comment from the department
investigators. Occupations of white and Negro women in
tobacco, glass and textiles, were entirely different, and largely
so in leather, and food products. The peanut industry was
exclusively theirs. The work was largely seasonal and wages
showed wide diversity between white and Negro workers.
Only 39 firms gave them the same work and equal opportunities

[1] *Negro Women in Industry*, U. S. Department of Labor, Women's Bureau, Bulletin No. 20.

with white women workers, and 7 of these made discriminations in their pay envelopes.

The Director of the Women's Bureau, Miss Mary Anderson, in 1928 undertook to compile for the National Interracial Conference, from the original forms of the general industrial studies for women which have been made by the Women's Bureau in 15 states, the figures relating to Negro women in each of these states.

The 15 state studies included 17,134 Negro women in 682 establishments. Of this number, 4,850 in 370 plants were not tabulated, since the interest of the present study centers in the Negro women in the newer manufacturing pursuits, while those excluded were known to be engaged in occupations that have been considered customary for Negro women, such as sweeping and cleaning, or they were in laundries, hotels or restaurants. Of the number remaining, 12,123 were in 251 manufacturing plants, and 161 were in 61 general mercantile establishments. It is probable that not quite all of the women in the more traditional types of work have been excluded, since some whose occupations were not reported are likely to have been sweepers or cleaners, as may also have been some whose departments were reported but whose exact occupations were not specified; but if the duties of these few were not especially unusual, at least the scene of their labors had been shifted into the manufacturing world. Most of those in stores were maids, as were also a very few in certain miscellaneous industries. The 12,123 in manufacturing for whom reports were obtained constitute a fair sample—11.5 per cent of the 104,983 Negro women that the 1920 census records in manufacturing and mechanical industries, and, if exact occupations could be analyzed, the census numbers would include some of the sweepers and cleaners who have been omitted from the Women's Bureau study.

The industries covered included clothing, drugs, food products, glass, house furnishings, paper products, textiles, tobacco, wood products, electrical supplies, toilet goods and several others. Only 13.6 per cent of all the women in these were working 8 hours or less. The shortest hours were in slaughtering and meat packing, glass and metal products; the longest were in cotton yard goods, tobacco, wood products and waste products.

Wages. The occupations with highest median weekly earnings were: Sausage makers, $22.35; oyster shuckers, $11.50; tobacco feeders, $14.00; tobacco twisters, $12.60.

The lowest median weekly earners were: Chicken pickers, $7.75; clothing machine operators, $3.80; tobacco pickers, $7.30; tobacco bunchers, $1.85; boxers and craters, $3.75.

The largest numbers of Negro women were found in tobacco, laundries, textiles and food products, and the Southern states employing greatest numbers were Missouri, Georgia, Tennessee and Kentucky. The striking discrepancy in wages paid is an outstanding feature of the compilation. In Georgia 88.9 per cent of the Negro women, and 20.9 per cent of the white women earned less than $10.00 a week; 35 per cent of the Negro women and 10.02 per cent of the white women earned less than $5.00 per week.

State	*Less Than $10.00 Weekly*		*Less Than $5.00 Weekly*	
	White	*Negro*	*White*	*Negro*
Missouri	26.71	80.71	26.71	50.0
Tennessee	40.62	84.94	11.69	27.76

The per cent of white earnings received by Negro women was 74.6 in Alabama, 76.4 in Arkansas, 51.0 in Georgia, 77.9 in Kentucky, 78.4 in Mississippi, 41.1 in Missouri, 69.1 in New Jersey, 72.1 in Oklahoma and 62.6 in Tennessee.

Home Work. Some employers have utilized the plan of giving to Negro women work that can be done at home. It solves the problem of work room space as well as racial contacts in the industry. Frequently this arrangement is preferred by these women because it does not seriously disturb household duties and the care of their children.

Myra Colson studied a group of 100 of these workers in Chicago who were drawing work from 40 employers.[2] She found that most of these women workers were migrants from the South; that the length of residence in Chicago of these women extended from less than one year (6 months) to 28 years, more than two-thirds having lived in the city 5 years or more; that rents paid were relatively high; that housing

[2] Colson, Myra, "Negro Home Workers in Chicago," *The Social Service Review*, Vol. II, pp. 385-413.

conditions were fairly good; that their ages centered around 20 to 35 with relatively few extremely young or old workers in the group; that they had been formerly employed in unskilled or semi-skilled occupations; that they presented favorable employment record from the point of view of length of time with their present employer; and that these interviewed had considerable experience at home work.

The list of occupations which they had followed previously ranged from farming and home dressmaking to nursing and teaching. Almost half of them had previously been engaged in some kind of needle work. Of the various reasons given by workers for doing home work the most frequent was that of supplementing the income of the husband, whose wages were too low or too irregular.

The wages received revealed the present lack of organization of this type of work, for they varied from 9 cents to $2.00 per hour, and there appeared to be neither a uniform rate of payment, nor an attempt to pay according to the amount of time required to do the work. Added to this, the work was seasonal, subject to capricious reductions in rates, and extremely long hours were required to make it pay.

Child Labor. The number of children between 10 and 17 gainfully employed in 1920 was about three times as great among Negroes as among native whites. In 1920, 442,585 Negro children, between 10 and 15 years of age were working. This was a percentage of 18.5 as compared with 8.4 for the country as a whole and 5.3 for native whites. It was twice as great in Georgia, Louisiana, Mississippi and South Carolina, although child labor in Southern states is generally high. Three careful studies of child welfare, one in Texas, one in Maryland, and another in Virginia, go beyond the bare figures of the census in attempting to measure the relation of several social factors. Hill and Rusk counties, of the cotton-growing areas of Texas, were found to be typical of those sections of the state with work in which children were used, and many children under 16 were engaged in field work. The median duration of field work, by months, of Negro boys and girls in Hill County was 5.9 months and of white boys and girls 4.5 months. The children of both races between the ages of 13 and 16 years averaged approximately 4 months. In Rusk County there was found a difference of one month favoring the white child in the total months of field work. Children of both races between the ages of 13 and 16 worked practically 4 months as in Hill County. In Hill County there were found 942 white children between 6 and 16 years of age, of which 370, or 39.0 per cent, were absent from school on account of farm work. In Rusk County 199 or 32.3 per cent of its 616 white children were out of school for the season. Of 124 Negro children studied in Hill County, 48 or 38.7 per cent were found absent from school as against 166, or 33.3 per cent, of the 499 Negro children in Rusk County.

Of a total of 644 white children in Hill County, 375 were retarded 1 year and 10 were advanced, while among the Negro children 38 out of 40 were retarded and none were advanced.

On the Maryland truck farms a Children's Bureau study [3] found 808 children working, of whom 328, or 40 per cent, were Negro children. These were used principally for picking, transplanting and hoeing. According to the reports given by parents, a majority of the white and the Negro children suffered a loss of schooling on account of farm work. Nearly one-fifth of the white children had been absent for farm work 30 or more school days, or 6 or more school weeks during the preceding year. Fewer Negro children lost as much actual time from school because of farm work for the reason that, following an old custom, their schools were closed during a large part of the busy season on the truck farms.

The Norfolk section of Virginia, which includes Princess Anne, Norfolk, Nansemond, Isle of Wight and York counties, is considered one of the most intensive truck-farming areas [4] in the United States. Eight hundred and ninety children under 16 years of age were working on these farms, of whom only 17 were white. These Negro children represented a low economic and social level. In two-thirds of the families one or the other parent could not read and write and in 20 per cent of the families both parents were illiterate. Although not all of these worked for long periods, one-fifth of the number had worked on at least 6 truck crops during the year. The major-

[3] *Child Labor on Maryland Truck Farms,* United States Department of Labor. Alice Channing, pp. 51-2.
[4] *Child Labor and the Work of Mothers, on Norfolk Truck Farms.* Children's Bureau Publication No. 130.

ity of them were under 14 years of age. Only 53.4 per cent of them had attended as much as 70 per cent of the school term. Since the study in 1924 the state compulsory school attendance law has been amended and may, if applied with less diffidence than before, bring about some changes.

CHAPTER VI

EMPLOYERS' OPINIONS OF THE COMPETENCE OF NEGRO LABOR

Although much discussion on the use of Negro labor has centered about their efficiency, practically no scientific measurements of relative industrial efficiency have been made. The opinions of employers have been relied upon as a measure of the quality of labor and these have varied with locality, time, and the type of work which Negroes have been permitted to do. Current demand for labor, the varied contacts and experience of employers with Negroes in this relation, and the accidental selection of workers from among the Negro working population may seriously affect these opinions.

Efficiency and Regularity. In 1891 *The Tradesman,* a Southern publication edited by George W. Ochs, sent out a questionnaire on Negro labor designed to draw information regarding wages, efficiency and the effect of training on Negro labor. Replies were received from 1,196 employers in Southern states using a total of 7,393 Negro workers, 978 of whom were skilled, and about 2,000 semi-skilled. The trend of the replies expressed satisfaction with Negro labor and a practically unanimous decision was made to continue the employment of Negroes and to advance them to more skilled positions. Sixty-seven plants employing 2,414 laborers reported an increase in efficiency; 43 using 2,279 workers, reported no improvement, and 15 employing 1,369 workers were in doubt as to whether or not there had been any improvement in efficiency.

An investigation in 1893 by the *Manufacturers' Record* of Baltimore revealed that the majority of manufacturers thought that Negro labor was at that time unfitted for work in manufacturing, but that training and discipline would undoubtedly fit them for this work. In 1902, *The Tradesman* in cooperation with Dr. W. E. B. DuBois extended the scope of its inquiry to 500 leading manufacturers of the South, 334 of these concerns employing Negro as well as white laborers. Of 36,404 workers 16,489 were Negroes. In the heavy work of these plants, Negroes were found to be superior to other laborers, but they were thought not so good in the skilled factory work. General satisfaction with Negro labor was expressed by the manufacturers, and practically all of them planned to continue using it. A rather larger number said that they wanted "all the Negro skilled labor" that they could get.

Dr. DuBois in 1906 in an article in the American Economic Association series [1] expressed the feeling that the average Negro worker at that period was probably less efficient than the average European. Katherine Coman,[2] writing in the American Statistical Association Journal from census figures of 1900, came to the conclusion that "the Negro farmer expends less per acre than any other agriculturist in the United States except the Indian and Hawaiian, and gets a higher return than any except the Chinese and Japanese."

The study of women in Georgia industries by the Women's Bureau, in 1918, cites one plant owner as saying, "The Negro girls receive a lower rate than the white, but produce about as much and do not complain at having to sweep around their own machines." Continuing, the report comments that "the danger is not that the Negro women will be able to do the work better than the white women, but that they will work for wages below the minimum accepted by the white workers."

A recent study of Negro women as industrial workers in Philadelphia observed that 23 of 64 employers interviewed were entirely satisfied with their colored employees, 16 thought them "slow," "careless," or "unreliable," 5 considered them "inferior" to white workers, 7 were satisfied with those they had, but did not care to employ more, or to try them in other departments, 2 employed them on one process, but had found them inefficient on others, and 11 were satisfied with the quality of their work, but found them unsatisfactory in other respects, principally in regularity of attendance. The garment industry itself, it might be noted, is notorious for irregu-

[1] DuBois, W. E. B., American Economic Association, series 3, Vol. VII, 1906.
[2] Coman, Katherine, "The Negro as a Peasant Farmer," *American Statistical Association Journal*, July, 1904.

larity of employment, holding one of the most prominent places in the list of industries described as "seasonal."

The West Virginia report of the Bureau of Negro Welfare and Statistics, 1925-26, gives the results of an inquiry among employers of the state regarding Negro efficiency, regularity, and "loyalty." There were 70 favorable and 39 unfavorable replies.

Missouri employers of Negro women report [3] that on the whole they were less steady than the whites and less skilled. One of the Phelps-Stokes Studies [4] observes significantly that "it is true that there are many white employers of the state who regard highly the skill of Negro tradesmen, but, on the other hand, the vast majority regard the Negro tradesman as a marginal man and perhaps below the margin of effective employment as compared with available whites in the same trades."

The Westinghouse Electric and Manufacturing Corporation employed 514 Negroes in 1923 and 990 in 1920, in each year 4 per cent of the total numbers of workers [5] The personnel manager gave as his opinion that the Negro workers were both dependable and punctual.

The Mayor's Interracial Committee of Detroit in 1926 sent out questionnaires in which were included questions regarding efficiency, regularity and turnover. The following table gives a more detailed picture of the results:

TABLE II

EFFICIENCY OF NEGROES AS COMPARED TO WHITE WORKERS ACCORDING TO OPINIONS OF EMPLOYERS

Degree of Efficiency	Firms	Employing
More efficient than white	11	5,102
Same efficiency as white	68	12,631 (approximate)
Less efficient than white	24	2,729
Not given	16	1,109
Total	120	21,571

[3] *Women in Missouri Industries,* Women's Bureau, Bulletin No. 35.
[4] Pinchbeck, Raymond, *The Virginia Negro Artisan and Tradesman,* Phelps-Stokes Study No. 7, 1927.
[5] McClelland, Edward S., "Negro Labor in the Westinghouse Electric and Manufacturing Corporation." *Opportunity,* Vol. I, pp. 22-3.

TABLE III

REGULARITY OF NEGRO AS COMPARED TO WHITE WORKERS ACCORDING TO
OPINIONS OF EMPLOYERS

Degree of Regularity	Firms	Employing
More regular	7	199
Same	68	8,864
Less	33	11,587 (note)
Not given	12	921
Total	120	21,571 (one approximation)

NOTE: These tables indicate that two-thirds of the employers hiring 82 per cent of the Negro men rated their Negro workers as efficient or more efficient than white workers; that although some employers reported that Negro workers were more regular, or just as regular as whites, the majority felt that Negro workers were slightly less regular than white workers. The recent migration was felt to be responsible for the high rate of irregularity. Labor turnover for Negro employees was thought to be generally less than for white employees.

Questionnaires were also sent to employers in Minneapolis, by Abram Harris [6] in his survey of the Negro population of that city. Eighty-three plants had at some time employed Negro labor. Of these 40 said their Negro labor was "regular" and 11 said that it was not, while 32 did not reply to the question. Of these same employers, 37 said that the Negroes were efficient; 13 said that the Negroes were not efficient, and 33 did not reply to the question.

Of the 137 plants questioned by the Chicago Commission on Race Relations [7] in 1920, 118 reported that Negro labor had proved satisfactory; 19 reported that it had not.

In such an array there is little certainty that the fact of efficiency or inefficiency has been established, but for the present at least employers' opinions of fitness rather than scientific measurement are most important in determining plant policy. The closest approach to actual comparison of white and Negro efficiency is provided in the study conducted by Dr. George E. Haynes [8] for the Division of Negro Economics of the U. S. Department of Labor in 1918-19.

Comparative Industrial Ability. Using as a measure of comparative industrial ability, average number of hours worked per

[6] Harris, Abram, *The Negro in Minneapolis.*
[7] *The Negro in Chicago,* Chicago Commission on Race Relations.
[8] Haynes, George E., director, *The Negro at Work During the World War,* U. S. Department of Labor, Division of Negro Economics, 1921.

week, average earnings per week and average earnings per hour, the study covered 4,260 white men and 2,722 Negro men in 194 occupations of 23 establishments. Six basic industries

TABLE IV

NEGRO LABOR SATISFACTORY OR UNSATISFACTORY IN ESTABLISHMENTS

CLASSIFIED BY INDUSTRIES

Industry	Total Number Establishments	Total Negroes Employed	Establishments Reporting Negro Labor Satisfactory		Establishments Reporting Negro Labor Unsatisfactory	
			Number	Number of Negroes Employed in These Establishments	Number	Number of Negroes Employed in These Establishments
Manufacturing:						
Clothing	0	203	8	191	1	12
Food products	8	7,597	7	7,547	1	50
Iron and steel	27	3,879	22	3,750	5	129
Tanneries	7	462	6	421	1	41
Miscellaneous [9]	18	713	13	464	5 [10]	249
Totals	60	12,854	56	12,373	13	481
Non-manufacturing:						
Railroads	16	5,408	16	3,408	..	...
Hotels	9	923	8	911	1	12
Laundries	20	763	16	587	4	177
Mail order	2	1,773	2	1,773	..	...
Public Service	4	42	4	42	..	...
Taxicab upkeep	1	250	1	250	..	...
Miscellaneous	16	323	15	296	1	27
Totals	68	9,482	62	9,267	6	216
Totals, all industries	137	22,356	118	21,640	19	697

were included in these establishments. In the skilled units of foundry work Negro workers showed a higher average number of hours worked per week than white workers and higher average earnings per hour in one unit. In 3 units Negro work-

[9] Includes a scattering list of industries represented by one to three establishments—Negro labor not important factor in these industries.

[10] Includes 3 paper-box manufacturing plants with 10, 20 and 113 Negro employees, largely women; and cooperage plant with 96 Negro employees and 1 sausage-casing plant with 10 Negroes. These plants reported Negro labor "slow," "lazy," or unreliable.

ers showed a lower average number of hours worked and in 5 units a lower average of earnings per hour. In the skilled occupations of the slaughtering and packing industry Negroes showed higher average hours and earnings than white workers. In semi-skilled work in 5 foundries Negroes showed higher hours and earnings per hours in three units, and lower average in 2. In automobile establishments Negroes showed the same average hours and earnings per hour as white workers. The semi-skilled group as a whole with 25 total units of comparison showed Negro averages higher in 8 units, lower in 5 units and the same as whites in 12 units. In the unskilled occupations studied there were 52 units of comparison. In 23 of these Negroes showed a higher average of hours worked per week, in 18 a higher average of earnings per hour. In 16 they showed lower hours per week, and in 22 lower earnings per hour. There were the same hours worked in 13 units and earnings per hour in 12 units. Comparisons for all work in a total of 85 units may be represented as follows:

```
Negro higher average hours worked per week ............ 35
Negro lower average hours worked per week ............. 25
The same average hours worked per week ................ 25
Negro higher average earnings per hour ................ 28
Negro lower average earnings per week ................. 33
The same average earnings per week .................... 24
```

Objections to Negro Labor. Some of the causes of exclusion of Negroes from plants may be summarized as follows:

1. Traditional policy of the plant not to employ Negroes.
2. Fear of racial difficulties if whites and Negroes are introduced into the same plant.
3. Fear of the objection of white workers and resultant labor difficulties.
4. Traditional beliefs about the Negro which concern their mentality and character, and general inability to perform the work required.
5. Fear of bringing Negroes into contact with white women workers.
6. Lack of training of Negroes for certain jobs.
7. Unsatisfactory experience with Negro workers in the past.

8. Advocacy of certain jobs as belonging exclusively to the white race.

9. Expense that would be involved in making alterations in the building to accommodate white and Negro workers separately.

10. Objection of labor unions.

Absenteeism and Turnover. Complaints of employers regarding Negro labor have stressed absenteeism, incompetence, the practice of drawing pay in advance, high labor turnover, requirement of more supervision than white workers, and shiftlessness. All of these have been observed of some Negro workers. It should be noted, however, that when Negro labor is referred to, it is rather as a group than as individuals, some of whom are poor, some fair and others good workers. White workers, on the other hand, are usually considered as individuals. An unfortunate experience with one does not preclude the employment of others of the same race. This doubtless accounts, in a measure, for the extremes of opinion as well as experiences of employers. Most frequent among the complaints is that of absenteeism.[11] This is thought to be characteristic of Southern Negroes recently inducted into Northern industry. The habit of irregular work in the South and tolerance of this as a Negro trait, has been offered as the explanation of irregularities in attendance. The fact is frequently observed, particularly in the almost anonymous unskilled jobs of large plants. On the employer's side it introduces problems of production as well as bookkeeping. Ninety-two employers in Chicago were asked about the reliability of their Negro workers. Sixty-three thought that they did not require more supervision than white; twenty-eight thought that they did. About three-fifths of the firms considered their absenteeism no greater than the whites while the others regarded their absenteeism greater than the whites.

D. T. Farnham[12] offered in *Industrial Management* an estimate of the values of Negro labor based upon thirty years'

[11] The Quarterly Report of the Welfare and Economic Work in the Detroit plant of the American Car and Foundry Company gives in unusual detail the causes and percentages of Negroes lost to the service of the company during a period—October 1, 1918, to January 1, 1919.

[12] Farnham, D. T., "Negroes as a Source of Industrial Labor," *Industrial Management,* August, 1918.

experience as a plant manager with them. Because of their "type," he maintained, Irish foremen are deemed the best bosses of Negro labor. Firmness is absolutely necessary with them. He found that labor turnover among unskilled Negro workers is about 50 per cent higher than among whites; that the Negro needs someone to think for him; that he tends to slow down to the speed of the slowest members of his gang; that he will seldom work under a Negro boss; that he often has trouble with his feet "because he hates to spend money for shoe leather"; that he takes to bathing naturally; that a certain amount of segregation is needed in the plant to preserve the peace; that the Negro "cannot stand the idea of missing Christmas away from home"; that he minds the heat less than the cold; and that work with periodic rest periods is the better type in which to employ them.

A compilation of returns by the Department of Public Welfare of Pennsylvania shows the following comparisons of Negro labor with whites:

EFFICIENCY AND REGULARITY OF NEGRO WORKERS IN PENNSYLVANIA

| | Efficiency | |
	Number of Establishments	Negroes Employed
Better than white	14	1,780
As good as white	32	6,400
Poorer than white	10	1,120
	56	9,300

	Regularity	
Better than white	3	431
As good as white	28	6,321
Poorer than white	25	2,548
	56	9,300

A statistical account of the work history of 996 Negro men in the employ of the Detroit plant of the American Car and Foundry Company [13] showed an average absence for personal reasons of 3 men a day from October 6th to January 1st. During that time 4 per cent of the Negro work force

[13] Quarterly report of the Welfare and Economic Work by the Assistant Director of Negro Work, American Car and Foundry Company, Detroit plant, from October 6th, 1918, to January 1st, 1919.

died from influenza. Fifty-four per cent of the force had been employed from 3 to 6 months.

The Director of Personnel for the Westinghouse Electric and Manufacturing Corporation in New Jersey, while stating that the Negro has been given little real chance for advancement in the plant, noted that 22 out of 35 Negroes took all their money out of the savings fund and cancelled their group life insurance just to have their money. However, he found that "Negroes lose no more time because of sickness, in fact not as much as the average white worker; they are obedient in every sense of the word, industrious, and, all in all, the Westinghouse Electric and Manufacturing Company is well impressed with them." [14]

The National Malleable Castings Company of Cleveland, Indianapolis and Chicago employed Negroes for 30 years at common labor. It now employs them as molders, coremakers, chippers, fitters, locomotive crane operators, melting furnace operators, general foremen, foremen, assistant foremen, clerks and timekeepers. It is the belief of the company that the Negro's record of absenteeism is a little better than the shop average. [15]

George T. Odell, [16] of Cleveland, published in *Tradewinds,* the results of certain inquiries in the state regarding Negro labor.

A superintendent of a rolling mill in Youngstown had reported an annual turnover of 1,250 for a force of 150 Negro laborers. The Negro temperament had been found exasperating to two other plants. This temperament involved indifference to the virtue of sustained labor, and a "tremendous penchant for funerals." The latter was important because of the frequent absences of "lodge members."

A second article on this subject, by John B. Abell, [17] based upon the experiences of Cleveland manufacturers, appeared two months later in the same publication and provided an employer's opinion which appears to have been based upon wider experience with Negro workers.

[14] McClellan, Edward S., "Negro Labor in the Westinghouse Electric and Manufacturing Corporation." *Opportunity,* Vol. I, pp. 22-3.
[15] House, I. O., "Negro Labor and the Industries." *Opportunity,* Vol. I, pp. 20-2.
[16] Odell, George T., "The Northern Migration of the Negro." *Tradewinds,* January, 1924.
[17] Abell, John B., "The Negro in Industry," *Tradewinds,* March, 1924.

Some 75 large employers of Negro labor had been questioned regarding their efficiency. It was noted that there were classes of Negroes, some intelligent, skilled and unskilled; others ignorant and inefficient.

The objections charging "lay-offs," "lack of ambition," "natural laziness," "craving for entertainment," when examined were found to have warrant in so far as they involved the inevitable shiftless element in any group. Moreover, the first contact of the Southern Negroes with Northern industries carried over to a degree some of the working customs of the South. It was a process of adaptation.

As they have become more accustomed to their new freedom here and the customs of the North, they have shown no tendency to become shiftless, but rather have they become more independent of charity and more regular at their work. Social agencies find that the Negro is more readily adaptable to new social conditions than most races.

Regarding turnover, some plants with as many as 25 per cent Negroes in the total working force reported that they were responsible for 75 per cent of the turnover. However, this was in unskilled work where turnover generally is high, and an equal number of firms stated that the Negro turnover had not been, even at the start, any greater than for other racial groups.

Too often the employer has turned to the Southern Negro simply in the hope that he could be pulled out of a tight labor difficulty in this fashion. The result is that the employer puts the newcomer on what might be termed turnover work—work not fitted to the man's training, and upon which there would be a constant change of employees under any circumstances.

Adaptability. The Director of the Bureau of Employment for the Pennsylvania Department of Labor and Industry tried to learn from 1,000 firms the extent to which Negroes are found adaptable to their work. They are adaptable, he discovered, in all lines ranging from common labor to skilled work but not in the same places. Whereas, one firm employing 30 Negroes found their adaptability limited, another employing 50 found them an absolute necessity. Another could use them only on concrete work, another only as laborers, another only on furnaces, another on asphalt work, and still another found them average workers in any line.

An interesting chart of racial adaptability to various types of plant work was assembled from the experiences of a large group of plants in the Pittsburgh district, by an employer's association to serve as a guide in selecting workers from some 36 different races and groups. The measure of the Negro worker's adaptability is given as follows:

Good	Fair	Poor
Concrete	Pick and shovel	Machinist's helper
Road repairing	Hod carrier	Carpenter's helper
Carrying material	Wheelbarrow	Blacksmith's helper
Cleaning and care	Tank cleaning	Pipe fitter's helper
taking	Trucking	Engineer's helper
Building demolition	Track repairing	Work requiring preci-
Coal passer and fireman	Shovelling material in	sion
Work requiring speed	bulk	Cold and wet work
Hot and dry work	Stills and furnaces	Work exposed to
Hot and wet work	Rigger's helpers	weather
Dusty work	Boilermaker's helpers	Work in variable tem-
Smoky fumy work	Closely confined work	peratures
Oily work	Dirty work	
	Night work	
	Shift work	

The American Management Association [18] concludes after its own inquiry in 1923 that the tenure of the Negro in Northern industry depends principally upon the employer. The Negro has certain advantages over foreign labor in that he understands English and is at once amenable to the influences of discipline, trade training and health education.

Plant Policy. In a survey of the industrial status of Negroes in Los Angeles, California, in 1926, by the writer, for the Department of Research and Investigation of the National Urban League, 456 plants of widely varying character were reached. Equally as interesting as any of the figures on Negro inclusion in industry, skill, wages and comparative efficiency, were the various configurations of policy, in each case declared to be founded upon the same racial instincts. The most frequently encountered policy was one based upon the belief that "Negro and white workers will not mix." They did "mix," however, in over 50 of the plants studied. In certain plants where Mexicans were regarded as white, Negroes were not allowed to "mix" with them; where Mexicans were classed as colored Negroes not only worked with them but were given positions over them. In certain plants Mexicans and whites worked together;

---

[18] American Management Association, Survey Report No. 5, 1923.

in some others white workers accepted Negroes and objected to
Mexicans; still in others white workers accepted Mexicans and
objected to Japanese. White women worked with Mexican and
Italian women, but refused to work with Negroes. Mexicans
and Negroes worked under a white foreman; Italians and Mexicans under a Negro foreman; and Mexicans in some places
were refused entirely because of plant policies against "mixing."
In a hospital Negro nurses attended white patients, but were
segregated from white nurses in the dining halls; in a manufacturing plant white workers refused to work with Negroes,
but worked under a Negro foreman. Brick manufacturing was
declared too hot and dusty for Negroes, yet the Negroes were
reputed to be the best brickworkers and were given a better scale
of wages than Mexicans; people from Southern climates were
regarded as better adapted to work in the presence of heat than
those from colder climates, but the Consolidated Ice Companies
found the Mexicans best fitted for handling and storing ice.
Because white elevator men and attendants in a department
store disturbed the morale of the organization by constant chat-
ting and flirtations with the salesgirls, Negro men were brought
into their places and morale was restored, in spite of the fears
that the races would not "mix." The solution is not untypical
and suggests the importance of plant policy in Negro industrial
relations.

Ralph W. Immel,[19] who is connected with a large industrial
concern near Baltimore, argues, in an article in *Industrial Management* that a large part of the ill success of the companies'
Negro labor is due to an inefficient labor policy. His company,
in his judgment, has been successful and he sets down this
policy as responsible for the successful experience with Negro
workers:

1. Segregation—The workers were not segregated.
2. Responsibility—A Negro welcomes responsibility and
   possesses a higher degree of faithfulness in following
   orders implicitly than many white or alien workmen.
3. Types of work best suited—Tasks demanding extra exer-
   tion but having periods of rest; taken with spectacular

[19] Immel, Ralph W., "The Negro and His Opportunity," *Industrial Magazine*, July, 1919.

but intermittent display of strength; work that possesses rhythm and which can be accompanied by song.

4. Supervision—Use white until colored foremen are available.

5. Lassitude—"The Negro is the original efficiency engineer."

6. Thrift and Health—He can develop a better status in these affairs.

General Observations from Plant Experience with Negro Labor. So far as the ordinary industrial jobs, unskilled and skilled, are concerned there are many instances of non-employment of Negroes, but no evidence that Negroes are incapable of performing the tasks, as indicated by the fact that for practically each job for which they are declared incapable in some plants they are actually working on them in others. There is an understandable fear in many plants that use of Negroes and whites in the same plants will bring unfavorable results, but no evidence that the fear is always well founded in fact, since there are many plants that employ Negroes with white workers in the same sections without conspicuous friction. The varied experiences of the plants may reasonably be traced to peculiarities of plant management and to the types of Negro workers secured.

The quality of Negro labor has not been uniform, and there is evidence that in many places where poor opinion is entertained concerning them, it is well deserved; but the opinion unfortunately and erroneously extends from one inefficient group of Negro workers to include the entire Negro working population. There are lines of work which are not attractive to Negro workers in which many of them have given indifferent service. Circumstances which should be taken into account in judgments of Negro "ambition," "reliability," "speed," "carefulness," etc., in particular plants are: the relative wages, opportunities for promotion, regularity of attendance on the basis of distance from the restricted area, methods of handling working crews, types and character of work assigned to Negroes in the particular plants. The inexperience of rural and small town Negro workers in industry and consequent lack of training have aided in establishing the convictions about Negro inefficiency. Generally, the frequent barrier to promotion and advancement has been observed to foster indifference among Negro workers, and a loss of what has been described as "hope on the job." The use of Negroes as marginal workers has the effect of producing the features of "casuals" in industry.

The trend of information indicates that where wages are good and some prospect of bettering conditions is present, Negro labor is regarded as more satisfactory than in plants in which Negro working crews are separated from other workers on grades of work which the others are unwilling to do. The objection of white workers to Negro workers is understandable as a basis for employers' exclusion of Negro workers, but there is evidence that this objection is not a permanent or deeply serious contingency, and further evidence that the objection has faded after a short period of contact. The fear of the competition of Negro workers on the part of the white workers is in known instances based upon the fear that Negroes will be paid less wages, thus either lowering their living standards or pushing them out of jobs. When this evidence is seen in a situation an essential part of the truth is omitted in the statement of employers, unqualifiedly that "white workers object to the bringing in of Negro workers."

On the surface of facts, Negro workers seem to have a special usefulness in iron and steel production, slaughtering and meat packing, in chemicals, longshore work, and generally where strength must be combined with agility and a certain amount of deftness. Despite the strength of opinion to the contrary they show an unexpectedly large number of crane operators, sand blasters, cupola tenders and rip saw operators, asphalt workers, and drivers of heavy machinery.

There is probably no more actual truth in the belief that they are better adapted than most races to work in the presence of heat than that they cannot do skilled work; rather the probability is that having been permitted "heat" jobs on this assumption, a normal success has provided support for the assumption. The chances are that the course of local policy and practice in industry has been shaped more by economic forces than racial ones. Rapid growth of industries recently has encouraged and drawn quantities of cheap labor from Europe, Mexico and the rural sections of America. Severe competition, even after the restriction of European immigrations, is at present observed in the lower grades of work, where Negroes are principally found, and between Negroes, European immigrants, Mexicans and a class of native whites without skill.

A reasonable conclusion is that since such widely different experiences are reported by different plants with the same race of workers, the problem is probably one of individual differences among Negro workers. No studies have been located which attempt in any way to measure the differences in individual industrial ability.

Negroes as Skilled Workers. The bulk of Negro labor has been unskilled and valuable to industry largely as bulk labor. Beyond unskilled lines of work more competition is encountered. During the period of slavery, when the population fell pronouncedly into the two divisions, master and slave, little concern was felt over the effects of Negro slave workers upon non-slave-holding whites. The more intelligent of the Negro slaves were trained as artisans and after supplying the needs of the plantations and domestic duties of town life, were leased for work requiring special skill. It has been a strange irony of history that the white workers who once protested the preference of skilled Negroes by contractors, leaving them starving and miserable, may now assert that Negroes lack even the capacity for skill.

The war forced the drafting of Negro workers into all grades of work. Negro men as well as white and Negro women were used during this emergency for semi-skilled and skilled work. A study by the Division of Negro Economics, under Dr. George E. Haynes, covers some of the results of this new induction of Negro men into skilled lines. The Emergency Fleet Corporation, in which Negroes were used as carpenters, boilermakers, calkers, blacksmiths, and in other lines, yielded excellent figures by race and employment. The division into skilled and unskilled workers for the eight districts is given on p. 83.

Of 38,723 Negroes employed in the divisions 8,835, or 22.81 per cent were skilled. In several places they established notable records for speed on skilled processes.

An inquiry undertaken in New York City, 1921-23, by Karl Y. Phillips, through the Department of Labor (unpublished) included 3,007 Negro workers, in 7 lines of work, of whom 31.53 per cent were classed as skilled. Of 42,159 skilled workers reached through a group of selected industries 948, or 2.25 per cent were Negroes. In glass, automobile repairing, laundry work, stevedoring and on common carriers they were above this proportion. In other fields they were below.

TABLE V

NEGRO EMPLOYEES WORKING AT PLANTS UNDER THE JURISDICTION OF THE UNITED STATES SHIPPING BOARD—EMERGENCY FLEET CORPORATION—DURING AND AFTER THE WAR, IN THE EIGHT PRINCIPAL SHIPPING DISTRICTS, 1918-19.

(Columns 1, during the war; columns 2, after the war)

	Southern District		Middle Atlantic District		Delaware River District	
	1	2	1	2	1	2
Total number employed	11,991	5,504	4,506	5,223	5,165	2,230
Skilled	3,578	3,078	117	114	....	99
Unskilled	8,413	2,426	4,389	5,109	5,165	2,131

	Northern Atlantic District		Gulf District		Southern Pacific District	
	1	2	1	2	1	2
Total number employed	371	297	1,830	309	582	399
Skilled	258	218	541	109	309	171
Unskilled	113	79	1,289	200	273	281

	Northern Pacific District		Great Lakes District		Total		Grand Total
	1	2	1	2	1	2	
Total number employed	176	96	27	17	24,648	14,075	38,723
Skilled	140	72	20	11	4,963	3,872	8,835
Unskilled	36	25	7	6	19,685	10,203	29,888

Raymond B. Pinchbeck,[20] Ph.D., a Phelps-Stokes Fellow, 1923-25, at the University of Virginia, is responsible for one of the most valuable studies, thus far published, of Negro skilled workers. He found the rate per 10,000 population of white artisans in excess of the Negroes for the 31 trades studied in all but 6. These were bakers, coopers, firemen (exclusive of locomotive and fire department), painters, sawyers and tailors. These are, incidentally, the trades most rapidly disap-

[20] Pinchbeck, Raymond, The Virginia Negro Artisan and Tradesman, University of Virginia, 1925.

pearing. The greatest excesses were found among carpenters where the rate per 10,000 for whites was 291.7 and Negroes 89.2, and machinists where the white rate was 155.6 and the Negro rate 17.2.

The Department of Labor found, in 1923, that Negro skilled workers had increased as a result of the northward migration on an average of 34 per cent in the industries to which the largest number of migrants went between 1920 and 1923. Mr. John B. Abell,[21] giving the result of an inquiry in Cleveland industries, says:

". . . Of 442 Negroes employed in one plant, making materials which require accuracy and rather complicated skill, 237 of them are engaged in the most skilled portion of the production. There are 128 on semi-skilled, or routine machine jobs, and but 77 doing common labor. The firm has used colored labor for nearly 10 years, and their people have developed from the ranks of the laborers.

"The manager of the plant reports the following as some of the different classes of work upon which the colored people are succeeding, and on which there has been no indication of the Negroes' physical make-up serving as a drawback: Drop hammer men, rolling machines, hot work presses, up-setters, shearmen, cranes, auto repairs, bending machines, belt men, carpenters, heat treating and grinders."

The reactions of present employers on the question of skilled Negro workers may be grouped as follows:

(a) Those who think they cannot perform other than unskilled work because of limited intelligence;
(b) Those who think they can perform other than unskilled tasks but lack both training and the opportunity for training;
(c) Those who entertain the belief that Negro workers are inherently incapable of jobs requiring skill and responsibility, but who have not tested these beliefs by any experiment;
(d) Those who believe that they are capable of skilled responsible work; because they are at present engaged upon it, or have been known to perform it satisfactorily.

[21] Abell, John B., "The Negro in Industry," *Tradewinds*, March, 1924.

Two factors are requisite in the development of skilled workers: (a) apprenticeship, (b) vocational schools. Only about 65 Negro apprentices are recorded for the manufacturing industries. It is indicated in the figures given in another part of this volume that so far as industry is concerned, the majority of Negroes go into the building trades, iron and steel, lumber, and, according to special geographical sections, textiles, petroleum refining, slaughtering and meat packing. Acquirement of skill except in crises is largely a personal matter and custom is making this more difficult for Negroes who wish to move out of unskilled work. The trades of carpentry, bricklaying and painting are gradually leaving the hands of Negroes, and with these the chances for training apprentices are diminishing.

Several suggestions are possible: the first is that of isolating special lines of work, beginning with those in which there is least social resistance to Negro workers, and developing specializations within these, leading to prestige and preference over purely racial handicaps. There are fields for specializations which do not require prohibitively elaborate equipment for training even within educational institutions:

Decorator, tinsmith, tile setter, electric wirer, tool-maker, pattern maker, metal pattern maker, draftsman, molder, core maker, dye sinker, welder, compositor, pressman, lithographer, plate printer, copper etcher, power press embosser, photo-engraver, knitting machine adjuster, weaver, warper, auto electrician, auto painter, wire weaver, meat cutter, stonecutter, photographer, retoucher, paper ruler, stone and metal artist, artificial-limb maker, junior engineer, furrier and upholsterer.

A second possibility is that of increasing the value and desirability of their labor by conscious development of a superior technique in the old lines.

Industrial Training and Specialization. Industrial education in general has reached a point of importance demanding consideration as a problem. There was no problem of training for industry for anyone when the occupational activities of the country were largely agricultural, when apprenticeship for the hand trades was functioning through the natural father and son relationship, adoption, and the practice of binding out for periods. With the coming of machinery and the disappearance

of the guilds this arrangement was broken up. Processes became simpler and the fragile substitute for apprenticeship de-
generated notoriously into the abuses of child and woman labor.
Inventions have multiplied, industry has been rapidly becoming
more specialized, the hand trades of artisans have been destroyed, and the occasions for use of rounded skill diminished.
The field now is practically new and more than Negroes are
caught. It is not alone true that Negro workers find it difficult to secure skilled work because of a lack of training opportunity; practically no formal training opportunities exist.
Neither through the trade schools, handicapped by isolation
from modern plants, nor the public schools founded upon another principle, nor corporation schools almost impossible to
sustain, nor correspondence schools, too utterly remote from
work, can this training be secured. Of necessity such "breaking in" as is accomplished becomes a personal, casual matter,
and in this Negro workers, except under the stress of an employer's emergency, fare hard.

There is striking similarity between the attitudes of labor
generally and Negro labor on the question of this industrial
training. There has been the fear that special training for industry was an anomaly in a democracy because it trained children into a working class. The schools have only recently been
accorded a dignity. On the other hand the unions have not
been over-zealous to train apprentices because it increased the
number of skilled men in theoretical competition. So the situation rests. Ever mounting specialization is bringing these far-
reaching changes which will be important both to Negro and
woman labor generally: The continued specializing of process
and product is throwing within the range of these two classes
of labor work which calls not so much for a long and unpleasant relationship of learning with a skilled worker, as for
some specialized competence, such as dexterity, strength, en-
durance, and divided skill. The continued use of machinery is
creating an increasingly large body of work of the grade to
which Negro and women workers are most frequently limited.
The provision, largely experimental at present, of training opportunities in evening, continuation and trade schools, in vesti-
bule schools and through private effort, can contribute to the
Negro workers an individual advantage in a system which is
growing more and more impersonal.

CHAPTER VII

THE NEGRO WORKER

The attitude of Negro workers toward their jobs and their employers can no more be generalized than that of their employers toward them. It·is reflected, at times, in unexplained discontinuance of service, in the restless moving about between unskilled jobs for greater comfort and wages, as compensation for a general situation which denies advancement and promotion. Not infrequently the quality of service is a measure of this attitude. Among the problems, exclusive of the normal ones of newcomers to an industry, may be enumerated hostility of white fellow workers and foremen, limitation of work to the most disagreeable kinds, poorest pay, exclusion from many of the unions where membership is essential to employment, and a long array of fixed conceptions and misconceptions about themselves and their race, which may become both annoying and distracting.

The difficulties, however, are not alone those from without: the comparative newness itself to industrial work, the large amount of illiteracy and bare literacy, their indiscriminate classification within and without the plants with the actually shiftless of their race; mental habits and musculature, in many instances adjusted to the simpler processes of agriculture; living and working habits adjusted to seasonal work, all of these may be included in personal handicaps. The pressure of unwholesome and uncomfortable surroundings together with the distance of the segregated residence areas from work, may register conspicuously in the character of the work performed and the opinions established regarding them as workers.

Attitude Toward Work. Flashes, selected at random from interviews with Negro workers, are suggestive.

(a) —— has been working as a stocker at a rolling mill (a stocker keeps material on hand for the heaters). For this he received $.37 an hour for a 5-day week. Formerly he was a cook.

He thinks that the foreman over his section at the Rolling Mill is a Klansman. "He seems to want everything white." The electrician, he says, boasts of being a Klansman. The white men in the section frequently gather in bunches to discuss things which seem not to have any relation to the work. "Any chance the electrician gets to do Negroes dirty, he appreciates it very highly." The work of the Mill is to make old scrap iron into new. The Negro common laborers and helpers receive from $.37 to $.39 per hour. The majority of the white men, he says, work on tonnage scale and average about $8.00 a day. These white men are heaters and rollers. Labor on the yard gets 5 days a week of 9 hours. The work of the Negroes consists largely in wheeling, running the shearers (that is, cutting up scrap iron), putting on packages, hauling off refuse (that is, pushing buggies and wheelbarrows loaded with scrap iron). He feels that the Klan has done much to keep Negroes out of work. For a long period they barred, whenever they could, Negroes, Jews and Irish. At the Rolling Mills are two colored oilers, this man says, and every time work is scarce, one of these Negroes is laid off and a white worker switched to his job. Every time the foreman can lay off a Negro, he does.

(b) —— works in a car shop of the Pennsylvania Railroad in a mid-western city. They were rebuilding steel cars and at that time earning $.87½ an hour. "The foreman laid on us colored fellows always, but he didn't quarrel with the Pollacks working there. These Pollacks did everything they could to show up the colored workers. A Polish worker had the job of throwing hot rivets to me and was deliberately careless. One of the rivets burned my hat off. This Pollack pretended then, that he couldn't talk English. One job I had required heating about 20 sizes of rivets in the furnace and whenever the foreman came around these fellows would always try to call for rivets that they knew I didn't have."

(c) —— is a car wheel inspector in a Foundry (inspects wheels after they are made; there is one other inspector under him). He has been employed in the plant 27 years, and as a wheel inspector for 18 years. By trade he is a wheel roller. The plant pays $.45 an hour for 10 hours, but the day's work can be completed in 4 or 5 hours. —— thinks it would be better to pay them at the rate of $.60 an hour for the 4 or 5 hours of actual work. The Negro core makers at the Foundry get $.45 an hour. Ordinarily this is considered a white man's job. There are 2 colored molders, 5 colored molders' helpers. When work is slack, the Negro molders are put on the helper's jobs. The helper can average $6.50 a day, the molder $8.50 a day when business is good. In the best periods there are from 12 to 15 Negro molders. They have more white molders than Negroes. The plant has been known to make stock they did not need immediately, just to keep the men in some kind of work.

(d) —— is a shipping clerk in a wholesale house where he has been working since 1919, at a salary of $30.00 a week. He is a graduate of the local high school and of Wilberforce University. The owners of this concern are Jewish, and he found less difficulty, on applying for the job in response to an "ad," in being considered for it. His relations with his employers are pleasant, although he does not believe that there is any promotion for him beyond his present job. His duties require that he come in contact with the trade each day in sales and although he has waited upon many classes of people, he has heard, so far, no complaints.

(e) "As reward for ambition, this official states that there are no other jobs open to Negroes. They are kept at their original occupations because white employees will not work with the moor under them. Of course it is unfair—you can't expect them to be ambitious if you won't promote them, but since white employees and buyers feel such a strong prejudice against having them around, what can the employer do? About a year ago a very intelligent young Negro was employed in the drug department weighing and classifying drugs, a position requiring skill and careful attention to the work. The boy proved to be highly satisfactory and had an agreeable personality but complaints came in so frequently from business associates that the boy had to be discharged. (His whereabouts since that time are not known.) This was an unusual boy. In other cases employees have objected to working with Negroes, however skilled (tried them at one time in the laboratory—good workers, but other employees objected)." [1]

The Chicago Commission study took occasion to investigate conditions in a foundry against which certain Negro workers interviewed had made complaints:

A foundry company employing 20 Negroes out of a total of 80 employees was one of the establishments reporting Negro labor unsatisfactory. Negroes interviewed there complained of harsh and unfair treatment by bosses and said that Negroes usually did not stay longer than 30 days. The employment manager of a large foundry employing 427 Negroes out of a total of 2,488 employees told the investigator that the foremen in the plant would refuse to

[1] From field records in the Department of Research and Investigation National Urban League.

use Negroes if white labor could be obtained, and if such a time should come the foremen would have their way, because it took years to make a foreman, but a laborer could be picked up any day. The investigator was not permitted to interview any of the employees at this plant, but he visited some of them at their homes. They complained of harsh treatment by foremen, reduction in piece rates without notice, and discrimination in favor of white workers. The labor turnover reported by this plant was 70 per cent for Negro as compared with 14 per cent for white workers. This contrast is readily accounted for when the attitude of foremen toward Negroes is known.

In contrast with conditions in the preceding case, the investigator found no complaints of mistreatment by foremen or other causes for dissatisfaction among Negro workers at another foundry which employs 125 Negroes out of a total force of 466 employees. Negro labor in this foundry was reported "satisfactory" and as efficient as white labor. The attitude of foremen evidently contributed to the contentment and success of Negroes in this plant.

Attitude Toward White Fellow-workers and Employers. The Department of Labor [2] commenting upon the high Negro turnover rate in the cotton mills says: "The per cent of separations in relation to the total number of full-time workers is 366.9 for 47.7 women and 180.2 for 86 men. The per cent for Negro women is more than twice as high as that for white women. This difference may be due to the unskilled character of their work, to low compensation, or to the restlessness resulting from long and continuous hours of work."

A mortar mixer in Springfield, Illinois, born in Arkansas, had been a farmer in the South and left the section because income was too uncertain. He belonged to the Hod Carriers' Union but felt that the advantages were doubtful. When the mines of this locality close down the men will work outside of their regular jobs for less than the union rates of the hod carriers, and this increases their unemployment. If the unions did not discriminate against colored workers they would be useful. As it is, they can't give you assignments and prevent you from working on your own terms.

The interesting reactions, as given to Miss Ophelia Settle, by Southern Negro workers in a Southern city help to explain their

[2] U. S. Dept. of Labor, Bulletin of the Women's Bureau No. 52. *Lost Time and Labor Turnover in Cotton Mills.* A Study of Cause and Extent, 1926.

relation to their work, as well as some of their groping aspirations and fears.

(a) —— Jones came from the country and had been in the city about 7 months. He brought his wife who is just 31, and children. He got a job as an Ash Pan Cleaner at one of the Railroad shops. "What do I like about it?" "Nothing, except that it is a steady job, and a man is sure of his money. It's hot, and the wages are too low, and I don't like the Sunday work. I am going to get another job if I stay here. I heard that they had unions here, but I don't know whether it would be the best for me or not; but if it comes into effect, out there, I guess I'd join. Yes, I see the whites are using steam drills and things where you never saw whites working before." He pays $14.00 per month for rent and is trying to keep all of the children in school. This was his chief reason for coming to town. Now, he thinks he would like to go to Chicago for better work and wages, but is afraid that he "cannot make it with all the children." He owned his home in the country, but the wife is determined not to go back because, "You can't give the children any schooling there. They have to go to work so early, they just can't stay in school."

(b) The husband in this family is 57 years old and has worked 11 years as a Car Builder's Helper. His weekly wage is $14.40. The work is hazardous and he sees no chance of promotion. He stays there because it is steady and dislikes both the low wages and the danger. He was not in the strike which they had there a few years ago because he was afraid that he would lose his job. The wife says, "The whites done taken all of our men's jobs; they are street workers, scavengers, dump fillers, and everything. All white men got the jobs around the city hall that colored used to have. We women have to help out; if I hadn't gone to work and helped my husband, we never would have got this house paid for. Now they're trying to cut down women's wages and they are running taxes so high look like they do that to keep us down. The city taxes are so high they almost take your home, and they leave us with an old toilet outside and no sewerage or streets. My husband's work is dangerous. He got hurt twice since he been there. He broke a bone in his hand this year, and just went back to work last week. Of course he is insured. The railroad sees to that. He has to pay for the insurance there. I get $1,000 if he dies naturally and $2,000 if he is killed. They pay him half wages when he is sick and they pay his doctor's bill. The whites are taking all of our jobs; right back over there they're filling up a dump and there are only 2 colored men on the job. The whites are doing all of their work now, and even cutting out the women and girls. If they want you, it's only for a half day or something." The wife is 55 years old, and does enough laundry work to "pay the insurance." The husband's job is at the Railroad Shop.[3]

The Chicago Commission investigators found, however, that a very small proportion of Negro workers actually complained against their white fellow workers, a situation which may indicate some reticence. Dr. Charles H. Wesley has tabulated 50 strikes of white workers in protest against the employment of Negro labor between 1882 and 1900. Eleven of them were successful and 39 failed. The troubles of Negro workers come as well from other Negroes. In one of the automobile plants in Detroit where large numbers of Negroes have been employed, on two occasions individual Negroes have engaged in fights in this plant. The management has threatened to discharge the entire force.

Industrial Housing for Negro Workers. What appears to be the most comprehensive survey of industrial housing developments was made by Leifur Magnusson and published in the Bulletin of the United States Bureau of Labor Statistics, No. 263 in 1920. Concerning Negro housing the investigator found "a certain amount of segregation" in housing in a few company towns. Negroes in Alabama are separated, although two company towns in that state stated that they made no separation of Negroes and whites; a steel town in western Pennsylvania alternated the migrant races with Negro families in order, it states, to prevent too great clannishness among the European immigrants, and similar arrangement is observed in an iron-mining town in Michigan.

Among the miscellaneous industries it was found that one town provided houses for native whites and bunks for Negroes and immigrants. Colored families lived in barracks with a matron and entertained their men friends on the porch in the summer, while no arrangement was made for winter calls. The racial composition of this community is given on p. 93.

To each of the concerns responsible for housing developments the Research Committee of the National Interracial Con-

[3] From a study in preparation in the Department of Social Science, Fisk University.

ference directed a special inquiry concerning Negro housing and replies were received from 34.

The Youngstown Sheet and Tube Company had built in 1918 for Negro workers 135 concrete 2-, 3- and 4-room houses. The Westinghouse Air Brake Company had built 50 model 3-, 4- and 5-room houses with rentals of $12.00, $15.00 and $18.00 a month. The Republic Cotton Mills which owns the town of Great Falls, South Carolina, has "a section of the village devoted exclusively to housing Negroes," providing also a school and a moving picture theatre. Older developments are located at Birmingham. Generally, the employers expressed relief that

Items	White	Colored
Dwellings for families	....	....
Number occupied	1,949	515
Occupants		
Men	3,637	515
Women	2,492	499
Children	3,352	840
Total	9,481	1,854
Dwellings for unmarried	....	....
Number occupied	51	40
Occupants		
Men	1,052	1,540
Women	102	56
Total	1,154	1,596
Total—all occupants	10,635	3,450

though employing Negroes they "have not had to give any consideration to the housing of Negro employees." Other aspects of the problem of workers' homes are discussed under the section devoted to *Housing*.

Breaking Economic Deadlines. Urban League Industrial Secretaries from 15 cities in conference in Louisville, Kentucky, in 1929, thus summarized the means by which Negro workers have succeeded in breaking through present economic "deadlines" in industry. (1) Through the personal interest of some member of the management in a particular Negro, or his family; (2) superior efficiency; (3) labor shortage; (4) the elimination of employer or employee prejudice in individual instances; (5) the practice of "passing for white"; (6) political influence; (7) "shading" or the process of graduating Negro workers beginning with those of very fair complexion and adding successively darker ones; (8) accepting completely segregated facilities; (9) accepting lower pay; (10) opportunism; (11) training and apprenticeship; (12) strike breaking.

Unemployment. During the periods of business depression workers released are usually those who were added most recently to the pay roll. The entrance of Negroes to industry has been recent and as a consequence they are seriously affected as mass workers by this policy. Moreover, the most drastic reductions as well as the first ones considered are in the unskilled lines of work. The Negroes have a larger proportion of unskilled workers than any other group.

The introduction of machinery has been more rapid in work done by unskilled labor. Thus the permanent reductions in man power tend to strike Negro workers heavily. They are located in seasonal industries—fertilizer manufacturing, lumber, building, long shoring and similar lines. This occurs so constantly that one might almost regard it as a condition of Negro employment. How seriously this population is affected by periods of unemployment is difficult to determine. Philip Klein [4] in a general discussion of unemployment considers the Negro's part in it.

Negro day labor in the South was frequently obtainable in the winter of 1921-22 at $1.00 or $1.25 a day, and this competition brought white labor down to $2.50. It is reported that Negroes generally fared worse in cities visited. Generally the Negro population suffered more seriously. The deflation struck the Negro hardest and first.

In the discharge of workers they were the first to go. In any resumption of activities they were the last to be called back, both because of existing prejudices and because of their low standing in seniority. Not only was the ratio of unemployment among them high, but their natural resources were comparatively low. Standards of health, sanitary and living conditions among them, never too high, were depressed still more.

The expected re-migration of Negroes to the South whence they had poured into Northern cities during the industrial boom, failed to take place on a scale sufficiently large to relieve the congested cities or their impoverished and incomeless Negroes. Few ap-

[4] Klein, Philip, *The Burden of Unemployment.*

peared to have cared to return, and fewer still had the means to do so.

The recent period of serious unemployment in 1921 was followed in seriousness by 1924, 1925 and to some extent 1927 and 1928. During 1921, in one intensive survey of unemployment, it was found that 13.4 per cent of the working males were idle.[5]

A study in Baltimore, Maryland, in 1928 by the Bureau of Labor Statistics of the state, however, gives data by race, and the Negro unemployed were 2.2 greater than were the whites.

The study located 15,473 men and women unemployed, or about 13,000 families out of an approximate number of 175,000 families. Of the 15,473 unemployed, there were 5,042 Negroes (4,316 males and 726 females) or 32.6 per cent of the unemployed, although the Negro population is 14.7 per cent of the total population.

Displacement by Machinery. The extent to which Negroes are being or may be displaced by machinery is a subject requiring present study. In general it is true that those fields of work in which common labor is most seriously affected by the introduction of machinery, Negro labor as a whole will feel the effects acutely. Negroes have been employed in the Pittsburgh Plate Glass Company in rather large numbers. It is pointed out by Secretary of Labor Davis, however, that the industry is undergoing a complete change through the introduction of machinery:

Take, for example, the revolution in the glass industry. A single machine—not a single plant, but a single machine—can turn out all the carboys, five gallon containers, that the United States can use. Not long ago hundreds of skilled men were needed to blow these carboys. Now a single machine has released the majority of these men to other fields.

The introduction of cotton-picking machinery threatens to affect most profoundly the strongholds of Negro workers, since this is the largest single group of Negro workers in the entire United States.

The International Harvester Company has developed a cot-

[5] United States Bureau of Labor Statistics, Bulletin No. 409. A Study of Unemployment in Columbus, Ohio, 1921, 1925.

ton-picking machine and a stripper which meets many of the essential requirements and has placed a limited number in various sections of the South where the experimental operation is being watched with more than common interest. Because cotton picking has been so stubbornly a hand process, the perfection of such a machine has a profound effect upon the entire economic and social life of the cotton area, and, indeed, the South. Two men are required for its operation, but it is expected to do in 1 day work equivalent to what 2 pickers can do in 8 to 10 days, or from 4 to 7 times as much.

Displacements by Other Workers. There is evidence, at points, of a situation of displacement of Negro workers by white workers in lines which have hitherto been considered "Negro jobs." A part of this has been a natural result of the emergence of the white working classes. A part, however, appears to be due to the use or misuse of racial propaganda intended to reduce normal competition between the working groups giving the advantage to white labor.

The effects have been indirect and it is possibly true that reports have been exaggerated. Such reports have mentioned secret organizations, outstanding among which is the Ku Klux Klan. It is a fact that Klan ritual demands that Klansmen actively oppose any job for a Negro that will place him on "social equality" with a white person, or in any position of authority in relation to any white person. Public service positions even of the menial character of street cleaning and garbage removal are passing over into the hands of white workers and some Southern cities are stressing the advantages of a pure Anglo-Saxon working class in their Chambers of Commerce publicly. Many hotels and public service positions long counted as secure to Negroes are being committed to white workers. Organizations seeking to have Negroes employed at plants have been met with the objection that Negroes cannot be taken on so long as there are white workers idle. Other factors have entered. In Atlantic City the threat of supplanting Negroes in the hotels has been due to political forces. Being a year round population, they have magnified their voting importance over the transients and owners and are thus becoming *persona non grata.*

Loss of Traditional Occupations. There is a justifiable concern over the apparent losses sustained by Negro workers. But there are certain observations which deserve mention in the interest of intelligent appreciation of the whole problem involved.

An important concentration of interest should be upon what is happening in those industries which have in the past provided largest proportions of work for Negro workers.

(a) Agriculture has accounted for 44 per cent of the Negro workers, and the concentration has been in cotton. Since 1923 there has been a serious per capita decline in crop production and this has had the double effect of limiting returns for agricultural workers and forcing migration from the country to the cities and industrial centers.

(b) Bituminous coal mining has absorbed in West Virginia, Alabama, Tennessee, Illinois and some parts of Pennsylvania, thousands of Negroes. The industry is seriously upset by overproduction, excess of miners, and this in the face of a curtailed use of coal. One instance will suffice. Increased economies in the use of coal in power production in public utilities plants have resulted in a decrease of 43 per cent in consumption.

(c) The lumber industry has been slow in recovering from the war slump and for several years has actually declined.

(d) Iron and steel work in which Negroes have found employment readily has declined consistently since 1923.

(e) Building construction has been noticeably unsteady and although highway construction has increased it has scarcely served to compensate for losses.

These are fields in which Negroes have found largest employment. But some other factors are to be likewise noted: The fields which have not been open on a large scale to Negroes have also experienced a slump, or are destined for it. Among these are the textile industry, and food products. The petroleum industry which alone was expanding at a rapid rate, as a result of the opening of new wells, has come under the observation of President Hoover and his zeal for conserving these natural resources—a result is restriction of output. All of these industries in their suspended activity have thrown labor upon the market. Add to these factors the rapid introduction of labor-saving devices during the past ten years, and as one economist has pointed out, the rearrangement in plant layout, the simplified routing of materials which under the old system required common labor, and the substitution of machinery for hand labor, and the problem of excess labor begins to assert itself. There are actually fewer factory laborers than there were in 1920.

Since the war the entrance of women in increasing numbers to industry has brought new complications, not because they have no business there, but because their usefulness in untried lines has been proved to the displacement of the traditional male. A paradox is observed at this point in the two observable phenomena which can be measured: High wages appear along with increasing unemployment, and this is a manifest contradiction of the law of supply and demand. The speculation is that there is some absorption in the new industries.

There are as yet no means of determining with accuracy the extent of this absorption, or whether, really, instead of absorption there is a widening fringe of unemployment. William A. Berridge, economist of the Metropolitan Life Insurance Company, has made certain estimates which prove valuable here.

Using 1923 as a base year he estimates the unemployment for that year at 1,000,000, the increase in supply of employables through population growth at 3,000,000, the number of farm workers moving to town as 1,000,000, the decline in employment at 1,200,000, as against possible new employment for 2,100,000, leaving a net unemployment of about 4,000,000. Assuming then that the Negro workers are affected by these same forces in the same degrees there would be expected a displacement of at least 400,000, or 300,000 more than were unemployed in 1923. The proportion of workers to the population is higher among Negroes than for any other class and this would contribute to the seriousness of these purely non-racial forces affecting the Negro workers. Moreover, Berridge's estimates do not take into account immigration. Negro labor is more seriously affected by this than other classes because they, like the immigrants, represent simple new recruits to industry and are in harshest competition. We think of immigration, however, in terms of the quota restrictions which do not include the heavy immigration of common labor from Mexico which has reached nearly a half million during the past ten years.

The causes behind the displacement of Negro workers are not far to seek. Where their old traditional positions have not been affected by the pressure of excess white labor from other fields, from rural sections and from normal population expansion, willing to accept any grade of work and almost any pay, it has been affected at least some by a decline in jobs. It appears then that discussion of certain insidious and concerted forces at work to oust Negroes from jobs stops too short. One comment that it seems safe to make on this is that the insidious forces are not necessary so long as the economic ones are in action. The one outstanding speculation at present that is as vital to labor in general as to Negro labor is to what extent this known excess created by reduced man power is being absorbed in new lines. Some of these general new lines are the partial by-products of the automobile industry, such as garages, service stations; the radio industry, road construction, and moving pictures.

The conclusion seems warranted that Negro workers are being displaced in certain fields. The process is not in all localities the same. Different lines of work are affected in different areas. The degree of displacement is not the same in all communities, and in one or two rare instances it was noted that Negro workers are gaining more rapidly than in others. The lines most commonly affected by other workers are the skilled trades of carpentry, bricklaying and plastering; unskilled public service jobs; truck driving, hotel work, and barbering, particularly for the white trade.

The lines of work most recently affected by machinery are: ditch digging and excavating, hod carrying (by hoisting machines), tobacco, transporting of materials, painting, laundering, and mortar mixing. The lines most seriously limited by labor unions are carpentry, bricklaying, molding, metal working, longshoring, printing, plumbing, tobacco work and garment making. There is definite evidence apart from the circumstances mentioned, of the absence of adequate measures of the industrial training of Negroes which, if not remedied, will undoubtedly result in greater displacement on grounds of inefficiency or insufficiency in numbers of skilled workers to support such opportunities for them as might be considered.

Absorption Into New Occupations. What then are the Negroes doing, if anything? As a convenient though admittedly limited test of this, the industrial records of 200 Negro families representing about 1,000 persons in Nashville, Tennessee, have been examined. This city has a Negro population which is over 30 per cent of the total. The data cover the period from January to March, 1929. Of the 200 there were 190 male heads of families and chief bread winners, selected by the random sampling method of every tenth family; less than 8 per cent were involuntarily unemployed, and there were noted 53 persons, or 27.8 per cent of the group, engaged in occupations that might be described as "new" to Negroes.

There were 11 truck drivers, 4 contracting carpenters, 4 grain weighers and workers, 3 concrete finishers for road work, 2 garage workers, 2 bootleggers and a string of such other occupations as mortar mixer, concrete mixer, automobile mechanic, gas pipe layer, car washers, floor waxer, telephone lineman, ice and coal dealers, acid testers, hosiery mill packer, blue print operators, junkman, linotype setters, insurance agent, machinist's helper, boilermaker's helper, chiropodist, embalmer, and sales manager.

The avenues for expansion, it would appear, have been distributed inconspicuously among many lines. Negro accessions have usually been considered in the mass. As with labor in general the "service" occupations associated with the automobile have provided work for Negroes, although of an unskilled character for the most part, as car washers, garage attendants, greasers, chauffeurs, truck drivers and mechanics. The road work has absorbed some as laborers and concrete workers. Negro business itself has made some minor contributions. The number of insurance salesmen and office workers has increased. In the elevation of the entire group through special training a small portion of the would-be excess has been removed through the schools to the professions of teaching and medicine.

Negro Business. Economic speculation has, not infrequently, turned to Negro business both as a possible expression of improved status, and an accessory outlet for Negro skilled clerical and managerial service rejected in the general market, on purely racial grounds. The dominant direction of this interest has been more racial than economic. Attention has been centered more upon Negro business for Negro patronage than upon this business as a purely economic venture for profit. The direction may, indeed, have been determined by the relative strength of the incentives to individual enterprise. It has been observed, for example, that the first and the present largest businesses of Negroes are in a sense "defensive enterprises." The insurance companies grew out of burial and mutual societies and later secured a strong foothold as a result of the policy of exclusion, or larger premium charges, of companies operated by white persons. The banks which, despite a number of failures, rank close to the insurance companies, have as one of their chief arguments for existence, the fact that Negro individuals and small business men are refused credit, or credit on the same terms as others. Where racial segregation is most rigid Negro businesses succeed more easily. The largest number of successful enterprises are personal service fields, in which racial discrimination is rather universally practiced. These are restaurants, beauty parlors, barber shops, undertaking establishments and, to a lesser extent, grocery stores.

The amount of money annually expended from wages by Negroes is, after all, considerable, and the disposition to ignore this element in community wealth has unquestionably proved a provocation to economic policies colored by racial philosophy. The principal objection to the policy is its apparent insistence upon an exclusively racial economy.

There are now, it is estimated, about 70,000 Negro business enterprises of various kinds.[6] The most numerous of these businesses are the restaurants; the most heavily capitalized, the insurance companies. In 1927, there were 28 Negro insurance companies with assets of $11,170,791 and a gross income of $13,856,742. These 28 companies have $243,534,500 insurance in force and employ 9,100 persons.

In banking, as Arnett Lindsay, himself one of the younger Negro bankers, points out, Negroes have, curiously enough, a longer history. Individual Negroes were skilled traders in

[6] Cited by Monroe N. Work, *The Annals of the American Academy of Political and Social Science,* November, 1928, p. 144.

money long before the Civil War. Although banking institutions were established soon after the war, and some 137 have been attempted to the present, only about half of them have survived any considerable period. This mortality has been greatest among the commercial types of institutions.

W. G. Pearson of Durham, North Carolina, where an unusually large number of Negro businesses flourish, reported to the 1927 Durham Conference on the American Negro, that there are now about 33 savings and commercial banks exclusive of the stock savings and commercial type; between 30 and 50 building and loan societies, mutual savings and loans or investment associations. The 33 stock banks in 14 states showed, as of July 31, 1927, total assets of $15,292,820. The liabilities were, total capital $2,086,369, total surplus $485,911 and total deposits $11,900,250.

It is difficult to estimate the extent to which these various businesses are providing employment for Negroes. Three of these: "merchants," "insurance employees" and "barbers and hairdressers," total approximately 50,000. Mr. Albon L. Holsey, Secretary of the National Negro Business League, estimates that a reasonable control by Negroes, over the expenditures by Negroes for food and clothing, would result in the creation of 125,000 jobs for themselves.

The most promising step taken recently has been the deliberate study in 1928 of the field of Negro business by the Negro Business League,[7] an organization founded in 1900 by Booker T. Washington. This study covered 2,757 concerns employing 12,459 Negroes.

More than 3.2 per cent of these establishments had been in business over 5 years, a record which Dr. Cherington observes compared favorably with the longevity of any similar group of retailers. The most profitable field for Negro employment among Negro businesses is with contractors who used 20.5 persons per enterprise.[8] These were 1.1 of the businesses.

Next in order of importance were the printers and publishers employing 8.6 persons and constituting 2.6 of the enterprises,

[7] Report of the Survey of Negro Business, conducted by the National Negro Business League, 1928. Containing an introduction by Dr. Paul T. Cherington.

[8] The Insurance Companies and Banks were covered by a special questionnaire and were not included in this total.

and the next, undertaking, using 6.1 persons and constituting 5.6 of the enterprises. The groceries were the largest group, 19.0 of all enterprises studied, employing 3.06 persons each. Restaurants followed, being 11.0 per cent of the businesses and employing 4.6 persons each. The average for all businesses was 4.5 persons. Interestingly enough the Negro contractors with the largest volume of non-Negro business employed the largest number of Negro workers per establishment.

Sixty financial institutions employed 5,090 persons (principally on a commission basis), or an average of 83 persons per enterprise and yielded for these workers an average annual salary of $930.00.

The tendency, it appears, is in the direction of an increase both in number and stability in these businesses. An active new interest in this field is manifested in Negro colleges which are extending rapidly their courses in business administration. Intensive training, thus, may in time offer some compensation for the natural handicaps of the situation.

Some Problems Indicated. Although it is recognized that an important part of the present Negro industrial problem is one of employer and employee attitudes, there are conspicuous barriers to adjustment and to the intensive development of this working group, upon which attention might well be centered. Among these are the problems of an adequate substitute for apprenticeship for Negro workers; a practical, functioning relationship between vocational schools and present vocations; training of Negro workers for special positions of skill not yet controlled by white workers; re-entry of old positions in industry; the development of Negro business as a training ground for Negro skilled workers; elaboration of current lines of work into new directions, as for example, iron workers into metallurgy and industrial chemistry, nurses into governesses, cooks into caterers; the development of technical high schools; regulation of the movement of Negro industrial workers; registeries of skilled workers not employed at their trades; relations with labor organizations; improvement of personnel work and methods of recruiting Negro labor; and development of a community of interests with means of reducing competition based upon race.

Studies Required. Although the literature of this field is fairly large it does not adequately provide the results of careful study of many fundamental issues in the present question of Negro industrial status. As an aid to further understanding, research in the near future should attempt to throw more light upon the following: Negroes in skilled trades; methods by which Negro workers acquire trades, as a basis for intelligent vocational guidance; a scientific measure of Negro industrial efficiency and adaptability to certain lines of work; an index of wages for Negro labor, semi-skilled and skilled; the relation of Negro to Immigrant labor; cost of living for Negro workers' families in selected Northern and Southern cities; employers' attitudes toward Negro labor; the Negro workers (a study of personal attitudes toward employers and white fellow workers) ; a detailed study of the use of Negro labor in selected basic industries (automobiles, iron and steel, railroad and mining) ; extent to which Negro workers are being displaced as a result of racial propaganda; employment of Negroes in new industries (the radio, motor bus, aeroplane, etc.) ; Negro workers in unemployment crises; strike breaking; Negro workers and speed jobs; racial traits in relation to industrial fitness; turnover of Negro labor and unskilled labor generally; income of Negro families; physical fitness and stamina of Negro workers; and present trends in Negro occupations.

CHAPTER VIII

THE NEGRO WORKERS AND ORGANIZED LABOR

Accurate information regarding the extent of Negro inclusion in Labor organizations has been scarce because of the extreme difficulty of getting the particular data regarding Negroes from the general records, which in themselves were not conveniently kept. A study [1] has been under way by the National Urban League supported by the American Fund for Public Service.

This study was prompted by an almost utter absence of any reliable and, at the same time, comprehensive information about this matter. That material should be lacking is not surprising. The American Federation of Labor itself did not until very recently know [2] its own membership, and even now does not know it except by approximations. Although its members number more than 3,000,000 it has only been directed on its present policy since 1880, and came into its greater importance with the same social upheaval of war that swept Negroes from the South into industry, where their troubles began. The surest index to numbers is records, and although the system of organization is feasible, the practice in keeping and reporting is at the mercy of at least the handicaps of an unwieldy volume, and the disinclination of many locals to keep written accounts. There are 33,800 locals affiliated through nationals and internationals, or directly with the American Federation of Labor. No central body of data or records exists and probably for this good reason. Changes are gross and constant. During 1919, for example, 6,742 new charters were given and 1,719 lapsed or were surrendered. Except for the men in the upper skilled trades writing is a difficult and unfamiliar duty. The same

[1] Johnson, Charles S., *The Negro and Labor Unions,* National Urban League.
[2] It has known only the total number paying dues, but not the details about its members.

uncertainty about women and organization exists. Their entry is as recent as the Negroes, and about them almost as little is known.

Particular difficulties enter into the Negro situation. Where relations are most friendly, there the disposition has been to disregard the item of particular race and specific color, merging the workers under the classification, Americans. This policy itself, which is the ultimate objective of those who insist upon full inclusion of Negroes in labor unions, makes excessively difficult the gauging of the present numerical volume of this Negro inclusion. The United Mine Workers Union, which at one time reported a membership of 500,000, the United Garment Workers, and, to a lesser degree, the International Brotherhood of Longshoremen, and the Hod Carriers and Building Common Laborers are cases in point. With the mine workers the liberal policy is enforced by a fine of $100.00 for refusal to work with a Negro union miner. Negro numbers increase more rapidly in the liberal unions and the full extent of organization is difficult to determine.

This study has encountered these difficulties, and although the results at this point are uneven, it is possible, we feel, to draw from these scattered and obscure sources, a working basis in information on the question.

The area covered by the first part of the survey included the locals of 49 National and International unions affiliated with the American Federation of Labor with a combined membership of 1,527,248, the Negro membership in locals of Chicago, New York City, Detroit, and Washington, D. C., the states of New Jersey, Delaware, Minnesota, Idaho, Connecticut, Maryland, Pennsylvania, and Ohio; the mine workers of West Virginia and Pennsylvania organized under the United Mine Workers Union; the three large independent Negro unions: the Railway Men's Independent Benevolent Association, the Dining Car Men's Association and the forming Pullman Porters organization. The total Negro membership in these was 65,492. (This figure includes estimates of the number of miners, counted as 12,000; Hod Carriers counted as 8,000; and Pullman Porters counted moderately as 4,000 although the organization, while refusing to give exact figures stated that 50 per cent of the 12,000 porters are organized.)

There are in New York City 14,000 Negroes in unions, in Chicago about 13,000 and in Detroit 2,000. The largest numbers of Negroes are members of the Longshoremen's Union, with about 15,000 (in New York City alone, there are 5,000 Negro members); the Miners with 5,000; the Hod Carriers and Building Laborers with about 8,000; the Musicians with 3,000; the Garment Trades with about 6,000; the Hotel and Restaurant Employees with about 1,000; the Freight Handlers, Teamsters and Drivers, Tobacco Workers, Asphalt Workers. The total figure of 65,492 for Negro Union members, while derived from different sources, may be safely regarded as a minimum figure. It is not improbable that the full returns when the South has been included and the scattered groups further combed will show a total Negro membership close to 100,000.

The question of the Negro and Trades unions has just recently assumed a new importance. Strangely enough, the questions heard today are much the same as those arising shortly after the emancipation of Negro slaves, when they became a sudden menace to free labor. The Knights of Labor, the organization which preceded the American Federation of Labor, received them more cordially than they are now received. The policy, it is true, was prompted as much by fear as fellow-feeling. The debate on the admission of Negroes before the historic Baltimore Congress just after emancipation brought out the fear that: "Negroes will take possession of the shops if we have not taken possession of the Negroes."

There was a prototype of the Chicago Negro Labor Congress of 1927, in the National Colored Labor Convention which met in Washington, D. C., in 1869, when Sella Martin, laborite from Massachusetts, and the distinguished Negro, John M. Langston of Ohio, clashed and Martin first dramatically voiced the plea that "the interests of the laboring classes white and black on this continent are identical. We should work harmoniously together for the furtherance of the causes of labor." The limitations upon Negro numbers in the North imposed by foreign immigration and the gradual crowding out of Negro skilled workers in the South for many years lessened the menace of Negro workers. The first organizations were skilled crafts and many of these in the beginning were social and fraternal organizations—lodges, which excluded Negroes on the broad principle of social inequality. This meant two things: (a) The organizations first took form in lines of work in which Negroes were not engaged. In 1910 over 75 per cent of working Negroes were in agriculture and domestic service, occupations which are not now and never have been organized. (b) The organizations took form in sections of the country in which there were extremely few Negro skilled workers. Whereas, there were, for example, Negro carpenters, bricklayers, and plasterers in the South in 1900, and in 1910, the strongest organizations of these crafts were located in the North and, where they existed at all in the South, the taboo against joint unions most rigidly obtained.

Although at earlier conventions the American Federation of Labor had expressed its disfavor of those unions which excluded Negroes from membership, it was not until 1919 that the significance of these changes was seriously noted by labor groups when at the Atlantic City Convention nearly 50 of the 110 National and International Unions affiliated with the American Federation of Labor, in response to the urging of the Executive Council and this Convention, reported that they raised no barrier against Negro workers, and the convention authorized the formation of Federal locals of all colored workers refused membership in any international. Although only 8 of the nationals and internationals of the American Federation of Labor now expressly bar Negro members, the status of Negro workers in unions has not changed greatly in those fields from which they were originally barred. The sentiment of the American Federation of Labor as expressed in its convention resolutions and in other official pronouncements, within the past 7 years, has more strongly supported the unionization of Negroes. This policy has been a coldly logical one with neither the force of general agreement nor official power behind it.

Types of Union Relations

Unions Which Exclude Negro Workers. Twenty-two international and national labor organizations exclude Negro workers by constitutional provision. Eleven of the International unions which are known to have exclusion clauses in their constitutions or rituals have a total membership of 436,200 and control a field in which are employed a minimum of 43,858 Negroes.

These unions are:

Carmen of America, Brotherhood of Railway
Clerks, Freight Handlers, Express and Station Employees, Brotherhood of Railway and Steamship
Conductors, Brotherhood of Dining Car
Conductors, Order of Sleeping Car
Conductors of America, Order of Railway
Engineers, Grand International Brotherhood of Locomotive
Expressmen, Order of Railway
Express Workers, American Federation of
Firemen and Enginemen, Brotherhood of Locomotive
Mail Association, Railway
Masters, Mates and Pilots, National Organization
Neptune Association
Railroad Workers, American Federation of
Station Employees and Clerks, Brotherhood of Railroad
Switchmen's Union of North America
Telegraphers, Order of Railroad
Telegraphers' Union of America, Commercial
Train Dispatchers Association, American
Trainmen, Brotherhood of Railroad
Wire Weavers' Protective Association, American
Yardmasters of America, Railroad
Yardmasters of North America, Railroad

To this list might be added the Blacksmiths and Helpers' Union which, though permitting auxiliary locals of Negro helpers, insists that they shall not be promoted to blacksmiths; they shall not transfer except to another Negro helpers auxiliary, and that they shall not be admitted to shops in which white helpers are now employed. In certain agreements drawn between this union and employees it is specified that "none but white, English-speaking helpers are to be employed." [3]

The Brotherhood of Maintenance of Way Employees and the National Rural Letter Carriers' Association, while admitting Negro members, specifically bar them from representing themselves in conventions or holding office.

Unions Which Discourage Negro Membership. There is but

[3] Agreement between the Main Central Railroad Company of Portland Terminal and the International Brotherhood of Blacksmiths and Helpers, in effect November 12, 1927. *Blacksmiths Journal*, December, 1927.

small difference between this group and the next one which, while having nothing in its constitution against Negro membership yet discourages it, and actually succeeds in keeping the numbers low. Most outstanding of such unions are the Electrical Workers with 142,000 members and practically no Negroes although there are at least 1,343 Negro electricians; the Sheet Metal Workers with 25,000 members and no known Negroes; the Plasterers Union with 30,000 members and less than 100 Negroes, although there are 6,000 Negro plasterers; the Plumbers and Steam Fitters with 35,000 members, no Negroes, and a long history of successful circumventions to avoid Negro membership although there are 3,500 Negro workers in this trade (the case of the Negro plumbers in Chicago who for over 6 years have been attempting to get into the unions, is a notable instance of this).

There are also the Flint Glass Workers with 6,100 members who have no law against Negroes, but who object to them universally on the grounds that the pipe on which glass is blown passes from mouth to mouth and "no one would use it after a Negro." The Journeymen Tailors, with 9,295 members and less than 100 Negro members, assert that there are few Negro tailors capable of making coat, vest and pants of a suit.

Unions Which Do Not Encourage Negro Membership. A third group of unions admit but do not encourage Negro memberships. These include the carpenters with 340,000 members and only 592 Negro members although there are 34,217 Negro carpenters; the painters with 120,604 members and only 279 Negroes although there are 10,600 Negroes in the trade. There are numerous other organized trades of lesser importance.

Another reason for low membership in the unions of this class is a situation for which the unions are not wholly responsible. It is the blunt fact of experience, testified to by scores of skilled Negro workers working in independent crafts outside of factories, that when they place themselves under union jurisdiction and cease bargaining individually for themselves, all other white workers are given preference over them both by employers and officials who have in their hands the assignments of jobs. The unions regard this, coldly, as the Negro workers' "hard luck" and make no effort to do anything about it. If the Negro works for other than union rates, in order to work at all, he is subject to a fine or suspension. The net result is virtually punishment for a sacrifice. The attitude of the union is evident in the comment of one official that "the Negroes expect us to get jobs for them." Where these unions are in control and in demand in cities, it is extremely difficult for Negro workers to get admittance. The total membership of the 11 organized trades which while admitting either discourage or do not encourage Negro membership is 783,959.

Unions Admitting Negroes Freely to Separate Organizations. A fourth group consists of those unions which admit Negroes freely but only to separate unions. These include the musicians with 125,000 members and 3,000 Negroes; the Hotel and Restaurant Employees, with 38,503 members of which over 1,000 are Negroes; the Journeymen Barbers, the Laundry Workers, Tobacco Workers, United Textile Workers, and Cooks and Waiters. The most successful of these are the musicians who find an advantage in separate organization and the regulation, which applies to certain locals, to the effect that the Negro Union or its special charter from the American Federation of Labor shall be subservient to the laws of the white local, but must not mix in bands or orchestras or play in the same organizations, does not seem to interfere with the freedom and opportunity of the Negro members. In other cases like the Barbers there is a different clientele; in the case of the Federation of Teachers there are separate schools, but with the textile workers there is the fact that the work is divided between New England, where there are few Negroes and communities of foreign workers are in control, and the South, where relations must be as separate as the fingers of the hand.

Unions Admitting Negroes Freely to Mixed and Separate Organizations. There is a fifth group composed of unions which admit Negroes freely to mixed or separate unions. In this is included the largest Negro membership. They are, The Longshoremen, The Hod Carriers, and Common Building Laborers, and Tunnel Workers.

John R. Commons observed of the Hod Carriers, Building and Common Laborers of Pittsburgh:

In 1908 the hod carriers and mortar mixers secured $3.00 a day, or a scale of $.37½. Two dollars a day was the standard wage at this time. So this rate was due to the institution of the building laborers and hod carriers union established by American-born, English-speaking common laborers, white and colored, to protect themselves against the "greens," Slavs and Italians.

Two items are worth noting here: These are not skilled trades of a sort which require apprenticeship; and they are lines of work in which Negroes are freely employed. There will be found numerous separate unions, as when the preponderance of Negroes automatically makes it a Negro union; or when geographical distribution of locals establishes one where only Negroes live, or where, as in New Orleans, the white and Negro Longshoremen, although in separate locals, meet in Executive sessions and follow a rigidly fair policy of work distribution. Negro preponderance in these lines may also be explained in part by the rigidness of barriers to advancement by promotion; white hod carriers may more easily become helpers and advance from helpers to carpenters or bricklayers. In these 3 organizations there are probably 24,000 Negro members. Beside those mentioned are the Boot and Shoe Workers, whose policy is determined by geography; the National Federation of Federal Employees; and the Mail Carriers; the National Federation of Post Office Employees, which allows but one local under the jurisdiction of one postmaster. What happens in the South is that where there are Negro members the whites withdraw and are permitted to affiliate with a white local of any near-by city.

Unions Admitting Negroes to Mixed Organizations Only. A sixth group is made up of those unions which admit Negroes only to mixed unions. These include the United Mine Workers and the Garment Workers Unions. In the first union discrimination among members and locals is discouraged with the threat of a fine. In the second, because the clothing industry centers about New York City and Chicago, and is largely Jewish and foreign in membership, racial sentiment against Negroes is not strong. There are probably 11,000 Negroes in these two unions.

Independent Negro Unions. The seventh group is composed of independent Negro unions. Among these are the Railroad Men's Independent and Benevolent Association with headquarters in Chicago, a protest union composed of railroad men barred from the regular unions of their crafts; The Dining Car Men's Association with headquarters in Washington, and the Pullman Porters' Organization just forming. These, together, have a membership of about 8,000. The Railroad Men assert that they will affiliate with the American Federation of Labor as soon as restrictions are removed and they are admitted to full membership. The Dining Car Men feel that they have nothing to gain by paying assessments to an organization which can offer them no aid; that they distrust white-controlled unions; that practically all Dining Car men are Negroes and there is no question of competition. The recent appearance of President Green before the Pullman Porters and his new attitude of friendliness indicates that this situation is approaching a more comfortable adjustment for the porters.

There is another group, composed of unions which are organized in lines in which few or no Negroes are employed—for example, the Pattern Makers, Operative Potters, Leather Workers, Metal Engravers, Granite Cutters, Plate Printers and Dye Stampers. Here the lack of skill, the lack of opportunity of gaining skill through the restrictions imposed both by employers who will not hire, and union members who will neither instruct nor work with Negro aspirants for these jobs, are responsible for the absence of Negroes.

Unionists and Negro workers see quite differently the problem of unionization. To the first it means improvement; to the other "getting something in the first place." The Stock Yards workers strike for an increase of 50 cents a day in wages and 8 hours instead of 12; the Negroes to whom the entrance rate of pay in the stock yards was twice the sum they were getting at home, are actually bettering their conditions in larger measure than the others. Men of any race or station may be expected to follow the direction in which their best interests lie. As living standards among workers approach each other the same demands are to be expected. Where the trade unions have been open to Negroes they have entered freely with the white workers. In Chicago the proportion of Negro men in organizations is more than twice their proportion in the total population. This, of course, is partly because there is relatively a larger proportion of Negroes engaged in industry.

But most important is the fact that the great masses of Negro workers are employed in fields which are not organized. A differential eligibility is in these figures: For all classes those in agriculture and domestic service, unorganized lines, constitute 34.5 per cent of the working population; for the Negroes, 67.3. In other words, just about twice as many of the working Negroes relatively are actually ineligible for unions as other classes. Again, the greatest degree of organization is to be found in the North and four-fifths of the Negroes live in the South. The skilled trades are most thoroughly organized but three-fourths of the Negroes are unskilled. These factors must be kept in mind in considering their organizability.

Negroes as Strike Breakers. One source of hostility of white union workers to Negro workers is the fear of them as strike breakers. But this hostility has little to do with the exclusion of Negroes from the unions of these lines. The fear is warranted, for not only is there a menace to union objectives in the availability of Negro workers, but it has so happened that many of the greatest advances which Negroes have made in industry—many of them first opportunities, are due to strikes and their part in breaking them. They were used to break the Stock Yards strike, and they have been employed there since; they were largely responsible for the failure of the Steel Strike and they have since been used in a proportion of 17 per cent in the Steel Mills; they were used effectively in the great Railroad Strike of 1922 and about 700 mostly skilled are still working in one system alone. In New York in 1910 they broke the Teamsters strike, although 5 or 6 years later, they were organized; in the Shopman's strike they got their first opportunity as machinists; they were used in the Anthracite Coal Strike in Pennsylvania, several hundred having been brought from the South, and in the strike of Bakers and Confectionery Workers in Chicago. The list could be continued indefinitely.

Negroes as Union Members. Precisely the opposite situation has occurred when Negroes have been inside the Unions. In the West Virginia Coal strike of 1922 there was the peculiar situation of the Mine Owners looking to the Negro recruits to hold their position and the Mine Workers Union looking to the stamina of its Negro members to sustain its position. The strike lasted several months. As fellow unionists they struck with Musicians, with the Textile Workers in Columbus, Ga., and the Tobacco Workers in the strike of 1900. As Longshoremen, they stayed with their organizations in periods of difficulty and in spite of the fact that there were Negro strike breakers. Union officials tend to agree that as union men they are as faithful to their obligations as white members.

Labor Union Practice. Among the Unions which admit Negroes there are to be found immense differences in practice and unwritten policy. Without dealing with this question in too much detail there is revealed in a few instances one serious discouragement to Negro membership. Whereas the carpenters of New York have a Negro organizer it is impossible for Negro carpenters in cities of Ohio to get into unions except by transfer of card. In Kansas City, Missouri, recently, as a Negro union man got into a Bricklayers union and went to work, white union men struck in protest; while in Mobile, Alabama, they functioned well together in mixed locals. The secretary-treasurer of the Machinists says that if Negroes are organized he fears they will be used by employers "to break the ranks of white unionists." The Sheet Metal Workers allow Negroes to work 9 and the whites 5 hours and there is a different wage scale. Fifteen years ago there were 200 Negroes in the Railway Mail Association and now they refuse to admit Negroes and even to respect the insurance feature in relation to the old Negro members. In Philadelphia the Hoisting Engineers Union and Cement Finishers refused to work even with union Negroes on the same jobs. While the Barbers employ a Negro organizer in Chicago, those in California try to discourage Negro membership. In Akron, white bricklayers will not work with Negroes; the riveters in California initiating a Negro thought to be white asked him to swear that he would never knowingly introduce a Negro for membership. The Plumbers' union in Chicago has persistently refused to admit Negroes who have several times passed all examinations required. The Cooks and Waiters initiate Negroes into the white local and push them off forthwith into a colored auxiliary with no power or vote. In Boston the separate locals of Waiters fought so continuously and were used with such disastrous effects by employers to break the powers of each other that they merged.

Labor union practice, in Los Angeles, California, for example, traced the pattern of plant practice. Negroes were admitted freely when they were a menace to white workers, and when it was conceded that they held distinctly favorable positions with employers. The bricklayers were indifferent to Negro membership and refused to "mix" with them until they discovered that Negro bricklayers were "working independently for whatever wages they could get." The Asbestos Workers bar Negroes, Mexicans and Italians. These are the three reasons they give: "Negroes cannot stand the heat of the work"; "there are no Negroes in the trade"; and "if we begin mixing the races they will get all of the good jobs." The iron workers are certain that their work is "too dangerous for Negroes" besides, "the work pays well." So they are kept out. On the other hand, in these days when Negro musicians are favored by the public and frequently given preference over white musicians, the urge to preserve working standards for all musicians disregards many of the otherwise insistent "racial instincts." The white painters could not have Negroes or Mexicans in their locals, but they frequently worked for Negro contractors.

One hundred and twenty-seven Negro men picked at random in 10 cities were asked their attitude toward Labor Unions. About half were then or had been union members. The advantages and disadvantages to them may be summarized as follows:

Among the advantages are: better wages since contractors know the scale; protection; sick benefits; and an equal chance with whites. Among the disadvantages are: union Negroes are boycotted by employers; unions keep one out of work by giving preference to their white men; fees too high; unions do not help laborers; unions cannot help in particular trades.

The really important fact is that it is only just now that Negro workers, one million strong, in the North and exposed to industry for more than 12 years, with the source of other recruits limited, are having their first real contact with skilled jobs. They are eligible in larger volume for admission to the old craft organizations which are still disposed to think of them as usurpers taking white men's jobs. The gaps being made in skilled lines by promotion, retirement and death cannot be filled entirely by white workers, or the reduced immigration. The situation is taut and vital, and upon its final determination will probably hinge both the fate of Negroes in the skilled trades and the ultimate security of labor unionism itself.

CHAPTER IX

THE AGRICULTURAL NEGRO

According to Census figures, there has been a marked decrease in the number of Negro farmers in the North, including the New England, the Middle Atlantic, the East North Central, and the West North Central sections but there was a slight increase of Negro farmers in the West and South. In 1920 there were 360 less Negroes owning their farms than in 1900 for the country as a whole. In the North this decrease in ownership, 1910-20, was 1,749; in the South there was an increase in ownership of 1,278. In the number of white 'managers, there was an increase of 1.2 per cent the decade, 1900-10, and of 17.1 per cent in the 10 years, 1910-20. Negro managers decreased 17.7 per cent during 1900-10 and increased 41.3 per cent 1910-20. White tenants increased 14 per cent during 1900-10 and 3.8 per cent 1910-20, while Negro tenants increased 20.8 per cent between 1900 and 1910 and 4.7 per cent between 1910 and 1920. The trend is toward decrease in ownership and increase in tenantry among Negroes; the same is true of whites in Northern states, but in the South white owners show an increase of only 0.6 per cent during 1910-20, but a decided increase of managers, 47.8 per cent during that same period. On the whole, the trends for whites and Negroes are similar.

A comparison of the 1900, 1910, 1920 and 1925 figures on Negro ownership, managership, and tenantry in the Southern section is given in the accompanying table.

TABLE VI

TABLE SHOWING NEGRO FARMERS BY CLASSES FOR THE YEARS 1900-25

	1900	1910	1920	1925
Owners	179,118	211,087	212,365	188,945
Managers	1,561	1,190	1,759	638
Tenants	551,383	668,559	701,471	612,250
Total	732,062	880,836	915,595	801,833

There was an increase in the total number of Negro farmers in the South up to 1920, then a drop of 113,762 over the 5-year period. The number of owners decreased 23,420 between 1920 and 1925;[1] the managers show a decrease of 1,121, and the tenants a decrease of 89,221. Some of the decrease is due to the migration to Northern states. This is notably true of ownership, but a great part of the remaining is undoubtedly due to the development of industries in the South and the consequent movements of both white and Negro populations to the cities.

Agriculture is still the occupation engaging the largest number of Negroes. In 1900 the per cent so engaged was 53.7; although in 1920 this had decreased to 44.4 the position of this occupation was still maintained.

Mr. Monroe N. Work, editor of the *Negro Year Book* prepared for the National Interracial Conference a compilation of significant statistical shifts in the Negro farm population which reflects careful study of statistical sources of data regarding the Negro farmer.

In the period 1920-25, the 5 states, Delaware, Virginia, Maryland, West Virginia and Florida showed an increase in Negro farm owners, and the number of Negro tenants increased in Maryland, Virginia, West Virginia, North Carolina, Oklahoma, and Texas. Seven states showed an increase in the number of white farm owners and 4 states a decrease in number of white tenants. A study of Changes in Population and Land Tenure in counties of the South, under way in the Department of Research and Records at Tuskegee indicates already that the tendencies of the white and Negro farmers are on the whole about the same. For example, in 224, or 53.7 per cent of the 417 counties in Alabama, Georgia, Tennessee and North Carolina, the white and Negro population trends were identical. The population had increased for both in 161 and decreased in 63. This was true for both owners and tenants. Information on the movement of tenants in 1920 indicates that white tenants move more often than Negro tenants.

The age distribution for both races differs from that of the urban and village population. The largest numbers of the farm

[1] Because of different methods of gathering the figures for inter-censal years these differences may not hold their apparent significance.

population are found in the age group 5 to 14, whereas the largest urban and village numbers are in the age group 25 to 44 years. Precisely this division appears also in the Negro population between North and South. In all sections of the country the Negro males outnumber the females in the farm and village population; but in the urban Negro population of the North and West there are more males than females. The reverse of this is true for the South.

When the size of all the farms is taken into account the greatest increases have been in the group ranging in size from 10 to 49 acres. This has been rather consistent for some 45 years. The larger farms have in recent years shown important decrease in number. The average size in acres of both white and Negro farms in the South is decreasing. For white farmers it was 172.1 in 1900 and 135.2 in 1920; for Negro farmers the acreage dropped in the same period from 52.1 to 44.8.

Between 1920 and 1925 the decrease in the white farm population totalled 1,009,531 and the Negro 789,736. Georgia lost the largest numbers from its farm population, followed by Alabama. The two Southern states, South Carolina and Georgia alone, however, lost a total of 344,231 Negroes.

The Negroes are 16.2 per cent of the farm population of the United States as compared with 9.9 per cent of the total population. They are 26.9 per cent of the total population of the South and 30 per cent of the farm population. Regarding crop production Mr. Work has this to say:

It would appear that there has been no marked increase in the acreage production of the staple crops raised in the South. The average yield per acre of cotton in 1899 was 183.8 pounds per acre: the average yield in 1926 was 182.6 pounds per acre. The average yield of corn per acre in 1899 was 17.1 bushels per acre: the average yield in 1919 was 18.3 bushels per acre.

It would appear that we shall have to look in other directions than the average yield per acre to ascertain whether progress is being made in agriculture in the South. It is found that in spite of the loss in farm population the agricultural products of the South are not decreasing. Certain factors have helped to maintain and in some instances increase production. The increasing use of machinery has resulted in an increase in production per man. The number of acres cultivated per farmer increased from 48.7 in 1910 to 49.0 in 1920 and to 50.4 in 1925. The development of cooperative marketing is an important factor because it is enabling both the white and Negro farmer to find a dependable profitable market for their poultry, swine, cattle and other products. Another important factor is the great increase in the extent to which farm boys in the South are being educated, through 4-H clubs and in other ways, for farming.

Carl Kelsey's study of the *Negro Farmer* in 1903, though not a definitive volume, continues to provide, in its description of the natural divisions of the agricultural South, the background which makes more intelligible present movements of the Negro. These divisions of the section which are important for the Negro farmer are:

The Tidewater Section of Virginia, Central Virginia, the Sea Coast, the Central District, the Alluvial District and the Sugar Region.

In the Tidewater Section, agriculture is supplemented by the fishing and oyster industries. The farm suffers because the owner is in one of these industries.

Central Virginia, not nearly so prosperous, is the greatest tobacco region. The soil is often rolling, rocky and sandy. The Negro in this section has to get advances to carry him over, and this permits a more varied diet than the traditional corn meal and pork. There is a little diversification, but tobacco tends to usurp much more than its share of the average and is for everyone the chief crop. There are various odd jobs, such as cutting cord wood, that yield some cash returns in short seasons, and some families manage to live comfortably. The Alluvial District in Mississippi is very rich, and not yet densely populated. Cotton is the chief crop and is usually raised by tenants on a plantation. The soil is heavier and requires a great deal of cultivation; new land is sometimes brought into cultivation by offering it rent free to a Negro tenant for three years. The land of the Sugar Region in Louisiana is worked by hired hands who are under an overseer. There are no tenants, but the hired man lives on the farm in houses which are provided for him and his family free. The areas described constitute in large measure the home of the agricultural Negro. The change occurring in these should prove of value in interpreting the shifting populations.

The Negro Farmer. The statistical division of the Negro farmers into owners, managers and tenants, provides a cold picture. The bulk of these, who are tenants, are parts of a system the features of which admit of considerable exploitation, both deliberate and undeliberate.

Slavery was dependent upon the plantation system, which formed, as Dr. U. B. Phillips phrases it, "the social and industrial frame of government in the black belt communities." It was "the factory system applied to agriculture," and provided for the employment of large gangs in large scale production of five staples. While it could draw upon the productive labor of the Negro, it limited the white laborer, prevented diversification, and rather generally restricted economic efficiency.[2]

Several Southern writers have insisted that the present high proportions of Negro farmers have tended to hold down the standard of living of farmers generally. Roland Harper[3] argues that standards of living are not generally or necessarily related to soil and other environmental factors but are related to the proportion of superior and inferior races, and differences among individuals among the same race. Although Carver and Vogt in their books on rural economics and sociology assert that high standards of living are correlated with fertile soil, there are exceptions, he holds, for while it is true for small areas with a homogeneous population, for widely separated regions and different races this does not hold. China and Denmark, the mountains of North Carolina and the Rocky Mountains in California and Colorado stand to the contrary. On the same spot the prevailing standards may change. Where the pioneer farmers of Illinois and Iowa once lived in primitive abodes there are now one- and two-house farms. A little reflection, he feels, will show that people of low standards as, for example, Chinese and Negroes, will get little out of rich soil, while progressive farmers will get much out of poor soil.

There is much to be said of the wasteful methods of Negro farmers, who, however, received their training in the South. There is as much, indeed, to be said of the normal life of the

---

[2] Phillips, Ulrich B., "Decadence of the Plantation System," *Annals of the American Academy of Political and Social Science,* January, 1910.

[3] Harper, Roland M., "Rural Standards of Living in the South," *Social Forces,* November, 1923.

soil which is beyond the control of these farmers. Alfred Holt Stone, a Southerner and a student of Southern life, has set down the dreary routine of the Negro agricultural worker under the characteristic systems of labor, with such objectivity that its features remain now with scarcely a change.

In the cultivation of cotton we have in the Delta nearly every system of labor to be found in the South. They are roughly divisible into two classes, the more general being the true metayer, or some modification of it, and the other the fixed cash rental. Where the Negro does not own the soil he cultivates, his relation to it is either that of a renter or a cropper. The share system presents no peculiar features. The cropper furnishes his labor in planting, cultivating, and gathering the crop; the land owner furnishes the land, the team and the implements; and the crop is divided equally between them. The planter advances to the cropper such supplies as are needed during the year, to be paid for out of the latter's half of the crop. As soon as a quantity of cotton sufficient to pay this account has been delivered to the planter, the cropper usually receives his portion of the cotton, to be disposed of as he sees fit. The extent to which the cropper exercises control over his cotton varies with the locality.

The features of land-renting by Negroes vary according to the nature of the tenancy, where the land is part of a plantation under white supervision, or a small tract, or part of a plantation entirely rented by a non-resident landlord. In the first case the land is rented for a fixed sum per acre, varying with cotton prices and the character of the soil, from $5 to $7. Where a lint rent is taken it varies from 80 to 100 pounds. Generally speaking, the supervision over a renter is not as strict as that over a cropper, and as soon as his account is paid his cotton is at his own disposal. More privileges and a larger measure of independence are considered by the Negro as incident to this tenure, and as he becomes the owner of a mule it is his ambition to become a renter. It frequently happens that a planter will rent a mule to a Negro who has nothing at all, the uniform rent being $25. Under each of these systems certain general features obtain. The planter takes no deed of trust, for the state statutes give him a lien on the crop for rent and supplies. Nor is it usual to have any written contract other than a mere memorandum.[4] There is generally no definite

---

[4] Within the past few years labor conditions have grown worse, and it is safe to say that probably 90 per cent of the plantation labor of this region is now under written contract. Specific agreements as to supplies are now the prevailing rule.

understanding as to the amount of supplies to be advanced, and it is well within the truth to say that usually the planter is engaged in an effort to keep the Negro's account within such limits as will make it safe, while the Negro is equally anxious to obtain as much as he can on credit.[5]

When the Negro tenant hires out to the landlord he signs a contract. The arrangement has brought endless misunderstanding, for the tenant usually finds himself wholly at the landlord's mercy. The system has encouraged at times both dishonesty and wastefulness. "It tended," says Ray Stannard Baker,[6] to make landlords cruel and greedy, and increased the helplessness, hopelessness and shiftlessness of the Negro." Peonage, of which so much has been heard, was a natural development of the system. The great volume of discontent is, however, in those milder cases which usually attract no attention.

The story of one ex-farmer in a Southern city reveals along with the pressure of low income a type of relations with land owners which is not wholly unique.

I just got tired of trying to farm and not making nothing either. I tried it awhile after I left my papa's place, and I worked on two men's places, but I couldn't get along with them. The first man I worked for made a trade with me to work on halves and he furnished the team and every day I worked for him he would pay just like everybody else. When the time come to settle up, he didn't want to keep his part of the deal. I finally got him to come across with all he owed me. When we got through settling up, he told me I was the best man he ever had on the place; I'd made more for him than anybody he'd had, but he didn't want me no more.

I worked for another man the next year and he told me I could have hogs and a garden. I had them too. I can raise hogs. It ain't everybody that knows how to handle hogs; my hogs never have no cholera, they can feed right along with hogs what got cholera and they never take it. All you have to do is get you some of this hog lye, lye with a hog on the can and give them 1 tablespoonful in enough slop for 10 hogs. They'll never have no cholera. I had such pretty hogs. He come to me and wanted me to let him have all of them but one. He said I didn't need but one, and if I needed any more I could buy meat from him. I told him that was all right if he wanted more meat than he had, he could

[5] Stone, Alfred Holt, *Studies in the American Race Problem*, pp. 99-100.
[6] Baker, Ray Stannard, *Following the Color Line*, pp. 94-5.

buy meat from me. Well, he got mad because I wouldn't let him have them, and wouldn't give me no work when mine was through with, expecting me to have to sell them hogs to get something to eat. But I just stepped over the fence and went to work for the man next to him. He didn't like that and come and told me he was going to turn the stock out and if I wanted to keep my garden, I'd have to put a fence up. I told him no, I wasn't. I had kept my part of the agreement, and he hadn't, and he was just trying to get my hogs. He got mad and threw a clod of dirt in my eyes and we had a scrap. Well, I left there and come to town. I would like to go back to the country if I ever get money to have my own place but I can't work for no white man. Course, I think I'll go to Chicago and work for my cousin. He says he's got a sausage factory and he gives all his folks work what comes up there. Everybody he got working for him now is his kinfolks.[7]

It would be unfair to regard this as the full picture; it is rather an index to the frequent abuses which figured so largely in the Negro discontent.

Of vital interest here, however, are those factors affecting both Negro and white tenant farmers, reflecting a restlessness which the census figures so dispassionately reveal.

A given area of soil can be made to yield greater production only in proportion to the intensive cultivation it gets and the added machinery and materials for working it. This applies whether the area is 1 acre or 1,000,000 acres. In addition to this, the law of diminishing returns limits even this proportion when the soil is condemned. On the other hand, as has been pointed out by one economist, it requires no more effort for 250,000 couples to produce 1,000,000 babies than for 1 couple to produce 4 babies. The Negroes, no more indeed than the whites, have not been able to compete with this principle. Instead of the productivity of the land increasing it has actually decreased while the instruments of improvement have increased in price over 60 per cent and land over 100 per cent. Unfortunately for the Negroes they have been producing cotton, which they could not eat, while the price of foodstuff, which they had to buy, has been rapidly and constantly increasing. Their work has been in large measure for cash and,

[7] From a Study in Preparation in the Department of Social Science, Fisk University.

whereas the exigencies of cotton have made the credit system notorious through loan extensions, crop uncertainties, failure, the boll weevil, droughts, floods, and long periods of unemployment, the actual buying power of the dollar has not improved. This credit system incidentally has worked inestimable damage to the economic independence of the Negro tenants.

There is further to be considered the general disorganization of agriculture in this country. The recent Agricultural Board appointed by President Hoover is a forceful recognition of this situation. This movement is not primarily political, but economic with social and political reactions. The farmers realize among other things that the period of expansion in new areas is practically at an end and that further expansion must be made by the movement on the part of the individual worker of the land, and in material through expansion in number and areas. For 20 years our economic statisticians have been telling us that agriculture is not keeping pace in its growth with other national industries. The exhaustion of the soil has brought further dangers. Those who are familiar with Southern farming conditions know that for the past 10 or 15 years there has been an hysterical emphasis upon crop diversification to preserve the life of the soil and give balance to its productivity.

The per cent of tenant farmers, instead of changing into owners, actually increased in practically every Southern state, while the per cent of owners decreased. Although this was to some extent true of white farmers, the proportion among Negroes was very much greater. Two forces are in operation: (a) the wealthy plantation owners are gradually taking over the land; (b) whites and Negroes are deserting the soil.

Bizzell [8] offers this explanation of the increasing control of land by a few owners. He says:

It may indicate that the high price of land has resulted in the consolidation of farm areas under capitalists' management where cultivation is in the hands of tenants or laborers; or it may indicate that the number and areas of abandoned farms have increased in this 10-year period. There is reason to believe that both factors enter into the explanation. Private monopoly in land and the

[8] Bizzell, W. B., *Farm Tenancy.*

inequalities that accompany it largely explain the problem of land tenantry. At least the immediate causes of farm tenantry have been conditionally the unequal bargaining power between land owners and land cultivators.

The farm tenant's labor income has generally been inadequate to supply his needs for maintaining a normal standard of living and to enable him to save a sufficient sum to apply on the purchase of a farm home. The tenant's labor income varies greatly with the type of crop production, acreage under cultivation and the amount of capital invested. Usually the farm tenant's investments are too small to leave a. margin of profits that may be used in making a farm purchase of a farm home. The tenant farmer depending solely on his labor income found it impossible owing to land specu- lation in land values to pay for a home without jeopardizing his economic independence. The tenant's ability to acquire a farm de- pends not only on the rate of income but upon the conditions under which he secures credit for his farm operations. The hazards con- nected with agricultural production and economic conditions have made the tenant farmer a poor financial risk. He concludes that the greatest progress in solving the farm problem is through legis- lation relating to rural credit.

In 1925, W. S. Scarborough,[9] formerly president of Wilber- force University, was sent by the Department of Agriculture into Virginia to study the changing tenure of Negro farmers. In that state with 19,000,000 acres of its territory in farm lands, the Negro farm population had decreased between 1910 and 1920 by 3,328 and white farmers had increased.[10]

In 1880, according to Dr. Scarborough, 45 per cent of all farms in Southampton County were operated by tenants. The number of these tenants decreased to 31 per cent in 1890; in- creased again to 56 per cent in 1900 and 59.2 per cent in 1910.

The intimate study made possible direct inquiries concerning the decline in Negro population. It had been assumed, of course, that the general tendency to migration northward was partially responsible. But the provocation to migration was re- garded as more important.

It was found that accumulations were very slow, particularly

---

[9] Scarborough, W. S., *Tenancy and Ownership Among Negro Farmers in Southampton County, Virginia*, U. S. Dept. of Agriculture Bulletin, No. 1404, April, 1926.

[10] *Negro Yearbook—1925-26* and U. S. Census of Agriculture, 1925. Sum- mary of Statistics by States.

in the tenant class. Sixty-one and six-tenths per cent of the tenants had accumulated less than $50 per year on the average since they began their earning life. Only 0.9 per cent of the tenants had been able to accumulate $200 or more per year, and 33.6 per cent of the owners.[11]

The factors were dismally inter-related, and reacted one upon the other. Lack of sufficient equipment was one of the penalties for failure to accumulate, but it also limited income and made the chances of accumulation less.

E. C. Branson in the *Journal of Social Forces* makes the situation more realistic. In the North and West tenant farming, he points out, is a capitalistic enterprise on the part of men with money; in the South it is a social estate on the part of moneyless men. The current notion of the North and West is that farm tenancy in the cotton belt is mainly a black man's problem; on the contrary it is a white man's problem. He uses Chatham County, North Carolina, as an example. In 1860 in this county there were 729 slave-holding families and nearly 1,800 white families who owned no slaves. Today the descendants of these 1,800 families are almost entirely the farm owners of the county. In 1922 Mr. J. A. Dickey, of the State University, spent the 3 summer months of 1922 in 329 farm homes of Baldwin and Williams townships in the northeast corner of Chatham County. The results of his observations point to a future which cannot be ignored in the present rural problems of the South. The tenants interviewed numbered 153; white 51; and Negro 102.

TABLE VII

All Farms	Sale of Farm Products	Other Cash Income	Total Money Income	Average Per Family
135 white owners	$ 72,218	$12,325	$ 84,553	$626.24
41 Negro owners	18,706	3,002	21,708	329.46
102 Negro tenants	17,867	8,396	26,263	257.49
51 white tenants	8,077	3,439	11,517	225.80
329 farmers	$116,868	$27,162	$144,041	$437.81

The ratio of tenants to all farmers is therefore 46.5 per cent or nearly half, against 35.8 per cent in the county-at-large, and

[11] Scarborough, W. S., *Tenancy and Ownership Among Negro Farmers in Southampton County, Virginia*, U. S. Dept. of Agriculture Bulletin, No. 1404, April, 1926.

43.5 per cent in the state-at-large. The 51 white tenants had accumulated personal property amounting to $23,277 which is an average of only $456 per family. The 102 Negro tenants held property amounting to $31,430, an average of $308 per family. The families of the Negro and white tenants were thus not very far apart in worldly goods. Neither could handle much money during the year.

The average daily cash income of these farmers was 34 cents for white owners and 32 cents for Negro owners; 14 cents for white tenants and 16 cents for Negro tenants; 8 cents for white croppers and 10 cents for Negro croppers. The situation regarding farm tenants in Chatham County, he maintains, is indicative of every other state of the South. Farm property is concentrated in the hands of land owners. (1) A little more than half of all the farmers, both races counted into the total, are land owners, but they own more than nine-tenths of all the property. (2) The black farm owners are a little more than a fourth of all the Negro farmers, but they own three-fourths of all the Negro property. (3) The white farm owners are nearly three-fourths of all the white farmers, but they own 97 per cent of all the white property.

His conclusion is most significant: "White farm tenancy in the South breeds poverty, poverty breeds illiteracy." [12]

H. Snyder, another Southern writer, in the *North American Review,* says that cotton, debt and boll weevil are the despots that rule the South. There is no other place where a single crop controls the destinies of so many people as in the South. Although in the hill regions there is some diversified farming, in the real cotton regions such as between the Yazoo and Mississippi rivers there is scarcely a hay-stack, orchard, or dairy. Oats from the North feed the mules. The tenant who cultivates the crop is supplied through the overseer with mules, feed, clothing, groceries, fuel, land, and everything for making a crop. He receives for his labor half of the crop. If the landlord is honest when cotton is high priced the tenant may have several hundred to two or three thousand a year net profit. As a rule, he is kept in debt. Interest is charged at a high rate by the capitalists who are constantly collecting the security given

[12] Branson, E. C., "Farm Tenancy in the South," *Social Forces,* Vol. I, pp. 213, 450-7, 1923.

and the vast army of tenant farmers both white and colored is constantly increasing. The cotton grower is not a farmer in the sense of the Northern farmer who produces a wide variety of agricultural products both for sale and for use at home. The Negro tenant as well as the white is dissatisfied and the shiftlessness does not produce the poverty of the South but the poverty produces the laziness. The tenant is always looking for some place where he can do better; thus the constant moving. Expert agriculturists and highly skilled labor, he feels, might cultivate a single crop with success but the average field Negro is rarely dependable, cunning and deceitful. "Especially do the cash renters in the less prosperous parts of the Cotton Belt till their acres in a disinterested, shiftless manner. Very frequently do they fail to pay for their 'furnish,' as they call their supply of provisions, and are forced to give up their mules and cows." The present-day South under the pall of debt should not be confused with the old South with its gay social life. The ill-balanced diet furthers the development of hook-worm, pellagra, and tuberculosis. . . . The 'migration, it is speculated, will change the status of the white man in the South for never before have so many entered the ranks of common laborers and sought opportunities in the North. What is to become of the plantations and the single-crop system which requires vast armies of men is the problem of the South today. The Negro continues to migrate to the cities and to the North.[13]

The desertion of the soil which cannot yield returns in proportion to population increase, thus is, perhaps, the strongest and yet the least obvious urge behind the restlessness and migrations of both Negroes and whites.

General results appear in the actual social condition of the farmer. Economic pressure prompts Negroes to use their children in farm work, and as E. E. Miller notes, white cotton growers have decided it necessary to work their children and often their wives in order to make a living. The white farmer has the competition of the Negroes who have been accustomed to low wages and standards of living. In individual cases this has been of great help but the labor of the children has helped to reduce prices. Any product made by cheap labor should sell

[13] Snyder, H., "Negro Migration and the Cotton Crop," *North American Review*, January, 1924.

at low prices. Whatever makes for industrial development in the South gives the cotton grower better chance for fair wages.

This clear conclusion is forced: "Anything done to advance educational interest in the rural South or to aid the Negro to a higher plane of living brings nearer the better day." [14]

As to remedies for the Negro farmers' plight, perhaps one of the first suggestions is that of a remedy for the farmers' plight generally. Obvious needs are education in scientific farm methods, credit facilities to aid in securing of land, animals and tools, development of cooperative marketing methods; improvement of certain of the harsher pictures in their social life in the rural sections—better schools, some forms of recreation, better homes. For after all these factors appear as motivating forces in migration.

Two projects have recently been launched in the South with a view to understanding these problems more thoroughly, and offer hopeful prospects:

(1) An agricultural study involving two counties in Georgia (Green and Macon) has been under way about two years, to determine the economic processes at work behind the following facts:

With approximately the same soil conditions and during the same period one county has experienced no change while the other has lost large numbers through migration. The factors involved are the operation of the tenant farmer system, crop diversification, schools, plantation management, and the ratio of tenants and croppers to owners.

The study is being conducted by Mr. Raper, a graduate of the University of North Carolina, under the auspices of the Commission on Interracial Cooperation in Atlanta.

(2) An agricultural experiment has been projected jointly by Tuskegee Institute and Alabama Polytechnical Institute, at Auburn, which contemplates the conducting of a controlled agricultural venture in farm purchasing, soil development and marketing, involving Negro and white farmers.

Monroe Work from the center of one agricultural area, at Tuskegee, sounds a note of encouragement when he says:

[14] Miller, E. E., "Cotton, a National Crop," *Review of Reviews*, Vol. LXXIV, pp. 70-73.

If one confined himself to the facts on agriculture in the South as presented by the census reports he might be inclined to believe that the Negro farmers are not making progress. When, however, one becomes acquainted at first hand with the farmers themselves, sees them in their meetings, hears them discuss in an intelligent way the technical aspects of their problems, if he visited the many county and community fairs which were held this year in various sections of the South and saw there the quality and quantity of the products which the Negro farmers placed on exhibit, he would conclude that in spite of their handicaps they were making some progress.

CHAPTER X

THE NEGRO'S HEALTH

A Story of Survival. Just as Negro dialect turns out to be a repository for the early seventeenth-century speech of the first English colonizers, the medical lore adopted by Negroes, and the conceptions of the origin and nature of disease reflected in the treatment of their ailments, are quite distinctly survivals of earlier American theory and practice. In the folk remedies, whether based upon Martin Luther's dogma of the scourge of demons or Cotton Mather's dogma of the scourge of God, the effect has been practically the same. In spite of the African background, with the known universality of belief in magic and witchcraft, it becomes tedious to separate these origins from those of common English and early American practice to which they are exposed. Dr. N. N. Puckett [1] devotes a large volume to Negro folk beliefs, gathered over a wide area, and concludes that "the tendency is for the Negro to take over English practice in regard to the direct maintenance and perpetuation of life, while in things relating to pleasure his customs seemingly have more of an African turn."

Conditions attending the first coming of Negroes to America prevented survival of many of the essentially African traditions. Few remembered even the parts of Africa from which they came. The policy of prompt distribution, both as a practical matter of sales and to guard against insurrections; the forbidding of communication in the native tongue; the varied tribal sources of slaves; and the strict regimentation of slave life generally contributed to a physical and cultural detachment well nigh complete. Contrary to the common notion, the majority of slaves were distributed in small numbers, and the close association with the early American settlers gave rare opportunity for taking over the most intimate features of the essen-

[1] Puckett, N. N., Ph.D., *Folk Beliefs of the Southern Negro*, p. 78.

tial beliefs of their masters. For the entire cotton area of the South at its highest point of development the average was no more than six full hands to the farm, and half of the total cotton crop was actually made by farmers whose slaves were on the average scarcely more numerous than the white members of their own families.[2]

The history of Negro mortality is a story of the persistence and inheritance of folk superstitions, magic and witchcraft; of theories of racial differences successively altered or abandoned; of economic factors, first operating to encourage their sensible care as property and later to limit their hold on life in the competitive struggle for survival following their emancipation. A seventeenth-century English pharmacopœia, not unknown to our early settlers, suggests among other things that the lungs of foxes will cure asthma, that moss from the skull of a person who has met with violent death is beneficial to persons suffering from certain diseases, and that cat ointment, oil of puppies boiled with earthworms, will cure dysentery. When Olmstead made his famous tour of the Seaboard States he reported a nerve medicine in use compounded of a Scottish mineral and steel filings.

The full African responsibility for Negro conceptions of disease, so important in the early mortality rates, becomes questionable even though there were numerous slave doctors with reputations for accomplishing remarkable cures among slaves and others. Cæsar, a South Carolina slave, became famed for a cure for poison which was a compound of plantain, hoarhound, golden rod roots, rum and lye, and in 1750 the legislature of the colony ordered it published for the benefit of the public. The differences in the Negro and white medical formulæ are in most cases quite minute. A Negro cure for backache, for example, was a live toad. frog; settlers from Devonshire, England, believed the cure was effected by a dead toad burned and the ashes carried about the neck in a silk bag.[3]

For whooping cough the Negroes used mare's milk, drawn from the left side, or horse manure placed on the chest; the Herefordshire people in America in the early eighteenth century used milk from a she-ass mixed with hairs from her back and

[2] Phillips, U. B., *American Negro Slavery.*
[3] Puckett, N. N., *Folk Beliefs of the Southern Negro.*

belly, and instead of the manure plaster the child was carried to a stable to inhale the breath of a piebald horse.[4]

With Negroes diseases were thought to be prevented by using some odoriferous substance "intended to keep the disease spirit away." Most commonly this was asafœtida. Similarly, in Europe and America, it was carried in the pocket to prevent small-pox, and faith in it survives even today among the isolated white Kentucky and Tennessee mountain folk.

Two significant features may be observed: (1) The earlier conceptions of disease and its cure reflected obviously the undeveloped state of medicine, before the epoch-making discoveries of Pasteur; and (2) the folk beliefs have survived longest among the Negroes who, despite contact, represent distinct and observable degrees of isolation in their intimate life. The general mortality rates as late as the beginning of the nineteenth century in Europe and America show this difference startlingly. The span of life then was 35 and 40 years. The life expectancy in Europe and America as late as 1900 was less than that of Negroes today. The real gains have come since the beginning of the twentieth century when there has been noted an increase of 10 years, from 48 in 1901 to 58 in 1925.[5] The assumption seems warranted that the change has been due to an improved understanding of disease and to purposeful public health efforts.

Early Records. Into the record of Negro mortality go, moreover, along with the potent folk beliefs, pages from the early history of medicine and anthropology. The development of the institution of slavery helped and was aided by the crystallization of the notion of physiological as well as physical differences. The ingenious explanations of this difference gave birth to a special order of observations for medical science. Seventy-five years ago, Dr. Samuel A. Cartwright of New Orleans, one of the most widely known physicians of his period, was appointed by the physicians of Louisiana to study the diseases and physical peculiarities of the Negro race. One of the most significant findings of his study, aided by an instrument called a spirometer, was that "Negroes are sometimes, though rarely, afflicted with tubercula pulmonum, or phthisis, prop-

[4] Leather, E. M., *Folklore of Herefordshire*. Also see Leans Collectanea, Vol. II.
[5] *Whither Mankind*, edited by Charles A. Beard. Chapter on Health, by C.-E. A. Winslow, p. 188.

erly so called"; that phthisis is, par excellence, a disease of the
sanguineous temperament, fair complexion, red or flaxen hair,
blue eyes, large blood vessels, and a bony encasement too small
to admit the full and free expansion of the lungs; that phthisis
is a disease of the master race and not of the slave race—that
it is the bane of the master race of men, known by an active
hæmatosis, by the brain receiving a larger quantity of aërated
blood than it is entitled to, by the strong development of the
circulatory system, by the energy of intellect, vivid imagination,
and an indomitable will and love of freedom. The Negro constitution, he found, being the opposite of all this, is not subject
to phthisis, although it partakes of what is called the scrofulous
diathesis; and this condition is due to the fact that the pulmonary apparatus of the Negro is adjusted to the consumption
of less oxygen, a conviction which had the support of no less
a person than Thomas Jefferson.

Guenebault,[6] writing in 1835, observed that several diseases
of the Negro were quite different from those of the white man,
and although contagious among Negroes could not be communicated to white men because of differences in their constitutions, on the same principle that contagious diseases which
affect one species are not communicated to another.

The infections most common to Negroes in the early nineteenth century were listed as abscess, furuncles, fluxions, tume-
factions of glands, erysipelas, false peripneumony, worms,
œdemia, bilious gastritis, dysentery and visceral obstructions,
but seldom liable to icterode typhus. Chamallon observed that
gout, gravel stone and apoplexy were unknown among them,
and that their affections were produced altogether by bad diges-
tion. Meckel in 1757 stated as a fact that the color of the
Negro child when first born is yellow, which becomes a shiny
black in manhood, and this observation was practically repeated
in 1852 by Dr. Cartwright of New Orleans, who claimed as a
fact that "Negro children and white children are alike at birth
in one particular—they are both born white, and so much alike,
as far as color is concerned, as scarcely to be distinguished from
each other."[7] Malpighi, Stubner, Meckel, Pechlin, Albinus,

[6] Guenebault, J. H., *Natural History of the Negro Race.*
[7] *Cotton Is King,* edited by E. N. Elliot. Paper on Ethnology by Samuel
A. Cartwright, M.C., p. 708.

Soemmering, Virey and Ebel, all learned men of medicine, testified to the darker secretions, blood and membranes as well as flesh of Negroes. The instrument called the "spirometer" measured a difference in the Negroes' consumption of oxygen, representing a deficiency of about 20 per cent. Thomas Jefferson is authority for fixing a difference in the amount of calories extricated from the air by respiration. The interesting proof of less oxygen consumption was propounded in an analogy between Negroes and the owl and flounder. Their motions, it was claimed, are slower and there is want of muscular and mental agility. The flounder's slow motion is due to smaller gills, the owl's and Negroes' to small oxygen consumption.

One efficacious remedy for this condition was found to be blistering the nape of the neck, or in the case of Negroes, some other part of the body. This was expected to relieve defective respiration and dispel that sluggishness and inactivity "almost approaching to asphyxia and resulting from the diminished quantity of oxygen consumed." The work of M. Dazille,[8] accepted as standard by medical men in the South, was responsible for the belief that Negroes were not so liable to inflammatory diseases of the lungs as the white races, because the "white fluids, or lymphatic temperament" predominated in them. However, he conceded, due to superabundant viscidities and mucosities of their mucous surfaces they were more liable to pulmonary congestion, pneumonia. Following these medical theories, now strange museum pieces, was the natural conviction that Negro constitutions required different remedies. This conviction survived for many years after emancipation. Into the history of Negro mortality, thus, should go the sober observations of Soemmering and Lichtenberg [9] of larger nerves with the inference by analogy of smaller brains than the European, a larger medullary spinal cord, an occipital foramen a third longer than the Caucasian, smaller lungs, larger liver and kidney, a brain one-tenth lighter than Europeans; the "lymphatic temperament" of Dr. Rudolph Matas, the "peristaltic" movements and reactions, "fibroid diathesis," and the famous notion of the closing of the frontal sutures at puberty.

[8] M. Dazille, *Observations sur les Maladies des Negres.*
[9] *Ueber die Körperliche Verschiedenheit des Negers von Europaer.*

Although the old prosoposcopia of Hippocrates served in most instances to diagnose the ailments of the Negro slaves, the health of their bodies was always essential as an economic measure. The careful regimentation of plantation life, the control exercised by the slave owners over food, alcohol and narcotics, the enforced regularity of habits, the exercise of work, and the encouragement of fertility even at the cost of certain moral concepts, contributed a factor which reflects itself statistically. Rates of mortality for Negro slaves and freedmen differ significantly as do the white and Negro rates when available for the early period. The mortality of Negro slaves was considerably less than that of the non-slave-holding whites of the South. Physicians' bills figure prominently in the accounting of practically all of the larger plantations, and although physical mistreatment of slaves was frequent and notorious it was recognized that attention to their well-being was as essential as to that of their beasts. The rules framed by Fowler's plantation in the Yazoo-Mississippi delta prescribed that "the health, happiness, good discipline and obedience, sufficient and comfortable clothing, wholesome and nutritious food for both man and beast are indispensably necessary to successful planting, as well as for reasonable dividends for the amount of capital invested." [10] Duties of pregnant women and sucklers were lightened at periods, a fact which both encouraged fertility and added to capital in new slaves. The diet while rough was regular and perhaps accounts for the absence of many diseases attributable to overeating. As in the matter of work the economic imperatives of the institution created for the slaves physical well-being superior to that of the poor whites in the South and the Irish immigrants in the North. Olmstead comments upon the poor whites of the North Carolina turpentine forests:

They are poor, having almost no property but their own bodies; and the use of these, that is, their labor, they are not accustomed to hire out statedly and regularly, so as to obtain capital by wages, but only occasionally by the day or job, when driven to it by necessity. A family of these people will commonly hire, or "squat" and build, a little log cabin, so made that it is only a shelter from rain, the sides not being chinked, and having no more furniture or pre-

[10] Phillips, U. B., *American Negro Slavery*, p. 262.

tension to comfort than is commonly provided a criminal in the cell of a prison.[11]

The slave-holder of North Carolina who wrote urging an immigration of Irish and Germans to Virginia and North Carolina, bears testimony to the necessity for physical care for Negro slaves not considered in the case of free labor.

". . . A good able-bodied Negro costs nowadays $1,000, and at this price is very unprofitable property. A mortgage on a flock of partridges is almost as certain. He may die, be maimed for life, or be induced by his philanthropic Northern friends to vamose; whereas, if 'Paddy' or 'Hans' shuffles off his mortal coil, you suffer no pecuniary loss; you don't even bury him, or pay his doctor's bill, but get another hand in his place." [12]

The absolute control over the slaves and the relations of the sexes conceivably exercised a selective influence. Mates could be deliberately selected with a view to improvement of the stock. Tillinghast thinks this was an important factor in adapting the race to a new environment. From such records as are available the mortality of Negro slaves was less than that of free Negroes. There is preserved in the letters of Professor E. A. Andrews [13] a record of the comparative mortality of slaves, free Negroes and whites for the city of Baltimore from 1824 to 1834. The deaths annually among the slaves averaged 1 to 44 of the whole number, among the whites 1 to 38 and among the free Negroes 1 to 29. The chances for life among the slaves were thus greater than among either the whites or free Negroes.

Dr. Frederick L. Hoffman,[14] in the first extensive research into Negro mortality trends, states that "the opinion of Southern physicians who practiced among Negroes before the (Civil) War was almost unanimous that consumption was less frequent among the colored population than among the white." Mortality records extend backward to an early period in Charleston, South Carolina; Mobile, Alabama; Savannah, Georgia; and

[11] Olmstead, F. L., *A Journey in the Seaboard Slave States,* Vol. I, pp. 388, 389.
[12] *Ibid.,* Vol. II, p. 386.
[13] *Slavery and the Domestic Slave-trade in the United States.*
[14] Hoffman, Frederick L., "Race Traits and Tendencies of the American Negro," American Economic Association, p. 69, 1896.

New Orleans, Louisiana. In Charleston the death rate for whites and Negroes from consumption between 1822 and 1848 was as follows:

Period	White	Colored
1822-1830	457	447
1831-1840	331	320
1840-1848	268	266
1822-1848	347	342

General mortality rates calculated by Dr. Hoffman from existing records show the following:

	Period	White	Colored
Mobile, Alabama	1843-46	45.83	23.10
	1847-50	42.53	31.19
	1852-55	54.39	34.70
Savannah, Georgia	1856-60	37.19	34.07
New Orleans, Louisiana	1849-60	59.60	52.10

The number of rejected recruits per 1,000 examined for the Civil War [15] was for white recruits 264.1, and for colored recruits 120.2; for consumption the number of rejections of white recruits was 11.4 and the Negro recruits 4.2. The curious consistency of the figures in different cities may in some degree balance their defectiveness otherwise. Immediately following emancipation when the Negroes were thrown suddenly, and in their vast unlettered helplessness, upon their own economic resources their mortality took an abrupt and startling upward trend. Coincident with this was the release of the hundreds of thousands of poor whites from the economic domination of slavery. The comparative records become almost uncanny in their story.

Mobile, Alabama				Charleston, South Carolina		
Period	White	Negro		Period	White	Negro
1843-46	45.83	23.10		1822-30	32.73	28.16
1846-80	24.64	39.74		1866-75	25.56	41.98

Savannah, Georgia				New Orleans, Louisiana		
Period	White	Negro		Period	White	Negro
1856-60	37.19	34.07		1849-60	59.60	52.10
1866-70	33.16	57.26		1871-73	28.63	44.61

The racial ratios shifted for consumption in Charleston, South Carolina, from 268 for whites and 266 for Negroes in

[15] Medical Statistics of the Provost Marshal General's Bureau, Vol. II, p. 431.

the period 1841 to 1848 to 198 for whites and 411 for Negroes in the year just following the Civil War. In 1890, the year for which the most recent figures were available for Dr. Hoffman, the white consumption rate was 355.4 per 100,000 and the Negro rate 686.3. The dismal conclusion of Dr. Hoffman's [16] book was: "In the plain language of the facts brought together the colored race is shown to be on the downward grade, tending toward a condition in which matters will be worse than they are now, when disease will be more destructive, vital resistance still lower, when the number of births will fall below the deaths, and gradual extinction of the race take place."

Later Records. The changes in mortality after the Civil War, while mirroring fundamentally altered economic conditions, are significantly related to improvements in the science of medicine. In 1865 Pasteur began his epoch-making discoveries in bacteriology through the indirect route of the silk industry. There followed the germ theory of disease, and between 1860 and 1880 some of the most vital contributions of the nineteenth century were made to the foundations of a new science of medicine.[17] During the last 50 years some 1,500 kinds of bacteria have been discovered. Not only has the knowledge of disease improved but the whole attitude toward disease has changed. Public health programs began with vigor around 1890 and the more advanced communities deliberately initiated their campaigns to control communicable diseases through the purification of water and food supplies, vaccines, the pasteurization of milk, and later through toxin-anti-toxin immunization. These results have been carried further of late years in programs for the control of infant mortality, venereal and mental diseases. During the past 50 years the general mortality rate has been reduced 60 per cent in spite of a concurrent high migration to cities, European immigration and the consequent concentration in smaller areas. The changed attitude regarding Negro disease and mortality has been slower than the rest, probably because the bulk of this population resided in those sections in which health progress generally was slow. Their mortality

---

[16] Hoffman, Frederick L., F.S.S., "Race Traits and Tendencies of the American Negro," p. 312, American Economic Association, 1896.
[17] Bossard, James H. S., *Problems of Social Well Being,* p. 158.

was at its peak when Dr. Hoffman's dark forebodings were announced. A dull fatalism dominated the speculation regarding their future. It is a strange irony that the Negro death rate today is almost precisely that of the white rate when the alarming comparisons were made 30 years ago.

In 1920 at a conference of the Urban League, in Newark, New Jersey, Dr. Louis I. Dublin, statistician of the Metropolitan Life Insurance Company, spoke on Negro health and observed the high but correctable mortality of Negroes from specific diseases. The frankness, curiously enough, constituted a sort of *faux pas*. The implications of the cold stark graphs and figures were resented. This incident serves well to mark dramatically the period of turning for Negroes and whites on the question of Negro mortality. For 60 years phthisic decimation had been accepted by most white students as inevitable to the constitutionally inferior physique of this race. The Negroes had refuted the facts defensively and uncritically along with other allegedly scientific findings which helped to fix their social status in America as inferiors.

Despite the relative imperviousness of sections of the Negro population to the new programs of health, through their isolation, educational backwardness, concentration in less advanced sections, sluggishness prompted by the attitude of futility to attempting to change their vital index, and the characteristic marginal status of Negroes in health programs of any sort, they have not escaped, during the past 30 years, many of the benefits from such general measures as water purification, vaccines, the pasteurization of milk, general economic improvement and the particular economic results of their mass migration during the World War. Always, however, the *lag* has persisted. And although the disparity between Negro and white rates is still considerable, the rate of decline for Negroes, during the past 20 years, has in certain notable respects been more rapid. As late as 1911 out of every 100,000 living Negroes 418 died of tuberculosis and 46 died of typhoid fever. In 1926 the tuberculosis deaths had dropped to 235, or about 40 per cent, and the typhoid deaths to 9.

Fifty years ago tuberculosis, diphtheria, typhoid fever and diarrhea were the chief causes of death for the population of the United States considered as a whole. Tuberculosis has fallen to fifth place and the fatal importance of the rest has disappeared. The new ogres are heart disease, nephritis, cancer and pneumonia. The *lag* of the Negro rates persists with a dogged faithfulness. Tuberculosis held first place with them as late as 1924. The new chief causes of death for Negroes are heart disease, nephritis and pneumonia, and since 1911 deaths from cancer and diabetes have increased. These changes, general and specific, emphasize the fundamental nature of the Negro health problem. They emphasize its relationship to education which is conditioned by health and in turn affects it; to industry and the standard of living which the wage determines; to housing, the full rôle of which is just beginning to be sensed in the new urbanization; to recreation which offsets fatigue and sets in motion the forces which make for health; and to that vast and restless universe of race attitudes and relations which, quite as much as science, are regulating the span of Negro life and reducing the ravages of preventable diseases.

GENERAL VITAL STATISTICS OF THE NEGRO POPULATION

General Mortality Data. The Negro death rate in the United States in 1925, the last year for which figures are available on the entire registration area, was 18.2; in 1924 it was 17.6 and in 1923 it was 17.7. It was 48 per cent higher than the white rate in 1924 and 62.5 per cent higher in 1925.

The Negro death rate, urban and rural, in the North is higher than in the South. The average death rate per 1,000 for 9 Southern states was 16.9 and for 10 Northern states it was 22.4. In the North the larger proportions of Negroes are found in cities. Urban deaths for this population are uniformly higher than rural death rates. These rates were 23.5 per 1,000 for urban and 15.2 for rural sections. The disparity between white and Negro death rates is greater in urban than in rural sections, the Negro rate being 94 per cent greater for the first and 50 per cent greater for the second. The Negro death rate is greater for Southern than for Northern cities. In 1925 it averaged 25.7 per 1,000 in the cities of 9 Southern states and 22.1 per 1,000 in the cities of 10 Northern states. On the other hand the Negro rural death rate is greater in the

North than in the South. For the North it was 23.4; for the South it was 14.8.[18]

The disparity between Negro rural and urban rates is over two and a half times greater than the disparity between white urban and rural deaths. The urban mortality rate decreases for whites and Negroes alike, the further north the area, and the rural rates increase. That is to say, the highest urban rates are in the lower South, the next highest in the upper South and the lowest in the Northern States; the lowest rural rates, on the other hand, are in the lower South and the highest in the North.[19]

Based upon the 11 registration states the expectation of life increased 8 years for Negro males and 7.3 years for Negro females between 1900 and 1920; for white males it increased about 5.9 years and for white females 5.3. An analysis of the 1919 and 1920 tables by R. H. Britten shows that both white and Negro females have a greater expectation of life, and that during the past 10 years Negroes have shown a greater improvement than whites in expectation at birth. There is still a large disparity, however. Gover and Sydenstricker[20] of the United States Public Health Service, basing their calculations upon the original registration states, find the mean age at death of all persons for the last three decades, as follows: white males, 48, 50 and 54 years; white females, 51, 54 and 56 years; Negro males, 33, 34 and 41 years; Negro females, 35, 38 and 42 years. The mean age for Negroes, thus, is about 15 years earlier than for whites. The calculation is based upon the original registration states, which, incidentally, contain less than 4 per cent

[18] The explanation is offered for the direction of these trends that economic conditions of the Northern city Negro, particularly since 1910, are superior to that of the Southern city Negro. Better clothing, food, housing, sanitation, medical attendance are possible. The rural Southern Negro is in the most favorable environment. The chances of escaping death are better through natural advantages; food is plentiful; there is unlimited fresh air and sunshine; more physical exercise for the great majority; life is simple and free from strain, devastating amusements and hazardous occupations. These tend to outweigh, in great part, poorer water supply and drainage and other disadvantages associated with life in the country. The Northern Negro living in the rural areas is exposed to severe weather during the winter months from which the Southern Negro is fairly exempt.

[19] *Mortality Among Negroes in the United States,* Public Health Bulletin, No. 174, 1928.

[20] *Some Tendencies Indicated by the New Life Tables,* Public Health Reports, April 11, 1924.

of the Negro population and include the highest Negro death rates in the entire registration area. They tend accordingly to represent a minimum and, probably, an artificially constricted life expectancy of Negroes. Mortality from all causes for Negroes, adjusted for age, shows smaller rates for rural Negroes than for urban whites in Florida, Louisiana, Mississippi, North Carolina and South Carolina.

The most serious disease among Negroes has been tuberculosis. In 1920 the rate was 202 per 100,000 as compared with 85.7 for whites. Pneumonia, lobar and bronchial combined,

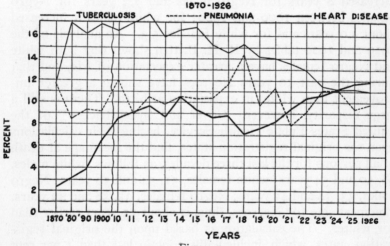

PERCENT OF NEGRO DEATHS FROM TUBERCULOSIS, PNEUMONIA AND HEART DISEASE IN THE UNITED STATES
1870-1926

Figure 9

came second with 145.9 as compared with 97.1 for whites, while acute nephritis and Bright's disease came fourth with 104.3 for Negroes, 28.0 for whites. In 1925 the importance of organic diseases of the heart was revealed as the leading cause of death. Following this, in numerical order of seriousness, were tuberculosis of the respiratory system, pneumonia, external causes (excluding suicide and homicide), congenital malformations and diseases of early infancy, cerebral hemorrhage and softening, and cancer. These eight diseases were responsible for over 58 per cent of Negro deaths.

In the Negro city population, the order was as follows: organic diseases of the heart, pneumonia, tuberculosis of the respiratory system, nephritis, congenital debility and diseases of early infancy, cerebral hemorrhage, cancer and external causes. In rural sections tuberculosis leads, followed by heart disease, nephritis, pneumonia, external causes, congenital malformation, cerebral hemorrhage, diarrhea and cancer. The diseases which, authorities agree, are due largely to unfavorable sanitary conditions and low economic status, show the greatest disparity between Negro and white rates. These are pulmonary tuberculosis, typhoid, malaria, pellagra and puerperal conditions.

Mortality from tuberculosis among Negroes has its heaviest incidence at younger age periods than for whites. It is greatly in excess of the white rates between the ages of 20 and 45 and reaches the highest point of disparity at the age of 25. Mortality from tuberculosis has declined rapidly during the past 15 years. It was 463 per 100,000 in 1910 and 239 in 1921. In New York City it declined from 617 in 1910 to 299 in 1921 while the white rate dropped from 202 to 97. It is six times as high among Negro boys and girls as among white boys and girls. Control of tuberculosis alone, it is estimated, would increase the Negro life span by 5 years. Negro mortality from all causes has increased about 59 per cent per 100,000 since 1923, and this increase has been distributed over all except the infectious diseases. The Negro crude death rate is less than that of Austria, France, Italy, Roumania and Spain.

The high Negro death rates in 1920 for specific diseases were paralleled most closely by the Irish in America, with the highest rates among whites for tuberculosis (194.6), nephritis and Bright's disease (190.5), cerebral hemorrhage and softening (99.9), and organic diseases of the heart (283.2).[21]

Adjusted Mortality Rates. Gover and Sydenstricker of the United States Public Health Service, in their study of Negro vital statistics from government sources, in 1928, had the cooperation of the Census Bureau beyond that usually accorded private individuals. The most recent year in which both the population and deaths were known was 1920. The Negro urban mortality for that period shows extraordinary fluctuations in seriousness by age groups. It varies for the years under 5 from 34.4 in Michigan to 100.9 in South Carolina.

[21] Carpenter, Niles, *Immigrants and Their Children,* Census Monograph, Vol. VII, p. 199, 1927.

Dean Deutcher's study [22] of the Negro population movement indicates what might be expected, that the percentage of children tends to increase with the number of Negro women migrating. Michigan is highly industrialized, and the labor demand has been primarily for men.

Wide differences appear in other age groups between states. For the age group 15-19 the rate of difference, measured in terms of standard deviation, is 2.78; for the group 0-4 it is 13.9; for the group 20-29 it is 1.53; but for the group 80-89 it is 39. These offer problems for study and may throw light upon the effect of migrations of various age groups upon general Negro mortality rates.

When adjusted, urban death rates for Negroes and whites are highest in South Carolina, Mississippi and Louisiana. Adjusted rural rates show lowest Negro rates in the Southern states.

TABLE VIII

White and Colored Mortality from All Causes for [23] Urban and Rural Areas of States, Adjusted for Age, 1920

State	Total White	Total Colored	Urban White	Urban Colored	Rural White	Rural Colored
Florida	11.7	17.3	13.7	24.0	11.1	15.4
Illinois	12.4	24.5	13.9	24.9	10.5	24.1
Kentucky	11.0	19.1	14.4	24.3	10.3	17.2
Louisiana	11.2	17.0	15.8	30.6	8.8	13.5
Maryland	13.0	22.6	14.1	26.8	11.6	19.5
Michigan	13.2	29.2	15.2	30.0	11.5	29.4
Mississippi	9.9	16.4	18.8	35.8	8.9	....
Missouri	11.5	22.5	14.9	29.9	9.7	18.0
New Jersey	13.0	23.6	13.8	25.7	11.7	20.3
New York	13.6	23.8	14.3	25.0	11.8	17.6
North Carolina	11.8	17.4	17.9	27.2	11.0	15.9
Pennsylvania	13.5	25.0	15.1	26.2	12.1	21.3
South Carolina	12.6	15.8	21.4	37.4	11.3	17.2
Tennessee	11.0	19.0	17.2	28.0	9.9	15.5
Virginia	11.6	18.9	14.5	25.6	10.7	16.8

NOTE. States used are those in the death-registration area of 1920 which contained 90 per cent or more of the total colored population and in which, with the exception of Michigan, the total number of Negroes was 100,000 or more. The Negro population of Michigan was 60,082 persons.

Using the 4 states, Mississippi, North Carolina, Ohio and Michigan as typical of different localities, death rates from all

[22] Deutcher, Dean, *Changes in Distribution of the Negro Population in the United States.* Unpublished manuscript.

[23] *Mortality Among Negroes in the United States,* Public Health Bulletin, No. 174, p. 16, 1928.

causes are high between the ages of 15 and 40 in Michigan and in Ohio between 15 and 30. In North Carolina and Mississippi death rates are higher during middle age than in the Northern states. The age specific rates would indicate, since the high Negro rural rate for old age is due to excessively high rates for early middle age, that tuberculosis has been the cause responsible for the high mortality from all causes among the rural Negroes in Northern states.

Non-census Statistics of Negro Mortality. The Metropolitan Life Insurance Company insures about 2,500,000 Negroes. Most of these are in its industrial department. While there is a certain selection of risks the records of the Company are most carefully kept. The data are more complete and less open to challenge than those of the Census Bureau, and they have, until recently, embraced an area more representative of the country than the registration area. Dr. Louis I. Dublin, statistician of the company, has given particular attention to these mortality trends and the bulletins issued constitute perhaps the most valuable data available regarding trends in Negro mortality. The experience of the company as late as 1927 indicates that at every age period and for each sex, the death rate for Negroes is in excess of that for whites.

TABLE IX

DEATH RATE PER 100,000 FROM ALL CAUSES—EXPERIENCE OF METROPOLITAN LIFE INSURANCE COMPANY, INDUSTRIAL WEEKLY PREMIUM-PAYING BUSINESS, 1927

Age	Males White	Colored	Per Cent Colored of White	Females White	Colored	Per Cent Colored of White
All ages	846.8	1,508.7	178.1	770.5	1,416.4	183.8
Under 1	3,413.9	5,574.6	163.3	2,761.6	4,621.3	167.3
1-4	553.7	1,035.3	187.0	483.5	853.3	176.5
5-14	213.7	334.8	156.7	172.9	298.8	172.8
15-24	310.9	753.5	242.4	315.2	875.2	277.7
25-44	661.7	1,233.0	186.3	514.7	1,168.0	226.9
45-64	2,369.9	3,005.1	126.8	1,646.8	2,628.9	159.6
65 and over	7,148.3	7,962.6	111.4	5,797.1	6,845.4	118.1

The excess is more pronounced among females than among males for all but one group. The Negro infant mortality rates are nearly two-thirds above the whites. From age 5 to adolescence the margin of excess of Negroes is 57 per cent for males and 72 per cent for females. Between 15 and 25 years of age the Negro rates are nearly two and one-half times that of the

whites.   Between 25 and 44 the difference is not so great but
still unfavorable to the Negroes.   The margin narrows during
the later ages.   The life expectation calculated from these
figures shows 44.24 for Negro males and 46.39 for Negro females as compared with 54.16 and 58.64 respectively for the
whites.

Tuberculosis was the chief cause of death among the Negro
policy holders.   In 1927 the rate was 226.2 per 100,000 or
about three times the white rate of 73.4 per cent.   Organic
heart disease followed with a rate of 211.6, or about twice that
of the whites.   Chronic nephritis (122.1) was third.   These
three, with cerebral hemorrhage, pneumonia and fatal accidents
accounted for two-thirds of the mortality of Negroes.   Their
rates for typhoid, pneumonia, whooping cough, bronchitis, puerperal conditions, influenza, acute nephritis, malaria, pellagra
and homicides were from three to eleven times higher than the
insured whites.   The acute communicable diseases of childhood,
such as measles and scarlet fever, occur less frequently among
Negroes.   The same is true of all forms of cancer, of erysipelas,
diabetes, anemia, locomotor ataxia, diseases of the ears, gall
stones, spleen and urinary calculus.   Dr. Dublin thus sum-
marizes :

After evaluating all of the relatively unfavorable items the fact
still stands out that a remarkable decline in the mortality of the
American Negro has taken place in a little less than two decades.
In 1911, the mortality of the colored industrial policy holders of the
Metropolitan was 17.5 per 1,000.   In 1927, the death rate of these
insured Negroes had declined to 14.0, which represents a drop of
approximately 20 per cent in this period.   There would have been
more than 8,000 deaths of colored policyholders than actually occurred in 1927 if the 1911 death rate had prevailed in that year.
This marked decline is due, for the most part, to improvements in
the death rates from tuberculosis, pneumonia, malaria, typhoid
fever and pellagra, and in some smaller degree, Bright's disease.
A number of factors are clearly at work which are operating favorably on the life and health of our Negro population.   Particularly
noteworthy has been the great development of health activities in
the South and Southwest.   The general economic status of Negroes
has been better, both during the War period and in the decade since.
The betterment has been a broad one, affecting virtually all areas,
with scarcely a state (in which there is a significant Negro popu-

lation) failing to show a decided decline in the total death rate. While it is true that the mortality among Negroes is still high, reflecting marked deficiencies in the health provisions for them, we cannot but conclude that the public health movement is making a favorable impress upon our colored population.

Sources of Mortality Statistics. It is pointed out by the most careful students of Negro vital statistics that returns from the registration area, until recently, have been most unsatisfactory as a true picture of mortality trends. The original states of this area: Maine, New Hampshire, Vermont, Massachusetts, Connecticut, Rhode Island, New York, New Jersey, District of Columbia, Indiana and Michigan, contained only 4 per cent of the Negro population.[24] Alabama, Oklahoma, Texas, West Virginia and Arkansas, with a combined Negro population of 2,350,315, have not yet qualified for admission. The United States Public Health Bulletin No. 174 (1928) discounts many of the racial comparisons from the figures of the death registration area which, until the last few years, has included few states having a large enough Negro population to warrant drawing very definite or broad conclusions. Moreover, few Southern states and municipalities have published statistics in sufficient detail to permit of an intelligent inquiry into the mortality experience of the Negro population.

Negro Population Estimates. A frequent source of difficulty has been the calculation of Negro death rates for inter-censal years. The Negro migration involving over a million persons has made it impossible to estimate increase with any great reliability. The Census estimates of the population would thus tend to provide a low Negro population base for Northern cities, exaggerating the death rates, and a high base for the South, reducing the rate. The death rate for New York City in 1926, for example, is given as 30.5. This rate is based upon a supposed Negro population of 170,400. The Negro mass migration after the war is responsible for a total population in that

[24] The additions to the area since 1900 have taken place as follows: California, Colorado and Maryland, in 1906; Pennsylvania, 1908; Washington and Wisconsin, 1908; Ohio, 1909; Minnesota, Montana and Utah, 1910; Kentucky and Missouri, 1911; Virginia, 1913; Kansas, 1914; North Carolina and South Carolina, 1916; Tennessee, 1917; Illinois, Louisiana and Oregon, 1918; Delaware, Florida, Mississippi, 1919; Nebraska, 1920; Georgia, Idaho, Wyoming, 1922; Iowa, 1923; North Dakota, 1924.

year of not less than 220,000. If the rate were based upon a
Negro population of 220,000, which is nearer to the actual
population, it would be 20.0. The 1920 Census itself was
doubtless affected seriously by the movement of several hundred thousand Negroes during 1919. It separated thousands
of families for long periods, introducing the possible new factor
of interrupted reproduction in the normal population increase.
In the South this tendency is checked somewhat by the movement from rural sections to Southern cities. When this occurs,
however, the rural death rate is minimized. The laxity in reg-
istering deaths in rural sections and greater laxity in recording
births is recognized. The extent to which these accidental factors operate has not been determined. The authors of the
United States Public Health Bulletin No. 174 think that "birth
registration is still poor for the Negro population, and birth
and infant mortality statistics are by no means complete."

Inaccuracy in Diagnosing Causes of Death. There is, as is
well known, considerable caprice in the assignment by physicians of primary and contributory causes of death. In the case
of Negroes diagnoses have not infrequently been made loosely
and with indifference. Largely because of this, death statistics
are not comparable over certain periods and between sections.
These dangers are very particularly pointed out by George H.
Van Buren, of the Metropolitan Life Insurance Company. The
classification of deaths before 1900 was essentially different
from the first International Classification. This was revised in
1909 and the Census Bureau warns specifically against attempts
to compare death rates for certain diseases and groups for years
of the period 1900-09. Deductions regarding tuberculosis, particularly, are liable to error. For, despite the greatly increased
classification under the head of tuberculosis of diseases which
formerly were concealed under such terms as "hemorrhage,"
"chronic bronchitis," "pulmonary congestion," "undefined diseases," and "other diseases of the respiratory system," the published rate for tuberculosis has continually decreased. The decline has in all probability been much greater than the figures
show, for between 1900 and 1915 the apparent death rate from
"hemorrhage" alone declined from 4.3 to .4, and that from
"chronic bronchitis" from 19.3 to 7.7. The influence of inaccurate or indifferent diagnosis of disease in the case of Ne-

groes is apparent. There is less efficient medical service and fewer hospital and clinical facilities; larger numbers are without physicians, particularly in the early stages of illness, and without doubt popular notions regarding the incidence of certain diseases among them influence the study of individual cases of illness. The most convincing evidence of difference in this respect is in the comparative rates per 100,000 in 1925 for that group of "un-defined diseases." For the white population the rate was 8.4 and for the Negro population 91.8.

CHAPTER XI

LEADING CAUSES OF DEATH AMONG NEGROES

The 75 cities with largest Negro population proportions were taken as representative of the important centers of Negro population in the United States. These proportions vary widely between sections. For the year 1925, comparable data could be secured from the local health departments of 58 cities. In 25 of these, or 48 per cent, the leading cause of death was heart disease. In 10, or about 20 per cent of the cities, it was tuberculosis.

The leading cause of death in 1925 was tuberculosis in 6 of 19 Northern and Midwestern states (New Hampshire, New York, Ohio, Wisconsin, Minnesota and North Dakota); in 5 of 13 Southern states (Alabama, Mississippi, North Carolina, Tennessee and West Virginia); and in 7 or 8 Far Western states. It was heart disease in 9 of the Northern and Western states; and in 7 of the 13 Southern states. It was pneumonia in 3 Northern, 1 Southern, and 1 Far Western state.

Nineteen of the 25 cities in which heart disease was the leading cause of death, or 76 per cent, were Southern cities. Tuberculosis deaths lead in New York; Jacksonville, Florida; Cleveland, Ohio; Cincinnati, Ohio; Macon, Georgia; Little Rock, Arkansas; Fort Worth, Texas; Los Angeles, California; Kansas City, Kansas; and San Antonio, Texas. Three of these are Northern; the others are Southern and Western. Pneumonia led in Philadelphia, Baltimore, Birmingham, Atlanta, Memphis, Richmond, Detroit, Pittsburgh, Kansas City, Missouri; Columbus, Ohio; Winston-Salem, Chattanooga, Newark, Beaumont, Tampa and Omaha. Five of them, about 31 per cent, were Northern, 9 of them were Southern and 2 Western. Nephritis led in Charleston, South Carolina; Dallas, Texas; and Roanoke, Virginia. Homicide led in Miami, Florida; malforma-

152

tion in Wilmington, North Carolina; and cerebral softening in Portsmouth, Virginia.

TABLE X

CITIES IN WHICH LEADING CAUSE OF DEATH IS TUBERCULOSIS

City	Negro Population	Per Cent Total	Mobility[1]	General Negro Death Rate	Excess Over White	Infant Death Rate	Excess Over White	Birth Rate
New York, N. Y. ...	170,000	4.9	+ 83.8	30.5	16.0	118.4	56.4	36.9
Jacksonville, Fla. ...	90,347	37.0	+ 11.3	21.2	10.9	117.6	62.0	17.9
Cleveland, O.	49,400	5.2	+ 19.0	23.8	14.2	111.7	49.4	31.0
Cincinnati, O.	34,800	8.5	+ 14.1	27.2	12.3	105.3	31.8	28.9
Macon, Ga.	25,100	43.1	+ 33.0	25.2	11.1	....	....	....
Little Rock, Ark. ...	18,600	25.0	+ 10.6	35.5	17.6	....	....	....
Fort Worth, Tex. ..	19,000	12.2	— 5.4	15.1	5.8	....	....	....
Los Angeles, Cal. ..	......	5.8	+ 13.2	....	....	67.5	9.8	....
Kansas City, Kan. ..	19,398	16.7	+ 19.7	21.8	9.1	180.8	106.9	17.7
San Antonio, Tex. ..	16,700	8.4	+ 11.7	17.1	2.0	....	....	....

CITIES IN WHICH LEADING CAUSE OF DEATH IS HEART DISEASE

City	Negro Population	Per Cent Total	Mobility[1]	General Negro Death Rate	Excess Over White	Infant Death Rate	Excess Over White	Birth Rate
Chicago, Ill.	149,800	6.7	+ 20.1	29.3	13.8	115.4	43.8	28.5
Washington, D. C. ..	123,500	20.4	+ 9.5	22.0	11.0	131.7	70.0	23.2
New Orleans, La. ..	107,900	25.9	+ 9.2	31.6	16.8	....	....	....
St. Louis, Mo.	85,300	10.4	+ 16.6	22.8	10.0	....	....	....
Norfolk, Va.	61,100	36.1	+ 11.1	15.4	7.7	157.7	98.3	16.1
Louisville, Ky.	46,100	15.2	+ 11.2	22.1	9.3	128.2	51.5	25.7
Savannah, Ga.	42,300	45.4	+ 17.1	23.8	12.4	....	....	....
Nashville, Tenn.	38,900	28.6	+ 5.6	24.8	10.5	....	....	....
Indianapolis, Ind. ...	42,300	11.8	+ 11.6	18.9	5.8	113.2	50.3	21.5
Houston, Tex.		8.1	+ 12.5	....	....	....	....	....
Augusta, Ga.	23,100	41.8	+ 14.8	25.9	9.6	....	....	....
Montgomery, Ala. ..	20,100	....	+ 6.2	24.3	12.8	....	....	....
Shreveport, La.	21,500	37.8	+ 9.7	38.7	23.2	....	....	....
Boston, Mass.	18,700	2.4	+ 15.6	23.9	9.3	117.6	33.5	25.5
Charlotte, N. C.	16,300	30.6	+ 7.0	25.0	13.2	163.9	92.5	33.7
Newport News, Va. .	19,200	40.7	+ 4.4	11.1	6.2	120.7	65.9	15.1
Petersburg, Va.	15,100	92.3	+ 4.0	20.5	9.3	165.7	84.1	24.0
Knoxville, Tenn.	12,000	12.5	+ 6.7	27.2	15.4	....	....	....
Atlantic City, N. J...	11,700	21.8	+ 14.4	20.7	0.6	95.6	25.3	21.5
Wilmington, Del. ...	11,700	9.6	+ 9.0	19.7	8.8	137.9	56.8	14.4
Galveston, Tex.	11,000	22.7	+ 15.8	22.2	9.8	....	....	....
Lynchburg, Va.	7,700	22.0	+ 2.1	27.0	13.3	115.2	31.5	28.2
Oakland, Cal.	14,800	3.8	+ 19.9	— 9.7	— 0.5	45.3	— 8.0	19.4
Charleston, W. Va. .	5,300	10.8	— 42.0	28.1	13.0	131.6	37.6	21.5

[1] As a rough index of population shifts within cities the deviation from the normal age groups 20-45 in a population pyramid is measured. The age group distribution of the total Negro population is regarded as the "normal" distribution.

TABLE XI

CITIES IN WHICH LEADING CAUSE OF DEATH IS PNEUMONIA

City	Negro Population	Per Cent Total	Mobility*	General Negro Death Rate	Excess Over White	Infant Death Rate	Excess Over White	Birth Rate
Philadelphia, Pa. ...	163,500	8.2	+ 15.6	22.5	10.2	127.6	57.7	28.6
Baltimore, Md.	117,100	14.7	+ 11.5	25.0	12.2	122.2	50.3	27.9
Birmingham, Ala. ..	81,000	39.3	+ 7.3	23.7	11.0	....	....	....
Atlanta, Ga.	......	41.8	+ 9.1	....	....	....	....	....
Memphis, Tenn.	63,300	36.1	+ 12.9	28.7	14.7	....	....	....
Richmond, Va.	54,700	29.9	+ 7.5	21.4	9.4	131.7	74.3	27.5
Detroit, Mich.	82,700	6.6	+ 22.0	19.7	9.3	128.2	51.5	25.7
Pittsburgh, Pa.	45,600	7.2	+ 14.3	23.7	9.5	102.0	22.6	31.2
Kansas City, Mo. ...	34,500	9.4	+ 19.7	26.0	13.4	....	....	....
Columbus, O.	28,200	10.0	— 9.0	21.6	8.5	168.0	99.4	22.6
Winston-Salem, N. C.	30,200	43.7	+ 34.0	16.9	7.4	169.2	6.7	29.4
Chattanooga, Tenn. .	17,600	26.4	+ 11.5	43.2	28.1	....	....	....
Newark, N. J.	22,100	4.8	+ 13.6	29.0	18.2	154.8	95.2	41.2
Beaumont, Tex.	16,400	32.4	+ 8.1	14.0	4.3	....	....	....
Tampa, Fla.	18,602	19.6	+ 13.1	23.7	12.6	173.3	119.1	23.0
Omaha, Neb.	13,700	2.3	— 17.1	15.6	2.5	121.8	56.8	14.4

CITIES IN WHICH LEADING CAUSE OF DEATH IS NEPHRITIS

City	Negro Population	Per Cent Total	Mobility*	General Negro Death Rate	Excess Over White	Infant Death Rate	Excess Over White	Birth Rate
Charleston, S. C. ...	33,100	45.3	....	31.0	19.5	....	....	....
Dallas, Tex.	26,100	....	+ 14.1	23.9	11.8	....	....	....
Mobile, Ala.	24,500	37.1	+ 53.9	21.2	7.9	....	....	....
Roanoke, Va.	10,000	17.1	+ 6.1	23.0	10.4	139.8	46.9	32.9

CITIES IN WHICH LEADING CAUSE OF DEATH IS CEREBRAL SOFTENING

City	Negro Population	Per Cent Total	Mobility*	General Negro Death Rate	Excess Over White	Infant Death Rate	Excess Over White	Birth Rate
Portsmouth, Va. ...	26,700	45.2		6.7	14.7	7.0	124.0	55.2	18.1

CITIES IN WHICH LEADING CAUSE OF DEATH IS CONGENITAL MALFORMATION

City	Negro Population	Per Cent Total	Mobility*	General Negro Death Rate	Excess Over White	Infant Death Rate	Excess Over White	Birth Rate
Wilmington, N. C. ..	14,000	37.7	+ 3.3	21.1	10.1	144.3	67.6	28.7

CITIES IN WHICH LEADING CAUSE OF DEATH IS HOMICIDE

City	Negro Population	Per Cent Total	Mobility*	General Negro Death Rate	Excess Over White	Infant Death Rate	Excess Over White	Birth Rate
Miama, Fla.	22,078	31.6	+ 11.9	23.7	5.4	155.4	90.2	41.4

* See footnote on p. 153.

Changing Mortality. Employing the figures for the registration area 1910-20, Professor Howard Woolston,[2] of the University of Washington, calculated the rates of change for various causes of death in different racial and local groups.

The index used was: *The ratio of* $\dfrac{1920 \text{ rate}}{1910 \text{ rate}}$ *for the total popu-*

[2] Woolston, Howard, "Changing Mortality," *Amer. Jour. Soc.,* Vol. XXXII, pp. 937-46.

lation in the registration area is .884 = 1.00. Indices for sub-

$$\text{divisions of population and territory} = \frac{1920}{1910} \div .884.$$

A first statistical observation was that Negro urban and rural deaths though higher than whites show a greater rate of improvement.   In comparisons by specific causes of death the range of variation was considerable, and makes possible prediction, of a sort, of the possibilities of further reduction in mortality.   Measured in terms of variation of change, city Negroes have shown most improvement in typhoid, diabetes, puerperal septicemia, diphtheria and tuberculosis, and the rural Negroes in scarlet fever, measles, whooping cough, diphtheria, nephritis and heart disease.   City whites achieved considerable improvement over city Negroes.   Rural Negro rates improved more rapidly than white rural rates, and urban white rates more rapidly than either Negro or white rural rates.   The conclusion that white urban dwellers are more resistant to urban conditions or more successful in changing them than Negroes is thus paralleled by the conclusion that city whites, "whether by nurture or by art, are in some respects capable of greater progress in health than rural whites."

Tuberculosis.   The Negro race is and has long been regarded as peculiarly susceptible to tuberculosis.   According to one somewhat popular theory, the disease is the penalty paid by the human race for violating the laws of nature in the process of civilization.   The greatest penalty is paid by the newest convert.   Such as the Jews, the English, and the Germans, give better prognosis than the Irish, the Negroes and the American Indians.   The question of the immunity and susceptibility of certain racial stocks to the disease has controlled much of the discussion and practice in regard to the exceptionally high Negro rates.   Dr. Hoffman's notable study in 1896 helped to set the pattern of thinking.   "Its susceptibility to consumption, alone," he held, "will suffice to seal its fate as a race."   Albert Bushnell Hart [3] in 1910, sensed the questionableness of the deductions and pointed out that they were based upon a meagre selection of unreliable statistics, and that where tuberculosis was increasing among Negroes it was increasing for the same reason that it was ravaging the Indians in Alaska.   They were

[3] Hart, Albert Bushnell, *The Southern South.*

living in close houses which became saturated with the virus of the disease.

Medical science more recently has set down new principles which tend to emphasize social and economic factors more and purely racial factors less except in so far as economic and social status is conditioned by race. Dr. Milton J. Rosenau, Professor of Preventive Medicine and Hygiene at Harvard University, and at one time Director of the Hygienic Laboratory, United States Public Health Service, and a foremost authority, regards it as a class disease.

It is more prevalent among the poor than the well-to-do. Hence the prevention of tuberculosis has become a sociological problem. Poverty with its attendant hardships, poor food, bad housing, crowding, overwork and worry, diminishes resistance to the infection; while prosperity, which buys good food, rest, change of air and scene, choice of occupation, and diversion, increases our resistance to the infection, and avoids contact with it. An increase of wage or decrease of the cost of living; shortening the hours of work; improving the conditions of industrial hygiene; adding to the number of holidays; playgrounds, parks, and wholesome recreation, all help to increase our resistance against and diminish the prevalence of tuberculosis.

The fact that between 50 and 90 per cent of the population are infected when they reach adulthood, that it is now declared not hereditary, and that its incidence is heaviest among the poorer classes raises the question of a racial lack of resistance among Negroes which is more economic than biological.

The medical literature on the subject is large and the greater volume of it stresses the shorter period of contact of the Negro race with tuberculosis as responsible for the prevalence. Paisseau observes that tuberculosis in the native African reveals the character of a primary infection similar to that seen when infants are infected. Carter [4] of the Virginia Sanatorium made a similar observation. Most of the Negro cases were 20 to 30 years of age while those of whites were between 28 and 34. This is statistically substantiated in both the registration area

[4] Carter, H. G., "Pulmonary Tuberculosis Among Negroes," *Am. Rev. of Tuberculosis*, pp. 653-61, Vol. XIV, December, 1926.
———, "Further Observations on Pulmonary Tuberculosis in American Negroes," *Am. Rev. of Tuberculosis*, Vol. VI, pp. 1002-7, January, 1923.

and Metropolitan Life Insurance Company records. Borel [5] has stated that in the areas of Africa where there has been no important contact with Europeans. tuberculosis is practically unknown. Again this is, in a measure, supported by the experience of African troops in the World War. Although carefully examined before leaving Africa the death rate from the disease contracted in France was 56 as contrasted with 5.7 for other British troops. The American Negro troops who had been exposed in the United States did not have an excessive tuberculosis mortality in France. Studies at Bellevue Hospital in New York indicate that when tuberculosis attacks offspring from non-tuberculous parents a greater toll is taken than among those descended from tuberculous parents. It is presumed that in the first group the bacillus is implanting itself in virgin soil, in the second it finds greater resistance. Differences have been noted between the resistance of blacks and mulattoes to the disease but the data are as yet meagre for convincing results. Inheritance in tuberculosis, according to Dr. Godias J. Drolet of the New York Tuberculosis Association, is not in the direction of a predisposition to the disease but toward the acquirement of immunity itself. Without discounting entirely, therefore, the possible influence of heredity, which is slow and frequently life-costing, it is now demonstrable that more rapid gains may be made through modification of environment, betterment of living conditions, improved changes in education in personal hygiene and all that the public health movement stands for.

Prevalence of Tuberculosis Among Negroes. The extreme difficulty of determining the number of cases of tuberculosis in a community has made it necessary to rely heavily upon mortality rates for the prevalence of tuberculosis. However, the Community Health and Tuberculosis Demonstration in Framingham, Massachusetts, has given a reasonably sound basis for estimate. It would appear that there are 4 cases of tuberculosis for every 100 Negroes. Each year about 35,000 Negroes die from the disease. At the incidence rate of 4 per 100 approximately 440,000 Negroes are ill at all times with the disease.

The report of the Surgeon-general on recruits for the World War, however, indicates certain untypical trends in Negro mor-

[5] Borel, Ann. Inst., Pasteur, Vol. XXXIV, p. 105, 1920.

tality from tuberculosis. An analysis of army recruits in "The World War," Vol. XV, part 1, Army Anthropology, shows that the ratio for pulmonary and suspected tuberculosis per 1,000 cases in a group was lower for the agricultural Negro than for the agricultural native white of the South.[6]

In Alabama the rate for pulmonary tuberculosis was highest in a section with 69 per cent of Negro blood. That a smaller proportion of Negroes showed tuberculosis at the time of examination than the whites was due, it was thought, to the fact that tuberculosis runs a much more rapid course in Negroes than in whites, so that a smaller proportion of them would be found to be affected on a particular day, or that pure-blooded Negroes suffer less from tuberculosis than the hybrid Negroes of the white section.

The "black belt" of Georgia, comprising 1,250,000 people, 61 per cent of whom are Negroes, showed that in the Negro area of the state only half as much tuberculosis was prevalent as in the white area. The conclusion of this report is to the effect that about 10 per cent more tuberculosis is recorded for native whites than for Negroes. An attempt to account for it was made by assuming that the examiners at local boards in the Negro sections were inferior to those in the native white sections.

There has been a noteworthy decline in the disease even though the rate for Negroes continues high. This rate is about that of the white population 30 years ago. The rates of decline for white and Negroes, in the experience of the Metropolitan Life Insurance Company for the period 1911-26 were 62.7 per cent for white males, 54.9 for white females; 44.3 for Negro males and 43.0 for Negro females. The rate of decline among Negro children between 5 and 14 has, on the whole, been greater than the white.

Dr. Hoffman, in 1927, reviewed his earlier findings regarding Negroes and this disease, and while observing that the rates were uniformly and apparently above those for the white population, concluded that there was a hopeful decline:

The mortality from pulmonary tuberculosis, especially, has been very considerably reduced, although the prevailing rate among the

[6] The classification appears to have been made by population proportions of sections rather than on the race of individual recruits.

Negro population is still 203.2 per 100,000 in contrast to a rate of only 67.8 per 100,000 for the whites. This extraordinary reduction in pulmonary tuberculosis is primarily the result of better wages, yielding better nutrition, shorter hours, yielding a larger measure of rest and recreation and last but not least, better working conditions involving a reduction in dust and an improvement in light and ventilation. All of these factors operate in a like manner to better results, leaving the disparity in the rates due to racial conditions still unchanged.

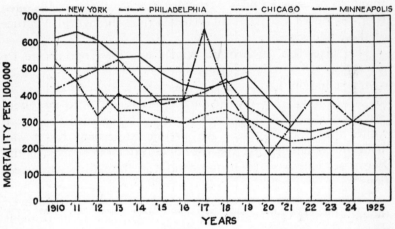

TRENDS IN NEGRO MORTALITY FROM TUBERCULOSIS IN FOUR CITIES
PER 100,000 POPULATION

Figure 10

Specific figures for several important cities indicate that the pulmonary rate is higher in Southern than in Northern cities, and appears to be declining more rapidly in Northern than in Southern cities. For a brief period the Negro rate in New York City was lower than that of rural New York, due probably to better control of environment.

The conclusions of the major studies of tuberculosis among Negroes may thus be summarized:

1. Negroes were tuberculized during slavery, while their high mortality rate after freedom was due to unhygienic existence fostered by low economic status.
2. The American Indian reacts to tuberculosis in a manner similar to that described for the Negro.

3. The prognostic significance of race depends more upon the habits of the individual than upon other racial characteristics.

4. The peak of the Negro tuberculosis death rate comes in the early twenties or ten years earlier than the peak for white cases.

5. The disease advances more rapidly in Negro than in white cases.

COMPARISON OF NEGRO AND TOTAL PULMONARY DEATH RATE
MINNEAPOLIS, 1910-1925 PER 100,000 POPULATION

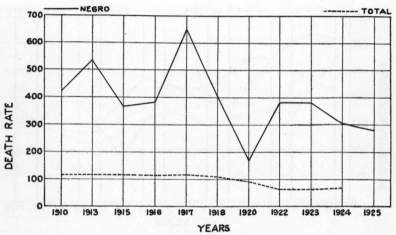

Figure 11

6. The danger of tuberculosis infection depends upon the length of time the people have been exposed.

7. There is no absolute racial immunity to any disease. The Negro is not more susceptible to tuberculosis because of physical make-up or inherent racial traits, but because his resistance has not had time to develop.[7]

8. There is not a great difference between the Negro tuberculosis rate and that of the Irish—both recent comers to urban conditions.

9. There is convincing evidence that the Negroes' tuberculosis rate is related to their living and working status.[8]

[7] Garvin, Charles H., "Immunity to Disease Among Dark-skinned People," *Opportunity*, August, 1926.
[8] Public Health Reports, Vol. XLIII, No. 11, March 16, 1928.

Heart Disease. The Anti-tuberculosis organizations are now well established, but the corresponding organization interested in a campaign against heart disease (The Association for the Prevention and Relief of Heart Disease) is only recently established, and little known. Heart disease, however, has mounted seriously within the past 25 or 30 years both for the white and the Negro population. During the main age periods the rates for Negroes are about double those for whites. According to trends marked by the United States Public Health Service there has been a steady increase in this disease since 1884. From 1918 to 1922, the period following the influenza epidemic, there were unusually low rates. Afterwards, however, the curve began to mount again.

The experience of the Metropolitan Life Insurance Company shows an increase for both white and Negro persons, with notable differences in the incidence according to age groups; that is, the age period 1-4 shows a Negro mortality nearly twice that of the whites; from 5-9 a rate less than that of the white; the period 10-14 less than white and from 20 years onward the Negro rates tend to be in excess of the white.

Heart disease has its heaviest incidence in the later age periods. The assumption is that the lessening of the rate of mortality of other diseases and the longer span of life affect statistically the mortality rates from this disease. For the Negro population it has been suggested that the high prevalence of such diseases as malaria, typhoid and syphilis plays a part in creating this excess. Other racial differences are apparent in the statistical trends. Russian Jews, Italians and Austro-Hungarians show a low mortality rate from this disease, while English, Scotch, Welsh, German and Irish show high mortality rates. The Irish rate very closely approximates that of the Negro.

Although this disease has reached the position of the leading cause of death among Negroes there have been few studies apart from compilations of trends. However, there is reported a statistical study of types of heart disease in the Negro in progress, under Dr. George R. Hermann of the College of Medicine of Tulane University. There is also being studied by him the responses to treatment of a damaged heart in Negroes doing heavy labor, and of the syphilitic heart in Negroes.

Bulletin No. 174, prepared by Grover and Sydenstricker, avoids the use of "heart disease" and refers to cardio-renal disease, because of the manifest difficulty of distinguishing between the breakdown of the heart and the kidneys, thus to determine which was primary and which secondary. In the group of diseases classified as cardio-renal are included heart disease, endocarditis, pericarditis, myocarditis, angina pectoris, Bright's disease, nephritis, uræmia and dropsy.

Dr. H. A. Callis of the United States Veterans' Hospital at Tuskegee suggests that too little attention is paid as yet to environmental factors. Negroes as a race spend their lives in hard manual labor. Hard work is quite as potent a factor in cardio-renal diseases as syphilis. Even so apparently trivial a factor as tenements without elevators in the larger cities, and the worry over the continuous necessity for economic and social adjustment may exercise stress.

Cancer. The greater number of persons surviving to age 40 and beyond, and the improved skill in diagnosis, have contributed to the increase in cancer mortality rates for Negroes as well as whites. The rise in rates for Negroes, however, *lagged* for many decades. Raymond Pearl's investigations,[9] in which the higher white cancer rates were observed, led him to suggest a possible antagonism between tuberculosis and cancer. The percentage increase or decrease in cancer death rates per year by age divisions for the period 1911-22 in the experience of the Metropolitan Life Insurance Company [10] was as follows:

	White		Negro	
Age Period	*Males*	*Females*	*Males*	*Females*
25 and over	plus 1.43	plus .19	plus 2.84	minus .09
45 and over	plus 1.54	" .32	" 3.09	plus .05

This volume per cent increase of cancer, it appears, is higher among Negroes, and Dr. Frederick Hoffman in his volume *The Mortality from Cancer Throughout the World,* published in 1925, asserts this to be true. Grover and Sydenstricker found Negro rates from the registration area higher than white up to 50 years of age, and thereafter considerably lower. The rise in rates appears to be constant.

[9] International Clinic, Vol. III, pp. 53-77, Institute of Biological Research, Johns Hopkins Hospital, Bulletin, Med., 1028.

[10] "Color, Sex, Age Constant, 'Standardized' death rate," Statistical Bulletin, Vol. IV, No. 9, 1911-22.

DEATH RATES PER 100,000 PERSONS EXPOSED [11]

White			Negro		
Jan.-Sept.	*Jan.-Sept.*	*Jan.-Sept.*	*Jan.-Sept.*	*Jan.-Sept.*	*Jan.-Sept.*
1927	*1926*	*1925*	*1927*	*1926*	*1925*
73.4	73.7	70.3	71.6	69.2	69.6

In every age group from 25 upwards, the white and Negro female rates exceed those of the male, and in practically every age group, the white rate exceeds the Negro. The minimum death rate from cancer is for the age period from 10 to 14. The maximum height of the curve is reached between 25 and 45 years of age. The Negro female rate often exceeds the white female rate between the ages 15 and 45, but the rate for Negro males is lower than that for whites at all ages. The average rate for white males in cancer of the buccal cavity is 4.5; for females .9; for Negro males 2.3; females 1.3. In cancer of the stomach and liver, the white male rate is 23.9; females 28.0. The Negro male rate is 17.4; the female rate 19.1. The white male rate for cancer of the peritoneum, intestines and rectum is 6.7; the female rate 10.8; the Negro male rate 3.9 and Negro female rate 8.1. For cancer of the female genital organs the white rate is 24.9 and the Negro rate 38.4. Cancer of the breast for white males is .1; white females 11.7; Negro males .2; and Negro females 14.6. Cancer of the skin for white males is 2.1, and white females 1.6; for Negro males .7; Negro females .8. Cancer of other organs shows a white male rate of 13.5 and female rate of 9.2; Negro male rate of 9.4 and Negro female rate of 7.5.

Negro women lead in cancer of the genital organs, but otherwise the white population rates are in excess. The Detroit Health Study [12] shows a decrease in the Negro cancer rate as a cause of death, over a 5-year period, from 61.5 per 1,000 to 37.8 per 1,000, and it drops from sixth to twelfth as an important cause of death. In the Tampa, Florida, study [13] cancer is not important enough to be listed as a major cause of death. The Chicago study,[14] conducted by Dr. H. L. Harris, in 1926,

[11] Dublin, Louis I., "Mortality Experience of the First Nine Months of 1927," *Metropolitan Life Insurance Company Bulletin,* 1927.
[12] *The Negro in Detroit*—Section IV, Health, Detroit Bureau of Governmental Research, 1926.
[13] *A Study of Negro Life in Tampa,* Y.M.C.A and Urban League, 1927.
[14] Harris, H. L., Report of a Health Survey and the Recommendations of Advisory Committee to the Commissioner of Health, City of Chicago, 1926.

for the Chicago Health Department, shows a white cancer death rate of 106.78 per 100,000 and a Negro rate of 89.38 per 100,000. Among whites heart disease and nephritis only outrank cancer as a cause of death. Among Negroes tuberculosis, pneumonia, convulsions, nephritis, homicide, congenital debility and malformation, and external accidents outrank cancer as a cause of death. It is not yet a major cause of Negro mortality generally, although it has risen from fifth to third place as a cause of white deaths in Chicago.

Venereal Diseases. Considerable speculation has entered into the estimates of the extent of venereal diseases among Negroes. The natural difficulty of detection in the general population, the careful efforts at concealment, failure of cases to come to official attention and the difficulty of controlled studies of prevalence, favor uncritical speculation. Most of the studies have been made under circumstances which reveal little representativeness for the general Negro population. The Venereal Section of the United States Public Health Service has conducted several studies which have provided the most reliable data thus far. However, it has considered these unsatisfactory as a true picture of prevalence and is now engaged upon a study in Tennessee which utilizes the records of all physicians as well as clinics.

Syphilization of the Negro is variously estimated at from 3.2 per cent to over 75 per cent. Authoritative syphilographers like Boas, Hazen and Fox agree that a fair average is estimated to be one and one-half times the rate for the whites. Jamison of New Orleans in a series of medical cases in colored women found 16.6 per cent syphilitic. Young of Louisville found that 25 per cent of the Negro women attending the obstetric clinic were positive for syphilis; Schurman and Barnes of Philadelphia General Hospital found 27.8 per cent in the same class of patients. Williams of Johns Hopkins found 16.2 per cent. Bartholomew of Atlanta, "where approximately half the colored children of Atlanta are born," demonstrated that pregnancy is complicated by syphilis in 4 per cent of all patients applying for delivery, and he did not consider a reaction less than three plus as positive. Later, McCord, working with a similar group in the same place, found 22.5 per cent.

E. P. Boas (*Social Hygiene* 1914-1915), feeling that there was an inadequacy of reliable statistics on the prevalence of syphilis in the Negro, made a collection of as many statistical studies as he could find. Most of these investigations were made in hospital dispensaries and insane asylums. For general purposes conclusions cannot be drawn for insane asylums, because of the frequency with which syphilis appears as the cause of insanity. In 1916 Wender stated that of 106 colored male patients admitted to the Government Hospital for Insane, Washington, D. C., during the past year, 50 per cent had syphilis. As a result of his studies, Boas found that 5 per cent to 6 per cent of Negro patients in hospitals are diagnosed as syphilitic, while 3 per cent to 4 per cent of the white patients in the same hospitals are diagnosed as syphilitic. The army admission rate for syphilitics was 3.2 per cent for Negroes and 2.2 per cent for whites.[15]

Perhaps the most thorough study of local prevalence of venereal disease is given in Venereal Disease Bulletin No. 79 of the United States Public Health Service. The study was made by Dr. W. J. V. Deacon of the Michigan Department of Health. According to the census of 1920, 1.64 per cent of the population of Michigan was Negro, whereas it was found that 16 per cent of all cases of venereal disease were Negro; 20 per cent of the syphilis and 11 per cent of the gonorrhea. He warns, however, that it would be unwise to accept this statement without further inquiry, because of the large immigration of Negroes into the state during the few years preceding, and the fact that it is the young adults who are most likely to move from place to place seeking employment. The portion of the white population in the group of 15 to 54 years of age represented 52.2 per cent white males, and this per cent furnished 61.7 per cent of the venereal disease cases; while among the Negro males 1.3 per cent of the population furnished 10.2 per cent of the cases. It appeared further that 45.6 per cent of white females furnished 21.6 per cent of the cases, while less than 1 per cent of the Negro females furnished 6.5 per cent of the cases. It was observed that the Negro is very likely, for economic purposes and reasons, to visit the public clinics more freely than the whites, where the case is most likely to be reported, and, owing to the fact that his social position is not

[15] Granger, W. R. R., "A Neglected Health Problem," *Opportunity*, March, 1928, pp. 72-73.

likely to give him material prestige, physicians would not hesitate to report these cases as such, as they might in cases among their white friends.

Doctors Belding and Hunter in a series of Wassermann Tests in Boston, to determine the influence of race and nationality, report that clinical evidence of syphilis was as frequent in Negroes as in whites. The Surgeon-general of the United States Army in his report on recruits publishes comparative figures which do not show wide differences.

STATISTICS FOR 1912—ENLISTED MEN IN THE ARMY

	Number	Admission for Syphilis	Ratio Per 1,000 Men Strength
Whites	76,135	1,725	22.66
Negroes	4,631	150	32.39
Serving in United States:			
Whites	57,912	1,215	20.98
Negroes	1,696	36	21.23
Serving in Philippines:			
Whites	9,377	303	32.31
Negroes	1,811	68	37.35

Dr. Howard Fox found 621 cases among 15,000 whites and 1,900 among 32,000 Negroes. He observed that syphilis is milder in the Negro. McNeil of Galveston found evidence among children under puberty low and assumed that infection is largely acquired. Dr. Hazen of Washington found prevalence among school children; and Noble reaches the conclusion that immunity is being rapidly acquired. The high mortality from certain diseases appears to be connected with previous syphilitic infection; among these are heart disease and nephritis. However, it appears that the rate of syphilitic infection among white people of the same social class as the Negroes is about the same as that among the Negroes.

Of peculiar significance is the fact that despite the high estimates of venereal disease prevalence among Negroes the number of cases of blindness is small. Miss Kate Hubbard [16] of the Blind Association of Mississippi was prompted to make a survey in the state, since 54.4 per cent of all educable children in Mississippi in 1923 were Negroes, and since the white institution for the blind was crowded. This survey revealed only 30

[16] Hubbard, Kate, "Are There Any Blind Black Babies"—*Survey*, Vol. LII, p. 91, 1924.

cases of blindness throughout the state among 418,481 educable Negro children in Mississippi between 5 and 21. Moreover less than 20 cases of these children could possibly have been made blind by infection at birth. Of white children in the blind schools nearly 17 per cent were blinded by ophthalmia neonatorum.

Doctors Plaut and Kraepelin of Berlin were impressed by the frequent mention of differences in the symptomatology of syphilis between Negro and white patients made by American writers and were prompted to a study of Negro and Indian cases for their possible aid in solving the question of what produces general paralysis in some types of syphilitics and not in others. The studies made by the Johns Hopkins Hospital, at Baltimore, included in this survey, show that the chancre produces no marked induration in the Negro patients, a conclusion independently sustained by Morrison. All authors agree that extragenital chancre is rare among Negroes, and this rare occurrence was attributed to the more adequate cutaneous protection.

In secondary syphilis the follicular papulous and pustulous rashes are more frequent and marked in the Negro, while the macular and maculopapular rashes are more frequent among white syphilitics. Annular syphilids around the nose and mouth, and moist papules and condylomata are more prevalent among the Negroes, especially the women. Malignant syphilis is rare among Negroes. Gummata of the testicles and of the sternoclavicular region, and lymphatic involvement are considered typical of syphilis in the Negro. Aortitis in Negroes is twice as frequent as in white syphilitics, according to the medical literature covering this field. The general opinion is reached that Negroes did not suffer from tuberculosis and syphilis extensively before their emancipation, and the occurrence of insanity among them is considered rare. However, many factors enter to confuse the clinical picture. It cannot be proven that general paralysis occurred much more rarely among Negroes than white people in the second half of the nineteenth century. Dr. Pollock, of the New York Institution for the Insane, warns against believing that insanity is more frequent among the white than among the Negro population. He holds that there are relatively more Negro than white persons in the asylums except in the South, where few institutional provisions exist. The personal studies by Professors Plaut and Kraepelin at the St. Elizabeth's Hospital revealed that the differences between the Negro type of paralysis and that seen by the German scientists in Europe were not marked. The studies as a whole showed that differences in the clinical picture do not warrant the conclusion that they have an influence upon the etiology of paralysis. They are partly due to insufficient treatment taken by the Negro.

Diphtheria. According to the figures compiled by the Metropolitan Life Insurance Company,[17] the white death rate from diphtheria was 16.6 and 30.0 per thousand for 1923 and 1911 respectively, for Negroes 5.1 and 9.2 per 100,000 for 1923 and 1911 respectively. This shows a decline of 44.7 per cent for white and 44.6 per cent for Negroes over the 12-year period.

Statistics for 1927 show a continued decrease in white rates but a slight increase in Negro rates, although the white rate is still higher than the Negro rate. The tables [18] quoted give the death rates per 100,000 persons exposed from January to March, 1925-26 and 1927:

	White			Colored	
Jan.- *Mar., '27*	*Jan.-* *Mar., '26*	*Jan.-* *Mar., '25*	*Jan.-* *Mar., '27*	*Jan.-* *Mar., '26*	*Jan.-* *Mar., '25*
12.6	10.9	14.4	8.1	5.6	5.8

The largest Negro increases were in Alabama and Oklahoma. The age rates are also interesting. Grover and Sydenstricker [19] found that the age of highest mortality from diphtheria for white is 2-3 years; for Negroes under 1 year.

There is, then, a lower Negro than white diphtheria rate, and although there has been a slight increase in the Negro rate for 1925-27, there had been a steady decline in the rate for both races up to that period. Dr. Dublin [20] believes that there is a racial factor in immunity to diphtheria and found that "Negro children living in crowded neighborhoods show a high proportion of positive Schick reactions. Children of Italian extrac-

---

[17] Dublin, Louis I., *Recend Trends in Negro Mortality*, 1924.
[18] Dublin, Louis I., *Mortality Experience for the First Quarter of 1927*, 1927.
[19] "Mortality Among Negroes," United States Bulletin No. 174.
[20] *Metropolitan Life Bulletin*, Vol. II, No. 6, June, 1927.

tion, living in the crowded East Harlem section, gave the lowest percentage of positive reactions. Jewish children also living in congested 'sections of the city of New York showed a low percentage of positive reactions and children living in the less crowded areas a high percentage of positive reaction. Not only is the actual death rate from diphtheria lower among Negro children, but a study of 5,884 white children and 1,906 Negro children in Baltimore revealed that the Negro child has a slightly lower carrier rate than the white child.

Hookworm. In Southern states hookworm is thought to be more common among Negroes than among whites. Soil pollution through privies is one of the causes of hookworm infection. An examination of several hundred farms in North and South Carolina, Georgia and Alabama showed that twice as many farms without privies are occupied by Negroes as by whites.

Dr. Wardell Stiles' study [21] under the United States Public Health Service concluded that the Negro presents relative immunity to the direct effects of hookworm infection when compared with whites; that there is a probability that the Negro brought the disease from Africa to America; that hookworm infection has an indirect effect in increasing the death rate from pulmonary tuberculosis; and that hookworm is a severe handicap to the mental advancement of the Negro. The Rockefeller Sanitary Commission [22] a few years later, after examination of 2,092 white school children from various localities in 8 counties of North Carolina found an infection percentage of 34.1. In the same communities an examination of 1,337 Negro school children showed only 15 per cent infected.

INFANT MORTALITY

The infant mortality of Negroes is greater than that of whites in the published records of every state in the registration area except Maine and New Hampshire. The disparity is

[21] Stiles, Ch. Wardell, "Hookworm Disease in Its Relation to the Negro," U. S. Public Health and Marine Hospital Service, reprint No. 36 from the Public Health Reports, Vol. XXIV, No. 31, 1909.

[22] Glasson, William H., "Rural Conditions in the South," Rockefeller Sanitary Commission, Trinity College, Durham, N. C., *Jour. Amer. Stat. Assoc.*, Vol. XIII, p. 76, 1911.

least in California where in 1926 the white rate was 62.5 and
the Negro rate 64.5; it is greatest in Idaho where the white rate
is 60.0 and the Negro rate 284.6.

Some of the excess in the Negro rates is undoubtedly due to
poor birth registration in the Southern states where most of the
Negroes live. Only recently have the Northern states begun to
approach accuracy in this respect. Such is indicated in the
figures for increase in the Negro birth rate in Pennsylvania,
from 17.5 in 1916 to 23.8 in 1921 and this in spite of a notable
tendency in recent years to declining birth rates. The natural
increase of the Negro population is faster than whites in California, New York, Washington and Wyoming. The infant
death rate is lower for Negroes than for·whites in Los Angeles,
Oakland, San Francisco, California; St. Petersburg, Florida;
Goldsboro and Wilmington, North Carolina; and Seattle,
Washington. The lowest infant mortality rate for Negroes in
the year 1925 was in Montclair, New Jersey, where it was 18.9
per 1,000 births, while that of the whites was 10.0. The Negro
population of Montclair is 4,000. There were 53 births and 1
death under 1 year. The highest recorded rate was among the
Negro population of Leavenworth, Kansas, where the population was 3,183 and the infant mortality rate 615.4. The number of births was 13, of which 8 died before reaching the first
year.

The principal cause of infant deaths for white and Negroes
is premature birth; for Negroes the second cause is respiratory
diseases and for whites ·gastro-intestinal diseases. Measles,
scarlet fever, diphtheria, injuries at birth, are more serious for
whites than for Negroes; while the reverse is true of whooping
cough, convulsions, syphilis, and congenital debility. In 1925
the infant mortality rate was 110.8 per 1,000 births for Negroes and 68.3 for whites. In 1910 the rate was 261 for Negroes and 129.7 for whites. The infant mortality is greater in
cities (125.0) than in the country (100.5). The Negro infant
mortality rate, however, is lower than that of Austria, Belgium,
France, Germany, Italy, Roumania, Hungary, and Spain.

The studies dealing with Negro infant mortality have, for
the most part, been compilations of figures showing merely
trends in rates. In some instances attempts have been made to
establish racial comparisons. Such, however, have been widely

scattered, and in spite of a certain particular interest have lacked comparable data for a more comprehensible picture. In general the studies have taken three directions : statistical, medical and social.

The study of 22,967 live births by Robert Morse Woodbury [23] for the Children's Bureau, covering the period 1915 to 1921, shows marked variations for various nationalities.

TABLE XII

INFANT MORTALITY RATES, BY CAUSE OF DEATH AND COLOR AND NATIONALITY OF MOTHER [24]

Live Births in Eight Cities
Infant Mortality Rates from Specified Causes

Color and Nationality of Mother	All Causes	Gastric and Intestinal Diseases	Respiratory Diseases	Early Infancy	Epidemic Diseases	Other Causes
Total	111.2	32.4	19.6	36.1	7.1	16.1
White	108.3	32.6	17.9	35.1	6.4	16.4
Native	93.8	25.2	13.0	36.1	5.4	14.1
Foreign born	127.0	42.2	24.2	33.7	7.7	19.2
Italian	103.8	21.7	27.3	33.7	7.7	13.3
Jewish	53.5	10.5	8.9	22.7	4.9	6.5
French-Canadian	171.3	64.2	25.1	44.7	6.5	30.7
German	103.1	27.1	18.0	30.9	11.6	15.5
Polish	157.2	64.0	33.2	28.7	3.9	17.4
Portuguese	200.3	101.6	50.8	20.9	14.9	12.0
Other	129.6	38.5	20.6	35.8	8.1	26.7
Colored	154.4	28.1	44.6	52.2	17.2	12.4

Negro rates were less than those of the Portuguese, Poles and French-Canadians, but nearly three times greater than the Jewish and nearly one and one-half times that for the native whites.

Dr. J. V. dePorte [25] sought to determine, from mortality tables worked out in detail from the entire birth registration area for the period 1916-21, what racial elements of the American population are most likely to have the highest survival value and hence most likely to provide the bulk of future generations. Immigration into the United States, he felt, is now restricted

[23] Woodbury, Robert Morse, Ph.D., *Infant Mortality and Its Causes,* p. 48, Baltimore, 1926.
[24] *Ibid.,* p. 109, Baltimore, 1926.
[25] DePorte, J. V., "Interracial Variations in Infant Mortality," *American Journal of Hygiene,* Vol. V, No. 4, 1925.

and all races likely to provide an appreciable number of immigrants are already well represented. His results showed racial variations in infant mortality from all causes as follows:

Infant Death
Rates
Per 1,000   Racial Stock
  69-69 ....Scandinavians
  70-79 ....British, Native-born Americans
  90-99 ....Hungarians, Irish, Italians
  100-   ....Austrians, Canadians, Poles, Negroes

Calculating rates for deaths from respiratory diseases, congenital malformations and diseases of the digestive system he concluded that for the period under study there has been a definite decline in infant mortality rates for all racial groups.

Knox and Zental, in a study of infant mortality among Negroes in the registration birth area, from 1921 reports [26] conclude that Negro infants died four times more frequently from pulmonary tuberculosis, 4 times more frequently from syphilis and 2.3 times more frequently from pneumonia, than whites. They found no marked racial differences in deaths from diarrhea and enteritis. Congenital malformations and injury at birth were twice as frequent among whites as among Negroes. Twenty per cent of all Negro deaths under 1 year were due to tuberculosis, syphilis, or diseases of the respiratory system, as contrasted with 10 per cent of all white deaths during 1 year from these 3 causes. The 4 diseases, tuberculosis, pneumonia, syphilis and premature birth caused 42 per cent of deaths of Negro infants and 28 per cent of deaths of white infants. The births and deaths as compiled by Knox and Zental for the period 1916-21 revealed an increase in Negro births and a decrease for whites, and a more pronounced decline in deaths for Negro infants.

BIRTHS EXCLUSIVE OF STILLBIRTHS

	1922	1921	1920	1919	1918	1917	1916
Total	22.5	24.3	23.7	22.3	24.6	24.7	25.0
White	22.0	24.0	23.5	22.1	24.6	24.7	25.1
Colored	26.0	27.9	27.0	25.2	24.5	24.7	20.4

[26] Knox, J. H. M., and Zental, Paul, "The Health Problem of the Negro Child," *American Journal of Public Hygiene*, Vol. XVI, p. 805, 1926.

DEATHS AT ALL AGES EXCLUSIVE OF STILLBIRTHS

	1922	1921	1920	1919	1918	1917	1916
Total	11.9	11.7	13.1	13.0	18.3	14.2	14.8
White	11.6	11.4	12.8	12.6	17.8	13.8	14.6
Colored	16.3	15.9	18.4	18.5	26.8	21.3	21.8

According to J. H. Mason Knox [27] in the registration area, syphilis and tuberculosis were 3 times more frequent in Negroes than white; pneumonia 2.3 times as often. Diarrhea and enteritis were not conspicuously prevalent. Tuberculosis, syphilis and pneumonia accounted for 29 per cent of all Negro infant deaths and 7 per cent of whites. He concludes that the greatly diminished life expectancy of Negro infants is due to lower average of moral, economic and educational standards, resulting in unhygienic living.

Special compilations of figures on Negro infant mortality have been made in 5 cities in which studies have been conducted recently. In Chicago [28] the rate for whites was 64.6 and for Negroes 94.7 per 1,000 births. In 1900 Negro deaths were 2 per cent of the total from congenital debility and malformation; in 1926 it had risen to 7 per cent. The rates for diseases peculiar to early infancy and premature births were practically the same for both groups. However, tuberculosis caused 7.8 per cent of the Negro deaths and only .08 per cent of the deaths of other children. The Detroit, Michigan study in 1926 by the Mayor's Interracial Committee, indicated a decline from 297.0 for Negroes and 102.0 for whites in 1915 to 121.0 and 77.5 respectively in 1925. The decline was attributed to the definite encouragement by the Board of Health of Negro confinements in hospitals.

The survey of the Negro population in Minneapolis, Minnesota (1926), by Abram L. Harris in its report observed that the number of births had been lower than the deaths. In 1914 the infant mortality in the Negro population was 126.3; 208 in 1915 and 261 in 1916. The rate dropped to 96 in 1917 and to

[27] Knox, J. H. Mason, "Morbidity and Mortality in the Negro Infant," *Arch. Pediat.*, Vol. XLII, p. 292, 1925; "Causes of Mortality, Prematurity, Tuberculosis, Syphilis, Secondary Pneumonia," *Rev. Amer. Jour., Dis. of Children*, Vol. XXX, p. 437.

[28] Harris, H. L., Report on a Negro Health Survey and the Recommendations of the Advisory Committee to the Commissioner of Health, City of Chicago, 1927.

74.6. in 1918 but in 1919 it rose to 120, and in 1920 it fell again, though slightly. In 1922 the rate fell to 101.4, then to 81 in 1923, and to 59.7 in 1924. In 1924 the Negro rate was just 5 points above that of the total population. However, in 1925 the Negro infant rate soared to 151.9 which was higher than it had been since 1916. To what extent this increased infant death rate was due to an increased population of marriageable females resulting from migrations of Negro families to Minneapolis between 1920 and 1925 could not be ascertained. More than 23 per cent of the infant deaths among Negroes during this period (1910-25) were due to respiratory diseases and 37 per cent to diseases peculiar to early infancy. Among the gastric and intestinal diseases diarrhea and enteritis were responsible for the greater number of deaths. Pneumonia was responsible for one-half of the deaths that occurred from the respiratory diseases. Premature births caused more than three-fourths of the deaths grouped as peculiar to early infancy. Over half of the deaths which occurred from epidemic and communicable diseases were due to congenital lues.

A study in Philadelphia by the Armstrong Association [29] follows the course of the mortality for 1915-26. The infant mortality rate computed on the basis of 1,000 living births was 63.78 in 1927 as compared with 77.37 in 1926 and 144.4 in 1908. The decrease was most pronounced in deaths from pneumonia and diseases commonly called "summer complaint." The infant mortality rate for both whites and Negroes showed a decrease. The city had been engaged upon an extensive program of preventive medicine with increased facilities and large corps of health workers for child care.

Causes of Infant Mortality. Statistics of the Negro birth rate in the birth registration area,[30] as compiled by Dr. William Travis Howard of Johns Hopkins in 1921, attempt to compare the influence of race stock. He concludes that accidents of pregnancy are higher among whites, and that accidents of labor

[29] "Health Conditions Among the Negro Population of Philadelphia"—A Study by the Research Department—Armstrong Association of Philadelphia, February-March, 1928.
[30] Howard, William Travis, "The Real Risk-rate of Death to Mothers from Causes Connected with Childbirth." Papers from the Dept. of Biom. and Vital Statistics, Johns Hopkins University, No. 26.

are higher among Negroes. Statistics for Maryland, Kentucky, North Carolina, Virginia, Washington, D. C., and Baltimore show total rates for important rubrics much higher among Negro women. Dr. J. Ross Snyder,[31] after clinical observation of 1,529 white and 499 Negro babies concluded that the number of Negro mothers unable to nurse infants was rapidly increasing; that malnutrition is universal among artificially fed Negro babies; that malnutrition is general among Negro children between the first and second year, and that malnutrition is common among older Negro children. Rickets plays an important rôle in Negro mortality, particularly in affected bone structure and chest deformities in later life, which increase susceptibility to other diseases.

The study conducted in the Columbus Hill District, New York City [32] in 1923 under the direction of the New York Association for the Improvement of the Condition of the Poor, provides important figures on the effects of syphilis on infant mortality. Of 339 children born alive to untreated and unsupervised syphilitic mothers 131 died within the first two years, a mortality of 383 per 1,000.

Economic Status of Parents. The Children's Bureau has found that while there is little difference between the death rates for different economic classes among infants under one month of age; for infants over that age the rate in the United States in the lowest income group is ten times the rate in the highest income group. In one outstanding study which compares like economic groups for whites and Negroes, the infant mortality rates were about the same. "In families—of the groups studied by the Children's Bureau—where fathers earned less than $450 per year the infant mortality rate among Negroes was 163.7 as compared with 164.8 among whites of the same group." Striking figures are offered in the Woodbury [33] study from records of investigations in 7 states of infant mortality rates by per capita income from fathers' earnings.

[31] Snyder, J. Ross, "The Problem of the Negro Child," *Southern Medical Journal,* Vol. XVI, No. 1, 1922. Chairman's address, Section in Pediatrics, Southern Medical Association, Chattanooga, Tenn., November 13-16, 1922.
[32] "Health Work for Mothers and Children in a Colored Community," 1924. Publication 131 of the New York A. I. C. P.
[33] Woodbury, Robert Morse, *Infant Mortality and Its Causes.*

The infant mortality rate, as measured by fathers' earnings was 215.9 for those earning less than $50 monthly; 141.8 for those earning between $50 and $100, and 60.5 for those earning $400 and over. Similar trends are found for congestion, rentals, and working mothers.

The Children's Bureau studies, while affording no basis for conclusion as to racial differences in innate vitality, indicate that low income is undoubtedly a decisive factor among the causes accountable for the high infant and maternal mortality of the Negro. The report on Infant Mortality, Baltimore, 1915, in comparing rates for the whites and Negroes, states: "A large part of the difference in mortality, but not all, is evidently due to the greater poverty of the colored families." In a statistical study of causal factors of infant mortality by the Bureau, based on investigations in 8 cities, the conclusion is reached that the high mortality among the Negroes seems to have been largely a reflection of their low economic status. Grace Abbott, chief of the Bureau, points out that there has been a general health gain among the Negroes since the writing of these reports. The infant mortality rate has fallen from 181 (1915) to 100 (1927). This decrease of 45 per cent is greater than the corresponding decrease (38 per cent) for the white, with rates of 99 in 1915 and 61 in 1922. However, the Negro infant mortality rate remains relatively high, and it is suggested that it is still influenced by economic conditions, although not to the extent of a decade ago, for facilities for the public protection of maternity and infancy have been greatly increased during that period, and being free to all tend not only to reduce the infant mortality rate but to lessen its dependence upon economic conditions.

A study by the Public Health Service of absence from school in certain cities in Missouri in 1919-20 showed a consistently higher sickness rate among the children of the lower paid workers in all age groups between the ages of 6 and 16. A similar study of sickness among school children in Florida, in 1921-22, showed the same general tendency, for absence on account of sickness to increase with the decrease in economic well-being.

Comparison of child mortality rates among specific occupational groups and in various cities and counties shows that there is a constant tendency for the mortality to increase among the children of the lower paid groups of workers, although in some cases this tendency was not quite so marked in rural communities. In regard to specific diseases it appeared that diphtheria and scarlet fever vary less in the different classes than measles and whooping cough, both of which occur more frequently among the poorer children.

Although these data are scattering and are for varying periods, the practical uniformity in the results in showing a higher sickness incidence and mortality rate for both children and adults among the lower paid income groups indicates that sufficient income to insure reasonable physical comfort, proper nourishment, and care in the event of sickness, is of the utmost importance.

The Problem of Midwives. The very large number of Negro midwives and the dependence of Negro families upon them have prompted measures to offer some elementary training for them, as a safeguard against the extremes of insanitation and ignorance. The cost of physicians, and their scarcity in many sections of the South tend to continue midwives as an institution. There appear to be no specific studies of this phase of the infant mortality problem, although there are scattered compilations of births and mortality, classified by the attendants at birth. A compilation made by the Department of Welfare of North Carolina showed that in 1925 of 57,904 white births, 8,163, or 14.09 per cent, were attended by midwives; of 25,270 Negro births, 17,825, or 70.55 per cent, were attended by midwives. Where midwives were most common it happened also that there were the highest death rates both of infants and mothers.

Dr. E. C. Terry [34] points out that the toll of babies in Jacksonville, Florida, delivered by midwives is about twice as high as for physicians. However, Lucy Oppen, of the American Child Health Association, does not recognize in this the Negro problem as such, but regards it as a vital social problem, involving education of more doctors and nurses; raising the standards of midwifery and providing proper hygienic surroundings. "It happens that in the South it is chiefly the poorer and less economically and socially fortunate families—that is the Ne-

[34] Terry, E. C., "The Negro: His Relation to Public Health in the South," *Amer. Jour. of Public Health,* Vol. III, p. 300, 1910.

groes—who patronize the midwife." In Mulberry District Station in New York City, which is not Negro, 70 per cent employ midwives at delivery.

With regard to maternal mortality, the Children's Bureau report on that subject published in 1926 states:

An important cause of the heavier puerperal mortality among the colored is probably the poorer medical and midwifery service which they receive. Their excessive death rate from puerperal septicemia was undoubtedly due to poor quality of confinement care and a considerable part of their high mortality from other diseases connected with pregnancy and confinement was probably due to lack of skilled attention during pregnancy as well as at confinement.

Vital Index of the Negro Child. Dr. Frank L. Roberts and Dr. James A. Crabtree,[35] in a study of 1,564 white and 1,254 Negro children forming 25 per cent of the total school population of a Tennessee County, ascertained the standing height in centimeters, weight in pounds, stem length and age, using the Sonborn wet spirometer. They concluded: (1) On the basis of sitting height there is no difference between the white and Negro child; (2) Negro children have vital capacities lower than white of the same ages; (3) The index is lower for body weight; (4) The index is lower for standing height; (5) For stem length the vital capacities of white and Negro children were practically the same. They maintain that this study shows that the vital capacity of the Negro race, both sexes, is lower than the white—15 per cent to 20 per cent in children, 25 per cent to 30 per cent in adults; and that the growth curves of weight and standing height of whites and Negroes correspond closely.

[35] Roberts, Frank L. and Crabtree, James A., "Vital Capacity of Negro Child," *Journal A.M.A.*, Vol. LXXXVIII, No. 25, pp. 1920-32, 1927.

CHAPTER XII

RACIAL SUSCEPTIBILITY AND IMMUNITY

The Problem Summarized. For a number of years it was assumed that there was so pronounced a susceptibility among Negroes to tuberculosis that expenditures for preventive or corrective measures were practically useless. On the other hand, it was thought that there was a corresponding immunity to such diseases as cancer, malaria and diabetes, and that no special measures of relief were necessary. The course of experience has shown a reduction in the first and an increase in the latter diseases. The problem has been summarized by Dr. Dublin [1] as follows:

I do not believe that there is such a thing as absolute racial immunity to any disease. But racial color doubtless does exert more or less influence over the prevalence of, and the death-rate from, many diseases. Just how much of this influence is due to racial immunity or susceptibility and how much to racial customs, economic status and environment is difficult if not impossible to determine. The factor of the "crossing" of the white and Negro bloods also beclouds the issue—since the mulatto, the octoroon, etc., have both white and Negro blood, although they are classified as "colored."

The Negro death-rates for practically all diseases in the prevention or cure of which care and sanitation are of paramount importance are much higher than among whites; but this does not prove that the Negroes are, inherently, more susceptible to such diseases —or, for that matter, that they are less resistant to them. It is probable that their higher death-rate is due more than anything else to ignorance, poverty and lack of proper medical care. Pulmonary tuberculosis, typhoid fever, pellagra, malaria and puerperal conditions are examples of such diseases in which the mortality rates are much affected by unfavorable or unsanitary environment—or by

[1] Dublin, L. I., "The Health of the Negro," *The Annals of the American Academy of Political and Social Science,* Vol. CXL, 1928.

low economic status—and all of them have higher death-rates among Negroes. But there is no convincing evidence that the Negro is necessarily more susceptible than the white man to any of the above diseases.

There is some evidence, however, in a number of diseases of either *"relative* immunity" or *"relative* susceptibility" of Negroes. Medical authorities do not yet understand the comparative absence of locomotor ataxia in Negroes, since the disease is recognized as of syphilitic origin and the records indicate a higher incidence of syphilis among Negroes than whites. Moreover, the Army medical investigators after examination of many recruits state that the nervous system of Negroes shows fewer cases of instability than that of whites. There were found only about a third as many cases per thousand examined, of neurasthenia and "psychopathic state." There was also less diabetes, only half as many functional cardiac disturbances of nervous origin, and there were fewer eye and ear defects. The skin of the Negro was found more resistant to micro-organisms than that of whites; there was less gall bladder infection and fewer cases of urinary calculus. Only about a third as many acute abscesses and infections of the connective tissues of the skin appeared. Summarizing the study of 500,000 army sick reports, Love and Davenport [2] observe that:

"Army officers have ascertained . . . that colored troops are relatively less resistant to diseases of the lungs and pleura as well as to certain general diseases." As a result of a less unstable nervous system the Negro shows less neurasthenia, psychopathic states and only half as much alcoholism. Nutritional disorders are common among Negroes but the uninfected Negro metabolizes better than the white.

Although these carry rather strong indications of immunity there is the fact that the past few years have disclosed the growing importance of diabetes and diseases of the heart, and in urban centers there is a very high morbidity and mortality rate from these diseases. Dr. Dublin finds in the experience of the Metropolitan Life Insurance Company that Negroes are more resistant to the organism of caries; there is less prevalence of

[2] Love, A. C., and Davenport, C. B., "A Comparison of White and Colored Troops in Respect to Incidence of Disease," *Journal of A.M.A.,* Vol. LXXII, No. 20, p. 1468, and National Academy of Science, Vol. V, p. 58.

diphtheria, scarlet fever and German measles, and that they are less apt to be attacked by the organism of acute anterior poliomyelitis. On the other hand the Negro appears more susceptible and less resistant to whooping cough. Mental defects appear to have the form of acute mania and run sooner into imbecility. There is some evidence that Negroes have extraordinary power to survive both wounds and major surgical operations, and that once convalescent, they are less liable to the reactions of fever and other complications. One of the most important recent contributions to this subject is the discussion of biological factors in Negro mortality by Dr. Raymond Pearl of Johns Hopkins, which is carried as a special paper in Part II of this volume.

The contradictory nature of much of the existing evidence leads Dr. Dublin to doubt "whether we really know how important a part racial immunity or susceptibility plays in the life of the Negro—or whether we are in reality concerned with the effects of racial customs and environmental conditions."

The persistent high tuberculosis rate constitutes a challenging problem.

The observations of Dr. Milton J. Rosenau on this point, while analytic, point to no final conclusion. He says:

There is a temptation to assume that the Negro must be especially susceptible to tuberculosis. This is not believed by all students of the race, though we are almost entirely without exact statistical data on the question. There are some who think that the unhygienic living conditions of the colored people, the bad housing, the low wages, and the poor ventilation, together with lack of knowledge of health and sanitation, are the fundamental causes of the high Negro death rate from tuberculosis.

The tuberculosis death rate among Negroes today is not as high as was the tuberculosis death rate in New York City 33 years ago.

(a) At that time New York had a tuberculosis death rate for all forms of tuberculosis of 442 per 100,000 which was 24 per cent higher than the Negro rate for the registration area in 1917.
(b) The tuberculosis death rate of Paris in 1916 was 381 per 100,000, which is considerably higher than the Negro rate for that year in a number of American cities.
(c) The tuberculosis death rate in 13 departments of France in

1916 was higher than the rate for Negroes in either North Carolina or South Carolina. Thirteen departments of France, 281 ; North Carolina Negroes, 229; South Carolina Negroes, 201.

On the other hand, there are strong arguments in favor of a racial susceptibility in the case of Negroes, undoubtedly increased or aggravated by the poor economic conditions that prevail among so large a part of the race. Whenever Negroes live in the same community with white people, they have a higher tuberculosis death rate. If living conditions alone were the cause of the high tuberculosis death rate, we would expect to find high mortality rates among other groups, such as the Italian, who lives under conditions often as unfavorable as the Negro.

Yet the Italian death rate is low (a) while the Negro rate is high. (b) Fishberg believes the fact that primitive races, when first brought into contact with tuberculosis, readily fell prey to it, and cites the experience of the American Indian and the Negro as proof.

Dr. Charles R. Grandy of Norfolk, Virginia, probably expressed the sentiment of many on both sides of the question when he said, "The physical conditions, which surround the majority of Negroes, would conduce to tuberculosis in any race, though probably not to the same extent as in the Negro."

Other studies, principally medical, offer fragmentary evidence of racial immunity. Doctors T. K. Young and M. B. Cooperman report only one case on record of a Negro affected by Osteitis Fibrosa. Dr. J. T. Corson finds a peculiar absence of myopathic muscular atrophy in the Negro. Doctors Stokes, Hogan and Ewing, from a study of death rates in New Orleans, Newark and Baltimore, conclude that Negroes appear less susceptible to diphtheria, but that this may not be natural immunity; rather the failure to recognize the disease because a physician was not called or no cultures taken. Dr. E. P. Fisher attributes the apparent immunity of Negroes to urolithiasis (calcareous concretion in urethra, kidney urethus or bladder) to the fact of a comparative immunity to bacterial infections, since bacterial infection may be at the bottom of the calculus foundation.

Examples. An analysis of 150 cases of Granuloma Ingunale by Dr. Howard Cox disclosed 135 of them to be Negroes and only 15 whites. The majority of these Negroes were from the South. Trachoma is regarded as a rare disease among Negroes. There appear to be few cases of Exophthalmic goiter among Negroes. The Barnes Hospital in St. Louis to which 29,000 Negroes and 63,000 whites had been admitted between 1914 and 1920 disclosed 88 white and only 9 Negro cases, representing percentages of 0.13 and 0.03, respectively. A large amount of anorectal cases in the Negro is attributed to two contrasting factors: the fibroplastic diathesis; and the incidence of syphilis which is not attributed in turn to any predisposition or lowering of resistance but to earlier adolescence, living conditions, sex standards and poor hygiene.

Analysis of 160,044 patients in hospitals as reported by Dr. I. L. Lemmonn shows an incidence of diabetes of 1.4 per 1,000 for whites and only 0.86 for Negroes. This is regarded as a peculiar circumstance since syphilis may play an important rôle in producing diabetes. A case of malignant melanoma in a Negro woman reported by Dr. L. A. Sutton in the *Archives of Dermatology and Syphilology* raised the question of the possibility of a new growth derived from the chromatoblasts of the Negro's skin. Dr. F. G. DeSansure of Charleston, South Carolina, observes that the child-bearing period for Negro women is longer than that of white women; that Negro women seem less liable to eclampsia, septic poisoning and puerperal fever.

Dr. Smillie of the Rockefeller Institute for Medical Research gives the results of the studies of that Institute on the question of immunity and susceptibility:

The studies of the Rockefeller Foundation in the field have been limited in great part to hookworm disease, malaria, and yellow fever. The work of the Foundation is largely administrative and advisory. However, its work has clearly shown that the Negro in the United States, and apparently also in many parts of the world, is less susceptible to *Necator Americanus* than is the white man. A given number of worms will produce the same amount of injury in the Negro as in the white, but under similar conditions the Negro does not acquire as heavy infection as does the white. The reason for this is not known.

Another study of the Foundation, conducted by Dr. Augustine and myself, has shown that the Negro race has a lower vital capacity than the whites, and this observation has now been confirmed by other workers.

The Foundation has also some definite information showing that the Negro is less susceptible to malaria and its sequelæ than is the white, and there are certain data available in relation to the susceptibility of the Negro to yellow fever. If these additional data will be of value to you, I am sure that they can readily be compiled for you.

There has been, of course, a large amount of work done on the susceptibility of the Negro to rickets, tuberculosis, pneumonia, and other respiratory diseases, as well as studies showing higher homicide and lower suicide rates among the Negro than among other races.

Of particular interest to this discussion is the summary of data [3] on Negro Anthropology by Dr. Ales Hrdlicka of the Smithsonian Institution. Inasmuch as this includes the important studies of physical differences in the brain, craniology and osteology, and anthropometry, and takes into account the significant medical studies, it has an important bearing upon the question of racial immunity and susceptibility. His conclusion may be taken as an acceptable estimate of the value of the scattered studies to this point, in settling the problem to the satisfaction of science. These studies numbering several hundred, show, he says, "that scientific anthropology of the American Negro is still barely above its beginnings. Almost everything remains to be done, or done over, and better or more fully, according to present standards and requirements."

[3] "Anthropology of the American Negro, Historical Notes," *American Journal of Phys. Anthrop.*, Vol. X, No. 2, April-June.

CHAPTER XIII

HOSPITALIZATION, DOCTORS AND NURSES

Hospitals for Negroes. There are, according to the *Journal of the American Medical Association,* 6,807 hospitals of all kinds in the United States, with bed space of 853,318 and an average of 671,830 patients daily. This gives 1 bed for each 139 of the population. Estimates of the facilities available for Negro care in 1926, presented in a conference at the headquarters of the American Medical Association, placed the number of known hospitals of all kinds for Negroes at 210, of which 7 had been approved for interneship by the National Hospital and National Medical Associations, and the number of beds available 6,780 or an average of 1 bed for each 1,941 Negroes. For tuberculosis patients there was one-twenty-fifth the opportunity for sanitarium care for Negro as for white cases.

The problem of hospitalization for Negroes is shared by Negro hospitals, certain private and public hospitals in the North and in the South, the Negro wards of cities, counties and states. The varied policies regarding Negro patients of all except the exclusively Negro hospitals make extremely difficult any completely accurate check upon the total hospital facilities for Negroes. The difficulties experienced by Negro physicians in treating their patients in other than Negro hospitals, the limitation of beds in the special Negro wards, and the frequently encountered objection to Negro patients in the smaller hospitals or those not connected with schools of medicine, have focused the problem largely upon the separate institutions for Negroes and their adequacy.

The National Hospital Association, a Negro organization, attempted a survey of facilities among its memberships supplemented by such information from states and private institutions as could be secured. The list includes 178 hospitals for Negroes distributed as follows:

Alabama	15	Michigan	2
Arkansas	7	Mississippi	5
Arizona	1	Missouri	4
California	1	New Jersey	2
District of Columbia	4	New York	5
Florida	9	North Carolina	9
Georgia	15	Ohio	2
Illinois	7	Oklahoma	6
Indiana	7	Pennsylvania	6
Kansas	4	South Carolina	13
Kentucky	7	Tennessee	13
Louisiana	7	Texas	7
Maryland	2	Virginia	8
Massachusetts	1	West Virginia	7

Of these there are 10 which have been made "standard" by the American Medical Association, and in addition are certified by states but not by the American Medical Association. The total interne capacity is 70. Certain other of these hospitals are recognized by states, not in the sense of requiring that they meet adequate hospital standards, but to the extent that nurses in such hospitals, *as individuals* are permitted to take the state board examinations and are given the certification of Registered nurses, in that state only. After 1930 it is understood that this practice will be discontinued.

Under the direction of the Council on Medical Education and Hospitals of the American Medical Association, a survey of 120 hospitals for Negroes by Dr. Algernon B. Jackson, of the School of Public Health at Howard University, was completed in 1928. The report before being issued was reviewed by Doctors C. C. Bass of New Orleans, John E. Boyd of Jacksonville and James S. McLester of Birmingham, all of whom have a record of long experience in medical and hospital service for Negroes in the South. The 120 hospitals were 68 per cent of all known Negro hospitals, including those conducted by whites, and 29 others which were discovered in course of the survey. The 63 hospitals not covered were for the most part in the Northern states. In the 120 hospitals were 9,027 beds of which 6,451 on the average were occupied. Sixteen were graded at A, 43 at B, 30 at C, and 27 at D. Four were not graded. Ninety-three of them were regarded as worthy of support and

67 of the 93 were already receiving fair support. The staffs of 11 were entirely white; of 41, the majority were white; of 42 the staffs were entirely Negro physicians; and of 21 the majority of the staffs were Negroes. In a total of 999 physicians 482 were white and 515 were Negroes. Twenty-five hospitals were under white control and 95 under Negro control. Seven of these were city and county institutions, 2 under national federal control, 4 under state control, and 53 were private. Sixteen of these were in cities having between 200,000 and 500,000 inhabitants; 16 in cities between 100,000 and 200,000; 58 in cities between 10,000 and 100,000 and 30 in cities of less than 10,000.

Nurse training was found in 60 of these hospitals with a total of 690 nurses. In all 296 registered nurses were employed.

The hospitals visited ranged in capacity from two to two thousand beds and the range in organization and management was almost as great. So serious were some that the study recommended closing of the hospital; and there were others which met all essential requirements. The small towns offered little hospitalization for Negroes, the larger cities ample provisions for indigent Negroes, but poor facilities for the Negro pay patient. This latter is regarded as a serious problem for the Negro physician also; for the patient in a crisis turns away from the doctor who is limited in his service to one who can enter the better equipped institutions. Wherever Negro physicians, either through their own or other hospitals admitting them for surgical work, can provide a measure of the essential hospital equipment, there is no difficulty in holding the confidence of their Negro patients. The scarcity of trained hospital executives and administrators is held responsible for the unsatisfactory condition of many of these institutions, and indirectly, for the reluctance of philanthropy to give important support to them.

The recommendations of the survey suggest certain gross conditions requiring prompt attention.

Recommendations. 1. In order to determine the exact status of the matter of hospitalization for Negroes in the South, it is recommended that a careful study be made, state by state, of hospital

beds available, from all sources, for Negroes: the standard of
service rendered and the proportion of pay and indigent patients.

2. The conditions under which Negro nurses are trained in
Negro hospitals are deplorable. It is recommended that a definite
campaign be instituted to have each state adopt legislation requiring hospitals to obtain a license before operating a training school
for nurses. The present regulations are inadequate. The problem
of the inefficient nurse is as much the concern of the state as is the
problem of the inefficient doctor.

3. It is believed that a survey of some of the most likely institutions, with the purpose of instructing them in methods of administration and routine procedure, would be a valuable philanthropy.

4. Negro hospitals should not necessarily have Negro executives and a Negro hospital staff. Public hospitals, with beds for
Negro patients, should still have white executives and a white hospital staff, at least in the South.

5. Negro hospitals in general should be controlled by Negroes,
but at present in the South the assistance of the white people is
often needed.

Concerning the present hospital situation for Negroes generally these facts are evident: There is a shortage of Negro
doctors due in part to the opportunities for interneship, and
limited facilities for adequate nurse training. This latter is
yet a very unorganized and uncertain field. Clinics and out-
patient departments are yet exceedingly inadequate and hospital social service which is, perhaps, needed most for Negroes
is almost entirely undeveloped. In the hospitals, X-ray service
and Roentgenists are needed. This is a fact which disqualifies
most Negro hospitals for approval. The duplication of small
and undermanned hospitals at points preventing the development of a single adequate hospital which will permit necessary
specializations constitutes a serious but obviously remediable
situation.

Before any more exact picture of the situation can be obtained it will be necessary to study further the number of beds
available for Negroes in white hospitals, and the morbidity
rates among Negroes.

Negro Physicians and Dentists. The Council on Medical
Education and Hospitals of the American Medical Association
in 1928 compiled the following list of Negro medical students
and graduates in all institutions during the session 1925-26:

Name of College	Students	Graduates
College of Medical Evangelists	I	...
University of California Medical School	I	...
Howard University School of Medicine	226	54
Northwestern University Medical School	10	3
Rush Medical College	14	2
Chicago Medical School	24	3
Loyola University School of Medicine	15	...
Indiana University School of Medicine	5	I
University of Kansas School of Medicine	I	...
Boston University School of Medicine	I	...
Harvard University School of Medicine	7	2
Tufts College Medical School	4	...
University of Michigan Medical School	3	2
University of Nebraska College of Medicine	I	...
Columbia University College of Physicians and Surgeons	I	...
Long Island College Hospital	I	...
Western Reserve University School of Medicine	I	...
Ohio State University College of Medicine	4	...
Temple University School of Medicine	2	I
Woman's Medical College of Philadelphia	I	...
Dalhousie University Faculty of Medicine	4	4
McGill University Faculty of Medicine	16	3
Meharry Medical College	225	47
University of Toronto Faculty of Medicine	6	...
Total for 1926	574	122
Total for 1925	543	126
Total for 1924	471	85

Number and Distribution. The census of 1900 showed 1,734 Negro physicians; in 1920 the number was given as 3,495. At the annual rate of increase indicated it is probable that the number at present exceeds 4,500. This is 1 physician for each 2,600 of the Negro population. These are disproportionally distributed. The preference in location seems to be for cities of the North despite the fact that the bulk of the Negro population is in the South. The 5 cities, Chicago, Cleveland, New York City, Philadelphia and Washington, have as many physicians as are located in all the Southern states combined. Howard and Meharry, the two Negro medical schools, furnish 83 per cent of all the Negro physicians. The number of Negro graduates annually, from all medical schools, can supply just 58 per cent of the number required to meet the demands of Negro population increase without affecting the existing ratio to their racial population.

The amount of Negro illness and death attributed to dental and oral maladies is not known, but there stand the facts of excessive mortality, and much of this from diseases which may have as their source the focal infections, impaired nutrition and systemic disorders related to the health of the teeth and mouth. There are at present about 1,300 Negro dentists. The number increased greatly from 1885, when the first dental class of Negroes was graduated, to 1920. Since then the numbers have declined, probably as a result of increased requirements of pre-medical work for dental graduates.

The study of Dental Education [1] in the United States, published by the Carnegie Foundation for the Advancement of Teaching in 1926 includes an important discussion of the deficiencies of dental service for the Negro group. The ratio of white dentists to the population is 1 to 1,700; of Negro dentists, 1 to about 8,500. The mass migration of Negroes to cities of the North has served to deplete the already small numbers in active practice in the South, and this in the face of increased demands for trained oral hygienists to cooperate with school boards and public health authorities in the promotion of the welfare of Negroes.

As in the case of physicians the number of dentists being graduated is insufficient to keep pace with the yearly increase in the Negro population. From 1885 to 1925 the total Negro dental graduates from all institutions was 879 or an annual average of about 22. The 2 Negro schools, Howard and Meharry, graduated 73 in 1925, and these 2 schools have been responsible for 80 per cent of all Negro dentists. The report observes significantly that general growth of sentiment for segregation has increased the tendency, in many dental schools, to restrict the attendance to white students, or to admit only the small number of Negro students that may be useful for treatment of a few Negro patients in the infirmary. Some of the schools object to Negroes in their infirmary; others separate Negro patients, while several admit them without discrimination.

However, the 2 Negro dental schools are too severely handicapped by lack of equipment and facilities and even teachers to render adequate training for the few who are admitted.

Education and Service of Negro Nurses. A summary of the

[1] "Dental Education in the United States." A report to the Carnegie Foundation for the Advancement of Teaching by William J. Gies, Bulletin No. 19, p. 88.

result of a study of educational facilities for colored nurses made in 1924 by the "Hospital Library and Service Bureau" of the American Conference on Hospital Service gives these figures:

Accredited nurse training schools admitting colored students   54
Accredited nurse training schools not admitting colored students 1,588
Hospitals using colored graduate nurses   66
Hospitals using colored graduate nurses as "specials"   60
Hospitals not using colored graduate nurses regularly 1,576
Hospitals not using colored graduate nurses as "specials" 1,582
Departments of health not employing colored nurses—58 plus per cent
  replies   489
Departments of health employing colored nurses   59
Health departments reporting insufficient supply of colored nurses to
  meet the demand   24
Health departments reporting sufficient supply of colored nurses   132
Visiting nurse associations reporting use of colored nurses   19
Those stating preference for colored nurses for visiting nursing among
  colored   9
Hospitals using colored internes   21
Hospitals not using colored internes 1,640

Recent years have marked the rise of hospitals and nurse training schools for Negroes. Because of the number of nurses sent out among the people and the facilities afforded for caring for patients, hospitals and nurse-training schools are undoubtedly becoming important factors in the improvement of the health of Negroes.

CHAPTER XIV

SOME REMEDIAL MEASURES

Anti-tuberculosis Work. Wide variations appear in the remedial as well as preventive health work among Negroes. The most deliberate campaigns recently have been in anti-tuberculosis work under the general impetus of the National Anti-tuberculosis Association. The extent of local work among Negroes, however, depends upon the temper of the community. Pulaski County Tuberculosis Association at Little Rock, Arkansas, has for many years borne much of the expense of a Negro tuberculosis clinic. The Arkansas Tuberculosis Association has initiated and, with the aid of the Arkansas Negroes, made some progress on a legislative campaign for a Negro state tuberculosis sanitarium. In Atlanta the Anti-tuberculosis Association has a group of white physicians covering clinic needs of Negroes, and for many years they have paralleled this with a summer group work for Negro physicians. A Negro health education worker is employed for service among the Negro schools.

An interesting tendency in Negro tuberculosis work is the turning over of discarded sanatoria for Negro use. New ones would be better, but under present stress those so secured have been clear gain. This is illustrated by the Colored Pines Sanitarium being established when the White Pines was rebuilt by the Shreveport, Louisiana, Tuberculosis Association. Some social work is also done for pre- and post-patients of this institution by a representative of the local tuberculosis association.

The Kansas City, Missouri, Tuberculosis Association has developed and is conducting a Negro tuberculosis clinic which is being taken over by the city government in an effort to make some sanatorium provision for Negro patients. The Missouri Tuberculosis Association, in St. Louis, aided by the Kansas City and other local associations succeeded in having additional beds for Negroes opened in the State Tuberculosis Sanatorium.

The New York Association for the Improvement of the Condition of the Poor operates extensively in the Columbus Hill district of New York City, where some 95 per cent of the population are Negroes. Social hygiene, tuberculosis and infant welfare work are being done and tuberculosis patients are cared for by the Tuberculosis Department of the Association. This association intends later to place much of this supervision and service in the hands of trained Negro workers.

Negro physicians in Baltimore, under the Maryland Tuberculosis Association, have for several years through clinic work in a Baltimore hospital received special practice and training in the early diagnosis of tuberculosis. In Ohio, the Cincinnati Anti-tuberculosis League and the Shoemaker Health and Welfare Center are engaged in tuberculosis work in Cincinnati. The Henry Phipps Institute in Philadelphia conducts what is perhaps the most advanced Negro tuberculosis program under Dr. H. R. M. Landis, himself an authority in this field. The Davidson County Anti-tuberculosis Association, with the aid of Meharry Medical College and the Tennessee Tuberculosis Association, has begun Negro tuberculosis clinic work in Nashville.

Through an appropriation of the Laura Spellman Rockefeller Memorial Foundation the Tennessee State Department of Health, under Dr. Bishop, and the Social Science Department of Fisk University engaged in 1927 upon a tabulation of mortality statistics of Tennessee, with reference to the differential mortality of whites and Negroes over a period of 10 years. This project was the initial step in what will be without doubt the most comprehensive study of the public health problems of Negroes that has yet been carried out in the South. The statistical attack on the first question has been completed under Mr. Elbridge Sibley, a competent statistician. The cost of this study has been borne chiefly by Fisk; the State Department of Public Health has provided not only the raw materials of the study but the clerical service and mechanical tabulation of the data. The investigation has been carried further into the field, where both white and Negro workers, trained in epidemiological investigation, are seeking the causes of differences in the mortality and morbidity of the two races. Paralleling the medical investigation, Fisk University's Department of Social Science is engaged upon studies of the social-economic backgrounds of the people as they are related to public health problems. This extension of the work has been made possible by the Rosenwald Fund.

The Texas Public Health Association, at Austin, maintains a full-time Negro education worker. In Norfolk, Virginia, Dr. Charles R. Grandy, President of the Anti-tuberculosis League of Norfolk, is and has been providing active clinic and nursing work for Negroes.

Negro tuberculosis sanatorium beds are not listed. While some are known to be in Federal, state, county, city, private and semi-private sanatoria, it is a fact attested almost universally that the number is notoriously inadequate.

National Negro Health Week. Under the leadership of Tuskegee and the National Negro Business League one week is set aside each year for concerted campaigning against disease. Health sermons and lectures by ministers, doctors, and other qualified persons are provided in as many cities as find it feasible to cooperate. These speakers urge cooperation with organized health agencies, emphasize mother and infant welfare work to reduce high mortality, and these lectures, health films and exhibits stress personal and home hygiene, social hygiene education and venereal disease control measures.

A campaign is instituted to destroy the breeding places of flies and mosquitoes, and popular talks are given on the spread of disease by insects and rats, and methods of destroying them. Homes, markets, bakeries, and food establishments are urged to be screened against flies and cooperation with local health departments in this endeavor sought.

The National Urban League. Through its 37 local branches, under the policy of the organization to provide programs where conspicuous inadequacies appear in localities, health work is accomplished by the Urban League. This work is usually in cooperation with local health departments and agencies and occasionally of the nature of a survey to determine the prevalence and social factors responsible for excessive Negro mortality.

Health Centers and Clinics. There were in 1927 some 5,700 health centers and clinics in the United States. In the Northern cities many of these are open to Negroes and whites alike.

Local health centers for Negro mothers and babies are now appearing in some cities of the South where such service has been maintained for white mothers. In Northern cities, while Negro babies may be treated at the general clinics, these are not always convenient to the Negro residence areas and organizations interested in Negro work, notably the Urban Leagues, are sponsoring the placing of these where they can be reached by more Negro families.

The Whittier center in Philadelphia established in 1914 employed the first Negro nurses in that city. There is now a staff of doctors and nurses practically all of whom are supported by the Philadelphia Health Council.

In New York City clinics and health centers are for the most part open to all, but the largest Negro work is done in the Negro sections. Nurses working out from the Lincoln Center and the New York Urban League offices cover the majority of Harlem cases. The professional service at the New York Urban League is voluntary.

Cincinnati is in advance of most cities in organization for Negro health. During 1926-27 the Shoemaker clinic served 5,377 persons. There are in attendance 7 white and 11 Negro physicians, 10 Negro dentists and a registrar, 2 full-time nurses, a part-time nurse and a dental assistant. It conducts prenatal, tuberculosis and venereal clinics and a family service department under a budget of $25,000. Four other health centers are operated by this organization, 3 of which are at public schools. Fresh air classes are conducted with daily bath and diet supervision. There is now 1 Negro nurse to every 8,000 Negroes as compared with 1 white nurse to every 17,000 white persons. The family is stressed as a health unit and a notable improvement in Negro health and living has resulted.

In Washington, D. C., the Department of Health in 1927 showed a total of 12,596 visits of Negro children to child hygiene stations and 8,855 visits of nurses to homes. Of the 7 public health nurses in East St. Louis 3 are Negroes and working at Negro Health Centers. In Virginia 40 counties have Negro public health nurse service. The Virginia Anti-tuberculosis Association conducts venereal disease clinics in large cities with free chest examination clinics. Alabama has 1 Negro nurse who lectures on health among Negroes. Arkansas is employing temporarily a Negro nurse to assist the medical supervisor, and to conduct a special campaign for birth and death registration in counties having a large Negro population. Florida held during 1927 48 children's health and prenatal conferences for Negro children with 3,147 examinations. In the prenatal classes, 1,410 Negro mothers were given instruction. Three hundred and fifty-eight midwives' classes were also held, and more than 300 Neighborhood Institute meetings. There are now 9 dental clinics in the state for Negroes. Georgia has 1 staff nurse, and 5 county nurses. However, more than 4,000 midwives are registered in the state and most of them are Negroes.

Throughout the South one of the greatest difficulties in Negro child and maternal care is the general use of midwives. The Commonwealth Fund speaks of these as being as much in need of training as the mothers. The fact that these Negro midwives attend a great number of white cases has made the demand for supervision more insistent.

North Carolina has recently been vigorously developing a welfare program which includes the Negro. Community Improvement Leagues have been established in many counties in the state, and regular institutes are held for Negro social workers. In 1926, $20,610 was paid in salaries to the Negro welfare workers of the state. In Winston-Salem, though the Negro district is separated from the whites, an attempt was made to keep the same standards by maintaining a staff of efficient Negro physicians and nurses. There is a portable dental clinic carried between schools, a baby health center operating since 1919, and an attempt is now being made to secure a nutrition expert for the Negro schools.

In Nashville clinics, mother clubs and welfare stations operate from Bethlehem Center, supported by the M. E. Church South. Professional service is rendered by physicians from Meharry Medical College. This center has an interracial board. City health nurses work out from this center.

The American Association for Social Hygiene has a Negro field worker and lecturer, and under his direction has conducted summer courses in Sex Hygiene at Hampton and Tuskegee Institutes and several smaller schools. The Circle for Relief although national in scope and devoted entirely to Negro health has found its programs limited largely to the placing and maintenance of nurses in a few Southern states. The Metropolitan Life Insurance Nurses and the Visiting Nurses Association have provided important health instruction, and in some instances, care for the Negro sick. The Julius Rosenwald Fund which has been interested in health as well as other problems of the Negro population has now on its staff a competent student of public health in Dr. Michael Davis as advisor for the health programs of the Fund. For a period the venereal section of the United States Public Health Service maintained a Negro worker. The annual conferences at the John M. Andrews Hospital at Tuskegee serve in an interesting manner to keep alive a public health interest among Negro physicians. In this connection also should be mentioned the 78 national, state and city Negro medical associations and the journal of the National Medical Association.

Recent discussions of the high mortality rates of Negroes have been shifting somewhat, from a complete medical emphasis to consideration of problems of economic status and physical environment. The significant bearing of these social factors upon the rates discussed in this chapter is necessary to any adequate view of the health status of Negroes. Social problems are inter-related and nowhere in this inter-relation more noticeable than in the Negro population.

Further Studies of Negro Health Required. Review of the available literature on Negro health discloses many inadequacies in the statistical data. For a more faithful picture of the significant factors in Negro health and differential racial mortality, at least the following studies should be made:

An investigation of Negro mortality in rural areas.
An investigation of Negro mortality by income classes.
Study of facilities available for the health education of Negroes, and for the care of the Negro sick.
An inquiry into the extent of mental diseases among the Negro population; cases in institutions and cases requiring institutional care.
A comprehensive study—in two or three typical localities—of the social background of Negro mortality.
Study of the effect of migration from South to North upon Negro rates of death and birth.

A study of mortality by occupation and race.

The relative effects upon infant mortality of delivery by physicians and midwives.

The relation of changing diagnoses and classifications to trends in Negro mortality.

The relation of amounts spent in localities for Negro health to Negro mortality rates.

Effects of climate on mortality.

Study of Negro diet in relation to Negro mortality.

Study of Negro morbidity rates by important diseases.

An inquiry into the relation of diseases of early life to the excess mortality among Negroes from certain diseases.

The influence of superstition and magical practices upon Negro health.

The character of congenital malformations in Negro infants at birth.

Finally, medical research may profitably concern itself with:

(a) Causes of the high incidence among Negroes of nephritis in certain localities.

(b) Immunity and susceptibility, particularly with reference to *Tubercle Bacilli.*

Records of mortality slowly improve and several important studies are under way. In 1928 Colorado, Georgia and Oklahoma were admitted to the birth registration area, South Carolina re-admitted, and Georgia to the death registration area. The Carnegie Corporation, Rockefeller Foundation, the Julius Rosenwald, Commonwealth, Russell Sage and Twentieth Century Funds, are providing grants for important experimental and pioneer health enterprises. Four national health agencies in cooperation with the United States Public Health Service are launched upon a 5-year study of the cost of medical care, utilizing a research staff of physicians, sociologists and economists.

Dr. Harry H. Moore of the Public Health Service, commenting upon the continuing high mortality from preventable deaths, quotes William H. Welsh significantly as saying: "We know how to do a lot of things, which we don't do, or do on a wretchedly small scale." What is most disturbing is the fact so obvious that the scale for Negro work is still smaller.

CHAPTER XV

THE PROBLEM OF HOMES

There are few cities without Negro sections, and few of these sections that are not located within a stone's throw of the city's business district. It is one of the most curious phenomena of city growth. In Chicago it is the second ward, beginning where the "loop" ends; in Philadelphia it skirts along two blocks from Broad Street; in Atlanta Auburn Avenue of business breaks suddenly into Auburn Avenue of the Negroes and gradually fades into whiteness again; Beale Street of Memphis, famed for its "Blues" of "low" Negro origin, traces a similar course. In Richmond, Virginia, the Negroes' Leigh and Clay streets are just two blocks from Broad Street, the center of business; in Savannah, the Negro district begins across the street from the new Union station, so placed to indicate the center of transportation activities. Even in New York City, which has taken a somewhat untypical city growth, there is Columbus Hill around 58th Street within sight of Fifth Avenue and Broadway; and the remnants of the migration to Harlem may still be seen moving in and out of the archaic dwellings not yet destroyed, and not three blocks removed from the heart of the theatre district.

The course of a consistent tendency is marked in these. For it develops that in each case the Negro residence area is located on approximately the first residence sites of the city. As the city grows and the encroachments of business render the original areas less desirable for residence, the first owners move farther out, to newer developments. They are followed in turn, in the old dwellings, by successively lower income classes, as owners or renters. The buildings become older and more difficult to keep in repair; boarding houses and lodging places appear. Exclusiveness is gone. Low income foreign groups may move in. If their economic level is not improved sufficiently to allow individuals to move out, it becomes "Little Italy," or

"Little Ireland." Not infrequently the indiscriminateness of these transitional areas permits the entrance of houses of prostitution, or the milder iniquity of "buffet flats," and, in the more modern parlance "bootleg joints." These are the areas, generally, that become the Negro centers. For a greater income in rent may be secured from this social group than from the economic class of whites next in order of succession. Unlike the native or immigrant white, the elevation of economic status alone does not make possible movement to a different or newer area. The property is potentially valuable for business, depending, of course, upon the capricious direction of the city's growth. Carter Woodson's [1] compilation of free Negro heads of Negro families in 1830 shows New York City Negroes living on Wall, Nassau, Sullivan, Canal and Rector streets, holdings now of prohibitively high value. Abyssinia Baptist Church remained in the old Negro center on 50th Street until a few years ago before it moved to Harlem. Of the homes now occupied in Harlem practically none have been built by Negroes. They have been inherited and among these are rare examples of the architectural stamp of Stanford White. The Harlem dwellings are more habitable because they are relatively newer. The measure of general Negro housing in enough cities to make it a rule, becomes the quality of the property inheritance.

Housing for Negroes involves at least four important questions: (1) racial segregation, which may introduce or contribute to the seriousness of availability of houses, congestion, ownership, depreciation of property value and like matters; (2) factors of city growth and the natural distribution in residence areas of groups of like economic status; (3) the physical condition of structures occupied by the majority of the Negro population with its bearing upon sanitation and health; and (4) home ownership and its implications for the stability of the Negro family.

Residential Segregation. The factor of racial segregation both voluntary and involuntary may and frequently does contribute an angle to Negro housing as acute as segregation by income classes may contribute to the housing problem of small

[1] Woodson, Carter G., *Free Negro Heads of Negro Families in the United States in 1830.* Association for the Study of Negro Life and History.

income groups. For even though a city may have a sufficient number of dwellings for its total population, there can still be an acute problem of available homes for Negroes. This factor has been marked by the following :

(a) The tendency of the Negro population to concentrate in fewer wards of cities, particularly in the North;

(b) Segregation laws designed to delimit areas of white and Negro residence by legislation;

(c) Restrictive compacts entered upon by white property owners to prevent occupancy of certain areas by Negroes;

(d) The question of property depreciation;

(e) The problem of financing home buying by Negroes in areas designated *Negro*.

Studies of urban zones tend to stress the almost inevitable and unique racial concentrations linking them with certain economic implications. The urban studies at the University of Chicago, conducted under the direction of Robert E. Park and Ernest W. Burgess, have gone far towards reducing these observations to a pattern. Cities tend to expand and become organized on a pattern approximately that of concentric zones. These zones, as described by Dr. Burgess are: I. The Central Business District Zone; II. The Zone in transition; III. The Zone of working men's homes; IV. The Residential Zone; and V. The Commuter's Zone.[2]

The interstitial regions between residence and industry hold the Negro and immigrant groups. The concentration and scatter of these two groups is similar for as many cities as available data permit of study. The Negro, however, tends to have the highest percentage of concentration.

The acquiring of residence sites by new groups of imputed inferior status has been observed to follow a pattern which can now be described almost as a sociological process: (1) *invasion,* beginning often as an unnoticed or general penetration, followed by (2) *reaction,* or the resistance mild or violent of the inhabitants of the community, ultimately resulting in (3) the *influx* of newcomers and the rapid abandonment of the area

[2] Burgess, Ernest W., "Residential Segregation in American Cities." *The Annals of the American Academy of Political and Social Science,* Vol. CXXX, 1928.

by the old-time residents, and (4) *climax,* or the achievement
of a new equilibrium of communal stability.

Although there are areas in most cities in which the Negro
population is concentrated to the point of being regarded the
"black belt," there is in no large city, with the possible exception of Tulsa, Oklahoma, a concentration approaching absolute
segregation. The "black belt" of Chicago had at the time of
the study by the Chicago Commission on Race Relations only
about 51 per cent Negro population. Various cities have different types and degrees of segregation, determined by the
Negro population ratios, distribution of Negro employments,
the growth of the city, the general availability of low-priced
properties, and local attitudes toward segregation.

Dr. T. J. Woofter,[3] assisted by Mrs. Madge Headly Priest,
a housing investigator of rare experience and training, in 1927
studied the various patterns of Negro residential segregation in
some 17 Northern and Southern cities. Four types of segregation are described:

The first group is typified by New York and Chicago, where
the concentration of Negroes is great and yet where it affects only
a small part of the whole city area. In Chicago this pattern seems
to be changing as the Negroes spread more southward. In New
York 96 per cent of the white people are in concentrated white
areas and 28 per cent of the colored people are in concentrated
colored areas.

The second group is typified by Richmond, and includes most of
the large Southern cities where Negroes are highly concentrated in
several rather large parts of the city and lightly scattered in others,
thus leaving a large proportion of the white people in areas from
10 to 90 per cent Negro. In Richmond 53 per cent of the white
people are in concentrated white areas and 25 per cent of the Negroes in concentrated Negro areas.

The third group is typified by Charleston, and is limited to the
older Southern cities and towns which have a heavy percentage of
Negroes in their total population, and consequently a heavy scattering of Negroes throughout the city. In Charleston there are no
enumeration districts that have a population less than 10 per cent
colored, and none that have a population less than 10 per cent
white, placing all members of both races in districts from 10 to 90
per cent colored.

[3] Woofter, T. J., and others, *Negro Problems in Cities,* p. 38.

Group 4 is composed of cities with light-colored infusion, where the diffusion of Negroes affects only a very small area of the city, and is somewhat scattered within this area. In Gary, 89 per cent of the white people are in concentrated white areas and no Negro districts are more than 90 per cent Negro.

A significant difference appears between Northern and Southern cities. The location of many Negro homes in the South, near places of employment as domestics, has established tolerance in large degree of Negro neighbors, and it is possible, frequently, for them to purchase and improve the property. Moreover, in many cities of the South Negroes have preceded white populations in sites desired as new developments and, owning the property, have remained as these sites developed. Border cities, like Baltimore, Maryland; Louisville, Kentucky; St. Louis, Missouri, with an uncertain mixture of traditions of both the North and the South, have attempted to fix relations artificially through legislation. In successive instances, however, segregation ordinances limiting the residential areas of Negroes and of whites have been declared unconstitutional by the higher courts. In Northern cities, prior to the large migrations of Negroes from the South, the Negro population was a negligible factor. Economically hard pressed it lived in the abandoned sites of early white residents along with or in close succession to other racial groups of similar economic status. With the sudden influx of newcomers and the over-running of areas generally associated with Negroes, reaction to expansion was acute. In many instances racial factors were given an importance much out of proportion to their actual place in the natural course of the properties in question. The Chicago riot had as one of its aggravating causes this feature of the housing problem. Other cities have had similar, if somewhat wider, experiences, and may therefore be taken as more representative of a large area.

Detroit, the automobile center with its high wages and skilled workers, has since 1915 attracted thousands of workers from all sections of the country. It bid for Southern Negro labor in a war-time emergency and got it. With practically no foreign immigration Detroit's population increased from 993,678 in 1920 to 1,242,000 in 1925, and the Negro population from 5,741 in 1910 to 40,838 in 1920, and to 81,831 in 1925. The small Negro population had been living in many sections of the city, with a moderate concentration around St. Antoine Street, down town, and in other spots where their churches and other meeting places had been settled. The sudden population increase forced expansion beyond the familiar limits, and with a similar increase in the white population housing problems became more vexatious. The rate of Negro increase, however, was many times in excess of the rate for whites and despite the constant growth of the size of the city the limits of the Negro area remained fixed about the first sites. In 1920 Dr. A. L. Turner, a Negro physician, moved to Spokane Avenue, a white neighborhood in which were also many Southern whites. His house was stoned, windows broken out, and he was otherwise intimidated by a mob numbering several thousand. He moved. Dr. O. H. Sweet, another Negro physician, during 1925 found a home 8 miles east of the scene of Dr. Turner's experience. The same intimidations of the mob followed, and this time one white man among the mob was killed and another wounded. The doctor and his wife, 2 brothers and 4 other men were held without bail, all charged with homicide. Simultaneously, the Klan was waging a fierce political battle for control of the city Council. Established there in 1923, it increased in strength with the volume and intensity of racial clashes. The Mayor and Mr. Clarence Darrow were retained by the American Civil Liberties Union and the National Association for the Advancement of Colored People to defend the Negroes. After a long dramatic trial they were freed.

Cleveland, Ohio, offers another example. In September of 1925 copies of a printed hand bill, 9 x 11, were distributed among white residents of Cleveland Heights:

BE SURE AND READ THIS

Certain niggas have recently blackmailed certain residents of the Cleveland Hts. and other sections of the city.

They are now trying to erect a house at 11114 Wade Park Ave. to Blackmail us.

BUT THEY WILL NOT

The Residents of the neighborhood will not give one cent to these blackmailers.

Appoint your committees to oppose and eradicate this group of
Black Gold Diggers.

Let them know we can duplicate Riots in Tulsa, St. Louis, Chicago and Baltimore.

During this period there were noted 17 cities from Virginia
to California experiencing similar situations.

The opposition to Negro occupancy of certain areas has been
motivated by at least two factors:

(a) *Sentimental motives*—manifest in the objection to prox-
    imity to Negro neighbors. This is partly a question of
    racial tradition and group tastes, and partly a question
    of the implication of an inferior status for the whites
    who lived close by a group associated with an inferior
    economic status.

(b) *Economic motives*—manifest in the conviction and fear
    that Negro occupancy brings actual depreciation to prop-
    erty values.

The first of these is a question requiring study. The second
has been examined with some thoroughness by the Chicago
Commission study made in 1922.

Property values in the Hyde Park district of Chicago, it was
explained by real estate men, had been destroyed by the "invasion" of Negroes, the loss being placed at $200,000,000. The
Commission investigators, however, pointed out that the houses
there originally costing $50,000 and $75,000 to erect had been
consistently declining in value for 20 or 30 years before there
had been a threat of Negro residence. Otherwise, they could
not have been purchased by the Negroes, who, with a few exceptions, could not afford them. Owners had left because they
did not like the odors of the stockyards a few blocks off, the
smoke and dirt of the Illinois Central trains, or the cheaper
apartments placed there after the World's Fair, or the encroachment of the automobile industry with its display of shops. The
wear and tear of the elements had *deteriorated* them. The
homes had changed hands 4 or 5 times and when they reached
the level of the Negro purse, were being rented at a loss.
Negro tenants were brought in by white realtors to enable them
to boost rents. One Negro home, 4 times bombed, had been,

until its sale to a Negro family, registered by the police as an "immoral resort." It was explained by the Commission's report that property values are largely psychological, and this element is even more pronounced when the two races are leveled off to the same economic class.

Restrictive Compacts. Since the segregation ordinances have been declared unconstitutional it has been found most effective to band white residents of an area in a legal agreement not to rent, sell, give, lease or in any way convey to Negroes the properties. In one sense this is a social extension of the principle of zoning which has held the favor of municipal associations.

In some cities the exclusion has had less direct application to Negro families, as such, than to indifferent or economically inadequate families of any race which might give an uneven aspect to a site which made exclusiveness a chief value.

In the compacts races have in instances been specified, and various communities have included among undesirables, Orientals, Mexicans, "Balkan" races, and South Europeans, as well as Negroes. One of the most notable of the protests against this came in the "Curtis Case" in Washington, D. C., which has been before the courts in the District of Columbia supported there by the National Association for the Advancement of Colored people.

The Physical Condition of Negro Neighborhoods. One inescapable item with serious features, in the inherited properties of Negroes, is their advanced age.

(a) The dwellings, being no longer desirable for residence, while the land is potentially valuable for business, are as a rule difficult to buy.

(b) They are difficult to put or keep in repair.

(c) The area attracts few new dwellings.

(d) The dwellings are out of date and frequently fall within the class tolerated as "old law" houses, with few of the sanitary provisions required in new structures for the preservation of health.

(e) The dwellings were erected for purposes and family habits different enough from the habits and necessities of the new Negro families to introduce difficulties. For example the intimate arrangement of the early houses

for private families is dangerously unsuitable for the
new families which must take lodgers into their households. Privacy is destroyed and other social problems
introduced.

(f) Where this population is set off without influence there
is a temptation for the city government to neglect it in
matters of street cleaning, garbage disposal, paving, as
police protection, interest and available funds center
upon the improvements in new areas.

Congestion. Among the first and most dismal of the social
problems encountered by migrants from the South was that of
housing congestion. Negro residence areas expand very slowly,
and when these are hemmed in, as frequently happens, by other
social or natural barriers the result immediately registers in
overcrowding. Normally, the homes of Negro families have a
margin of space. The old institution of the unused "parlor"
frequently survives, even where there is overcrowding in the
sleeping rooms. The necessities of the new urban life, however, are forcing it out. In Cleveland, investigators in the summer of 1917 found such an acute situation that a special sub-
committee of the Welfare Federation was created to handle it.
The Real Estate Board estimated that some 10,000 new houses
were needed. For a period many hundreds of newcomers, principally men, lived in box cars, on railway sidings. In Newark,
New Jersey, old and discarded dwellings without heat, bath, or
toilets, were forced into use. One study of a group of 53 families indicated that they were crowded into "unsanitary, dark
quarters averaging 4⅞ persons per room." [4] In St. Louis, abandoned residence sections of whites provided shelter at an increased rental of 25 per cent. Epstein, in Pittsburgh, found of
318 families, 50 per cent living in rooming houses, and about
12 per cent in camps and churches. Kitchens, attics, basements
and dining rooms became sleeping rooms, and in the more
crowded sections beds were rented on a double shift basis. [5]

The extreme congestion of the first influx was softened as
new areas relented stubbornly. In 1919, James H. Robinson
in Cincinnati, however, found Negro families living in the

[4] Pendleton, H. B., in *The Survey*, February, 1917.
[5] Epstein, Abraham, "The Negro Migrant to Pittsburgh."

oldest model tenement houses in the city, 85 per cent of them fire traps; 1 out of 3 toilets out of repair, and 54 per cent of all of the houses without baths. Dr. Bernard J. Newman, of Philadelphia, in 1924 found in the old Negro areas a congestion expressed at points in an average of 5 persons to a room. The outlying areas were less crowded.

The study of Negro housing by Woofter and his assistants is the most recent one and offers a chart of present densities for white and Negro population in 15 cities.[6]

TABLE XIII

DENSITY OF POPULATION, 1925

City	White Population	Net Residence Area (Acres)	Density Per Acre	Negro Population	Net Residence Area (Acres)	Density Per Acre
New York (Manhattan)	1,926,985	8,644	223	148,081	441	336
Philadelphia	1,815,460	64,387	28	163,250	1,468	111
Chicago	2,966,200	94,464	31	154,800	2,329	67
Charleston	34,700	1,851	19	31,056	544	57
Richmond	131,254	11,840	11	57,770	1,247	46
Buffalo	529,216	34,596	15	1,800	245	40
Lexington	33,111	......[7]	..[7]	13,400	335	40
Louisville	218,781	9,486	23	40,505	1,362	30
New Orleans	304,700	22,038	14	109,380	3,671	30
Indianapolis	316,702	21,256	15	42,980	2,100	21
Knoxville	83,523	14,460	6	13,842	5,737	24
Gary	68,739	14,760	5	9,700	472	21
Memphis	114,703	8,737	13	69,394	3,340	21
Winston-Salem	39,200	2,075	19	34,400	1,746	20
Dayton	161,502	9,415	17	11,440	582	20

There was observed considerable variation in density between cities. From 336 per acre in New York City it falls to 21 in Indianapolis, Gary and Memphis. The large cities in the North show a tardy expansion more plainly. It is more than merely picturesque to describe this expansion of present Negro areas in New York, Philadelphia, or Detroit as vertical rather than horizontal. Density between sections of the same city has, perhaps, even more importance and as a test of this Dr. Woofter has related this with tuberculosis and infant mortality.

[6] Woofter, T. J., and others, *Negro Problems in Cities.*
[7] Not available.

TABLE XIV

NEGRO DENSITY AND DEATH-RATES BY WARDS, PHILADELPHIA, 1924 [8]

Ward [9]	Density Per Acre	Deaths Per 100,000 Tuberculosis	Deaths Under 1 Year Per 1,000 Births
14	63.6	230	8.9
22	78.8	127	10.6
34	80.0	241	6.7
38	89.6	195	8.1
28	96.3	116	10.3
26	106.7	188	9.8
36	109.0	198	11.0
40	110.5	215	14.2
24	111.3	203	8.9
32	114.6	203	9.1
47	116.6	206	12.2
13	118.9	253	15.2
20	120.3	272	10.7
15	121.4	308	11.2
14	123.0	290	13.7
30	140.9	299	10.7
7	164.2	463	12.5
2	169.2	408	15.7
3	170.2	341	8.3
4	170.4	400	13.2

The New York Urban League's study of "Twenty-four hundred Negro families in Harlem" [10] extended from 110th Street to 150th Street and from Lexington Avenue to Convent Avenue. In the 2,326 apartments covered, there were 12,501 persons, 24 per cent of whom were children under 14 years of age. There were in these apartments, 3,314 lodgers, an average of more than 1 per household. The high percentage of adults is thought to be due partly to the migration. Among the 2,326 homes studied, 45.9 per cent had 4 persons, or less, per household; 52.1 per cent had from 5 to 10 persons; and 2 per cent more than 10 persons. The average size of the household was 5.

In the study by the Mayor's Inter-racial Committee [11] in Detroit, of 924 houses 493 had 1 family only; 274 had 2 families, 77 had 3 families, and 49 had 4 families. One hundred

[8] Woofter, T. J., and others, *Negro Problems in Cities.*
[9] Hospital deaths in 37th ward omitted. Deaths from report of Philadelphia Board of Health.
[10] "Twenty-four Hundred Negro Families in Harlem—An Interpretation of the Living Conditions of Small Wage Earners," New York Urban League, 1927.
[11] *The Negro in Detroit.* Prepared for the Mayor's Inter-racial Committee, 1926.

and three of the 1,000 families kept 1 lodger, and 453 of the 924 houses kept none. The number of lodgers in the other families ranged from 2 to 27. The average number of children was 1.96. The average number of lodgers was 2.07.

The Chicago study [12] revealed that of 274 families in all types of neighborhoods studied, 170 had lodgers and 104 had none. The percentage of families having lodgers varied from 36 per cent of. the families in Woodlawn, an out-area, to 72 per cent of the families in the more congested district between 31st and 39th streets, where the lodger problem actually constituted an evil. The percentage of lodgers in these families was 35.0 and of children 22.7. The problem was complicated by migrants from other cities who lived with friends or relatives until they could get homes in which to live, and by the enormous rents charged which made the taking of lodgers necessary.

Elizabeth Hughes [13] of the Chicago Department of Welfare in 1924-25 investigated the living quarters of groups of Negro, Mexican and white families of the low income levels. Over 40 per cent of the Mexican and Negro 1-family households contained lodgers. The medium-size household among native whites numbered 4; among Negroes and foreign-born, exclusive of Mexicans, 5; among Mexicans, 6.

Using as a standard a 4-person household in a 4-room house, Mary Louise Mark [14] in Columbus, Ohio, noted about 54 per cent overcrowding in 1928.

A survey of Negro housing in Richmond, Lynchburg, and Charlottesville, Virginia, made by C. L. Knight,[15] under one of the Phelps-Stokes Fellowships, in 1927 showed an average density for Richmond of 6,894 families per square mile. This varied by sections of the city from 2,642 to 13,071. The density was 46 persons per acre in the Negro sections as compared with 11 per acre in the white sections. In some sections the density reached 78 persons per acre. Despite both organized and unorganized efforts on the part of the white residents to keep the Negroes in well-defined areas several "white" sec-

[12] *The Negro in Chicago.* By the Chicago Commission on Race Relations.
[13] Hughes, Elizabeth, "Living Conditions for Small Wage Earners in Chicago," Department of Public Welfare, Chicago, 1925.
[14] Mark, Mary Louise, *Negroes in Columbus.*
[15] Knight, C. L., *Negro Housing in Certain Virginia Cities,* 1927.

tions fell to Negro occupancy. The greatest number of Negro
families, 7,900, lived in a section north of Broad Street, part
of which was one of the old aristocratic white areas. These
homes were as a rule well kept, with practically no overcrowding. There had been, however, since the coming of Negroes,
a neglect of street cleaning and repairing.

The average number of persons per household was 4.4 among
owners and 4.6 among renters in Richmond; 4.8 among owners
and 4.3 among renters in Lynchburg; and 4.5 among owners
and 5.1 among renters in Charlottesville. The average number
of rooms among the Richmond owners was 6.4; renters 4.7; in
Lynchburg among owners 5.6; renters 3.7; and in Charlottesville 5.7 among owners and 4.1 renters.

Physical Condition of Negro Occupied Dwellings. The varied standards and rating methods of investigators complicate
the estimate of the physical character of dwellings occupied by
Negroes. Some of the studies, however, are sufficiently precise
and objective on the point to serve as examples of the general
findings where studies have been made. There has been a tendency to approach Negro housing as pathology and to limit inquiry either because of the greater ease of interviewing the less
fortunate families, or the desire to point out extreme cases of
poor housing, to those sections which represent the worst types
of housing in the city. It frequently occurs, too, that the most
favorable homes of Negroes are not to be found in the thoroughly settled Negro areas where studies are made, and escape
inclusion unless separately known about, even when the intention is to be general. Thus caution is necessary in reviewing
the findings of housing inquiries.

In New York 20 per cent of the Negro families studied in
1926 lived in cold water flats, more than half of these had no
baths, and many of those who did have tubs were unable to use
them because they were in need of repairs. In all of these flats,
coal stoves or gas heaters were used. As to the condition of
the apartments of the 2,326 families, 22 per cent were classed
as "good"; 18 per cent "fair"; 12 per cent were not reported
on, and 48 per cent were grouped as "bad," "poor" or "needed
cleaning."

The study in 1926 in Detroit covered 1,000 houses occupied
by Negroes. Here the chief Negro districts were in the older

deteriorated areas, and neither streets nor houses were well kept up. Of the 1,000 houses studied 549 were of the detached "style" type; 568 were two-storied and 367 one-storied. In 533 cases, or slightly over half, the condition of the toilets was reported as "good"; in 195 cases "fair"; in 77 cases "poor"; and in 56 cases "bad." About half of the houses, 500 and 473 respectively, were in good repair inside and outside; 133 and 141 were in poor condition, and 84 were in bad condition both inside and outside. In 805 cases, the interior cleanliness was good or fair. The number of rooms per house varied from 1 to 23 with the largest group living in 5- or 6-room houses. Only 689 of the 1,000 families reported no dark rooms. The others reported from 1 to 9 dark rooms. Of the 1,000 families studied 657 were renters, 312 owned their homes, 101 rented from Negro landlords. The largest number was rented from Jewish landlords. The types of houses ranged between extremes. Falling porches, dangerously bad floors, lack of ventilation, defective plumbing appeared with refusals of landlords to make any repairs. A number of the smaller houses of obviously small income families were kept in commendable tidiness, and some were beautifully appointed and kept.

In the survey of the Negro population of Fort Wayne, Indiana, by the National Urban League in 1926, some record was made of the neighborhood as well as the house. Of the 50 blocks in which Negroes lived, 26 were paved and 24 unpaved. About 30 per cent were accounted as being in poor or very poor condition. Sixteen per cent were without running water, 19 per cent were without toilets, and 74 per cent were without bathtubs.[16] A scale was worked out for grading the buildings as to state of repair, conveniences, and sanitation. A building which was in excellent repair, which had gas or electricity or bath, a toilet in the house, sound plumbing and a neat and clean general appearance would have a full value of 100. State of repair was given a value of 30; conveniences 40; and sanitation 30. Of the 139 schedules giving full information, 33 or 24 per cent were graded at 90 and above; 21 of these 33 were noted as sound and complete, well-kept homes. Twenty-eight

[16] "A Survey of the Negro Population of Fort Wayne, Indiana," 1928. Unpublished Manuscript, National Urban League.

per cent were graded at 50 and below and 48 per cent between 50 and 90.

The classification made of the houses in Chicago, by the Commission, is found convenient. They were graded from "type A" houses, the best homes, objectively described, to the poorest, "type D." Approximately 5 per cent of Chicago's Negro population lived in "type A" houses, 10 per cent in "type B." That is, only 5 per cent lived in houses with excellent physical surroundings, in good repair, and with modern conveniences, and only 10 per cent in houses that could be called "good" in these respects. The other 85 per cent lived in houses without many of the ordinary comforts, and more than half of these without the necessary conveniences to make them even a decent shelter for their inhabitants.

The Woofter housing study concludes that the migrant section in practically all Northern cities has an extremely poor type of housing, and there is at least one central district in most American cities where the majority of Negroes live. Municipal improvements are usually slow and very inadequate in many Negro sections, and even in cities where streets are paved and lighted, the sewers are often inadequate for the increased density in population. A table was prepared classifying the equipment and conditions of houses as "A," "B," "C," and "D": "A" meaning a good small dwelling adequate in size and equipment for the family occupying it; class "B" meaning houses lacking in 1 major or 2 minor items; class "C" houses lacking in 2 or more major respects or 3 minor; and class "D" houses lacking in at least 5 respects, and in many cases uninhabitable. This table gives condensed analysis of the findings of the study.

TABLE XV

NEGRO DWELLINGS BY CLASSES—FIFTEEN CITIES

Number	A	B	C	D	Total
Owners	434	1,150	570	44	1,998
Renters	171	1,247	2,019	801	4,238
Total	605	2,397	2,589	845	6,236
Per cent					
Owners	21.7	57.6	18.5	2.2	100
Renters	4.0	29.4	47.7	18.9	100
Total	9.7	38.4	38.3	13.6	100

In Minneapolis it was found, in 1925, that 97 per cent of the Negro families studied had water, 90 per cent had sewer connections, 95 per cent had gas and 74 per cent electricity. There was no overcrowding. Of 208 flats, 28, or about 9 per cent, were in "good" condition, 49 "fair," 60 "poor" and 71 unclassified. Of 249 single family detached dwellings 73 were classed as "good," 38 as "fair," 56 as "poor" and 82 as unclassified.

Housing for Negroes in many of the Southern cities cannot be generalized upon. There are individual homes which meet every requirement of neatness, sanitation and not infrequently luxury. Many of the homes of professional and business men are expensive, richly and tastefully furnished, and decorously kept. Extremes, however, holding larger proportions, exist beyond a condition which would be countenanced in a city with an active Sanitary Bureau and a public opinion intolerant of exaggerated insanitation. It is probable that housing conditions in the most backward of these towns have not been studied at all. "Red Quarters," in Tampa, Florida, corresponds to sections not unfamiliar in common observation and a description is cited here from a survey of this city by B. E. Mays.[17]

"Red Quarters" (condemned by the City Health Department) is made up of dilapidated houses, with three or four small rooms each. This group of houses is particularly unsightly, to say nothing of unhealthful. Practically everyone leaks; the porch roofs fail to stop even the sunshine. A cluster of eight chronically stopped-up outside water closets are available. Nine houses have cans for garbage, four have boxes, while eight have no receptacles at all. Fourteen families reported that garbage was collected weekly, while seven said that it was never collected. Several of the inhabitants stated that they disposed of garbage by burying it. Two surface wells, one out of commission, provide water for 22 families. One hundred and thirty-five persons use this well, including 23 lodgers and 37 children under 15 years of age. Rents average $3.05 per week.

Rents. The amounts paid by Negroes for rents vary according to several well-known conditions. Considered generally a larger proportion of Negro income is spent for rent than is true for any other large group of the population. Rents are higher

[17] A Study of Negro Life in Tampa, 1927. Made at the request of the Tampa Welfare League, the Tampa Urban League, and the Tampa Young Men's Christian Association.

in the North than in the South, and in the North Negroes, as a rule, pay more than white persons for the same dwellings. Rent increases to Negroes during one year were noted in St. Louis as $5.00 to $10.00 a month. In 1917 in Chicago these increases were from 20 to 50 per cent. Successive increases with the growing demand for houses in numbers of cities carried the increase in time to 100 per cent and beyond. Rentals, however, are not uniform throughout the country. Where rents are low generally Negro rentals are low, but slightly higher than that paid by the same economic class of whites. Where rents are generally high, Negro rents are high but the extent of excess over that paid by whites is determined by the factors limiting artificially the availability of dwellings for Negroes. A compensation for this has developed in the practice of taking in lodgers. One result not always noted is that with the contribution of lodgers Negro net rent payments are frequently less than those paid by similar economic classes. The absence of hotels and, to a large extent, of formal boarding houses among the population, has established the taking in of lodgers as a matter of course.

Recent studies in Negro housing in cities offer information on the actual amounts paid by them. In New York City in 1926 the rent per room of 86.8 per cent of the heated apartments was over $10.00; for unheated apartments the average rental was $7.80. The most common sizes of apartments were 4 and 5 rooms.

Mary Louise Mark,[18] of Ohio State University, found in 1928 that four-fifths of the Negroes studied in Columbus, Ohio, paid an average of between $3.00 and $6.00 a room, but the households paying $6.00 a month per room were 5 times as numerous as those paying less than $3.00. Among the owners only 8.4 per cent had from 1 to 3 rooms; 64.4 per cent had baths; 60 per cent had toilets inside; 74.7 per cent of the houses were in good repair inside and 72.8 per cent outside. Among the renters it was found that 32.6 per cent had only 1 to 3 rooms; 45 per cent had bath tubs; 33.6 per cent had inside toilets and in only 30.8 per cent of the dwellings was the state of repairs inside considered good.

In Philadelphia in 1924 one day's inspection of 63 of the

---

[18] Mark, Mary Louise, *Negroes in Columbus.*

old type dwellings used by Negroes, revealed 90 violations of the sanitary provisions of the Housing Law.

Rent increases are frequent in New York. They are most notable when Negro tenants follow white tenants into apartments. An example of these increases appears in the Harlem study made in 1927:

TABLE XVI

SHOWING INCREASE IN RENTALS PAID BY NEGROES OF NEW YORK CITY

No. Rooms	Past Rental	Present Rental	When Raised
3	$22.00	$42.00	1926
5	35.00	55.00	1925
5	40.00	60.00	1926
4	27.00	32.00	1926
6	50.00	90.00	1925
4	39.00	44.00	1926
4	21.00	30.00	1926
3	20.00	30.00	1926
4	30.00	46.00	1925
6	55.00	73.00	1926
4	35.00	47.00	1925
3	28.00	35.00	1925
5	35.00	65.00	1925
5	36.00	50.00	1925
4	23.00	33.00	1925
6	60.00	90.00	1925

Between 1919 and 1927, although average rentals in New York increased about 10 per cent, in one block selected as typical the average market rent for Negroes increased from $21.64 in 1919 to $41.77 in 1927.

In the study of small wage earners in Chicago, by Elizabeth Hughes in 1925, it was found:

As a group Negroes are paying much more for shelter than other classes in the community. A similar difference was found in the heated apartments where the median rental for white families was $55 to $60, but for Negro families $65 to $70. Several things have contributed toward making Negroes subject to higher rentals. In districts which are almost without exception occupied by Negroes, the competition for housing which is hard to obtain because scarce has forced up the price of rent; in districts where whites are moving out and Negroes are moving in, the inciting cause with more than one landlord in giving a building over to colored tenants is the greater income which it can be made to yield. Conversely, owners who wish to keep white tenants will often hold them at a sacrifice in rentals. Many agents with whom property has been placed for renting feel there is an added risk about a colored tenant which justifies asking him to pay a higher rental than a white tenant.

TABLE XVII

PER CENT OF HOUSEHOLDS OF SPECIFIED NATIVITY PAYING SPECIFIED AMOUNTS OF RENT PER ROOM PER MONTH FOR UNHEATED APARTMENTS

Nativity of Head of Household	Total Number of Households	Per Cent Paying Specified Rental Per Room Per Month			
		Less Than $5	$5 But Less Than $10	$10 or Over	Amount not Reported
Total	3,071	52.0	44.0	1.6	2.4
Native white	177	48.6	44.1	1.1	6.2
Mexican	307 [19]	65.1	30.9	2.0	2.0
Other foreign-born ..	1,363	61.8	35.0	0.2	3.0
Negro	1,224	28.0	57.0	3.0	2.0

Rentals in the South are, according to the studies available, considerably less than in other sections. C. L. Knight's study of Negro housing [20] in Richmond, Charlottesville and Lynchburg, Virginia, draws the conclusion that the number of Negro homes renting for more than $5.00 a week is small. This was true of all three cities studied, Richmond, Charlottesville, and Lynchburg. In the first city only about 20 per cent were paying more, and in the two others less than 10 per cent. The average weekly rental per room was 77 cents in Lynchburg and Charlottesville, and 92 cents in Richmond.

However, as in the Northern cities when better grades of houses are related to white rentals for the same homes, significant differences appear.

According to one prominent real estate agent in Richmond, whose firm is said to handle more Negro property than all the other real estate firms and dealers in the city combined, property values in this section advanced, as Negroes moved in, from 50 to 75 per cent. Houses on these streets that rented for about $25.00 per month when occupied by whites rent for $35.00 to $50.00 per month since Negroes began to occupy them. Some of the white property owners on these streets took heed of the trend of values and profited by not selling their property at the first approach of the Negro. Others saw the speculative opportunity which the

[19] Includes three American Indian households.
[20] Knight, Charles Louis, *Negro Housing in Certain Virginia Cities*, pp. 91-2.

situation afforded and bought property to hold for the rise in price.

Few studies have been made of those persons with incomes somewhat above that of common laborers. Such an inquiry was recently made in Chicago as the basis for an important housing project. These rentals are distinctly of a different level and represent persons corresponding to the class of whites who so frequently get the aid of large real estate concerns and boards and the city itself in developing new residence communities.

The average rental for Northern cities found by Woofter [21] and associates was $7.19 per dwelling per week and for Southern cities $3.74 per dwelling per week. By cities, this rent per week was $9.02 in Buffalo; $7.95 in Philadelphia; $7.20 in Gary; $7.19 in "Harlem," New York City; $6.00 in Dayton, Ohio; $5.68 in Indianapolis; $4.54 in Louisville; $4.52 in New Orleans; $4.46 in Richmond, Virginia; $3.73 in Memphis; $3.55 in Lexington; $3.37 in Knoxville; $3.11 in Charleston; $3.06 in Charlottesville; and $2.06 in Lynchburg, Virginia.

Rents in Relation to Earnings. It has been estimated that about 20 per cent of normal earnings can be comfortably applied to the rent item of an average family budget. Two studies offer reasonably representative data under this head. In New York it was found that of 2,160 Negro families, 4.7 per cent were paying less than 20 per cent; 21 per cent were paying between 20 and 30 per cent; 26 per cent were paying between 30 and 40 per cent; and 48 per cent were paying over 40 per cent. This study, however, does not take into account supplementary earnings of the families or the contribution of lodgers. What it shows most strikingly is the practical impossibility of maintaining normal family life in Harlem without lodgers and without income other than that of the chief bread winner's. In Chicago,[22] for the small wage earners the results were as appear in this table:

[21] Woofter, T. J., and others, *Negro Problems in Cities.*
[22] Hughes, Elizabeth A., "Living Conditions for Small-wage Earners in Chicago," Bureau of Social Surveys, 1925.

TABLE XVIII

	Total Reporting	Total Reporting	Per Cent Reporting Whose Monthly Rental Is Specified Per Cent of Monthly Earnings [23]			Not Reporting	Households not Renting
Total	1,526	886	43.9	2.6	53.5	425	215
Native white	122	60	....	...	....	41	21
Mexican	266	157	75.2	1.9	22.9	109	...
Other foreign-born..	468	249	61.8	3.6	34.6	101	118
Negro	668	419	20.4	2.4	77.2	173	76
American Indian ...	2	1	....	...	....	1	...

The investigator felt it necessary to explain that:

. . . The higher rentals paid by Negro families affects the proportions in this table very noticeably. Partial explanation lies in the inclusion of more heat-furnished apartments of the better grade among the Negro homes visited. Possibly some further explanation may lie in a larger amount of unemployment among Negroes or in smaller earnings.

Care of Property by Negro Renters. A circumstance not to be ignored in Negro housing is that of indifference to the care of dwellings where there is not ownership and particularly where there are large numbers of lodgers. The extent to which this applies to Negro renters has not been included in any of the studies. Generalizations have usually been in the direction of indifference or helplessness. Particular references in studies to untidiness, tolerance of physical disorder dangerous to health and reparable with little effort, and to cleanliness and tidiness in spite of the deteriorated condition of dwellings and in spite of the indifference of landlords, suggest the need of some measure of this essential trait in Negro families. Generally considered, there is the fact that the buildings which Negroes get are usually in such an advanced state of disrepair that more attention is required of them than of other groups of the population. At the same time there is less willingness on the part of landlords to make expenditures.

Home Ownership. The percentage of ownership ranges from less than 4 per cent of the 186 families in Wright's study of Pittsburgh, to 95 per cent of the Negro residents of Beckley, West Virginia, 1928, studied by Professor W. C. Matney of

[23] Per cent not shown where base is less than 100.

the Bluefield Institute. There has been a small but steady increase in Negro homes owned in the United States since 1890.

TABLE XIX

PERCENTAGE OF NEGRO HOMES OWNED AND RENTED IN THE UNITED STATES,
1910, 1900, 1890

	1910	*1900*	*1890*
All homes			
Percentage owned 23.3		21.7	18.7
Percentage rented 76.7		78.3	81.3
Farm homes			
Percentage owned 25.2		25.4	22.0
Percentage rented 74.8		74.6	78.0
Other homes			
Percentage owned 22.0		19.0	16.7
Percentage rented 78.0		81.0	83.3

The increase in the ownership of homes and the decrease in the proportion rented are noteworthy. Steady progress toward ownership is shown for "farm homes" and "other houses."

The homes owned in Beckley, West Virginia, range in value from $1,000 to $15,000. The value of the average home is $2,632.50. Thirty-nine and three-tenths per cent of those owning homes own other property. Five per cent of the residents live in rented property. But 22.8 per cent of those living in rented property own property in other cities. Sixty-two and one-half per cent of the 5 per cent who are living in rented homes rent them from Negro landlords. Thirty-seven and five-tenths per cent of the renters rent from white landlords. The average amount paid by renters was $17.43.[24]

In Bluefield, West Virginia, the same investigator found that 62 per cent of the families visited owned their homes, 12 per cent were buying and 26 per cent renting. These homes range from comfortable dwellings with adequate space, modern conveniences, situated in pleasing surroundings on wide, paved, lighted streets, to 2-room houses hung against a practically inaccessible hillside, and offering barely more than a shelter from darkness and weather, the value ranging from $15,000 to $500 or $600. Forty-seven per cent of the group studied own

[24] A Survey of Negro Housing and Home Ownership of Beckley, West Virginia, made by Professor W. C. Matney of Bluefield Institute, May, 1928, under the auspices of Bureau of Negro Welfare and Statistics, Charleston, West Virginia, J. W. Robinson, Director.

other property aggregating $75,200. Seventy-one per cent carry life insurance averaging $4,296 per individual.

James H. Robinson of the Negro Civic Welfare Committee of the Council of Social Agencies reported in 1919 that Cincinnati Negroes owned approximately 1,100 homes valued at $3,250,000. The Negro population was 30,079. One real estate dealer had sold 200 homes to Negroes and in but one case had the buyer failed to meet his full obligations. A study in Wheeling,[25] West Virginia, in 1926 showed 43 per cent of the Negroes owning homes valued at $708,800.

Home ownership in other cities of the state was given as 45.8 in Charleston, 60 per cent in Huntington and 54.7 in Clarksburg.

General Observation on Negro Home Ownership. 1. Home buying in Northern cities has about doubled since 1920.

2. In certain cities of the South the increase in Negro home buying has been more rapid than the increase for the cities as a whole.

3. In Northern cities there has been a rapid increase in home buying, but the dwellings purchased by Negroes have been, in large part, old and difficult to keep in repair.

4. Special difficulties are encountered in financing of Negro homes.

5. New housing developments are not freely open to Negroes, either in the North or South, except where they are sponsored by Negroes, or exclusively for them.

6. When these developments are sponsored by Negroes, the lack of capital, the difficulty of securing municipal improvements, and the enforced removal from proximity to work render them too hazardous to encourage full Negro financial support.

Housing Projects for Negroes. The Cincinnati Model Homes Company was among the first to experiment on a large scale with providing homes for Negroes. It began in 1918 with apartments for about three hundred Negro families. The project included white families also, although the developments were in different groups. Beginning as a risk it was found that receipts exceeded estimates.

25 "The Negro in West Virginia." Report of the Bureau of Negro Welfare and Statistics, 1925-26.

TABLE XX [26]

HOME OWNERSHIP, FIFTEEN CITIES *

City	Total 1920	Number 1910	Colored Homes Number Owned 1920	1910	Per Cent Owned 1920	1910	Change	All Homes Per Cent Owned 1920	1910	Change
Philadelphia	30,995	18,095	3,778	905	12.2	5.0	7.2	39.5	26.6	12.9
New York	36,412	22,452	1,163	545	3.2	2.5	.7	12.7	11.7	1.0
Chicago	25,684	10,421	1,912	662	7.4	6.3	1.1	27.0	26.2	.8
Gary	1,414	**	135	**	9.5	**	...	34.8	...	...
Indianapolis	8,754	5,818	1,525	853	17.4	14.7	2.7	34.5	33.0	1.5
Dayton	1,959	1,324	564	302	28.8	22.8	6.0	41.9	38.1	3.8
Richmond	13,307	10,507	2,010	1,646	15.1	15.7	—.6	25.9	24.0	1.9
Lynchburg	2,121	2,296	686	615	32.3	26.8	5.5	36.7	33.3	3.4
Louisville	12,456	10,962	1,190	708	9.6	6.5	3.1	29.8	26.6	3.2
Lexington	3,852	3,158	796	644	20.7	20.4	.3	32.2	29.7	2.5
Memphis	19,132	14,878	2,867	1,672	15.0	11.2	3.8	28.9	25.2	3.7
Knoxville	2,698	1,835	722	324	26.8	17.7	9.1	40.4	23.1	17.3
New Orleans	24,942	22,064	2,103	2,438	8.4	11.0	—2.6	23.1	23.1	.0
Charleston	9,858	9,387	1,016	836	10.3	8.9	1.4	20.2	17.6	2.6
Winston-Salem	4,763	**	820	**	17.2	**	...	29.8	...	...

* Data from the Federal Census. Includes less than 1 per cent other colored than Negro.

** Not shown by color in 1910.

[26] *Negro Problems in Cities.* A study made under the direction of T. J. Woofter, Jr., p. 137.

The most notable ventures, however, are two recent ones just beginning: The Paul Lawrence Dunbar Garden Apartments in New York City, financed by Mr. John D. Rockefeller, Jr., and sold on a cooperative basis, and the Michigan Avenue Garden Apartments in Chicago, financed by Mr. Julius Rosenwald, and to be rented. Both of these apartments are in the most desirable localities available to Negroes, are solidly and beautifully constructed and include in their structure substantial modern equipment and provisions for light and air and play space for children. About five hundred families can be accommodated in the former and four hundred in the latter. Apart from the provision by such a method of the initial capital for the economies of gross purchase and new quarters, these ventures represent experiments in two directions which may soon be tested: the first in cooperative buying and joint control of property; the second in demonstrating that apartments can be built for Negroes, rented at a moderate figure, and still yield a fair return on the investment.

CHAPTER XVI

THE BEGINNINGS OF NEGRO EDUCATION

Thomas Jefferson, in one of his notable opinions on the mentality of Negroes observed that "one could scarcely be found who was capable of tracing and comprehending the investigations of Euclid," and the redoubtable John. C. Calhoun asserted that if a Negro could be found capable of giving the syntax of a Greek verb, only then would he be disposed to call him human. The uneducability of Negroes has been a vital issue from the very beginning of slavery. For upon it rested much of the justification of their enforced labor. The conscience of the nation could not with comfort or consistency countenance the denial of mental improvement to persons like themselves, and the necessities of the economic system easily prompted rationalizations of unlikeness. Moreover, it was excellent political science as well as economics to control the interests and desires of those needed for the peculiar station which the Negroes had been selected to fill. Education tended to make them less useful as workers. The danger was too great of disturbing a social order already menaced by the imperatives of moral law, humanitarian sentiment, and the inherent qualities of the economic system itself. Education fostered discontent, the threat of insurrection and of a reversal of current social doctrines.

Chancellor Harper of South Carolina argued:

If as Providence has evidently decreed, there can be but a certain portion of intellectual excellence in any community, it is better that a part should be *unequally* divided. It is better that a part should be fully and highly cultivated, and the rest utterly ignorant.[1]

The slave holder asserted his belief in the mental incapacity of the Negro, and promptly, it would seem, advertised his lack

---

[1] "Slavery in the Light of Social Ethics" in Eliott, *Cotton Is King.*

of faith in his assertion by making laws to prevent slaves from acquiring knowledge. South Carolina while still a British Province led in legislating against the instruction of Negroes. In 1740 its legislature made it an offense punishable by a fine of 100 pounds to teach or cause to be taught any slave, or to employ one "as a scribe in any manner of writing whatever." Georgia followed in 1770 with a law modelled after South Carolina, adding to the fine of $500 imprisonment in the common jail, and a whipping of the free person of color or the slave instructed. Similar laws were enacted by Mississippi in 1823; Alabama and Virginia in 1832; North Carolina in 1835, when it abolished the existing separate schools for free persons of color and decreed that descendants from Negroes to the fourth generation should not share its public school system; and Missouri in 1847. The border states of Kentucky, Delaware and Maryland did not specifically oppose Negro education but restricted their facilities to "white children alone." The school laws of Illinois and Ohio specify "white children" throughout and do not mention persons of color.[2]

In Pennsylvania, Massachusetts, Connecticut and Rhode Island the Negroes, while permitted to attend the schools and in some cases to recover damages in an action of *tort,* for exclusion on account of race, frequently received such harsh treatment that they themselves petitioned for separate schools.

In Connecticut the school established by the gentle Quaker, Miss Prudence Crandall, at Canterbury, was first protested in solemn town meeting and later mobbed by intolerant neighbors. She was arrested and placed in the "murderers cell," and state legislation enacted to defeat her enterprise. A school for slaves was opened in New York in 1704 by the Frenchman, Elias Neau, a catechist of the Society for the Promotion of the Gospel of Foreign Parts. The famous Negro plot of 1712 turned a storm of hostility toward him although the trial proved that none of his pupils had been implicated in the plot. He continued it until his death in 1722 when the work was assumed in turn by various individuals until the formation of the New York African Free Schools in 1786.

[2] Woodson, C. G., *The Education of the Negro Prior to 1865.* Association for the Study of Negro Life and History.
Williams, George W., *The History of the Negro Race in the United States.*

Three illiterate Negroes who had been slaves in Virginia established the first school in Washington, D. C., in 1807 and secured a white teacher. Anthony Benezet established the first school for Negroes in Pennsylvania in 1750 and taught it without charge. He interested the Society of Friends in Negro education and in 1770 a special committee employed an instructor. In 1859 there were in Philadelphia alone 2,321 Negro pupils in various public and private schools.

After the emancipation of the Negro slaves, the most advanced elements of the Southern white citizens realized that the passing to freedom of 4,000,000 black slaves demanded some sort of education, although they doubted the ability of the Negroes to profit greatly by it. The "poor whites," released for the first time from the economic pressure of slavery, viewed the matter differently and, although temporarily awed by the show of military power after the war, looked with suspicion upon any means by which the Negroes might be given in their new status independent economic and cultural advantage over them.

One of the first acts of the Reconstruction governments, in which these liberated Negroes participated, had been the establishment of free schools. John R. Lynch, one of the few surviving Negroes who were public officials during the Reconstruction period, was one of the first to advocate compulsory education both in his state and in congress. P. B. S. Pinchback, onetime Lieutenant-Governor of Louisiana, James W. Hood, Assistant State Superintendent of Public Instruction in North Carolina, W. H. Steward of Kentucky, Thomas W. Cardoza, who served for a period as Superintendent of Schools in Mississippi, Wright Cuney in Texas, Peter G. Morgan in Virginia and Frederick Douglass in Washington left records of a feverish advocacy of common schools which survive amid the unhappy memories of political turbulence.[3] This interest manifested by the freedmen in common schools brought the terrible threat not only of racial inter-mingling and social equality, but depleted treasuries to meet such vast, unprecedented, and apparently reckless drafts for universal education. There was opposition to the establishment of the Freedmen's Bureau, based

[3] Noble, "Forty Years of Negro Education in Mississippi."
Newboldt, N. C., "Schools for Negroes in the South"; *Annals of the American Academy of Political and Social Science,* November, 1928.
Lynch, Jno. R., *The Facts of Reconstruction.*

upon a bitter objection to Northern teachers, described as "radical emissaries in disguise," with different social doctrines, and, in a more generalized manner, there was opposition to the idea itself of the education of the Negro. These attitudes were not softened by the disposition of the Negro leaders to favor mixed schools as the means of securing and maintaining equal advantages with the whites. With the removal of the Reconstruction governments reaction to their policies was reflected in radically new legislation. The public school systems in the new adjustment were almost sacrificed in refutation of all that the Reconstruction régime had suggested, and Negro education was in a large measure abandoned. The summary laws passed, however, could be justified by the necessity for curtailment of expenses; for the first zeal of the Reconstructionists for universal education had not always taken into account the poverty of the section following the war. Opposition to Negro education less intense but of more enduring character began to crystallize under the new objection of expense. Sentiment which was capable of abolishing the school system itself could not be expected to deal gently with Negro education. And as a consequence a great portion of the cost of this education fell upon the Freedmen's Bureau and private philanthropists. The thoroughness with which this salvaging was undertaken under General O. O. Howard and the trembling zeal of the ex-slaves themselves for learning are marked in an almost explosive expansion of schools.

In the first five years after the close of the war there were 4,239 schools established, 9,307 teachers employed and 247,333 pupils instructed. The Negroes themselves had sustained 1,324 schools and purchased 592 school buildings. The Bureau had provided 654 school buildings, and in addition to the elementary schools had established 74 high and normal schools with 8,147 students; and 61 industrial schools with 1,780 students. Of the $1,002,896 expended by the Bureau, the Negroes themselves, with a five-year margin of freedom, raised $200,000.

In 1860 there were 4,441,830 Negroes in the United States. Of these, 226,216 were in the North and 4,215,614 were in the South. The free Negroes who were reported by the Census as able to read and write numbered 151,245 or about 3 per cent of the Negro population. Although a few slaves could read and write, it is probable that emancipation found not more than 5 per cent of all the Negroes literate. In 1870, when that generation was born to which belong W. E. B. DuBois, James Weldon Johnson, Robert R. Moton, John Hope and others, now at the full tide of brilliant careers, 80 per cent of the Negro population were still illiterate.

SOCIAL FACTORS IN THE REDUCTION OF NEGRO ILLITERACY

The Decline in Illiteracy. The report of the Census Bureau for 1880 returned a total of 3,320,878 Negroes who were illiterate. This number constituted 70.0 per cent of the entire Negro population. The 4 succeeding decennial reports have in each instance returned a substantial decrease both in the total number and in the percentage proportion of illiterates. By 1890 the number of illiterates had declined to 3,042,668, and the percentage had dropped to 57.1. In 1900 these figures were, respectively, 2,853,194, and 44.5 per cent; in 1910, 2,227,731, and 30.4 per cent; while the last current report for the 10-year period concluded in 1920 gave a total of 1,842,161 Negro illiterates, who constituted 22.9 per cent of the total population.

While the Negro population was thus reducing its illiteracy by more than two-thirds in this 40-year period, the white population of the country, beginning at a much higher base of literacy, had cut its illiteracy percentage in half. The reduction in this case had been from 9.4 per cent in 1880 to 4.1 per cent in 1920. Negroes numbered only 9.9 per cent in the total population, but contributed 37.3 per cent to the number of illiterates.

Rural illiteracy is about twice that of urban illiteracy for Negroes, the per cent being 28.4 and 13.4 respectively. Further, the rural illiteracy in the 10- to 15-year group is about five times as great as for urban sections. One of the first factors to be noted in the great reduction in Negro illiteracy, then, is that of urbanization. Only 19.4 per cent of Negroes lived in cities in 1890, whereas 34.0, or nearly twice as many, were in 1920 living in urban communities. The influence of city life for increased educational opportunities is apparent in higher enrollment, more regular attendance, and the superior efficiency of the schools.

Effect of Migration and Urbanization. Another influential factor in the decrease of Negro illiteracy is one that will probably be more noticeable when the next census figures are made available. This is the effect of the migration in bringing Negroes into areas where better educational opportunities can be secured. The greatest frequency of Negro illiterates is in the seventeen Southern and "Border" states which maintain separate school systems for the races. Of the 8,053,125 Negroes in the entire country ten years of age or over, 6,792,507, or 84.3 per cent, resided in these states. The illiteracy rate for these states was 25.9 per cent, while that of the rest of the country was 6.3 per cent for Negroes ten years of age or over.

The problem then may fairly be said to be sectional. The highest illiteracy rate for the entire country is that returned by the 536,362 Negroes of Louisiana in the age-periods of ten years and upward. No less than 206,730 Louisiana Negroes in this class are illiterate, or 38.5 per cent. Conditions are almost as bad in such states as Alabama, with a rate of 30.1 per cent, South Carolina, with a rate of 30.3 per cent, Mississippi and Georgia with 29.3 per cent, and North Carolina with a rate of 29.1 per cent.

Another basic factor which appears to be closely correlated with Negro illiteracy is that of the relative wealth of the various states. If the states are ranked in order of wealth per child, Delaware has a rating of 27, Missouri a rank of 28 among all of the states. The other fifteen states maintaining separate systems, and falling at the bottom of the illiteracy list, come in order with the one exception of Vermont, which ranks thirty-fourth in wealth per child. The eight states with the highest illiteracy rates for Negroes all fall in the lowest quartile of the ranked order of wealth per capita child. Virginia, with a per capita wealth of $8,907 per child, heads the states in this group, which ranges on· down to Mississippi with $4,616 per capita child in taxable wealth. When it is considered that the average for the United States in 1922 was $14,241, the effect of this factor upon illiteracy is significant, especially when it is noted that New York returned a rate of only 2.9 per cent for its Negro illiteracy, and had a per capita wealth per child of $19,756; almost two and a half times higher than the figure for Virginia, which returned a Negro illiteracy rate of 23.5 per cent.

The greatest reductions in Negro illiteracy between 1880 and 1920 were made, of course, in the South, where the greatest number of Negroes lived. If the period was one in which Negroes were becoming more literate, it was also one in which the increase in wealth was proportionately as large as the decrease in illiteracy. Louisiana, for example, with an estimated wealth per child of $1,517 in 1880, reported as its figure for 1922, $7,772. While its wealth per capita child was thus increased more than 500 per cent in the forty-year period, the illiteracy rate of its Negro citizens decreased more than 200 per cent. Mississippi had an increase in wealth of 460 per cent and decreased its Negro illiteracy rate 300 per cent.

The Rosenwald School. The tremendous stimulation of the Rosenwald schools in the South should be accounted in the decline of both Negro and white illiteracy. With this aid more than 4,138 school buildings accommodating about 511,290 Negro children were planted in the South. In a total of $20,-000,000 expended in fourteen years, $3,000,000 came from Mr. Rosenwald, $4,000,000 from Negroes, $1,000,000 from white persons directly and $12,000,000 from public tax funds. Not only was the burden of taxation thus lightened, making possible a degree of development which public opinion would have retarded, but the provision for Negroes undoubtedly encouraged provision of more public funds for white children.

Psychological Factors. Other factors may be traced in the steady decline of Negro illiteracy, but they do not, however, always yield to such tangible expression. The intense passion of the Negro freedmen for educational advancement following the Civil War was one of these. Booker T. Washington has given an interesting discussion of this social conviction which motivated the Negro to become literate, in his autobiographical account, *Up from Slavery.* He stated that the attainment to a literate status was looked upon by many of the recently emancipated Negroes as the solution of their vexing problems.

Again, with urbanization, industrialization, and generally higher standards of employment and requirements for labor, the ability to manipulate the tools of written expression, and communication, becomes more highly prized and necessary as marketable equipment in the labor market. That this factor has also aided cannot be doubted, although it is so inextricably bound up with other trends already mentioned that its weight cannot well be determined. The improvement in the condition of the school systems in those states showing the largest proportion of Negro illiterates, the effect of increased enrollment and more regular attendance may also be mentioned here. And along with these factors which reflect the greater efficiency of the schools is the emphasis upon adult schools which are reaching annually many illiterates and converting them to the ranks of the literate.

In spite of progress achieved the conviction grows as the material on the subject is studied that the principal way through which reduction of illiteracy may be attained is by making sure that the younger generation of Negroes are not illiterate. If the present high figures of non-attendance continue to prevail, thousands of those, who now fall within the proper limits of required school attendance will become illiterate adults who may be reached at best only with much difficulty. It should also be clear that the Negro population suffers much more from this cause of high illiteracy than the white population, for if the number of persons listed as "white illiterates" be reduced by a subtraction of foreign-born who are literate in another language, or who have never had the opportunity afforded by a universal system of free public education, that of the native-born American white stock is almost inconsiderable. The only exception to this rule is furnished by certain Southern states where the school facilities for whites, although far superior to those for Negroes, are yet inferior to systems of public education in other states of the Union.

The fact that public opinion in the South does not make obligatory upon the officials of the schools the duty of enforcing compulsory school legislation, so far as Negro children are concerned, is a contributing factor to a high illiteracy rate that must not be forgotten in evaluating causes for the present excessive rate. That illiteracy has declined as rapidly as it has, however, is an indication of the growth of a public consciousness favorable to the enforcement of such laws, and an increase in the schools to which it might be required that children be sent. A large beginning has already been made in bettering this condition of affairs in the cities, and the passage of legislation in many Southern states of finance acts by which the amount of state appropriations is prorated on the basis of attendance is serving as a stimulant upon the growth of this opinion. Much depends now on the provision of adequate school facilities, for if the mandate of the law is obeyed strictly, and all Negro scholastics required to enroll and attend, there would yet be no place for them, as the existing equipment and plants are not extensive enough to take care of the number which would otherwise attend.

Effect of School Attendance. It may be noted from the following table that the percentage of Negro children attending school in 1920 was equal to that for whites of the year 1900, suggesting that in this respect the Negro population in education as in the matter of health is twenty years behind the white. The illiteracy for the Negroes decreased from 70 per cent in 1880 to 22.9 per cent in 1920—a fair measure of the effect of school attendance.

TABLE XXI

SCHOOL ATTENDANCE IN THE UNITED STATES FOR PRINCIPAL POPULATION CLASSES, 1850-1920 *

Year	Total Population, 5-20 Years White	Negro	School Attendance White	Per Cent	School Attendance Negro	Per Cent
1920	29,333,533	3,796,957	19,644,508	67.0	2,049,741	54.0
1910	25,992,293	3,667,860	16,279,292	62.6	1,670,650	45.4
1900	22,441,947	3,499,187	12,231,004	54.5	1,096,734	31.3
1890	19,250,565	3,126,497	10,667,171	55.4	999,324	32.0
1880	15,618,617	2,633,683	9,905,485	58.2	856,014	32.5
1870	12,528,178	1,958,237	6,414,740	51.2	180,372	9.2
1860	10,099,266	1,859,370	5,660,325	56.0	32,629	1.8
1850	7,681,163	1,524,829	4,063,046	52.9	26,461	1.7

* Fourteenth Census, Vol. II, p. 1043.

Another picture of the effect of school attendance upon illiteracy is provided in a table which gives the illiteracy figures as of the 1920 census for both races, together with the percentage of white and colored children in school and out. Although the table is limited to the eighteen states with separate Negro school systems, all of which are located in the South, the trend is unmistakable. Mr. Monroe Work has compiled the material on school attendance upon which this table is based.[4]

TABLE XXII

PERCENTAGE OF ILLITERATES AND CHILDREN IN SCHOOL AND OUT FOR BOTH RACES IN EIGHTEEN STATES IN THE SOUTH

	Percentage of Illiterates Native		Percentage in School		Percentage Out of School	
State	Whites	Negroes	Whites	Negroes	Whites	Negroes
Texas	3.0	17.8	93.7	88.7	6.3	11.3
Oklahoma	2.3	12.4	87.3	88.0	12.7	12.0
North Carolina	8.2	24.5	85.1	83.8	14.9	16.2
Missouri	2.0	12.1	81.4	78.7	18.6	21.3
Georgia	5.4	29.1	89.5	74.2	10.5	25.8
Virginia	5.9	23.5	84.8	72.7	15.2	27.3
Tennessee	7.3	22.4	80.3	71.6	19.7	28.4
West Virginia	4.6	15.3	80.6	70.8	19.4	29.2
Arkansas	4.5	21.8	73.4	69.6	26.6	30.4
Delaware	1.8	19.1	70.1	67.1	29.9	32.9
South Carolina	6.5	29.3	77.2	65.8	22.8	34.2
District of Columbia.	...	8.6	65.5	61.9	34.5	38.1
Maryland	1.8	18.2	69.5	61.2	30.5	38.8
Florida	2.9	21.5	81.3	60.9	28.7	39.1
Kentucky	7.0	21.0	65.0	60.9	35.0	39.1
Alabama	6.3	31.3	84.9	58.8	15.1	41.2
Louisiana	10.5	38.5	70.3	57.9	29.7	42.1
Mississippi	3.6	29.3	68.9	53.0	31.1	47.0

The attendance figures in this table for such states as Maryland, the District of Columbia, as well as others to a less degree, should be corrected to include the large number of children attending parochial schools. However, the attendance of Negroes upon private schools is hardly considerable enough to affect the figures here given. The three states with the highest percentage of Negro illiteracy also have the largest number of Negro children out of school. Here again is the potential school for illiterates, and it is probable that the next generation, far from finding illiteracy extinct in these states, will discover the presence of large numbers of adult illiterates graduated from the ranks of scholastics and untouched by the schools. The problems of adult and child illiteracy cannot be separated. A more detailed investigation of the organized effort of the states to reduce illiteracy furnishes proof of this fact. A significant study, based on the experience of two Alabama counties, shows how these factors are correlated.[5]

[4] *Negro Year Book*, 1925-26, p. 292.
[5] Lambert, J. S., "Make the Parents Literate." *The State Normal Journal*. Montgomery, Alabama, pp. 27-30, 1929.

In 1920, the United States Census Report showed that 51 per cent of Sumter County's Negro population, 21 years of age and over, was illiterate, a total of 4,705 adults. In the same year the school census report gave Sumter's quota of illiterate Negro children, 7 to 20 years, at 4,445. It is interesting to note that the number of illiterate children almost equalled the number of illiterate adults and that 47.3 per cent of the Negro school population was illiterate.

From 1920 to 1928, Sumter County reduced the illiteracy of her Negro children by 2,900, or 65.2 per cent. In 1920, 47.3 per cent of Sumter's Negro school population was illiterate. In 1928, only 16 per cent of Sumter's school population is in like condition.

During this period, the "Opportunity Schools" for adult illiterates had an enrollment of 2,483 Negro adults, a number almost exactly proportionate to the number of children removed from the illiteracy list to that for literates. A neighboring county, Dallas, had a different experience.

In 1920, Dallas County had 10,682 illiterate Negro adults, 51.2 per cent of her Negro population 21 years of age and over, a slightly larger percentage of illiteracy than that prevailing in Sumter County. In Dallas County, there were 5,910 illiterate Negro children (the largest number in any county of the state), 40 per cent of the Negro school population. Dallas had then in 1920 a slightly larger per cent of adult Negro illiteracy than Sumter possessed, but a slightly smaller percentage of children's illiteracy. Should Dallas not have reduced children's illiteracy more rapidly than Sumter did in the eight years from 1920-28? At the end of eight years, Dallas had 2,251 fewer illiterate children than her school census reported in 1924, but Dallas had not equalled the record of Sumter, a reduction of 2,900 in 8 years. Could the fact that Sumter made continuing and increasing effort throughout the period from 1920-28, with the exception of one year, to teach the illiterate adults be considered a reason for the difference in the numbers of illiterate children taught in the two counties? Could the fact that Dallas was handicapped in 1920 with a larger per cent of illiterate adult population have had its influence in making a difference in the numbers of the children taught in the two counties?

Dallas, at the time of taking of the 1928 school census, had conducted only two campaigns against illiteracy, one in 1926 and one in 1927.

The study concludes that "from the studies of reduction of illiteracy in Dallas and Sumter, it is reasonable to suppose that the 1930 census reports will afford strong evidence that the reduction of illiteracy among parents guarantees the reduction of illiteracy among children."

The final elimination of Negro illiteracy thus depends upon a number of factors. The efficiency of the rural schools and their coverage must be improved and extended to reach the standard achieved already by many city systems. In line with this improvement must come an equalization of educational opportunity among the various sections of the country. The variant ratios of wealth for the states and the communities within the states emphasize the need for some such equalization if illiteracy is to be effectively combated. Public opinion, both for whites and Negroes, must be brought to bear in the creation of a social consciousness which will result in the enforcement of the compulsory school attendance statutes. The part played by organized attempts to diminish adult illiteracy, as a means of inspiring the younger generation to renewed efforts, and awakening the community to the necessity for taking advantage of existing school facilities, cannot well be neglected. With this gradual infusion of the spirit of progress in the mind of the community, both white and black, and the growing necessity for the possession of the tools of literate expression by the individual in every-day adjustments to a more complex social organization, the eventual disappearance of adult illiteracy among Negroes may be confidently predicted.

CHAPTER XVII

COMMON SCHOOLS FOR NEGROES IN THE SOUTH

Attention was first drawn forcefully to the inequalities in expenditures for white and Negro education in the South, by the Report on Negro Education issued by the U. S. Bureau of Education in 1916, representing the investigations of Thomas Jesse Jones.[1] It was pointed out that on the basis of per capita expenditures for education in the Southern states the average amount for whites was $10.32 and for Negroes $2.89. Further, it was discovered that this inequality became greater as the counties were more densely populated by Negroes. By far the larger amount of funds expended for Negro education in the South is devoted to the salaries of teachers. It is possible, therefore, to obtain a fair picture of the situation as it has since developed from an inspection of the salary rates for teachers in counties with variant proportions of Negro inhabitants. Such a comparison is furnished by Table XXIII.

TABLE XXIII

COMPARATIVE EXPENDITURES FOR WHITE AND NEGRO EDUCATION IN COUNTIES WITH VARIANT PERCENTAGES OF NEGROES IN THE POPULATION

County Groups, Percentage of Negroes in the Population	White Teachers' Salaries	Negro Teachers' Salaries	Per Capita, White	Per Capita, Negro
Counties under 10 per cent	$ 7,755,817	$ 325,579	$ 7.96	$7.23
Counties 10 to 25 per cent	9,633,674	1,196,788	9.55	5.55
Counties 25 to 50 per cent	12,572,666	2,265,945	11.11	3.19
Counties 50 to 75 per cent	4,574,366	1,167,796	12.53	1.77
Counties 75 per cent and over ...	888,759	359,800	22.22	1.78

It developed, further, that while the Southern states appropriated $6,429,991 for higher schools for whites, only $350,000 was appropriated for a like purpose for Negro schools. Certain Southern states, notably North Carolina, found in these dis-

[1] *Bulletin No. 39,* Department of the Interior, Bureau of Education— Negro Education.

236

closures a suggestion for the improvement of instruction for Negroes. The widespread prevalence of illiteracy, both among the adult population and the scholastic enumeration, and its strong implication of sectional backwardness undoubtedly suggested to the South the need for better schools for Negroes. The conviction gradually became general, also, due largely to the insistence of such leaders as Booker T. Washington, that the continued ignorance and illiteracy of the Negro was bound to result in high crime rates and low civic standards for both races.

The paucity of official records makes difficult a full and accurate picture of educational status. In many instances the records which have been preserved and published are incomplete and even inaccurate.[2] Such information as is available, however, indicates a constant improvement in the course of the last few years. For purposes of greater clarity, the general field of Negro common school education in the South is discussed under certain leading heads in this section of the report.

School Population, Enrollment, and Attendance. Using Newbold's figures for 1912-13,[3] a partial picture of these fundamental aspects of the school problem is exposed. The figures given here are not wholly satisfactory because the ages within which the enumeration of scholastics is taken differ among the various states. It is thus not possible to make a comparison of the percentage of scholastics actually enrolled. The census figures are needed for such an age-enrollment comparison. The figures for 1920 have little of value, because of the shifts of population due to migration, and other causes. If with this table we remember the implications of the condition which finds a much larger proportion of the Negro school population neither enrolled nor attending regularly, the necessity for a larger provision for those out of school becomes evident. If, as will be shown, existing facilities for Negroes are already largely overcrowded, a prerequisite for the efficient handling of a larger enrollment is the development of physical

---

[2] In this connection it might be suggested that no greater immediate service could be done for the cause of Negro education than the standardization of the methods by which these data are gathered and preserved.

[3] Newbold, N. C., "Common Schools for Negroes in the South," *The American Negro.* Annals of the American Academy of Political and Social Science, November, 1928, p. 209.

facilities sufficient to meet the greater need which would result.
  The Negro Teacher. In the period immediately after the
Civil War, perhaps the greatest difficulty experienced in the development of a public school system for Negroes was that of
obtaining competent teachers. The need was first filled through
the channels of the various missionary associations, and for
the most part the teachers in these schools, jointly financed by
the Freedmen's Bureau and the religious organizations, were
Northern white men and women who volunteered to come to
the South and render service in the cause. In some parts of the
South, as for example, Charleston, South Carolina, and Richmond, Virginia, the Negro schools were taught by native
whites, a condition which prevailed for a number of years, until
these teachers were replaced by Negroes. As the high schools,
normal institutes, and colleges for Negroes began to function in
the graduation of numbers of persons qualified, Negro teachers
were substituted for whites.

  Standards were, of necessity, low, and as a result salaries
were deplorably low. This in turn reacted to establish a type
of teacher in the schools whose preparation was at best fragmentary and uncertain. As long as schools were conducted for
terms of three and four months, and salaries rarely exceeded
$20-$25 per month, it was impossible to insist upon higher
standards of certification, for well-equipped persons would not
be attracted to the school room under such conditions. However, as the financial condition of the Southern states became
more satisfactory, and more funds could be devoted to Negro
education, it became possible for state departments of education
to take the privilege of certification away from the local boards
of education, or the county superintendents, and set up a general state standard which demanded a more regular course of
study and greater efficiency from those desiring to enter the
teaching profession. The additional support given to local
boards of educational administration by state grants has also
permitted the state central department to set up higher standards, and to require the local units to meet these standards, with
regard to the employment of teachers, before financial aid is
granted.

  The lack of adequate records is here, again, responsible for a
condition which defies any evaluation of the training of Negro

teachers that will include in generalized form the entire South. It is only possible to make comparisons for specific states.[4]

The comparative figures show large discrepancies between salary rates for white and Negro teachers. The averages of $292, for elementary school teachers, and $661, for high school teachers, in the state of Louisiana, may, as an example, be compared with the corresponding sums for white teachers of $1,007 and $1,419, respectively. A like comparison for Arkansas gives the sums of $434 and $696 for the Negro elementary and high schools, respectively, and $634 and $1,236 for the white school teachers on these two salary levels.

Salary figures based on monthly payments are largely confusing, because the length of the school term is not given. Low salaries are also usually correlated with short school terms, and frequently a condition results in which teachers receiving an average monthly salary of $25-$30 are employed for only four or five months. The kind of educational leadership possible through this expenditure is obviously of an inferior grade. A qualifying factor not indicated by the statistical tables is introduced by the prevalence of community supplements in order to obtain good teachers where the state appropriation is too meager. In this way the Negro patrons raise money by various devices, charades, suppers, lotteries, and "shows," by which an extra month or so is added to the school term, and the teacher's salary brought to a living wage scale. In addition, the custom of furnishing free board for the teacher still prevails in many communities, thus allowing the community to secure the services of teachers who would otherwise be unable to subsist on the official salary paid for the work.

Apart from general effects mentioned, the low salaries result

[4] A word of caution is even necessary here, for it cannot be denied that where the certification of teachers is left in the hands of local agencies, less stringency is exercised in granting certificates to Negro teachers than to white teachers. Nor is this condition entirely the fault of these certificating agencies. In the past, to insist upon identical standards for both races would have been to deprive the Negro schools of perhaps the greater number of their teachers, for had they been required to meet standards identical with those for whites, large numbers would have been disqualified. With the increased efficiency of the state normal schools, however, it appears now possible to insist upon identical standards for the teachers of both races, and such states as Florida, Georgia, and Alabama have instituted such a system, by which salaries are graduated more and more upon the basis of training, and Negro teachers required to meet these high standards.

TABLE XXIV

Number of Teachers, Average Monthly Salaries and Average Term

State	Number of Teachers			Average Monthly Salary		Average Term [5] (in Days)	
	Elementary School	High School	Total	Elementary School	High School	Elementary School	High School
Alabama	3,183	290	3,473	$ 286	$ 779	116	164
Arkansas	2,251	132	2,383	434	696	137	137
Delaware	196	13	209	1,065	....	183	183
District of Columbia	591	137	728	....	....	180	180
Florida	....	....	2,148	393	....	123	123
Georgia	4,576	358	4,934	289	....	134	....
Kentucky	1,159	180	1,339	....	892	140	160
Louisiana	....	....	2,700	292	661	103	....
Maryland	....	....	1,320	985	2,003	177	184
Mississippi	5,117	108	5,125	30 (monthly)	....	94	94
Missouri	796	189	985	(no data)	....	(no data)	
North Carolina	4,362	1,453	5,815	68 (monthly)	....	137	160
Oklahoma	1,099	176	1,275	85 (monthly)	120	120	160
South Carolina	....	....	4,339	306	....	116	....
Tennessee	2,496	225	2,721	65 (monthly)	....	145	170
Texas	3,641	218	3,859	87 (monthly)	112	110	140
Virginia	3,528	263	3,791	(no data)	....	148	180
West Virginia	621	165	786	81 (monthly)	....	170	....

[5] The length of term for Delaware, Mississippi, Louisiana and Florida is not separate for grammar and high school divisions.

in a great deal of inbreeding, as only a native might be attracted to teach in some communities, tempted by the obvious advantage of living at home. This does not always conduce to greater professional ability or effort.

Although the lack of uniformity in the kind of certificates granted, and the amount of preparation required for their issuance, makes almost impossible a generalized picture, it is possible to list several instances of the kinds of certificates held by white and Negro teachers, and in this way determine the relative preparation of the two classes of teachers.

In Louisiana, to obtain a First Grade Certificate, the white applicant must present two years of college credit, or one year of college work with two years of experience. The Negro teacher who presents a high school diploma, with an additional one year of work done in a teacher-training institution, usually a school with low standards, may obtain the same certificate. Both are valid for five years. Even this discrimination, which it would be difficult to classify as for or against the Negro teacher, or the school taught by him, does not prevent the holding of lower certificates by a much larger number of Negro teachers than by whites. Of the Negro teachers 31.3 per cent hold certificates inferior to the grade of Professional-Elementary rank, which is granted on evidence of two years of college work (for Negroes), and a minimum of two years of college work and four years of teacher-training work for whites. Of the white teachers 22.68 per cent hold certificates below this rank, although the requirements for their admission to these upper grades are higher for Negroes. Only 6.6 per cent of the Negro teachers hold Professional certificates, which are granted on submission of one year of graduate work above the four year college, or four years of college work with nine hours of educational units and three years of experience. The holder of this certificate may teach for life in the Louisiana system, on its recommendation. More than twice as many white teachers, or 15.9 per cent, have qualified for this certificate.

The situation in Florida is similar to that found in Louisiana. Of the 4,541 certificates listed for white teachers in the biennium ending June, 1928, 73.5 per cent were of the three upper grades, namely, Graduate State, Life Graduate State, and Teacher Training Certificates. Only 29.9 per cent of the 849

Negro teachers in the state held certificates in these three classes, while 48.4 per cent of the Negro teachers held only temporary certificates, as contrasted with a percentage of 10.2 per cent for whites. Of the whites, 15.8 per cent were listed as having no certificates, as against 20.8 per cent for the Negro teachers.

Another index to the comparative standards maintained by the teachers of the two races is furnished by the Uniform Examinations for Teachers given annually in Florida. Of the 7,115 white examinees, 5,336, or 74.9 per cent, were successful in passing, while of the 2,311 Negro examinees, only 904, or 39.1 per cent, were successful in the examination.

19.9 per cent of the white examinees merited third grade certificates;
43.2 per cent of the Negro examinees merited third grade certificates;

18.6 per cent of the white examinees merited second grade certificates;
26.1 per cent of the Negro examinees merited second grade certificates;

4.5 per cent of the white examinees merited first grade certificates;
2.4 per cent of the Negro examinees merited first grade certificates;

2.86 per cent of the white examinees merited primary certificates;
0.66 per cent of the Negro examinees merited primary certificates;

5.52 per cent of the white examinees merited special certificates;
1.10 per cent of the Negro examinees merited special certificates;

0.01 per cent of the white examinees merited professional certificates;
0.01 per cent of the Negro examinees merited professional certificates;

48.9 per cent of the white applicants were successful in meeting the constitutional requirements;
26.2 per cent of the Negro applicants were successful in meeting the constitutional requirements.

Those Negro teachers who achieve certification by the presentation of diplomas from high schools, normal schools and colleges, while possessing on paper equivalent credentials with those presented by white applicants, are themselves the products of an inferior system as compared with that for whites from the primary department on through the college itself. There is, in fact, a vicious circle which begins with the first grade and ends with the graduation of the prospective teacher from the higher institutions of learning. The schools are poorly taught, for a short term, in inadequate buildings. Standards are low, and the result is the graduation of many persons from the grammar schools who are very incompetent. The Negro schools, as a matter of fact, do not appear to eliminate students on the basis of inability, and there is no evidence that under present conditions the more able students are retained while the less efficient are dropped out of the schools. The immense "mortality" among Negro school children in the later grades seems to take its toll as much from the fit as the unfit. These grammar school graduates are passed on to poor high schools, where the same conditions found in the grammar school prevail: poor teaching, low salaries, lack of standards. Graduation becomes a matter of being able to stay in school for four years, rather than intellectual ability. The high schools are so clogged with poor material that they either cannot, or will not, assume the responsibility of weeding out the unfit. Their graduates in turn are admitted to the normal schools, or go directly into the teaching profession, and the vicious circle begins to repeat itself. These poorly trained teachers, although they may bear diplomas showing standard preparation, will inflict the accumulated deficiencies of the system in which they have been trained upon their pupils, and so perpetuate it.

The states are awake to this condition. Teachers are being required to attend summer schools in order to renew, or extend, the life of low-grade certificates, and the proportion of teachers attending these summer schools is very large. In 1926, 23,686 Negro teachers were enrolled in summer schools in fourteen states. In Alabama alone, the State Normal School, headed by H. Councill Trenholm, maintains two branches, one at Birmingham and one at Mobile, in addition to the central school at Montgomery, and enrolled in these three divisions 2,226 teachers during the summer session of 1928. When the additional number of Alabama Negro teachers attending Tuskegee Institute, other summer schools in the state, and schools outside of the state is considered, it is probable that more than 70 per cent of the public school teachers in Alabama attended summer school in 1928. Further improvement is disclosed by a recent study of Alabama teachers made by President Trenholm. He found that the teachers holding examination certificates, the lowest grade obtainable, numbered only 1,417 in 1928-29, or 36 per cent of the total. Of the teachers whose answers were obtained in a survey made, 2,124 reported that they were graduates of high schools of ten, eleven, or twelve grades. Three hundred and fifty, or 10 per cent, reported that they were normal school graduates, while 149 (approximately 5 per cent) indicated that they were college graduates.

Certain of the states have utilized the Extension Courses to raise the educational standard of the teacher-in-service. They serve the purpose of developing professional interest in the teaching group and enlightening the teachers with regard to more recent trends in educational practice. Alabama is again in the forefront of this movement, and during the school year 1927-28, 1,276 Negro teachers were enrolled in these courses, conducted and supervised by members of the regular staff of the State Normal School. While the records for the past year are not yet available, indications point to an increased enrollment of more than 20 per cent for the year 1928-29. Florida, Oklahoma, and Texas are other states with an extensive program for reaching the teacher-in-service through an extension division.

Students Per Teacher. The need for more Negro teachers, as well as for those with better training is to be seen in the excessive number of children per teacher, both in the enrollment and attendance.

Alabama, with 3,473 teachers, has 52.4 enrolled pupils, and 35.6 pupils in average daily attendance per teacher.

Arkansas, with 2,383 teachers, has 47.9 enrolled pupils, and 30.3 pupils in average daily attendance per teacher.

The District of Columbia, with 728 teachers, has 30.7 enrolled pupils, and 28.1 pupils in average daily attendance per teacher.

Florida, with 2,148 teachers, has 43.5 enrolled pupils, and 33.3 pupils in average daily attendance per teacher.

Georgia, with 4,934 teachers, has 49.0 enrolled pupils, and 33.9 pupils in average daily attendance per teacher.

Kentucky, with 1,339 teachers, has 30.4 enrolled pupils per teacher.

Louisiana, with 2,700 teachers, has 50.6 enrolled pupils, and 38.2 pupils in average daily attendance per teacher.

Mississippi, with 5,125 teachers, has 53.6 enrolled pupils, and 36.9 pupils in average daily attendance per teacher.

North Carolina, with 5,815 teachers, has 43.5 enrolled pupils, and 32.6 pupils in average daily attendance per teacher.

Oklahoma, with 1,275 teachers, has 38.7 enrolled pupils, and 23.5 pupils in average daily attendance per teacher.

South Carolina, with 4,339 teachers, has 51.8 enrolled pupils, and 35.8 pupils in average daily attendance per teacher.

Tennessee, with 2,721 teachers, has 41.3 enrolled pupils, and 31.3 pupils in average daily attendance per teacher.

Texas, with 3,859 teachers, has 51.7 enrolled pupils, and 40.3 pupils in average daily attendance per teacher.

Virginia, with 3,791 teachers, has 40.1 enrolled pupils, and 29.5 pupils in average daily attendance per teacher.

In 1924-25, the average number of pupils enrolled per teacher for the entire United States was 31.94. It will be noted that only Kentucky and the District of Columbia had fewer children per teacher in 1927-28. Considering 30 pupils enrolled per teacher as a fair total, the following estimates indicate the number of teachers which would be needed to bring these Southern states up to this standard.

Alabama, with 3,473 teachers, would need 6,069, or 2,596 more.

Arkansas, with 2,383 teachers, would need 3,805, or 1,422 more.

Florida, with 2,148 teachers, would need 3,117, or 969 more.

Georgia, with 4,934 teachers, would need 8,062, or 3,068 more.

Kentucky, with 1,339 teachers, would need 1,342, or 3 more.

Louisiana, with 2,700 teachers, would need 4,487, or 1,787 more.

Mississippi, with 5,125 teachers, would need 9,164, or 4,039 more.

North Carolina, with 5,815 teachers, would need 8,436, or 2,621 more.

Oklahoma, with 1,275 teachers, would need 1,646, or 371 more.

South Carolina, with 4,339 teachers, would need 7,494, or 3,055 more.

Tennessee, with 2,721 teachers, would need 3,753, or 1,032 more. Texas, with 3,859 teachers, would need 6,625, or 2,766 more.

In the 12 states listed above, there are at present 40,111 Negro teachers. If the Negro schools were staffed on the estimated efficient basis of 30 pupils per teacher, the services of 23,729 additional teachers would be required. It may be remembered, also, that if the enrollment of scholastics was proportionately as large for Negroes as for whites, increased estimates would be in order.

Buildings. Mr. N. C. Newbold, Director of the Division of Negro Education for the state of North Carolina, is responsible for the statement that in the last 10 years 8 Southern states alone have expended upwards of $30,000,000 upon new construction for Negro common schools. During the same period $270,547,343 was spent for new schools for white children. Negroes constitute 30 per cent of the population in these 8 states. They received, therefore, 10 per cent of the monies expended for building purposes, a percentage far below that which their proportion in the scholastic population warrants. Much hope is held out for the future, however, by such an evidence, as the condition which existed only a few years back was so unrelieved by such expenditure that present conditions are by far more favorable than formerly.

Negro School Housing. Mere statements of value with regard to school property are of little value, as the appraisals are in many instances made with not even an attempt at accurate approximation. A better understanding of the situation may be obtained from considering the degree to which existing facilities meet the need of the present school population. A recent survey made in Delaware [6] suggested that the building program of a community should plan provision of additional class-rooms on the basis of 40 pupils per class-room. An estimate of the number of Negro pupils in a typical cross-section of the South shows that this optimum standard is reached only in the District of Columbia and the state of Oklahoma. The 12 states listed above with the detail of number of class-rooms have in all 28,379 rooms actually available now. To care properly

[6] Annual Report, Department of Public Instruction, Dover, Delaware, p. 58.

for the enrollment of 1,374,778 Negro children in these states as of the present date, 34,369 rooms would be needed, or a total of 5,990 more than now exist. The additions necessary would vary, of course, with the states. Based on an estimated capacity of 40 pupils per room, on the basis of present enrollment:

Arkansas would need 2,854 rooms, an addition of 808.
Florida would need 2,338 rooms, an addition of 569.
Georgia would need 6,047 rooms, an addition of 2,171.
Louisiana would need 3,415 rooms, an addition of 1,024.
North Carolina would need 6,325 rooms, an addition of 668.
Tennessee would need 2,815 rooms, an addition of 293.
Texas would need 4,969 rooms, an addition of 469.
Virginia would need 3,807 rooms, an addition of 151.

These "needs" are based on the present enrollment. A much smaller percentage of Negro scholastics is enrolled in the schools in the states here listed than white. This means that if the enrollment of Negroes is raised to the level of the enrollment of whites, a much larger room-capacity would have to be provisioned. Estimating the cost per room at approximately $1,250, the expenditure of some $7,000,000 or $8,000,000 in these 10 states would be required to meet the need of the present Negro school enrollment.

However, overcrowding, because of the lack of sufficient class-room space is not the only difficulty to be faced in solving the problem of Negro school housing.[7] Perhaps the greatest handicap of the Negro schools in this direction is the *kind* of housing now provided. In the state of Georgia, for example, the close of the year 1926 found 2,967 buildings listed as being used by Negroes. Of these, only 58, or 1.9 per cent, were of brick or stone construction. Contrasted with this condition is the fact that of the 3,900 buildings used by whites for school purposes, 723, or 18.5 per cent, were of brick or stone construction. Furthermore, 1,782 of the Negro school buildings, or 60.0 per cent, were owned by private interests and were rented by the state. This was true of only 21.0 per cent of the white

[7] Fifty-fourth and Fifty-fifth Annual Reports of the Superintendent of Education to the General Assembly of the State of Georgia for the Biennium ending December 31, 1926, p. 202 ff.

schools. The schools not owned by the state are usually lodge halls or churches, totally unsuited for educational purposes.

Moreover, of the 2,967 school buildings used by Negroes, 2,331, or 78.5 per cent, were 1-room structures and this is not untypical of conditions in the majority of Southern states. Only 32.8 per cent of the white school buildings had one room. While white schools are being consolidated, with all of the advantages consequent upon such a process, such as higher salaries for better teachers, better buildings and transportation, and an enlarged community program, the 1-room school has continued to be the principal source of educational inspiration for the Negro child. A striking example of this is furnished by the system of public education of Montgomery County, Alabama. Here the white population throughout the county is served by a consolidated system considered by educational experts as the best in the entire United States, with a few large, centrally located schools reached by an excellent transportation system. The Negro school population of more than 15,000 in the same rural districts is served by 73 isolated 1-room schools, supervised by an overworked Jeanes Supervisor. Only in the states of Louisiana, Texas, Oklahoma, and North Carolina has the consolidation of Negro schools resulted to any marked degree in the elimination of the inadequate 1-room buildings and the substitution of large and commodious schools of greater capacity.

Length of Term. The average term, in days, ranges from 94 in Mississippi to 183 in Delaware. If 20 days of school attendance constitute a scholastic month, it is evident that school opportunity, judged by this criterion, is limited to 4¾ months of education for the average Negro school child in Mississippi, while the Negro school child in Delaware has almost exactly twice as long a period for attendance in school. Granting a standard course requiring 8 years of 9 months each to complete the grammar grades, under the old 8-4 plan, the Mississippi child would be obliged to attend school for 16 years to obtain as full a coverage as that of the Delaware child. The system implies that the pupil will finish an equivalent amount of work, regardless of the shorter term; although it is obvious that the students in the better system would have a better chance of doing more in a short time than the pupils in the poor system. Here, again, we strike upon an arc of the vicious educational circle to which we have referred before, for the Mississippi children who will be graduated from an 8-grade course after 8 years of school attendance will have spent but 38 months in the school room, under conditions far from ideal, while the Delaware child will have spent more than 73 months in school. While the condition is aggravated in Mississippi, the average length of the school term being lower than any state in the South as far back as 1912-13, with the exception of Tennessee, South Carolina, and Alabama, there are other states where the condition is serious. Estimated on the basis of the present school term in days, the average graduate of the elementary school course will have spent

37.6 months in school in Mississippi
41.2   "   "   "   " Louisiana
44.0   "   "   "   " Texas
46.4   "   "   "   " Alabama
46.4   "   "   "   " South Carolina
48.0   "   "   "   " Oklahoma
49.2   "   "   "   " Florida
53.6   "   "   "   " Georgia
54.8   "   "   "   " Arkansas
54.8   "   "   "   " North Carolina
56.0   "   "   "   " Kentucky
58.0   "   "   "   " Tennessee
59.2   "   "   "   " Virginia
68.0   "   "   "   " West Virginia
70.8   "   "   "   " Maryland
72.0   "   "   "   " the District of Columbia
73.2   "   "   "   " Delaware

Philanthropic Aid. The cause of Negro education in the South has been given a tremendous impetus through the stimulus, encouragement, and substantial assistance given by special funds. A full account of the work done by these philanthropic foundations is given by N. C. Newbold in his story of the Negro Common Schools in the South previously referred to in the *Annals of the American Academy of Political and Social Science.* The general aggregates of their appropriations include:

Summary of Appropriations by Special Funds.

1. John F. Slater Fund:
   a. Religious and private institutions ....$ 2,081,899.00
   b. Public institutions 1,039,949.00
2. General Education Board 18,872,442.36
3. Anna T. Jeanes Fund 626,598.28
4. Phelps-Stokes Fund 153,000.00
5. Julius Rosenwald Fund 3,333,852.00
6. Pierre S. duPont Gift (for Delaware only).... 2,500,000.00

   Total $28,589,736.64

Certain Duke gifts added to the totals above make a total sum of more than $30,000,000 contributed by special funds for Negro education in the South.

The General Education Board has contributed to county training schools, state agents for Negro rural schools, with the vast bulk going to colleges and schools. The Anna T. Jeanes Fund has supported traveling teachers. who introduced into small county schools simple home industries and gave lessons in sanitation and cleanliness. The Slater Fund was established to encourage county training schools and high schools. The Julius Rosenwald Fund beginning modestly in 1914 has loomed as one of the most significant educational programs in the South. It provided the much-needed buildings within which the agents of the other active funds operated. Further, it stimulated contributions from public tax funds and from Negroes. The duPont gifts have been restricted to Delaware where through this aid modern school buildings have been placed in every Negro school district.

School Attendance—General. The following table (Table XXV) gives comparative data on school population, enrollment, and attendance for certain states in the South where such information is obtainable.

A word of caution is necessary in the interpretation of this table. The enumeration of the school population in the various states is hardly comparable, as various age limits are employed in the different states in the making of the school census. Alabama, for example, enumerates all individuals between the ages of 6-20 as falling in the school population, while Mississippi is required by statute to enumerate its school population from the age-group 5-21. The age-group included in the census of the scholastic population in Florida is from 6-21. The table given on page 233 of this report, referring to the number of Negro and white children in school and out, based on the government census of 1920, is the latest available. That table (XXII) should be referred to in considering the problem of Negro school attendance.

TABLE XXV

PERCENTAGE OF NEGRO SCHOOL CHILDREN ENROLLED AND ATTENDING SCHOOL DAILY IN CERTAIN SOUTHERN STATES

State	Year Data Reported	School Population	Enrollment	Per Cent Census Enrolled	Average Daily Attendance	Per Cent Census Average Attendance	Per Cent Enrollment Attendance
Alabama	1926-27	327,563	184,438	56.3	127,463	38.9	69.1
Arkansas	1927-28	156,785	110,853	70.7	78,121	49.8	70.4
Delaware	1927-28		6,489	...		...	87.3
Dist. of Columbia	1926-27		22,409	...	20,458	...	91.2
Florida	1926-27	141,094	90,302	63.0	67,235	47.6	74.4
Georgia	1926-27	376,217	241,884	64.2	167,497	44.5	69.2
Kentucky	1925-26	56,749	50,652	89.42		...	...
Louisiana	1926-27	255,470	136,634	53.4	103,322	40.4	75.6
Maryland	1925-26	68,949	49,165	71.3	36,457	52.8	74.1
Mississippi	1925-26	464,748	274,932	59.1	189,379	40.7	68.8
North Carolina	1926-27	306,270	253,095	82.6	169,373	55.3	66.9
Oklahoma	1927-28	53,922	49,401	91.6	30,035	55.7	60.7
South Carolina	1926-27	300,000	224,823	74.9	155,523	51.8	69.1
Tennessee	1926-27		112,610	...	83,398	...	74.0
Texas	1926-27	228,460	198,763	87.0	155,614	68.1	78.2
Virginia	1927-28	216,803	152,293	70.2	112,139	51.7	73.6

Nor is it far-fetched to question the accuracy of the figures on school attendance given in the reports of county superintendents to state boards, and appearing in the reports of the state superintendents as official. An investigation of the recording of the data for school attendance in Oklahoma [8] disclosed the fact that the figures reported by the county superintendents for Negro scholastics were in many instances grossly

[8] Bond, Horace M., "Survey of Negro Education in Oklahoma," reported in *The Crisis*, May and July, 1928.

exaggerated. In several instances attendance percentages as high as 90 and 95 per cent were reported, while the original reports for the individual schools when checked yielded attendance rates from 20 to 30 percentage points lower. Confirmation of this suspicion is given by the reported attendance figure for such a state as North Carolina, whose official report gives an attendance rate of only 66.9 per cent; yet, in such a state as Mississippi, where the Negro educational system is admittedly far inferior, a higher attendance rate of 68.8 per cent is reported.

One important analysis has been made of school attendance of Negro children in relation to the familiar problems of retardation and failures of promotion in the state of Delaware.[9]

The investigators found that there was a fairly even age distribution from 7 to 13 years, but that 34 per cent of the total enrollment was in Grade I and one-half in Grades I and II. After reaching the age of 12 they nearly all had fallen behind and more than half were over 2 years retarded. Further study of promotions and this striking retardation revealed that they began to fail in their first year in school and the further behind in age the slower the progress in school. A clue to the non-promotion was found in attendance. The promoted children had attended 138 days and the non-promoted children only 78 days. Non-attendance was charged by teachers in 63 per cent of all failures; and, moreover, it appeared that pupils more than 2 years behind made no serious effort to attend school. Going a step further non-attendance increased with distance of pupils' homes from schools. The factor of distance operated seriously with the younger pupils. The nine causes of non-attendance listed were: agricultural work, other work, weather, illness, quarantine, out of town, poverty, parental indifference and truancy.

Summary of School Attendance. The greatest obstacles to regular school attendance of Negro children in the South appear to be (a) seasonal occupations, such as the agricultural labor required in the planting and harvesting of the cotton crop in the spring and fall; (b) occasional occupations, which seriously affect the school largely because of public indifference to

[9] Cooper, Richard and Herman, *Negro School Attendance in Delaware.*

the enforcement of compulsory attendance laws; and (c) general community apathy, both on the part of the school authorities and the Negro patrons. One device to meet the first obstacle is that used in the state of Oklahoma, known as the 'Divided Session Plan." The schools in the rural districts meet for a short session of from 6 weeks to 2 months in the late summer, and recess in order to allow the children to help harvest the cotton crop. School is then resumed after the cotton-picking season; if the district maintains a 7-months school, two months of the summer session and five months of the winter session constitute the school year. This has proved most unsatisfactory. The amount of wastage due to even one long summer vacation is too familiar to need repetition here. Where the school year is thus split up into two parts, with two long vacation periods, this wastage in learning becomes so serious as to invalidate largely the work done during the short session. One solution suggested is the substitution of some other labor supply for the school children now utilized, or the alternative of sacrificing the educational future of the children to the immediate necessity of garnering the cotton crop. This problem of seasonal employment is aggravated in such states as Arkansas, Oklahoma and Texas because of the comparative lateness of the cotton-picking season in these states which are the northern section of the Southern Cotton ·Belt.

The other two obstacles can only be met by arousing public opinion, both white and black, to active support of the existing compulsory education statutes. This is being done, notably in Alabama, by the enactment of regulations by which appropriations from the state school fund to local units of administration are conditioned upon school attendance. Instead of making blanket appropriations per capita enrollment, or school population, the state equalization funds are now appropriated on the basis of the number of children attending school regularly, and this measure has been remarkably effective in stimulating teachers, administrators, board members and parents to renewed diligence in making school attendance more regular.

Supervision. In the rural districts of the South, supervision of the Negro schools is meagre and indifferent except where some special supervisory agency has been set up. The county

superintendents may or may not make a casual visit to the small
1-room schools throughout the entire term, and in many instances this visit is announced in advance and the occasion
assumes, in preparation and ceremony, the dignity of a rite.
Most effective work, however, has been done in those counties
which employ regular supervisors for the Negro schools.   At
first these workers were paid by the Jeanes Fund on a cooperative basis with the state or county.   Gradually the Jeanes Fund
has been able to withdraw its support from fields in which the
type of work done has attracted enough public support to assure
its continuance with state or local financing alone, and thus de-
vote its energies to the cultivation of areas hitherto untouched.
In this way the Fund has served a most valuable function in
stimulating community enterprise and interest in efficient supervision.[10]

In Alabama, for example, there are supervisors, 21 of whom
are paid partly by the Jeanes Fund and partly by the county in
which they are employed.   The others are paid by various
funds, including the state, county, Tuskegee and the Phelps-
Stokes.   Their activities entail class-room supervision through
elementary grades, industrial supervision, community projects,
and general teacher-training.   In rural schools an industrial
course in 3 units gives girls a knowledge of the care and use
of tools used in sewing, a knowledge of the fundamental and
decorative stitches, ability to recognize materials, to make common seams and finish edges in garments neatly, and cleanliness
and attractiveness in home setting.   They conduct "opportunity" schools for adults, Negro health week and assist in conducting health clinics and physical examinations.

County Training Schools. | Practically all Southern states
have developed a system of county high schools to meet the demand for secondary education on the part of the white rural
school population.   The institutions which meet the same general need for the Negro population are designated the County
Training Schools.   They began first as boarding schools with
a small nucleus around which teacher-training curricula on the
high school level were constructed.   As the normal schools have
taken over the teacher-training function, the county training

[10] McDavid, Mary Foster (Mrs.), "Facts Concerning County Supervision
in the Colored Schools of Alabama," *The State Normal Journal,* p. 25 ff.,
Montgomery, 1929.

schools have been restricted more and more to the sphere of high school preparation for higher work. The following figures, released by the officials of the John F. Slater Fund, indicate the coverage of the schools and their rapid growth during the last decade, especially.

Beginning with the Session 1911-12, at the request of 4 County Superintendents, the Slater Fund aided in establishing county training schools in these 4 counties. There was evident need for at least one good central public school in each county. The plan immediately met with the approval of State and County Superintendents. Fuller information about these schools will be found in the Annual Reports of the John F. Slater Fund.

The following facts show the steady progress:

TABLE XXVI

DEVELOPMENT OF COUNTY TRAINING SCHOOLS FOR NEGROES, 1912-28

Year	Number of Schools	Number of Teachers	Pupils in High School Grades	For Salaries from Public Tax Funds	For Salaries Through Slater Fund	Average Amount for Salaries from Public Funds	Amount Contributed by General Education Board for Building and Equipment
1912	4	20	77	$ 3,344	$ 2,000	$ 836	
1913	4	23	74	4,612	2,000	1,153	
1914	8	41	184	10,696	4,000	1,337	
1915	17	85	267	17,986	8,091	1,058	
1916	27	135	404	37,395	13,500	1,385	$ 5,488
1917	42	252	630	55,020	18,660	1,310	8,618
1918	52	308	948	78,533	25,840	1,510	11,656
1919	70	402	1,130	131,158	39,037	1,874	18,477
1920	107	624	1,649	239,252	52,894	2,236	36,733
1921	142	848	2,247	340,821	61,500	2,400	75,271
1922	156	964	3,782	401,949	59,750	2,577	60,689
1923	179	1,102	4,723	513,193	63,300	2,867	56,000
1924	204	1,297	6,189	594,268	69,300	2,913	54,292
1925	233	1,563	7,555	767,172	70,028	3,292	60,461
1926	275	1,889	9,483	970,935	97,875	3,530	65,930
1927	306	2,161	11,810	1,104,510	106,000	3,610	64,801
1928	328	2,379	14,092	1,269,228[11]	100,675	3,869	45,164[12]

[11] Total amount for session 1927-28 for all purposes from public tax funds $1,433,431.

[12] In 1927-28 the General Education Board contributed $52,000 for salaries. As these become fully accredited High Schools, they are dropped from the list of Training Schools.

High Schools. Most of the development of high schools for Negroes has been crowded into the past 10 years. Prior to 1918 there were but few scattered accredited high schools in the South. Sixteen Southern states in 1925 had 166 with 1,006 graduates, and in 1927 [13] there were 251 such schools with 4,910 graduates. North Carolina leads with 56 accredited high schools for Negroes of which number 33 are public and 23 private. Texas follows with 31 and Mississippi with 26. In the latter state more of these schools are private than public. South Carolina and Alabama in 1927 had neither public nor private Negro high schools.

Urban Versus Rural School Problems. Because of the fact, in general, more money is available in the support of urban education than for rural education, Negro schools in the cities of the South may be regarded as far in advance of the rural schools. Comparatively, it may be said that they tend more nearly to approximate the white rural schools, for as large a gap separates them from the white city schools as exists between the white and Negro rural schools. The concentration of the population in cities has resulted in better supervision, higher salaries, and, on the whole, better buildings than are enjoyed by the Negro rural school population. Because their need was not as great, however, they have been for the most part deprived of the aid furnished by the large foundations, and as a result have been obliged to subsist on such funds as were available from the local community tax fund. The greatest handicaps of urban schools for Negroes in the South may be summarized as follows: (a) Overcrowding. In many cities the building facilities available for Negro children are so inadequate that the school authorities have resorted to the expedient of having two, and in some cases, as many as three, short sessions per day. Under this system, one group of children report for school at an early hour, are hurriedly carried through an abbreviated schedule, and dismissed to make room for another group. Besides the manifest inefficiency which results from this hurried, breathless arrangement of the program, the immense drain upon the resources and strength of the teachers is obvious. It should also be remembered that these teachers re-

[13] Newbold, N. C., "Common Schools for Negroes in the South," *Annals of the American Academy of Political and Social Science,* November, 1928, p. 214.

TABLE XXVII

Four-year Accredited High Schools for Negroes in Eighteen Southern States *

States	1924-25				1925-26				1926-27			
	Public	Private	Total	Graduates	Public	Private	Total	Graduates	Public	Private	Total	Graduates
Alabama	0	0	0	0	0	0	0	0	0	0	0	0
Arkansas	4	3	7	....	3	3	6	227	6	6	12	194
Delaware	No data											
Dist. of Columbia	No data											
Florida	1	0	1	...	2	0	2	6	2	0	2	0
Georgia	2	9	11	...	3	9	12	422	6	14	20	739
Kentucky	11	0	11	...	14	0	14	122	14	0	14	....
Louisiana	3	0	3	...	3	1	4	196	3	2	5	138
Maryland	5	2	7	...	10	2	12	520	14	2	16	360
Mississippi	.	.	10	...	7	8	15	**	11	15	26	....
Missouri	8	0	8	...	7	3	10	**	10	0	10	....
North Carolina ...	20	23	43	1,006	25	24	49	1,220	33	23	56	1,575
Oklahoma	9	0	9	...	8	0	8	**	10	0	10	....
South Carolina ...	**	**	**	...	0	0	0	....	0	0	0	....
Tennessee	9	0	9	...	12	0	12	117	12	0	12	138
Texas	4	3	7	...	15	10	25	943	20	11	31	1,075
Virginia	9	9	18	...	8	11	19	507	10	10	20	428
West Virginia	12	1	13	...	15	1	16	327	16	1	17	263
Total	98	52	166	1,006	134	71	205	4,750	167	84	251	4,910

* Newbold, N. C., "Common Schools for Negroes in the South." The American Negro, Annals of the American Academy, November, 1928, p. 214.

** Figures not available.

ceive the same salary for this double service which they are expected to receive for the single-session day, and that their salary schedule is seldom higher than one-half that granted the white teachers, doing much less work. In spite of this device, which saves money for the system by reducing by one-half the number of Negro teachers that would ordinarily be required, much effective work is being done by the over-worked Negro teachers.

In those communities where the double-session is not used, the class-room space is woefully inadequate. Many teachers, especially on the primary level, have as many as 50 and 60 children in average daily attendance per room. This condition extends on through the upper grades and is repeated in the high school. It results in making promotions more mechanical than based on actual achievement, for, as one superintendent of instruction phrased it, "the children must be promoted to make room for those entering school next year." Repeated year by year, this process has no eliminating feature, and, of course, no special technique for caring for the mentally deficient is possible. Colleges receiving graduates of high schools of this type are obliged to limit admission to those in the upper third of the class, for the mere diploma of graduation represents little more than so many years of perseverance in school attendance.

(b) New buildings are seldom occupied by Negro children. When a system outgrows a structure, it is handed over to the Negro children if the movement of population has brought the building within the limits of this group-area. When a new bond issue for the replacement of old structures or for additions are voted by the city electorate, the Negro school population seldom, if ever, receives that share which its proportion would demand. A notable instance is furnished by the city of Atlanta, where Negro citizens voted time and again against a bond issue which was intended to rebuild the Atlanta school system. An agreement was finally effected by which the Negroes were offered a share of the proceeds of the issue if they would give their support to it. The issue was passed, but of the total amount expended, Negro schools received less than one-tenth, whereas the agreement had promised more than one-third. Such discriminatory tactics are usually justified on the familiar basis of the small amount of taxes paid by Negro citizens.

This reasoning neglects the obvious fact that if applied to the school population generally wide variations would appear in the types of educational institutions maintained for various classes of whites. It should also be kept in mind that while, apparently, the Negro does pay an inconsiderable portion of the public tax fund, actually, in his rôle of renter, consumer, and "man lowest down," he bears a considerable share of the taxing burden in the indirect impost of higher rents, prices and lower wages which in turn enable his white employer to pay the taxes under consideration.

In general, however, the city schools for Negroes maintain longer terms, return a higher percentage of scholastics enrolled and in average daily attendance, pay higher salaries and are better supervised and housed than rural schools. Their general rank appears to be in direct relation to the efficiency of the white school system, as well as to the number of Negroes in the total population. If the white city system is excellent, the Negro system will tend to be so; and a better provision is made for a small number of Negroes than where their number approaches that of the whites. All in all, like the rural schools the problems of the urban Negro schools can be traced back to the facts of financial ability and effort.

Finances of Negro Common Schools. It is certain that most, if not all, of the defects of educational facilities for Negro children can be traced to inadequate financial support. It is important, therefore, to make an analysis of this fundamental matter if the existing situation is to be understood.

The schools in which Negro children are enrolled fall roughly into three classes. There is first the kind of school which operated under a specific constitutional requirement of the state that the races be separated. In the second class fall such schools which are separated so far as races are concerned, either by virtue of a provision in the data of state constitution making segregation optional, or by the gradual solidification of custom and opinion which makes local segregation the will of the majority, regardless of constitutional limitations. It is interesting to note that residential segregation inevitably contributes to this casual school segregation.

The third class will include school systems which make no legal or extra-legal attempt to segregate the children of different races. As representatives of these classes, Alabama with mandatory segregation may be taken as a type of the first; Indiana as an example of the second; and Massachusetts as the type for the third class.

According to the Census of 1920, 86.9 per cent of the entire Negro population resided in the 17 states and the District of Columbia, where educational segregation has been made mandatory by state constitutions or other legal enactments for a period dating back almost to the founding of the state systems of public instruction in the South. No allowance, however great, for the migration of Negroes from that section since 1920, can seriously bring in question the fact that the crux of the problem of Negro education is in the first group of states here referred to as requiring racial segregation by constitutional enactment.

The effort and ability of these states in the support of Negro education is therefore considered here in detail.

Wealth Per Child as an Index of Ability to Support Education. The extension of authority to the state as the unit for taxation in the support of education has been universal in the South. Since the state presents, in addition, a comparable unit, the wealth of the state per child is considered here as an index of its ability to support education.[14] With other indices of economic power, this criterion has correlations of from .812-.9841. It may therefore be regarded as a safe guide to the real ability of a state to support education.

Selection of Age-group 6-13 as an Index of Educational Burden. The age-group 6-13 is used here in making per capita comparisons. To use school census figures is to involve any comparative study in a certain confusion; (a) a variety of age-limits are used by the states in reporting educables; (b) school attendance or enrollment figures are of limited utility for this purpose because the number of children enrolled by the school system is in itself a function of the factor we are trying to isolate, namely, the financial effort and ability shown by these states in supporting efficient schools.

From the table that follows it will be noted that the heaviest

---

[14] Based upon the study by the Research Division of the National Education Association, "The Ability of States to Support Education."

educational burden, as represented by the number of Negro
educables, is to be found in the poorest states. Of the 17
states listed in the table, only 2 have per capita wealth per child
aged 6-13 above the average for the entire United States. One
fundamental fact in the financing of Negro education, accordingly, is that Negroes live in the poorest states, and in the
natural course of events, even granted an equalization of opportunity within these states, would have the poorest schools.
Despite the fact, however, that Negroes live in the poorer sections, there is considerable disparity in such amounts as are
available for education and what they receive. The average
expenditure per educable child in the United States as a whole
is $81.19. Using the index as developed by the National Edu-
cation Association's study of the ability of states to support
education, the expenditures for the various states, per Negro
and white educable child are as follows:

	Negro	White
South Carolina	4.48	45.45
Alabama	5.45	37.63
Georgia	7.44	35.34
Louisiana	8.02	46.67
Mississippi	9.34	42.17
North Carolina	11.06	36.70
Florida	11.41	75.07
Arkansas	11.60	21.15
Virginia	14.86	54.21
Tennessee	20.15	33.47
Kentucky	26.57	26.57
Texas	28.34	40.04
Maryland	29.58	59.70
Oklahoma	31.65	50.04
West Virginia	51.59	52.79
Missouri	51.90	67.30
Delaware	53.40	47.16

The disproportion in number of scholastics and funds received for school purposes is shown in Table XXVIII. From
this table one can note that while in South Carolina 54.9 per
cent of the population between the ages 6-13 are Negroes, only
10.66 per cent of the money devoted to all of the educables in
the state is expended on this majority Negro group. Stated
otherwise, the white children of South Carolina, who are 45.1
per cent of the total, receive 89.14 per cent of the money spent
for education in the state.

TABLE XXVIII

PROPORTIONS STATE EDUCATIONAL FUNDS DEVOTED TO NEGRO EDUCATION
COMPARED WITH PROPORTIONATE DISTRIBUTION OF NEGRO EDUCABLES IN
SEVENTEEN STATES

State	Per Cent of Total Population 6-13 That Negroes Are	Per Cent of Total Expenditures for Education Received by Negroes
South Carolina	54.9	10.66
Mississippi	53.0	10.51
Georgia	43.5	13.33
Louisiana	39.3	9.98
Alabama	38.9	8.40
Florida	36.9	7.91
North Carolina	31.5	12.13
Virginia	31.3	11.09
Arkansas	25.9	15.99
Tennessee	22.9	11.93
Maryland	17.8	9.67
Texas	16.2	12.00
Delaware	14.4	13.78
Kentucky	8.2	8.02
Oklahoma	7.2	4.73
West Virginia	4.7	4.65
Missouri	4.1	3.15

Consequences to the Type of Educational Opportunity Afforded Under This System to Negroes. The following extract from the State Report of Education [15] of Georgia (1926) offers a typical cross-section of the conditions one may expect to find.

1. No state or county school system is meeting its obligations and economic needs until it has made some fully adequate provision for Negro education. It is beginning to be realized more and more throughout the state that in order to retain our best Negroes on the farms and in other places where they may properly serve, educational facilities must be furnished for the training of their children. We are glad to note an encouraging attitude on the part of the boards of education and others toward Negro education.

Recommendations

2. The Negro schools are usually inefficient because hundreds of them are still taught in lodge halls, churches and buildings unsuited for school work and unequipped. It would be almost impossible to have efficient school work in these buildings. For that

[15] Fifty-fourth and Fifty-fifth Annual Reports of the Commissioner of Education to General Assembly of the State of Georgia for the Biennium Ending December 31, 1926.

reason it is recommended that county boards of education adopt the policy of building at least one Negro school a year. ./. .

The needs of the Negro children should be considered when bonds are issued. Many towns and rural districts that have built schools for white children with bonds, should now take some provision for a suitable building for the Negro children.

Another cause of inefficiency in the Negro schools, especially the rural schools, is the poor teaching, due to meager salaries paid. No improvement can be expected in this respect until the better-prepared Negro teachers are paid better salaries. It is true that many Negro teachers are so poorly trained that they should not be allowed to teach at all, but better pay will attract better teachers to the schools.

After 50 years had passed since the establishment of the State public school system, Georgia had, in 1926, only one public accredited colored high school in the state. This is rather a poor showing, and there are many cities in Georgia that should develop the Negro school to the reasonable standard of the accrediting commission.

The state institutions for Negroes at Savannah, Albany, and Forsyth should be better equipped and supported. The Savannah school is in need of increased maintenance funds. The Forsyth school gets only $5,000 a year and is greatly in need of building, also maintenance funds.

It has been suggested that one of the principal difficulties in the financing of Negro schools is the poverty of the states in which by far the greater number reside. That this poverty will not be suddenly transformed into wealth is the conclusion of the Research Division of the National Education Association, which states that

Figures bearing on this point seem to indicate that existing differences in ability (i.e., to support education) are not peculiar to this decade and that similar differences will probably be found in the future. There is also some evidence that a state's comparative position, with respect to its ability to support education, is relatively permanent. In the majority of cases it has shown no tendency to fluctuate widely since 1880.

Of the 12 richest and 12 poorest states in which there has been little fluctuation since 1880 in the amounts available per capita for education, the largest Negro populations are to be found in 11 of the poorest states.

Possible Programs. From the data presented above, it is evident that (a) the efficiency of Negro schools coincides with the ability of states to support education; (b) the largest number of Negro educables is found in states with the smallest wealth per capita; and (c) there is little likelihood that these states will in the near future place Negro education on a parity with white schools, so far as expenditures are concerned, for to do so would call for a rate of taxation which these states would probably find unbearable.

Several years ago the Sterling-Towner Bill was proposed to equalize the existing inequality in school opportunities afforded to educables in various states, due to the reasons of low wealth per capita referred to above. This bill was proposed with special reference to white schools, and because it became and contained the provision that the funds which were to be appropriated, under the provisions of the bill, were to be expended according to the same ratio characterizing the expenditure of state monies in the past, it elicited violent opposition on the part of many interested in the betterment of Negro education on the ground that it would tend to perpetuate, rather than alleviate, the glaring disabilities of the Negro schools. The other provision of the bill found objectionable which had nothing to do directly with the matter of race was its provision looking forward to the establishment of a Department of Education, with an executive head sitting as a member of the President's cabinet. The objections to this feature of the bill emphasized current fears of centralization as a menace to educational freedom and federalization as an invitation to a deadening process of standardization.

Regardless of the worth of these objections, it is obvious that the education of Negroes, if left in the hands of the states for financial support, will for many decades remain far behind. Nor will it be entirely the fault of the states involved, for they have both more educables and less wealth in proportion than other states.

The urgency and present hopelessness of the situation have turned the attention of some to the advisability of sponsoring legislation looking toward the granting of assistance to the states in the education of the Negro population.

The fact that states vary in their ability to support education becomes more or less obvious. More needs to be known, however, of the inequalities in ability existing within the states, so far as the smaller units for educational administration are concerned. Whatever programs or steps are considered for the future, it is certain that they should be preceded by study of the inequalities of Negro education resulting within states by reason of variations in taxable wealth of smaller educational units, and study of the educational legislation of various states to see how the units of control and administration, and the units of taxation and appropriation actually affect the efficiency of Negro schools.

CHAPTER XVIII

NEGROES IN THE COMMON SCHOOLS OF THE NORTH

Variant Educational Policies. The majority of Northern states maintain no separate schools for Negroes: some of these keep separate records, others do not. In the states of the North there are various practices. In Illinois and New Jersey, for example, there are mixed schools in some parts of the state and separate schools in others. In Indiana the elementary schools are separate and high schools unseparated, with the exception of such cities as Indianapolis, where a separate high school was recently established. In still other cities the concentration of the Negro population and school districting produce the effect of separate schools. Cities like Philadelphia and Trenton, New Jersey, have, by appointing full staffs of Negro teachers and principals, brought the complete separation of the elementary schools and both states have state schools which are devoted exclusively to Negroes (Cheyney Normal School, of Pennsylvania, and the Bordentown Manual Training and Industrial Institute, of New Jersey). New York City represents, perhaps, the most cosmopolitan of all the cities in this regard, placing Negro teachers in the system without regard to the racial composition of the school and keeping no separate record of the Negro students. New Jersey, however, just across the river, employs several policies toward bi-racial education within the state. Mr. Lester Granger [1] of the New Jersey Manual Training and Industrial School at Bordentown has given an apt description of these in an attempt to measure the efficiency of different systems.

The northern section of New Jersey, which is industrial, has a thickly settled foreign population, and located close to New York and its cosmopolitan atmosphere there is democracy in its

[1] Granger, Lester B., "Race Relations in the School System," *Opportunity,* p. 327, November, 1925.

schools. Negro Normal School graduates are appointed to teaching positions solely on their merit, and it is not an infrequent sight in Newark and Jersey City to find a Negro teacher in charge of a class composed entirely of white pupils. White and Negro children attend school together from the kindergarten through the high schools, and the practice is not questioned. In suburban residence cities, such as East Orange or Montclair, sporadic efforts have been made to establish separate classes or separate buildings for Negro pupils. These efforts have regularly failed sooner or later, more for lack of intelligent, influential support than because of concerted, active opposition from Negroes. A Newark small separate school which was maintained some twenty years ago was discontinued on the death of its Negro principal, and the existence of it is barely remembered. North Jersey has felt no need for separate schools and is not interested in them; as a result there is no "racial problem" as such in the school system, as is constantly engaging the attention of school heads in the southern part of the state.

In the section of New Jersey, extending from Trenton and Asbury Park to Cape May, and lying across the river from Pennsylvania and Delaware, public sentiment takes on a good deal of the neighboring provincialism and intolerance. In the counties of Monmouth, Burlington and Gloucester, the Ku Klux Klan is particularly strong. It was pointed out by Mr. Granger that it was strong enough in Burlington County to buy the old county fair ground and to convert it into a pleasure park for Klansmen. In the rural township of Columbus, the local superintendent of schools is Kleagle for the county. Restaurants and theatres, and the public school system reflect a different racial attitude from that of the northern section. From the university town of Princeton, including the capital city of Trenton, southward to Cape May, every city or town with a considerable Negro population supports the dual educational system, with a building for its white and a building for its Negro pupils of the grammar grades. In the high schools the races are mixed. In no town south of Elizabeth does a Negro teacher have a class with white children in it, though wholly Negro classes are sometimes found with a white teacher in charge.

The Negroes are by no means in agreement for or against segregation, this study revealed. The intense discussions in Pennsylvania over the Cheyney Normal School, a separate Negro institution, and Philadelphia's separate public schools are indications of this difference of view. Some Negroes view the segregation as an unmitigated evil, dangerous to the status of the Negro in northern sections, while others see many benefits to the race in the form of closer racial solidarity, greater inspiration to Negro youth, and more positions for Negro teachers. The effect of the segregated school system upon the attendance and progress of the Negro student has not often been studied in this connection and Mr. Granger's data become particularly valuable here.

At the invitation of the Committee on Information of the New Jersey Organization of Teachers of Colored Children he instituted an investigation into the high school attendance of Negro children throughout the state.

With relatively larger numbers enrolled in the grades and smaller numbers in the high schools, Negro students in New Jersey appear to remain in and graduate from high school in larger proportions than whites. Studying separately the mixed and separate schools, it is revealed that Negro students enter high school in larger proportions from the separate schools. The conclusion is scarcely warranted, however, that this fact constitutes an argument in favor of the separate schools. For while Trenton, one of the larger cities, erected a building exclusively for Negroes at a cost of nearly $1,000,000, and secured superior Negro teachers to conduct the school, other cities have fallen into the practice most feared where separate schools exist, of providing grossly inferior accommodations and instructors. In Asbury Park, for example, there are two schools built jointly for white and colored children; with the races divided off into "wings," one of which is for white, the other for Negro, children. The white principal is in charge of the building; the Negro principal has the status of "head teacher" in charge of the colored wing. A high iron fence divides the playground. The interest of Negro teachers in the Negro children to the point of urging them to continue in school, while affecting favourably the figures of attendance, is conceivably no more than should be expected in any other institution from any interested teacher.[2]

With regard to racial disturbances arising from the presence of both races in the same school, it may be interesting to note that two cities in Indiana, Gary and Indianapolis, have witnessed in the last several years outbreaks within the schools themselves. The first culminated in a strike of white students because a small group of Negro high school students for whom no adequate separate high school could be properly built were placed in the existing high school.

In the latter instance agitation was rife on both sides for the establishment of a separate high school to care for the Negro pupils. The Negroes who advocated the building of a separate high school stated in defense of their position the belief that such a move would (a) result in the employment of educated young Negroes who were not, under existing conditions, able to capitalize upon their educational preparation; (b) result in a larger number of Negro pupils remaining in school, due to the greater encouragement and kindlier atmosphere found in an all-Negro school, with Negro teachers. Opponents of the proposed new high school expressed the fear that segregation would lead ultimately to discrimination in the kind of educational effort exerted in the upkeep of the Negro schools, and a relaxation of vigilance on the part of school authorities with regard to the standards maintained in the Negro school. The high school was finally built and has been placed in operation.

In many instances, the failure of official records to include separate statistics makes any estimate of the status of the Negro in Northern schools hazardous, at best. The sources from which material may be gleaned of any comparative value consist principally of special studies and surveys. A brief reference, however, may be made to some of the important problems disclosed by these surveys.

Intelligence and Retardation. It is usually customary to refer the retardation of school children to their intellectual status, as shown by existing psychometric instruments. This has not been done here, first, because in the section on Educability, and The Achievement of Negro Children, to follow, at-

[2] Granger, Lester B., "Race Relations in the School System," *Opportunity,* November, 1925.

tention is paid to the problem. In the second place, there are enough factors besides that of intelligence alone which may serve as an explanation of the greater retardation of the Negro child in Northern schools than his white school-fellow. Principal among these is the factor of migration. It has been indicated that the school term in certain Southern states was extremely short when compared with the standard school term existing in Northern states. When it is considered that by far the greater number of Negro children in Northern schools received their first classification and early preparation in these inefficient, short-term Southern schools, some explanation is provided of the high retardation rates for Negroes in Northern schools. The figures for such a city as Detroit, as shown in the chart that follows, may be used here. The Negro population of Detroit increased more than 611 per cent between 1910 and 1920. Children born in Michigan show only 4.76 per cent retardation while those born in the South show proportions closely approximating the state of the school systems.

THREE OR MORE YEARS RETARDATION BY PLACE OF BIRTH OF NEGRO PUPILS
IN THE DETROIT PUBLIC SCHOOLS

Place of Birth	Per Cent of Retardation
Michigan	///// 4.76
Indiana	////// 6.25
Pennsylvania	//////// 8.00
Illinois	/////////// 10.83
Kentucky	//////////// 11.32
Missouri	///////////// 12.70
Florida	/////////////// 14.28
Ohio	//////////////// 15.12
Texas	////////////////// 18.17
Louisiana	////////////////// 18.28
Alabama	////////////////// 18.50
Arkansas	/////////////////// 19.50
South Carolina	/////////////////// 19.71
Tennessee	/////////////////// 19.77
Virginia	//////////////////// 20.00
Georgia	///////////////////// 21.30
North Carolina	///////////////////// 21.63
Mississippi	///////////////////////// 25.00

A table culled from the Minneapolis report giving median ages at entrance for Negro and white pupils further indicates the degree to which retardation affects the two groups in a Northern city system. In the fifth grade the entering age for Negro pupils was more than a year higher than for whites, and while the difference in ages tends to decrease with further progress through the grades, it remains a large breach.

TABLE XXIX

MEDIAN AGES AT ENTRANCE OF PUPILS IN THE MINNEAPOLIS
SCHOOL SYSTEM

Grade	B5	A5	B6	A6	B7	A7	B8	A8
1921, all pupils	11.24	11.26	12.14	12.56	13.01	13.42	13.83	14.16
1921, Negro pupils..	12.33	12.54	13.04	13.52	13.88	14.18	14.78	14.97

The report in question, however, indictated that the median ages of entrance for Negroes showed a tendency to decrease from year to year.

The Superintendent of the Schools of Trenton, New Jersey, states that: [3]

The problem of retardation is more serious among colored children than among any other racial group. I am inclined to believe that the further extension of segregation and a real social welfare program is the only real practical solution when we consider the present economic and social burdens which are placed on the colored group. The over-ageness and the low educational age of most of those coming from the South and other cities adds materially to our problem. The economical status of our adult Negro population which, in a real way, controls the housing situation, is in itself a serious problem and contributes materially to retardation causes.

E. George Payne comments upon this situation by saying that:

There are several other factors that account for the status of the Negro in the schools in the North which can only be mentioned here. In all the studies the Negro showed greater irregularity of attendance and a less amount of attendance than the white. The situation is brought about by the requirement that Negro children help at home, aid in the economic support of the family, by the greater number of broken homes which indicate inadequate family control, and distance of residence from school.[4]

Dr. Payne's concluding summary from the article referred to, may well be quoted: [5]

[3] Report from Superintendent, Trenton, N. J., quoted in "Negroes in the Public Elementary Schools of the North," *Annals of the American Academy of Political and Social Science*, November, 1928, p. 230.
[4] *Ibid.*, pp. 231-32.
[5] *Ibid.*, p. 233.

The study of Negro experience in the educational institutions of the North led to the conclusion that the rapid influx of Southern Negroes into the North was creating a problem which taxed the intelligence of the best educational leadership to solve; that the problem of incorporating the Negro into the civic life of the North is complicated by color as well as customs and previous history, but must be faced; that equal educational opportunity is not present in the North and that the problem now facing the educator is that of providing for *every* child, white and black, the opportunity for personal growth and social adaptation in the interest of the general welfare.

CHAPTER XIX

PROBLEMS OF EDUCABILITY

One important question determining community interest in Negro education has been that of mental fitness for the same education given whites, or even for any important measure of education at all. Reference is frequently made to results of the various intelligence tests which gave results interpreted significantly as racial difference in ability to learn. This literature is critically reviewed in the following pages. It may be noted that despite the frequent and unquestioning use of these results, none of the tests so far made has been sufficiently free from vitiating conditions to warrant the conclusions which have gained currency. Unanimity of conclusion on the question of an innate mental inferiority of the Negro race appears to be the most consistent point of agreement. The findings of the various studies leading to this conclusion, however, more frequently than not, contradicted themselves.

Race Differences as Shown by Intelligence Tests. Dr. A. H. Arlitt,[1] a psychologist of wide experience in testing, reviewing studies in this field has been prompted to this cautious conclusion, regarding judgments of race differences found upon the intelligence tests as administered.

These differences are important to know, but almost no studies of this type provide any means for evaluating the contributions of nature and nurture. The environment of low-testing races or nationalities is generally inferior to that of high-testing races, but we do not know whether this environmental difference is a cause or an effect. Until we can have controlled experiments upon children of various races *transplanted at infancy* into uniform environments, precise knowledge regarding native racial differences may be impossible to secure.

[1] Arlitt, A. H., "On the Need of Caution in Establishing Race Norms." *Journal of Applied Psychology*, Vol. V, pp. 179-83, 1921.

Some thirty or more studies of race differences in intelligence are reviewed by Barbara Burks [2] in the 27th Yearbook of the Society for the Study of Education, 1928.

Her comments upon each of these indicate significant inadequacies either in data, or method or circumstances of investigation for any final conclusions at this stage.

It is perhaps desirable to give in brief outline what are considered the more important studies in this field for their value in indicating the present conclusions of the investigators, if not to suggest the further work to be done. In noting findings it must be remembered that many factors involving a high percentage of errors were either not considered or not adequately considered, among the most important of which were: psycho-social status, reading and learning habits, educational achievements of parents and subjects, selection, and social status.

Arlitt,[3] in 1921-22, using the Stanford-Binet Tests on 191 native-born whites, 87 Italians and 71 Negroes, in Louisiana, found:

Social status apparently more important than race in determining scores: median I. Q. of whites, 106; of Italians, 85; Negroes, 83. Median I. Q. of Negroes decreased with increasing age, 6 to 10-15, combined. At ages 5 and 6 Negroes of same social status of whites are superior; afterward uniformly inferior. Sex differences slight except at 5 and 6 when girls are markedly superior.

Brigham,[4] in 1923, using the Army Alpha and Beta Tests with wide samplings—large per cent of draftees of all races— found:

Negroes inferior to whites; mental age of 9 or 10 years compared with 13.1 for whites; investigation of Brigham's data shows Northern Negroes superior to Southern whites (pure-bred Anglo-Saxons). Brigham believes mulattoes account for superiority of Northern Negroes, with selection as another factor. Schooling and its influence on the tests he depreciates, although analysis shows high correlation.

[2] Burks, B., N.S.S.E., Yearbook.
[3] Arlitt, A. H., "On the Need of Caution in Establishing Race Norms." *Journal of Applied Psychology*, Vol. V, p. 183, 1921.
[4] Brigham, C. C., *A Study of American Intelligence.*

Clark,[5] in 1922, at Los Angeles, using the National Intelligence Test, found:

Los Angeles children (Negroes) in 5 schools did practically as well on the National Intelligence Test and a battery of achievement tests as did white children. The children were from 15 representative Los Angeles schools. Commentator for N.S.S.E. report believes selection the deciding factor here; there is strong evidence, however, which points toward influence of educational background and experience, social status, as explanatory.

Goodenough,[6] in 1926, in Tennessee, Louisiana and California, using the Goodenough Primary Intelligence Tests (Drawing Scale), with 2,457 in all of which number approximately 35 per cent were Negroes, found:

Because the test used is non-verbal, the inferiority of Negroes cannot be explained on the basis of linguistic handicap; although test is completely independent of language, order of races with Negro at bottom is same as highest for Negroes (due to mulattoes), lowest for Jews. Median I. Q.'s Jewish, 106.1; Chinese, 104.1; California Negroes, 85.5; Southern Negroes, 78.7.

W. H. Pyle,[7] in 1915, using the Ebbinghaus Completion Test, Controlled Association, Free Association and Ink Blot Test with Missouri children, found:

In general Negroes made scores two-thirds as high as whites. The difference between whites and Negroes decreased with age. In more difficult tests of controlled association, Ebbinghaus Completion Tests, etc., the Negroes are very inferior; while in the easier tests (Free Association and Ink Blot Tests) the Negroes equal the whites. Separating the Negroes on the basis of social status, the Negro boys are four-fifths of white boys, the girls three-fourths of white girls.

Pressey[8] and Teter, in 1919, using Pressey Cross Out (Group) Test with 187 Negroes in Indiana, found:

[5] Clark, W. W., "Birth Rate and Native Intelligence," *Pychological Clinic,* Vol. XIV, pp. 111-15, 1922.
[6] Goodenough, Florence L., "Racial Differences in the Intelligence of School Children," *Journal of Experimental Psychology,* Vol. IX, pp. 388-97, 1926.
[7] Pyle, W. H., "Mentality of the Negro Compared with Whites," *Psychological Bulletin 12,* Vol. XXII, p. 71, 1916.
[8] Pressey and Teter, "Comparison of Colored and White Children," *Journal of Applied Psychology,* p. 277, 1915.

With age-groups, Negroes average two years younger (mentally). The colored children average a score one grade below that for white children. The Negroes are best in tests of rote memory, poorest on a test differentiating between abstract terms and a test of verbal ingenuity. Negroes do fairly well in dealing with concrete and routine problems, and poorly with abstractions or mental reconstructions.

Pressey and Thomas,[9] in 1919, using Pressey Cross Out (Group) Test with 538 white school children from good and poor rural sections of Indiana, concluded that:

For the four ages used in comparisons, 20 per cent of the children in District 1 rate above the medians for the city children as compared with 36 per cent in District 22, which is the better district; 6 per cent in the poor district score above the 75 percentile for the city children, as compared with 11 per cent in the better district; 48 per cent in the poor districts rate below the 25 percentile for the city children, as compared with 28 per cent in the better district.

A. C. Strong,[10] in 1913, in Columbia, South Carolina, tested 72 Negroes, 60 white children from the mill section, 95 white children from the good section of the city, using the Goddard Revision of the Binet-Simon scale:

Of the children tested in Columbia, 60.8 per cent colored and 25.2 per cent white were below the norm, while 9.2 per cent colored and 26 per cent white were above the norm. Dividing the white group into a "mill section group" with unfavourable background, the mill whites show 48.3 per cent below the norm, and only 15.6 per cent above the norm. In addition the only subjects four years under age were found in the mill section group. Negroes did poorly in verbal description.

T. R. Garth and C. A. Whatley,[11] in 1925, in Arkansas and Texas, using the National Intelligence Test with 1,300 Negroes, found that:

[9] Pressey and Thomas, "A Study of Country Children," *Journal of Applied Psychology*, pp. 282-6, 1915.
[10] Strong, A. C., "Three Hundred and Fifty White and Colored Children Measured by the Binet-Simon Measuring Scale of Intelligence," *Pedagogical Seminary*, pp. 485-512, 1913.
[11] Garth, T. R. and Whatley, C. A., "The Intelligence of Southern Negro Children," *School and Society*, Vol. XXII, pp. 501-4, 1925.

The average I. Q. on the National Intelligence Test for 1,300 Negro children was 75. Although social status and educational experience of Negroes in this study are admitted to be inferior, the authors do not believe that this educational inferiority is sufficient to explain the results; the necessary conclusion arising from data, accordingly, is that Negroes are inherently inferior.

Helen L. Koch and Rietta Simmons,[12] in 1920, selected typical Texas cities and rural sections, and applying the National Intelligence Test, Myers Pantomime, Detroit First Grade, Pintner-Cunningham Primary to large samplings of three races, whites, Negroes and Mexicans, concluded that:

City whites and city Negroes far excelled rural whites in Pantomime tests, whites having margin over all others, including rural whites. No data for rural Negroes. Educational background of city whites best, that of city Negroes and Mexicans poor.

M. J. Mayo,[13] in 1913, in New York City, used school marks as indices of the mental ability of 150 Negroes and 150 whites. His results were:

Of 150 Negro high school pupils under economic conditions similar to those for 150 white high school pupils, 29 per cent of Negroes exceeded the white median of high school marks. School grades were thus used to measure mental capacity. The conclusion reached is that even selected Negroes are far inferior to whites.

L. D. Lacy,[14] in 1926, in Oklahoma City, employing the Stanford-Binet and Otis Self-administering Test of Mental Ability to 817 Negroes and 5,199 whites, found that:

Negroes are inferior. Average I. Q. by Stanford Revision of first three grades is 91. Average I. Q. above these grades is 82. Achievement test scores show Negroes inferior in reading; given as possible explanation of low score of Negroes in Otis test (verbal). Stanford-Binet tests support theory that mental growth of Negroes is slower than whites, but denied by Otis Self-administering Test in the upper grades.

12 Koch, Helen Lois, and Simmons, Rietta, *A Study of the Test Performance of American, Mexican and Negro Children.* (In *Psychology Monographs,* Vol. XXXV, No. 5, whole number 166.)
13 Mayo, M. J., "The Mental Capacity of the American Negro." (*Archives of Psychology,* No. 28.)
14 Lacy, L. D., "Relative Intelligence of White and Colored Children," *Elementary School Journal,* Vol. XXVI, pp. 542-6, 1926.

Katherine Murdoch,[15] in 1920, in New York City, used the Pressey Group Tests with 500 Italians, 500 Jews, 500 native-born Americans, and 230 Negro boys. Her general summary of results with conclusions are as follows:

Hebrew, American and Italian children of approximately the same economic status and all known to have no language handicap showed medians as follows: 57.7 per cent of Americans surpassed median of Hebrews; 30.3 per cent of Negroes, and 15.5 per cent of Italians; Negroes equal or exceed the Jews at 9 and 10 years, falling below from 11-12 inclusive. By grade comparisons Negroes and Italians make better showing, equalling or surpassing Americans at many points.

Joseph Peterson,[16] during 1925 and 1928, studied rural and urban sections of Tennessee, Arkansas, and North Carolina, using Pressey Tests, and Peterson's Rational Learning Test. His subjects were 739 white, 734 Negro rural and urban groups; 284 Negro and 274 white children from sections of Tennessee, Arkansas and North Carolina; 119 Nashville white, and 87 Nashville Negroes. His general summary of results is:

Verbal Group tests showed Negroes about 1.5 D. E. units inferior to white children. The Peterson Rational Learning Test showed a smaller, yet consistent difference. Scores of Nashville whites considerably lower than Pressey's Indiana norms; rural whites lower than city whites.

Joseph Peterson and Lyle Lanier, in 1929, studied 119 whites and 86 Negroes in Nashville; 17 whites and 40 Negroes in Chicago; 60 whites and 187 Negroes in New York, using Binet, Myers Mental Measure International Group Tests, Ingenuity Tests (devised by Peterson), Yerkes Point Scale. Their general summary of results is:

The group intelligence tests showed the wide racial variations. Nashville whites scored above New York City whites and Negroes on intelligence tests used, surpassing Nashville Negroes by far. New York Negroes equaled New York whites in general in these tests. The authors conclude that such intelligence tests are too much

[15] Murdoch, Katherine, "A Study of Race Differences in New York City," *School and Society*, Vol. II, pp. 147-50, 1920.
[16] Peterson, Joseph, *The Comparative Abilities of White and Negro Children, Comparative Psychology Monographs*, Vol. I, No. 5.

affected by school background, social experience and linguistic factor. New York City Negroes are superior to whites on ingenuity tests (Rational Learning). The authors conclude that the greater tendency of whites to have an existing "speed set" handicaps them when compared with Negroes who have a hesitation which amounts to "mental lethargy"; nevertheless, this peculiarly aids them in making higher scores than the whites. The authors conclude that the New York Negroes represent a very high selection of the "genes" (intelligence?) of the race in America and the West Indies, the tendency of migration being to concentrate this superior type in such cities as New York.

R. A. Schwegler and Edith Winn,[17] in 1920, applied the Stanford-Binet Tests to 58 whites and 58 Negroes.

Fifty-eight white boys and girls in a Kansas City Junior High School tested 10 points higher on the Stanford-Binet than 58 Negro boys and girls.

Dagne Sunne,[18] in 1917, 1924, and 1925, studied over 1,000 Negroes in New Orleans and a Northern city, using Stanford Revision, Yerkes Revision, National Intelligence Test, Myers Mental Test.

Negro average on National Intelligence Test 1½ years below whites; mental age lower by Myers Test; Yerkes-Bridges gives sex differences between boys and girls higher than race differences although whites were consistently superior. Negro children inferior to whites in tests requiring immediate retention of numerals, estimation of lines and weights, some forms of reasoning; better in tests demanding verbal analysis and facility and constructive imagination.

Dr. E. L. Thorndike,[19] in 1923, studying 349 Negroes and 2,635 whites in "A North Central City," using the I.E.R. Tests of Selective and Rational Thinking, found:

[17] Schwegler, R. A. and Winn, Edith, "Comparative Study of White and Colored Children," *Journal of Educational Research*, pp. 838-48, 1920.
[18] Sunne, Dagne, "Intelligence of Negroes," *Journal of Applied Psychology*, pp. 71-83, 1917; "Comparison of White and Negro Children by Terman and Yerkes-Bridges Revision of Binet Tests," *Journal of Comparative Psychology*, pp. 209-19, 1925; "A Comparison of White and Colored Children," *School and Society*, pp. 469-72, 1924.
[19] Thorndike, E. L., "Intelligence Score of Colored Pupils in High Schools," *School and Society*, Vol. XVIII, pp. 569-70, 1923.

Less than 4 per cent of the colored passed the median white score for the corresponding grade; and this percentage would be a little decreased if the two tests were increased to an infinite number. Of special importance is the difference in the upper range of scores. No colored pupil of all of these 150 scored above 530, and only one above 490. The colored pupils gain only three-fifths as much as whites from year to year of growth.

The diversity of these conclusions, the varied methods employed, the frequent points of contradiction and inadequacy of checks for accuracy, dependableness of selection and the influence of social factors, indicate the difficulty of arriving at definite and final conclusions regarding Negro intelligence.

Educational Standards in Common Schools and the Efficiency of Negro School Children. The intelligence test has been used to determine the capacity of Negro children to learn. The actual efficiency of Negro children under school conditions as they exist today carries still further the task of determining the degree to which potential ability is reflected in actual achievement. Sources which may be drawn upon in discovering this fact are: retardation and elimination figures for both races; the "holding power" of the school system as determined by the percentage of enrollment for the upper grades; and the testimony of such studies as have been made of the comparative achievement of white and Negro school children in the fundamental school subjects, using for this purpose certain standardized educational tests.

Under the section devoted to the common school systems in the North in which Negroes are enrolled, reference has been made to the general existence of much higher retardation for Negroes than for whites, and the partial explanation of an initial mediocre background given for this fact. In this section of the report, typical school surveys and specific studies have been used in obtaining material relating to the other factors to be considered under the general heading of school and student efficiency.

The educational achievement comparisons made between white and Negro children in the report of the Public Schools of Winston-Salem make it especially valuable for studies.

For convenience in interpreting the facts presented here the comparative efficiencies of the two school systems measured in terms of combined factors of facilities, teachers, and teaching equipment expenditures per capita, have been computed from the data given in this report.

The Negro school system is found to be about 66 per cent as efficient as the white. This fact should be kept in mind in considering the comparative ·data given.

TABLE XXX

THE BEGINNING AND THE END OF THE CLASS OF 1923—HIGH SCHOOL DEPARTMENT (WHITE)

Grade	1	2	3	4	5	6	7	8	9	10	11	Graduates
1912-13	429											
1913-14		489										
1914-15			453									
1915-16				440								
1916-17					353							
1917-18						281						
1918-19							253					
1919-20								204				
1920-21									184			
1921-22										152		
1922-23											97	
												81

THE BEGINNING AND THE END OF THE CLASS OF 1923—HIGH SCHOOL DEPARTMENT (COLORED)

Grade	1	2	3	4	5	6	7	8	9	10	11	Graduates
1912-13	610											
1913-14		217										
1914-15			161									
1915-16				197								
1916-17					175							
1917-18						137						
1918-19							103					
1919-20								108				
1920-21									35			
1921-22										49		
1922-23											46	
												39

In the colored schools the elimination along the route began at the second grade. There were 400 children eliminated at the end of the first grade. Of the 610 who were enrolled in 1912-13 only 39 remained to graduate. Principals and teachers must take this high "mortality" into consideration. Every effort must be made to give more children more education.[20]

[20] Tenth Annual Report of the Public Schools of the City of Winston-Salem, North Carolina, 1922-23.

Nineteen per cent of the white and 6.4 per cent of the Negroes finished school. It should be noted, however, that previous to this year the Negro schools ran only 8½ months as compared with 9 months for the whites, and that this is the first year that Negro pupils graduated from a full high school course, it being limited in previous years to the 2nd and 3rd years. The rate of elimination in the Negro schools was more than 3 times as great as that in the white schools of the city, for the high school grades, and for the lower grades from 50 per cent to 75 per cent higher. The same condition is reflected in the age-grade conditions of the schools, as indicated in the following table:

TABLE XXXI

THE AGE-GRADE CONDITIONS IN THE WHITE AND COLORED SCHOOLS

Per Cent	Grades	1	2	3	4	5	6	7	8	9	10	11	Average
Over age	White	31	44	51	56	65	62	65	61	60	63	50	52
	Colored	62	83	85	85	76	78	73	73	74	67	74	74
Normal age	White	69	55	42	42	35	37	33	37	38	36	49	47
	Colored	38	17	15	12	20	23	25	23	24	25	22	25
Under age	White	0	1	3	2	0	2	2	2	2	1	1	1
	Colored	0	0	0	3	2	4	2	4	2	8	4	1

Transmuting the average per cent retardation into efficiency scores, the Negro pupils represent a level of achievement 77.5 per cent that of the whites. This fact should be noted in the light of the relative school efficiency of the Negro school system of 65.8 per cent.

Testing the Results of Instruction. Standardized tests in spelling and handwriting indicate that the efficiency of the Negro pupils is about 75 per cent that for whites. It is an interesting and inescapable fact that comparative school achievement follows closely comparative school efficiency.

TABLE XXXII

AVERAGE SCORES MADE BY WHITE AND COLORED PUPILS OF VARIOUS AGES

NATIONAL INTELLIGENCE TEST

	Ages	7	8	9	10	11	12	13	14	15	16	17	18
Winston-Salem	White	45	46	54	66	79	92	101	120	123	119	109	116
	Colored	33	31	38	40	48	48	62	67	67	64	77	51

SPELLING

	Grades	3rd	4th	5th	6th	7th	8th	9th
Winston-Salem	White	48	64	71	72	73	68	..
	Colored	50	59	66	70	49	55	42

HANDWRITING

	Grades	3rd	4th	5th	6th	7th	8th	9th
Winston-Salem	White	28	32	38	43	61	47	..
	Colored	45	73	77	78	86	83	78

A survey of the Baltimore public schools was made in 1919-20.[21] Two problems of especial significance were found: first, the age-grade progress of white and Negro pupils; and, second, the educational achievements as indicated by the results of standardized tests.

The increases for the whites were in every case larger than for Negroes. In the case of the Negro high school enrollment there was an actual decrease. These disparities were due to two causes: first, the lack of an adequate compulsory attendance law and its less rigid enforcement in the case of Negro pupils; and, second, the then very inadequate facilities to that period for high school education of Negroes which resulted in a decided increase where a high school was provided—e.g., since 1920 the high school enrollment of Negroes has increased 137 per cent and 157.4 per cent over 1913. The white high school enrollment has increased 82.6 per cent over 1920 and 110.7 per cent over 1913.

An analysis of the comparative results of retardation reveals a more or less typical situation. In 1920, the following situation was found:

Elementary Schools

	White			Colored			42 Groups and Cities	
	Boys	Girls	Total	Boys	Girls	Total	1918	Total
1. Under age	1.4	1.6	1.5	1.8	2.8	2.3	12.0	...
2. Normal age	55.0	60.0	59.0	34.0	40.0	37.0	67.0	...
3. Over age	43.0	38.0	39.0	64.0	57.0	61.0	21.0	...

The retardation of the Negro pupils is greater than that of the white but, significantly, the disparity is paralleled by the disparity in the two systems. Measured by the Ayres scale the Negro system here represented is about 80 per cent as efficient

21 *Baltimore School Survey*, Parts III and IV, Vol. II, George Drayton Strayer, Director, 1920-21.

as the white. Transmuting grade loci into indices of school achievement, it is found that the Negro pupils are almost 86 per cent as efficient as the whites. The validity of the contention that retardation is a primary function of school efficiency is further established by comparison with other school systems. In St. Louis, where the system (including white and Negro together) is more efficient as measured by the Ayres index, and where the disparity between the white and Negro systems is not as great, it is found that the retardation of the system, as a whole, is less than Baltimore, and that the disparity in retardation of the system, as between white and Negro pupils, is considerably less. Secondly, in 1926, the Negro pupils had reduced their "normal ageness" by 16.4 per cent. The white pupils during the same period decreased their "over-ageness" by 5.5 per cent, and increased their "normal ageness" by 14.7 per cent.

With reference to the colored pupils the survey report comments as follows:

The non-promotions of colored children show that irregular attendance accounts for practically 50 per cent, both in the elementary and in the high schools.

Irregular attendance is a more frequent cause of non-promotion for boys in the high school than for girls and a less frequent cause in the elementary school. In the elementary school, indifference is also a much more frequent cause of non-promotion among boys than girls. . . . There is less difference between boys and girls in all of these causes among colored children, with the exception of indifference which again affects the promotion of boys more than that of girls.

In 1920, the per cent failing all grades and all subjects for white and colored pupils were as follows:

	Boys	Girls	Total
White	15.0	12.0	14.0
Colored	26.0	22.0	24.0

The survey further reports that:

The tabulation of subject failures for the colored children in the elementary schools shows the same general tendency as for white children. In reading a much larger percentage of colored children fail in the first grade. In all years, except 1920, it represents more than 33⅓ per cent and in 1920 31 per cent. Reading seems to continue more difficult through the second, third, and fourth grades than for white children. A smaller percentage of colored children fail in spelling in the lower grades than for white children, the point of greatest difficulty coming in the third and fourth grades for colored children. Composition, language and grammar and the English branches, when grouped together, follow very much the same tendencies as for white children. In 1920 the percentage of colored children failing in arithmetic fails to show as much improvement over preceding years as does the percentage for white children. During most of the preceding years, arithmetic has been very little more difficult for colored children than for white children, as judged by the percentage failing. The difference between boys and girls is more noticeable among colored children.

Two points should be noted: first, as will be seen later, the poor work done in arithmetic accounts for the poor showing of Negro pupils on the Curtis Arithmetic Test; second, the relative failure of the two groups as indices of scholastic achievement is markedly paralleled by the comparative school efficiencies. The Negro school system is approximately 80 per cent as efficient as the white; the achievement of Negro pupils as measured by subject failure is approximately 87 per cent of that of the whites.

The measurement of spelling ability gives the advantage to the white children, but by no such extreme margin as is characteristic of the divergence in arithmetic scores.

While the intelligence test scores of Baltimore Negro children tend to be lower, relatively, than the scores made in the fundamental educational tests, there is an appreciable trend following the ratio of the efficiency of the system, as compared with the white children.

TABLE XXXIII

COMPARISON OF INTELLIGENCE SCORES IN BALTIMORE AND ELSEWHERE BY AGE

NATIONAL SCALE A

	Ages 8	9	10	11	12	13	14	15	16
Baltimore, White	65	69	83	91	102	111	112	118	123
Baltimore, Negro		55	53	71	73	74	78	103	114
Washington, D. C.	65	73	82	98	113	119	132	122	130

TABLE XXXIV

COMPARISON OF INTELLIGENCE SCORES IN BALTIMORE AND ELSEWHERE
BY GRADE

NATIONAL SCALE A

Grades	4	5	6	7	8
Baltimore, White	67	84	105	123	139
Baltimore, Negro	44	61	84	106	110
Washington, D. C.	63	87	104	118	138

The study investigated the comparative reading abilities of 223 pupils of the Mosley School, Chicago, Illinois, on the basis of the Gray Oral and Silent Reading Tests. The pupils were divided into three groups as follows:

1. Native whites, 86.
2. Northern colored, 80—(those colored pupils who were either born in the North or South, but who were going to school in the North before the 3rd grade in school was reached).
3. Southern colored, 57—(those colored pupils who were either born in the North or South but who received more than three grades of schooling in the South).

The factor of environment was evaluated in the following manner: First, all groups attended the same school and were taught by the same teacher in the same grade; second, since the public school law of Chicago provided that all pupils residing in a certain geographical area shall attend the school in that area, it was assumed, and in this case generally verified, that the socio-economic status of these pupils was practically the same.

The following facts were found:

1. That when the white pupils were compared with the total Negro group (both Northern and Southern combined) they were superior in both oral and silent reading.
2. That when the white pupils were compared with the Northern Negroes the latter did just as well as the whites, and in a few cases excelled them. It was shown quite strikingly that the difference between the whites and the total Negro group combined was considerably greater than that between the Northern Negro and white groups. (The investigation rightly concludes that the environmental differences are considerably in evidence, although the racial factor does not affect the rating of children.)

From the data presented here, the conclusion seems warranted that the efficiency of Negro children as measured by achievement tests in the fundamental school subjects is less than that of white children. This disparity in achievement may be due to one, or both, of the following factors: (a) lower mental capacity of the Negro children; (b) lower efficiency ratio of the Negro school system. Studies, quoted above, indicate that there is a high correlation between school efficiency and the educational efficiency of the pupils. As the efficiency of the school system for Negroes approaches that of the system for whites, the divergence in achievement ratios becomes less noticeable. The assumption holds, at least tentatively, that the inefficiency of Negro pupils is at least as much a function of a poor educational system and an inferior background, as of an inferior, inherited mental constitution.

CHAPTER XX

NEGRO COLLEGES AND
UNIVERSITIES

It is an apt phrase that "the Negro college was named before it was born." The institutions established by missionary effort immediately after the Civil War, of necessity limited their curricula to the literacy status of the recently freed slaves. For 60 years there has been, however, gradual expansion of grades and subjects accompanied by considerable "institution mortality," and the addition of new institutions. At the time of the sweeping study of Negro colleges by Dr. Thomas Jesse Jones, in 1916, only 33 of the 653 existing secondary private and state schools were teaching any subjects of college grade, and only 3, Howard University, Fisk University and Meharry "had student body, teaching force, equipment and income sufficient to warrant the characterization of 'college.' " Nearly half of the college students, and practically all of the professional students were in these institutions. Fifteen others were classed as "secondary and college" with a wide variation in the essentials of college work.

The rating was the first important one for the Negro institutions, and, although proceeding according to definite criteria, was largely based upon an individual determination. The Bureau of Education, for purposes of comparison, mentions 31 Negro institutions in 1916 offering college work and an enrollment of 2,132 students. Since 1916 there has been a pronounced growth in students and standards and the list has been considerably modified. The American Medical Association undertook at this period to classify these colleges for purposes of admission to medical schools into classes I, II, and III. The first class included those Negro colleges accepted "year for year for purposes of admission"; the second, those required to present 50 per cent more work for admission; and the third, those required to present just double the amount of work as Class I.

Only two colleges were given Class I rating. In an interlocking arrangement through membership with the Bureau of Education Committee on the Study of Negro Colleges, the rating is being revised. As a general basis for the new rating the committee has an increase from 31 to 77 (of 79) institutions now doing college work and an increase from 2,132 to 13,860 college students, or 550 per cent.

The paucity of facts about Negro educational institutions prompted the Bureau of Education to initiate a study of Negro colleges.[1] This study made available in 1928 constitutes the most dependable recent data. Seventy-nine institutions were covered in this analysis: 22 publicly supported under state ownership and control including land grant colleges, 9 owned and controlled by independent boards of trustees and privately supported; 31 under white church ownership and control and 17 under Negro denominational church organizations and conferences.

Institutions Governed by Independent Boards of Trustees. In this first group are nine institutions: Tuskegee Normal and Industrial Institute, Tuskegee Institute, Alabama; Howard University, Washington, D. C.; Atlanta University, Atlanta, Georgia; Lincoln Institute of Kentucky, Lincoln Ridge, Kentucky; Morgan College, Baltimore, Maryland; Lincoln University, Chester County, Pennsylvania; Fisk University, Nashville, Tennessee; Hampton Normal and Agricultural Institute, Hampton, Virginia. These showed a total annual income of $2,349, 732 of which 9.63 per cent was from federal appropriations, principally to Howard University, 36.2 per cent from interest on endowments, 30.0 per cent from gifts for current expenses and 19.5 from student fees. The capital investment in the properties of the group amounts to $8,329,507 or $925,500 per institution. Land owned by the institutions totals 3,953 acres, with 384 used for educational activities and 3,269 for non-campus purposes. The management of these schools under independent trustees is regarded as effective and economical.

Publicly Supported and Controlled Negro Institutions. Under this group were included the following 22 schools: Arkansas Agricultural, Mechanical and Normal School, Pine Bluff,

[1] *Survey of Negro Colleges and Universities,* Bulletin No. 7, Bureau of Education, 1928.

Arkansas; State College for Colored Youth, Dover, Delaware; Florida Agricultural and Mechanical College, Tallahassee, Florida; Georgia State Industrial College, Savannah, Georgia; Agricultural and Mechanical College for Negroes, Forsyth, Georgia; Georgia Normal and Agricultural College, Albany, Georgia; Southern University and Agricultural and Mechanical College, Baton Rouge, Louisiana; Princess Anne Academy, Princess Anne, Maryland; Alcorn Agricultural and Mechanical College, Alcorn, Mississippi; Lincoln University of Missouri, Jefferson City, Missouri; Negro Agricultural and Technical College of North Carolina, Greensboro, North Carolina; North Carolina State Colored Normal School, Elizabeth City, North Carolina; State Normal School for Negro Race, Fayetteville, North Carolina; Winston-Salem Teachers' College, Winston-Salem, North Carolina; Colored Agricultural and Normal University of Oklahoma; Cheney Training School for Teachers, Cheney, Pennsylvania; Agricultural and Industrial State Normal College, Nashville, Tennessee; Prairie View State Normal and Industrial College, Prairie View, Texas; Virginia Normal and Industrial Institute, Ettricks, Virginia; West Virginia Collegiate Institute, Institute, West Virginia. These have a combined annual income of $3,201,575 which is the largest of any group because publicly supported. However, the group is larger and individual institution budgets are less than that of the first group. The value of plants and the 5,751 acres of land owned by this group is $10,443,746.

Colleges Controlled and Administered by Negro Church Organizations or Conferences. Seventeen Negro church schools showed capital invested of $6,369,174 and a total annual income of $1,071,636, of which $280,160, or 26.1 per cent, represented state appropriations. They are: Miles Memorial College, Birmingham, Alabama; Selma University, Selma, Alabama; Shorter College, North Little Rock, Arkansas; Edward Waters College, Jacksonville, Florida; Morris Brown University, Atlanta, Georgia; Paine College, Augusta, Georgia; Simmons University, Louisville, Kentucky; Coleman College, Gibbsland, Louisiana; Kittrell College, Kittrell, North Carolina; Livingstone College, Salisbury, North Carolina; Wilberforce University, Wilberforce, Ohio; Morris College, Sumter, South Carolina; Lane College, Jackson, Tennessee; Roger Williams University, Nashville, Tennessee; Paul Quinn College, Waco, Texas; Texas College, Tyler, Texas.

Colleges Owned and Controlled by Northern White Church Boards. This group is divided under the control of several church denominations. The Board of Education of the Methodist Episcopal Church is responsible for: Philander Smith College, Little Rock, Arkansas; Bethune-Cookman College, Daytona Beach, Florida; Clark University, Atlanta, Georgia; New Orleans University, New Orleans, Louisiana; Rust College, Holly Springs, Mississippi; Claflin University, .Orangeburg, South Carolina; Walden College, Nashville, Tennessee; Morristown Normal and Industrial Institution, Morristown, Tennessee; Samuel Houston College, Austin, Texas; Wiley College, Marshall, Texas; and Bennett College for Women, Greensboro, North Carolina; with a total annual income of $527,795 of which practically none comes from the state appropriations. Their properties are valued at $4,403,014. The American Baptist Home Mission Society controls Benedict College, Columbia, South Carolina; Bishop College, Marshall, Texas; Jackson College, Jackson, Mississippi; Shaw University, Raleigh, North Carolina; Morehouse College, Atlanta, Georgia; Virginia Union University, Richmond, Virginia; with an aggregate income of $465,897, and properties valued at $3,265,290. The American Missionary Association controls Talladega College, Talladega, Alabama; Straight College, New Orleans, Louisiana; Tougaloo College, Tougaloo, Mississippi; Brick Junior College, Brick, North Carolina; LeMoyne Junior College, Memphis, Tennessee, and Tillotson College, Austin, Texas; with an annual income of $408,969 and properties valued at $2,867,538. The Board of National Missions of the Presbyterian Church in the United States of America controls Barber College for Women, Anniston, Alabama, and Johnson C. Smith University, Charlotte, North Carolina; with total annual revenues of $174,260, which are to be considerably augmented as soon as one of the colleges commences to receive the yield on its endowment, estimated at from $500,000 to $750,000. The present value of the two plants is $1,129,000. Other colleges under the jurisdiction of Northern white church denominational boards are: Southern Christian Institute, Edwards, Mississippi; Jarvis Christian Institute, Hawkins, Texas;

St. Paul Normal and Industrial School, Lawrenceville, Virginia; St. Augustine's School, Raleigh, North Carolina; and Xavier College in New Orleans, Louisiana.

The annual income of all Negro universities and colleges increased from $2,283,000 in 1918 to $8,560,000 in 1926-27, or about 275 per cent; and the total capital investment in the real properties of the institutions from $15,720,000 to $38,680,000, representing a gain of 146 per cent. Productive endowments increased from $7,225,000 with an annual yield of $361,250 in 1917 to $20,713,000, with an annual yield of $1,701,300 in 1927, a gain of approximately 185 per cent.

Development of School Standards. If normal schools are included in the list, there were in 1926 in all schools of higher training 17,506 Negro students. Fifteen in every 10,000 Negroes as compared with 90 in every 10,000 white were attending college. Of the 1,046 college teachers, 903, or 86 per cent, have obtained degrees earned in course and 139 hold no degrees. There are 883 with undergraduate degrees such as Bachelor of Arts or Bachelor of Science; 107 with professional degrees such as Doctor of Medicine, Bachelor of Laws, and Bachelor of Theology, and 305 hold graduate degrees such as Master of Arts, Doctor of Philosophy, and Bachelor of Divinity.

Teachers' Salaries. One of the notable disclosures of the study was that of the discouragingly low standard of teachers' salaries. These fall into three general classes, which describe the usual range of salaries: the upper, middle and lower salary groups. The institutions under the control of independent boards of trustees pay the highest average salary to the upper third of their teachers, the average being $2,702. The publicly supported institutions which include the land grant and teacher training colleges, pay the second highest, the average amounting to $2,151. Ranking third are the Northern white church institutions, averaging $1,744, and the last on the list is the Negro church college with an average of $1,518.

"An examination of the salaries paid the lower third of teachers, however, shows a situation so discouraging as to demand immediate attention. Although the average salary in the lower third of teachers in the publicly supported institutions is higher than in any other group, it amounts to only $1,141."

Institutions under the control of independent boards of trustees pay even a lower salary to this group of teachers, the average being $1,113, while the average salary of the lower third of teachers in the Northern colleges of church boards and Negro church colleges amounts to but $851 and $828 annually.

Fifty-four of the 79 schools granted degrees in 1926-27. Those that did not were junior colleges and other institutions that lacked a year or more of graduating their first college classes. In 1921-22 there were granted 497 degrees and 169 graduate and professional degrees. In 1925-26 the number of first degrees was 963, an increase of 94 per cent. The graduate degrees numbered 211 in 1925-26, an increase of 25 per cent.

The lack of coordination of the work of the Negro colleges has been a drawback to administrative efficiency in the individual schools and to educational programs generally. Boards have lacked knowledge of one another and their work; there has been little uniformity in the names of schools doing the same grade of work; methods of rating students have been capricious and involved; and, due to the variety of separate controlling boards there has been wasteful duplication of work, funds and physical plants.

The American Missionary Association has taken the lead in reducing the number of small institutions under its supervision and in centering its attention upon the larger and stronger colleges. With the tendency observed in several of the larger universities of the North, to restrict the number of Negro students, and, in the state universities especially, to limit admissions largely to natives of the state, the elevation of standards of Negro colleges in the South has become increasingly important. The movement now is definitely in the direction of developing a few centers of Negro education in the South doing work which can be fully accredited by the highest rating agencies, within the same area but under different boards of control, and the movement has been favored by the philanthropic agencies which have been making large contributions to Negro education. In Atlanta, Morehouse College, Atlanta University, and Spelman College have combined in a stronger institution with a graduate school, under the historic name of Atlanta University, with John Hope of Morehouse as president. In New Orleans, Straight College, New Orleans University and the Flint Goodrich Hospital have been merged into the new James H. Dillard University, named for the present director of the Slater and Jeanes Funds, for many years a passionately active leader in the efforts to lift the level of Negro education. In Nashville, Tennessee, Meharry Medical College and Fisk University, while retaining their separate identities, have made possible the use of certain joint facilities through closer physical proximity.

Negro Doctors of Philosophy. At the end of 1928 there had been awarded to Negroes 44 degrees of the rank of Doctor of Philosophy from 13 American and 4 foreign universities. These have been awarded in Social and Natural Science, Philosophy, Classical Languages, Education, Religion and Modern Languages. Many of these have made notable contributions. W. E. B. DuBois, Harvard, 1895, in the field of History, Economics and Government has published *The Suppression of the Slave Trade, The Negro, Souls of Black Folk;* sociological studies among which were *The Philadelphia Negro;* several important monographs in the Atlanta University Series, and two novels. Since 1910 he has been Editor of the Crisis. Carter G. Woodson, Harvard, 1912, in the field of History, is responsible for important researches in Negro History, among which are *The Education of the Negro Prior to 1861, The Negro in Our History, A Century of Negro Migrations, History of the Negro Church, The Mind of the Negro as Reflected in ·Letters, Negro Orators and Their Orations,* and *Free Heads of Negro Families in the United States in 1830.* He is director of the Association for the Study of Negro Life and History and Editor of the *Journal of Negro History.* George E. Haynes, Columbia, 1912, was for a period Director of the Bureau of Negro Economics in the Department of Labor, Professor of Sociology at Fisk University and is now Secretary of the Interracial Commission of the Federal Council of Churches of Christ in America. He has published *The Negro at Work in New York, The Trend of the Races* and other smaller monographs. Ernest E. Just, Chicago, 1916, is the outstanding Negro scientist in the country and has won international reputation for his researches in biology. Julian Lewis, Chicago, 1915, in Pathology, is an assistant professor at the University of Chicago. St. Elmo Brady, Illinois, 1916, is a research professor at Fisk University and recognized as an authority on alkaloids. Alain Leroy Locke, Harvard, 1913, in Philosophy, is a professor of philosophy at Howard University. One of his noteworthy publications is the volume *The New Negro.* Charles H. Wesley, Harvard, 1925, is a professor of History at Howard University. He is the author of *Negro Labor in the United States from 1850 to 1925.*

R. R. Wright, Jr., the first Negro to receive his degree in Sociology, at the University of Pennsylvania in 1911, is the Editor of *The Christian Recorder,* a publication of the African Methodist Episcopal Church. Francis C. Sumner, Clark, 1920, Charles H. Thompson, Chicago, 1926, W. A. Daniel, Chicago, 1925, Jane McAllister, Columbia, 1928, and others are making valuable contributions, principally in the teaching profession.

Until very recently a problem has been that of finding congenial positions for these scholars. Few of them so far have gone into or remained long in the South. The pay has not been commensurate with the expenditure in education, and with one or two exceptions the character of the institutions has not been attractive. The new emphasis on educational standards, however, in the expanded colleges and consolidated universities has suddenly increased the demand for their services and more are needed than are available.

Industrial Schools. Martin R. Delany, a Pennsylvania Negro of prominence in 1828, in criticizing the current notions about Negro education objected that a beginning had been made "at the superstructure of the building instead of the foundation.—We should first be mechanics and common tradesmen, and professions as a matter of course would grow out of the wealth made thereby." Frederick Douglass, when discussing with Harriet Beecher Stowe 25 years later the best type of educational institution for Negroes, insisted that they needed "more to learn how to make a good living than to learn Latin and Greek." The early industrial schools began as institutional substitutes for apprenticeship. Under the stimulation of the extraordinary personality and leadership of Booker T. Washington their usefulness became clearly apparent.

They have run a gauntlet of white and Negro opinion. Beginning with a practical objective for the newly emancipated Negroes, who needed to learn first how to earn a livelihood, the idea of learning to work with the hands seemed to Negroes superfluous, after the terrible discipline of slavery. Moreover, it lacked the lure and glamor of spectacled erudition, and fell in time under the suspicion of the sensitive freedmen. This suspicion was enlivened by the disposition of many white patrons either to support only the industrial education with its implication of limited capacity, or to insist that the function of the schools should be the preparation of domestics. Many of the smaller struggling institutions boldly and shamelessly exploited this appeal and their activities went far towards coloring the concept of this type of training for Negroes. Thus, the fundamental features of value in the institutions were for a period obscured by an emotional conflict over motives. The spread of technical education, the demands of industrial expansion and the utilization of this base in the educational philosophies of Montessori and John Dewey had in time the effect of imputing greater dignity. Negro sentiment, however, had not been changed sufficiently on this point before many of the schools had responded to the pressure by expanding their college subjects. The trade training has not been abandoned; rather the training has been intensified by the addition of theory and general cultural subjects. The increased requirements of the state departments in the South for Negro teachers would have forced the same changes in the curricula independently of any other factor, and in some instances actually did. Tuskegee and Hampton now award the degree of Bachelor of Science.

There were in 1925, 323 Negro Normal and Industrial Schools large and small, which (if Hampton Institute is added) had a total of 2,883 teachers and 73,557 students. The State Agricultural and Normal Schools commonly referred to as the Land Grant Colleges have another large group of students.

The total industrial and non-college students in these schools in 1925 was 9,245. Since this period the number has of course materially increased. The land grant college survey undertaken in 1928 by the Bureau of Education will reveal data comparable to that provided in the survey of Negro colleges. Impetus has been given to industrial education for Negroes and whites by this federal cooperation with local governments as well as by the passage of the Smith-Hughes Act in 1917 which provided actual joint support from state and federal funds for vocational education.

TABLE XXXV

State Agricultural and Mechanical Colleges

Organized	Name of Institution	College Courses	Other Courses
		Per Cent of Students in Particular Colleges	
1875	Agricultural and Mechanical College for Negroes (Normal), Ala.	2.6	97.4
1875	Agricultural, Mechanical and Normal School (Pine Bluff), Ark.	5.1	94.9
1895	State College for Colored Students (Dover), Del.	...	100.0
1887	Florida Agricultural and Mechanical College for Negroes	14.1	85.9
1891	Georgia State Industrial College	3.1	96.9
1886	Kentucky Normal and Industrial Institute for Colored	13.1	76.7
——	Southern University (Baton Rouge), La.	14.1	85.6
——	Princess Anne Academy, Md.	...	100.0
——	Alcorn Agricultural and Mechanical College, Miss.	11.1	88.9
1866	Lincoln University, Mo. ....,......	31.2	68.8
——	Negro Agricultural and Technical College, N. C.	11.3	88.7
——	Colored Agricultural and Normal University, Okla.	4.3	95.7
——	Colored Normal Industrial and Mechanical College, S. C.	28.6	71.4
——	Agricultural and Industrial State School, Tenn.	42.4	57.6
1881	Prairie View State Normal and Industrial College, Texas	16.3	73.7
——	Virginia Normal and Industrial Institute	5.8	94.2
——	West Virginia Collegiate Institute	24.6	75.4

Total—Those taking college courses 17.7
   Those taking other courses 82.3

There has been a revival of complaints among Negro educators, but in a different direction. They are protesting the disposition of public school officials to ignore vocational training for Negro youth in Negro schools, and the sudden and disturbing willingness of these authorities graciously to grant Negroes the inexpensive "classical" training, while centering the expensive equipment of vocational training in the white schools alone. The failure of the Negro teachers, of school officials, and parents to impute sufficient dignity to this type of education is being recognized as responsible for a vast social and economic waste.   President W. D. Bluford of the Agricultural and Technical College of Greensboro, North Carolina, instituted a survey of 3,000 Negro high school students to determine the careers for which they were preparing themselves.   Only 41 were planning to enter agriculture, although 75 per cent of the Negroes of the state were engaged in agriculture; 9 planned to enter science, 16 engineering, 52 the ministry and social service; 83 business; 207 trades; 249 "clerical work," and 2,062 the professions of medicine and law.   Faced with the fact that over 90 per cent of the population at the high school age level eventually fall into the non-professional work and are for the most part unprepared for it, the disproportion in occupational objectives becomes indeed disquieting.

CHAPTER XXI

WHERE NEGRO CHILDREN PLAY

Interest in recreation as a formal problem for study is of comparatively recent development. This, no doubt, accounts in part for the fact that few studies and no important general statistics appear to be available. To this fact, however, must be added the circumstance of a small amount of actual work in this field for Negroes.

In order that some reasonably adequate picture of Negro status in this field should be presented, it became necessary to go beyond available studies and scattered reports, and make specific inquiries in the 75 cities with largest Negro populations selected as most important for the purposes of this study.

The problem of recreation for Negroes appears to take this general aspect:

(a) In the larger cities of the North, where long established Negro communities are in proximity to city parks and playgrounds, the Negro children have access to them along with other children. Parks are freely open; however, it most frequently occurs that difference in management, population ratios, and equipment, influence in various ways the use of the playgrounds.

(b) In cities of the North where new Negro residence areas are in proximity to parks and playgrounds, there is access to these, but frequent racial friction tends to influence attendance adversely.

(c) In certain Northern and "border" cities playgrounds have been designedly located near Negro residence areas, and special attendants, sometimes white, sometimes Negro, placed in charge. These are used chiefly and freely by Negro children, but the number of children benefiting by them is an almost negligible proportion of the number of children of playground ages.

(d) In cities of the South recreation facilities are meagre for whites as well as for Negroes. However, there are several cities in which special provisions have been made for Negroes, but space and equipment are inadequate in nearly all of them.

(e) The most common point of racial friction in the recreation field has been in the use of the swimming pools.

(f) Where expenditures have been made for Negro recreation in cities of the South they bear a relationship to expenditures for white children similar to the relation which expenditures for Negro education bear to expenditures for white education.

(g) Where there are public parks in the South, unless specifically set aside for Negroes, it is usually assumed that they are for the exclusive use of the white population.

Thirty-two of the 75 cities of largest Negro population responded to the queries regarding parks, playgrounds and other recreation centers for their Negro population, and 23 of them yielded information of some value. Baltimore, Maryland, has one playground and several playfields for Negroes, a swimming pool and tennis courts in Druid Hill Park. During the summer there are 119 school yard leaders for white and 17 for Negro children. The average daily attendance during 1928 for Negro children was 250. The Negro population of Baltimore is about 110,000. Brooklyn, New York, and New York City had no separate playgrounds set aside for Negro children. In Brooklyn they play together. In New York City there is one small plot used as a playground in Harlem. School yards are employed during the summers. Charlotte, North Carolina, has 16 playgrounds of which 4 are used by Negroes, and 4 parks none of which are used by them. Chicago has 4 fairly well-equipped playgrounds, which employ a total of 14 leaders. Three of them have skating ponds for winter play, and 1 a baseball diamond. These are in the Negro residence areas. Concerning the parks, the report states:

The Commissioners of Lincoln Park have no separate parks or playgrounds set aside exclusively for the use of Negroes. We have 6 small parks attached to the system and Negroes are welcome to use any and all of the recreational facilities offered.

One of our parks, Seward, is located in a fast-changing district, white to colored, and we estimate that about one-third of the attendance at this park is now colored. Many of the athletic teams of this park are composed of Negro athletes.

A few Negroes play golf at the Lincoln Park public golf course and some use the bathing beaches, mixing in with the whites. They are not over-welcome by the whites but as yet we have had no serious trouble.

Of 81 playgrounds in Cleveland 8 are used by Negroes. They have access to all of the 9 parks of the city. In Denver 2 of the 27 city playgrounds are used. In Knoxville, Tennessee, they use 2 of the 14 playgrounds. The city has 20 parks which, however, are not used by them. Philadelphia has 90 Board of Education playgrounds of which 24 are used by Negro children. The median daily attendance is 85. Waco, Texas, has 7 playgrounds and 18 parks. Negroes have 2 playgrounds and may not use the parks. The daily attendance at these playgrounds is 550, and there are 1 paid worker and 2 volunteer supervisors.

Twelve cities providing fuller information are grouped:

TABLE XXXVI

	Estimated Number Negro Children	Average Daily Attendance	Per Cent Attendance	Total Number Paid Negro Workers
Atlantic City	4,425	150	3.3	..
Baltimore	5,100	200	3.9	14
Dayton	2,910	500	17.0	8
Detroit	15,713	400	2.5	26
Houston	3,700	309	8.0	0
Los Angeles	3,284	130	4.0	7
Lynchburg	3,310	508	21.6	4
Macon	8,283	300	3.6	3
Memphis	11,543	100	.08	2
New Orleans	24,817	300	1.0	1
San Antonio	5,010	400	7.0	3
Savannah	12,143	600	4.0	3

In all the cities reporting, except Denver, Philadelphia, Baltimore, and Houston, Texas, support of recreation was derived from municipal funds. Denver and Philadelphia conduct recreational activities through the Board of Education which has a tax levied. Baltimore gets one-half of its support from city taxes, and the rest from the Community Fund, and Houston, Texas, received her support jointly from the City Council and Community Fund.

Summarizing these returns briefly, it appears that in both the North and South one important condition of free participation in play facilities is separation; that where public support is not sufficient for an adequate dual system, the Negro facilities suffer; and that in 28 of the cities there are means for accommodation of not more than 8 per cent of the Negro children. Lynchburg, Virginia, and Dayton, Ohio, of the cities reached, appear to offer the largest recreation opportunities to Negroes.

A feature which should be noted is the consistent opposition to Negroes in swimming pools and on golf courses. There is here the possibility of a question for study in the former, inasmuch as the Chicago riot was touched off by an incident at a bathing beach; difficulties at Atlantic City centered around the use of the beaches by Negroes which threatened to dislodge Negro workers from their positions as waiters in the resort hotels; and questions have been raised in the Young Men's Christian Associations, Young Women's Christian Associations, Physical Training Departments of colleges and universities, as well as public swimming pools. Detroit, New York, Minneapolis, Philadelphia and Washington have registered specific objections to the playing of golf by Negroes on the public links.

In the summer of 1927 Forrester B. Washington of the Atlanta School of Social Work undertook a study of recreation facilities for Negroes. His data include returns from 57 cities, 40 of which were located in the North and 17 in the South. This material which was prepared for the joint use of the National Interracial Conference and the volume on the *American Negro* issued by The Annals of the American Academy of Political and Social Science, is presented here in abstract.

Southern Cities

Atlanta, Ga.	Lexington, Ky.	Orlando, Fla.
Baltimore, Md.	Macon, Ga.	Richmond, Va.
Birmingham, Ala.	Memphis, Tenn.	Savannah, Ga.
Columbus, Ga.	New Orleans, La.	Tampa, Fla.
Houston, Texas	Norfolk, Va.	Washington, D. C.
Jacksonville, Fla.	Nashville, Tenn.	

Northern Cities

Atlantic City, N. J.	St. Joseph, Mo.	Philadelphia, Pa.
Berkeley, Cal.	Kansas City, Mo.	Pittsburgh, Pa.
Burlington, Iowa	Lansing, Mich.	Rock Island, Ill.
Buffalo, N. Y.	Milwaukee, Wis.	South Bend, Ind.
Canton, Ohio	Montclair, N. J.	Sandusky, Ill.
Colorado Springs, **Col.**	Minneapolis, Minn.	Springfield, Mass.
Cincinnati, Ohio	Morristown, N. J.	St. Louis, Mo.
Cleveland, Ohio	Mason City, Iowa	Scranton, Pa.
Decatur, Ill.	New Bedford, Mass.	Toledo, Ohio
Detroit, Mich.	Newark, N. J.	Van Wert, Ohio
Duluth, Minn.	New York City	Wichita, Kan.
Des Moines, Iowa	Oakland, Cal.	Watertown, N. Y.
Fort Wayne, Ind.	Port Huron, Mich.	Zanesville, Ohio
Indianapolis, Ind.		

These returns are summarized in the following tables:

TABLE XXXVII

PUBLIC RECREATION—SEVENTEEN SOUTHERN CITIES

	Whites Only	Segregation			No Facilities
		Complete	Some	None	
Playgrounds	o	8	o	o	3
Parks	4	13	o	o	o
Recreation centers	3	3	o	o	11
Bathing beaches	3	11	o	o	4
Swimming pools	10	6	o	o	1

TABLE XXXVIII

PUBLIC RECREATION—FORTY NORTHERN CITIES

	Whites Only	Segregation			No Facilities
		Complete	Some	None	
Playgrounds	o	o	7	33	o
Parks	o	o	o	40	o
Recreation centers	o	2	23	12	3
Bathing beaches	5	11	12	o	12
Swimming pools	3	2	29	3	3

TABLE XXXIX

PRIVATE RECREATION (SOCIAL SERVICE)—SEVENTEEN SOUTHERN CITIES

	Whites Only	Segregation	No Facilities
Recreation centers, settlements, community centers	7	3	7
Playgrounds	9	2	6
Y.M.C.A.	2	15	o
Boy Scouts	14	3	o
Swimming pools	10	6	1
Summer camps	12	5	..
Camp Fire Girls	15	2	o

TABLE XL

PRIVATE RECREATION (SOCIAL SERVICE)—FORTY NORTHERN CITIES

	Whites Only	Segregation Complete	Some	None	No Facilities
Recreation centers, settlements, community centers	5	24	6	5	..
Playgrounds	0	1	34	5	..
Y.M.C.A.	2	22	6	10	..
Boy Scouts	0	14	14	12	..
Swimming pools	..	4	30	6	..
Summer camps	..	13	9	18	..
Camp Fire Girls	..	18	22	10	..

TABLE XLI

COMMERCIAL AMUSEMENT—SEVENTEEN SOUTHERN CITIES

	Whites Only	Segregation Complete	Some	None	No Facilities
Moving-picture theatres	4	3	10	0	0
Pictures and vaudeville houses	2	2	10	..	3
Outdoor amusement parks	2	10	0	0	5
Legitimate theatres	3	0	11	0	3

TABLE XLII

COMMERCIAL AMUSEMENT—FORTY NORTHERN CITIES

	Whites Only	Segregation Complete	Some	None	No Facilities
Moving-picture theatres	0	0	33	7	0
Pictures and vaudeville houses	0	0	24	16	0
Outdoor amusement parks	3	0	19	11	7
Legitimate theatres	0	0	26	14	0

Other Data. Recreation facilities for Negroes as recorded by the Playground and Recreation Association of America and supplied through E. T. Atwell include the following outdoor playgrounds.

Open year round (42 cities), 82; open summer months (85 cities), 181; open other seasons (9 cities), 17; total number of playgrounds for Negro children open in 1927 for first time (28 cities), 37.

Indoor recreation centers for Negro citizens are reported to the number of 103; open year round (24 cities), 44; open school year (24 cities), 45; open other seasons (7 cities), 14; total number of indoor recreation centers for Negro citizens open in 1927 for first time (9 cities), 9.

Community houses for Negro citizens as reported included 36; open year round (24 cities), 27; open school year (2 cities), 3; open other seasons (6 cities), 6.

The major activities were: music, athletics, social recreation, dramatics, games, handicraft, literary and civics groups.

Local Studies of Negro Recreation Needs. The Mayor's Inter-racial Committee in 1926 included in its survey of the Negro population of Detroit, a section on recreation needs. Detroit, incidentally, is among the most advanced of the cities in this regard, having increased its provisions from 1 paid play director in 1915 to 5 in 1927. In April of 1928, the City Council voted the expenditure of $268,000 for a recreation center for Negroes in the heart of the Negro community. The survey in 1926 revealed the following:

52 playgrounds and playfields having recreation center buildings;
118 swimming pools included in these centers;
151 recreation centers in schools, churches, etc.;
4 community buildings;
1 bathing beach;
1 summer camp;
8 other play areas.

And other tables show the number and race of play directors:

NUMBER AND RACE OF PLAY DIRECTORS

	1915		1920		1925		1926	
	White	Colored	White	Colored	White	Colored	White	Colored
All year	40	1	60	2	80	5	80	5
Summer	100	3	175	5	300	12	325	16

The Y.W.C.A. and Y.M.C.A. are particularly active among children and form the chief private agencies in this field. The Y.W.C.A. is in need of suitable buildings for recreational work.

Among the other active agencies are the Franklin Street Settlement, the Sophie Wright Neighborhood House, the Highland Park Community House, the Tau Beta Community House, the Urban League Center, the St. Augustine Community House, and the Baptist Christian Center, which has an attendance made up entirely of colored people. Some of the churches also have social programs that take the children on outings of various kinds. Of 1,000 colored heads of families responding to study schedule cards sent out, the majority said that they patronized theatres regularly. All of the theatres are open to Negroes, though in some there are restrictions in seating. Pool rooms also figure here as a big source of amusement and seem to be free from gambling and unwholesome atmosphere. Sports, such as baseball and automobile races, are patronized by Negroes.

Professor William H. Jones, of Howard University, published in 1927 the results of a survey of recreation and amusement among Negroes in Washington, D. C. The study includes both commercialized and non-commercialized recreation, and an attempt was made to trace certain behavior sequences to inadequate recreation and amusement facilities. "Six of the 25 playgrounds supported and supervised by the city government are for Negroes." Only one of these is equipped with a swimming pool. The playgrounds are well supervised and equipped. In addition there are 12 school yards opened as playgrounds in the summer. Among the pathological consequences which he thought might be attributable to inadequate recreation in Washington were forms of community disorganization, prostitution, gambling, alcoholic orgies, and hidden night life. The rigid exclusion of Negroes from the theatres of Washington, Mr. Jones feels, has stimulated the practice of "passing for white."

The Chicago Health Survey, in 1927, stated, regarding recreation facilities for Negroes generally, that "in the city as a whole, the average population to each acre of park area is 507.4. However, in the second and third wards where the population is largely Negro there is an average population of 8,059.9 per acre of park space. Two of the city's largest parks, however, Jackson and Washington, are at no great distance from these wards. The two playgrounds which at present serve the Negro communities are totally insufficient, although they represent significant and important beginnings in providing adequate recreational facilities for Negroes in Chicago."

The recreation section of the Fort Wayne survey of the Negro population, made by the National Urban League, reports 9 playgrounds with a registration of 3,000 children or about

30 per cent of the school census enumeration. White and Negro children use all playgrounds, and only in one has there been racial friction. The order on all other playgrounds was satisfactory. There was some evidence that conditions surrounding the Holman grounds (nearest the Negro community) were largely responsible for its difficulty. The Wheatley Center is the only formal recreation center for Negroes in the city. It organizes clubs, provides inside recreation hours and arranges camping parties. A program which sponsored social dancing had to be discontinued because of protest from the Negro ministry. Pool halls seem to furnish much of the recreation for young men, and they are usually conducted in an orderly fashion. The inadequacies in the field of public recreation are largely responsible for the seeking of illegitimate recreation, according to the report. "The family histories revealed in answer to the question 'where do you spend your leisure time' that the majority of them spent it at home."

The recent study of Negro problems in cities, made under the direction of T. J. Woofter, carries the summary of recreation by Henry J. McGuinn: "In general, Negro playgrounds are less numerous, smaller, poorer in equipment and less adequately supervised than playgrounds for white children in the same city." One important observation was that of actual programs in these playgrounds: The programs offered young children, it was found, were decidedly more attractive than programs offered preadolescent boys and girls. "The reason for this is not hard to seek. Programs in most instances are not provided because, so far as the needs of Negro youths are concerned, most of the cities studied have not yet supplied adequate play space for this group of boys and girls."

In Cincinnati, according to a first published report of the Public Recreation Commission in 1927, there are more than 100 white and 26 Negro park supervisors, instructors and attendants. There were also 6 community centers for whites and 2 for Negroes; 7 public school gymnasia for white and 2 for Negroes, which are open on certain nights during winter weeks.

Playground, the monthly magazine of the Playground and Recreation Association of America, summarizing advances made in recreation in various cities in the South, called attention to Negro participation in new developments in Lynchburg,

Virginia; Durham, North Carolina; and Columbus, Georgia. In Lynchburg a new Community Center was opened at a church, and football and basketball leagues organized to correspond to the white group. In Durham a Negro club gave $500.00 for a wading pool for the one Negro playground.

Ernest T. Atwell, of the Playground and Recreation Association, pointing to the need for further recreational programs for Negroes, observed that "of the nearly 4,600 play centers reported, there were 147 used by colored children exclusively."

In the general recreation movement it is estimated that there are about 11,000 paid supervisors of recreation. Of this number, some 2 per cent are Negroes.

Some Special Recreation Programs. The one outstanding organization in the field of recreation for Negroes is The Playground and Recreation Association of America through its colored work division, of which E. T. Atwell is the director. The policy of the association is that when a city-wide program is organized it should plan to include opportunities for all groups.[1] Special examples are cited alongside those reported in previous tables.

The Festival of Negro music given by the Community chorus in New Haven was made up entirely of music by Negro composers. A concert of Negro spirituals rendered in Syracuse by 200 local Negroes after a few weeks' training was most favorably commended by the press. In New Orleans a similar production was given successfully by a group of 275 colored musicians. Sufficient funds were raised through this concert to employ an assistant colored recreation director and in addition a special worker to direct the future music program of the colored chorus which is to function permanently. Through such events it is the aim to develop special benefits of lasting value to both the colored people and for the entire community.

"The Mile Stones of a Race," a pageant depicting the achievements of Negroes was given by a cast of 500 under the leadership of a colored worker from the Association. "Ethiopia," "The Spirit of Education," and "Loyalty's Gift," are other pageants and tableaux creditably given by amateur talent in local communities. "Loyalty's Gift" has been given by colored people in a number of cities in various sections of the country, but its rendition at the

[1] Playground and Recreation Association of America Maintaining Community Service, Bulletin No. 91.

Sesqui-centennial in Philadelphia made an outstanding impression. Such work by the Association has developed a wealth of talent, valuable to the community and to the colored people themselves as a phase of wholesome expression and activity.

Each year the Association has conducted an institute for the training of colored playground and recreation center workers. In the 8 schools held thus far 217 colored men and women have been trained and are now serving the recreation needs of their own people in cities and towns throughout the country. During 1926, 28 requests for such leaders were cared for by the Association.

Many and varied methods have been used by the colored people to obtain funds with which to provide their community play and recreation facilities. To an increasing degree municipal appropriations and community chest contributions have been secured. In most cases, however, group plays, musical programs, and social entertainments with the colored people themselves furnishing the talent, have been the chief source of revenue. Especially in the initial stages of their work is it necessary to depend upon such means of financial support. Their resources are extremely limited and the community at large does not always respond to their efforts until time has demonstrated their benefits.

Perhaps the most valuable by-product of this work with the colored groups has been the bringing together of important white and colored leaders, thereby building better inter-racial understanding.

The Young Men's and Young Women's Christian Associations. The most extensive institutionalized recreational work for Negro youth is conducted by the two above organizations.

The Young Women's Christian Association reaches young Negro girls through 65 local branches composed of Negro members and governed by interracial boards. Special emphasis has been placed upon the South, and in all, some 135 secretaries are employed. Through the Girl Reserve movement, industrial and business clubs and its regular institutional features, an important measure of service is provided in communities for a somewhat limited number of girls.

The Young Men's Christian Association. The "Association" movement among Negroes dates back to 1907, when George Foster Peabody's gift of a building in Columbus, Georgia, was followed by a gift of a building in Washington. Four years later, however, it received its greatest impetus when

Mr. Julius Rosenwald made a contribution of $25,000 for a building in Chicago and offered, for a period of five years, to contribute a similar amount to any other city that would raise at least $75,000 from Negro and white citizens. Eighteen cities have profited by this offer and in 1928 the organizations had developed to the point that there were 78 city and 140 student associations, 4,469 directors and committeemen and a membership of 40,000. Some 75 Hi-Y clubs, 18 employed boys' brotherhoods and 44 young men's divisions associated with local organizations are counted. The property valuation of the Negro associations is $4,894,000 and the operating expenses amount to $683,800, of which amount 90 per cent is raised through income-producing features of the work. The recreation features during 1928 as listed by Mr. Channing H. Tobias, included promotion of 2,292 "socials" for men and boys, 532 motion picture exhibits, 1,126 boys sent to summer camps, and some 5,000 taught swimming and life saving. In the regular gymnasium classes were 9,658 men and boys.

Some Recreation Needs. The director of Colored Work for the Playground and Recreational Association offers these as acute recreation needs: (a) Facilities for small Negro populations of from 1,000 to 10,000, and rural towns. These are the greatest sufferers for lack of any program. Large cities provide something even though commercial and debilitating activities are more highly financed and available. (b) It is most desirable that interracial interest be secured, so that more serious and real consideration be given to provision and support of facilities and employment of trained colored leadership where groups for major activities are for some reason not including or welcoming the Negro. This effort might invite a more equitable disbursement of present tax funds and chest funds in this more important factor in social, economic and citizenship improvement.

CHAPTER XXII

LAW OBSERVANCE AND ADMINISTRATION

Since the emancipation of the Negroes practically all the records agree that, with certain recent and notable exceptions, the Negro crime rate has been greatly in excess of the white. Explanations of this have come from three directions. One of these is based upon convictions of a native lower level of intelligence and civilization which renders Negroes less sensitive to the ordinary interests of society; another is based upon the feeling that disturbed social conditions following emancipation were responsible for the larger infractions of the law. This carries the implication of correctability through education, through strengthened economic foundations and increased social responsibility. Finally, there is the explanation that these higher rates are due to a greater willingness on the part of the administrative machinery to suspect, arrest and convict a Negro. Studies of Negro crime have accepted as a starting point one or the other, and sometimes two of these explanations.

The Negro Crime Rate. From the single record of prison populations, the only comprehensive census data on this point, it is not possible to secure an uninvolved picture. One of the most widely known of the crime studies involving Negroes is McCord's *The Negro as a Dependent, Defective and Delinquent.* It is not recent but represents in large measure the data employed in similar studies of the period. McCord holds that "the average Negro is a child in every essential element of character, exhibiting those characteristics that indicate a tendency to lawless impulse and weak inhibition." He cites figures for Atlanta, Georgia, of arrests by race from 1906 to 1913, for crime which show the Negro average per cent to total population as 26.03 in 1906 and 21.23 in 1913, while that of the white was only 7.95 and 5.83, respectively.

He concludes that there are more Negro convicts in Georgia

than there are Negro college graduates in the United States; that there are more than five times as many Negro convicts as college graduates; that there are more feeble-minded Negroes in the United States than there are Negro school teachers; that there are twice as many insane Negroes in hospitals as college graduates; that the Negro race is a child race as indicated by the fact that he loves praise, respects power without malice; kindness is soon forgotten by him; he is brutal; impulsive; revels in the marvelous; is a victim of his own appetites and

TABLE XLIII

PERCENTAGE OF NEGROES IN PRISON POPULATION, 1910

	In Total Population	Among Prisoners and Juvenile Delinquents	
		Enumerated Jan. 1, 1910	Committed During Year
United States	10.7	30.6	21.9
The South	29.8	70.1	58.9
South Atlantic	33.7	72.0	61.6
East South Central	31.5	73.1	63.6
West South Central	22.6	62.4	46.0
The North	1.8	13.1	9.6
New England	1.0	4.6	2.6
Middle Atlantic	2.2	12.8	9.4
East North Central	1.6	14.7	11.0
West North Central	2.1	20.8	14.4
The West	0.7	5.9	3.2
Mountain	0.8	7.8	4.4
Pacific	0.7	4.6	2.5
United States Penitentiaries	...	31.3	24.6

fancies, is lacking in foresight; is the victim of itinerant agents; thinks laboriously; is imitative, childlike in his moral conceptions; and is ever open to mental suggestion.[1]

Statistics of Negro crime left the following impressions: While "colored people" contributed 12.1 per cent of the general population in 1900, he points out, they contributed 32.6 per cent of the prisoners enumerated in 1904. This was about three times as many as the white. Between 1890 and 1900 the proportion of Negroes in the total population decreased from 11.9 to 11.6, the percentage of criminals increased from 30.4 to 32.6.

In 1904 the prisoners in 1,337 prisons were enumerated by

[1] McCord, Charles H., *The American Negro as a Dependent, Defective and Delinquent.*

the Census Bureau.   There were in these prisons, at the time, 50,111 white and 26,661 colored persons.   There were committed to these prisons that year, 125,093 white persons, and 24,598 colored persons.   In 1910, the prisoners in 3,198 prisons were enumerated.   There were in these prisons at that time, 72,797 white and 38,701 colored persons.   During the year there were committed to these prisons 368,468 white persons and 110,319 colored persons.

The rate for Negroes is much higher in the Northern than in the Southern states.   Attention is called to this by Reuter.

Although the Negro crime rate, based upon the record of commitments is three to four times that of the whites, it is considerably lower than that of certain other groups in the population.   In 1904, Reuter notes,[2] the commitments per 1,000 for certain nationalities were: Mexican 4.7, Italian 4.4, Austrian 3.6, French 3.4, Canadian 3.0, Russian 2.8, Poles 2.7, and the Negroes 2.7.

TABLE XLIV

COLORED PERSONS IN PRISON

Year	Northern States	Southern States
1870	2,025	6,931
1880	3,774	12,973
1890	5,635	19,244
1904	7,527	18,530
1910	10,081	28,620

PRISONERS PER 100,000 OF COLORED POPULATION

Year	Northern States	Southern States
1870	372	136
1880	515	221
1890	773	284
1904	765	220
1910	722	323

Ninety and two-tenths of all committed in 1910 were males and 9.8 females.   For Negroes these percentages were 80.9 for males and 19.1 for females.   For whites the ratio of men to women was 13 to 1; of Negroes 4 to 1.

Judging by the figures alone per 10,000 Negro population, the commitments were 88 in the South, 283 in the North and

[2] Reuter, E. B., *American Race Problems.*

366 in the West. "In other words, the Negro is three times more likely in the West to be committed to prison than he is in the South." [3]

The percentages of Negroes for total commitments were slightly more than one-fifth in 1910, but for grave homicide it was over one-half, and for lesser homicide 49.0 per cent; for assault, 41.1 and for burglary about one-third.[4]

In 1923, according to the most recent figures of the Bureau of the Census, Negroes formed 31.3 per cent of the prison population and 23.3 per cent of the commitments. Their population proportion was 9.3 per cent.

Statistics of prison populations present an unrepresentative picture when studied comparatively by race. If these are over-weighed by the fact of longer sentences for one of the groups involved, it follows that there will always be a larger residuum of one set of prisoners each year to increase the total for this group.

In 1910 the percentage of Negroes who received prison sentences of over one year was about three times as high as the percentage of the white commitments. In 1900 approximately one-third of all Negroes committed to prison received sentences of one year or more; of the white commitments for the same year less than 10 per cent received sentences of one year or more. The percentage distribution of Negro and white commitments under sentence of imprisonment only for the year 1910 appears in the following tabulation.

Length of Sentence	Percentage Distribution	
	Negro	White
Total	100.0	100.0
Life	1.7	0.2
One year and over	28.3	8.2
Less than one year	58.8	74.3
During minority	4.5	5.6
Indeterminate	5.9	11.2
Not reported	0.7	0.4

Of the total number of persons sentenced for one year or longer 40.9 per cent were Negroes, while of those sentenced to terms of less than one year only 13.4 were Negroes. This difference is in part sectional rather than racial. In the South where the bulk of the Negroes reside the proportion of long

[3] Reuter, E. B., *American Race Problem.*
[4] Comparison of prison sentences by term of Commitments, 1910.

prison sentences for both races is greater than in the North. This, however, does not explain the entire difference, for within the same section and state the percentage of Negroes among those committed for long terms is greater than among those sentenced for short terms, and the percentage of Negroes increases as the length of the term of imprisonment increases.

Police Reports of Negroes Arrested. Although attempts were made to secure data from the chiefs of police of seventy-five cities on Negro and white arrests and convictions, satisfactory returns were not available. The records were not separately tabulated, or if separately tabulated not given out, or if given out, sparse. Methods of keeping records were varied and unstandardized, making the task of obtaining a full picture essentially impossible. Fairly comparable reports as provided by police officials of ten cities for the year 1927 are given in the following table:

TABLE XLV

	Year	Number of Negro Arrests	Total White and Negro Arrests	Per Cent[5] Negro Population to Total	Per Cent Negro Arrests to Total
Cincinnati, Ohio	1927	3,638	25,495	7.5	14.2
Atlantic City, N. J.	1927	2,869	6,864	21.3	29.4
Columbus, Ohio	1927	4,630	10,481	9.4	29.8
Cleveland, Ohio	1927	6,763	25,156	4.3	21.1
Milwaukee, Wis.	1927	1,582	30,985	0.5	4.84
Detroit, Mich.	1927	7,112	25,065	4.1	22.1
Minneapolis, Minn.	1927	432	10,834	1.0	3.83
Washington, D. C.	1927	38,061	53,302	25.1	41.6
Wilmington, Del.	1927	2,155	6,442	9.8	25.0
Baltimore, Md.	1927	24,547	108,745	14.8	22.5

In Dayton, Ohio, the Negroes formed 8.5 per cent of the population, but contributed 43 per cent of the total arrests; in Pittsburgh, from December 1, 1922, to May 31, 1923—"The number of Negroes arrested represented 9 per cent of their population, while the number of white persons arrested represented only 4 per cent." In Detroit, the rate is more than twice as high for Negroes as for whites. In the District of Columbia, the total number of arrests among Negroes exceeded that of whites in the majority of felonies and misdemeanors. In Baltimore, Maryland, in 1927, of 108,745 arrests 24,547 were Negroes. The chief offenses by race were:

[5] Per cent Negro population as of 1920.

Chief Offense	White	Colored
Disorderly conduct	8,665	7,307
Disturbing the peace	3,579	6,873
Larceny	1,421	1,615
Suspicious characters	425	515
Burglary	386	640
Drunkenness	4,335	1,140

Examination of available records of Negro crime prompts these observations as a preface to further analysis:

1. It is difficult to secure dependable data on Negro crime, because (a) general crime records are poor and comparative figures less dependable, and (b) racial factors enter, influencing the agencies of law enforcement most frequently to the disadvantage of the Negro and the Negro records of crime.

2. The Negro crime rate as measured by all comparative records is greater than that of the white.

3. The difference varies widely and according to geographical location and population ratios; it also varies by types of offenses.

4. There is a much higher Negro rate for homicides than white, even when the emotional factors referred to are taken into account.

5. Negro arrest rates are higher than white for petty offenses and lower than white in commitment to prison for serious offenses.

6. There is obvious discrimination in the administration of laws on the part of the police, magistrates, judges, and pardon boards, which explains an undetermined degree of the disparity between white and Negro rates.

7. It is possibly true that Negro rates of crime are more nearly actual crime rates of Negroes than white recorded rates are of crimes committed by whites.

8. Illiteracy, unfavorable environment, age distributions, and unfamiliarity with city and urban life, are factors to be seriously studied in relation to present Negro crime.

Special Studies of Negro Crime. During the period, January 1, 1924, to June 30, 1924, there were 15,734 arrests made in Philadelphia;[6] 3,842, or over 24.4 per cent, of those were Negroes, while the Negro constituted 7.4 per cent of the total population. Seven out of every 1,000 whites and 29 out of every 1,000 Negroes were arrested during this period. Two factors promptly appeared to temper the figures: (a) many of these arrests do not indicate crime; and (b) many were, on

[6] Thompson, A. J., *A Survey of Crime Among Negroes in Philadelphia.*

trial, discharged or proved not guilty. Convictions prove not a fair index to Negro crime for there were many Negro convictions on trivial offenses, for which whites would not ordinarily be arrested. Cases are cited illustrative of this fact. Only .6 per cent of the total Negroes were charged with rape, and .6 per cent with murder. Of 98 persons charged with crimes of serious enough nature to be held without bail for higher court, 28 were charged or suspected of highway robbery, 14 for rape, 10 for forcible entrance and larceny, 9 for aggravated assault and battery, and 6 for murder. The other charges were less serious. The greatest number of males were arrested for attempted or suspected larceny. The next largest number of arrests was for violation of prohibition ordinances and laws. The rate of arrests for males was 48 out of each 1,000 males, for females, 8 out of each 1,000. The greatest number of arrests occurred between the ages of 20 and 25, and the next greatest between 25 and 30.

Of the 3,842 Negro arrests, 1,282, or 33.1 per cent, of the total Negroes arrested were discharged. Strong suggestion that many of these arrests were unwarranted is found in the detailed account of what disposition was made of these arrests; 26.2 per cent were held for higher court; 13.9 per cent were sentenced to from 5 to 30 days in the county prison; 9.6 per cent were fined, and 3.2 per cent got sentences of from 3 months to 3 years in the House of Correction. No uniformity was found in the disposition of the other cases.

Lack of adequate housing, the vicious environment of the "Negro section," and the lack of recreational facilities, are cited as contributing factors to the high rate of crime. These are reinforced by the fact that many unwarranted arrests are made of Negroes; that it is difficult for the Negro arrested to prove his innocence. These facts explain in part but do not alter the situation of a larger proportionate share of crime by Negroes.

Ruth M. Miller [7] in 1924 based a study upon police records in Pittsburgh covering a period from December 1, 1922, to May 31. Newspaper clippings and case studies of offenders handled by the Associated Charities, the Urban League and Morgan Community House were used to supplement these figures.

In Pittsburgh, as in Philadelphia, the number of arrests

[7] Miller, Ruth M., *Negro Delinquency in Pittsburgh.*

among Negroes was greater than among whites. During the period studied, there were 26,476 arrests of which number 3,678, or 13.8 per cent, were Negroes. The number of Negroes arrested represented 9 per cent of their population in Pittsburgh, while the number of white persons arrested represented 4 per cent. In Pittsburgh more Negroes were discharged because of lack of sufficient evidence to hold them than whites. The percentages were 36.7 for the Negroes and 33.2 for the whites. More Negroes were penalized than whites.

The environmental factor is again pointed to in the Negro crime rate. Poor housing conditions, inadequate recreational facilities, an insufficiency of positive forces to counteract the evil influences of the communities in which they are forced to live, and exploitation by white criminals and politicians are underlying causes of Negro delinquency.

The ages at which arrests were most frequent were between 18 and 30; there was an extremely small percentage of arrests under 15 and a sharp decrease after 30. Seventy-one per cent of the male delinquents, and 49 per cent of the females were unmarried. Ninety-five per cent of the total delinquents were laborers and practically all of them were from the lower economic strata. Sixty-five per cent of the males and 55 per cent of the females were employed; 85 per cent of the males and 93 per cent of the females claimed residence in Pittsburgh. Ten per cent of the males and 5 per cent of the females were immigrants and 5 per cent of the males and 2 per cent of the females were homeless.

A grouping of the types of offenses committed by Negroes reveals the fact that most of them were petty offenses. Thirty-one and seven-tenths per cent of the total number of Negroes arrested were arrested for drunkenness.

As to what the police figures actually tell when published the findings of the investigator are most illuminating. Instances of the overlapping of the classifications of charges were seen, in the cases of those who are charged with disorderly conduct, who in reality were guilty of a variety of offenses: carrying concealed weapons, cutting other persons, attempting suicide, abusing family, petty theft, or who were merely witnesses of some offense. Even a greater variety of offenses are booked under the Suspicious Person charge. There seemed to be no distinction made between a bawdy house and a disorderly house, or between a disorderly house and a gambling house in charging persons with keeping or visiting the same. Gambling, loitering, reckless driving and vagrancy, are all violations of a city ordinance and are included under charges named after the respective offenses, as well as under the charge, "violation of City Ordinance." The disposition in most of the cases seemed to indicate the whim of the magistrate rather than the merits of the case, and were often out of proportion to the offense committed. Negro delinquents were more frequently single young men between the ages of 18 and 30 of the laboring class. They lived for the most part in congested lodging areas and lacked sufficient influence to protect themselves if they would from the encroachment of vice. Although a larger percentage of Negroes was arrested for petty offenses, a higher percentage of them was penalized than of whites. Both police and the magistrates, the study indicated, were guilty of discriminations.

Dr. W. T. Root [8] in 1927 made a psychological and educational survey of 1,916 prisoners in the Western Penitentiary of Pennsylvania, under the Board of Trustees of the Western Penitentiary. The Negroes' share in various crimes as revealed by his study was as follows:

TABLE XLVI

PERCENTAGE OF CRIME [9]

	Native White		Negro	
	I	2	I	2
Robbery	38.1	16.8	35.1	10.5
Larceny	17.4	7.6	11.7	3.4
Burglary	5.6	2.5	6.7	2.0
Embezzlement	2.0	.8	....	....
Forgery	4.0	1.7	0.4	.1
Rape	12.3	5.4	3.5	1.0
Sodomy	1.9	.8	2.4	.7
Pandering	.5	.2	....	....
Homicide	12.3	5.4	28.2	8.4
Felonious assault	4.1	1.8	11.8	3.5
Labor trouble	.4	....	....	....
Arson	....	.6	....	.05
All crime	44.1	44.1	30.0	30.05

[8] Root, W. T., Jr., *A Psychological and Educational Survey of 1,916 Prisoners in the Western Penitentiary of Pennsylvania.*
[9] No. 1 based on total racial groups; No. 2 based on prison groups.

The report shows that the Negro commits 13.69 times as much crime as the native white group, and four times as much as the Italian group; 13 times as much predatory crime as whites; 5.48 times as many sex crimes; 34.22 times as many crimes of violence; and has 13.69 times as many cases of sodomy charged against him.

Concerning types of crime and the mental ages of prisoners committing them by race, the findings of the study were as follows:

TABLE XLVII

Crime	White	Negro	Mental Age White	Negro
Robbery	86.4	71.3	13-10	11-5
Larceny	84.8	68.0	13-7	10-11
Burglary	88.2	71.5	14-1	11-5
Rape	77.9	66.0	12-5	10-7
Sodomy	80.0	65.5	12-10	10-6
Homicide	82.7	67.0	13-3	10-9
Felonious assault	80.5	64.3	12-2	10-3
All crimes	77.4	69.3	12-5	10-11

It was estimated that about 15 per cent of the Negro group was psychopathic.

Interesting data are given on birthplace, age of leaving home, marital and religious status and native factors of crime.

The Negro rate as in the other studies is high as compared with that of other races:

When incidence of population is taken into consideration, the Negro has committed more crime than any other racial group. He surpasses every group in every specific crime except embezzlement and 'labor trouble' offenses in which he does not figure at all. In the majority of cases, the frequency is many times that of any other race, and the peak is reached with felonious assault, with a frequency 41.07 times that of the native whites.[10]

Nature and Factors of Crime

Drink	25.4 per cent	21.7 per cent left home under 16
Women	20.4 " "	41.2 " " were married
Gang	9.8 " "	67.8 " " " Protestant
Gambling	9.5 " "	5.1 " " " Catholic
Emotional	28.8 " "	27.1 " " " indifferent
Out of work	56.0 " "	
Circumstance	?	

[10] Root, W. T., Jr., *A Psychological and Educational Survey of 1,916 Prisoners in the Western Penitentiary of Pennsylvania*, p. 215.

Of those Negroes in the prisons 50 per cent appeared to have been there for some reason connected with unemployment; about 80 per cent came from outside of Pennsylvania, while 10 per cent came from city and county in Pennsylvania.

Root gives these causes for the high rate of crime among Negroes: (1) unfavorable social conditions such as poor housing and environment and social humiliations produced by the caste system; (2) the larger number of unmarried "floaters" drifting into the city from other districts; (3) the tendency of the law to allow white offenders to go unpunished and to give heavier sentences to Negro offenders in some cases; (4) lack of education for definite trades and general habits of mind which would unsuit the Southern migrant for life in a Northern city; (5) the low mental ability of a large number of these "floaters" which makes them more liable to exploitation; (6) their illiteracy which makes them unsuitable for some jobs, and race prejudice which bars them from others; (7) the effect of the American caste system's application to the entire race. Dr. Root thus concludes:

The Negro criminal is a victim of a vicious circle of social, biological and economic causes; lack of education, no trade training commensurate with the intelligence he has; a set of moral, social and leisure habits adjusted to a rural Southern community; a victim of caste, forced to live in discarded houses of the dominant race; restricted in employment and social opportunity, the Negro is forced daily to feel inferiority and humiliation in a thousand ways. All this must be given consideration if judging his status in the criminal world.[11]

The report of the Detroit Bureau of Governmental Research, 1926, devotes a section to crime which provides a summary of all crimes, felonies, and misdemeanors committed by Negroes in Detroit for the periods January 1 to June 30, 1926, and for 1913-19.

[11] Ibid., p. 217.

ARRESTS AND CONVICTIONS FOR 1913-19

(A study made by the Bureau of Government Research)

	Arrests Per 10,000 Population	Ratio Colored to White	Convictions Per 10,000 Population	Ratio Colored to White
MALE				
Colored	4,008.0	2.59	1,015.5	1.92
White	1,554.0	1.00	526.9	1.00
FEMALE				
Colored	1,676.7	5.6	843.00	8.56
White	299.4	1.0	98.44	1.00

ARRESTS AND CONVICTIONS FOR JANUARY 1 TO JUNE 30, 1926

(Present Survey Study)

MALE				
Colored	1,450.4	2.57	600.9	2.03
White	563.0	1.00	294.7	1.00
FEMALE				
Colored	1,008.4	6.93	506.7	9.57
White	147.5	1.00	52.9	1.00

From the table it is obvious that (a) the ratio of arrests and convictions of Negro women has uniformly increased; (b) while there seemed to be fewer male arrests in 1926 than in 1913-19, convictions have been more frequent in the case of both males and females.

Of serious crimes the largest number of Negro arrests was for larceny, 142.2 per 10,000 population as compared with 17.7 per 10,000 for whites; the highest percentage, however, was for unarmed robbery—61.2 per cent of total arrests for that crime and 61.3 per 10,000 population as compared with 38.7 and 3.3 for the whites. Murder came next with 57.1 per cent of total arrests for that crime, and 13.1 arrests per 10,000 population. In every crime listed, the Negro rate was higher than that of the white; the rate per 10,000 varied from .5 for Negroes and .4 for whites in manslaughter and negligent homicide to 424.8 per 10,000 for colored and 37.6 for whites for accosting and soliciting.

The greater number of criminals charged with accosting and soliciting in the Detroit Study fall within the ages of 20 to 40. The same is true for convictions, and of inmates of the House of Correction. There is a high percentage of arrests and convictions among single men and women: The rate is 53.7 per cent of total arrests for Negro males and 63.4 for white males; 63.2 per cent for Negro females, and 80.4 for white females. About the same ratio is found in convictions.

Among the causes listed as important in the high rate of crime were: the abnormal increase of the Negro population including a number of migrants from the South, with their differences in manners and customs and difficulty of adjustment to a Northern urban environment; overcrowding, poor social environment, economic pressure, and the tendency to arrest Negroes for slight offenses, or without warrant and to convict them for minor charges.

Discussion of the treatment of Negroes by the police revealed unnecessary brutality on the part of the police, and that often the police were in league with houses of prostitution and crime.

The study of Chicago Negroes found that although the Negro population increased from 2.1 of the total in 1910 to 4.5 in 1919, over 100 per cent, the Negro crime rate for that period increased 50 per cent, or less than half as rapidly as the Negro population. The Commission discussed critically the difficulty of securing accurate statistics on Negro crime, and after receiving the testimony of judges and other officials that Negroes were [12] consistently more readily arrested, and convicted than whites and received larger sentences, concluded that such data as were available for examination would be both inaccurate and misleading. While, for example, the figure for Negroes might be a reasonable measure of the serious offenses committed by Negroes, it is not so accurate a measure of the serious offenses committed by whites with whom they are compared. The Chicago Crime Commission found in 1919 that while the police records showed only 1,731 total burglaries or persons arrested for burglary, during the first eleven months of the year 5,509 actual burglaries had been reported.

An example of the uncertain character of ordinary official statistics of Negro crime is afforded in two Minneapolis studies covering the same period. The first, by Charles Davis, of the Hennepin County Law Enforcement Society, found that in 1924, 930 adult Negroes were convicted in the Municipal Court,

[12] *The Negro in Chicago.*

and that in 1925, 892 were so convicted. A series of cases of pandering, involving Negro men and white women was cited. Employing the record of the indictments of the Grand Juries for the first ten months of 1926 an extremely high percentage of Negro criminals in the major offenses was found. The study concluded as follows:

This condition is bad and is rapidly growing worse. Unless some method is devised to at least subdue the activities of these Negroes, there is certain to be a series of race riots in Minneapolis, followed by the usual lynchings and killings which always disgrace any civilized community when these outbursts occur.

Maurine Boie's study grew out of the report made by the Grand Jury in October, 1925, which expressed alarm over the findings in Mr. Davis' study. The number of arrests for colored people were noted. Five hundred and twenty-three for 1923; 389 for 1924; and 478 for 1925. It will be remembered that the first study by Davis, quoted above, gave 470 convictions in 1923, 930 in 1924 and 890 in 1925. It was discovered further that there had been errors in the handling of the statistics by clerical workers. Moreover, "arrests" had been counted as "convictions" by the first study without obvious excuse. Police officials when questioned in the conviction that there had been serious errors accepted the later study as more nearly correct. Of the 389 arrested in 1924, 310 were convicted; 50 cases were dismissed, 2 found not guilty, and the disposition of 27 not handled by the municipal court. The majority of arrests were made for vagrancy, or for being found in a disorderly house or in a gambling house. A large number of arrests were for prostitution. Few violent crimes had been committed.[13]

Carl M. Rosenquest of the University of Texas attempted an analysis of crime in Texas by occupational status. To quote the premise of this study:

In the struggle for a living each man develops characteristic methods which he finds successful or are forced upon him by the limitations of his ability and training. These methods . . . constitute his "occupation" and represent the adaptations he has made to the demands of competition. . . .

[13] An analysis of Crime Statistics for Minneapolis for 1923, 1924 and 1925.

The study included 1,531 Negroes, 1,468 whites and 361 Mexicans. The modal age for whites and Mexicans was 22 and for Negroes 21. The most common white and Mexican crime was. burglary, followed by violations of the liquor law. The most common Negro crime was murder. The rate was twice that of the white. Total illiteracy was 18 per cent of the convict population; the general rate for Texas was 8.5. Separately considered in relation to the Census:

	Convicts	Census
White	6.7	2.4
Negro	24.5	18.7
Mexican	36.5	34.1

Of the literates the modal grade passed in school was for whites 7th, Negroes 4th, and Mexicans 2nd. Crimes against persons correlated with illiteracy. Of burglars 25 per cent had been unemployed, of thieves 16 per cent, of forgers 9.2 per cent, of murderers 3.3 per cent, suggesting some relationship between unemployment and certain types of crime.

One of the most thorough and careful studies of Negro crime is carried in the *North Carolina Chain Gang* by Jesse F. Steiner and Roy M. Brown.[14]

On October 1, 1926, there were approximately 2,500 prisoners in all the county chain gangs in the state of North Carolina. Only 48 of the 100 counties at the present time chain gangs, but these cover slightly more than half of the total area of the state and comprise two-thirds of the entire population, including nearly all the more progressive and wealthy counties which have taken an active interest in the construction of good roads. Of the total number of prisoners on October 1, 1926, more than 1,600 were Negroes and about 800 were white. This statistical study includes 1,521 prisoners—1,036 Negroes, 469 whites, and 16 Croatan Indians. These prisoners were in 33 prison camps in 20 counties. The study, therefore, includes about five-eighths of the county chain gang prisoners in the state. The proportion of white to Negro prisoners in the group studied is approximately the same as that for the whole state.

Of the 1,052 Negroes and Croatan Indians, 496, or 47 per cent, were unskilled laborers; 230 or nearly 22 per cent farmers; 117, or 11 per cent, belonged in the skilled trades, mechanics, plasterers,

[14] Steiner, Jesse F. and Brown, Roy M., *The North Carolina Chain Gang.*

etc.; 85, or 8 per cent, were workers in factories, chiefly factories of tobacco; 75 individuals were in domestic service; the remaining 49 prisoners belonged to various occupations.

The Negro offender appears more liable to commit crimes of violence. The Negro does not get sentenced to the roads for fighting with his hands any more frequently than the white man, but assaults with a "deadly weapon" form a larger percentage of his offenses, and he is more frequently convicted of violence against women. Housebreaking, including all breaking and entering, constitutes 8 per cent of his crimes; and larceny 31 per cent; the white prisoner's record in these two offenses is 4 per cent and 25 per cent respectively. The white man, on the other hand, appears more prone to forgery and check passing, to offenses against morality, and to violation of the prohibition law.

The prisoners were used chiefly for road construction without attempt to classify them according to types of work for which they were best fitted, or degrees of criminality, or recidivism. Discipline was extremely harsh. It was believed that no improvement in character could come to persons given such a system of treatment.

In 1915 Dr. Frederick Hoffman began the publication of *The Homicide Records of American Cities*. This rate for Negroes was recorded as excessively high; in Memphis, Tennessee, in 1915 the number recorded was 115. Durett and Stromquist followed this with a study of violent deaths registered in the cities of Atlanta, Birmingham, Memphis and New Orleans for the years 1921 and 1922. These authors point out among other things that Dr. Hoffman's figures were in error. Instead of 115 Negro homicides in Memphis for the year in question the number was 79. The homicide rates for the four cities over a 2-year period were quoted:

TABLE XLVIII

HOMICIDE RATES PER 100,000 POPULATION IN ATLANTA, BIRMINGHAM, MEMPHIS AND NEW ORLEANS, 1921-22 [15]

	Per Cent Colored Population	White	Homicide Rates Colored	Total
Atlanta				
1921	31.0	14.7	99.4	40.9
1922	30.3	15.2	107.0	43.0
Average	30.7	15.0	103.2	42.0

[15] Durrett, J. J., and Stromquist, W. G., "A study of violent deaths reg-

	Per Cent Colored Population	White	Homicide Rates Colored	Total
Birmingham				
1921	39.2	29.2	86.4	51.6
1922	39.2	26.7	108.0	58.6
Average	39.2	28.0	97.2	55.2
Memphis				
1921	37.3	35.6	94.3	57.3
1922	36.9	23.6	139.2	66.3
Average	37.1	29.6	116.8	61.8
New Orleans				
1921	26.2	7.2	47.2	17.8
1922	26.2	9.5	46.2	19.0
Average	26.2	8.4	46.7	18.4

Oxley [16] reports that of the 199 men and 1 woman "committed to the penitentiary at Raleigh, North Carolina, for execution by electrocution, 148 were Negroes and 52 whites" (p. 3). Of the convictions represented by this number, the frequency distribution was:

	White	Per Cent	Colored	Per Cent	Total
Rape	4	7.7	37	25	41
Murder	46	90.3	104	69	150
Burglary	1	1.9	8	5.4	9

It is the opinion of the North Carolina study that the prevalence of illiteracy has contributed largely to the high crime rate for Negroes. Sixteen per cent of the white and 34 per cent of the Negroes in penal institutions were totally illiterate. One hundred and fifty-one Negroes between the ages of 14-20 years were unable to read a newspaper, and Oxley points out the fact that they are all within the school age and have grown up since the adoption by the state of North Carolina of a compulsory school attendance law. Not one of the Negro prisoners convicted of a capital crime had gone beyond the sixth grade in school.

Rape. A great part of the concern about Negro crime, particularly in its bearing upon lynchings in the South, centers around the question of rape. The table below gives the rate of commitments for rape by race in 1910, the last year for which the detailed data are available for all persons in prison:

istered in the cities of Atlanta, Birmingham, Memphis, and New Orleans for the years 1921-22."
[16] Oxley, L. A., "Capital Punishment in North Carolina," Special Bulletin No. 10, Raleigh, North Carolina, 1928.

Commitments for Rape Per 100,000 Population in 1904

Whites	0.6	Austrians	3.2
Colored	1.8	Hungarians	2.0
Italians	5.3	French	1.9
Mexicans	4.8	Russians	1.9

The Negro rate is lower than that of any group except native whites. An interesting comparison of the Negro rates for rape was made a few years ago by James Weldon Johnson of the National Association for the Advancement of Colored People.

When the Congressional Committee on Immigration in 1911 made its study of crime in the United States, an investigation was made of 2,262 cases in the New York Court of General Sessions, and in that investigation it was found that the percentage for the crime of rape was lower for Negroes than for either the foreign-born whites or native whites.

Contrast these records, bad as they may appear, with the records for New York County, which is only a part of New York City, and we find that in this one county in the single year of 1917, 230 persons were indicted for rape. Of this number 37 were indicted for rape in the first degree.

That is, in just a part of New York City the number of persons indicted for rape in the first degree was 9 more than the total number of Negroes lynched on the charge of rape in the entire United States during the period of 1914-18. Among these 37 persons indicted by the New York County Grand Jury, there was not a single Negro. The evidence required by the Grand Jury of New York County to indict a person charged with rape must be more conclusive than the evidence required by a mob to lynch a Negro accused of rape.

Professor Thorsten Sellin of the University of Pennsylvania has this to say about the figures of Negro arrests and convictions in Detroit:

The conviction rate was higher for the whites for the crimes of larceny, unarmed robbery, assaults, murder, drunkenness, gaming, begging and vagrancy, but since the rate was based on arrests, and not on cases brought to trial, it is clear that the higher rate of convictions for the white is primarily the result of unwarranted arrests of Negroes, particularly since the white rate was shown to be higher for some of the offenses for which the Negro is commonly arrested, such as gaming, drunkenness, vagrancy, etc.

For the period covered by the survey 48.6 per cent of the colored defendants in the Recorder's Court were convicted of felonies, as compared with 43.8 per cent of the whites. Of the colored, only 7.1 per cent were given the alternative of a fine or a prison sentence, while 13.5 per cent of the whites were so sentenced. Only 7.2 per cent of the Negroes were given probation, while 12.2 per cent of the whites got it. The fact that probation may have been refused to the Negroes because of lack of facilities for proper probation work with them, or because their social environment made them extremely bad risks does not alter the situation much, since, in the last analysis, discrimination was responsible for the existence of these conditions. A slightly larger proportion of Negroes received a suspended sentence, very likely as a substitute for probation. Altogether, 30.9 per cent of the Negroes and 15.5 per cent, or half as many, whites were sentenced to imprisonment. Some of the discrimination portrayed here is in itself apparent only and may be due to a larger proportion among Negroes of serious offenses calling for heavier penalties. When misdemeanors alone are studied, the Detroit survey shows that a larger proportion of Negroes than whites were given the alternative of a fine or imprisonment, but 8.5 per cent of the Negroes and 5 per cent of the whites were given jail sentences, and twice as many whites as Negroes were given a suspended sentence or placed on probation.

He points to a similar situation in the record of cases decided in the circuit courts of Alabama in 1920-22.

The percentages of acquittals, based on cases brought to trial, proved much lower for the Negro than for the white for all serious offenses, except for robbery. For the biennium 1924-26, arson took the place of robbery as the only serious crime in which the Negro acquittal rate showed to advantage.

CHAPTER XXIII

JUVENILE DELINQUENCY

For general figures on Negro juvenile delinquency the most comprehensive are provided by the Bureau of the Census, 1923. These, however, relate only to children in institutions, and. provide no clue to actual extent. The cost of institutional care is one considerable factor. Another more confusing one is the tendency in the direction of placing children in homes, which goes hand in hand with the tendency of institutions to accept "child" delinquents who in earlier counts were not included as delinquents. The detailed information provided by the institutions is valuable, however, in pointing to the major elements in the delinquency problem.

Extent of Delinquency Among Negro Children. In all institutions for delinquents on January 1, 1923, there were 29,468 children of which number 5,412 were Negroes. This was about 18 per cent of all children in institutions. Of those in prisons and reformatories, however, there were 1,031 white and 619 Negroes, and of those in jails and workhouses, there were 293 whites and 287 Negroes.

While the Negroes were 18 per cent of the delinquents, they were 37 per cent of all children in prisons and reformatories and 49 per cent of those in jails and workhouses.

Colored delinquents, says the official report, more often than white, were imprisoned for nonpayment of fine—50.7 per cent of the colored as compared with 26 per cent of the white. Twenty boys under 18 years of age were sentenced to imprisonment for life. Eleven of these boys were white and 9 were Negro. Two and three-tenths per cent of the Negro children received sentences of 5 years and more, and 1.4 per cent of the white children received sentences of this length. Fifty per cent of the Negro children and 26 per cent of the white were imprisoned for nonpayment of fine during the first 6 months of 1923.[1]

[1] Children Under Institutional Care, 1923, Department of Commerce, Bureau of the Census.

Regarding illiteracy and school attendance the percentage was much smaller in 1923 than in 1910—3.5 as compared with 8.6. Illiteracy among white juvenile delinquents decreased from 6.8 per cent to 2.4 and among Negro children from 18.5 per cent to 10.7. Among boys illiteracy was reduced from 9 per cent to 4.1, and among girls from 6.3 per cent to 1.6.

In the lower ages the percentages not attending school before commitment were much higher for the Negro children than for the white. Almost one-fourth (23.1 per cent) of the Negro children under 12 years had not been attending schools, as compared with 6.3 per cent of the white children under 12. The percentage of Negro 12-year-old children not attending school was more than twice as high as the corresponding percentage of white children practically the same age; somewhat larger percentage of white than of colored children 17 years of age were not attending. Of the Negro children 14 and 15 years of age, 2.9 per cent had never attended school, and 37.3 per cent had failed to reach the fifth grade. The corresponding percentages for white children were 0.4 and 17.4. In the age group 16 years and over, 3.8 per cent of the Negro children never attended school, and 33.1 per cent had not reached the fifth grade, the corresponding percentages for white children being 1.7 and 15.2.

Using the census figures available only as late as 1910, it appears that both white and Negro delinquency is increasing, the Negro rate, however, more rapidly than the white. By sectional divisions it is evident that those sections with greatest facilities for handling delinquents are those with highest recorded rates per 100,000 population.

TABLE XLIX

JUVENILE DELINQUENTS PER 100,000 OF POPULATION [2]

Divisions	White			Colored		
	1890	1904	1910	1890	1904	1910
United States	23.5	29.7	25.7	25.5	34.4	39.2
North Atlantic States	39.6	48.6	34.9	215.4	208.9	199.0
North Central States	21.8	26.9	27.6	147.9	200.7	226.0
South Atlantic States	13.9	20.9	19.2	15.7	23.9	25.1
South Central States	2.8	4.3	7.4	4.3	4.6	10.8
Western States	12.1	28.4	24.0	4.7	45.9	244.5

[2] Reuter, E. B., *The American Race Problem.*

Judges of children's courts in 12 cities were asked in course of this compilation in 1928 for an estimate of Negro delinquency as reflected in the cases coming to their attention. Two of these have comparable data :

PER CENT OF ALL CRIMES COMMITTED BY NEGRO BOYS AND GIRLS

Year	Ramsey County, St. Paul, Minnesota	Children's Court, New York City
1914	2.6	2.8
1915	2.6	3.9
1916	1.5	3.9
1917	1.3	3.3
1918	1.2	3.3
1919	.62	4.2
1920	.5	4.2
1921	2.0	4.5
1922	2.6	4.9
1923	2.6	5.5
1924	1.2	5.7
1925	1.2	7.9
1926	1.1	8.4
1927	3.7	7.9

With the exception of Knoxville, Tennessee, the 11 cities for which there were reports show a higher percentage per 100,000

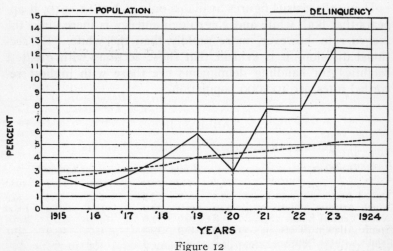

NEGRO PERCENT OF TOTAL CASES OF JUVENILE DELINQUENCY AS COMPARED WITH PERCENT TOTAL POPULATION CLEVELAND, OHIO, 1915-1924

Figure 12

population among Negro delinquents than among native whites. The Knoxville study explains that there are no Negro probation officers to report cases, and no institutions in which to place them and so they are not arrested. In St. Louis, Missouri, the Negro population is approximately 10 per cent of the total population; however, there were 1,074 Negro juvenile arrests or 26 per cent of the total for 1927.

The table listed below traces the increase in Negro and white delinquency in Cleveland between 1915 and 1924.

TABLE L

INCREASE IN NEGRO JUVENILE DELINQUENCY IN CLEVELAND, 1915-24

Year	Number of Delinquents			Per Cent of Delinquents		Cases Per 1,000	
	Colored	White	Total	Colored	White	Colored	White
1915	60	2,136	2,196	2.7	97.3	2.9	3.2
1916	47	2,540	2,587	1.8	98.2	2.1	3.7
1917	89	2,857	2,946	3.0	97.0	3.3	4.0
1918	157	3,277	3,434	4.5	95.5	5.3	4.5
1919	207	3,295	3,502	5.9	94.1	6.4	4.4
1920	110	2,998	3,108	3.5	96.5	3.1	3.9
1921	195	2,300	2,495	7.8	92.2	4.9	2.9
1922	190	2,243	2,433	7.7	92.3	4.2	2.7
1923	314	2,232	2,546	12.3	87.7	6.2	2.6
1924	291	2,088	2,379	12.2	87.8	5.2	2.4

Woofter and McGuinn [3] in a discussion of delinquency emphasize the lack of recreation as a cause of delinquency to the extent that juvenile delinquency is discussed under the heading "Recreational Needs." They found the rates for several cities as follows:

JUVENILE DELINQUENCY IN SEVEN CITIES

	Estimated Negroes in Total Population Per Cent	Negroes in Total Juvenile Cases Per Cent
Richmond (average 1921-24)	31.5	41.0
Chicago (1925)	5.0	16.0
Indianapolis (1925)	12.0	35.0
Gary (1925)	14.0	41.0
Dayton (1923)	6.0	27.0
Memphis (1925)	31.0	48.0
Charleston (1925)	47.0	75.0

Causes Assigned for Negro Juvenile Delinquency. In all of the reports and studies which attempt to assign causes for the high rate of Negro juvenile delinquency, and for juvenile delinquency in general, these are cited: low wages, making it

[3] Woofter *et al, Negro Problems in Cities.*

necessary for both parents to work away from home leaving the children without proper supervision; broken homes; and lack of supervised recreation. In the reports of the Negro delinquency in Northern cities, migration also counts as a contributing cause, as does forced proximity to houses of prostitution, "bootlegging joints" (which find it easy to thrive with little molestation from authorities in or around the Negro districts), together with the usual crowded housing conditions in the Negro sections of most cities to which Negroes have migrated. To this list of causes Reuter adds "illiteracy of parents" and, especially in the South, "race prejudice."

Offenses. The studies analyzed, excluding the Detroit Survey, give the most frequent delinquencies as disorderly conduct, desertion of home, waywardness and ungovernable habits. "These three charges," says the New York City study of Delinquent and Neglected Children, "are ordinarily regarded as among the less serious offences, and more attributable to improper parental control, from whatever cause, and to unpleasant home surroundings than to a dangerously anti-social nature." They constitute 60 per cent of the total in the New York study. Stealing ranks next in importance for boys; while for girls, "ungovernable and waywardness" and "desertion from home" are the charges usually given, these two accounting for 58 per cent of their delinquencies. In Detroit it was found that larceny ranked highest for Negro boys representing 20 per cent of the total for Negro offenders; incorrigibility ranked second with 14.2 per cent and unlawful use of automobile third (13.3 per cent). For Negro girls immorality is the highest charge being 76.4 per cent of the total. The migrant population is believed to have affected this rate, and environmental conditions are again emphasized.

An ultimate problem upon which all the studies agree is that of inadequacy of institutional care for Negro delinquents and dependents, or of sufficient provisions for placing them in homes. Practically all of the judges and agencies report overcrowded conditions and long waiting lists. The New York and Brooklyn Society for the Prevention of Cruelty to Children has an average of 2 to 42 days of waiting in the Society Shelter by Negro children who had been committed to various institutions. One girl waited 104 days before there was room for her in the institution to which she had been assigned. In Knoxville it was found that some of the Negro children deliberately committed offences because they knew that the court could not sentence them because of lack of institutions to which they could be sent.

The "Study of Delinquent and Neglected Negro Children" is summarized in some detail because it happens to be a thorough study in a representative Northern community:

1. In 1925, of a total of 11,512 cases in the New York City Children's Court, 890, or 8 per cent, were cases of Negro children; of these 61 per cent were delinquents; Negro boys brought into court for delinquency outnumbered the girls three to one.

2. On the basis of population the proportion of juvenile delinquents among Negroes is considerably greater than among the whites, but whereas the most common charge against white boys is stealing, that against Negro boys is disorderly conduct; the offence second in importance among Negro boys is desertion of home, whereas among white boys who are brought to the Children's Court it is burglary.

3. In approximately 85 per cent of the Negro girl delinquency cases the charge is "ungovernable and wayward" or desertion of home.

4. Of the 890 Negro children arraigned, 802 were Protestants, 86 were Catholics, and in two cases the faith was not ascertainable.

5. Of the 543 Negro children arraigned in 1925 as delinquents, 107 or approximately 20 per cent were committed to institutions; of the rest some were placed on probation. Of 34 cases of assault one resulted in commitment; of 78 cases of stealing 14 were committed.

6. Contributing causes of delinquency among Negro children the Committee found to be:
   a. Lack of opportunities for supervised recreation.
   b. Lack of parental control commonly where mothers work outside the home.
   c. Retardation in school and resulting tendency to truancy.

7. The largest number of neglected Negro children were under 7 years of age; the largest number of delinquents, boys and girls, were between 13 and 16 years of age.

8. Of 50 cases picked at random only one child was found to have had any contact with organized recreation; in two-thirds of this group there was practically no attendance at church or Sunday School by either child or parents.

9. Whereas there is considerable provision for mild delinquents among the white children, there is less for colored. children than for white, and even this limited provision is decreasing.[4]

In general there is a higher percentage of Negro than white delinquents; the contributing causes as pointed out are largely environmental; the offences committed by Negro children are among the less serious ones, largely attributable to improper parental control and to unpleasant home surroundings; the largest age grouping is between 11-16 for both boys and girls, and the problem of handling Negro delinquents is more difficult because of lack of proper institutions to which commitments can be made.

[4] *A Study of Delinquent and Neglected Negro Children,* Joint Committee on Negro Child Study in New York City, p. 6, 1927.

CHAPTER XXIV

THE QUESTION OF CITIZENSHIP RIGHTS AND PRIVILEGES

The question of citizenship is essentially one of law and government under the theory of democracy. Problems of Negro citizenship are bound up with questions of racial policy, tradition, and the various practices of government in the various states of the union. The question has its beginning in the Civil War Amendments which attempted through explicit provision to secure the full economic, civil and political rights for the emancipated Negroes which were already operative for whites.

The effect of Supreme Court decisions has been, according to Warren, in his *History of the United States Supreme Court,* to "leave the federal statutes almost wholly ineffective to protect the Negro, in view of the construction of the amendments adopted by the court, the lack of adequate legislation in the Southern states and the extremely limited number of rights which the court deemed inherent in a citizen of the United States, *as such,* under the Constitution."

As a matter of fact, the 14th. Amendment has been of less value to the group which it was intended to protect, than to business, if the number of cases dealt with is an indication. A compilation of United States Supreme Court opinions by Charles Wallace Collins of the Alabama Bar, shows 604 cases involving the 14th Amendment, of which 28 concerned the Negro.

The question as here discussed includes (a) distinctions in American laws based upon race; (b) the franchise; (c) the right to trial by jury, infractions of which may be found in the persistent instances of summary execution of Negroes without trial.

Race Distinctions in American Law. Attention is called by

Judge Stephenson [1] to the difference between race distinction and race discrimination; and between actual race distinctions practiced without sanction of law and legal race distinctions. The laws of certain states requiring white and Negro passengers to occupy separate coaches on railroad trains is recognized as a legal distinction, provided all facilities for travel—clean quarters, courteous service, etc., are equal for both races. It is objected, and frequently with full evidence, that the accommodations are not the same and thus a violation of the principle. It is, moreover, insisted that, taking into account the varied circumstances of population ratios, travel habits, railroad administrations, and the wastefulness of exactly dual accommodations, in so far as it is practically impossible for them to be the same without being identical, the laws requiring it are an infraction of Negro citizenship. These objections have been pressed in scattered cases, but in general custom, which preceded the laws, has controlled the practice. Between 1881 and 1907 all Southern states, except Missouri, enacted legislation requiring that white and colored persons occupy separate seats, compartments or coaches in transportation. The years in which these laws were passed were: Tennessee, 1881; Florida, 1887; Mississippi, 1888; Texas, 1889; Louisiana, 1890; Alabama, Kentucky, Arkansas, Georgia, 1891; South Carolina, 1898; North Carolina, 1899; Virginia, 1900; Maryland, 1904; and Oklahoma, 1907. Parallel with this development, Civil Rights legislation was passed almost simultaneously in 16 Northern and Western states as follows:

Connecticut	1884 and 1905	Minnesota	1885, 1897 and 1899
Iowa	1884 and 1892	Nebraska	1885 and 1893
New Jersey	1884	Rhode Island	1885
Ohio	1884 and 1894	New York	1893, 1895 and 1913
Colorado	1885 and 1895	Pennsylvania	1887
Illinois	1885	Washington	1890
Indiana	1885	Wisconsin	1895
Michigan	1885	California	1897

The first two or three decades following the War between the states may be considered under two general periods. In the first of these periods, the Negro exercised the right of franchise under the guarantees of the so-called "War Amendments." This was the Reconstruction Period. It came to an end about

[1] Stephenson, G. T., *Race Distinctions in American Law.*

the year 1875. For more than 20 years afterward the Southern states were content to disfranchise the Negro by direct intimidation and overt measures. Mississippi, in 1890, formulated a Constitution whose specific purpose was to make the existing disfranchisement of the Negro coincide with legal forms. The other Southern states followed Mississippi. South Carolina enacted laws with the explicit purpose of eliminating the Negro from politics in 1895. Louisiana in 1898, North Carolina in 1900, Alabama in 1901, Virginia in 1902, Georgia in 1908 and Oklahoma in 1910 successfully passed laws designed to exclude the Negro from electoral privileges by legal means. The method employed by these statutes vary. In general they are as follows: [2]

Tax Test.—Alabama, Arkansas, Florida, Louisiana, Mississippi, North Carolina, South Carolina, Tennessee and Virginia require the payment of poll taxes as a prerequisite to voting. In Georgia all taxes legally required since 1877 must be paid six months before the election.

Property Test.—The property requirement in Alabama is forty acres of land in the state or real or personal property worth three hundred dollars ($300) on which the taxes for the preceding year have been paid.

In Georgia it is forty acres of land in the state or five hundred dollars ($500) worth of property in the state.

The Louisiana requirement is three hundred dollars ($300) worth of property and payment of personal taxes.

South Carolina prescribes three hundred dollars ($300) worth of property on which taxes for the preceding year have been paid.

Mississippi, North Carolina and Virginia have no property test.

Educational Test.—Louisiana requires that the applicant must be able to read and write and must make an application for registration in his own handwriting.

In Mississippi he must be able to understand or reasonably interpret any part of the Constitution of the state.

In North Carolina the requirement of the ability to read and write the State Constitution in English.

The Constitution of Oklahoma says the applicant "must be able to read and write any section of the Constitution of the state."

South Carolina requires ability to read and write the Constitution.

[2] *Negro Year Book*, 1925-26, pp. 240-1.

Virginia requires that the applicant must make out his application in his own handwriting and prepare and deposit his ballot without aid.

Understanding and Character Clauses.—The Mississippi law permits one who cannot read to register if he can understand and reasonably interpret the Constitution when read to him.

In Alabama, South Carolina and Virginia the Understanding Clause is a part of the Grandfather sections and became inoperative with the "Grandfather Clauses."

Suffrage Restriction. In all cases the alternatives proposed for those desiring to qualify for voting were intended to eliminate Negroes without restricting the electoral privileges of white citizens. With reference to the Mississippi Constitution, which served as a model for other Southern legislatures struggling with the problem, Porter [3] says that:

Thus, it will be seen that this Constitution paved the way for wholesale exclusion of the Negroes on perfectly legal grounds. The strongest point, of course, was the discretionary power vested in election officials to decide whether or not an illiterate person understood the Constitution and could give a reasonable interpretation of it. Its weakness was that it did not fully protect the illiterate white from the same discrimination. For this reason the Mississippi Constitution was not entirely satisfactory, and it took several years to develop more effective measures. The ultimate ideal, of course, was to exclude all Negroes and no whites.

In the same study the opinion is expressed that the Negro himself is to be blamed on account of his apathy toward political participation. He speaks of "the palpable futility of trying to stimulate social consciousness and create capacity through mere alternations in political machinery. . . . The thought suggests itself that federal legislation or federal action in the interests of the Negro is almost hopeless and when he develops such capacity federal action will be quite unnecessary." [4]

In a more recent discussion of the qualifications which have been placed in State Constitutions to restrict the privilege of voting, Porter says that "aside from theoretical objections there is no justification for literacy tests." "Most states," he adds, "provide schools, therefore, if there is considerable illiteracy

[3] Porter, Kirk H., *Suffrage in the United States,* p. 210.
[4] *Ibid.,* p. 221.

they should have schools. Foreigners are taken care of in naturalization laws. The only remaining use for a literacy test is to discriminate against Negroes in the South and that need not detain us here." [5]

The statement is commonly reiterated that the Southern states are not nullifying the Constitution because there is no law which Congress has provided as an enforcing measure. These commentators object to the criticism frequently made of Southern Drys by Northern Wets, who assert that the South is insisting on the enforcement of the 18th Amendment (Prohibition) to the Constitution while declaring their "natural right" to nullify the "Civil War" Amendments which have reference to the suffrage of the Negro.

There are yet those who aver that the Constitution in this respect already has "teeth" and that it is the recalcitrancy of Congress which prevents their application. In spite of the apparent justice of the provisions in the State Constitution, the discretionary power which is given the registration boards affords grounds for the inquiry by the Federal Courts as to whether the registration officer is discriminating. A law passed by Congress many years ago providing that any officer or person charged with the summoning of jurors who failed to summon any citizen on account of race, color, or previous condition of servitude should be guilty of a misdemeanor and fined not more than $5,000. The Supreme Court upheld this law and in the case of a judge in Virginia who had been guilty said that he could be punished. [6]

Another means of enforcing the Amendments lies in applying the constitutional provision which says that if any state restrict the right of its citizens to vote on account of "race, color, or previous condition" that its representation in Congress will be reduced accordingly. As long ago as 1893 an advocate arose who held that Negro suffrage was a failure, that the 15th Amendment should be repealed, and that the states should be allowed to restrict their suffrage without federal interference if they wished to do so. This writer believed that the Southern

[5] Porter, Kirk H., "Suffrage Provisions in State Constitution." *American Political Science Review*, Vol. XIII, p. 577, 1922.
[6] "Negro Suffrage—The Constitutional Point of View." *American Political Science Review*, Vol. I, pp. 17-43, 1906.

states would willingly suffer reduction in their congressional representation if they could gain the exclusion of the Negro in this manner.[7]

This point of view has practically disappeared as the next few decades witnessed the South achieving the end of eliminating the Negro politically with no sacrifice of representation. The possibility of invoking the constitutional penalty for this wholesale disfranchisement of the Negro still is heard after the lapse of years. Although Garner[8] states in 1914 that the South has the sympathy of the entire nation behind it in the disfranchisement of the Negro, and that Roosevelt had stated in a letter in November, 1904, that no one seriously dreamed of cutting down Southern misrepresentation, the recent agitation over the 18th Amendment has brought it again to the fore. The session of Congress, June of 1929, witnessed a gesture in this direction when Representative Tinkham of Massachusetts had an amendment tacked on to the Census-Reapportionment Bill and to the surprise of the country found it receiving an overwhelming vote in the Congress, although this action was soon overruled.[9] How far this agitation will lead is dependent upon the possibility of prolonged agitation for repeal or modification of the 18th Amendment.

Many commentators have decried the policy of active agitation for political participation of Negroes as one lacking in wisdom, fomenting race prejudices and hatreds. They express the belief that if the Negro is patient and prepares himself diligently for the exercise of the balloting right the South will present no bars to his full enjoyment of the rights of citizenship. A former governor of South Carolina, the Honorable Charles B. Aycock, defended Negro education, stood out against mob violence and insisted on fair treatment of the Negro as an imperative duty of the dominant white race in relation to the inferior Negro group. He said that agitation for the political

[7] Wickliffe, J. C., "Negro Suffrage a Failure, Shall We Abolish It?" *The Forum*, Vol. XIV, p. 797, 1893.

[8] Garner, J. W., *Studies in Southern History and Politics*, Chap. XV; "Southern Politics Since the Civil War."

[9] Milton, G. F., Jr., "Black Ballots in the White South." *The Forum*, Vol. LXXVIII, pp. 906-13, 1927.

equality of Negroes handicapped him in his efforts for their betterment.[10]

The last quoted opinion is open to some doubt in view of the recent recrudescence of political consciousness, and the renewed efforts of Southern legislators to add new restrictions to those, such as educational and property qualification, which the developments of the Negro has rendered ineffective as bars to his exercise of the franchise.

There are no studies which give the actual extent of Negro voting. It is known that there is some voting by Negroes in practically all the Southern states, and it is known that particular efforts have been made to restrict it.

In most of the border states, such as West Virginia, Kentucky, Maryland, and even Tennessee and Virginia, there is a considerable amount of voting on the part of Negroes. This is probably due to the active two-party rivalry in these states. In Baltimore some 28,239 Negroes are registered.[11] There is much less voting, however, in other sections of the South. Dr. Woofter has estimated that about 3,500 Negroes are registered in Atlanta, 2,000 in Savannah, and 1,000 in Jacksonville. Mr. Kent states that there are only 595 Negroes registered in the entire state of Louisiana.[12]

The most effective of the restrictions has been the one-party system and its connection with the Democratic primaries, which came to a test in Texas, in the now rather well-known case of Nixon vs. Herndon. The point at issue was the right of a political party to exclude the Negro from its primaries in a state where those primaries virtually constituted the election. The case arose out of the passage by Texas of a law specifically excluding the Negro from Democratic primaries in that state, a law contested by Dr. L. A. Nixon, a Negro, and another duly qualified Democrat.

The case eventually was carried to the Supreme Court aided by the National Association for the Advancement of Colored People and the extraordinarily able counsel which it secured. Mr. Fred C. Knollenberg of El Paso and Mr. Arthur B. Spin-

[10] Poe, Clarence H., "Suffrage Restriction in the South; Its Causes and Its Consequences." *North American Review,* Vol. CLXXV, pp. 534-43, 1902.
[11] Giligan, Francis J., *Morality of the Color Line.* Chapter on "Political and Civil Discrimination."
[12] Kent, Frank, *The Great Game of Politics.*

garn of New York, chairman of the Association's Legal Committee, represented Dr. Nixon and the reply brief to the brief filed by the Attorney General on behalf of Texas, was prepared by Mr. Louis Marshall. On March 7, the Supreme Court declared the Texas law unconstitutional by unanimous decision. The opinion was handed down by Mr. Justice Oliver Wendell Holmes and in it the Supreme Court declared: "It seems to us hard to imagine a more direct and obvious infringement of the Fourteenth Amendment." The decision closed with the following paragraph:

The statute of Texas in the teeth of the prohibitions referred to assumes to forbid Negroes to take part in a primary election the importance of which we have indicated, discriminating against them by the distinction of color alone. States may do a good deal of classifying that it is difficult to believe rational, but there are limits, and it is too clear for extended argument that color cannot be made the basis of a statutory classification affecting the right set up in this case.

A new statute was enacted by the state of Texas which delegates power to the Democratic Committee to state the qualifications and prerequisites of the voter in any Democratic primary and under this purported delegation of power the State Democratic Committee did prohibit Negroes from voting in the primary which was held on July 28, 1928.

Council for Dr. Nixon and the National Association for the Advancement of Colored People responded with a move to bring action for damages against certain election judges in the city of El Paso, who refused Dr. Nixon the right to vote in a primary held during the month of October for the purpose of selecting candidates for office on the Democratic ticket.

Extent of Negro Disfranchisement. An attempt was made by Dr. W. E. B. DuBois to measure the extent of disfranchisement in the South and relate this to proportional representation of the various states of the Union. Tables are prepared from Census estimates of the population of voting age in 1920 and from figures on the number participating in the presidential elections of 1920. His summarized results are to the effect that in the Middle West and Southwest about 70 per cent of the voters vote, while about a third voluntarily disfranchise themselves.   It requires about 75,000 voters to secure the apportionment of a representative in Congress.   In the South with a population of 23,000,000 and a voting population of about 13,000,000 there were, in 1920, less than 2,000,000 votes cast, or less than 10 per cent of the total population and about 18 per cent of the male and female voters.   The Southern states, however, received 104 representatives in the 67th Congress, thus requiring only 21,248 voters for each representative.

The Northwestern states have between 60,000 and 70,000 voters for each representative and about 60 per cent of the voter's vote.   In New England and the Middle States, with a considerable foreign population, between 50 and 55 per cent of the voters vote.

If the South with its 104 representatives is properly represented, then the Middle West ought to have 479 representatives instead of 139; the Pacific and Northwestern states ought to have 91 instead of 32; the Southwest ought to have 35 instead of 10; the Border States should have 197 instead of 62; the Middle States should have 265 instead of 101; and New England should have 89 instead of 35.   Or, to put it another way, if the Middle West is properly represented, then the South instead of having 104 representatives ought to have 31.   These figures are, of course, tentative and may be criticised because of the assumptions made in estimating the voting population and the disfranchised foreigners.   Nevertheless on the whole they approximate a correct picture of the dangerous situation in this country.[13]

Further figures are cited from the 1924 elections:

In Louisiana the state furnished a fairly accurate official record. In the election for President in 1924, there were 274,529 white persons registered and 980 Negroes. The white population of the state in 1920 was 1,096,611; the Negro population was 700,257. Of these 564,933 whites were 21 years of age and over, and 359,251 Negroes. Of the adult Negroes 229,980 were reported as illiterate. This leaves 129,271 who can read and write. The statistics of illiteracy are inaccurate. Still, it would seem reasonable to suppose that at least 100,000 Louisiana Negroes were men of average intelligence, able to read and write. Nearly 80 per cent

13 "Disfranchisement of Colored Americans in the Presidential Election of 1920."   The National Association for the Advancement of Colored People.

of the Negro population, 10 years of age and over, is engaged in gainful occupations. Among the Negroes there were more than 10,000 persons who owned their farms, and in addition to these farmers, 28,906 Negroes owned their homes.

Yet out of all these people, only 980 were allowed to register and vote and the number of Negro registered voters has decreased almost by half in the last 16 years, as there were 1,743 registered in 1908. Manifestly Louisiana is disfranchising mainly by race and not simply for illiteracy or shiftlessness.

In Alabama, there were reported 269,847 Negroes 21 years of age and over who could read and write in 1920. Careful inquiry shows that "there are not more than 3,500 Negroes voting in the state of Alabama and less than 1,000 in the city of Birmingham."

In Macon County, for instance, where Tuskegee Institute is situated, there are 4,927 Negroes 21 years of age and over who can read and write, and of these 22 are registered voters.

In Montgomery County containing the capital of the state, out of 13,973 literate Negroes, 21 years of age and over, 41 are registered.

In Mobile County, out of 17,375 literate Negroes, 21 years of age and over, 958 are registered.

In the city of Birmingham, among the most progressive of the industrialized Negro group, out of 33,655 Negroes 21 years of age and over, who can read and write, less than 1,000 are registered voters.

In Mississippi, according to a careful inquiry made in 1927, there are at present 850 Negroes registered, out of a total literate Negro population, 21 years of age and over, of (1920) 290,278.

In Texas the difficulties are illustrated by one incident brought to my attention in 1918. Marion County, Texas, has a population of 10,886, of which 6,667 are Negroes. There are 2,146 whites 21 years of age and over, and 2,937 Negroes. Forty-three of the whites are illiterate and 855 of the Negroes. It would look as though at least 1,500 of the Negroes were persons of intelligence and thrift, because they owned, in 1918, 85 per cent of the cultivated land and paid, outside the corporation taxes, over 50 per cent of the taxes. Many Negroes owned farms of 1,000 acres and more —one owning 3,200 acres. The Negroes owned 23 cotton gins, 25 grist mills, 32 saw mills and 17 shingle mills. There were 25 small merchants and 1 colored physician whose practice was 50 per cent white. The 6-months colored county school was "fairly good." The town school in Jefferson ran 9 months and had 10 grades. And yet, in the face of that, the following election notice was issued Tuesday, September 3, 1918:

To the People of Jefferson:

The election to be held Tuesday, September 3, is for the purpose of voting to repeal the stock law or allowing it to stand as it is.

It was unanimously voted by the Council to allow all white Citizens, men and women in the city of Jefferson, 21 years of age, to vote on this question as the Council wants to know how the people stand on it. The people who are in favor of Repealing this law are willing that an Ordinance be passed allowing stock to run at large from 6 A.M. from 1st day of April until 1st day of December, which would be 8 months in the year and put them up the remaining 4 months. You are all interested.

So come out and vote.

The Committee.

It must be remembered that a Stock Law, which regulates the fencing of crops and the running at large of stock, is of great importance, both to the farmer and the small town worker.[14]

The questions involved in Negro suffrage, however, are related to Negro population proportions in sections, to problems and theories of race relations and to psychological factors which discussion has tended to aggravate quite as often as it has clarified. The prospect of any important early extension of Negro suffrage in the South is yet clouded. It is contended that the danger of Negro control of political machinery which has prompted the emotional reaction of the Southern states, no longer exists; that the section injures its influence nationally by the abrogation of constitutional principles; and that the votes of intelligent Negroes who are barred can possibly contribute more to good government than the votes of many of the less intelligent whites who exercise the franchise. Wisdom is seen by some of the Negro leaders in the participation of Negroes in local politics even when candidates may be selected from the Democratic party only. The contention is that more protection from such officials as judges, sheriffs and commissioners is insured when it is recognized that conspicuous unfairness in the administration of laws will jeopardize election or re-election.

One precedent of significance is present in the experience of

[14] Du Bois, W. E. Burghardt, "The Possibility of Democracy in America." *Crisis*, September, 1928.

the Populist party in the South. In Alabama the small farmers in resentment against the other sections of the state polled disquietingly large votes by what is, described as "an alignment between intelligent whites and Negroes." The white voters were split and the attitude toward the race problem somewhat modified, when in 1892 particularly, the Democratic party was not threatened (in Kolbs revolt) by the black counties, but had to rely upon them to stay in power.

Legal Action Involving Citizenship Rights. A large proportion of the questions involving "citizenship rights," which have been dramatized by attention and court action, has been handled by the National Association for the Advancement of Colored People. These have included the action involving the Emerson High School in Gary, Indiana, in which it contended that the transfer of Negro children was illegal in that they were discriminated against by being sent to a school which did not offer them an opportunity to complete a college preparatory course and the facilities of which were inadequate and unequal to those at Emerson; action against the school authorities of Atlantic City, New Jersey, for refusal to admit Negro children to the Pennsylvania Avenue School; mandamus proceedings on behalf of the Negroes of Charleston, West Virginia, to compel the library authorities to permit them to use the main Public Library, the theory of the case being that the denial of this privilege to Negroes is contrary to the laws of the state and that even though there are school laws providing for the separation of the races, this law does not cover public libraries; assistance in damage action brought by James West vs. A. C. Bliley, William Boltz and William Ricker who are, respectively, residents of Richmond, Virginia, and judges of the election district in which the plaintiff lives in the same city, which alleges that under a state law which delegated power to the State Democratic Committee, a seclusion act was passed by said committee which prohibited Negroes from voting in a Democratic primary; assistance in a damage action brought by H. D. Goode vs. Thomas A. Johnson, and Paul F. Riers, who are respectively resident of Pensacola, Florida, and judges of the election district in which the plaintiff lives, in the same city, alleging that although a qualified Democrat and he had applied for the privileges of voting in the primary held in that state for the purpose of selecting a nominee for the office of city commissioner, on the Democratic ticket, under a state law which delegated power to the State Democratic Committee, a resolution was passed prohibiting him from voting in the said primary. Other action has been taken in cases involving refusal to register Negro Republicans during registration period immediately preceding the general election which took place on November 6th, in two counties of Oklahoma; two cases in the District of Columbia, which involve legality of covenants entered into by property holders of a section or community, who contract among themselves against leasing, conveying, selling or occupying of any property owned by the parties to the covenants to Negroes; cases involving discrimination in Civil Rights Law in Asbury Park, New Jersey; the case of Ben Bess, a Negro who has been imprisoned since 1915 at the penitentiary of South Carolina, and who, in May, 1928, was granted a suspension of sentence and finally a full and unconditional pardon by the Governor of that state but returned to the penitentiary. It appears that the pardon was granted by the Governor after the complainant who, in 1915, had testified that Bess had committed rape upon her, had made an affidavit in which she stated that the testimony given in 1915 was untrue. This woman after being told that she would be prosecuted for perjury, signed a second affidavit which stated that in her first one she merely intended to forgive Bess of the crime which he had committed upon her. When this second affidavit was presented to the governor, he attempted to revoke the pardon.

Habeas Corpus proceedings raised the question of the governor's power to revoke a full and unconditional pardon which had been accepted.

Other cases handled suggest the type of alleged infringement of citizenship privileges protested by Negroes.

Will Brown was arrested in Columbus, Ohio, charged with being a fugitive from justice from the state of Missouri and charged with murder in that state. The Columbus, Ohio, branch with the assistance of the National Office investigated the case and was convinced that it was a case of mistaken identity.

The lynching records from 1889 to 1927 in the state of Missouri and the facts tending to establish that Brown was not the man wanted in Missouri, were placed before the Governor of Ohio and extradition was refused.

Mr. Scipio A. Jones, an attorney of Little Rock, Arkansas, reported the case of two Negro boys, Robert Bell and Grady Swain, ages 14 and 18 respectively, who were sentenced to the electric chair for murder. The conviction was based on alleged confessions which were forced from the boys under duress and torture.

The Supreme Court of the state has set aside the conviction on the ground that testimony was not sufficient and has remanded the defendants for a new trial.

Two Negroes, residents of Elmhurst, Long Island, a part of the greater New York City, have required police protection since moving into a block which had hitherto been occupied solely by whites. Their homes were stoned and some damages done.

Action has been brought by individual Negroes for alleged discrimination in public carriers, public service, stores, restaurants, schools, and theatres. The most successful of these have been in states of the North where there exist Civil Rights legislation. The damages awarded have been so small, and the cost of prosecution so considerable that only a few of these cases have been pressed.

Summary Execution Without Trial. The problem of organized lawlessness, taking the form of mob violence, appears to have resolved itself within the last five years into a test problem of great significance for good citizenship. This has been recognized in the recent Presidential messages to Congress.

In the 30-year period from 1889 to 1918, inclusive, 3,224 persons were lynched. Of this number, 2,522 were Negroes. The remaining number, 702, was principally of white persons, with an appreciable proportion of people of Mexican blood. An inconsiderable fraction was furnished by Indians and Chinese. The largest number lynched in any one year, counting both races, was 226 in 1892. The largest number for Negroes was also in 1892, 155 persons being lynched in that year.[15]

In the 10-year period since 1918, up to November 30, 1928,

---

[15] The Annual Releases of the National Association for the Advancement of Colored People have been used in this summary statement.

361 Negroes have been lynched .as compared with 38 whites. While the number of Negroes lynched in 1919—77—was the largest since 1908, the data show a marked decline in total number since that date. The greatest single decrease occurred between 1922 and 1923. The former year dated 56 lynchings of Negroes, while 1923 yielded only 26. Since 1923 lynchings have exceeded 20 in number only once—1926 with 28—and have dropped as low as 16, in 1924. The year 1928 returned the smallest number of lynchings in the history of this crime.

TABLE LI

NUMBER OF WHITE AND COLORED PERSONS LYNCHED IN THE UNITED STATES, 1889-1928

Year	Total	White	Colored	Year	Total	White	Colored
1889	175	80	95	1909	89	14	75
1890	91	3	88	1910	90	10	80
1891	194	67	127	1911	71	8	63
1892	226	71	155	1912	64	3	61
1893	153	39	114	1913	48	1	47
1894	182	54	128	1914	54	5	49
1895	178	68	110	1915	96	43	53
1896	125	46	79	1916	58	7	51
1897	162	38	124	1917	50	2	48
1898	127	24	103	1918	67	4	63
1899	109	22	87	1919	83	6	77
1900	101	12	89	1920	65	8	57
1901	135	27	108	1921	64	7	57
1902	94	10	84	1922	61	5	56
1903	104	17	87	1923	28	2	26
1904	86	7	79	1924	16	0	16
1905	65	5	60	1925	18	0	18
1906	68	4	64	1926	34	6	28
1907	62	3	59	1927	21	3	18
1908	100	8	92	1928	9	1	8

Taking the period 1889-93 as 100 per cent, it is of interest to note that every 5-year period since has shown a decrease in

TABLE LII

PERCENTAGE OF DECREASE DURING EACH FIVE YEAR PERIOD, 1889-1928

Years	Total Number	Per Cent Decrease	White, Per Cent Total	White, Per Cent Decrease	Negro, Per Cent Total	Negro, Per Cent Decrease
1889-1893	839	0.0	260	0.0	579	0.0
1894-1898	774	7.8	230	14.1	544	4.7
1899-1903	543	35.2	88	67.1	455	20.3
1904-1908	381	54.6	27	89.5	354	38.0
1909-1913	362	57.2	36	85.8	326	43.6
1914-1918	325	61.3	61	77.6	264	54.4
1919-1923	301	64.1	28	89.2	273	52.8
1924-1928	98	88.3	10	96.1	88	84.8

total number of individuals lynched.   Table LII on p. 351 illustrates this fall in total lynching, with percentages for each 5-year period.

From this table it will be seen that the number of Negroes lynched in the post-war period 1919-23 shows the only exception to a steady falling lynching curve for Negroes since 1889.

Alleged Offenses.   Murder is the cause most frequently alleged by mobs in the data here tabulated.   The following table indicates the nature of the causes for lynching with the number of individuals executed for each alleged offense.

TABLE LIII

The Alleged Causes for Which 3,224 Persons Were Lynched, 1889-1918

	White Victims	Negro Victims
Total lynched	702	2,522
Murder	319	900
Rape	46	477
Attacks	13	237
Crimes : person	62	253
Crimes : property	121	210
Miscellaneous crime	135	303
No crime	6	142

Of the 361 Negroes lynched since 1918, 116, or 32.1 per cent, were accused of murder; 114, or 31.3 per cent, were lynched for alleged attacks or attempted attacks upon white women.   This compares with a total of 38.8 per cent of the lynchings in the period 1889-1918 for alleged murder, and 28.3 per cent in the same period for alleged rape or assault.

Contributing Factors in Mob Violence.   On July 26, 1918, President Wilson said with reference to lynching: "It cannot live where the community does not sanction it."

Little more needs to be said.   Practically all analyses of the lynching problem locate its crux in the effect of community complaisance.   The responsibility and the potential influence in abating this evil rests with the individual citizen, according to practically all commentators on the matter.   From various pronouncements on lynching and mob violence, the following tendencies have been gleaned as representing a consensus as to the immediate contributing causes to mob violence:

(a) Negligence of peace officers, amounting in some instances to actual connivance.

(b) The influence of the press in stimulating race prejudice and mob action.

(c) The absence of local organizations of public-spirited citizens which might present checks to the mob spirit.

(d) Delays in executing judgments and legal technicalities which enable criminals to escape justice. Such a condition would necessarily result in a lack of public confidence in the regularly constituted instruments of justice.

Contributing Factors in the Decline of Mob Violence. It will be observed from the accompanying graphs and tables that at the present rate of decrease, lynching will apparently soon

NUMBER OF NEGROES LYNCHED IN THE UNITED STATES
1889 TO 1928

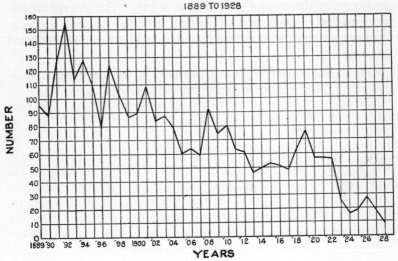

Figure 13

cease to be a problem in race relations, due to its disappearance. Reasons for this decrease have been variously stated. Associated factors with the decline are:

(a) The propaganda carried on by such organizations as the Interracial Committees of the South, the National Association for the Advancement of Colored People, etc.

(b) Agitation for control of lynching as a protective measure in the face of the threatened Federal Anti-lynching Legislation, such as the Dyer Bill. Many editorials from Southern newspapers and statements from Southern leaders opposed to lynching have cited the advisability of eliminating lynching in order to avoid federal interference.[16]

(c) The active functioning of local committees of white and colored citizens in anticipating mob violence.

Some commentators on the decline of lynching are inclined to be cynical, stating that several instances of hurried trial, conviction and execution indicate that the "mob spirit" still exists under the disguise of legal form. There are cases on record in which Negroes accused of capital crimes have been arrested, brought to trial, convicted and sentenced to death within thirty-six hours of the commission of the crime. The degree of advance in the dispensation of justice afforded by such a procedure as compared with avowedly extra-legal action is questioned by some.

[16] *Sic* the Foreword of "Mississippi and the Mob," by J. N. Flowers; State Bar Association of Mississippi, Jackson, Mississippi, 1926.

CHAPTER XXV

RACIAL ATTITUDES

Race contact is implied in each of the divisions of study discussed. Beneath the purely social problems of health, industrial relations, education, housing, law observance, there is the deep and scarcely plumbed world of racial attitudes which are responsible for much of the special stress encountered.

For the curious directions of behavior and beliefs there is always some reason. J. H. Oldham [1] quotes Graham Wallas as saying, "The future peace of the world largely turns on the question whether we have, as is sometime said and often assumed, an instinctive affection for those whose features and colour are like our own combined with an instinctive hatred for those who are unlike us."

The strength of tradition, the obvious features of physical difference, the ubiquitousness of the "colour problem" in one form or another point to the validity of the fundamental assumptions which ascribe race antagonism to instinct. As in other fields, however, the basic assumptions find effective challenge in contrary observations. Professor Ellsworth Faris of the University of Chicago points out, for example, that race prejudice is a phenomenon that is not essentially connected with race. The only sense in which it deals with race is in the naïve and untechnical fashion in which the United States Government lists races for the purposes of the immigration law, where one may read of the Irish, Welsh, Bohemian, African and Spanish-American race.

In this crude world in which we live, it is of importance to determine not what races are, but what men call races when they manifest racial antipathy.

Some Causes of Race Antagonism. The fact that race prejudice, being emotional, is not rational, has led to what Faris regards as the error of assuming that it is organic and native.

[1] Oldham, J. H., *Christianity and the Race Problem.*

355

This race prejudice is contingent upon a certain type of group consciousness which may have no defense whatever in scientific classification. Moreover this group consciousness has a beginning in each particular case. Reuter suggests that the first reaction of the American colonists to Negroes was probably "hygienic" rather than racial, for it required many years to reach the point of regarding all whites as essentially different from all Negroes.

There are numerous instances of group consciousness which have all the features of race prejudice when the element of race is actually absent. The "poor whites" in the South, although they belonged to the same race as the slave holders, were looked upon as almost a different species. As Broadus Mitchell of Johns Hopkins points out, nothing has been said of the Negroes' mentality, morals, religion or ethics that has not been said about the "poor whites" of the South by their blood cousins. When Olmstead[2] was in the South he met gentlemen who told him of the "poor whites." The girls, he was told, were unchaste and their fathers did not object to their reputation as harlots; a Southern physician expressed to him the opinion that if an accurate record of births were kept, as many illegitimate as legitimate births would be found. A South Carolina editor referred to them as "a curse instead of a blessing; generally worthless, unprincipled, enemies to our peculiar institution and formidable barriers to the success of our native mechanics," and these mechanics were the Negro slave artisans.

Other causes of race antagonism suggested have been: conflict of economic interest, differences in tradition, customs and "temperament," ethnocentricism, the fear of contamination of racial stock, and conflict of political interests. Most, if not all of these, may be observed in relations between persons of the same race. Where there are obvious physical differences, emotions excited by any of the complex causes are reinforced and each time they are evoked become more closely associated with the group.

Economic Foundations of Race Prejudice. The literature of this field is voluminous and in itself reflects an illuminating array of attitudes and sources responsible for them. One tangible field of evidence of possible value on this general question

---

[2] Olmstead, *A Journey in the Seaboard States,* Vol. II, p. 149.

points to those factors in race relations in America which are more economic than racial. It has been mentioned that the first Negroes brought to America for a considerable period were not very differently regarded from the white indentured servant; that racial attitudes after the crystallization of the institution of slavery fluctuated with the economic importance of Negro slaves to the system; that the most severe attitudes accompanied the agitation which threatened the loss of this property and capital in slaves; that the organization of slaves in slavery debased the "poor whites" and stimulated enmities; and that after the emancipation of these slaves the most intense racial difficulties developed in some form or other of economic rivalry. This suggestive trend may be developed further in the course of race relations during the past twenty-five years. Lynchings in the United States have been regarded as an index to community sentiments and the assumption has been that the migration of Negroes from certain sections of the South has been a response to the intolerable race hatred encountered. These lynchings when related by counties to migration, over a period of years, offer curious evidence.[3]

Of 10 Georgia counties, in which 5 or more lynchings occurred, the Negro population increased in 5. Of the other 5, in which the Negro population decreased, there was a corresponding decrease in the white population in 3, and an increase in the other 2 considerably less than the average. To use one example: in Montgomery County, in which 5 lynchings occurred, the Negro population decreased from 7,310 to 4,348 and the white population from 12,328 to 4,768. If decrease is a measure of persecution, the whites, it seems, are the greater victims.

In Jasper County, Georgia, there were 9 lynchings, the largest number for any county of the state in 30 years. The Negro population actually increased in this county between 1890 to 1920, while the white population during 1900 and 1910 actually decreased.

Or to take the state of Texas. Of the 6 counties with 5 or more lynchings, the Negro population increased in 4 and de-

[3] The compilation of lynchings over thirty years was taken from the handbook prepared by The National Association for the Advancement of Colored People.

creased in 2. Of the 2 in which there was a Negro decrease, there was a corresponding but more serious decrease in the white population. In Waller County, the Negro population decreased from 6,712 in 1910 to 4,967 in 1920; the white population decreased from 6,375 in 1900 to 5,426 in 1910 and to 4,082 in 1920. In Harrison County, with the largest number of lynchings (16), the Negro population showed a similar increase from 15,544 to 15,639.

In the state of Alabama, Jefferson County, with 10 lynchings, increased from 90,617 in 1910 to 130,211 in 1920—the largest recorded increase in any county. Dallas County, with the largest number of lynchings (19), lost only 1,246 Negroes, while Sumter, with no lynchings at all, lost 3,491.

/A plausible deduction is that the most frequent lynchings, as well as night riding and the raids of the white cappers, took place in the poorer areas where the poor whites had been established, where the population ratios were more evenly balanced; in other words, where competition was more severe./ Dr. Young of the University of California has made another grouping of lynching and found that they occurred in inverse relation to the size of the county. | In other words, the larger the county the smaller the lynchings.\ Whatever the other conclusions of the study might be two facts stand out : (a) Negroes live in greatest numbers in the most populous counties of the South, and (b) the most sparsely populated counties are sparsely populated largely for the reason that life is harder in them. Furthermore, in the smaller units it is increasingly difficult to deal impersonally with the occasions for conflict.

On the question of riots, it might be pointed out that they came suddenly and were crowded within the brief period following the Negro migration to the North. It is well known that the first of these clashes in East St. Louis was caused by the importation of Negro workers who began to menace the jobs of the white workers. Theodore Roosevelt threw the responsibility upon labor and labor organizations. The real bitterness of the Chicago riot centered in two spots : the area about the stockyards where Negroes had entered the industry in thousands and were accused of taking white men's jobs, while the whites were away in the army; and in the Hyde Park area where the chief grievance was the financial loss to white owners in Negro residence there through an alleged depreciation of property values. The Arkansas riots were instigated to curb the efforts of Negro cotton growers to get more for their cotton. The Tulsa riot had in its background the resentment against Negroes for their growing independence, their accumulation of money, their so-called arrogance and impudence, and the desire of certain interests to gain control of the valuable property and desirable sites which Negroes owned. In the Atlanta riot one of the chief stimulants was the circulation of cards showing Negro carpenters and bricklayers building houses and thus menacing the economic security of white men.

In one of the northern hill regions of Georgia in 1916, white residents of one county destroyed property valued at $90,000 belonging to farmers in an adjoining county who employed Negroes. In North Carolina in 1915 a bill was introduced into the legislature to prevent the employment of Negroes on railroads. In southeast Missouri for a long period, night riders busied themselves posting notices for successful Negro farmers to get out of the county and shooting into the houses of Negro tenants who, they felt, were holding down farm wages.

Another phase of the problem might be referred to in the effect of economic status itself upon other problems such as education, health, housing, from which discomforts classed as race prejudice come. With respect to education, it is perhaps fair to say that there is no state in the South with a notoriously low outlay for Negro education that is as able to sustain a school system as a Northern state, and the disparity in per capita outlay is in inverse proportion to the ability of states to support education. The outlay for Negro schools, further, can be correlated with the amount of white illiteracy in the states. Whether Mississippi would do better in the ratio of white and Negro support, if she could, is another question. It is reasonable to suppose that she would do better by her own education if her capital were greater. The heaviest educational burden as represented by the Negro educables, it has been indicated, is in the poor states. The professed reason for the limitation of Negro school funds, when the poor whites came into power was that of cost, and the feeling of bitterness toward such Negro facilities existed because they deprived the equally disadvantaged white children by that amount. One value of the Rosenwald schools has been that of stimulating an adjustment of this difference which could never have been done under the pressure of a dual school system; and of stimulating an improvement of white education, which in turn has dispelled some of the fears about facilities for Negroes. It is to be remembered, too, that education was opposed at first because it made Negroes less useful as slaves. Later the section was induced to support industrial education to make better domestics in positions which the whites regarded as Negro jobs and did not compete for. When industrial education became established as necessary to the requirements of the new industrial order we have the curious situation of bricklayers' unions petitioning the City Council of one Tennessee city to stop teaching the trade to Negroes in the public schools; and school boards being strangely willing to let Negroes have the inexpensive classical education while the expensive equipment for technical high schools is supplied to white children only.

The problem of Negro housing is one largely of property depreciation. Conversely, when Negroes invade white areas it is because other white persons have subordinated racial sentiment to increased profits from their property. The Chicago study revealed that where the biggest protests were made the white residents and white realtors themselves had sold some 1,100 homes to Negroes. And these cases could be carried further.

It is possible to regard peonage and the evils of contract labor as the direct effects of economic pressure. The economy of the South has been built upon a precarious credit system. For years the loans and banking capital of the Southern plantations were controlled by the North. The earnings were consumed by tariffs, freights, commissions and profits which the Southerners had to pay. In 1860 when the value of cotton reached $200,000,000, less than $30,000,000 of it was in the banks of the South. After emancipation when reverses came and the banks pressed the planters, the planters pressed the tenants and laborers farthest down. Peonage was a substitute for the enforced labor which was the only method by which the archaic plantation system could be supported.

The present situation of labor unions presents an excellent example of the force of economic laws. In lines of work in which Negroes are given preference by employers, by virtue of superior skill, strength or longer tenure, e.g., hod carrying and bituminous coal mining, it is pleasing to note how cordial and how lacking in race consciousness the men are. Where, on the other hand, there is no demand specifically for Negro labor, or there is opportunity to limit the available workers in the interest of better wages, or more exclusiveness, the chances of admission are poor or not at all. When white employers found it profitable through smaller wages to employ Negroes as strike-breakers, and the white workers found their jobs actually menaced, as Mr. Seligman observes, they very suddenly discovered the brotherhood of man.

Or, again, there has been occasional effectiveness observed in the economic boycott. A store in Richmond, Virginia, which had been profiting richly from Negro patronage inserted an advertisement in the daily paper which read, "Our white patrons need not fear trying on garments formerly tried on by Negroes as we have discontinued Negro trade." A few days of pressure and the manager was fired and an apology appeared in the papers.

In Nashville the Troy laundry carries a large sign on the door "No Negro Work Accepted," and their wagons haunt the Fisk University Campus.

It need scarcely be mentioned that in spite of several "unfortunate mistakes," the Negroes of means in the South enjoy considerable prestige and respect. There are few who cannot or do not evade the Jim Crow laws by getting Pullman accommodations.

Social psychologists have suggested that persons who are most in danger of losing status protest loudest. The securely wealthy as the securely cultured appear to be less disturbed by the advances of the Negro.

Without discounting a single crime of Negroes it may yet be said that most of the serious clashes in the past twenty years have had at bottom the resentment of changed status. And this, indeed, appears to be a large part of what is meant by teaching too smart Negroes a lesson; "keeping the Negro in his place"; "there must be no social equality." On the other hand the long period of Negro servitude and dependence is without a doubt responsible for the conviction of many persons that he is not an independent economic asset, that abets the feeling that a narrowing of economic statuses implies a relative loss of position.

In the first place, by recognizing a persistent factor in a troublesome situation it can be isolated for dispassionate attention.

Although only a part of the problem, these observations are drawn together for their possible value in assembling "non-organic" racial factors for study. Implicit in this is the possibility that once it is clearly enough seen it can be made apparent to anyone that poor wages, limited opportunities make for poor markets, and for greater profits there must be developed a higher buying power, new wishes and the means for satisfying them; that low wages for Negroes are a constant and insidious menace to high wages for white workers; that it is in the long run less expensive to permit a group of 12,000,000 persons to be increasingly productive than to support it by taxation of those permitted to work.

In so far as the features of race and class prejudice are very much the same, it is a clear step to change the visible evidence of inferior class as represented in unattractive neighborhoods, illiteracy and the other accompaniments of social inadequacy. It suggests further that a commonality of interest should be sought to destroy the bitter group competition which in a democracy is an anomaly, and which in any other form of united government is destructive to its highest ends.

Human nature is plastic; social customs are mutable; it is one clear lesson of history that new moral and social habits inevitably follow changes in economic codes.

Studies of Racial Attitudes. The question of race relations does not lend itself readily to study. Efforts in the direction of improving these relations may be tabulated, with, however, constant speculations regarding the ultimate efficacy of different programs employed. An attempt was made in the section on *Public Opinion in Race Relations,* of the volume prepared by the Chicago Commissioners to trace group behaviour in racial crises to their responsible origins. The principle employed was that of isolating persistent *beliefs* concerning the Negro race, with or without adequate foundations, and tracing their relationship to controlling points of view in current social and racial situations; stereotyped opinion in measuring the contribution of the press, general literature, the stage, in gossip, jokes and pseudo-scientific literature. The attitude of articulate Negroes toward themselves and the white population was similarly sought. The conclusions of this study were about as follows:

We are convinced by our inquiry: (a) that measures involving or approaching deportation or segregation are illegal, impracticable and would not solve, but would accentuate, the race problem and postpone its just and orderly solution by the process of adjustment; (b) that the moral responsibility for races rioting does not rest upon hoodlums alone, but also upon all citizens, white or black, who sanction force or violence in interracial relations or who do not condemn and combat the spirit of racial hatred thus expressed; (c) that race friction and antagonism are largely due to the fact that each race too readily misunderstands and misinterprets the other's conduct and aspirations.

We therefore urge upon all citizens, white and Negro, active opposition to the employment of force or violence in interracial relations and to the spirit of antagonism and hatred. We recommend dispassionate, intelligent, and sympathetic consideration by each race of the other's needs and aims; we also recommend the dissemination of proved or trustworthy information about all phases of race relations as a useful means for effecting peaceful racial adjustment.

Since rumor, usually groundless, is a prolific source of racial bitterness, and strife, we warn both whites and Negroes against the acceptance or circulation by either of reports about the other whose truth has not been fully established. We urge all citizens, white and Negro, vigorously to oppose all propaganda of malicious or selfish origin which would tend to excite race prejudice.

We condemn the provocation or fostering of race antagonism by associations or organizations ostensibly founded or conducted for purposes of patriotism or local improvements or the like.[4]

One of the most active institutes concerned with methods of studying race relations is *The Inquiry*. Two volumes of special interest, *And Who Is My Neighbor,* and *Race Attitudes in Children,* attempt by a case method of presentation to plumb the well of hidden motives in the behavior patterns characteristic of racial situations. Of particular value in both studies is the guide for discussions leading to individual analysis.

[4] *The Negro in Chicago,* A Study of Race Relations and a Race Riot. The Chicago Commission on Race Relations, p. 644.

Dr. Donald Young, of the University of Pennsylvania, studied the effects of a course in American Race Problems on the prejudice of 450 undergraduates at the University of Pennsylvania. Testing the students before and after the course as to their opinions regarding inborn mental ability in a list of races, he found that the students showed no fundamental change of opinions.

In his volume *Immigration and Race Attitudes,* dealing with approach, origins and change, variation and adjustment, in race attitudes, Professor Emory S. Bogardus finds:

The races toward which there is the greatest growth of race friendliness in the United States are also in the main the races toward which there is also the greatest growth of race antagonism. Japanese, Negroes, Chinese, Germans, and Mexicans not only head the antipathy column but also are the races toward which friendliness has grown most—a surprising observation. Public opinion has been focussed on the antipathy facts but has entirely neglected the friendliness developments. "Race haters" are often loud in their denunciations, angry and dogmatic in their assertions, and reap the benefits of headline publicity in the metropolitan press. A candidate for United States senator emotionally declaring that the country's gates shall be closed to all Orientals "brings down the house" in tumultuous and violent, almost "heated applause," but who has heard of a senatorial candidate strongly urging oriental friendliness? The "race befrienders" secure a very limited hearing in the press, but the pulpit is usually open to them.

The fact remains that whatever attitudes control groups, classes or sections there are recognizable imperatives to some basis of mutual adjustment in moral law, the Christian principles professed, by an important portion of the nation, the theory of democratic government subscribed to, and the insistence of normal impulses to friendship among members of the human family. Dr. Reuter closes his extraordinarily valuable discussion of the American Race Problem with the observation that the problem now is that of "defining relations in terms tolerable to the members of each racial group." This is essentially the task set by the interracial associations which have been functioning with such effectiveness in recent years.

Race Relations Programs. Such organizations as the Urban Leagues with their interracial boards, the Young Men's Chris-

tian Association and Young Women's Christian Association
with special interracial features in their programs and the various committees associated with the Commission on Interracial
Cooperation should be counted among the major interracial organizations.

The National Urban League. One of the first social organizations developing the interracial feature in its program was
the Urban League, with L. Hollingsworth Wood as National
Chairman and Eugene Kinckle Jones as Executive Secretary.
The organization was a fusion of the programs and boards of
two smaller agencies, one concerned with the protection of
young Negro women coming to the city, the other with the
mounting problems of Negro urbanization. The Interracial
feature of its program is well expressed in the words of one of
its founders, Mrs. William H. Baldwin, Sr., when she said:
"Let us work not as colored people nor as white people, for
the narrow benefits of any group alone, but *together* as American citizens for the common good of our common city, our
common country."

Field programs were developed with considerable rapidity
during the war when the migrations of Negroes from the
South, unaccustomed to city life and ways, were placing strain
upon relations in the North. Each of the fields of interest
claiming its attention—industry, health, community organization, involves interracial action in the improving of Negro
status and in gaining recognition and opportunity for them
where they have been previously denied. Beginning 18 years
ago with a single clerk and a budget of $2,500.00 it now has a
combined personnel of 200 and a total budget for national and
local organizations, of nearly $500,000.

The Young Men's Christian Association. There are Negroes on all of the governing boards of the important national
features of the Association programs, and the local boards are
interracial. Nine Negroes are members of the National Council of the United States and they are represented on the World's
Committee of the Movement.

The Young Women's Christian Association. The personnel
of both local organizations and conferences is now mixed. The
Louisville Conference of the Association in 1915 gave this important judgment:

We believe that the time has come for the appointment of a committee composed of white and colored women from all over the South.

We recognize that the best method of cooperation in the city associations is through branch relationships.

In cities where such relationships are possible Negro and white girls attend national conferences as one delegation. Miss Eva Bowles, a Negro worker [5] of excellent judgment and experience, serves as official adviser of the National Board on all phases of work among women and girls; and Mrs. Elizabeth Ross Haynes is a member of the National Board.

Special Interracial Movements. In the South for many years there had been sporadic individual efforts to initiate organized adventures in interracial good will. The first pronounced program, however, grew out of the Conference for Education in the South, which was organized by Dr. J. L. Curry and Dr. Hollis B. Frissell. Out of the Conference came the impulse which brought to action in the section the Jeanes, Slater and General Education Boards. This organization was followed by the Southern Sociological Congress, organized in Tennessee with the aid of Mrs. E. W. Cole and Governor Ben Hooper, with J. E. McCulloch as Executive Secretary; the University Race Commission organized by Dr. James H. Dillard with the help of the Phelps-Stokes Fund, and the Southern Publicity Committee, having as its secretary, Mrs. John D. Hammond. This last was an attack upon public opinion through the press and general literature.

The Commission on the Church and Race Relations of the Federal Council of Churches of Christ has had as its secretary Dr. George E. Haynes whose activities were noteworthy in the organization of the first conference in Cincinnati, in 1925, which provided the seed for the National Interracial Conference in Washington, out of which this volume has grown. The forming of race-study groups among religious workers and church members, a publicity service, advice in critical interracial situations in localities, the conducting of the Harmon Awards for conspicuous service and talent, have been among the services contributed by this Secretariat. The volume, *The*

[5] Weatherford, W. D., *The Negro from Africa to America.*

Trend of the Races, prepared by Dr. Haynes, had reached some 60,000 readers a few years after publication.

The Commission on Interracial Cooperation. This organization, under the direction of Dr. Will W. Alexander has, since the period following the World War, gained a universal prominence, and prestige for its work in the field of race relations. Its headquarters are in Atlanta, Georgia.

It is composed of nearly 100 men and women, white and Negro, in positions of leadership throughout the South. Affiliated with the Commission there are in the South 13 state and several hundred local committees similarly constituted. Each of these groups is entirely autonomous, but close relations are maintained between them and the Commission through the latter's field staff, who set up committees and assist them to find and deal with their respective problems. The Commission also cooperates in an advisory way with 4 state and many local committees outside the South.

In general the purpose of the movement may be defined as two-fold:

1. The correction of interracial injustices and the betterment of conditions affecting Negroes;
2. The improvement of those interracial attitudes out of which favorable conditions grow.

The first end is sought through the activities of the state and local interracial groups, who look carefully into conditions that need attention, agree upon remedial programs, and endeavor to carry them out. Conference and cooperation between the white and Negro groups are fundamental principles in the work of these committees. It is characteristic of their methods also that they do not depend chiefly upon their own unaided efforts, but rather upon enlisting the interest of the powerful official and unofficial agencies of state and community which alone are equal to the larger objectives aimed at.

It has been found also that as a by-product of these cooperative efforts for immediate ends, the Commission's second objective—the improvement of interracial attitudes—is greatly advanced as well. The theory is that if enough people could be enlisted in interracial conference and cooperation, it would not be necessary at all to deal directly with attitudes.

In the effort to reach the mass public the Commission carries on a widely varied educational program through every available channel—the press, the colleges and public schools, the platform, the pulpit, and the programs of the great religious organizations.

The Commission's headquarters staff consists of the director general, educational director, director of woman's work, and 5 clerical assistants. The field staff consists of 7 state or regional directors, 2 of whom are colored. The states for which the Commission is primarily responsible are Virginia, the Carolinas, Kentucky, Tennessee, Georgia, Florida, Alabama, Mississippi, Louisiana, Texas, Arkansas and Missouri.

Probably the most significant and important gains of recent years have been the phenomenal increase in the support of Negro public institutions by state legislatures, and the general inclusion of colored welfare agencies in community budgets. In the attainment of these results, now fixed as unquestioned and permanent policies, the direct efforts and influence of the interracial movement have had no small part.

During 1928 the Commission was engaged on an exhaustive scientific study of the social and economic conditions of Negroes in two typical Georgia "black belt" counties, a study in which it has had the constant counsel of the Social Science Department of the University of North Carolina. So far as is known this is the first effort made to get an adequate picture of rural Negro conditions, and it is hoped that the study, when complete, will reveal the needs more clearly, and suggest also the best agencies and methods for their relief.

The pattern of race relations, like the pattern of attitudes, varies according to geographical area and the peculiar traditional background of these areas; it varies according to population ratios, to emotional "sets" frequently as determined by other than racial factors; to the degree of direct economic competition between the groups; and, not infrequently, according to the intensity and effectiveness of the direct activities of purposeful racial organizations. In the Southern section the concern of the interracial organizations has been with the grosser problems of welfare and interracial injustices. Public conscience, so far from regarding the absence of the simple facilities of healthful living and good citizenship as a question of group or individual relations, is frequently insensitive to the disparity, and sometimes hostile to it as a danger to the security of the dominant group. Nor are all the Southern states alike. The patterns change strikingly between states, and even between counties of the same state. In Georgia, for example, the concern of interracial bodies has been that of assisting helpless Negroes, trapped in the vicious system of peonage, to secure their freedom, and getting either court action or public censure for the responsible persons through publicity; of providing influential counsel for Negroes who faced serious and unseemly punishment for little or no offenses; of organizing to prevent lynching; of urging removal of sheriffs in cases of flagrant neglect of their duty to protect Negro prisoners; urging the use of State Constabulary and the rotation of judges; of getting a measure of health care, reducing gradually the inequalities in expenditures for education in counties of the state. During a year, for example, the work of the committees of one state ranged from phases of rural research to sending Dr. George Carver of Tuskegee on a tour of ten Southern white colleges for lectures, and incidentally for observation. Some of the most notable recent work in Southern sections has been the bold public campaigns against lynching, peonage, insanitation imposed by municipal neglect, tuberculosis, misrepresentation in press publicity, lack of adequate care for dependent and delinquent Negro children, and the vast inequality in appropriation of school funds. In Kentucky, through the legislature, $600,000 was secured to support Negro colleges. This is the largest amount thus far so appropriated for these schools. At the same time there was secured legislation calling for a tax to support a colored department of the University of Louisville, which was scheduled to be opened in 1929. Through the efforts of the Louisville committee the colored schools received a more equitable portion of a city bond issue of $5,000,000.

In Atlanta the interracial committee was able to defeat a proposed closing of Negro night schools, which had an enrollment of some 4,000 adults.

In Louisiana, bills have been urged by committees and passed for the creation of a first State Normal School for Negroes and a School for Delinquents, but because of a lack of funds neither of these institutions has been started. Likewise the Texas legislature passed a bill to establish a school for delinquent girls.

Through an investigation of one of the committees it was brought to light that some 3,000 colored children in Missouri were being kept from schools because of a particular legal provision. The state committee informed the legislature of that condition and made a request for relief. The Louisiana committee has been able to get a Negro representative on the State Board of Health, while the Tennessee organization has pointed out the need of public facilities for the training of Negro doctors and nurses, which situation was brought before the State Board of Health. The Shepherd-Towner maternity work in Texas has been largely carried on through federal funds, but the Texas committee has worked to get the legislature to take over the entire support of that program. The Savannah, Georgia, and Richmond, Virginia, committees are raising funds for the erection of colored charity hospitals, and the Missouri body has been interested in having provision made for a sanatorium for the care of colored tuberculosis patients, as well as provision for better care of the feeble-minded among Negroes. Through similar committee efforts a public health nurse has been employed in Albany, Georgia, while better provisions have been made for Negro tuberculosis patients in Mobile, Alabama, and bus accommodations for Negroes sought in North Carolina, Kentucky and Tennessee. Again, in Kentucky the committee has been working on the "Pullman situation," and in North Carolina the steamship discrimination is being protested. A paving and lighting program was put through in the colored sections of Greensboro; a police matron was put on in Augusta, Georgia; playgrounds were secured in Charleston, South Carolina, and in Americus, Georgia; a colored woman probation officer was installed in Atlanta, Georgia; and a program for extensive paving and a fire protection unit for the colored section of Mobile, Alabama, was initiated. Recreation plans are under way for Columbus, Georgia; the Newport News, Virginia, committee worked on a program in which streets, sewers, parks, playgrounds and a bathing beach are involved; a colored farm demonstration agent and a social worker were secured in Macon, Georgia, and in Louisiana the committee took on the task of gaining better recreational facilities for Negroes.

In Georgia, Texas and Alabama investigations have been

made and legal aid given in a number of cases, the most notable
being the Batchelor-Leonard murder case in Alabama, where
the quite evident effort to save the white principal by railroad-
ing the Negro agent to the chair was defeated. The former was
made to pay the death penalty while the latter, found to be mentally deficient and because it was known that he was forced to
commit the crime, received a sentence of life imprisonment.
Also, in Georgia, members of the committee helped to defeat
the move on foot for the pardon of Williams of "Murder
Farm" fame, and in Atlanta especially studies have been made
concerning residential conflicts, and conferences held between
white and colored leaders in the troubled sections. Similar
work has been done in Dallas, where there are also plans under
way by which it is hoped to meet the housing situation constructively. In Alabama an investigation was made of cases of
reported cruelty in a road camp, and the findings brought to the
state highway authorities, who appointed a special officer to
clear up the situation, with promises of a cessation of such
abuses, and in New Orleans the committee hopes to secure
fairer treatment for Negroes from police and in the courts,
while in Baton Rouge, particularly, it is sought to fight the economic exploitation of Negroes.

It is perhaps significant that, as a result of this range of
interest, a movement very similar is being developed in South
Africa with governmental approval and encouragement, councils of natives and Europeans having been set up in many important centers for the promotion of understanding and the
improvement of conditions.

Changing Racial Attitudes. The younger members of both
white and Negro races have, on occasion, broken away from
the earlier memories of bitterness and from the set attitudes of
indifference. This is observed particularly in the colleges in
such student organizations as the interracial discussion group
at the University of Chicago, the Negro-Caucasian Club at the
University of Michigan, and the informal relations at International House at Columbia University. In the South the University of North Carolina has entertained at least three Negro
lecturers, the student paper has devoted one entire issue for
three years to the best literary products of the younger Negro

writers, and the Duke University student publication, *The Archive,* has solicited and carried poetry by Negroes.

Significantly, the renaissance of art and letters in the South is taking a course not very different from that observed among the young Negro writers, and, what is yet more vital, both are finding artistic expression through the stark realities of Negro life itself. The most outstanding of the present writers of the new South—Julia Peterkin, DuBose Heyward, Paul Green, Howard W. Odum, Guy Johnson, and Roark Bradford—have not merely developed Negro themes, but, through their art, have made their subjects more humanly real. They have made the vital discovery that it is possible to interpret universal truth in terms of the portraiture of the Negro race. As an authentic recognition of these values Paul Green's "In Abraham's Bosom" in 1926 won the Pulitzer Prize for the play which contributed most to art, and at the same time, to a wholesome appreciation of American life; and in 1928 Julia Peterkin's "Scarlet Sister Mary" was awarded a similar honor. The discovering of the elemental force of Negro art "for re-vitalizing a tired civilization," as Albert C. Barnes puts it, has not been without its effect in creating a new prestige. Periodicals have begun to open their columns to discussions of the most intimate phases of the question, thus breaking the long grip of tradition and taboo. The Negro writers and artists, through poetry, fiction and trenchant essays, through song and the stage, have revealed both their own technical competence and the wistful beauties in the lives of their own race.

Robert E. Park, a sociologist of rare insight into the problems of race, was one of the first to point to the power of art in dissolving old emotional fixations, and Ellsworth Faris expresses further this idea in the observation that when an attitude changes it must disappear in the melting heat of an emotional experience, and the new attitude is moulded just as the one that it replaces.

The cure is similar to the cause. What art gives art can take away. *Uncle Tom's Cabin* produced emotional attitudes and occasioned epoch-making changes in the objects which men held in mind over a large section of the nation. *The Klansman* and *The Birth of a Nation* had identical tendencies in the opposite direction. Poetry, painting, the novel and the drama, to which may be added that-form of literature which we call history, are perhaps responsible for more of our prejudices and for more of the changes which take place in time than actual experiences. But actual experiences do modify us. An emotional situation can never leave us unchanged. Every interesting and sympathetic contact with an approved member of a despised group is a drop of water slowly wearing away the granite of collective attitude.

PART TWO

THE PROBLEM DISCUSSED

FOREWORD

METHOD OF THE CONFERENCE

The decision to hold the National Interracial Conference was made in the light of a report prepared by a preliminary Committee on Plans and Programs, which had set down the following aims to be achieved:

(1) The assembling of scientific data concerning actual conditions in the relations of white and Negro races today and the underlying causes of these conditions, so that the participating organizations may come to understand more accurately the problems with which they are confronted.

(2) Fuller insight into the fundamental principles. which should be kept in mind by all organizations in working out the wise and right solution to these problems.

(3) Understanding by all of them of the efforts by which each agency is contributing or can contribute to their practical solution.

(4) Appreciation of the fact that each organization is itself part of a larger group concerned in a common problem.

(5) The discovery of methods of helpful co-operation among them.

Implied in these objectives was the idea. that this was to be a conference of craftsmen to perfect both their technique and their understanding, rather than a gathering with a program directed primarily toward the public. The Conference was therefore to be kept small, designed to bring together staff workers in social organizations and educational institutions and others having active relationship to problems affecting the Negro race in the United States. The theme was defined as "Race Problems in the United States in the Light of Social Research."

The program for a survey of social research was designed, as shown in its origin, not as an end in itself but as preparation for the Conference. The Conference was to be the occasion for study of the data and discussion of it by craftsmen in the task of bringing about better race relations. By what methods could a Conference be organized in order to accomplish so ambitious a purpose? Fortunately, among the participating organizations was The Inquiry, an agency which has been exploring social problems in the United States through the method of conference and discussion. The aid of its representatives on the Executive Committee was sought in the development of a plan of procedure. Gradually a method was worked out which may be summarized in the following outline:

(1) The data gathered on every main topic of the program were first set forth in a fairly extensive report by the research secretary. This report was then placed in the hands of an expert on the subject, who was asked to study it, criticize it, and present its salient points to the Conference.

(2) These reports were then abstracted in the form of briefer memoranda, which were placed in the hands of all delegates in advance of the Conference. They constituted The Data Book.

(3) To summarize each main topic, covering both the presentation of data at the Conference and the discussion following it, a committee of two, including as far as possible representatives of both racial groups, was appointed in advance. One member of the committee was to present the summary to the Conference at the close of the day when the topic was discussed.

(4) To insure continuity in the proceedings, two presiding officers, Mordecai W. Johnson, president of Howard University, and Robert R. Moton, principal of Tuskegee Institute, were appointed to share the chairmanship at all sessions. A chairman of discussion, who had been chairman of the Executive Committee, was also appointed, to preside at the discussion by delegates at every session.

(5) The day before the Conference, a meeting was held at Howard University for detailed discussion of procedure. It was organized by the Committee on Plan and Procedure and was attended by the presiding officers, the chairman of discussion and the chairmen of the committees of summarizers. The results of the day's work were reported to the Conference itself at the introductory session on Sunday evening, when at the

same time the plan of research for the Conference was outlined by the research secretary. Thus before the beginning of the real program on Monday morning, the whole Conference was informed of the methods by which it was proposed to achieve its aims.

(6) The objective of all this planning was the delegate. Through it he was to be enabled on the one hand to be informed of the results of the survey and in turn to contribute his own views of the significance of the data in the light of his experience. Each abstract sent to him in advance contained a series of questions for discussion, together with an invitation to him to submit other questions.

(7) The test of all this planning was the discussion by delegates, and here a device was used which brought about a much wider participation than would have otherwise been possible. Following the presentation of data and interpretative comment by one or more other speakers, a brief period of silence gave opportunity to delegates to write questions or topics to be considered in the succeeding discussion period. During an intermission the Committee on Plan and Procedure, with the chairman of discussion, sorted the cards (3 by 5 inches in size, with one topic or question on each card) and arranged them in groups which constituted an agenda for delegates' discussion. Questions which could be answered as matters of fact were referred at once to the research secretary, who at the beginning of the discussion period answered them or indicated the need for further investigation to provide the answers. The chairman of discussion then presented the whole series of questions, allotting time for each main topic according to its importance and the interest displayed as measured by the number of delegates who had suggested it. The enthusiastic response of the Conference to this plan and its value as a method may be indicated by the fact that at the opening session, on Health, more than seventy pertinent and important questions or topics were presented. In contrast with the alternative plan of having these suggestions presented from the floor as they happened to occur to the delegates, this method made possible the participation of many more delegates through their written questions and also insured discussion of the whole range of subjects which had occurred to them in connection with the topic of the session.

(8) The presentation of data and the discussion which followed it took place at sessions during the mornings and afternoons. In the evenings, following the summaries of the day sessions by the committees already described, speakers were invited to present the topics of the day from their own standpoints or as a result of their own research. For example, on the first day, the topic of Health having been discussed in the morning, one of the speakers in the evening, Dr. Raymond Pearl of Johns Hopkins University, presented the results of his own research on the subject of "Biological Factors in Negro Mortality."

Thus the task of delegates at the Conference was to study the material and on the basis of it to answer three large questions:

I. In the light of social research, what do we now know about Negro life and race relations as affecting both the white and colored races in the United States?

II. What significance has this knowledge for the programs of social organizations whose purpose it is to improve these conditions?

III. What gaps in knowledge are revealed, calling for further study by universities and research organizations?

The answers to these questions came from representatives of well-nigh every school of thought and point of view on the subject. Commenting upon the Conference, one of its members, Alain Locke,[1] wrote: "No such representative body had in fact ever before convened for council and deliberation on the American race problem." After references to several earlier conferences which had given results in mutual understanding and tolerance, he added:

But never before had the entire gamut of social thought and programs connected with the race problem been spanned in an effective conference. . . .
The materials of the summarized reports had frequently been screened through several points of view. The result was that when interpretation was eventually sought it disclosed in most

[1] Locke, Alain, "The Washington Conference on the American Negro," in *The Survey Midmonthly,* January 15, 1929.

instances either an unexpected amount of substantial agreement between views generally thought hopelessly partisan and conflicting, or the vitality rather than the colorlessness of composite findings. A report, for example, on the subject of race relations which laid particular stress on the need for increased personal, cultural and professional relations between black and white citizens, came from an interracial, intersectional committee composed of two white southerners, one representing a liberal academic center, the other, a large corporate foundation, and a liberal northern Negro—and the report was a unanimous opinion. A scion of a prominent southern family with sympathy and apparent approval read the report of a veteran Negro reformer's analysis of the imperative need for full citizenship rights for the Negro. The successor of Booker T. Washington stressed participation in politics. The most vigorous examples of successful demands for an equitable distribution of public funds for schools and civic facilities came from a Negro minister of Louisville, Kentucky, and a Negro woman educator from Florida. At the closing evening session, Julius Rosenwald heard himself lauded at once as the man who had put, and stimulated putting, millions of dollars into the primary schools of the backward rural South, and on the other hand as a benefactor of research in biology by a Negro scholar and as a conference member who missed several of the afternoon sessions in order to intercede for larger governmental appropriations for Howard University.

An important result of the Conference, embodied in its procedure, was a heightened respect on the part of its white members for the achievements and the intellectual ability of leaders in the Negro race. The interchange of cultural feeling and spiritual values on the part of persons whose intellectual equipment was similar brought the members of the Conference to the feeling that a new stage had been reached in race relations in this country. In the next stage it will be more vividly realized that the task is not to be performed by a dominant race, however good its will and however philanthropic its spirit. It is a joint responsibility to work out on this continent something new in the history of the world. The disadvantages of a weaker race are the concern and the disadvantages also of a dominant race, because these disadvantages enter into the common civilization. Intellectual equality and responsibility, democracy based upon science and science devoted to social ends, were keynotes of the Conference, not in the sense of formulated conclusions but as realizations, the results of working together. They suggested the method of approach, in truly co-operative thought, research conference and action.

MARY VAN KLEECK,
Chairman, Executive Committee,
National Interracial Conference.

INDUSTRY AND AGRICULTURE
THE NEGRO IN INDUSTRY
NILES CARPENTER, PH.D.
University of Buffalo

CHAPTER XXVI

THE NEGRO IN INDUSTRY

Niles Carpenter, Ph.D.

As a background to our discussion of the Negro in industry we should always remember that we are still talking about a minority group. Very close to seven out of ten Negro males are still engaged in domestic and personal service. The occupations which the Negro men and women are filling most rapidly are in the first place the *semi-domestic occupations,* such as janitors, sweepers, porters. In the Southern textile mills a curious bi-racial situation has grown up: The mill operatives are largely white, but the various occupations which partake of the status of domestic service, such as sweepers and porters and janitors, are occupied by colored.

In industry proper we begin with the *bottom structure occupations,* which are the unskilled labor jobs in large-scale industry, particularly iron and steel, meat-packing and coal-mining. Those three industries are taking care of an enormous and an increasing number of Negro workers.

The various semi-skilled occupations of Negroes might be divided into two groups: For lack of a better phrase we will call these the *pushing up occupations* and the *vacuum occupations.*

By *"pushing up" occupations* I mean those which come just after the bottom structure; semi-skilled work in rolling mills, in steel works and similar industries. By the *"vacuum" occupations,* I mean those which are relatively new, such as the entire range of occupations centering around the automobile industry, including chauffeurs, automobile mechanics and filling-station men.

We find a considerably smaller proportion of Negroes engaged in these semi-skilled occupations than are engaged in unskilled labor, and a still smaller proportion engaged in the purely skilled occupations.

These skilled occupations, again, we can divide into three groups:

(1) The residue of the old skilled crafts.
(2) The *pushing up* occupations.
(3) The *vacuum* occupations.

The status of the Negro in the *old skilled crafts,* especially in the building trades, is a curious one. Before emancipation, the Negro was strategically located throughout the South in these skilled trades; and there are some very interesting data showing that the white skilled laborers were unable to compete with colored skilled laborers in spite of the fact that the colored help was more expensive, because the employers of the colored skilled laborer had to pay the laborer's board and lodging and also to pay his master his wages, whereas the white laborer kept himself and got about the same wage.

Since the close of that period of almost complete dominance, the Negro as a skilled craftsman has been losing ground steadily. There have been a good many reasons at work in this situation. The most important reason is that immediately after emancipation, the Negro was not able to bargain effectively. The bargaining had been done over his head by his master, and in competing against the white man, who was used to bargaining, he was at a disadvantage. And then, of course, there has arisen the whole range of trade union restrictions.

The fact is quite obvious that, excepting in certain very well-located industries, the skilled workers, *white and colored,* have had a very hard time of it in this country, especially those engaged in the old-line skilled crafts. The replacing of the older skilled crafts by machines has led to the substitution of unskilled laborers for skilled laborers and a net reduction of all grades of labor in the trades involved has occurred. So there has been a general demoralization and confusion throughout the whole of the older skilled crafts, and in any event the colored skilled worker in them is having a difficult time both in the South and in the North. And trade union restrictions are making his lot particularly hard.

In the *pushing up* occupations, on the other hand, we have a very different picture. We find, apparently, the beginning of the Negro's emergence into the skilled crafts in large mass-production enterprises, such as iron and steel, and the foundry industries, which he has invaded in large numbers. I am struck with one fact that was developed in a study of one city in the state of New York. The Negro crane and derrick men make up about 4 per cent of all the crane and derrick men which is a larger proportion than they constituted in the population at large of New York City.

A number of local studies which the Urban League and other groups have made show a similar situation. In Cleveland, 11 out of 12 of the foundries studied were promoting Negroes to their highest skilled grades, and one of those industries, the National Malleable Castings Company, had Negro foremen, clerks, time-keepers, locomotive engineers, crane men, and cupola men.

We must remember that in these industries we have almost a mass invasion of Negroes. These industries are, moreover, not strongly unionized and they require a relatively small number of highly skilled, highly paid men working with a large sub-stratum of unskilled labor. Let us hold that fact in mind and I will try to return to it later on.

The Negro migration has been discussed to a certain extent and we have not any very satisfactory figures on this and will not have until the 1930 census. It should be said here incidentally, that the Census Bureau should be urged to make an analysis of the migration figures in the 1930 census, so that it will be possible to know just what has happened in this Negro migration. The migration was just starting when the 1920 census was taken. But if we have a thorough enumeration and if there is expert analysis of the figures, so that we can see the long-time trend between 1900, 1910 and 1930, then we will know, as we have never known before, the extent of this significant movement. For example, in Buffalo in 1920 we only had about 4,000 Negroes. By 1926 or 1927 we estimated that there were 10,000 Negroes; and this is very typical of what has happened throughout the country, namely—that most of the migration has come after the 1920 census.

One or two things about the migration should be mentioned: There is, of course, the fact that we have all heard about, that the cutting down of immigration during the war, together with the rapid expansion in industry in the North set up a situation of stress which resulted in a widespread demand for Negro workers in the industries of the North, especially in the big munitions industries. But there is more to it than that. There is, in the first place, the habit that American industry has of using unskilled labor. By and large, American industry has put its brains into displacing skilled labor by machinery but has taken unskilled labor for granted. It is only within the last few years that American industry has begun deliberately to use machinery to replace unskilled labor. Heretofore it has depended upon unskilled labor from Europe for its rough jobs and has used machinery largely as a replacer of skilled labor. In the interval between the abandonment of this policy and the inauguration of the new one, the Negro became almost indispensable.

In the South, there have been many influences operating. They include that group of social conditions and attitudes which one Negro migrant had in mind when he wrote to his friends back in the South that he didn't "have to humble to nobody any more." These influences explain the fact that when the depression of 1920-21 came, the return tide to the South that everybody in the South expected did not come. Even after the great race riots in Chicago only a handful of Negroes returned South.

Besides these very strong emotional factors behind Negro migration, there was the agricultural distress in the South— the boll weevil devastation—the gradual decline in the numbers of independent farmers. All these things tended to bring about unrest among both white and colored populations in the South and to make it very easy to induce colored people to come North to the industrial opportunities that were awaiting them there.

What has happened to the colored man in Northern industry? I have suggested already one factor. Where he has entered industry in large numbers he has found his place, first of all, as a rough unskilled laborer, but he is beginning to get his head above water, so to speak, and is pushing into some of the skilled jobs.

What about his efficiency? The data on efficiency are not worth a great deal because they are based upon employers' own statements of opinion. Like the neurotic patient who had so many symptoms that she could not have them all at once, the employers' opinions are so contradictory that we cannot have them all at once. One group of employers puts Negroes to work on ice because they liked the cold; but up in Buffalo we were told they liked the heat, and they were put to work in hot jobs. They cannot be racially fitted for both kinds of jobs. It is like being at the North Pole and at the Equator at the same time!

The contradictions in the various statements concerning the efficiency of the Negro indicate that we are still in the realm of belief and opinion and not in the realm of ascertained fact.

In spite of that, we find that the majority of employers (when measured both by the number of employers and by the number of people employed) say that the Negro is about as good as the white worker, and that some say he is better.

With regard to the labor turnover of the Negro we are told in some quarters that he is unsatisfactory and not faithful and takes excessive time off. But a rather careful study has been made in certain localities and it is found that the Negro labor turnover is not so very much different from the white labor turnover. Moreover, we know that labor turnover depends largely upon management, and where we have a high turnover we do not talk about the worker any more; we want to know what is the matter with the employment policy of the industry concerned.

Besides, the Negro is put in the high-turnover jobs such as the unskilled work. He is out toward the economic margin; so that, in case of lay-offs, he is the first man to be laid off. He is also in many cases recently from the South and is totally unused to the time-clock routine of Northern industry.

All these factors make what turnover we have among the Negroes largely a matter of adaptation to special circumstances rather than of racial characteristics, and there are beginning to be instances in which it is reported that the Negro is more satisfactory and faithful than the white.

I wish to suggest just one further point concerning industrial efficiency. There may possibly be certain neuro-muscular characteristics in the Negro which make him fit for jobs requiring intermittent bursts of energy and great strength. I personally am much more interested in studying race differences in terms of the neuro-muscular side of the question than the so-called intelligence level. I think there is more scientific basis for investigation in this direction; and it may be that the Negro is a little more capable than the white of these sudden bursts of energy such as are required in the steel and foundry industry. But we are still largely in the realm of speculation here.

There are not a great deal of data about women and children, but there are one or two things that I want to suggest. First of all, is the quite obvious fact that Negro women are still engaged almost entirely in domestic and personal service and what we might call the border-line jobs between domestic service and industry. By the *border-line* we mean such occupations as chamber-maids in hotels, workers in laundries, and elevator attendants. There is in addition, a certain number of definitely industrialized trades which Negro women appear to have occupied for a great many years, such as the tobacco industries in the South, and the peanut-packing and canning factories. These industries especially, which by their nature have to be located near the crop and which are largely seasonal, have utilized Negro female help because of its accessibility and of the ease of securing it.

The development of home-work among Negro women is a very interesting one. It has the obvious characteristic of obviating all elements of race friction which might occur in a shop. Of course home-work ordinarily is considered a very bad thing, but home-work for the Negro woman, at least, gives the opportunity of gainful occupation without the embarrassment and difficulties presented by racially mixed groups in a shop.

The second main point that I want to suggest about Negro women and children in industry, concerns what I have called the *ratio of gainful occupation.* When I first began to study occupation statistics I was immensely impressed by the fact that Negro women and children showed the highest rate of gainful employment of any group in this country, not excepting the foreign-born. Out of a thousand Negro women, more of them were working for money than could be found among the whites or even among the foreign-born whites.

The evidence assembled in the report seems to suggest that there has recently been a very striking decrease in the ratio of gainful employment for women. In 1910, 54 per cent of women were gainfully employed. In 1920 the per cent dropped to 39; and in West Virginia we find the highest percentage of men employed and the lowest percentage of women employed. There is no reason on the face of it why there should be a decrease. If anything, the opportunities are advancing for women, and there does not seem to be any dearth of opportunity in domestic and personal service.

I think that the rate of gainfully employed women and children is a reverse index of the economic progress of the colored group. I suggest, and I cannot do any more than suggest, that to the extent that women are leaving occupations Negro men are advancing economically. All of these startling figures, especially as to women, seem to me to be one of the most outstanding facts of all the data we have. Women are preserved for making their homes more efficient. It means that these women are being released for home-making, and, economically, in the long run this fact means more efficient homes. The children are released for further education, and the general economic efficiency of the group is going to be to that extent greater in years to come.

If now we try to ask ourselves what all the assembled data show as to the prospect of the Negro in industry I think that perhaps we can line them up on the *plus* and *minus* sides.

The *plus* side I have already suggested. First of all, we have the fact that American industry will probably continue for some time to demand a large body of unskilled labor, and, the further fact that immigration is definitely restricted in this country. If anything, it will be more thoroughly restricted on the north and south borders. This means that there will continue to be a sort of economic hunger for unskilled labor of the kind that the Negro is extraordinarily well able to give.

The Negro seems to be having the greatest success in those industries where he is carrying on a kind of mass occupation. There are iron and steel plants today where the Negro makes up 90 per cent of the working group; especially is this true of the foundry industry. There is also a heavy invasion in the packing industry. There is beginning to be an invasion in the coal mining industry. The Negro seems to get a foothold in a certain industry and then to keep on going until he dominates its labor force. The same thing has been true of the Polish and the Italian and, earlier, the German immigrants. They tended to a certain extent to pick one industry and to flow into it very heavily.

There seems to be a bit less resistance to the Negro in what we call the vacuum industries—industries which are not already stratified by traditions of exclusion and of racial demarcation. Let us take, for instance, the oil refining industry. That industry began to exist about the time the new immigrants came to this country, and the new immigrants poured into that industry. Whiting, Indiana, was built about the time of the heavy immigrant invasion to that part of the country, and the whole town of Whiting, Indiana, an oil refining town, was practically an immigrant town. There is a possibility that this same sort of thing may occur with the Negro in such new industries as are now developing. And we have already noted the relative ease with which the Negro has entered into some of the automobile trades, particularly the great increase of Negro chauffeurs and the recent appearance of Negroes as taxi-cab drivers. Such evidence as this suggests that in these new and unstratified industries an opportunity arises.

Each year makes the Negro better adapted to industry. He has gone through the first and most fundamental processes of adjustment, and every year that he stays in the North and learns about American industrial ways and gets habituated to them, he is just so much more efficient and more likely to hold his job.

The Negro has an enormous advantage as compared with the immigrant in a knowledge of the American language. Also, there may be certain factors in the Negro temperament, factors of good nature, of cooperativeness, and so on, which have developed out of long experience as a domestic servant. Those things are spoken of by employers as factors that favor the Negro.

Now, we must consider the *minus* factors. There is the continued disruption of industry by machinery and the fact that, in all likelihood, unskilled labor will be more and more replaced by machinery as unskilled labor rises in price. There is some talk about cotton-picking machinery. Of course that would make a revolution in the South. In the long run it might prove beneficial because it might cheapen cotton so much as to widen the market. The cotton gin did just that thing. It caused more acres of cotton to be planted because the cheapened cotton widened the demand for it. And the machine cotton picker would do the same thing, probably. But we are again in the realm of speculation there.

The Negro is in the high turnover occupations, and when unemployment comes, he is the first one to go. He has been hired, often to tide over an emergency. There is a certain amount of friction and opposition by his fellow workers. The employer himself, especially the employment manager may feel race prejudice. All these influences increase the Negro's liability to unemployment.

But the most important factor is the opposition of his own fellow workers. Quite often an employer says he does not dare hire colored men because of the fear of opposition by his white workers. Of course in the South that attitude is quite clear-cut and is responsible for the situation in the textile industry there. In the North it is present and once in a while it flares up, as it did in the East St. Louis riots. It is not a constant factor. It fluctuates from factory to factory and from point to point and it varies tremendously with the attitude of the employer. If the employer really wants to, he can quite often override the opposition by the workers. Nevertheless, the situation is there. It offers the curious anomaly of the workers disagreeing among themselves to the immense advantage of the employer.

In this connection we have to make some mention of trade unions. I think I am not over-stating the case when I say that the trade unions have not helped the Negroes' economic advancement, and that the Negro has made his widest gain in trade unions in those industries where he could not be kept out. It is also fair to say that the Negro's difficulty in the skilled trades has been due, at least in part, to the fact that the skilled trades are very highly unionized.

In conclusion, we can say that to the extent that the Negro makes his way economically he demonstrates his ability and his capacity in a way that all the American people understand, and in a way that is quite unmistakable and cannot be gainsaid by anyone.

He has just begun to enter the testing period in this respect. In the North he is in industry. He has made the first step and got a foot across the threshold of American industry. It is beginning to look as though he was getting beyond the threshold

and doing what every other group has done before—pushing
up, slowly and steadily, into the skilled jobs that lie right ahead
of him.   It is beginning to look as if he were doing this gradually but implacably and that the next ten years are going to tell
a very interesting story.

INDUSTRY AND AGRICULTURE

QUESTIONS FOR DISCUSSION

Is there not a real danger that Negroes will be shut out of important jobs in industry more and more because of the white competitors?

Granted that opposition from fellow workers (white) plays an important part in keeping Negroes out of industry, need it be so important? That is, although many employers say that is their reason for not employing Negroes, are they perfectly honest, since they do many other things to which their white employees object?

What examples are there of companies that instead of "overriding" their white employees have educated them to welcome Negro fellow employees?

What can be done about changing the situation in places of industry where Negro women, regardless of their ability, can secure only what is known as menial jobs?

What types of work, if any, have been opened to the Negroes (a) in the South, (b) in the North?

Since the security of the Negro in agriculture and all other forms of industry is primarily a question of efficiency and since Negro vocational schools are usually handicapped for funds and equipment, what relation of schools to industry can be worked out for increasing the quality of vocational education of Negro youth?

In view of the increasing difficulty of the Negro to find employment in the skilled trades, due to the persistent introduction of machinery, the hostility of the Labor Unions, white workmen and employers, what will be the ultimate purpose of Negro Industrial Education?

Is Northern migration helping permanently or merely changing industrial conditions in the South?

The Negro comes from the rural South and becomes a city dweller. He gives up producing his food and purchases. Has there been any movement into market gardening so that the Northern Negro might become more self-sustaining in his special sense? Would not the possibilities of such cooperative effort be worth investigation?

Is Negro immunity to Organized Labor an advantage in the industrial field?

How can the Negro become more widely and effectively union-ized?

In view of the present dependence of Negro Labor, had he better remain unorganized temporarily?

Would the interests of the Negro be best protected by having his own labor unions? Or by being affiliated with the corresponding sections of the American Federation of Labor? Or by being accepted for membership in white unions?

Cannot the same complaint made against the trade union with reference to exclusion be made against the Negroes towards each other?

What can we learn from those trade unions on the Pacific Coast that include Orientals in their membership rather than run the risk of being wiped out by non-union Oriental labor?

Is it not to the economic advantage of the white trade unionist to accept Negro members rather than have the constant threat of employers who use Negroes as strikebreakers?

Since real moral and social advancement will be slow and almost impossible until Negro women and children are released from day labor and long hours what can be done to induce great industrial plants whose owners contribute to Negro charity and welfare to lift the industrial boycott and give the Negro jobs instead of charity?

Is it not true that the Negro female is losing out in personal service? So often newspapers are specifying white in their want ads.

Is it not desirable that our activities for the improvement of the Negro's position in industry should include specific efforts for a definite increase in efficiency along specific lines?

Is the relative success of the Negro in industry to which he is drawn in the mass due to an adaptation of industrial management policy and the absence of friction with white fellow workers?

Did home work of immigrants in the early days of the garment industry "obviate race friction"?

Is Negro capital growing at a sufficient rate to promise Negro employment in Negro enterprises as an important factor in the near future?

In the business world, should Negroes look forward to invading white business enterprises, banks, stores, etc., or to developing a segregated business system?

What phases of the Negro farmer's plight can be approached without awaiting a solution of the farm problem as it affects both races?

Figures show that the South has its share of agricultural depression but that some Negro farmers are making money and progress. What kind of people are these successful farmers? How does this phenomenon relate to education?

What effect does the tendency of the land owners of the South to keep the Negro tenant in debt have upon the turnover of the Negro tenant?

What may be done to induce young Negro men and women to prepare themselves for agricultural leadership?

Is it not true that the same forces that decrease the white farm population operate to decrease the Negro farm population aside from the causes of prejudice?

SUMMARY OF DISCUSSION

The competition of white labor is limiting the opportunities of Negro workers and resulting in a loss of traditional occupations. This tendency in industry is somewhat offset by the economic advantage of cheaper labor, individual white employers who override the objections of white workers or educate them to racial adjustment, and a few new opportunities in certain lines of work, as in filling stations. American industry will continue to demand a large amount of unskilled labor, and the greatest success will come where Negro labor is carrying on a mass invasion. Here the Negro has an advantage over the immigrant in language, cooperative spirit and adaptation.

As in the past, the skilled Negro worker is restricted though in this field also individual exceptions are encouraging. The problem of Negro industrial education is complicated by inadequate funds and equipment for Negro vocational schools, the failure of courses in industrial education for white workers to create openings, and the loss of opportunities for craft skill due to the use of machinery. Opportunities for apprenticeship and diversification of Negro occupations are necessary.

The advent of an increased Negro population in industrial centers, due to migration, has added to the problem of racial discrimination the problems of any mass labor. A possible adjustment may be worked out through a definite utilization of the Negro farmer in the North in truck gardening, cooperative marketing, and in the merchandizing of food in the large centers of Negro population.

In the field of group competition, the Negro is forced to lean toward capital rather than labor because labor organizations on the whole discriminate against competing racial groups, rather than welcoming them as workers with the same economic problems. In several instances in the South, in the West and in Northern industrial cities, white and Negro working groups have cooperated and eliminated racial friction. It was suggested that some permanent agency should be established out of the constituent organizations to carry on the study of Negro industrial opportunity, and promote the advantage of Negro labor individually and in group relations with organized labor.

The problem of Negro women and children in industry, while similar to that of white workers in some industries, in that the newest group in industry is the one given the least opportunity and must prove itself before being given more jobs, calls for particular efforts in the creation of more tolerant social attitudes, continued demonstrations of capacity, and the collection and publication of data on discrimination and records of efficiency. Negro women are being displaced in domestic service, and those that remain are subject to undesirable conditions and working hours.

Negro capital and experience are inadequate to supply any significant amount of employment for Negro workers.

The Negro farm population in the South has decreased by over 700,000 and a comparable loss has occurred among the white farm population. The total amount of agricultural products and the acreage under cultivation have nevertheless increased. The Negro farmers are faced with problems of profitably increasing production, cooperative marketing, the especially pressing difficulty of securing credit at low rates of interest from dependable sources, and education in better farming methods, through an increased staff of county agents from state and national departments of agriculture. Farmers' meetings, fairs and county demonstrations indicate progress among the Southern colored farmers.

Mr. T. Arnold Hill, National Urban League, New York.
Prof. Kelly Miller, Howard University, Washington, D. C.
Mr. Channing H. Tobias, National Y.M.C.A., New York.
Mr. W. A. Robinson, Principal, Knoxville High School, Knoxville, Tenn.
Mr. John P. Frey, American Federation of Labor, Washington, D. C.
Dr. George E. Haynes, Federal Council of Churches.
Mr. Paul Kellogg, Editor, *The Survey*.
Dr. Niles Carpenter, Committee on the Cost of Medical Care.
Mr. J. F. Fletcher, National Council of the Protestant Episcopal Church.
Mr. Bellman, Longshoreman's Union, Norfolk, Virginia.
Mr. Israel Mufson, Workers Education Bureau.

Miss Mary Anderson, Women's Bureau, Department of Labor.

Miss Nannie Burroughs, Vocational Training School, Washington, D. C.

Mr. Monroe N. Work, Department of Research and Records, Tuskegee Institute.

HEALTH

THE HEALTH OF THE NEGRO

Louis I. Dublin

Statistician, Metropolitan Life Insurance Company

BIOLOGICAL FOUNDATIONS OF A NEGRO HEALTH PROGRAM

Raymond Pearl

Johns Hopkins University

CHAPTER XXVII

THE HEALTH OF THE NEGRO

Louis I. Dublin

Health is as important to a race as it is to an individual. It affects a man's personal relations; for, obviously, the sick individual is rarely a good person to live with. A race handicapped by disease likewise finds it hard to adjust itself to other groups of the community. Without health the individual or the race is hampered at every point. Sickness means disability; it means dependence on others for care; it means also heavy expenditures during a period when income is entirely cut off or curtailed. Consequently, sick people are unable to progress or to reach the position to which their innate abilities entitle them. The psychological aspects of ill health are, moreover, of far-reaching importance and influence fundamentally a man's attitude towards both himself and his associates. The feeling of inferiority which ill health engenders makes a profound impress upon the mental and emotional life of a race. So I imagine no problem would loom larger on the program of a conference devoted, as this one is, to the inter-relations of races, than a discussion of health. This, I think, rests at the bottom of many of our racial troubles.

With regard to the Negro, health is even more important than among other groups. The Negro, in spite of his 300 years of residence in this country, still finds himself to a large extent in an alien environment. This is unquestionably a hard country to live in; meteorological conditions make life difficult and place disabilities on people whose natural habitat is in tropical or semi-tropical climates; and in that class belong the Negroes, the Italians, and other immigrants from Southern countries. People who are used to a warm climate and to abundant sunshine find difficulty in adjusting themselves, especially during the first few generations, to the long inclement seasons of our Northern

states. And so we find that the Negro must combat really
serious health disabilities which seriously obstruct his progress.

In order to estimate these limitations in concrete terms, it is
necessary to have some unit of measurement. The figure which
I will now use probably serves better than any other to indicate
the nature of the disabilities which the Negro must overcome.
In spite of the very considerable gains in health which the race
has made during the last 30 or 35 years—and I will go into
that in a moment—it still falls short by 14 years of attaining
the present expectation of life which its white neighbors have
reached. Please realize what that means. To determine the
expectation of life we take a large group of people, say 100,000,
at the moment of birth, follow them until all have disappeared
by death, and see how long, on the average, they have lived.
This figure of the average duration of their lives would be their
expectation of life.

Measured by that standard—and it is the best standard we
have—we find that the Negro people are now enjoying an expectation of life of 45 years, as compared with one of 59 years
for the white race. In both cases there are sex variations—
females live longer than males; but combining both sexes for
comparison, so that we need remember but one set of figures,
there remains a differential of 14 years in life expectation in
favor of the whites. To understand the significance of this
loss to the Negro race, contrast the death of a man of 45 with
one of 59. These 14 years constitute a most valuable period
of life—the time when a man has reached the height of his
powers and would be expected to produce his best work. The
difference between an expectation of 45 years and 59 years can
often be translated into terms of broken homes, widows, families without mothers, orphans and the aged left to become dependent upon the community. These years make a great difference in the social economy of a people.

Let us now analyze this difference of 14 years and see to
what causes it is due. The first item is easily located. We find
as we analyze our problem that we can distinguish very sharply
between conditions among Negroes living in the cities and those
living on the farms. Taken by and large, the rural Negro is
far better off, from the health standpoint, than his urban
brother. We find also that on the whole the Negro in the

South is better off, from the health standpoint, than the Negro
in the North. But in order not to be misleading, this statement
must be qualified to show that differences between North and
South result from the fact that many more Negroes in the
South are on the farms; and it is due to the rural character of
their life that the figures for the South are so much better than
those for the North.

But, on the other hand, Negroes living in the cities of the
North are better off, from the health standpoint, than Negroes
living in the Southern cities. The location of the cities makes
a lot of difference in our vital statistics. It is easy to put your
finger geographically on the sore spot and the sore spot in the
health of the Negro is in the Southern cities. It is not on the
Southern farms. If there were time, I could name the most
dangerous cities and dilate on their conditions with which I am
familiar. But briefly, it is in Savannah and Charleston, in
Macon, Atlanta and Birmingham that much of the trouble lies.

Now, analyzing our problems a little differently, what are
the conditions which bring about the excess of ill health and
the high mortality of the Negro? One thinks at once of the
large infant death rate which is still a major problem. In spite
of all of the improvement that has taken place in the last 30
years, infant mortality among the colored people is very high,
and unnecessarily so. There are some exceptions to which I
shall refer later. Here we are only considering its effect upon
life expectation—and a heavy infant mortality adversely affects
the general mortality and produces a much shortened life span.
For you can readily see that when a human being has been cut
off at the moment of birth, or within its first year of life, there
has been destroyed all possibility of that individual's rounding
out his complete expectation and 60 years of life have been lost
at one stroke. If you save a baby at birth or in the first year
you have the possibility of bringing that person to the age of
60; and as the hazards of life become constantly reduced with
advancing years, that is during childhood, adolescence and early
adult life, by saving life at its beginning you add materially to
the life span of the whole people.

If you look still further into the causes of death, you will find
outstanding the respiratory conditions. Pneumonia stands high
in the list of causes of death. Tuberculosis is a very serious

source of mortality and morbidity among the colored people. Maternal mortality and other causes growing out of the bearing of children, are extremely high among young colored women, and account for a very large part of the extra mortality. But I now come to a condition which, to my mind, underlies all of these that I have already mentioned (infant mortality, tuberculosis, pneumonia and maternal mortality), and that is the extremely high death rate for syphilis. Syphilis is the arch enemy of the colored people. If we could eliminate this one disease and the sequels of it, the mortality of the colored people in the next generation would probably become as low as among the whites. Syphilis is responsible for the disabilities of the colored people as is no other single condition. It decimates the children. It is often a cause of still-births, premature births, of congenital malformations, as obstetricians and social workers know. Syphilis underlies a great deal of the excessive tuberculosis mortality among the colored people. It drains vitality and makes the individual subject to infection and then causes him to succumb to diseases which otherwise he could throw off. When ordinary illnesses come they more often result fatally in the colored race than they do in the white race, because a much larger proportion of the colored people are afflicted with syphilis. I am not going into the causation of syphilitic infection. I am limiting myself to facts, not to theories, and have here no interest in the moral questions at stake. But the prevalence of syphilis cannot be gainsaid. The problem which faces us is, What are we going to do about it? As I said, this disease accounts as does no other single factor for the health disabilities of the colored race and constitutes one of the major issues upon which those interested in Negro well-being must concentrate attention. There is urgent need for an active and widespread campaign against the venereal diseases. The various social hygiene organizations have made some headway in this direction, but their efforts must be still further intensified.

As a result of these diseases which I have named, the mortality of the colored people is fully two-thirds higher than that of the whites. The death rate varies from place to place. In the cities, it is usually double that of the white race. In the rural areas it is only 50 per cent higher; but, generally speaking, the mortality of the colored people exceeds that of the white race by a figure ranging from 50 to 100 per cent; and in some communities it is 200 per cent in excess.

But we must not forget that there is another side to the picture. Even though there are many unfavorable items in the health situation which are responsible for a death rate still far too high, nevertheless, a very distinct improvement in mortality has occurred in recent years. The expectation of life of the Negro has increased almost 12 years since the beginning of the twentieth century. In 1900, it was only about 33 years; but now it has been extended to 45 years and is the same as that of the whites about 30 years ago. This means that virtually one-third has been added to the life span of a whole race in a period of less than 30 years—an amazing achievement. Another way of estimating the advance which has taken place is by comparing the death rate. During the Reconstruction Period, Negro mortality reached its most appalling height and was somewhere between 35 to 40 per 1,000. In 1911, the death rate of colored industrial policyholders insured in the Metropolitan Life Insurance Company was 17.5 per 1,000. The death rate of these insured Negroes had declined to 14.0 in 1927, which represents a reduction in mortality of 20 per cent in 16 years. Eight thousand more deaths would have occurred among policyholders in 1927, had the 1911 death rate prevailed. This result was due, for the most part, to improvements in the death rate from tuberculosis, pneumonia, malaria, typhoid fever and pellagra.

In 1911, the typhoid fever death rate among the colored Industrial policyholders of the Metropolitan Life Insurance Company was 46.2; by 1927 it had declined to 8.2. During the period under consideration, malaria was almost eliminated as a cause of mortality, the death rate declining from 26.3 at the earlier date to 3.9 at the later. In these two cases improved sanitary conditions are to be held fairly responsible for the change. Greater knowledge and better treatment have also slightly reduced the mortality from conditions of the puerperal state and have been even more successful in dealing with diarrhea and enteritis. Turning now to the most important cause of death, let us see what the situation is in regard to tuberculosis mortality. In 1927, the death rate was 228.0 which made it the leading cause of death among colored Industrial policyholders, this being a considerably worse showing than among whites of the same class. But in 1911, it was almost double the 1927 figure, or 418.4. Those familiar with the tremendous gains in the treatment of that disease which have been made in recent years do not despair. They feel that tuberculosis is amenable to control, that by securing proper treatment for the tuberculous, supplying them with the facilities of sanatoria, and the benefits of a suitable climate and environment, it is probable that this disease will fall low in the list of causes of death. It is strange, therefore, that though the anti-tuberculosis campaigns have proved so successful, it should still be necessary to fight against the inertia and in some cases the open hostility of those who claim that by curbing this disease we are interfering with Nature's method of dealing with the unfit. Anti-tuberculosis activities among the colored have been particularly handicapped on this account. I am confident, however, that in spite of the obstacles which have been placed in the path of those fighting tuberculosis, the accomplishment has been great. There is every probability that tuberculosis will fall lower and lower in the list of causes of death, with the progress of time.

This leads to a question which lies within the province of a conference like this one. Are the disabilities which tend to raise the figure of Negro mortality above that of the whites, inevitable? That is, are we dealing with inherent deficiencies and susceptibilities, or are we dealing with conditions subject to control? Obviously, it is important for those who are concerned with the well-being of a people to know in advance whether they are up against a stone wall, or whether their efforts may lead to success. That is a fundamental question with which I imagine you have all wrestled. There is no way of avoiding it. Our literature recently has been flooded with discussions of this subject, not only in relation to colored but also to white people. As you know, there are scientific fashions just as there are other fashions. At present, it is highly fashionable to discuss the inherent value of races, the innate worth of various classes of people and to list them in categories as either inferior or superior. Certain schools of eugenists seem to be having their day, and they tell us that health and longevity conditions are determined by heredity and hence are unavoidable;

that nothing that man can do "cuts much ice"; that we had better study Nature and be guided by her processes instead of hitting our heads against stone walls. They warn us against making these philanthropic efforts because they are afraid that we will only make fools of ourselves in the end and after it is too late to change the forces which we ourselves have set in motion.

This doctrine has been applied to the Negro situation. A fatalistic attitude has been adopted in some quarters regarding the whole question of Negro susceptibility to disease and the utility of public health measures. It is pointed out that the Negro race is particularly susceptible to a certain number of diseases and apparently immune to others. I believe there is some truth in this claim. Color does seem to exert more or less influence on the resistance of the Negro to skin infections. As a consequence, he is relatively free from acute abscesses, dermatitis, arising from traumatism, cancers of the skin, measles and scarlet fever. He is also remarkably free from locomotor ataxia in spite of the high prevalence of syphilis.

As against these immunities, Negroes suffer abnormally from the respiratory affections, such as pneumonia and tuberculosis. It is in connection with the last-named disease that we hear most about the futility of doing public health work among Negroes. There are many that claim that the Negro is suffering from an inherent disability and nothing that medical science can do will influence greatly the excessive mortality from tuberculosis. My answer to all this is that other races with similar low standards of life also suffer from high tuberculosis rates. But even more important is the fact that in the comparatively short period of 30 years, Negroes have been able to reduce their death rate from tuberculosis by more than half. All of the evidence points, in my judgment, to the conclusion that tuberculosis can be controlled in the case of Negroes as well as whites. We meet the same argument in connection with the high maternal and infant rates prevalent among Negroes. We are told that no matter what provision is made for the care of mothers and babies, their death rates will always remain very high. When it is pointed out that these high maternal and infant death rates always accompany poverty, low wages, and the industrial employment of mothers, we are told that these suggestions are

mere sentiment and folly; that we are putting the cart before
the horse, that low wages and poor living conditions result from
the fact that these people are of poor stock and that they would
show the same high death rates even if more money were put
into their pockets. In short, raising their living standards would
have no effect on their ability to survive. I consider these arguments entirely at variance with the facts, because they totally
disregard the highly encouraging experience of the last two or
three decades which prove that real advances can be achieved
through effort. We have learned how to control environment
to a considerable extent and by so doing have actually improved
this people's chances of survival. One demonstrated fact is
worth whole books of theory in this connection. I, for one,
resent, in the face of all of these facts, the persistent warnings
of those who would doom the Negro to oblivion as a factor in
American life. I am altogether in agreement with those who
see the Negro, like other disadvantaged people, suffering primarily from conditions well within control. It should be possible for them, just as it has been for others, to stand up like
men and to fight their disabilities with more than an even hope
of success.

The arguments of those eugenists who regard the American
Negro as inferior in physical stamina do not, in my judgment,
rest upon sound scientific foundations. This is merely the
opinion of those who are satisfied with the status quo and who
are placing a veneer of scientific phraseology over their own
prejudices. I am not here interested in discussing the biological
factors in Negro mortality because, to my mind, they are not
the predominant ones in the situation. Naturally they do enter
into the question, but the exact way in which they work is still
unknown. As a matter of fact, the whole study of human
genetics is in its infancy in spite of all the protestations of the
eugenists to the contrary. Though large and impressive-looking
books have been written on the subject, their premises are very
shaky, their logic faulty and their conclusions unsound. All
too often, whatever biological and genetic knowledge has been
discovered is used to ferment hatred instead of amity between
peoples dwelling side by side, and to arouse on the one hand
feelings of racial inferiority on the part of the "under dog" and,
on the other, a sense of overweening superiority—both of which

emotions are equally harmful and only result in intolerance, bigotry and ill-will.

I must, therefore, emphasize the need for humility, for expressions of ignorance in many fundamental matters relating to the inheritance of physical or mental characteristics. Being a practical man, living in a practical world, and seeing the benefits derived from applying the newest medical and sanitary knowledge to public health problems and how this has proved effective in reducing mortality from certain causes, I have concluded that the thing for us to do is to go full steam ahead and promote all those measures which are at the present time giving us relief. I do not mean for one moment to dampen the ardor of those who are engaged in research. By all means, let us utilize to the fullest extent the knowledge of the laboratory; let us encourage the anthropologist, the biologist, the chemist and the physicist in all their experiments. But let us realize also how little we actually know, how many gaps we must fill in, before we can lay down any rule as to how human qualities and traits are handed down from one generation to another. Likewise let the knowledge which will be brought to light be used in a constructive and not a destructive manner—to promote friendship between peoples and more cordial inter-racial cooperation, rather than the reverse.

In view of the spectacular progress which the Negro has made in reducing his death rate and in raising his expectation of life, the possibilities that the public health movement holds for him have been more than vindicated. The results which have already been achieved answer the scoffers and the skeptics who told us it could not be done. They confirm the wisdom of those who instigated health campaigns and encouraged new activities. We may now go ahead with increased energy. But let us remember this is not a task which one small group of people can accomplish single-handed. Public health work is no longer the plaything of philanthropy nor is it a task for "Lady Bountiful." It is an essential activity of a well-organized community operating for the benefit of all its people, irrespective of race, creed or color. Epidemics spread without respect for the color line. A health campaign such as we have in mind is costly; but fortunately, money is available. This is not a poor country, nor are we a poverty-stricken people. It is a matter of pride that the Negro partakes of our prosperity and is living under new and better conditions the country over. Certainly there is no better purpose to which some of our newly acquired wealth can be put than to spend it wisely for health promotion and life conservation.

BIOLOGICAL FACTORS IN NEGRO MORTALITY

RAYMOND PEARL

I

The fundamental basis of all health programs is biological, and must always remain so. Man is an animal with all the opportunities for pleasure and all the risks of misfortune which that fact implies. When we think of health programs as social forces, we are thinking soundly and pertinently, but nevertheless about secondary rather than primary variables, in considerable part. When such programs succeed in some measure, it is only because the basic, primary biological factors involved have permitted that degree of success to be achieved.

In attacking any biological problem the investigator is at once confronted by the difficulty of disentangling and evaluating the effects of heredity separately from those of the environment. What makes this difficulty so great is the fact that no living organism can be separated from the environment in general (that is, from any environment at all) and still continue to be a living organism. Or, to put the case in another way, for every living organism certain factors in its environment are *necessary* conditions for its continued living existence. For example, man cannot live in an atmosphere devoid of oxygen. The presence of oxygen in the environment is therefore a necessary condition for human life. Similar relations are true for other organisms, and other environmental factors.

Yet always what we want to know, when we are discoursing of health matters, is something like this: Mr. A. is, let us say, 82 years of age, and enjoys excellent health and has done so all his life. To what extent is this happy situation to be attributed to the manner in which Mr. A. has conducted his living, and to what extent is it to be attributed to the soundness of his inherited constitution? The same problem confronts us if we try to evaluate public or group health, as when we attempt to determine the causes of the individual Mr. A.'s well-being.

413

Now since we cannot study either Mr. A., nor a thousand of him, apart from the environment, we are forced to resort to indirect methods to get as much useful knowledge as possible regarding this great puzzle. One of the best of these indirect methods is to take advantage of a situation in which one of the basic biological variables involved is as different as possible in one group of individuals from what it is in another group, and then see how the secondary variables compare in the two groups. Such an opportunity is offered, in respect of health matters, by studying mortality and morbidity in two groups which are *racially* different. This opportunity has attracted the attention of a number of workers. I have myself been for some time rather actively engaged in the investigation of the pathology and mortality of Negroes as compared with whites. I want tonight to put some of the results of this work before you for discussion; not with any notion of finality, because the whole subject of comparative racial pathology is in its veriest infancy, but rather in the hope of interesting others to go into this fascinating field of human biology.

II

The first practical implication of the remarks made a moment ago is that the American Negro is to be regarded as a group racially distinct from whites. Is there sound foundation for such an idea? Everyone knows that there has been a great deal of intermixture of white and Negro races in North America ever since the Negro first came to this continent. Have we any right, under these circumstances, to speak of the American Negro as a race?

This has lately been re-investigated thoroughly and carefully by Dr. Melville J. Herskovits. It will be pertinent to quote his conclusions [1] on the point:

"What we see is that in trait after trait the average is about halfway between the averages for the white population and the African, so that what we have represented here is a blend, if the gross statistical analysis is correct. In the second place" . . . "there would have to be an increase in variability if the Mendelian hypothesis were operative in this case. But I need not repeat the

[1] Herskovits, M. J., *The American Negro*, pp. xiv, 92.

fact that the American Negro is homogeneous, and that the index of this homogeneity is the low variability of trait after trait when this variability is compared with that of the so-called 'pure' populations.

"If race means anything in the way of definite physical type, then the American Negro is a racial group. If it means anything in the sense that lowness of variation is associated with racial purity, then the American Negro is a pure racial group."

It should be clearly understood that the above quotations are not intended to imply that Dr. Herskovits regards the American Negro as a pure race. In fact he specifically states that this is not his opinion. The purpose of the quotations is merely to bring out the fact that his extremely careful and thorough investigation has shown that the American Negro, as a group, has some, at least, of the important biometrical relationships which are commonly found also to be characteristic of recognized racial groups. Doubtless the correct conclusion to be drawn from this circumstance is the one which has been drawn by Dr. Herskovits, namely, that we have yet to achieve a precise and unequivocal definition of what constitutes a pure race and what, if any, its invariant characteristics are.

Not only is the American Negro different in external body size and conformation, but the anatomy and physiology of his internal organs in some respects are different from those of whites. Bean, who has devoted much attention to this subject, claims to have found a number of quantitative differences. Thus he concludes [2] that the size of the temporal lobe of the brain is both absolutely and relatively smaller in the Negro than in the whites, and that the shape of the lobe is also different in the two races. The same investigator also reported that the spleen is smaller [3] in the Negroes than in whites, a result which Pearl and Bacon [4] were able to confirm. Bean and Baker [5] in

[2] Bean, R. B., "A Racial Peculiarity in the Pole of the Temporal Lobe of the Negro Brain." *Anatomical Record*, Vol. VIII, pp. 479-91, 1924.

[3] Bean, R. B., and Baker, W., "Some Racial Characteristics of the Spleen Weight in Man." *American Journal of Physical Anthropology*, Vol. II, pp. 1-9, 1919.

[4] Pearl, R., and Bacon, A. L., *Biometrical Studies in Pathology*, III. The absolute weight of the heart and spleen in tuberculous persons. Johns Hopkins Hospital Reports, Vol. XXI, pp. 297-377, 1924.

[5] Bean, R. B., and Baker, W., "Some Racial Characteristics of the Liver Weight in Man." *American Journal of Physical Anthropology*, Vol. II, pp. 167-73, 1919; "Some Racial Characteristics of the Weight of the Heart and Kidneys." *Ibid.*, pp. 265-74, 1919.

later papers found the liver to be smaller in Negroes, while there was no significant difference between the two races in respect of size of the heart or kidneys. Pearl and Bacon (*loc. cit.*) confirmed this finding so far as concerns the heart.

That the Negro body may react differently to organic disease

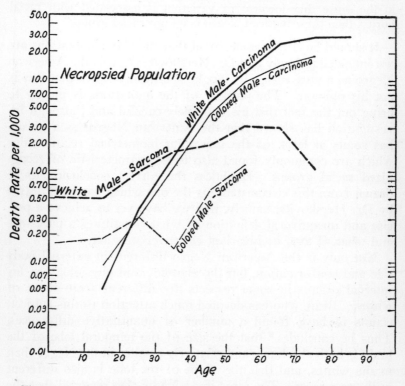

Figure 14. Comparing the death rates at ages among male persons autopsied in the Johns Hopkins Hospital (a) whites dying of carcinoma, (b) colored dying of carcinoma, (c) whites dying of sarcoma (or other malignant tumor, not carcinoma), and (d) colored dying of sarcoma.

than that of the white has lately been shown for neoplastic diseases by Pearl and Bacon [6] on the basis of the autopsy records of the Johns Hopkins Hospital. In the first place, whether tested by autopsy data, as in Fig. 14 and 15, or in general popu-

[6] Pearl, R., and Bacon, A. L., *Biometrical Studies in Pathology*, V. The racial and age incidence of cancer and of other malignant tumors. *Archives of Pathology*, Vol. III, pp. 963, 992, 1927; VI. The primary site of cancers and of other malignant tumors. *Ibid.*, Vol. VI, pp. 67-89, 1928.

lation death ratios, as in Fig. 16, or by general population death rates, cancer (and other malignant tumors) occur more frequently relatively among whites than among the colored. This racial difference is more marked in the cases of sarcoma than in the cases of carcinoma, but for all kinds of malignant tumors

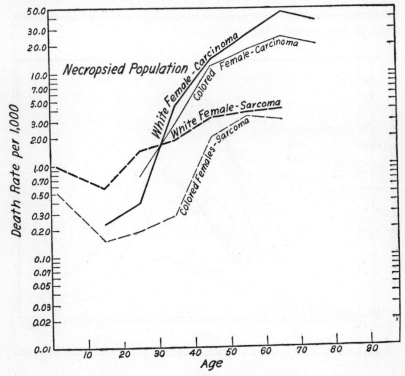

Figure 15. Like Fig. 14, but for females.

the relation holds in general. The only possibly significant exception is .found in colored women during the child-bearing ages, where the death rates are somewhat higher than in the whites.

But the differentiation of Negro from white in respect of cancer goes farther than mere incidence. Table I on p. 419 shows the distribution of malignant tumors in different parts of the body.

From Table I it is plain that the malignant tumors in this

autopsy material have their primary location in the alimentary tract and its associated glandular organs (pancreas, gall-bladder and ducts, and liver) more frequently than at any other site, in male persons, both white and colored. On the other hand, in females the organ system in which malignant growths most frequently occur is the reproductive system (including both primary and secondary sex organs together), with the alimentary tract in the second place.

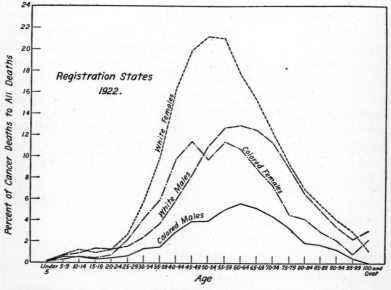

Figure 16. Cancer (and other malignant tumors) death ratios by color, sex and age.

In the Negroes the broad facts stated above as to location of primary tumors are emphasized more strongly than in the whites. Thus in the males it is seen from Table I that 50 per cent of all malignant tumors had their primary site in our class B (alimentary tract). But in the Negro males 64 per cent of all malignant tumors fell in this organ group. In the white females 45 per cent of all malignant tumors had their primary site in some organ of the reproductive system as here defined. But in the Negro females 63 per cent were so located. The racial picture afforded by Table I indicates that the susceptibility to malignancy of the different organ systems of the body is a more diffuse and widely scattered phenomenon in the whites than it is in the Negroes. What cancer the Negroes have tends to appear primarily in either the alimentary tract or in the reproductive organs, and not in the other organ systems, more constantly and regularly than is the case with the whites. The facts suggest that malignancy is, in certain respects, a different thing biologically in the whites from what it is in the Negroes. Or, to put it more precisely, whites and Negroes are biologically different—that is, have different constitutional patterns—in a great variety of respects, many of which have been defined and measured by anthropologists; and we now see that these constitutional differences are clearly reflected in the reactions of the two races toward cancer. The whites have more cancer in proportion to numbers exposed than do the Negroes. Their malignancy is also more diffusely spread over the body, in respect of the primary site. The Negroes give a different picture, both because of smaller incidence, and of greater concentration upon the two most important organ systems.

TABLE I

PERCENTAGE FREQUENCY OF MALIGNANT TUMORS BY SITE, SEX AND RACE—
AUTOPSY RECORDS

Location of Primary Tumor	White Males	Negro Males	White Females	Negro Females
A. Skin	2.90	....	1.28	3.80
B. Alimentary tract, liver and pancreas	50.24	64.04	33.33	22.78
C. Reproductive organs, primary and secondary	8.94	8.99	44.87	63.29
D. Excretory system	10.63	5.62	2.14	3.80
E. Respiratory system	3.62	7.87	0.85	1.27
F. Endocrine organs other than sex ..	2.90	1.12	2.14	....
G. Skeletal and muscular system	2.90	3.37	0.43	....
H. Nervous system and sense organs.	11.11	2.25	8.97	1.27
J. Lymphatic system	5.31	6.74	5.13	2.53
K. All other organs	1.45	....	0.85	1.27
Totals	100.00	100.00	99.99	100.01

This same principle of greater concentration of the primary tumors at the most-favored site in the Negroes, as compared with the whites, is further substantiated if we go to still more precise localization.

Table II shows that in males the most frequent site for a primary cancer anywhere in the alimentary tract is in the

TABLE II

CANCER OF THE ALIMENTARY TRACT

Location	Johns Hopkins Hospital Autopsies, Carcinoma Only		U. S. Registration Area, 1914, Deaths, Cancer and Other Malignant Tumors	
	White Males (Total Cases 182) Per Cent	Negro Males (Total Cases 45) Per Cent	White Males (Total Deaths 11,821) Per Cent	Negro Males (Total Deaths 302) Per Cent
Mouth (including lips and tongue).	16	9	16	14
Œsophagus	15	2	4	3
Stomach	48	67	58	67
Intestine (including rectum)	21	22	22	16
Totals	100	100	100	100

stomach. But again it is apparent that the concentration of primary tumors at this most frequent site is distinctly heavier in the Negroes than in the whites. This curious relationship is exhibited in practically the same degree quantitatively whether we deal with autopsy results or with the mortality records of the general population.

The same thing is true of the most prevalent cancers of females, as is shown in Table III.

TABLE III

CANCER OF PRIMARY AND SECONDARY SEX ORGANS

Location	Johns Hopkins Hospital Autopsies		U. S. Registration Area 1914 Deaths	
	White Females (Total Cases 105) Per Cent	Negro Females (Total Cases 50) Per Cent	White Females (Total Deaths 12,461) Per Cent	Negro Females (Total Deaths 795) Per Cent
Ovary	20	12	4	2
Uterus	50	56	55	73
Breast	30	32	41	25
Totals	100	100	100	100

It has already been noted that in females the most frequent site of primary cancer is the primary and secondary sex organs. Within this rubric, Table III shows that the uterus is the most frequent primary site. And again, whether we take autopsy statistics or the mortality records of the general population, the concentration of primary tumors upon this most frequent site is higher in the Negro than in the white race.

Finally, I wish to call attention to one further difference between whites and Negroes in respect to their reaction to malignant tumors. The whites exhibit secondary or metastatic growths somewhat more frequently than do the Negroes. Thus among the cases in white males 71.3 per cent showed metastatic growths, as against 66.7 per cent among the Negro males. The corresponding percentages for females are 67.4 per cent in whites and 62.5 per cent in Negroes. These differences are not large, and cannot be certainly regarded as statistically significant, but their trend is in accord with the other facts which have been presented.

Summing the whole case up, it has been shown that the difference in general biological organization, constitution, or pattern, which exists between whites and Negroes is clearly reflected in the incidence and distribution of malignant tumors in the two cases.

III

The extensive and penetrating reviews of the existing data on Negro mortality and its trends, derived from official vital statistics, presented to this Conference by Dr. Louis I. Dublin, and Dr. Charles S. Johnson and the Research Committee make it unnecessary to go further in that direction at this time. Instead I wish to continue the discussion of the biological factors involved in the differences between white and Negro mortality along somewhat different lines.

In 1920, in an attempt [7] to approach the problem of human mortality from a more directly biological standpoint than that of current vital statistics, I discussed the distribution of human deaths on the basis of an organological classification of the several statistically recorded causes. The underlying idea in the classification was to group all causes of death under the heads of the several organ systems of the body, the functional breakdown of which is the immediate or predominant cause of the cessation of life. The basis of the classification was not that of etiology, but rather that of the anatomical location of the

[7] Pearl, R., "Certain Evolutionary Aspects of Human Mortality Rates." *American Naturalist*, Vol. LIV, pp. 5-44, 1920.

principal breakdown. The matter was further discussed, and the original classification amended and corrected, in later publications.[8]

In these investigations there came to light evidence that the present characteristics and distribution of human mortality are in part—perhaps a considerable part—the results or consequences of the evolutionary history of the human body itself. It appears that the different organ systems of the body are not all equally capable of withstanding the environmental stresses and strains which they have to meet. The evidence on this point was necessarily suggestive rather than conclusive. Human vital statistics, taken by themselves, are for many reasons inadequate to elucidate such a point as this.

As the next step, attention was turned to the mortality records of lower forms of life in the London Zoological Garden over a period of four years (cf. Pearl, *loc. cit.*). The results are shown in Fig. 17 on p. 423.

It is seen at once that in reptiles, birds, and mammals, just as in man, the two organ systems having the largest mortality chargeable to them are the respiratory and the alimentary systems, with the circulatory system standing third. The other organ systems, which have a low mortality chargeable to them in man, also are concerned in a low mortality in the reptiles, birds, and mammals. This rough but still evident correspondence between man and the lower orders of vertebrates in the organological distribution of their mortality considerably tends to increase one's confidence that this classification has some real biological significance.

There is, however, another point in regard to which there is need for improvement in the evidence. In all previous discussions of the biological classification of human mortality the data used have been derived from official vital statistics; that is, registered mortality. But, as everyone knows, the diagnosis of the causes of death which are recorded upon death certificates represent, in the vast majority of cases, only the clinical judgment of the physicians signing the death certificates. Only in a small percentage of cases is the diagnosis confirmed by autopsy. It is obviously desirable, in the interest of accuracy

    [8] Pearl, R., *The Biology of Death*, Philadelphia, 1922; *Studies in Human Biology*, Baltimore, 1924, p. 653; "Evolution and Mortality," *Quarterly Review of Biology*, Vol. III, pp. 271-80, 1928.

and precision, to try the biological classification of the causes of death upon an autopsied population, in which there is as much known as can be, in the present stage of development of pathology, about the cause of each patient's death.

Such an experiment has been made, using the autopsy material of the Johns Hopkins Hospital, with the results which

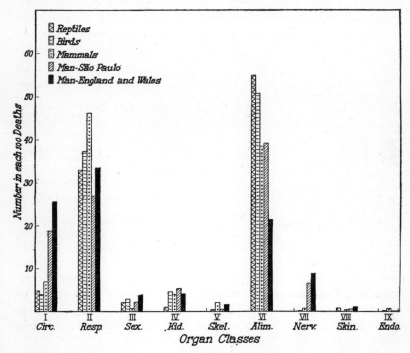

Figure 17. Bar diagram of the biological classification of the causes of death of persons and animals autopsied in the Johns Hopkins Hospital.

are here presented for the first time, in preliminary form. Later a more detailed analysis of the data will be published elsewhere.

The organological classification of the causes of death set up in the earlier publications cited, and followed in this present study is as follows:

    I. Circulatory system, blood, and blood-forming organs.

   II. Respiratory system.

 III. Primary and secondary sex organs.

IV. Kidneys and related excretory organs.
V. Skeletal and muscular systems.
VI. Alimentary tract and associated organs concerned in metabolism.
VII. Nervous system and sense organs.
VIII. Skin.
IX. Endocrinal system.
X. All other causes of death.

Table IV shows the absolute number of cases falling in each of the ten categories of this classification, in the autopsy material of the Johns Hopkins Hospital.   In distributing the autopsies into this classification a careful study was made of all doubtful cases, with multiple lesions, etc., and the final disposition of each case was made on the basis of the clinical history as well as the autopsy findings.   The cases falling in Class X are, in considerable degree, prematurely born babies who died within a short time of birth, and in which there were found at autopsy no specific anatomical lesions apparently adequate to cause death.   The other cases in this class represent incomplete autopsies, and cases in which no definite conclusions could be reached as to the organ system to which the death could be reasonably assigned.

TABLE IV

BIOLOGICAL CLASSIFICATION OF THE CAUSES OF DEATH OF PERSONS AUTOPSIED IN THE JOHNS HOPKINS HOSPITAL

Class Organ System	White Males	Colored Males	White Females	Colored Females
I. Circulatory system, blood and blood-forming organs	628	246	493	237
II. Respiratory system	365	175	440	237
III. Primary and secondary sex organs..	165	238	52	208
IV. Kidneys and related excretory organs	206	75	80	60
V. Skeletal and muscular systems	44	22	45	21
VI. Alimentary tract and associated organs	707	317	324	187
VII. Nervous system and sense organs..	84	153	144	107
VIII. Skin	30	8	5	7
IX. Endocrinal system	51	49	12	20
Sub-total—all biologically classifiable deaths	2,480	1,283	1,595	1,084
X. All other causes (unknown or unclassifiable)	111	37	55	25
Grand total—all causes	2,591	1,320	1,650	1,109

Omitting Class X, and reducing all other deaths to a percentage basis, we have the results shown graphically in Figs. 18 and 19.

While greater accuracy inheres in autopsy results than in general mortality statistics, so far as concerns diagnosis of the cause of death, hospital and autopsy data suffer from certain statistical peculiarities, some of which it will be well to consider before attempting to draw any conclusions from the data given in Table IV and Figs. 18 and 19.

The first of these peculiarities concerns the age distribution of the persons autopsied in the Johns Hopkins Hospital. Pearl and Bacon [9]

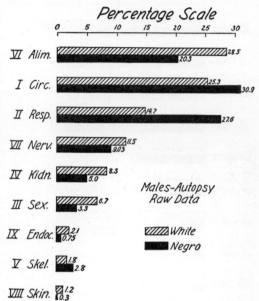

Figure 18. Bar diagram showing the proportionate mortality in white and colored males, in nine broad organ system classes. Johns Hopkins Hospital autopsies; actual data without correction for age.

have shown that this group of persons differs in respect of age from the general population out of which it came, in the following respects. The autopsied group has (a) an under-representation of infants and children under 5 years of age, (b) a marked over-representation of persons between 10 and 60 years of age, and finally (c) again a marked under-representation of persons more than 60 years of age. Now plainly this departure of the autopsied group from the general population in respect of ages at death will be reflected in some degree in the figures of proportionate mortality given in Figs. 18 and 19. The best way in which to

[9] Pearl, R., and Bacon, A. L., Biometrical Studies in Pathology. IV. Statistical characteristics of an autopsied hospital population. Archives of Pathology, Vol. I, pp. 329-47, 1926.

form an idea of the magnitude of this influence upon the results is to correct the percentage figures to allow for the deviant age distribution of the group from which they are derived.

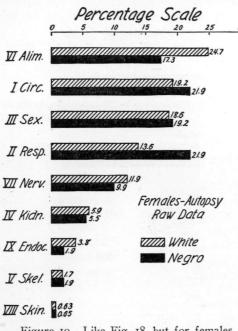

Figure 19. Like Fig. 18, but for females.

This has been done with the results shown in Figs. 20 and 21, the corrections being based upon the distribution of ages of all the biologically classifiable deaths of persons of known age in the U. S. Registration Area for deaths in 1925.

Confining attention on the present occasion solely to the differences between whites and Negroes in respect of the organological distribution of their mortality, it is seen that the Johns Hopkins Hospital autopsy material, whether adjusted to the same age distribution or not, shows in both sexes a *smaller* proportion of the total mortality assignable to the alimentary tract and its associated glandular organs in the Negroes than in the whites.

On the other hand, the mortality attributable to lesions of the circulatory system, and also that attributable to the respiratory system, both form a *greater* proportion of the total mortality of the Negroes than is the case in the whites.

The proportion of the total mortality attributable to lesions of the nervous system, the kidneys and associated excretory organs, and the endocrine system, is, in each case *smaller* in Negroes than in the whites, whether one considers the raw autopsy data, or those adjusted for age.

In the case of lesions of the skeletal and muscular systems

the absolute mortality is small, but the proportionate amount is *larger,* in this autopsy experience, in Negroes than in whites.

The proportionate mortality attributable to lesions of the skin is *smaller* in Negro males than in white males. In the female sex this relationship is reversed, but the excess proportionate mortality of Negro females over white is very slight.

In the case of the mortality attributable to the sex organs the situation is somewhat complicated. To begin with there is a differentiation of the sexes in this regard. In males the proportion of the total mortality attributable to the primary and secondary sex organs is absolutely small, and is less in Negroes than in whites. When corrected for age the mortality assignable to the sex organs is abnormally high in white males in this experience. This is due chiefly to the disproportionate number of prostatic patients in a hospital population.

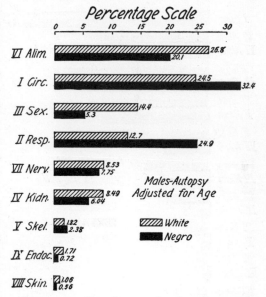

Figure 20. Bar diagram showing the proportionate mortality in white and colored males, in nine broad organ system classes. Johns Hopkins Hospital autopsies; adjusted to coincide in age distribution with all biologically classifiable deaths of persons of known age in the U. S. Registration Area, 1925.

In females, owing partly to the hazards incident to childbearing and partly to the great frequency of cancer of the uterus and the breast, the mortality assignable to the primary and secondary sex organs is higher than in males. Furthermore it forms a greater proportion of the total mortality in Negroes than it does in whites.

In Table V, 11,213,602 deaths occurring in the U. S. Registration Area between 1914 and 1925 inclusive, are distributed according to the biological classification. For the considerable labor involved in the preparation of this table, I am indebted to my associates, ·Dr. John Rice Miner· and Dr. Joseph̦ Berkson. The comparison of the results here shown for the general population with the more exact, if less extensive, data from autopsy records presents many points of interest, but on the present occasion attention will again be confined solely to comparison of the white and colored races. The proportionate mortalities of Table V attributable to the different organ systems are shown graphically in Figs. 22 and 23.

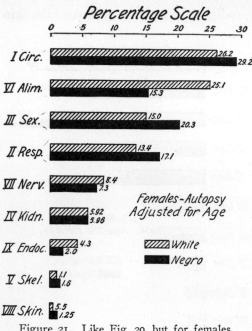

Figure 21. Like Fig. 20, but for females.

TABLE V

DEATHS IN THE UNITED STATES REGISTRATION AREA IN THE YEARS 1914-25

Class	White Males		White Females		Colored Males		Colored Females	
	Absolute	Per Cent	Absolute	Per Cent	Absolute	Per Cent	Absolute	Per Cent
I	1,088,200	20.90	954,363	20.00	97,830	15.82	91,865	14.92
II	1,588,479	30.50	1,345,065	28.19	249,298·	40.33	227,303	36.91
III	85,235	1.64	363,146	7.61	22,007	3.56	56,290	9.14
IV	483,560	9.29	438,761	9.19	60,563	9.80	56,570	9.19
V	43,756	0.84	39,781	0.83	5,743	0.93	4,891	0.79
VI	1,010,496	19.41	859,297	18.01	112,070	18.13	111,212	18.06
VII	779,739	14.97	621,623	13.03	64,288	10.40	60,115	9.76
VIII	47,756	0.92	33,822	0.71	2,838	0.46	2,263	0.37
IX	80,141	1.54	116,396	2.44	3,571	0.58	5,269	0.86
Total	5,207,362	100.01	4,772,254	100.01	618,208	100.01	615,778	100.00

In order to show more precisely the agreements and divergences between autopsy and general population data in regard to the proportionate organological distribution of mortality in the white and colored races Table VI has been prepared.

TABLE VI

SHOWING THE AGREEMENT AND DIVERGENCES OF DIFFERENT GROUPS OF MATERIAL RELATIVE TO THE ORGANOLOGICAL DISTRIBUTION OF CAUSES OF DEATH

+ MEANS HIGHER PERCENTAGE IN WHITES THAN IN NEGROES; — MEANS LOWER PERCENTAGE IN WHITES THAN IN NEGROES; O MEANS NO SENSIBLE DIFFERENCE

	Males			Females		
Organ Class	Raw Autopsy Data	Age Corrected Autopsy Data	General Population	Raw Autopsy Data	Age Corrected Autopsy Data	General Population
I. Circulatory	−	−	+	−	−	+
II. Respiratory	−	−	−	−	−	−
III. Primary and secondary sex organs	+	+	−	−	−	−
IV. Kidneys and other Exc.	+	+	−	+	O	O
V. Alimentary tract	+	+	+	+	+	O
VI. Skeletal and muscular.	−	−	−	−	−	O
VII. Nervous	+	+	+	+	+	+
VIII. Skin	+	+	+	O	−	+
IX. Endocrinal	+	+	+	+	+	+

While the classes of causes are distributed somewhat differently in Figs. 22 and 23 from what they are in Figs. 18-21, for reasons which cannot be gone into here, the differences between the white and Negro proportionate mortalities in the various organ system classes turn out to be in the main, though with some exceptions, similar in the general population to what they were in the Johns Hopkins Hospital autopsies. A higher proportion of the total deaths is assignable to the sex organs. With respect to the mortality assignable to the nervous system, the endocrine system and the skin, the proportion of the total deaths is definitely smaller in the Negroes than in the whites. The circulatory system and the alimentary tract proportionate mortalities, as well as that assignable to the kidneys, show somewhat different relations in the general population from those observed in the autopsy material, so far as concerns racial differences.

It is seen from Table VI that there is complete agreement between the three sets of data, in the case of males, in respect of six organ systems, respiratory, skeletal and muscular, ali-

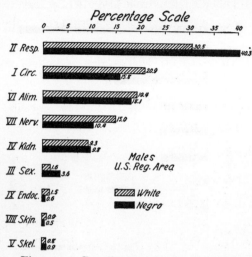

mentary, nervous, skin, and endocrinal. In the cases of the circulatory, reproductive, and excretory systems the general population data show an opposite result in males to the autopsy data. In the females four organ systems, the respiratory, reproductive, nervous, and endocrinal, show complete agreement in all three sets of data. In the case of the excretory system the general population and age corrected autopsy data

Figure 22. Bar diagram showing the proportionate mortality in white and colored males, in nine broad organ system classes. All deaths capable of organological classification, of persons of known age, in the U. S. Registration Area, 1914-25.

are in agreement. In the other four organ systems the general population and autopsy data are divergent in their indications in females.

The divergences between general population and autopsy data are probably due in part to more precise attribution of deaths to organ systems in the autopsied group, and in part to the selected character, in respect of pathology, of any hospital population. These are matters which cannot be discussed on the present occasion, but I hope to return to their consideration at another time and place.

IV

The purpose of this paper is simply to present evidence that biological differences between the Negro and white races, many of which have been demonstrated by various somatological studies, are also, to some extent, reflected in the comparative pathology of the two races. This object may fairly be said to have been accomplished, I think, by the data which have been discussed. The Negro reacts differently to diseases than the white, in a great many ways, including incidence, organological distribution of pathological lesions, etc. In some respects these racial differences in pathology are so great as to make it seem reasonable that they should be taken into account in planning health programs for the Negro. In some particulars he appears to enjoy a greater biological fitness than the

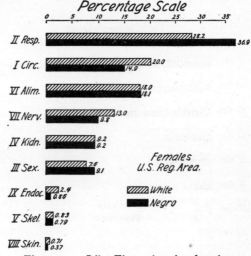

Figure 23.   Like Fig. 9, but for females.

white race, while in other respects he is apparently distinctly less well adapted to the general environment in which he must live and have his being. Is it unreasonable to suggest that specific health activities be directed toward helping him in regard to his specific biological disabilities? If by such methods a definite amelioration of Negro mortality can be accomplished the whole community of mankind, both white and colored, will be benefited.

HEALTH

Questions for Discussion

Why is the Negro death rate, urban and rural combined, higher in the North than in the South? Why is the Negro death rate greater for Southern than for Northern cities, while the rural death rate is greater in the North than in the South?

Can we depend upon our present vital statistics as an accurate guide for programs of social work and health agencies?

Are there any comparative death rates for other pioneer groups, e.g., for foreign-born Italians in one of the East Atlantic States as compared with native-born Spanish-Americans?

Where can we get data that will show that, if the Italian and the Negro had the same economic status as other Americans, the climate is still a handicap?

Do scientific evidence and experience bear out the contention, formerly widespread, that racial susceptibility to certain diseases "seals the fate" of the Negro race, giving to public health work only the opportunity for relieving pain without permanent improvement? Or does the fact that the diseases more prevalent among Negroes than whites are the ones due largely to unfavorable sanitary conditions and low economic status (pulmonary tuberculosis, typhoid, malaria, pellagra, and puerperal conditions) suggest that improvement of the health of Negroes is a problem of society quite as much as it is medical, and susceptible of solution without the obstacle of inherent racial predispositions?

Given the fact that the mortality rate for tuberculosis is now the same as the white rate was in New York City 25 years ago, is it likely that racial susceptibility may change in the course of a generation, and would this change be expected to be gradual or abrupt?

If it is true that the "dogma" of inherent disability is a fallacy, and that the high mortality among American Negroes is due rather to environmental causes, which cause seems to be the most important? What is the relative importance of the Negro's economic status as a cause? Is the economic status less important—as a cause—where Negro workers have bargaining power?

If there is a difference in the "immunity" of the different races, is there any assurance that the immunity can be overcome by medical or health measures?

How rapidly is the Negro as a race building an immunity to syphilis comparable to that of whites? In Africa, for example, this disease carried there by whites has decimated whole areas. Is the Negro in the United States becoming more immune?

Is not the health problem fundamentally an economic problem? Will not digging into the economic conditions and offering remedial measures there materially help the health situation?

What deductions as to biological or environmental causes of the high death rates of Negroes may safely be drawn from the fact that the disparity between the urban and the rural death rates for Negroes is twice as great as that between the similar rates for whites?

How can we quicken the interest of the health authorities of the South in the health condition of the Negro—as to health nurses, condition of public schools, hospital facilities, etc.?

What additions should be made to the efforts now being made to improve Negro health?

Would it be possible to take a unit of population where tuberculosis or some other disease is rampant, put in adequate hospital nursing and clinical service and then dramatize what can be done in the Southern community to prove that the disease is not inherent in the race?

What is the best health program in Northern states where the Negro population is scattered in small communities?

Rather than treat health as a separate entity in Negro life, does it not appear (through speeches and data) that Negro family life, or the Negro family organization, is the base from which all this emanates?

Do national health agencies consider the interracial situation as important in applying health programs?

Summary of Discussion

The higher death rates for the Negro in the North, rural and urban combined, compared with those for the Negro in the South, indicate the underlying causes of a general higher mortality rate for Negroes than whites—environmental factors of changed climatic conditions, and the economic conditions of clothing, food, housing and medical attention.

Present mortality statistics are fairly satisfactory for the country as a whole, but the span of ten years between the censuses makes the analysis and comparison of death rates, in their relation to the populations of small areas or race and nationality groups, inadequate. Such figures as are available on infant mortality and tuberculosis rates indicate marked variations between various racial and immigrant groups. In the experience of this group, these facts substantiate the conclusion drawn from the Negro rates, that the variation may be best explained by environmental conditions. Further scientific investigation is necessary before inherent racial predispositions can be accepted as the explanation of high mortality rates.

The theory of racial susceptibility to certain diseases is gradually being discredited by the emphasis on economic and social conditions, that is, controllable conditions, underlying the prevalence of diseases like tuberculosis as well as diphtheria and typhoid. The demonstrable results of controlled health education, such as the health facilities in cities like New York as compared with the lack of adequate facilities to meet increases in population in Chicago, Cincinnati and St. Louis, likewise point to the environmental causes underlying racial disabilities.

These new approaches to special health problems reveal the deplorable lack of health education and inadequate facilities for training health workers in the South. In the North as well, it is almost impossible for the Negro student to get an interneship in a hospital. In some sections of the South health programs are being initiated that may be examples for a supposedly more liberal and philanthropic North.

Bringing the attention of Health Commissioners and law makers to the facts regarding the health problems of the Negro, particularly those concerning hospitalization, public schools, nurse training, etc.; health instruction in teacher training institutions; county demonstrations in improved sanitary conditions, such as an experiment developed by the Arkansas Tuberculosis Association, and the improvement of standards for midwives in Mississippi under the Sheppard-Towner Bill, were suggested as methods of quickening the interest of health authorities of the South in the health conditions of the Negro.

The interracial situation, as it applies to health programs, is a national problem, deserving and requiring the help of national health agencies and national appropriations. The Rosenwald Fund plan to supplement the public health nurses in Southern counties, as it does the county schools, and the health work under the Sheppard-Towner Bill are efforts to compensate for the serious and particular lack of funds and facilities for health work in the South.

Dr. Louis I. Dublin, Metropolitan Life Insurance Company.
Dr. Joseph A. Hill, Bureau of the Census.
Miss Grace Abbott, Children's Bureau, U. S. Department of Labor.
Dr. Algernon B. Jackson, Department of Public Health, Howard
   University.
Mrs. Mary Bethune, Daytona-Cookman Institute, Daytona-Beach,
   Florida.
Miss Mary White Ovington, N.A.A.C.P.
Dr. George E. Haynes, Federal Council of Churches.
Dr. R. R. Moton, Tuskegee Institute.

EDUCATION

QUESTIONS FOR DISCUSSION

In formulating a policy of education for the Negro should the aim be to accentuate traits supposed to belong distinctly to the Negro, thus accentuating race pride and group consciousness, or to emphasize those traits which are supposed to belong to the best Americans?

As the largest numbers of Negro children to be educated are in states with the smallest wealth per capita, should we look forward to state action to raise the rate of taxation sufficiently to place Negro education on a parity with white schools, or must we look to Federal aid or philanthropy?

How can education of Negro children be made more a matter of Federal attention? Can the various agencies that distribute school funds be made to give Negroes their proper share?

Would not large Federal aid to Negro schools tend to create friction in the South and to remove from the states that major responsibility for the support of education which must be theirs? In a word, is it not dangerous to look to Uncle Sam to solve local financial problems?

If a new Federal bill is passed, will it not be like some of the other bills such as the Purnell Bill, for example, which is inoperative when applied to the Negro?

Will a Federal Department of Education reflect the prevailing attitude and result in continued disparity in appropriations between white and colored schools?

In case the Sheppard-Towner Bill became a law, would it not on the whole be administered by Southern whites? They seem to predominate in the Federal Bureau of Education. In such an event, Negro education South would not receive the benefit of Northern opinion.

If subsidies from the Rosenwald schools, the General Education Board and Jeanes Funds stimulate local giving and taxes, why wouldn't Federal aid judiciously given stimulate still more effectively? Is this not the same as helping in Boulder Dam, Flood Control, etc.?

What would be the attitude of the Southern states—their de-

436

partments of Education—toward an attempt on the part of the Federal Government to provide adequate educational facilities for Negro children? Has the South an open mind in this matter?

Can illiteracy in the South be eliminated in the same manner as James Yen is doing it in China?

Do we not need above all a revolutionary leader, who can command a hearing (Lenin? Gandhi? Sun Yat Sen? Mussolini?), who will really launch a cultural, if not an economic, fundamental change in our national life?

SUMMARY OF DISCUSSION

The formulation of a policy of education for the Negro may aim to accentuate traits supposed to belong distinctly to the Negro, such as faithfulness, good nature, musical talent, etc. These qualities are in no way opposed to "those traits which are supposed to belong to the best Americans," and in addition they would encourage race pride and consciousness important in development. The actual conditions of Negro education at the present time demand a recognition of the inadequacy and retardation of facilities and the necessity of policies to correct them and bring them up to the common educational ideals of the nation, at the same time that they provide special vocational training. On the other hand, if the Negro is to be absorbed into the mass of the population, whatever tends to create group consciousness and accentuate differences should be avoided. Sufficient race consciousness is stimulated by organizations outside the schools. Moreover, Negro students should be considered as individuals and future citizens, rather than as a special group, and emphasis placed on those traits which are American rather than racial.

To secure adequate educational facilities for Negro children in all sections of the country account must be taken of the fact that the largest number of Negro children to be educated are in states with the smallest wealth per capita. Either state action must raise the rate of taxation sufficiently to place Negro education on a parity with white schools, or Federal aid or philanthropy must supplement local provisions. Formerly the South opposed Federal aid because of political animosity between North and South, but that insistence on state rights seems to have died away and Federal control has been welcomed in other state activities. Federal aid for land grant colleges, agricultural research and general adult education has been accepted and successfully administered. However, there is a danger that a national education bill would overstandardize curricula and methods, remove the incentive for local interest and effort and invite political patronage. In the opinion of some people, local authorities could be depended upon to relieve the educational situation. Others felt that Southern administrators could not be depended upon to give the Negro a fair share in the educational appropriations of the state, especially as there is inadequate provision for the white children too; nor would they be fair with Federal funds, as the experience with the Smith-Hughes funds indicates.

The efforts of philanthropic boards, like the Rosenwald Fund, General Education Board, Slater Fund and Jeanes Fund have sometimes administered their appropriations through state departments, and have stimulated local departments to assist and finally take over most of the financial burden of the schools they have sponsored.

The impressive success of the efforts of James Yen in eliminating illiteracy in China suggests that if the various states in this country were sufficiently interested in education they could secure the necessary funds and eliminate illiteracy in the South without Federal aid. This suggestion would make the problem one of educating local public opinion rather than securing a national appropriation.

Miss Mabel Carney, Columbia Teachers College.
Dr. James E. Gregg, Hampton Institute.
Mr. William J. Clark, President, Virginia Union University.
Mr. Arthur J. Klein, Division of Higher Education, U. S. Department of Interior.
Mr. R. E. MaGill.
Mr. George Arthur, Julius Rosenwald Fund.
Mr. James H. Hubert, New York Urban League.
Mr. Allen B. Doggett, Editor, Southern Workman.
Mr. Fred Brownlee, American Missionary Association.
Dr. H. A. Miller, Ohio State University.
Mr. Kenyon L. Butterfield, American Country Life Association.
Miss Charl Williams, National Education Association.
Miss Erle Chambers, Arkansas Tuberculosis Association.
Miss Florence Reed, President of Spelman College.
Mr. Thomas Jesse Jones, Phelps-Stokes Fund.
Dr. Thomas Elza Jones, President, Fisk University.
Bishop G. C. Clement, A.M.E. Zion Church.
Mr. Monroe Work, Tuskegee Institute.
Mr. W. A. Robinson, Principal, Knoxville Colored High School.
Mr. Forrester B. Washington, Director, Atlanta School of Social Work.

Mr. Fred McCuistion, State Department of Education, Little Rock, Ark.

Mr. Leo M. Favrot, General Education Board.

Dr. Anson Phelps Stokes, President, Phelps-Stokes Fund.

LAW OBSERVANCE AND ADMINISTRATION

THE NEGRO AND THE PROBLEM OF LAW ENFORCEMENT AND OBSERVANCE IN THE LIGHT OF SOCIAL RESEARCH

THORSTEN SELLIN

University of Pennsylvania

CHAPTER XXVIII

THE NEGRO AND THE PROBLEM OF LAW OBSERVANCE AND ADMINISTRATION IN THE LIGHT OF SOCIAL RESEARCH

Thorsten Sellin

I

I have been asked to present to you some data concerning the problem of law observance and administration as it affects the Negro. Since I have already examined this particular question in some detail in the recent volume on "The American Negro," edited by Dr. Donald Young and published by the American Academy of Political and Social Science, and since the memorandum of the research committee has given the gist of several studies made in this limited field with observations or tentative conclusions suggested by them, it would be unprofitable to do more, in the time at my disposal, than to discuss certain general questions facing the student of Negro crime. In doing so I hope to place in relief certain matters, such as (a) the inadequacy of the data upon which some generalizations concerning the criminality of the Negro have been made; (b) the defects in these generalizations; and (c) some lines along which research may be profitably made in the near future.

The memorandum contains abstracts of studies, which have been made by students engaged in the search for truth. While they may, at times, have been led into errors of interpretation, they have been dominated by the spirit of scientific research. Unfortunately, there have been numerous other writers, who have given attention to this problem without being urged by motives of disinterested inquiry. The literature dealing with the social problems of the Negro is filled with statements which in no uncertain terms accuse the.Negro of excessive lawlessness. They have charged him with failure to appreciate, or utilize, the freedom which his emancipation from slavery gave him.

They have accused him of filling our prisons with dangerous criminals, because his inferior mentality and primitive emotions made it impossible for him to develop the self-control or the conformity to standards of conduct which life in a civil society demands. Occasionally his criminality has been laid at the door of the unequal struggle for existence under conditions which have encouraged crime. Whether biological or social inferiority has been stressed, the high, one might say the abnormally high, criminality of the Negro has been accepted as an established fact, supported by quantitative data which such writers are in the habit of using without inquiring too seriously into their validity.

The result of these popular assumptions, fostered or spread by persons without qualifications which would entitle them to consideration by a group such as this, has been that up to the present time the attention of the *students* of Negro criminality has been to a large degree focussed on the *amount* of that criminality and its relationship to that of the whites. They have consulted the records of the various agencies of criminal justice and have arrived at the general conclusion, explicit or implicit in various studies digested in the memorandum, that the Negro commits more crimes than the white. This is in harmony, then, with popular belief. I shall try to indicate that, considering the poverty of our source material, such a conclusion requires considerable modification.

Before entering upon the interpretation of data, such as those contained in our memorandum, let me for a moment bring to your attention the quality of the source material upon which statistical studies of the amount of Negro crime have been based. If you were to embark upon such a study you would naturally consult those agencies of criminal justice, from the police to the penal institution, which have come into professional contact with Negro offenders and have thus been in position to secure information about them and their offenses, information which can be expressed in quantitative terms for purposes of tabulation.

II

Presumably, all police agencies gather data concerning their work. Most of these data, however, never see the light of day.

Some of them are published in the form of annual reports, varying in length from a typewritten sheet to booklets of respectable size. The information they contain is designed to satisfy the administrative heads of the community. It is no exaggeration to say that in no case is any effort specifically made to give data of any value to the student of criminology. This situation has led the National Crime Commission, in a recent report, to make this facetious comment: "For the most part the annual police reports are little less than ridiculous. Information as to the number of horses, bushels of oats for the horses, pairs of puttees bought, days of illness, number of guns, and sometimes the number of arrests, can be had." Even for administrative purposes these statistics are woefully inadequate. There are, for instance, only a handful of police departments which publish (or, rather, dare to publish) the number of complaints or the number of crimes known to the police, absolutely essential administrative data for estimating the efficiency of a department's work.[1]

To permit him to develop arrest rates for Negroes and whites, the investigator should, of course, like to know the number of all arrests made by the police and the race of those arrested. He should like to know, in addition, the sex, the age, and the charge, for Negroes and whites respectively. This would give him some idea of the composition of the two groups and the nature of the criminality charged to each. This is the minimum of useful data.

By contrast, this is what he finds. Out of 75 cities, with a population of more than 100,000 in 1925, only half publish reports which aim at some completeness. Only a quarter give any information about the race of the arrestant and then not always for all complaints. Fewer than half a dozen of these cities are in the South. New York and Chicago, with large Negro populations, give no information in their relatively voluminous reports, regarding the color of all offenders. The New

---

[1] Since this was written, the splendid work of the Committee on Uniform Crime Records of the International Association of Chiefs of Police has resulted in the publication of a manual of police statistics, which undoubtedly will be widely used by the police. The International Association has already pledged itself to the annual reporting of data to a central bureau, which will, it is hoped, be established in Washington, in connection with the Department of Justice. Some of the conditions referred to in my paper may thus be remedied, in a measure, in the near future.

York report never mentions race. The Chicago report gives the color and the sex of those arrested who have been disposed of by the Municipal Court. In addition, it gives the sex and color of those arrested for homicide and of their victims. Philadelphia, although compiling information about color, sex and age, has not published a report since 1923. A couple of years ago, I asked a high police official of that city why the publication ceased. His answer was indicative of the value placed by many upon criminal statistics: "You see, it was very expensive and, furthermore, we used to have very few demands for it." If the circulation figure of a statistical report is to be the measure of its value, most of our statistical bureaus would have to be scrapped. The official in question apparently had no conception of the fact that police work is the public's business and that the public is entitled to consult the balance sheet even though it is not a best seller. The observations here made explain in some degree why the memorandum contains such meager information about recent arrest rates in the 75 cities studied by the research committee.

Very few students of Negro crime rates have used judicial statistics. I shall, therefore, spend little time in discussing them. I merely wish to emphasize that what has been said about police statistics is in a great measure true of judicial statistics. They have been compiled for administrative purposes, are not published except by a handful of states, or by a few municipalities, and even when thus made accessible the race of the defendant is only occasionally given.

Penal statistics are, in addition to police statistics, the most important source which has been used for the compilation of comparative crime rates. Theoretically speaking, these are statistics dealing with penal treatment, both non-institutional and institutional, from the suspended sentence to the death penalty, on the one hand, to imprisonment, on the other. Since data concerning suspended sentences, fines and probation are usually included in judicial statistics, these data become subject to the criticisms leveled against the latter. As a matter of fact, the investigator has relied mostly upon institutional statistics found in the annual reports of individual penal institutions, the reports of administrative state boards, and the census reports occasionally published by the Federal Census Bureau and constituting our only national criminal statistics. The last of these national reports was published for part of the year 1923, the one immediately before that, in 1910, another, in 1904, etc. In these reports the student finds two kinds of enumerations, a census of the institutional population taken on a given day, and the number of admissions, or commitments, to the institution during a given period. Like the earlier ones discussed, these reports have been compiled for administrative purposes. A great deal of space is given to the economy of the institutions, its labor problem, its staff, its religious work, reports by the teacher, the librarian, the parole officer, etc. As for the prisoner, his race is usually given, but rarely for each offense.

Upon data drawn from the above source, conclusions have been reached that the Negro is responsible for a "larger proportionate share of crime"; and that "the Negro has committed more crime than any other racial group"; and that "the Negro crime rate as measured by all comparative records is greater than that of the white." These are statements drawn from the memorandum of the research committee. Their inaccuracy will be made apparent in subsequent paragraphs. The data hitherto compiled from the sources discussed above permit only one conclusion, namely, that the Negro appears to be *arrested, convicted* and *committed to penal institutions* more frequently than the white. Any other conclusion would be based on the assumption that the proportionate number of arrests, convictions or commitments to the total number of offenses actually committed is the same in both groups. This assumption is untenable, for there are specific factors which seriously distort the arrest, conviction and commitment rates for Negroes without affecting these rates for whites in a similar manner. No measurement has as yet been devised for the evaluation of these factors. Besides, our inability to refine the crude rates mentioned should counsel prudence in their use.

III

The greatest of the disturbing factors to which reference has been made is the racial attitude of the dominant white group. Take arrest rates, for instance, employed by half a dozen of the studies abstracted in the memorandum. To what extent do unfavorable racial attitudes so distort the arrest rates as to invalidate any generalization regarding comparative criminality based upon them? It has been suggested that the Negro is arrested more frequently than the white on insignificant charges, and that the dragnet, a common device used by the police in their work of crime repression, has been frequently employed in a discriminatory manner. There is considerable truth in these charges. The very high rate of acquittals for Negroes on certain complaints brought into court would seem to support them. The way in which race discrimination affects the arrest rate of the Negro appears from the following illustrations. In a park of a Northern city, about a year ago, a young woman was assaulted. Her assailant, a young Negro, escaped. The police immediately determined upon a suitable campaign for the arrest of the criminal. Every Negro who passed that particular spot in the park during the five weeks subsequent to the event was arrested. The campaign ended when the young woman identified her assailant. Whether or not the identification was correct does not concern us here. What is significant for our purposes is that had the assailant been a white man, the method used by the police to apprehend him would hardly have been practical. Furthermore, the Negro arrest rate in the community was seriously raised. The Detroit survey referred to in the memorandum is rich in similar case material.

The police can hardly be blamed for this condition. A policeman is, of course, supposed to enforce the law equitably. On the other hand, he is the product of a group which has fostered in him the racial attitudes which characterize it. Knowing the strong emotional basis for such attitudes, it would be too much for us to expect a policeman to shed them when he dons his uniform. His failure to do so makes the task of the statistical criminologist so difficult that he cannot rely upon arrest rates as indexes of comparative criminality.

Such judicial statistics as have been studied would seem to lend support to the belief that unfavorable racial attitudes are reflected in the conviction rates as well. The Detroit study showed that the race of the defendant influenced the nature of the sentence. It also suggested that the high acquittal rate for Negroes for certain offenses proved the frequency of unwarranted arrests. It would seem perfectly natural that the treatment of the Negro at the hands of white prosecutors, juries and judges would be conditioned by popular feeling toward his race. The degree of this influence cannot at the present time be measured, one reason why judicial statistics are of little or no value as indexes of comparative criminality.

The same is true, with even greater force, of institutional penal statistics. Here the culminating effects of race discrimination are most clearly observed. As has already been mentioned, imprisonment is but one of several forms of penal treatment. There is evidence for the claim that the Negro is not granted a suspended sentence or probation so frequently as the white. Since he is as a rule in the lowest economic class, his inability to pay a fine opens still another road to prison. Unfavorable discrimination by our courts and the poverty of the Negro offender thus combine to increase the number of commitments to prison. As an index of comparative criminality, as it is used in some of the studies abstracted in the memorandum, institutional penal statistics are therefore of absolutely no value.

IV

The rates which have been used as crime indexes are deficient for other reasons than those discussed. Criminal statistics would be of no value for the purpose we are considering at the moment, if we had no general population statistics; in fact, the degree to which the former can be made useful depends on the quality of the latter. Once upon a time we used to see birth rates computed on a total population basis; we now prefer to compute them on the basis of the number of women of child-bearing age. In practice, we have not yet reached that stage in criminal statistics, as can be seen from an examination of the memorandum. Even when the student is conscious of the need for refining his rates, he is frequently unable to do so, due to the absence of population statistics.

Criminality, like the capacity for bearing children, is not evenly distributed over the entire population. There are no criminals at all among the infants, very few among children and the very old and relatively few among women. The majority of all criminals who reach our agencies of justice are young men. The proportion of men, particularly young men, in a given population group will consequently bear a direct relationship to the number of crimes committed by that group. Can we accuse a group of being more criminal than another, because it has higher proportion of adult males? With no greater justice than we can accuse of a low birth rate a group which has a small proportion of women of child-bearing age. In other words, we cannot estimate, for comparative purposes, the criminality of different groups unless we know at least the most elementary facts about the composition of these groups with regard to size and age and sex distribution.

The importance of these observations with reference to Negro crime need not be emphasized. Some of the most valuable studies of such crime have been made since the great war and the beginning of the northward migration of the Negro. The effect of this migration on the composition of the Negro population in the North, where most of these recent studies have been made, can be seen from an examination of the diagrams of age and sex distribution in Chicago, for instance, as given in the memorandum on population. That arrest, conviction and commitment rates from such communities need to be refined before they are used as a point of departure for theories on racial factors in crime is obvious. Failure to do so has led some investigators to completely erroneous conclusions, as can be seen from even a cursory examination of the comparative figures for rape, quoted in the memorandum.

No matter, then, how much we perfect the record systems of our agencies of justice and the tabulations made from them, the ultimate usefulness of these statistics as indexes of comparative criminality will depend upon the extent to which we can develop our general population statistics.

I hope that I have made clear the difficulties which face the student who wants to determine whether or not the Negro commits more crime than the white. First, he has to take his raw material from sources which are inadequate and not always accurate. Then, in interpreting his tables he must take into account disturbing factors for which he possesses no measurement, such as race discrimination. Finally he arrives at a crude rate, which he finds it practically impossible to refine for lack of necessary population data. These facts suggest the greatest discretion in the interpretation of criminal statistics. Until we have gathered more data and subjected them to a much more

searching analysis, it would be foolhardy indeed to draw any
other conclusion than the following: There is reason to believe
that the Negro as a group comes more frequently into contact
with criminal justice than does the white, but whether or not
this means that he is more criminal than the white, it is impossible to say with any degree of certainty.

It is unfortunate that the belief in the Negro's excessive
criminality has made students of Negro crime expend so much
energy in attempts to verify the charge. Attention has thus
been diverted from much more fundamental matters, such as
the causes of crime and the relationship of the Negro to our
agencies of justice. We all realize that if crime is to be prevented we must know what causes it. I am not unmindful of
the fact that many of the writers in, or out of, the memorandum
have enumerated causes of Negro criminality, but such statements have been based more upon the "common sense" of the
observer than upon conclusions derived from intensive scientific
study of the Negro offender or the conditions which made him.
Criminologists have been asserting for a considerable time that
such studies are essential for the intelligent development of programs of prevention. It may be argued that since the mechan-
isms of human behavior are the same regardless of race, such
studies need not take their clinical material specifically from the
Negro group. This argument is not without merit, but considering the fact that the social status of the Negro in our country
provides him with a sufficiently different environmental setting,
the constant accumulation of case material concerning him
would form an exceedingly valuable basis for specific preventive policies.

It would be unjustified to claim that statistical studies of the
type given in the memorandum lack all value. I have merely
criticized the assumption, explicit or implicit, in some of them
that it is possible today to determine the relative criminality of
the white and the Negro groups. These studies clearly demon-
strate the very high proportion of Negroes among those arrested, convicted and sent to prison for offenses against the
criminal laws. Furthermore, they suggest interesting depar-
tures for future research. In closing, may I suggest in a very
general way the problems which demand attention of the student in this field:

a. There is an imperative need for facts concerning the treatment of the Negro at the hands of the police, the courts and the penal institutions. Due to the unreliability or absence of statistical data for large areas, such studies should be confined to small selected type-areas, such as rural counties, villages, urban areas of different sizes, etc., both in the North and in the South. Social survey methods should be utilized or developed as the need arises.

b. By all methods known to modern criminology, the Negro offender should be studied, particularly the delinquent and the pre-delinquent, in order to acquire more definite knowledge regarding the causes of crime among Negroes and thus permit the formulation of preventive programs.

Here are rich fields awaiting the explorer, who can traverse the high mountain ranges of our ignorance.

LAW OBSERVANCE AND ADMINISTRATION

Does the larger recorded Negro crime rate point to a racial lack of emotional stability?

To what extent are crime figures a measure of Negro crime?

To what extent is unfamiliarity with city life a factor in the Negro crime rate?

Is there a growing tendency toward the administration of justice or does there seem to be an actual lessening of crime among Negroes?

Is it not true that a great many convictions of Negroes in the South are due to a need for road building or some other service rather than law enforcement?

Is the Negro crime rate as much a question of race as economic status?

Is there evidence to support the statement that there is better law observance by Negroes where they have a hand in its administration, through police force, judiciary, etc.?

How can the traditional concern of Christian churches in visiting the prisons be transformed into fuller cooperation with social agencies and scientific research in the modern approach to crime?

In what particular ways is it possible for social agencies to reduce Negro crime?

What can be done to secure justice for the Negro at the hands of the courts?

Is it not possible to select one state in which to promote a constructive program of the administration of criminal offenses?

Is it right to demand that a law or certain laws be obeyed and at the same time the lawmaker makes no provision for literary training of those whom they demand should keep the law?

Does the excess of recorded Negro crime with the evidence of greater willingness to suspect, arrest and convict Negroes and give them longer sentences, suggest that less severity is required for Negroes or that more severity is required for whites?

How far is the defect in treatment of Negro offenders dependent upon more enlightened treatment of all offenders?

What can be done to get the states to draft Negroes for jury service when members of their race are being tried?

Since statistics from official reports are so inadequate, why not promote the study of crime by taking a series of Negro and white neighborhoods and by securing cooperation of the police and social agencies, keep track of the actual offenses in the neighborhood and the social environment factors?

Would it be possible for some board or organization to select a sample of counties in representative states and make a detailed study of law observance and enforcement as these are conditioned by the health education and economic background of the persons involved?

Summary of Discussion

Note: Suggested topics for discussion were concerned almost entirely with further studies, indicating that the group believed considerably more research necessary in this field. The questions, however, seem useful as an index of community concern in phases of the problem.

HOUSING AND RECREATION

HOUSING AND RECREATION

Summary of Discussion

In most communities shelter and recreation for Negroes are utterly ignored, or only just being considered. Conditions vary from the unique facilities provided by the Dunbar Cooperative Apartments erected by John D. Rockefeller in New York City and the Michigan Avenue Garden Apartments erected by Mr. Julius Rosenwald in Chicago to the wretched housing conditions in the rural South. However, Negro home ownership has increased more in the last ten years than in the previous thirty. Real estate firms find Negroes good risks on mortgages and rents. In Northern cities Negroes have shown diplomacy and courage in securing and retaining homes in new districts. The successful experience of the Philadelphia Housing Association indicates that a great handicap could be eliminated if people of ability and money organized and financed building loans and mortgages whereby Negroes could in time own their own homes.

Recreation for Negroes in the rural sections of the South presents a tremendous problem in itself. In the cities of the South also there is inadequate provision for leisure time, though the Negro population has been increasing through migration and as a new group in city life particularly needs proper recreation facilities if ill health and crime are not to result. In most community plans for recreation, the Negro has been omitted, although such public provision is all the more necessary, as the Negro group in itself is not well enough established financially to support alone an inclusive program. There are some noteworthy exceptions in the attitude and provision for colored people, and the number of employed colored recreation workers has increased considerably within the last ten years. In a few instances, as in Louisville, and Daytona Beach, Florida, colored groups have secured recreation facilities by use of the ballot. Fear of race contacts, or a belief that general social agencies are adequate to meet the needs of colored children and adults, retard public support. A restricted but promising field for the development of cultural opportunities for colored people in the South lies in the cooperation between Negro colleges and city groups.

Mr. Forrester B. Washington, Director, Atlanta School of Social Work.

Mr. E. T. Attwell, Playground Association of America.

Mrs. Mary Church Terrell, Washington, D. C.

Bishop George C. Clement, A. M. E. Zion Church.

Mrs. Mary McLeod Bethune, Bethune-Cookman Institute, Daytona-Beach, Florida.

Miss Mary McDowell, University of Chicago Settlement.

Mr. Roscoe C. Bruce, Resident Manager, Dunbar Cooperative Apartments, New York.

CITIZENSHIP
THE NEGRO CITIZEN
W. E. B. Du Bois, Ph.D.
Editor, The Crisis

CHAPTER XXIX

THE NEGRO CITIZEN

W. E. B. Du Bois

It is the duty of this paper to ask what we know about the civil and political rights of Negroes in the United States; what significance this knowledge has for social organizations whose purpose it is to improve conditions; and what further study by universities and research organizations is called for.

The task of the Research Committee of the National Interracial Conference on Negro citizenship has not been difficult, for the simple reason that "this is a field in which there have been few direct studies."

Our general knowledge may thus be summarized: There is a system of color caste in the United States, based on legal and customary race distinctions and discriminations, having to do with separation in travel, in schools, in public accommodations, in residence and in family relations. There is discrimination in the kind and amount of public school education and in civil rights of various sorts and in courts, jails and fines. There is disfranchisement of voters by means of various tests, including restrictions as to registration, voting in primaries and the right of summary administrative decisions, and finally there is lynching and mob violence.

Over against this there are the war amendments of the Constitution and various civil rights laws of the states and the decisions of the courts in these matters.

The results of these discriminations have been pretty carefully studied in the case of education and lynching, but have received little systematic study in the matter of voting and civil rights.

I doubt if it would be worth while to examine any more fully than the summary of the Research Committee has done, the general and pretty well-known facts of Negro citizenship and caste. I therefore pass to the matter of the significance of this general knowledge for social organizations whose purpose is to improve conditions.

Here we are confronted not simply by lack of exact data but by a clear disposition not to investigate or even to discuss. I know of no organization that has ever proposed to study Negro suffrage. I distinctly remember when this recoiling from the facts covered other fields.

There was a time when social studies having to do primarily with the health, physique and growth of the Negro population were of pressing importance because of the widespread assumption that the Negro was not adapted to the American climate, to conditions of life under freedom, that he was of peculiar and unusual physique, that he was bound sooner or later to die out.

It was necessary, therefore, to test these assumptions by such scientific measurements as were available. Yet for a long time universities and social organizations refused to touch the matter, and philanthropists refused funds and encouragement when Atlanta University attempted its wretchedly restricted pioneer work. Times changed. Today tests and measurements have gone so far that there is no further question of the survival of the Negro race in America and the physical studies connected with him are no different and demand no different technique or organization from the general physical studies carried on in the nation. The real question narrows down to matters of sanitation, hospitals and income. What has Negro suffrage to do with these?

Again, between the years 1890 and 1910, the right of the American Negro to modern education had to be established and proven. It was assumed that the ability of the Negro to assimilate a college education was at least questionable, and it was dogmatically stated that the economic future of the Negro in America was such that all that he needed was industrial training to make him a contented laborer and servant; that this class of people did not need political power and could not use it, but that on the contrary their disfranchisement would free the South so that it could divide its vote on pressing political matters, and that the South could be depended upon to guard the rights of this working caste.

The fight was bitter and long-drawn out. Those of us who insisted that in modern industrial life no laboring class could maintain itself without educational leadership and political power were assailed, put out of court, accused of jealousy and of an overwhelming desire to promote miscegenation.

Today finds us with the educational part of our contention answered by facts. We have 19,000 college students, where we had less than 1,000 in 1900, and we are graduating annually 2,000 Bachelors of Arts, when in 1900 we sent out less than 150. It is admitted now without serious question that the American Negro can use modern education for his group development, in economic and spiritual life.

There is, however, still the feeling that the present problems of Negro education are problems of charity, good will, self-sacrifice and double taxation and not problems which depend primarily for their final solution upon political power.

So, too, in the matter of housing, recreation and crime we seem here to assume that a knowledge of the facts of discrimination and of the needs of the colored public are sufficient, with faith, hope and charity, to bring ultimate betterment; and that in presenting demands to the government of city, state and nation we have only to prove that Negro poverty, disease and crime hurt white citizens in order to induce the law-makers elected by white citizens to do justice to black citizens.

In the matter of occupation and income the need of political power in any laboring class is conceded by every social student. For the American Negro or his friends to dream that he can sustain himself as a peasant proprietor, an artisan or day laborer, and secure recognition from his organized voting white fellow worker and a decent wage from his employer, is extraordinary. It is simply a well-known and conceded impossibility in every other modern land.

We can point with some pride to what has been accomplished in the courts in breaking down caste and establishing Negro citizenship, and in the abolition of mob law and lynching. But we are still uncertain in estimating the cause and effects of such actions.

I have heard a number of plausible and attractive explanations of the decline of lynching from 226 in 1896 to 9 in 1928. Some attribute it to prayer, and others to interracial resolutions; but when I see the curve of mob murder fall lazily and indifferently for 25 years and then suddenly in a single year drop

75 per cent, I study the occurrences of that year, 1922. And that study leads me to believe that the effective check to lynching was the organized political power of Northern Negroes that put the Dyer Anti-Lynching Bill through the House of Representatives on January 26, 1922, by a vote of 230 to 119.

The bill was forced through a Senate committee and reported to a Senate with a majority pledged to its passage. The only way that the South accomplished its defeat was by refusing to allow the government of the United States to function. Knowing that such high-handed measures were going a bit too far, the South promised to stop lynching and it has pretty nearly kept its word. And yet consider the cost: there has not been in Poland or in Haiti, in Russia or in the Balkans, a more open, impudent and shameless holding up of democracy than the Senators of the Bourbon South, holding office on the disfranchised Negro vote, accomplished in November, 1922.

The success which we have had before the courts in abolishing the hereditary right to vote which the "Grandfather" clauses bestowed on white Southerners, the fight against the white primary, the fight against segregation in residence and its spread in schools, and numerous civil rights cases have not simply been brought to successful issue because of our present small but increasing political power, but are without significance unless they point to fuller political power.

I do not for a moment argue that political power will immediately abolish color caste, make ignorant men intelligent or bad men good. We have caste and discrimination in the North with the vote, and social progress in some parts of the South without it. But there is this vast difference: in states like New York, where we are beginning to learn the meaning and use of the ballot, we are building a firm and unshakeable basis of permanent freedom, while every advance in the South, unprotected by political power, is based on chance and changing personalities. I maintain that political power is the beginning of all permanent reform and the only hope for maintaining gains.

There are today a surprisingly large number of intelligent and sincere people, both white and black, who really believe that the Negro problem in the United States can ultimately be solved without our being compelled to face and settle the question of the Negro vote.

Nearly all of our social studies apparently come to this conclusion, either openly or by assumption, and do not say, as they ought to say, that granted impulse by philanthropy, help by enlightened public opinion and the aid of time, no permanent improvement in the economic and social condition of Negroes is going to be made, so long as they are deprived of political power to support and defend it.

Nowhere else in the world is there any suggestion that a modern laboring class can permanently better itself without political power. It may be a question; it certainly is a question, as to just how labor is going to use this power ultimately so as to raise its economic and social status. But there is no question but that such power must be had and today the world over it is being used.

With all the research that has gone on, and especially in the last few years, with regard to the American Negro, with singular equanimity, nothing has been said or done with regard to the Negro vote. I am therefore stressing in this paper the significance and the danger of this omission, and I am seeking to say that of all the questions that are before the National Interracial Conference, that of political power on the part of the American Negro occupies, to my mind, the key position, and is the question which peculiarly tests the sincerity of this meeting and the future problem of its constituent parts.

I listened day before yesterday with mounting astonishment to the discussion of school betterment in the South, after two excellent papers. I am convinced that in no other civilized country in the world could such a discussion have taken place. The crucial problem was that of raising local funds for schools and of having the national government supplement those funds in the poorer states; and the essential point in the whole matter was purely the selection of local officials who would spend the money as the local voting population wished, would raise funds by local taxation fairly placed on local wealth and would expend national monies equitably. In any other land the first point of the debate would have been the question of the selection of such proper officials and of the democratic control of their actions.

That question, day before yesterday, was never raised. It was assumed that, although there were to be schools for Negroes, Negroes were to have no voice in the selection of local officials, no control of their own taxation, no vote on expenditure, and that despite this, through philanthropy and good will you were going to get and maintain a decent and adequate school system for them.

If the present rulers of Russia had heard this debate they would have gone into gales of laughter; and if any government had attempted to carry on a debate on these lines in the English Parliament, the German Reichstag or the French Chamber of Deputies, the government would have been thrown out forthwith. Every Englishman, Frenchman or German would have said, without qualification, that education today cannot be carried on as a matter of philanthropy and good will, that it is the duty of the state and that back of the state must stand some effective control. Most nations would make this control the ballot in the hands of all adult citizens, and even Italy and Russia and Turkey would affirm that this is the ideal toward which they consistently and steadily march. It is of extraordinary significance that in an intelligent and open-hearted assembly like this, such a clear and obvious point was either not thought of or, worse yet, we did not have the courage to make it.

In the question of the lack of public funds for growing expense in education one cannot assume that members of this conference do not know what the public thought of the world in the most progressive countries is doing, in insisting that wealth bear a greater burden of taxation and that poverty be exempt. The United States is the one great country of the world where wealth is escaping taxation and where the burden of public contributions that falls upon the farmer, the small householder, the laborer, and particularly the black laborer, is crushing in its incidence; and yet no word was said of drafting by universal suffrage sufficient wealth for the public good to pay every reasonable expense, and of putting the people, black and white, back of such draft.

I hold this truth to be self-evident, that a disfranchised working class in modern industrial civilization is worse than help-less. It is a menace, not simply to itself, but to every other group in the community. It will be diseased; it will be criminal; it will be ignorant; it will be the plaything of mobs; and it will be insulted by caste restrictions.

So far we are upon old ground. This argument has been urged many times in the past. It has failed to impress the people of the United States, simply because so many folk do not care about the future of American Negroes. They once almost hoped that the problem would be settled by the Negroes dying out or migrating, or bowing in dumb submission to any kind of treatment that the people of the United States decided to give them.

But today the latter is changed, and it is changed because those Americans who have any ability to see and think are beginning slowly to realize that when democracy fails for one group in the United States, it fails for the nation, and when it fails for the United States it fails for the world. A disfranchised group compels the disfranchisement of other groups. The white primary system in the South is simply a system which compels the white man to disfranchise himself in order to take the vote away from the Negro.

The present extraordinary political psychology of the Negro in the South, namely, that the voluntary disfranchisement of intelligent and thrifty black men is helping to solve the Negro problem, is simply putting into the hands of black scoundrels and grafters the meager remains of those political rights which 200,000 black Civil War soldiers fought to gain.

All this had led to extraordinary results. In the past we have deplored disfranchisement in the South because of its effect on the Negro. But it is not simply that the Negro remains a slave as long as he is disfranchised, but that Southern white laborers are dragged down inevitably to the Negro's position, and that the decent white South is deprived not only of decent government but of all real voice in both local and national government.

Today, in the South, politicians have every incentive to cut down the number of voters, black and white. The Republican organization, in nine cases out of ten, becomes simply the tail to the Democratic kite. Party government disappears. Political power is vested in the hands of a clique of professional politicians, white and black, and there is nothing that has been done in dirty politics by Tammany in New York, by Thompson in Chicago or Vare in Philadelphia, that you cannot find duplicated by the political oligarchies which rule the southern South.

Political ignorance in the South has grown by leaps and

bounds. The mass of people in the South today have no knowledge as to how they are governed or by whom. Elections have nothing to do with broad policies and social development, but are matters of selection of friends to lucrative offices and punishment of personal enemies. Local administration is a purposely disguised system of intrigue which not even an expert could unravel.

Today a small group of western Congressmen, to the dismay of East and South, are investigating the sale of offices by a black Republican in the South; but offices from the highest to the lowest have been regularly sold by white Republicans and white Democrats in the South and are being sold today. And yet of all this there must be no criticism, no exposure, no real investigation, no political revolt, because the decent white South lacks the moral courage to expose and punish rascals even though they are white and to stand up for democracy even if it includes black folk.

I yield to no man in my admiration for what the new young South is doing in liberalizing race relations and humanizing thought, but I maintain that until the liberal white South has the guts to stand up for democracy regardless of race there will be no solution of the Negro problem and no solution of the problem of popular government in America. You cannot build bricks of molasses.

Nor is this all. Because of the rotten boroughs of the South, real democratic government is impossible in the North. The Democratic party cannot become a liberal body, because the bulk of its support depends upon disfranchisement, caste and race hate in the South. It depends on minimizing participation in politics by all people, black and white, and stifling of discussion. It is the only part of the nation where the woman suffrage amendment is largely ignored and yet the white women do not dare open their mouths.

So long as this party holds this grip on 114 electoral votes, despite argument, with no reference to dominant political questions and with no reference to the way in which votes are actually cast, this party cannot be displaced by a third party. With no third party corrective for a discredited minority, democratic government becomes simply impossible without something resembling revolution.

When in 1912 Roosevelt tried to appeal to liberal thought in the United States against the reactionary Republicans and the Bourbon Democrats, he only succeeded in putting the Democrats in power. When LaFollette tried to do the same thing in 1924, he simply scared the country into larger reaction, since it realized that it had to choose between Bourbon Democracy and organized privilege.

In 1928 we had an extraordinary spectacle. You know it too well for me to comment on it. I only remind you that the right of Southern white men to vote as they wished on public questions was openly and vehemently denied and the right of dominant political cliques, holding their power by disfranchisement of 4,000,000 white and black voters, to make their own election returns as to the vote cast, without state or national investigation or inquiry, was successfully maintained. This is the only modern nation in the world that dares not control its own elections.

How is all this going to be remedied? How are we going to restore normal democracy in the United States? It is not a question of the millennium; of being able, through democratic government, to do everything immediately. But it is a question, and a grave and insistent question, whether the United States of America is going to maintain or surrender democracy as the fundamental starting point of permanent human uplift. If democracy is still our corner stone, must it be smashed because of 12,000,000 Negroes? Better cut their throats quickly and build on.

On the other hand, if democracy fails in the United States, and fails because of our attitude toward a darker people, what about democracy in the world, and particularly in India, in China, in Japan and in Egypt? We have a chance today, and an unrivaled chance, again to rescue and guide the world, as we did at the end of the eighteenth century. And we have the same kind of dilemma.

In those days when we started to build a nation of equal citizens, Negro slavery could have been abolished. Its abolition was begun even in the South; but the respectable people, the smug people, sat down before it and organized the American Colonization Society, which was the interracial movement of that day, and instead of fighting evil were content to congratulate themselves on the good already accomplished. In the long run, they did less than nothing.

So today it is fortunate that people can sit down at inter-racial conferences and find so much to congratulate themselves about in the improved relation between races and the increased knowledge which they have of each other. But all of this is going to be of no avail in the crisis approaching unless we take advantage of the present desire for knowledge and willingness to study and willingness to listen, and attack the main problem, which is and has been the question of political power for the Negro citizens of the United States.

I do not for a moment minimize the difficulty of inaugurat-ing, in a land but a generation removed from slavery, universal suffrage which includes children of slaves. It is extraordinarily difficult and calls for patience and tolerance. But my point is that the sooner we face the goal the quicker we shall reach it. We are not going to make democracy in the South possible by admitting its impossibility and refusing to study and discuss the facts. Let us first of all say and broadcast the fact that all Americans of adult age and sufficient character and intelligence must vote and that any interference with or postponement of this realization is a danger to every American—a danger to be attacked now and continuously and with dogged determination, with a clear avowal of intention by every open-minded man.

What then is called for? Facts. A foundation of actual fact concerning the political situation of Negroes; their voting, their representation in local, state and national government; their taxation, their party affiliation and subservience to po-litical machines; the economic nexus between political power and occupation and income.

This study beginning with Negroes should extend to whites. We must lift the curtain from democracy and view it in the open. We must insist that politics is no secret, shameful thing known only to ward healers and political bosses, and to the cor-porations which buy and sell them. Here is the greatest and most insistent field of scientific investigation open to the social reformer.

CITIZENSHIP

Since citizenship is a pre-requisite to justice to the Negro groups, is the Federal Government actually responsible either through and by the war amendments, or without them, for the right and privilege of voting in the Negro groups in all and every state in the Union?

To what extent is the abstention of the Southern Negro from voting due (a) to laws (b) to intimidation (c) to habit?

What proportion of the total Negro population in the United States is not allowed to vote? In places where there is Negro suffrage is general advantage taken of it by the Negroes?

Why is it that in some parts of the South Negroes are allowed to vote and in others they are not?

If prejudice is a superiority complex on the part of white people, how can the ballot on the part of the Negroes change this inner attitude?

What movements, if any, are going forward in the South toward increasing the Negro franchise?

What may be done in areas where restrictions are operative against the Negro voting to develop among Negroes the will to vote? What may be done to encourage Negroes to vote intelligently and effectively?

Negroes of the North have full voting rights and yet they suffer serious social and economic disabilities. Please explain this. That is, why should they have these limitations if the voting power is fundamental?

What has been the result of the Louisville Segregation fight?

SUMMARY OF DISCUSSION

There is a system of color caste in the United States based on legal and customary race distinction and discriminations, having to do with separation in travel, in schools, in public accommodations, in residence and in family relations. There is discrimination in the kind and amount of public school education and in civil rights of various sorts and in courts, jails and fines. There is dis-

471

franchisement of voters by means of various tests, including restrictions as to registration, voting in primaries and the right of summary administrative decisions, and finally, there is lynching and mob violence. Over against this there are the war amendments of the Constitution and various civil rights laws of the states, and the decisions of the courts in these matters. To a great extent, the absence of research in the field of suffrage is due to the timidity of philanthropy and the practical necessity for conciliatory methods; the real challenge of democracy which the present situation presents is not being realized in a great part of the country and the consequences of this are contrary to the pretended principles of the American people and subversive of their realization. On the other hand, the necessity of conciliatory and slow action was emphasized. Much has been done in the direction of acquiring suffrage by the direct action of the courts and the active opposition to bond issues which discriminate against the Negro part of the community.

This problem should be attacked in a direct way, but nevertheless strategically. It is analogous to the fight made by women for suffrage which is a possible example of the combination of vigorous and cautious action.

The more local questions should be sought after first. It is not only easier to arouse interest in local problems, such as schools and sanitary facilities, but is easier to make the injustice of the situation evident to the group in power.

The necessity of full citizenship was recognized to be the only safe basis for any group and particularly among a group such as the American Negroes where a large proportion is of what we call the laboring class.

The effect of Federal legislation on the problem of lynching was emphasized. Many attempts to meet the problem of Negro citizenship have been to some extent successful, and if the democratic ideal is to be achieved in the future, no legal instrument can be left unused.

Mr. Clark Foreman, Julius Rosenwald Fund.
Dr. R. R. Moton, Tuskegee Institute.
Mr. James Weldon Johnson, National Association for the Advancement of Colored People.
Miss Mary White Ovington, National Association for the Advancement of Colored People.
Mr. G. Lake Imes, Tuskegee Institute.
Mr. Channing H. Tobias, Y.M.C.A.
Mr. W. A. Robinson, Austin High School, Knoxville, Tennessee.

RACE RELATIONS
RACE RELATIONS IN THE UNITED STATES
Herbert A. Miller
Ohio State University

CHAPTER XXX

RACE RELATIONS

HERBERT A. MILLER

When returning from Europe once since the war, I was telling a friend that I was optimistic about certain tendencies I had seen. "Yes," he said, "I also am optimistic about what is inevitable."

We all draw a line of distinction between the ethical and the inevitable. Most of our worry is over the ethical, but there are forces rampant that make the capacity of man to bring about what ought to be seem very insignificant. From Jesus' "the spirit indeed is willing, but the flesh is weak" to Huxley's "Evolution and Ethics," we have assumed that ideals and natural forces run counter to one another. But science, whether physical or social, is trying to find out the ways of Nature, and often it becomes obvious that all that ethics has to do is to bring the individual under the control of facts instead of trying to change the facts, which he sometimes thinks is his business.

A changing attitude is illustrated by this conference. It was originally promoted by a religious organization which certainly has its main interest in ethics, but the program and the data collected for use in connection with it consist merely of descriptions of conditions and their trends. No one would suspect any more ethical motive behind it than in a program of the American Association for the Advancement of Science. What optimism has been displayed has been derived from implications of the inevitable rather than from the setting up of standards of idealistic purpose.

My subject is the first one in the whole conference which might have ethical implications. Morality is exactly the problem of human relationship. I think, however, that our optimism cannot be derived even in this matter from any new norms that have been set up in our times. Everything that anyone can say about man's duty to man has been said ages ago.

Therefore I wish to discuss the subject as a cosmic dynamic process which is going on whether or not one thinks it ought.

This conference would not have been called if there had not been a mass of descriptive tendencies which need to be understood. I take it that what is desired of me is to justify the Commission on Race Relations of a religious organization for cooperating in a factual conference.

This does not mean that ethics is unimportant. The setting up of purposes and ideals is the one way of escaping from stereotypes, and no individual is entirely lacking in an interest in ethical objectives, however much he may be conventionalized and stereotyped. The one thing he needs to stir him up is to become aware of the facts.

In addition to what may be called the objective facts, such as are easily measured by statistics, are the psychological processes which are becoming more and more objective.

If we take just the headings of the subjects for consideration at this conference, we may find that they are intricately involved in race relations. If it were possible to keep a race in complete isolation, questions of race, health, education, industry, housing, recreation, crime and citizenship would have only an academic interest for any other race than the one concerned. Although this is an interracial conference, most of our data are about the colored race. This is perhaps proper for the present, because the process of relationship is incomplete, with the advantage, for various reasons, on the side of the white race. I asked a colored policeman if the colored community did not take a sneaking pride in the fact that a colored gang had held up a bank. At first he felt that he must condemn such a major crime, but he confessed that there was some satisfaction in the fact that the whites no longer possessed a monopoly on first-class villainy.

Let us consider health. Whatever may be one's theory about race superiority, practically all disease germs prove that, so far as they are concerned, whatever lies under pigmentation is equally meat for them. The killing off of one race by disease under any existing situation would jeopardize the other. It does not require a moral appeal to make it clear that race relations lean heavily on the side of constructive hygiene.

In education, likewise, since social organization is so inescapable, added intelligence anywhere accrues to the benefit of the whole, and deficient spots do not stay within the spots.

Since industry is concerned with producing goods, and though fellow workmen may have racial predilections, the goods produced are racially indistinguishable. Whether the silk of your stockings is made by Japanese, or from artificial silk which you cannot tell from the real, but whose raw materials have been produced by Negroes, makes no difference in the stockings. No one can tell or cares whether colored or white workmen made the excavation for this building. Since the object of industry is the product which goes to the consumer, in the long run it is the consumer who determines, by not caring who produces it, that a unit of labor is only a unit of labor. When I visited the Ford factory last year the man who was spraying paint on the Fordson tractors was a Negro, but the painting was neither better nor worse because of that fact. What I mean is that there is a force above the individuals concerned, which is merely economic, which is determining the relations in industry, and this force is working night and day, making things different than they have been.

Houses pay rent and taxes, and every Babbitt is a booster for population. If Negroes move into a section, it helps to boom a restricted subdivision, and sooner or later conditions change, and even the restriction bends or breaks. A bad housing section reflects on the good name of the city and a crusade is started.

Recreation quickly becomes sport, and the object of sport is to win. Delicacy as to means may prevail for a time, but even in the neighborhood of Sacco and Vanzetti Italians have played on football teams. If he is good enough to help the team to win, a Negro can get on most of the leading teams; and as competition becomes keener, the number will increase.

In citizenship the Negro may be undesirable to those he will not vote for, but he always might change. It has been interesting to me to see how kindly disposed to Negro citizens are the Governor, the Mayor, and the Chief Justice of the Supreme Court.

My own interests in this subject are more particularly in the field of anthropology and group organization.

The more the anthropologists study race questions, the less

clear it becomes what they are. The old categorical lines are disappearing so that when the new facts are discovered, such as have been brought out in this conference, they fit into a different situation than formerly prevailed. That is, art may now be just art, whether produced by Caruso or by Roland Hayes. It will not be long before we have as little interest in the color of the maker of a Victrola record as in the fact that the discoverer of the law of relativity was a Jew.

Even though the psychic contents of different races may be better or worse, a fact which is becoming less evident every day, the total psychic reactions of groups are the same.

The first step of an individual who has a disadvantage is to discover who is in the same boat with him, and thus begins group solidarity. Then the whole group undertakes to secure group self-respect. The Jews, Poles and other oppressed peoples called it "national self-respect." The Negro is now going through the same process. It always means a tremendous acceleration in activity. The best parallel to the Negro is the Jew, who has experienced most of the same social handicaps. It seems to be an eternal paradox that the best way to make people go ahead is to try to hold them back. While an individual by all the laws of ethics ought to stand on his merits as an individual, as a matter of fact he does not escape his group until his group has thrown off its handicaps, and the more he is limited as an individual the more value he may be to his group, especially if he be unhappy in his limitation. If the Jews had suffered from no limitation, the world would be much poorer, for the drive of his reaction to discrimination has given us eminent contributions. In the same way I venture to prophesy that in the next generation or two the group that will make far and away the most progress in America will be the Negroes.

There will be strains, and ups and downs, but as the process goes on the biological similarity will be demonstrated until the races will forget their differentiation. This at least is the indication which can be seen from every study of the cosmic process which is indifferent to the desires of a moment or a generation. If we can adjust our ethical standards to conform with things as they are going, rather than as we have thought they ought to go, we may be able to help progress and be less unhappy in the meantime.

The biological relationship always has run counter to ethics and will continue to do so for some time, but it is one of the cosmic forces that many people think to be the ultimate and inevitable solvent of race relations, although it is the one about which the strongest stereotypes now prevail. Some people even try to deny it at the very time when colors are fading out. That different mores can exist is proven by Mexico and Egypt, where interracial marriages attract no more attention than the intermarriage of tall and short people. I defy anyone in America to separate this audience on race lines. I myself have been taken for a Negro, a Chinese and an Indian, as well as for a Jew and a Roman Catholic.

The restriction of immigration has profoundly affected race relations by substituting the Negro for the European. He now finds himself occupying many of the positions of the immigrant, but more important is the fact that both the theory and the machinery which had been developed for dealing with the immigrant are being transferred to the Negro.

I have spoken twice before in this hall, both times at immigration conferences; and what I said, with changes of names, would have been just as appropriate for this meeting.

In other words, the vacuum produced by stopping immigration not only let in the Negro but focussed on him the momentum of interest that would have felt bereft if he had not fortunately fitted into the situation. We have theories, adult classes, special appropriations, conferences, mayor's committees, lectures to women's clubs, discussion groups, tours in the neighborhoods of Negroes, all just as ten years ago we were doing it for the immigrant, and I imagine that after the D.A.R. gets the Navy taken care of it will turn its attention to the Negro.

Books are now being written about race instead of about the immigrant, and the courses now given in our colleges are turning from Americanization to the Negro. Such new courses are being given in hundreds of colleges, and what was accepted five years ago as a matter of feeling is at least being psychoanalyzed, is approaching a real science. This is of the utmost importance, for while people do not much mind being called biased or even bad, for that is a matter of opinion, they do hate to be called stupid, for that can be proven.

The pressure of the problems discussed in this conference,

which may be called internal, and the world race relations, which make our own microscopic, have stimulated a tremendous popular interest which is measured by the books and magazine articles. More than 10,000 copies of the recent number of the Annals of the American Academy on the Negro have already been absorbed. The subjects discussed at this conference are not so important as the fact that it has been held.

Nor do we need to be discouraged because most people feel as they have always felt. New ideas always begin in a class and then penetrate up and down. The prestige of the class with the new facts guarantees that the penetration will take place.

The dominant note in this conference has been hope, but hope based not so much on faith in ideals as on the evidence of inevitable tendencies. Confirmed idealist that I am, I cannot but believe that new moral standards will greatly accelerate as a pulling force the dynamic drive of the inevitable tendencies which are going in the direction we want them to go because there are no inherent reasons why the problem of race relations cannot be solved.

RACE RELATIONS

Is it not unscientific to divide human beings into racial groups?

On what points should one counsel the postponement of commitments to specific policies or ways of conduct until after a more searching study of the various factors involved?

Can the decreases in lynchings be regarded as an index of improved race relations?

Are tolerable race relations and full Negro citizenship incompatible?

Is not the idea of inferiority planted early in the minds of youth the basic reason for the timidity and handicap of black youth?

What measure of contact between groups and individuals of different groups seems to you desirable to obtain a maximum of adjustment of cultural standards, with a minimum of danger to the safety of the highest standards so far attained?

In which departments of life do you consider fellowship and equality, in which separation and inequality, the most promising basis for bringing American culture as a whole to its highest flower?

On what points do you consider practicable immediate commitments on the part of Christian men and women, involving not only demands upon state or church, or society at large, but also upon their own personal conduct?

Has America a race problem that can be defined, analyzed, solved, or only a multitude of separate problems in the adjustment of different racial and national groups, requiring separate solutions? If the latter, what are some of these problems?

What are the major elements in the attitudes of the racial and national groups toward each other? Which of them are unchangeable and why; which of them are, can and must be changed to bring about a more harmonious living together of these groups?

SUMMARY OF DISCUSSION

Race relations have previously been regarded and discussed as an abstract ethical problem; but with the gradual growth of a

481

scientific attitude on the race questions, there is now a tendency to make race relations the subject of definite investigation and to construe the actual changes of group attitudes in society as not so directly influenced by reform or agitation as indirectly controlled by changes in the relationship of social groups and classes. What had been looked forward to as an objective of philanthropic reform in the matter of race relations is establishing itself rather definitely out of the new alignment of races in the world at large and the new attitudes of the modern mind as thus determined.

Of greatest importance in the change of attitudes are the demonstrations of cultural ability and superiority that are rapidly coming from a certain section of the Negro population tending to disprove and undermine the older stereotypes upon which unfavorable public opinion was based.

One of the new and important forces in the change of interracial relations must be the interest in interracial contacts in the universities and colleges, and this movement is really almost focused in the Southern and mid-Western universities and colleges. There are in the South more than a dozen forums consisting of white and colored students who are discussing regularly mutual racial, civic and social problems.

The approach of such interracial groups, especially among the younger college population, is factual and not controversial and is extending beyond the formal relations of their meetings, and in many cases leading to independent individual investigations of local conditions, even going over in some cases into the formation of definite friendships and other sustained contacts between the two race groups. The need was emphasized for mutual concessions; that Negro students had in their experience developed counter prejudices and attitudes which are negative, and it is quite important and useful for Negro students to have the opportunity for educating themselves out of such negative attitudes. On their side, there is quite as much constructively to be done, as there is in the case of the white student.

A considerable portion of the younger generation through such agencies and also on their own initiative are making voyages of exploration and discovery between the races and this is one of the most hopeful signs and trends of the present situation.

In connection with the growth and development of interracial associations it was felt that such work had grown up from mere philanthropic contacts and remedial temporary local councils, that sort of social coroner's jury out of which, of course, the interracial group meetings first came, into such definite organizations as the Southern Interracial Commission that we have now permanently organized, local and sectional conferences between the representative and better elements of the white and black citizenry; that the movement had gone step by step into social work conferences, into interracial university study groups, college study groups; and now even awakening interest in cultural and artistic activities. The latter, in fact, was one of the most hopeful of its phases, because there the interracial groups are brought together not in terms of direct attempt to modify race attitudes, but in terms of a common interest in common problems and common ideals. There should be more inter-race association and conference along the lines of practical, scientific and professional interests, especially, between the professional classes in the North and in the South, as, for example, between white and Negro lawyers and white and Negro physicians, and white and Negro ministers; that there is now in the demonstrated experience of at least certain intelligent sections of the American population the definite growing conviction that race prejudice, instead of being based on innate instinct, is now definitely recognized by thinking minds to be an acquired social attitude, and that as we confronted it in a scientific spirit we would come to understand that just as people could be indoctrinated into these negative social attitudes they could be educated out of them and that there was in this a very hopeful way of eventually bringing the better and more representative elements of the two races into full cooperative contact.

Dr. Alain Locke, Howard University.
Dr. Howard W. Odum, University of North Carolina.

BIBLIOGRAPHY

Books

Andrews, Ethan Allen. *Slavery and the Domestic Slave Trade in the United States.* Boston, 1836.

Bailey, Thomas. *Race Orthodoxy in the South.* New York, 1914.

Ballagh, James Curtis. *White Servitude in the Colony of Virginia.* Johns Hopkins University Studies. 13th Series, VI-VII, 1895.

Banks, E. M. *Economics of Land Tenure in Georgia.* New York: Columbia University Press, 1905.

Barnes, Albert C. *The Art in Painting.* New York, 1927.

Barnes, Charles B. *The Longshoreman.* New York: Russell Sage Foundation, 1915.

Basil, Joseph. *The Clash of Color.* New York, 1924.

Bassett, John Spencer. *Slavery in the State of North Carolina.* Baltimore: Johns Hopkins University Press, 1899.

Beard, Charles and Mary. *The Rise of American Civilization.* New York, 1927.

Beer, G. L. *The Origins of the British Colonial System, 1578-1660.* New York, 1908.

Bender, L. L. *The Negro in Paterson, New Jersey.* Columbia University Thesis, 1927.

Blyden, Edward. *Christianity, Islam, and the Negro Race.* London, 1887.

Boas, Franz. *The Mind of Primitive Man.* New York, 1922.

Bogart, E. L. *Economic History of American Agriculture.* New York, 1923.

Borel. *Annals Institute Pasteur.* Vol. XXXIV, p. 105, 1920.

Bossard, James H. S. *Problems of Social Well Being.* New York, 1927.

Bowers, Claude. *The Tragic Era.* Boston, 1929.

Brackett, Jeffrey R. *The Negro in Maryland.* Baltimore: Johns Hopkins University Press, 1889.

Notes on the Progress of the Colored People of Maryland. Baltimore: Johns Hopkins University Press, 1890.

Brigham, C. C. *A Study of American Intelligence.* Princeton: Princeton University Press, 1923.

Brawley, Benjamin. *A Social History of the American Negro.* New York, 1921.

Bruce, Phillips A. *Economic History of Virginia in the Seventeenth Century.* New York, 1896.

Bryce, James. *South American Observations and Impressions.* New York, 1902.

486 BIBLIOGRAPHY

Burgess, E. W. (Ed.). *The Urban Community.* Chicago: University of Chicago Press, 1926.

Burton, C. H. *Living Conditions of Negroes in New Haven, Connecticut.* 1913.

Calhoun, Arthur W. *A Social History of the American Family from Colonial Times to the Present.* Cleveland, 1919.

Callender, G. S. *Selections from the Economic History of the United States, 1765-1860.* New York, 1909.

Carpenter, Niles. *Nationality, Color and Economic Opportunity in the City of Buffalo.* University of Buffalo Studies. June, 1927.

Cartwright, Samuel A. *Paper on Ethnology.* New Orleans, 1852.

Catterall, Helen T. *Judicial Cases Concerning American Slavery and the Negro.* Washington: Carnegie Institute, 1926.

Chandler, Julian A. C. *The History of Suffrage in Virginia.* Baltimore: Johns Hopkins University Studies. 19th Series, VI-VIII, 1901.

Chicago Commission on Race Relations. *The Negro in Chicago.* Chicago: University of Chicago Press, 1922.

Child, B. G. *The Negroes of Lynchburg, Va.* Phelps-Stokes Fellowship Studies, University of Virginia, 1923.

Clarkson, Thomas. *History of the Rise, Progress and Accomplishment of Abolition of the African Slave Trade by the British Parliament.* London, 1808.

Collins, E. D. *Studies in the Colonial Policy of England, 1672-1680.* Washington: Government Printing Office, 1901.

Colson, Myra. *Industrial Home Work Among Negro Women in Chicago.* University of Chicago Thesis, 1927.

Commons, John Rogers and Others. *A Documentary History of American Industrial Society.* Cleveland, 1910.

Cox, Ernest. *White America.* Richmond: White America Society, 1923.

Cutler, James Elbert. *Lynch Law: an Investigation into the History of Lynching in the United States.* New Haven: Yale University Press, 1904.

Daniels, John. *The Negro in Boston: a Study of the Influence of Environment on Heredity.* Cambridge: Harvard University Press, 1908.

In Freedom's Birthplace. Boston, 1914.

Dazille, J. B. *Observations sur des Maladies des Negres.* Paris, 1776.

Detweiler, Frederick German. *The Negro Press in the United States.* Chicago: University of Chicago Press, 1922.

Deutcher, Dean. *Changes in Distribution of the Negro Population in the United States.* Unpublished manuscript.

Dew, Thomas Roderick. *Review of the Debate in the Virginia Assembly, 1831-1832.* Madison Pamphlets, Vol. XIV. Richmond, 1832.

Dewey, John. *Human Nature and Conduct.* New York, 1922.
Dowd, Jerome. *The Negro in American Life.* New York, 1926.
Dublin, Louis I. *Health and Wealth.* New York, 1928.
  Recent Changes in Negro Mortality. New York: Metropolitan Life Insurance Co., 1924.
DuBois, William Edward Burghardt. *The Gift of Black Folk.* Boston, 1924.
  The Philadelphia Negro. American Economic Association. Series 3, Vol. VII. Philadelphia: University of Pennsylvania Press, 1906.
  The Suppression of the African Slave Trade to the United States of America, 1638-1870. Cambridge: Harvard University Press, 1896.
DuBois, William E. B., and Others. *The Negro American Artisan.* Atlanta: Atlanta University Press, 1912.
Duncan, Hannibal. *The Changing Race Relationships in the Border and Northern States.* Philadelphia: University of Pennsylvania, 1922.
Durand, F. N. *Des Maladies Contagieuses et Infectieuses à Propos d'une Memoire de Aufourard, intitulé: Fièvre jaune et traite des Noirs.* R. Med. R. et Etrang., 1850.
Elliott, E. N. (Ed.). *Cotton Is King and Pro-Slavery Arguments.* Augusta, 1860.
Elwang, W. W. *The Negro in Columbia.* Columbia: University of Missouri Press, 1904.
Epstein, Abraham. *The Negro Migrant to Pittsburg.* Pittsburgh: University of Pittsburgh Press, 1918.
Finot, Jean. *Race Prejudice.* New York, 1921.
Fleming, Walter L. *Deportation and Colonization.* Studies in Southern History and Politics. New York: Columbia University Press, 1924.
Frazier, E. Franklin. *Negro Longshoremen.* New York: Russell Sage Foundation, 1921.
Gaines, Francis Pendleton. *The Southern Plantation.* New York: Columbia University Press, 1925.
Gayarre, C. *History of Louisiana.*
Garner, J. W. *Southern Politics Since the Civil War.* Studies in Southern History and Politics. New York: Columbia University Press, 1925.
George, J. Z. *The Political History of Slavery in the United States.* New York, 1915.
Gillette, J. M. *The Effect of Immigration upon the Increase of Population in the United States.* In *The Urban Community.* Chicago: University of Chicago Press, 1927.
Gilligan, Francis J. *The Morality of the Color Line.* 1928.
Goldenweiser, Alexander. *Early Civilization.* New York, 1922.
Gravely, William Henry. *Can the Water Be Made Fine. Southern Politics and Women; Primaries, Prohibition, Labor, the Negro Question and Remedy.* Roanoke, 1921.

Guenbault, J. H. *Natural History of the Negro Race.* Charleston, 1835.

Hakluyt, Richard. *Collection of Early Voyages, Travels and Discoveries of the English Nation.* London, 1856. *Discourses I.*

Hankins, Frank. *The Racial Basis of Civilization.* New York, 1926.

Hardy, Eric W. *The Relation of the Negro to Trade Unionism.* Chicago: University of Chicago Press, 1911.

Harlow, V. T. *A History of Barbados, 1625-1685.* Oxford, 1920.

Hart, Albert Bushnell. *Slavery and Abolition, 1831-1841.* New York, 1914.
The Southern South. New York, 1910.

Haynes, George Edmund. *The Negro at Work in New York City.* New York, 1912.
The Negro at Work During the World War. Washington: Government Printing Office, 1921.
The Trend of Races. New York: Council of Women for Home Missions and Missionary Educational Movement in the United States, 1922.

Helper, Hinton R. *The Impending Crisis.* New York, 1859.

Helps, Sir Arthur. *Life of Las Casas.* London, 1868.

Hening, William Walter. *Statutes at Large of Virginia, Vol. II.* Richmond, 1821.

Herarra, de Antonio. *Historia Generale des Voyages et Conquestes des Catillians.* Paris, 1771.

Hill, W. B. *A Rural Study of Clark County, Georgia.* Athens: University of Georgia, 1915.

Hoffman, Frederick L. *Race Traits and Tendencies of the American Negro.* American Economic Association Publication VII, Nos. 1, 2 and 3. New York, 1896.

Huntington, Ellworth and Whitney, L. F. *The Builders of America.* New York, 1927.

Jefferson, Thomas. *Notes on the State of Virginia.* Newark, 1801.

Jerome, Harry. *Migrations and Business Cycles.* New York: National Bureau Economic Research, 1928.

Johnsen, Julia E. (Comp.). *Selected Articles on the Negro Problem.* New York, 1921.

Johnson, Franklin. *The Development of State Legislation Concerning the Free Negro.* New York, 1918.

Johnson, Guy B. *The New Ku Klux Klan Movement.* Chicago: University of Chicago Press, 1922.

Johnston, Harry. *The Negro in the New World.* New York, 1910.

Kellog, Paul U., and Others. *Pittsburgh Survey: Findings.* New York: Russell Sage Foundation, 1914.

Kent, Frank. *The Great Game of Politics.* New York, 1923.
Kerlin, Robert. *The Voice of the Negro.* New York, 1920.
Klein, Philip. *The Burden of Unemployment.* New York: Russell Sage Foundation, 1923.
Knight, C. L. *Negro Housing in Certain Virginia Cities.* Richmond, 1927.
Koren. *Some Facts About the Prison Population of the United States.*
Lamar, Lucius Quintus Cincinnatus. *Speech of Hon. L. Q. C. Lamar of Mississippi in Senate of the U. S., June 14, 1880, on the Report of the Committee Appointed to Investigate the Causes of the Emigration of Colored People from the Southern to the Northern States.* Washington: Government Printing Office, 1880.
Langdon-Davies, John. *The New Age of Faith.* New York, 1925.
Las Casas, Bartholome. *Brevísima Relación de la Destruycion de las Indias Occidentales.* Seville, 1552.
Lasker, Bruno. *Race Attitudes in Children.* New York, 1929.
Lauck, W. Jett and Sydenstricker, Edgar. *Condition of Labor in American Industries.* New York, 1917.
Leather, E. M. *Folk Lore of Herefordshire.*
Locke, Alain Leroy. *The New Negro.* New York, 1925.
Long, Edward. *History of Jamaica.* London, 1774.
McCord, Charles H. *The American Negro as a Dependent, Defective and Delinquent.* Nashville, 1914.
McCullock. *Commercial Directory.* Vol. I, pp. 519-22.
Martineau, Harriet. *Society in America.* London, 1837.
Mayo, M. J. *The Mental Capacity of the American Negro.* New York, 1913.
Miller, Herbert. *Races, Nations and Classes.* Philadelphia, 1924.
Miller, Ruth M. *Negro Delinquency in Pittsburgh.* Carnegie Institute of Technology, 1924.
Millin, Mrs. Sarah Gertrude. *The South Africans.* New York, 1927.
Mims, Edwin. *The Advancing South.* New York, 1926.
Mitchell, Broadus. *Economic Effects of Slavery.* Baltimore: Johns Hopkins University Press, 1924.
Moton, Robert Russa. *What the Negro Thinks.* New York, 1929.
Münsterberg, Hugo. *The Americans.* New York, 1914.
Muntz, Earle. *Race Contact.* New York, 1927.
Nearing, Scott. *Black America.* New York, 1928.
Nott, Josiah Clark, and Glidden, C. R. *Types of Mankind; or Ethnological Researches,* etc. Philadelphia, 1854.
Odum, Howard. *Social and Mental Traits of the American Negro.* New York: Columbia University Press. 1910.

Odum, Howard W., and Johnson, Guy B. *The Negro and His Songs.* Chapel Hill: University of North Carolina Press, 1925.

Negro Workday Songs. Chapel Hill: University of North Carolina Press, 1926.

Oldham, J. H. *Christianity and the Race Problem.* Student Christian Movement. London, 1924.

Olmstead, Frederick. *A Journey in the Seaboard Slave States.* (Reprint.) New York, 1904.

Page, Thomas Nelson. *The Negro, the Southerner's Problem.* New York, 1904.

Phillips, Ulrich Bonnell. *American Negro Slavery.* New York, 1918.

Documentary History of American Industrial Society. Plantation and Frontier Documents, Vol. II. 1909.

Pinchback, Raymond. *The Virginia Negro Artisan and Tradesman.* Phelps-Stokes Fellowship Study No. 7, University of Virginia, 1927.

Porter, Kirk Harold. *A History of Suffrage in the United States.* Chicago: University of Chicago Press, 1918.

Puckett, Newbell Niles. *Folk Beliefs of the Southern Negro.* Chapel Hill: University of North Carolina, 1926.

Quillan, Frank. *The Color Line in Ohio.* Ann Arbor: University of Michigan Press, 1913. (Ph.D. Thesis.)

Ramsey, D. Heden. *Negro Criminology.* Phelps-Stokes Fellowship Study: University of Virginia, 1915.

Reed, Ruth. *Negro Illegitimacy in New York City.* New York: Columbia University Press, 1926. (Ph.D. Thesis.)

Reuter, Edward. *The American Race Problem.* New York, 1927.

The Mulatto in the United States. Boston, 1918.

Root, W. T., Jr. *A Psychological and Educational Survey of 1916 Prisoners in the Western Penitentiary of Pennsylvania.* 1927.

Scott, Emmett J. *Negro Migration During the War.* Washington: Carnegie Endowment for International Peace, 1920.

Seligman, H. J. *The Negro Faces America.* New York, 1924.

Shannon, H. J. *The Racial Integrity of the American Negro.* Nashville, 1925.

Siegfried, André. *America Comes of Age.* New York, 1927.

Simkins, Francis B. *The Tillman Movement in South Carolina.* Durham: Duke University Press, 1926.

Smith, Robert E. *Christianity and the Race Problem.* New York, 1922.

Smith, W. P. *Negro Suffrage in the South.* New York: Columbia University Press, 1914.

Soemmering, S. T., and Lichtenberg. *Ueber die Korperliche Verschiedenheit des Negers von Europaer.* Frankfurt am Main: M. Varrentz, App & Wenner, 1785.

Speer, Robert. *Race and Race Relations.* New York, 1929.
Spero, Sterling Denhard. *Labor Movement in a Government Industry.* The Worker's Bookshelf, Vol. VI. New York, 1924.
Steiner, Jesse F., and Brown, Roy M. *The North Carolina Chain Gang.* Chapel Hill: University of North Carolina Press, 1927.
Stephenson, Gilbert T. *Race Distinctions in American Law.* New York, 1910.
Still, William. *The Underground Railroad.* Philadelphia, 1872.
Stoddard, Lothrop. *The Rising Tide of Color.* New York, 192̈1.
Tannenbaum, Frank. *Darker Phases of the South.* New York, 1924.
Taylor, Alrutheus Ambush. *The Negro in the Reconstruction of Virginia.* Washington: Association for the Study of Negro Life and History, 1926.
    The Negro in South Carolina During the Reconstruction. Washington, 1924.
Turner, Edward Raymond. *Negro in Pennsylvania, Slavery—Servitude—Freedom, 1639-1861.* Washington: American Historical Association, 1911.
Vance, Rupert. *Human Factors in Cotton Culture.* Chapel Hill: University of North Carolina Press, 1929.
Van Evrie, John H. *Negroes and Negro Slavery.* Baltimore, 1854.
Weatherford, W. D. *The Negro from Africa to America.* New York, 1924.
Wesley, Charles H. *Negro Labor in the United States, 1850-1925.* New York, 1927.
Weston, George Melville. *The Progress of Slavery,* 1851.
White, Walter. *Rope and Faggot.* New York, 1929.
Wilcox, Walter F. *Economic Position of the Negro.* American Economic Association Publications. Series 7, 1906.
Williams, George W. *History of the Negro Race from 1619 to 1880.* New York, 1882.
Winslow, C. E. A. "Health." In *Whither Mankind.* New York, 1928.
Wolfe, French Eugene. *Admission to American Trade Unions.* Baltimore: Johns Hopkins University Studies, Vol. XXX, pp. 463-635, 1912.
Woodbury, Robert Morse. *Infant Mortality and Its Causes.* Baltimore, 1926.
Woodson, Carter G. *A Century of Negro Migration.* Washington, 1918.
    The Education of the Negro Prior to 1861. New York, 1915.
    The Mind of the Negro as Reflected in Letters Written During 1800-1861. Washington, 1926.
Woofter, Thomas Jackson, Jr. *The Basis of Racial Adjustment.* New York, 1925.

Woofter, Thomas Jackson, Jr. *The Negroes of Athens, Georgia.*
    Athens: The University of Georgia Press, 1913.
Woofter, Thomas Jackson, Jr., and Others. *Negro Problems in
    Cities.* New York, 1928.
Work, Monroe. *Negro Year Book.* Tuskegee: Negro Year Book
    Co., 1915-28.
Young, Donald, and Others. *The American Negro.* Annals of
    the American Academy of Political and Social Science, 1928.

Periodicals, Reports, Proceedings, Pamphlets

Abell, John B. "The Negro in Industry." *Tradewinds.* March,
    1924.
Adams, J. T. "Disfranchisement of the Negro in New England."
    American Historical Review, Vol. XXX, pp. 543-47. April,
    1925.
"Adaptation of the Negro to Northern Industrial Relations."
    Monthly Labor Review, Vol. XXIII, pp. 29-30. June, 1926.
"Agreement Between the Main Central Railroad Company of
    Portland Terminal and the International Brotherhood of
    Blacksmiths and Helpers in Effect November 12, 1927."
    Blacksmiths Journal, December, 1917.
Allen, Gerald E. "The Negro Coal Miner in the Pittsburgh Dis-
    trict." Unpublished Thesis. University of Pittsburgh, 1927.
American Association for Social Hygiene. Annual and Special
    Reports.
American Car and Foundry Company. "Quarterly Report of the
    Welfare and Economic Work in the Detroit Plant." October
    1, 1918, to January 1, 1919.
American Economic Association. "Publication of the Special
    Committee on the Economic Position of the Negro." Decem-
    ber, 1904.
American Federation of Labor. Convention Proceedings, 1915-27.
American Journal of Public Health.
American Management Association. "Survey of the Negro in
    Industry." New York, 1923.
Andrews, Norman P. "The Negro in Politics." *Journal of
    Negro History,* Vol. V, pp. 420-36. October, 1920.
Annals of the American Academy of Political and Social Science.
    Special Issues and Articles on the Negro. January, 1903;
    May, 1906; January, 1910; November, 1928.
"Anthropology of the American Negro. Historical Notes."
    American Journal of Physical Anthropology, Vol. X, No. 2.
    April-June, 1927.
Arkansas State Department of Education. "Biennial Report of
    the State Superintendent of Public Instruction," 1926-27;
    1927-28.

Arlitt, A. H. "On the Need of Caution in Establishing Race Norms." *Journal of Applied Psychology,* Vol. V, pp. 179-83. 1921.

Armstrong Association. Annual and Special Reports. "Colored Women as Industrial Workers in Philadelphia," 1927.

Atlanta University Studies of the American Negro. "Social and Physical Conditions of Negroes in Cities."

"Attacking the Fourteenth Amendment." *Opportunity,* Vol. II, p. 322. November, 1924.

"Attitude of the N.A.A.C.P. in Regard to Organized Labor." *Monthly Labor Review,* Vol. XIX, pp. 176-77. September, 1924.

Bacon, Alice M. "The Negro and the Atlanta Exposition." John Slater Fund, Occasional Papers, No. 7. 1896.

Baker, Ray Stannard. "Following the Color Line." *American Magazine,* Vol. LXIII, pp. 563-79. April, 1907.

"Problems of Citizenship." *Annals of the American Academy of Political and Social Science,* Vol. XLIX, pp. 93-104. 1913.

Beales, Le V. "Negro Enumeration of 1920; a Reply to Dr. Kelly Miller." *Scientific Monthly,* Vol. XIV, pp. 352-60. April, 1922.

Birmingham School Survey. 1923.

Bitting, Samuel T. "Rural Land Ownership Among the Negroes of Virginia." Phelps-Stokes Fellowship Papers. University of Virginia, 1916.

Bizzell, W. B. "Farm Tenantry in the U. S." Texas Agricultural Experiment Station, Bull. No. 278. October, 1921.

Boie, Maurine. "An Analysis of Crime Statistics for Minneapolis for 1923, 1924, 1925." *Opportunity.* June, 1927.

Bond, Horace M. "Survey of Negro Education in Oklahoma." *The Crisis.* May and July, 1928.

Bond, James. "Progress in Race Relations in Kentucky. Report of the Director of the Kentucky Commission on Race Relations for 1922." Atlanta, Ga.

Boy Scouts of America. "Report of Committee on Interracial Activities." 1927.

Branson, E. C. "Farm Tenancy in the South." *Journal of Social Forces,* Vol. I, pp. 213-24, 450-57. March-May, 1923.

Brawley, Benjamin. "Early Effort for Industrial Education." John F. Slater Fund, Occasional Papers, No. 22. 1923.

Burgess, E. W. "Residential Segregation in American Cities." *Annals of the Academy of Political and Social Science,* Vol. CXXX. 1928.

Busch, John. "Race Attitudes of Children." *Religious Education.* January, 1926.

Campbell, R. "South et al.; Reply to G. W. Harp." *Forum,* Vol. LXXVII, pp. 468-69. March, 1927.

Carter, H. G. "Tuberculosis Among Negroes." National Tuberculosis Association Transactions, pp. 226-33, 1920.
"Further Observations on Pulmonary Tuberculosis Among American Negroes." *American Review of Tuberculosis,* Vol. VI, pp. 1002-1007, January, 1923.
Chambers of Commerce. Reports and Bulletins, 58 Cities.
Christenson, Niels. "Fifty Years of Freedom: Conditions on the Sea Coast Regions." *Annals of the American Academy of Political and Social Science,* Vol. XLIX, pp. 58-66. September, 1913.
City and State Departments of Health. Annual and Special Reports.
Clark, Howard L. "Growth of the Negro Population in the United States and Trend of the Migration from the South Since 1860." *Manufacturers Record,* Vol. LXXXIII, pp. 61-63. January, 1923.
Clark, W. W. "Birth Rate and Native Intelligence." *Psychological Clinic,* Vol. XIV, pp. 111-15. 1922.
"Color, Sex, Age Constant—1911-1922." Statistical Bulletin, Vol. IV, No. 9.
Colson, Myra. "Negro Home Workers in Chicago." *Social Service Review.* Vol. II, pp. 385-413.
Coman, Katherine. "The Negro as a Peasant Farmer." *Publications of the American Statistical Association,* Vol. IX, p. 39. June, 1904.
Commission on Interracial Cooperation. "Cooperation Studies in Southern Communities." Atlanta, 1921.
Commonwealth Fund. "Child Health and County Health, Rutherford County, Tenn."
Comstock, A. P. "Chicago Housing Conditions." *American Journal of Sociology,* Vol. XVIII, pp. 241-57. September, 1912.
Conference on Racial Differences. Proceedings. Auspices of the Committee on Problems and Policies, Social Science Research Council and Division of Anthropology and Psychology, National Research Council. Washington, 1928.
Coulter, John Lee. "The Rural South." *Publications of the American Statistical Association,* March, 1912.
Cushman, Robert Eugene. "The Social and Economic Interpretation of the Fourteenth Amendment." *Michigan Law Review,* Vol. XX, p. 737. May, 1922.
Daves, J. J. "The Colored Population of Knoxville, Tenn." Knoxville Free Colored Library. 1926.
DePorte, J. V. "Interracial Variations in Infant Mortality." *American Journal of Hygiene,* Vol. V, No. 4. 1925.
Detroit Bureau of Municipal Research. "The Negro in Detroit." 1926. Detroit Commission on Race Relations.

Detroit Mayor's Interracial Committee. "The Negro in Detroit." 1927.

Dillard, J. H. (Ed.). "Five Letters of the University Commission on Southern Race Questions." John F. Slater Fund, Occasional Papers, No. 24. 1927.

Donald, Henderson. "Negro Migration of 1916-1918." *Journal of Negro History,* Vol. VI, No. 4. October, 1921.

Dover, Delaware, Department of Public Instruction. Annual Report.

DuBois, William Edward Burghardt. "The Possibility of Democracy in America." *The Crisis.* September, 1928.

DuBois, W. E. B., and Dill, A. G. (Eds.). "The Common School and the American Negro." Atlanta University Publications No. 16. 1911.

DuBois, W. E. B., and Stoddard, Lothrop. "Debate—Shall the Negro Be Encouraged to Seek Cultural Equality?" Chicago Forum Council. 1929.

Dublin, Louis. "The Health of the Negro." *Annals of the American Academy of Political and Social Science,* Vol. CXL. 1928.

"Life, Death and the Negro." *American Mercury.* September, 1927.

"Mortality Experience of the First Nine Months of 1927." New York: Metropolitan Life Insurance Company. Bulletin. 1927.

"The Reduction in Mortality Among Colored Policy Holders." Annual Conference of the National Urban League. 1920.

Dunne, William F. "Negroes in American Industries." *Workers Monthly.* April, 1925.

Durham Conference of the American Negro. 1927.

Durhman, John Stephens. "The Negro and Labor Unions." *Atlantic Monthly,* Vol. LXXXI, p. 22. 1898.

Durrett, J. J., and Stromquist, W. G. "A Study of Violent Deaths Registered in the Cities of Atlanta, Birmingham, Memphis and New Orleans for the Years 1921-1922." Memphis: Memphis Department of Health.

"East St. Louis Riots." "Report of the Special Committee Authorized by Congress to Investigate the Riots." House of Representatives Document. No. 1231.

Echel, Edwin C. "Negro Concentration in the South." *World Today,* Vol. IX, pp. 1215-20. November, 1905.

Edwards, T. J. "Tenant System and Some Changes Since Emancipation." *Annals of the American Academy of Political and Social Science,* Vol. XLIX, pp. 38-46. September, 1913.

"Employment of the Negro in Pennsylvania Industries." *Monthly Labor Review,* Vol. XII, p. 206. January, 1921.

"Employment of Negroes on Railroads." *Monthly Labor Review,* Vol. XIX, p. 161. November, 1924.

Evans, Wm. S. "The Negro in Chicago Industries." *Opportunity*, Vol. I, pp. 15-16. February, 1923.

Faris, Ellsworth. "The Mental Capacity of Savages." *American Journal of Sociology*, pp. 603-19. March, 1918.

"The Natural History of Race Prejudice," in *Ebony and Topaz*, edited by Chas. S. Johnson. New York: National Urban League. 1926.

"The Nature of Human Nature," in *The Urban Community*, edited by E. W. Burgess. Chicago: University of Chicago Press. 1926.

"Racial Attitudes and Sentiments." *Southwestern Political and Social Science Quarterly*, pp. 479-90. March, 1929.

Farnham, D. T. "Negro as a Source of Industrial Labor." *Industrial Management*. August, 1918.

Favrot, Leo Mortimer. "A Study of County Training Schools for Negroes in The South." John F. Slater Fund, Occasional Papers, No. 23, 1923.

Federal Council of Churches. "Report on the Coal Strike in West Pennsylvania." May, 1928.

Fleming, Walter Lynwood. "Plantation Life in the South." *Journal of American History*. April-June, 1909.

" 'Pap Singleton,' the Moses of the Colored Exodus, Baton Rouge." *American Journal of Sociology*. July, 1909.

Florida State Department of Education. "Biennial Report of the Superintendent of Public Instruction, for Two Years Ending June, 1928."

"The Fourteenth and Fifteenth Amendments." *Opportunity*, Vol. VI, pp. 67-8. March, 1928.

Fry, C. Luther. "A Census Analysis of Southern Villages." Institute of Social and Religious Research. New York, 1924.

Galloway, Rev. Bishop Charles B. "The South and the Negro." John F. Slater Fund, Occasional Papers, No. 11. 1904.

Gannett, Henry. "Occupations of the Negroes." John F. Slater Fund, Occasional Papers, No. 6. 1895.

Garth, T. R., and Whatley, C. A. "The Intelligence of Southern Negro Children." *School and Society*, Vol. XXII, pp. 501-04. 1905.

Garvin, Chas. H. "Immunity to Disease Among Dark-skinned People." *Opportunity*. August, 1926.

General Education Board. Annual Report. 1917-18.

Georgia Colored Citizens' Conference. "Outlining the Causes of Migration and Placing the Responsibility and Suggesting the Remedy. Address to the State Legislature."

Georgia Committee on Race Relations. "A Statement from Gov. Hugh M. Dorsey as to the Negro in Georgia." April 22, 1921.

Georgia State Department of Commerce and Labor. "Fifth Annual Report of the Commissioner of Commerce and Labor, Year Ending December 31, 1916."

Georgia State Department of Education. "54th and 55th Annual Reports of the Superintendent of Education to the General Assembly of the State, for the Biennium Ending December 31, 1926."

Gies, William J. "Dental Education in the United States." Carnegie Foundation for the Advancement of Teaching. Bulletin No. 19.

Glasson, William H. "Rural Conditions in the South." *Journal of the American Statistical Association.*

Goodenough, Florence L. "Racial Differences in the Intelligence of School Children." *Journal of Experimental Psychology,* Vol. IX, pp. 388-97. 1926.

Granger, Lester B. "Race Relations in the School System." *Opportunity.* November, 1925.

Granger, W. R. R. "A Neglected Health Problem." *Opportunity.* March, 1928.

Gray and Ellis, H. "On Certain Diseases of the African Slaves." *Medical Chirurgal Journal and Review.* 1816.

Green, Howard Whipple. "A. Comparison of the Death Rates from Tuberculosis in 23 Large Cities of the United States." *American Review of Tuberculosis,* Vol. XIII, No. 1. January, 1926.

"A Study of the Movement of the Negro· Population of Cleveland." 1924. Bureau of Statistics and Research, Cleveland Health Council.

Hammond, L. H. "Southern Women and Racial Adjustment." John F. Slater Fund, Occasional Papers, No. 19. 1920.

Harper, Roland M. "Rural Standards of Living in the South." *Journal of Social Forces,* Vol. I, p. 13; Vol. II, p. 253. November, 1923; January, 1924.

Harris, Abram L., Jr. "The Negro Population in Minneapolis." The Minneapolis Urban League. 1926.

"The Plight of the Negro Miners." *Opportunity;* Vol. III, p. 303. October, 1925.

"A White and Black World in American Labor." *Journal of Social Forces,* Vol. IV, pp. 376-83. December, 1925.

Harris, H. L. "The Health of the Negro in Chicago." Mimeographed Report. 1927.

"Report on a Negro Health Survey and the Recommendations of the Advisory Committee to the Commissioner of Health, Chicago." 1927.

Haynes, Mrs. Elizabeth Ross. "Negroes in Domestic Service in the United States." *Journal of Negro History,* Vol. VIII, pp. 384-442. October, 1923.

"Two Million Negro Women at Work." *Southern Workman,* Vol. LI, p. 64. February, 1922.

Haynes, George Edmund. "The Effect of War Conditions on Negro Labor." *Annals of the American Academy of Political and Social Science,* Vol. VIII, pp. 299-312. February, 1919.

Haynes, George Edmund. "Negro New-comers in Detroit, Mich." Home Mission Council. New York, 1918.

Hennepin County Law Enforcement Society. "The Black and Tan Situation in Minneapolis." 1926.

Herskovits, Melville J. "Age Changes in Pigmentations of American Negroes." *American Journal of Physical Anthropology.* July-September, 1926.

"On the Relation Between Negro-white Mixture and Standing in Intelligence Tests." *Pedagogical Seminary and Journal of Genetic Psychology,* Vol. XXXIII, No. 1, pp. 30-42. March, 1926.

"A Preliminary Consideration of the Culture Areas of Africa." *American Anthropologist,* Vol. XXVI, No. 1. January and March, 1924.

"Social Pattern: A Methodological Study." *Social Forces,* Vol. IV, No. 1. September, 1925.

"Some Effects of Social Selection on the American Negro." *Publications of the American Sociological Society,* Vol. XXXII. 1926.

"Some Observations on the Growth of Colored Boys." *American Journal of Physical Anthropology.* October-December, 1924.

Hill, T. Arnold. "The Negro in Industry." *American Federationist,* Vol. XXXII, pp. 915-20. October, 1915.

Hobson, E. C., and Hopkins, C. E. "A Report Concerning the Colored Women of the South." John F. Slater Fund, Occasional Papers, No. 9. 1896.

Johns Hopkins University. Studies in Political and Social Science. Baltimore, 1889-1902.

House, I. O. "Negro Labor and the Industries." *Opportunity,* Vol. I, No. 1, pp. 20-22. 1923.

Howard, W. Travis. "The Real Risk Rate of Death to Mothers from Causes Connected with Childbirth." *Journal of Hygiene,* Vol. I, pp. 197-233. 1921.

Hrdlicka, Ales. "Pigmentation in the Old Americans with Notes on Graying and Loss of Hair." Smithsonian Report for 1921; Publication 2696.

Hubbard, Kate. "Are There Any Blind Black Babies?" *Survey,* Vol. LII, p. 91. 1924.

Hughes, Elizabeth. "Living Conditions of Small Wage Earners in Chicago." Chicago Department of Public Welfare. 1925.

Ihlder, John. "Housing in the South." *Survey.* November, 1913.

Inquiry, The. "And Who Is My Neighbor?" New York, 1924.

Institute of Biological Research, International Clinic, Johns Hopkins University Hospital Bulletin, Vol. III, pp. 53-77. 1928.

Interchurch World Movement. Report on the Steel Strike of 1919.

"Industrial Condition of the Negro in the North." *American Academy of Political and Social Science Publication*, No. 498. 1906.

Johnson, Charles S. "Abstracts of a Group of Recent Studies with Conclusions Pertinent to Negro Problems." National Urban League.

"Black Workers and the City." *Survey*, Vol. LIII, p. 641. March, 1925.

"Letters and Documents Collected During the Negro Migration of 1917-1918." Unpublished Manuscripts.

"Los Angeles Survey." Department of Research and Investigations, National Urban League.

"The Negro and Labor Unions." National Urban League.

"The Negro Migration." *Modern Quarterly*, Vol. II, No. 4. 1925.

"Survey of the Negro Population of Fort Wayne, Ind." Department of Research, National Urban League. 1928.

Johnson, James Weldon. "The Gentleman's Agreement and the Negro Vote." *The Crisis*, Vol. XXVIII, pp. 260-64. October, 1924.

"Three Achievements and Their Significance." *The Crisis*, Vol. VII, pp. 222-24. September, 1927.

"Native African Races and Culture." John F. Slater Fund. Occasional Papers, No. 25. 1927.

Johnson, John Quincy. "Report of the Fifth Tuskegee Negro Conference." John F. Slater Fund, Occasional Papers, No. 8. 1896.

Jones, Eugene Kinckle. "Problems of the Colored Child." *Annals of the American Academy of Political and Social Science*. November, 1921.

Journal of Delinquency, Vol. I, No. 4. September, 1916.

Journal of the American Institute of Criminal Law and Criminology, Vol. XVIII, No. 3. November, 1927.

Journal of Negro History.

Keezer, Dexter M. "Low Wages in the South." *Survey*, Vol. LVII, pp. 226-28. November 15, 1926.

Keith, Arthur. "The Differentiation of Mankind into Racial Types." Smithsonian Report. 1919.

Kelsey, Carl. "The Negro Farmer." Ph.D. Thesis, University of Pennsylvania. 1903.

Kent, F. R. "The Negro and the Franchise." *Independent*, Vol. CXVII, pp. 291-92. September 11, 1926.

Knox, J. H. M. "Causes of Mortality, Prematurity, Tuberculosis, Syphilis, and Secondary Pneumonia." *American Journal of Diseases of Children*, Vol. XXX, p. 437. 1925.

"Morbidity and Mortality in the Negro Infant." *Archives of Pediatrics*, Vol. XLII, p. 292. 1925.

Knox, J. H. M., and Zental, Paul. "The Health Problem of the Negro Child." *American Journal of Public Hygiene,* Vol. XVI, p. 805. 1926.

Koch, Helen Lois and Simmons, Rietta. "A Study of the Test Performance of American, Mexican and Negro Children." Princeton Psychological Monographs, Vol. XXXV, No. 5. 1920.

Lacy, L. D. "Relative Intelligence of White and Colored Children." *Elementary School Journal,* Vol. XXVI, pp. 542-46. 1926.

Lambert, J. S. "Make the Parents Literate." *State Normal Journal* (Montgomery, Ala.), pp. 27-30, 1929.

Landis, H. R. M. "The Clinic for Negroes at the Henry Phipps Institute." Transactions 17th Annual Meeting, National Tuberculosis Association.

Lett, Harold A. "Migration Difficulties in Michigan." *Southern Workman,* Vol. LVI, No. 5. May, 1927.

Louisiana State Department of Labor. "Twelfth Annual Report of the State Commissioner, Department of Labor and Industrial Statistics." 1923-24.

Louisiana State Department of Education. "Special Report on Negro Education." Bulletin 104.

"Report on Special Activities in Negro Education." Bulletin 18. October, 1921.

Love, A. C., and Davenport, C. B. "A Comparison of White and Colored Troops in Respect to Incidence of Disease." *National Academy of Science: Proceedings,* Vol. III, pp. 58-67. 1919.

McClelland, Ed. S. "Negro Labor in the Westinghouse Electric and Manufacturing Corporation." *Opportunity,* Vol. I, No. 1, pp. 22-23. 1923.

McDavid, Mary Foster. "Facts Concerning County Supervision in the Colored Schools of Alabama." *State Normal Journal* (Montgomery, Ala.). 1929.

McKenzie, H. S. "South, the Cotton and the Negro; Reply to H. Snyder." *North American Review,* Vol. CCX, pp. 486-95. April, 1924.

Mark, Mary Louise. "Negroes in Columbus." Ohio State University Studies, Graduate School Series in Social Science, No. 2. 1928.

Maryland Interracial Commission. "Report with Recommendations to the Governor and General Assembly." 1928.

Marrs, S. M. N., Bludworth, G. T., and Taylor, D. B. "Negro Education in Texas." Texas State Department of Education. Bulletin No. 212. October, 1926.

Massachusetts Bureau of Statistics of Labor. 34th Annual Report, "The Social and Industrial Condition of the Negro in Massachusetts." Boston, 1904.

Medical Statistics of the Provost Marshal General's Bureau, Vol. II.

Metropolitan Life Insurance Company. Bulletins and Reports.

Miller, E. E. "Cotton, A National Crop." *Review of Reviews,* Vol. LXXIV, pp. 70-73. July, 1926.

Miller, Kelly. "Forty Years of Negro Education." *Educational Review,* Vol. XXXVI, pp. 484-98. December, 1908.

"I See and Am Satisfied." *Independent,* Vol. LXXV, p. 319. August 1, 1913.

"The Negro as a Working Man." *American Mercury,* Vol. VI, pp. 310-13. November, 1925.

"Race Adjustment—The Causes of Segregation." *Current History.* March, 1927.

"Is the American Negro to Remain Black or Become Bleached?" *South Atlantic Quarterly,* Vol. XXV, No. 3. July, 1926.

"The Negro in New England." *Harvard Graduates Magazine.* June, 1926.

Milton, G. F., Jr. "Black Ballots in the White South." *Forum,* Vol. LXXVIII, pp. 906-13. December, 1927.

"The South and 1924." *Outlook,* Vol. CXXXVI, pp. 29-30. January, 1924.

Mims, Edwin. "Law and Order in Tennessee." Interracial Commission. Atlanta, 1919.

Minton, Henry M. "The Part the Negro Is Playing in the Reduction of Mortality." *Hospital Social Service,* Vol. X, p. 10. 1924.

Mississippi State Department of Education. "Biennial Report and Recommendations of the State Superintendent of Public Education." 1925-26 and 1926-27.

"Mississippi and the Mob." Jackson Printing Co. Jackson, 1926.

Missouri Negro Industrial Commission. "Biennial Report." 1921-22.

Moffat, Adeline. "New Problems Caused by the Importation of Colored Labor into the North." National Federation of Settlements, Proceedings, pp. 18-20. 1918.

Monthly Labor Review.

Moss, R. Maurice. "The Negro in Westchester County." September, 1924. Westchester County Recreation Commission.

Mossell, Sadie. "Standard of Living Among 100 Negro Migrant Families in Philadelphia." *Annals of the American Academy of Political and Social Science,* Vol. XCVIII. 1929.

Moton, Robert Russa. "The Negro and the South's Industrial Life." *Southern Workman,* Vol. XLIII, p. 411. June, 1914.

Morton, Richard L. "The Negro in Virginia Politics." Phelps-Stokes Fellowship Papers No. 4. University of Virginia. 1919.

Murdock, Katherine. "A Study of Race Differences in New York City." *School and Society,* Vol. II, pp. 147-50. 1920.

"Nashville Plan of Interracial Work, The." Interracial Committee, Atlanta.

National Anti-Tuberculosis Association. Reports.

National Association for the Advancement of Colored People. Annual Reports. New York. 1926, 1927, 1928.

"Disfranchisement of Colored Americans in the Presidential Election of 1920."

"Thirty Years of Lynching in the United States, 1889-1918." April, 1919.

"A Year's Defense of the Negro's American Citizenship Rights." 1928.

National Education Association. "Research Division Report on the Ability of the States to Support Education," Vol. I, Nos. 1 and 2. January and March, 1926.

National Industrial Conference Board. "The Wage Earner in New York and Other States." 1928.

National Interracial Conference. Reports.

National Negro Business League. "Survey of Negro Business." 1928.

National Negro Health Week. "Fifteenth Annual Observance." U. S. Public Health Service Bulletin. 1929.

National Negro Insurance Association. "Proceedings of the Seventh Annual Session, April 20-22, 1927."

National Society for the Study of Education. "Twenty-seventh Yearbook," edited by Barbara Burks.

National Urban League. Reports.

"Negro Enfranchised Again." Independent, Vol. CXVIII, p. 305. March 19, 1927.

Negro in the South. "Lectures and Addresses." Phelps-Stokes Fellowship Papers. University of Virginia. 1915.

"Negro Labor. The Expressions of Southern Manufacturers." Tradesman (Chattanooga, Tenn.), Vol. XXVI, pp. 31-35. October 15, 1891.

"Negro Skilled Labor in the South." Tradesman (Chattanooga, Tenn.). October 15, 1902.

"Negro Voters and the Presidential Campaign." Opportunity, Vol. II, pp. 336-39. November, 1924.

Newbold, N. C. "Common Schools for Negroes in the South." Annals of the American Academy of Political and Social Science. 1928.

New Orleans Public Schools.

New Orleans Vocational Information Series.
No. 1, "The Colored Printer in New Orleans," by Lulie Westfeldt.
No. 2, "The Colored Beauty Worker in New Orleans," by Lulie Westfeldt.
No. 3, "Colored Registered Nurses in New Orleans," by Lulie Westfeldt.

No. 4, "The Colored Public School Teacher in New Orleans," by Virginia Peeler.

New York Urban League. "2,400 Negro Families in Harlem." 1927.

"Housing American Negroes in Harlem." 1917.

New York A.I.C.P. "Health Work for Mothers and Children in a Colored Community." Publication 131. 1924.

New York Committee on Negro Child Study. "A Study of Delinquent and Neglected Negro Children Before the New York City Children's Court." 1927.

"New Day for the Colored Woman Worker in New York City, A." Joint Committee for Study of the Colored Woman. Nellie Swartz, Chairman. March 1, 1919.

New York Times Magazine. May 18, 1924.

Nichols, Franklin O. "Some Public Health Problems of the Negro." *Journal of Social Hygiene,* Vol. III, No. 3. July, 1922.

Noble, S. G. "Education Values in Schools for Negroes." *South Atlantic Quarterly,* Vol. XVIII, pp. 116-24. April, 1919.

North Carolina State Department of Education. "Biennial Report of the Superintendent of Public Instruction." 1926-27, and 1927-28.

North Carolina State Board of Charities, Division of Negro Work. "Crime Among Negroes." 1928.

Odell, George T. "The Northern Migration of the Negro." *Tradewinds.* January, 1924.

Opportunity, A Journal of Negro Life. National Urban League, New York City.

Oxley, L. A. "Capital Punishment in North Carolina." State Department of Education. Special Bulletin No. 10. 1928.

The North Carolina Negro. Reprinted from the *Welfare Magazine.* November, 1927.

Pace, Harry H. "The Attitude of Life Insurance Companies Toward the Negro." *Southern Workman,* Vol. LVII, pp. 3-7. January, 1928.

Page, Thomas Nelson. "The 'Old Time Negro.'" *Scribner's Monthly,* Vol. XXXVI, pp. 522-32. November, 1924.

Parks, P. C. "The Passing of the Big Plantation." *Southern Ruralist.* September 15, 1922.

Park, R. E. "Concept of Social Distance as Applied to the Study of Racial Attitudes and Racial Relations." *Journal of Applied Sociology,* Vol. VIII, pp. 339-44. July, 1924.

"Experience and Race Relations." *Journal of Applied Sociology,* Vol. IX, pp. 18-24. September, 1924.

"The International Conference on the Negro." *Southern Workman,* Vol. XLI, p. 347. June, 1912.

Park, R. E. "Methods of Race Survey." *Journal of Applied Sociology*, Vol. X, pp. 410-15. May-June, 1926.
"Our Racial Frontier on the Pacific." *Survey*, Vol. III, pp. 192-96. March, 1926.
"A Race Relations Survey." *Journal of Applied Sociology*, Vol. VIII, pp. 195-205. March, 1924.
Pendleton, Helen B. "Cotton Pickers in Northern Cities." *Survey*, Vol. XXXVII, pp. 569-71. February 17, 1917.
Pennsylvania Department of Welfare. "Negro Survey of Pennsylvania." Harrisburg, 1927.
Peters, William H. "Negro Health and Race Relations." *Journal of Medicine*. May, 1925.
Peterson, Joseph. "A Comparison of the Abilities of White and Colored Children." Comparative Psychological Monographs, Vol. I, Series 5. July, 1923.
Peterson, Joseph and Lanie, Lyle H. "Studies in the Comparative Abilities of Whites and Negroes." Mental Measurement Monographs, Serial No. 57. February, 1929.
Philadelphia Housing Commission. "Housing of the City Negro." 1915.
Phillips, Ulrich Bonnell. "Decadence of the Plantation System." *Annals of the American Academy of Political and Social Science*, Vol. XXXV, pp. 37-41. January, 1910.
"Economics of the Plantation." *South Atlantic Quarterly*, Vol. II, p. 231. 1903.
Pickens, William. "Lynching and Debt Slavery." American Civil Liberties Union, New York. May, 1921.
Poe, Clarence H. "Enormous Wastes in Cotton Farming." *South Atlantic Quarterly*, Vol. V, pp. 128-33. April, 1906.
"Suffrage Restriction in the South: Its Causes and Consequences." *North American Review*, Vol. CLXXV, pp. 534-43. 1902.
"Politics and the Negro." *Harper's Weekly*, Vol. XLVII, p. 777. May 9, 1903.
Porter, Kirk Harold. "Suffrage Provisions in State Constitutions." *American Political Science Review*, Vol. XIII, p. 114. 1922.
Pressey, S. L., and Teter, G. F. "A Comparison of Colored and White Children." *Journal of Applied Psychology*, p. 277. 1915.
Pressey, S. L., and Thomas, "A Study of Country Children." *Journal of Applied Psychology*, pp. 282-86. 1915.
Pryor, R. A. "Sufficiency of the Constitutional Amendment." *Forum*, Vol. IX, p. 266. 1890.
Pyle, W. H. "Mentality of the Negro Compared with White." Psychological Bulletin No. 12, pp. 22-71. 1916.
Radin, Paul. "History of Ethnological Theories." *American Anthropologist*, Vol. XXXI, No. 1. January-March, 1929.

Randolph, A. Philip. "The Truth About the Brotherhood of Sleeping Car Porters." *Messenger,* Vol. VII, pp. 37-38. February, 1926.

"Reference List of Private and Denominational Southern Colored Schools." John F. Slater Fund, Occasional Papers, No. 20. 1925.

"Republican Consistency." *Nation* (New York), Vol. LXXVI, p. 164. February, 1903.

Robinson, James H. "The Cincinnati Negro Survey and Program." Proceedings of the National Conference of Social Work. 1919.

Rose, J. C. "Disfranchisement of the Negro in Maryland." *Nation* (New York), Vol. LXXVIII, p. 6. January 1, 1904.

"Negro Suffrage: The Constitutional Point of View." *American Political Science Review,* Vol. I, pp. 11-43. November, 1906.

"Politics and the Race Question in Alabama." *Nation* (New York), Vol. LIX, p. 211. 1894.

Satterthwait, L. "Why the Southern Election Fraud Was a Failure." *American Journal of Politics,* Vol. II, p. 412. April, 1893.

Schuyler, George S. "Negro Labor and Publication." *Messenger.* April, 1927.

Schwegler, R. A., and Wynn, Edith. "A Comparative Study of White and Colored Children." *Journal of Educational Research,* pp. 838-48. 1920.

Shaffer, E. T. H. "A New South—The Negro Migration." *Atlantic Monthly.* September, 1923.

Shields, Emma L. "Negro Women in the Tobacco Industry." *Life and Labor.* May, 1921.

Smillie, W. G., and Augustine, D. L. "Vital Capacity of the Negro Race." *Journal of the American Medical Association,* Vol. LXXXVII, pp. 2055-58. December 18, 1926.

"The Effect of Varying Intensities of Hookworm Infestation upon the Development of School Children." *Southern Medical Journal,* Vol. XIX, No. 1, pp. 19-28. January, 1926.

Snavely, Tipton Ray. "The Taxation of Negroes in Virginia." Phelps-Stokes Fellowship Papers. University of Virginia. 1916.

Snyder, H. "Negro Migration and the Cotton Crop." *North American Review,* Vol. CCXIX, pp. 21-29. January, 1924.

Snyder, J. Ross. "The Problem of the Negro Child." *Southern Medical Journal,* Vol. XVI, No. 1. 1922.

"Southern View of the Fourteenth Amendment." *Harper's Weekly,* Vol. XLIX, pp. 80-81. January 21, 1905.

Southern Workman. Hampton Institute, Hampton, Va.

Sozinsky, T. S. "Medical Aspects of the Negro Exodus." *Pennsylvania Monthly,* Vol. X, pp. 529-38. June, 1879.

State Commissioners of Labor. Reports.
Stemons, James S. "The Industrial Color Line of the North." *Century*, Vol. LX, pp. 477-78. June, 1900.
Stolberg, Benjamin. "The Pullman Peon—a Study in Industrial Race Exploitation." *Nation* (New York), Vol. CXXII, pp. 365-67. April 7, 1926.
Stone, Alfred Holt. "The Economic Future of the Negro; the Factor of White Competition." *Publications of the American Economic Association*, Third Series, Vol. VII, pp. 243-94. 1906.
Strayer, George Drayton. "The Baltimore School Survey," Vol. II. 1920-21.
Strong, A. C. "Three Hundred and Fifty White and Colored Children Measured by the Binet-Simon Measuring Scale of Intelligence." *Pedagogical Seminary*, pp. 485-512. 1913.
Sunne, Dagne. "Intelligence of Negroes." *Journal of Applied Psychology*, pp. 71-83. 1917.
"A Comparison of White and Negro Children by Terman and Yerkes-Bridges. Revision of Binet Tests." *Journal of Comparative Psychology*, pp. 209-19. 1905.
"A Comparison of White and Colored Children." *School and Society*, pp. 469-72. 1924.
Surface, G. T. "Negro Mine Laborers, Central Appalachian Coal Field." *Annals of the American Academy of Political and Social Science,* Vol. XXXIII, pp. 338-52. March, 1909.
Tampa Welfare League, Y.M.C.A., and Urban League. "A Study of Negro Life in Tampa." 1927.
Terry, C. E. "The Negro—His Relation to Public Health in the South." *American Journal of Public Health,* Vol. III, p. 300. 1910.
Thomas, David Y. "Tenancy as Related to the Negro Problem." *Manufacturers Record.* June 17, 1920.
"Negro Skilled Labor in the South." *Tradesman* (Chattanooga, Tenn.). October 15, 1902.
Thomas, W. I. "Race Psychology." *American Journal of Sociology,* Vol. XVII, pp. 725-75. May, 1912.
Thompson, Anna J. "A Survey of Crime Among Negroes in Philadelphia." *Opportunity,* Vol. IV, pp. 251-54. August, 1926.
Thorndike, E. L. "Intelligence Scores of Colored Pupils in High School." *School and Society,* Vol. XVIII, pp. 569-70. 1923.
Tobey, James A. "The Death Rate Among American Negroes." *Current History,* Vol. XXV, pp. 217-20. November, 1926.
Trenton, New Jersey, Public Schools. "Superintendent's Report on Negroes in the Public Elementary Schools of the North."
Tulsa Manufacturers. "List of Manufacturers Employing Negroes."

Tuskegee Institute. Department of Records and Research Reports.

Virginia State Department of Education. "Annual Report of the Superintendent of Public Instruction." 1928.

"Votes for Negroes." *The Crisis,* Vol. XXI, pp. 103-04. January, 1921.

United States Bureau of the Census.

Department of Agriculture, Bulletins.

"A Decade of Negro Extension Work, 1914-1924." Miscellaneous Circular No. 72. October, 1926.

"Extension Work Among Negroes." Department Circular. 1920.

Saunders, J. T. "Farm Ownership and Tenancy in the Black Prairie of Texas." Bulletin No. 1,068. May, 1922.

Scarborough, Wm. Saunders. "Tenancy and Ownership Among Negro Farmers in Southampton County, Va." Bulletin No. 1,404.

"Condition of Colored Farmers in the United States." American Association of Farmers Institute. Experimental Station Bulletin No. 251. 1912.

Department of Commerce, Bulletins.

Carpenter, Niles. "Immigrants and Their Children." Census Monograph VII. 1928.

"Negroes in the United States." Bulletin No. 129. 1915.

"Prisoners, 1923." Bulletin. 1926.

Department of the Interior, Department of Education.

Blose, David T. "Statistics of Education of the Negro Race." Bulletin No. 19. 1928.

"Hampton Normal and Agricultural Institute." Bulletin No. 27. 1923.

"Negro Education." Bulletin No. 38, Vol. II. 1916.

Phillips, Frank M. "Statistical Survey of Education, 1925-26." Bulletin No. 12. 1928.

"Statistics of City School Systems, 1925-1926." Bulletin No. 32. 1927.

"Statistics of Universities, Colleges, and Professional Schools, 1923-1924." Bulletin No. 45. 1925.

"Survey of Negro Colleges and Universities." Bulletin No. 7. 1928.

Thurber, Clarence H. "Fiscal Support of State Universities and State Colleges." Bulletin No. 28. 1925.

Department of Labor.

"Child Labor and the Work of Mothers in Oyster and Shrimp Canning Communities on the Gulf Coast." Children's Bureau. Publication 98. 1922.

Channing, Alice. "Child Labor on Maryland Truck Farms." Children's Bureau.

Department of Labor.
"Child Labor and the Work of Mothers on Norfolk Truck Farms." Children's Bureau. Bulletin No. 130.
"Lost Time and Labor Turnover in the Cotton Mills." Children's Bureau. Bulletin No. 52. 1926.
"Negro Migration in 1916-1917." Division of Negro Economics. 1919. By. T. R. Snavely.
"Negro Women in Industry." Women's Bureau. Bulletin No. 207.
"Women in Missouri Industries." Women's Bureau. Bulletin No. 25.
United States Coal Commission. Report. Part III.
United States Immigration Commission. 1911-28 Reports.
United States Railroad Labor Board. Proceedings. 1921.
United States Public Health Service.
"Disability Among Workers Caused by Respiratory Diseases," Vol. XLIII, No. 11. March 16, 1928.
Grover, Mary, and Sydenstricker, Edgar. "Mortality Among Negroes in the United States." Bulletin No. 174. 1928.
"Some Tendencies Indicated by the New Life Tables." Bulletin. April, 1924.
Stiles, Charles Wardell. "Hookworm Disease in Its Relation to the Negro," Vol. XXIV, No. 31. 1909.
Trask, John W. "Death Rates of the Colored Population." Bulletin No. 329. March 17, 1916.
University Commission on Race Relations. Proceedings.
Washington, Booker T. "The Negro and the Labor Unions." Atlantic Monthly, Vol. CXI, pp. 756-67. June, 1913.
Washington, Forrester B. "Study of Negro Employees of Apartment Houses in New York City." New York: National Urban League. Reports, Vol. VI, No. 5. December, 1916.
Weatherford, W. D. (Ed.). "Lawlessness or Civilization— Which?" 1917.
"Interracial Cooperation." Interracial Commission, War Work Council, Y.M.C.A.
Wesley, Charles H. "The Historical Basis of Negro Citizenship." Opportunity, Vol. II. pp. 356-59. December, 1924.
West Virginia Bureau of Negro Welfare and Statistics. Annual Report, 1929, 1925-26.
Matney, W. C. "A Study of Negro Housing and Home Ownership of Beckley, W. Va." May, 1928.
West Virginia State Department of Education. "Biennial Report of the State Superintendent of Free Schools, for Two Years Ending June, 1926."
"White Primary, The." The Crisis, Vol. XXX, pp. 33-35. May, 1925; Vol. XXXIV, pp. 9-10. March, 1925.
"White Primary—Fifth, The." The Crisis, Vol. XXX, pp. 123-24. June, 1925.

Wickliffe, J. C. "Negro Suffrage a Failure: Shall We Abolish It?" *Forum,* Vol. XIV, p. 797. 1893.

Williams, E. B. "The Negro in Michigan Industry." *Michigan Manufacturer and Financial Record.* April 3, 1920.

Williams, W. T. B. "Report on Negro Universities and Colleges." John F. Slater Fund, Occasional Papers, No. 21. 1922.

Wilson, Agnes E. "The Facilities for the Care of Dependent, Semi-delinquent and Delinquent Negro Children in Los Angeles." Community Welfare Federation. February-March, 1925.

Winston-Salem, North Carolina, Public Schools. "Tenth Annual Report on the Public Schools, 1922-1923."

Woolston, Howard. "Changing Mortality." *American Journal of Sociology,* Vol. XXXII, pp. 937-46. May, 1927.

Woofter, T. J., Jr. "Progress in Race Relations." Georgia Committee on Race Relations. 1922.

Wright, Richard Robert, Jr. "The Negro in Unskilled Labor." *Annals of the American Academy of Political and Social Science,* Vol. XLIX, pp. 19-22. September, 1913.

Young, P. B. "Adjustment of Race Relations." *Southern Workman,* Vol. LVII, No. 4, p. 147. April, 1928.

NATIONAL INTERRACIAL CONFERENCE,
DECEMBER 16-19, 1928

Abbott, Miss Grace, Washington, D. C., United States Children's Bureau.

Alexander, Dr. Will W., Atlanta, Ga., Commission on Interracial Cooperation; National Council Y.M.C.A.

Anderson, Miss Mary, Washington, D. C., United States Department of Labor, Women's Bureau.

Arthur, George R., Chicago, Ill., Julius Rosenwald Fund.

Attwell, Ernest T., Philadelphia, Pa., Playground & Recreation Association of America.

Banks, W. N., Prairie View, Texas, Prairie View State College.

Battle, Wallace A., New York City, American Church Institute for Negroes.

Bethune, Mrs. Mary McLeod, Daytona Beach, Fla., National Association of Colored Women.

Bishop, Rev. Shelton H., New York City, Fellowship of Reconciliation.

Blanton, Mrs. Carolyn S., Louisville, Ky., National Board Y.W.C.A.

Bloom, Dr. W. Knighton, Washington, D. C., Missionary Education Movement; Congregational Church Extension Boards.

Bluford, President F. D., Greensboro, N. C., Agricultural & Technical College, Greensboro, N. C.

Bond, H. M., Nashville, Tenn., Fisk University.

Bowles, Miss Eva D., New York City, National Board Y.W.C.A.

Brady, Miss Mary Beattie, New York City, Harmon Foundation.

Brooks, Rev. R. W., Washington, D. C., Lincoln Temple; Chairman, Hospitality Committee of Conference.

Brown, Thomas I., Baltimore, Md., Morgan College.

Bruce, Roscoe Conkling, New York City, Paul Laurence Dunbar Apartments, Inc.; speaker.

Bryan, Miss Helen R., Philadelphia, Pa., American Friends Service Committee.

Burroughs, Miss Nannie H., Washington, D. C., National Association for the Advancement of Colored People; Council of Women for Home Missions.

Butcher, Mrs. Harriet S., New York City, Delegate-at-large.

Butterfield, Kenyon L., Atlantic City, N. J., American Country Life Association.

Carney, Miss Mabel, New York City, Columbia University.
Carpenter, Dr. Niles, Buffalo, N. Y., University of Buffalo.
Carter, E. C., New York City, The Inquiry.
Chambers, Miss Erle, Little Rock, Ark., Arkansas Tuberculosis Association.
Chapin, Miss Caroline B., Englewood, N. J., Commission on Race Relations, Federal Council of Churches.
Clark, Miss Adele, Richmond, Va., National League of Women Voters.
Clement, Bishop George C., Louisville, Ky., Federal Council of Churches.
Coleman, Mrs. Maude B., Harrisburg, Pa., Pennsylvania Department of Welfare.
Cook, Dean George W., Washington, D. C., Delegate-at-large.
Craver, William C., Raleigh, N. C., Shaw University.
Darby, Dr. W. L., Washington, D. C., Washington Federation of Churches.
Davage, Dr. M. S., Atlanta, Ga., Clark University.
Davis, Dean Carroll M., New York City, Home Missions Council.
Davis, Jackson, Richmond, Va., General Education Board.
Davis, President John W., Institute, W. Va., West Virginia Collegiate Institute.
Davis, Milton C., Philadelphia, Pa., American Friends Service Committee.
Deffenbaugh, W. S., Washington, D. C., Visitor.
Devine, Dr. Edward T., Washington, D. C., American University.
Dickerson, Mrs. Addie W., Philadelphia, Pa., Commission on Race Relations, Federal Council of Churches.
Dill, Augustus Granville, New York City, Fellowship of Reconciliation.
Doggett, Allan B., Hampton, Va., Hampton Institute.
Dumas, Dr. M. O., Washington, D. C., National Medical Association.
Dublin, Dr. Louis I., New York City, Metropolitan Life Insurance Company.
DuBois, Dr. W. E. B., New York City, National Association for the Advancement of Colored People.
Edwards, Prof. Paul K., Nashville, Tenn., Fisk University.
Edwards, Thomas C., New York City, National Health Council.
Eichelberger, Dr. James W., Chicago, Ill., International Council of Religious Education.
Eleazer, Robert B., Atlanta, Ga., Publicity Advisor of Conference.
Elliott, Dr. John Wesley, Philadelphia, Pa., International Council of Religious Education.
Embree, Edwin R., Chicago, Ill., Julius Rosenwald Fund; speaker.
Exner, Dr. M. J., New York City, American Social Hygiene Association.
Favrot, Leo M., Baton Rouge, La., General Education Board.

Fisher, Galen M., New York City, Institute of Social and Religious Research.

Fledderus, Miss M. L., The Hague, Holland, International Industrial Relations Association.

Fletcher, J. F., New York City, American Church Institute for Negroes.

Foreman, Clark, Atlanta, Ga., Phelps-Stokes Fund.

Frey, John P., Washington, D. C., American Federation of Labor; speaker.

Fry, Dr. C. Luther, New York City, Institute of Social and Religious Research.

Gandy, President John M., Petersburg, Va., Virginia Normal & Industrial Institute.

Gardner, Miss Katherine, Englewood, N. J., Commission on Race Relations, Federal Council of Churches.

Garrison, Lloyd, New York City, National Urban League.

Gaumnitz, W. H., Washington, D. C., Visitor.

Gilman, Miss Elizabeth, Baltimore, Md., Baltimore Open Forum.

Glenn, John M., New York City, Russell Sage Foundation; speaker.

Gosselin, Miss Grace, New York City, National Federation of Settlements.

Graham, Miss Irene J., Buffalo, N. Y., Local Community Research, University of Chicago.

Greene, Miss Amy Blanche, New York City, Fellowship of Reconciliation.

Greene, Lorenzo J., Washington, D. C., Association for the Study of Negro Life and History.

Gregg, President James E., Hampton, Va., Hampton Institute.

Grossley, President R. S., Dover, Del., State College, Dover, Del.

Guild, Arthur A., Richmond, Va., Richmond Community Fund.

Guild, Mrs. June Purcell, Richmond, Va., Richmond Council of Social Agencies.

Haines, Dr. Blanche M., Washington, D. C., United States Children's Bureau.

Haynes, Dr. George E., New York City, Commission on the Church and Race Relations, Federal Council of Churches; Executive Secretary of Conference.

Hill, T. Arnold, New York City, National Urban League.

Hill, Dr. Joseph A., Washington, D. C., United States Census.

Hines, Prof. George W., Nashville, Tenn., Fisk University.

Hobbs, Rev. G. Warfield, New York City, National Council Protestant Episcopal Church.

Holloway, Dean William H., Bricks Junior College, Bricks, N. C.

Holmes, Dean D. O. W., Washington, D. C. Howard University.

Hope, President John, Atlanta, Ga., Morehouse College.

Hovey, Dr. George R., New York City, Home Missions Council.

Hubert, James H., New York City, New York Urban League.

Huffington, J. W., Baltimore, Md., Maryland State Department of Education.

Hughes, Dr. W. A. C., Philadelphia, Pa., Methodist Episcopal Church, Board of Home Missions and Church Extension.

Hunt, H. A., Fort Valley, Ga., American Church Institute for Negroes.

Hunton, Mrs. Addie W., Brooklyn, N. Y., Delegate-at-large.

Hurst, Bishop John, Baltimore, Md., National Association for the Advancement of Colored People.

Imes, G. Lake, Tuskegee Institute, Ala., Tuskegee Institute.

Jackson, Dr. Algernon, Washington, D. C., Howard University Medical School.

Jackson, James A., Washington, D. C., United States Department of Commerce.

Jackson, Dr. W. C., Greensboro, N. C., North Carolina College for Women.

Jacobs, Dr. F. M., Brooklyn, N. Y., African Methodist Episcopal Zion Church.

Jernagin, Dr. W. H., Washington, D. C., National Baptist Convention, Inc.

John, Walter C., Washington, D. C., United States Department of the Interior.

Johnson, Campbell C., Washington, D. C., Twelfth Street Y.M.C.A.

Johnson, Charles S., Nashville, Tenn., Fisk University; Research Secretary of Conference.

Johnson, Mrs. Georgia Douglass, Washington, D. C., United States Department of Labor.

Johnson, Guy B., Chapel Hill, N. C., University of North Carolina.

Johnson, James Weldon, New York City, National Association for the Advancement of Colored People.

Johnson, President Mordecai W., Washington, D. C., Howard University; joint chairman of Conference; speaker.

Jones, Eugene Kinckle, New York City, National Urban League.

Jones, President Thomas Elsa, Nashville, Tenn., Fisk University.

Jones, Dr. Thomas Jesse, New York City, Phelps-Stokes Fund.

Johnson, President William Hallock, Lincoln University, Pa., Lincoln University.

Kellog, Paul U., New York City, Delegate-at-large.

Keeny, S. M., New York City, The Inquiry.

Kester, Howard A., New York City, Fellowship of Reconciliation.

King, Dr. W. R., New York City, Home Missions Council.

Klein, Arthur J., Washington, D. C., United States Department of the Interior.

Kleinschmidt, Dr. H. E., New York City, National Tuberculosis Association.

LaFarge, Father John, New York City, Delegate-at-large.

Langvick, Miss Mina M., Washington, D. C., Visitor.

Lasker, Bruno, New York City, The Inquiry.
Lathrop, Dr. Charles N., New York City, Department of Christian Social Service, Protestant Episcopal Church.
Lathrop, Miss Edith A., Washington, D. C., Visitor.
Lester, Robert M., New York City, Carnegie Corporation.
Locke, Alain, Washington, D. C., Delegate-at-large.
Long, Miss Willie L., Orange, N. J., Orange (N. J.) Y.W.C.A.
McDowell, Miss Mary E., Chicago, Ill., National Federation of Settlements.
Magnusson, Mr. Leifur, Washington, D. C., Washington Branch International Labor Office (Geneva, Switzerland).
Matthews, Miss E. N., Washington, D. C., United States Children's Bureau.
Matthews, Joseph B., Washington, D. C., Fellowship of Reconciliation.
Mead, Miss Margaret P., Plainfield, N. J., National Board, Y.W.C.A.
Medford, H. T., Washington, D. C., African Methodist Episcopal Zion Church.
Miller, Prof. Herbert A., Columbus, Ohio, Columbus Urban League; speaker.
Miller, Dr. Kelly, Washington, D. C., Howard University.
Miller, Spencer J., New York City, Workers Education Bureau of America.
Millner, George W., Norfolk, Va., International Longshoremen.
Mitchell, Dr. Broadus, Baltimore, Md., Johns Hopkins University.
Morton, Miss Helen, Boston, Mass., National Federation of Settlements.
Moton, Dr. Robert R., Tuskegee Institute, Ala., Tuskegee Institute; joint chairman of Conference; speaker.
Mufson, Israel, Philadelphia, Pa., Workers Education Bureau of America.
Nelson, Mrs. Alice Dunbar, Philadelphia, Pa., American Interracial Peace Committee.
Newbold, N. C., Raleigh, N. C., North Carolina State Department of Education.
Nichols, Franklin O., New York City, American Social Hygiene Association.
Niebuhr, Miss Hulda, New York City, Fellowship of Reconciliation.
Norment, Miss Carolina G., Baltimore, Md., American Friends Service Committee.
Olden, Dr. J. C., Washington, D. C., National Interdenominational Ministers Alliance.
Ovington, Miss Mary White, New York City, National Association for the Advancement of Colored People.
Oxley, Lawrence A., Raleigh, N. C., North Carolina State Board of Charities and Public Welfare.

Pearl, Dr. Raymond, Baltimore, Md., Johns Hopkins University; speaker.
Pendleton, Miss Helen B., Washington, D. C., National Federation of Settlements.
Pierce, Dr. Jason Noble, Washington, D. C., Delegate-at-large.
Pratt, Dean Butler, Washington, D. C., Delegate-at-large.
Preble, Dr. Paul, Washington, D. C., United States Public Health Service.
Randolph, Miss Jeannette, New York City, The Inquiry.
Read, Miss Florence M., Atlanta, Ga., Spelman College.
Regan, Miss Agnes, Washington, D. C., National Conference of Catholic Women of the National Catholic Welfare Conference.
Reid, Ira DeA., New York City, National Urban League.
Reynolds, L. R., Richmond, Va., Commission on Interracial Cooperation.
Rhodes, I. B., New York City, National Council Y.M.C.A.
Richards, Miss Bertha, Raleigh, N. C., Bishop Tuttle School of Social Work.
Robinson, J. W., Charleston, W. Va., West Virginia State Bureau of Negro Welfare.
Robinson, W. A., Knoxville, Tenn., Austin High School; speaker.
Rogers, J. F., Washington, D. C., Visitor.
Rosenwald, Julius, Chicago, Ill., President Julius Rosenwald Fund; speaker.
Russell, Dr. J. Alvin, Lawrenceville, Va., St. Paul's School, Lawrenceville, Va.
Schoellkopf, Mrs. A. H., Buffalo, N. Y., The Inquiry.
Scott, Mrs. Bobbie Beatrix, Washington, D. C., Tougaloo College, Tougaloo, Miss.
Scott, Dr. Emmett J., Washington, D. C., Howard University.
Scott, Mrs. Minnie M., Washington, D. C., National Association of Colored Women.
Seligman, Herbert J., New York City, Publicity advisor of Conference.
Sellin, Dr. Thorsten, Philadelphia, Pa., University of Pennsylvania; speaker.
Shepard, Dr. J. E., Durham, N. C., North Carolina College for Negroes.
Shipley, Miss Elizabeth Taylor, Harrisburg, Pa., Pennsylvania State Department of Welfare.
Sims, Miss Mary S., New York City, National Board Y.W.C.A.
Slowe, Dean Lucy D., Washington, D. C., National Board Y.W.C.A.
Smart, P. J., Washington, D. C., Visitor.
Snodgrass, Miss Pearl, Raleigh, N. C., St. Augustine's College.
Spaulding, C. C., Durham, N. C., North Carolina Mutual Life Insurance Company.

Spingarn, Arthur B., New York City, National Association for the Advancement of Colored People.

Stokes, Dr. Anson Phelps, Washington, D. C., Washington Interracial Committee.

Sullivan, Verne R., Washington, D. C., Brotherhood of Railroad Trainmen.

Taylor, Mr. Graham R., New York City, Commonwealth Fund.

Terrell, Mrs. Mary Church, Washington, D. C., National Association of Colored Women.

Tobias, Channing H., New York City, National Council Y.M.C.A.

Trenholm, H. Councill, Montgomery, Ala., Alabama State Normal School.

Trigg, H. L., Raleigh, N. C., Delegate-at-large.

Valentine, W. R., Bordentown, N. J., National Council Y.M.C.A.

van Kleeck, Miss Mary, New York City, Russell Sage Foundation; chairman of Executive Committee of Conference.

Villard, Oswald Garrison, New York City, Delegate-at-large.

Wagner, H. Milton, Ruxton, Md., Visitor.

Wagner, Mrs. H. Milton, Ruxton, Md., Women's Interdenominational Missionary Union of Baltimore.

Wallace, Roy Smith, New York City, Playground and Recreation Association of America.

Ward, Patrick J., Washington, D. C., National Catholic Welfare Conference.

Warrick, Miss Marie E., Germantown, Pa., Fellowship of Reconciliation.

Washington, Forrester B., Atlanta, Ga., Atlanta School of Social Work.

Watkins, George W., Richmond, Va., National Council Y.M.C.A.

Watson, Mrs. Grace, Philadelphia, Pa., Fellowship of Reconciliation.

Wesley, Charles H., Washington, D. C., Howard University.

West, Hon. Roy O., Washington, D. C., Secretary, United States Department of the Interior; speaker.

White, Walter, New York City, National Association for the Advancement of Colored People.

Wilcox, Mrs. F. W., New York City, Council of Women for Home Missions.

Williams, Miss Charl O., Washington, D. C., Visitor.

Wilson, G. R., Cambridge, Mass., Delegate-at-large.

Wood, L. Hollingsworth, Mt. Kisco, N. Y., National Urban League.

Wood, Mrs. L. Hollingsworth, Mt. Kisco, N. Y., American Friends Service Committee.

Woodson, Dr. Carter G., Washington, D. C., Association for the Study of Negro Life and History.

Woofter, T. J., Jr., Chapel Hill, N. C., University of North Carolina.

Work, Prof. Monroe N., Tuskegee Institute, Ala., Social Science
    Research Council, Committee on Interracial Relations.
Wright, W. L., Lincoln University, Pa., Lincoln University.
Young, Donald, Philadelphia, Pa., University of Pennsylvania;
    American Academy of Political and Social Science.
Young, Miss Willa R., New York City, National Board Y.W.C.A.

NATIONAL INTERRACIAL CONFERENCE
FOR THE STUDY AND DISCUSSION OF
RACE PROBLEMS IN THE UNITED STATES
IN THE LIGHT OF SOCIAL RESEARCH

WASHINGTON, D. C.
DECEMBER 16-19, 1928

Sponsoring Organizations

American Friends Service Committee, Interracial Section
American Social Hygiene Association
Commission on Interracial Cooperation
Council of Women for Home Missions
Federal Council of Churches, Commission on Race Relations
Fellowship of Reconciliation
Home Missions Council
The Inquiry

National Association for the Advancement of Colored People
National Board Y. W. C. A.
National Catholic Welfare Conference
National Council Y. M. C. A.
National Federation of Settlements
National Urban League
Phelps Stokes Fund
Protestant Episcopal Church, Department of Christian Social Service

Officers

Mary van Kleeck, Chairman
Eustace Seligman, Treasurer

George E. Haynes, Executive Secretary
Charles S. Johnson, Research Secretary

Executive Committee

The Officers and
Will W. Alexander
Eva D. Bowles
E. C. Carter
Samuel McCrea Cavert
Carroll M. Davis
A. G. Dill
M. J. Exner
Clark Foreman

Grace Gosselin
Amy Blanche Greene
John Hope
James Weldon Johnson
Eugene Kinckle Jones
Margaret E. Jones
Thomas Jesse Jones
William R. King
Charles N. Lathrop

Grace Lindley
Margaret P. Mead
Franklin O. Nichols
Channing H. Tobias
Elizabeth Walton
Patrick J. Ward
Walter White
Mrs. F. W. Wilcox
L. Hollingsworth Wood

Research Committee

Graham R. Taylor, Chairman

Gertrude E. McDougald Ayer
Glenn A. Bowers
Louis I. Dublin
Joseph A. Hill
George W. Kirchwey
Broadus Mitchell

Howard W. Odum
Leonard Outhwaite
Robert E. Park
Forrester B. Washington
Leo Wolman
Monroe N. Work

Committee on Plan and Procedure

E. C. Carter, Chairman

Charles S. Johnson

Channing H. Tobias

Committee on Membership

Eugene Kinckle Jones, Chairman
Will W. Alexander
Samuel McCrea Cavert

John Hope
Margaret P. Mead
Walter White

Committee on Arrangements

Franklin O. Nichols, Chairman

Robert W. Brooks
W. L. Darby

Mordecai W. Johnson
Anson Phelps Stokes

Committee on Hospitality

Robert W. Brooks, Chairman

W. L. Darby
Clark Foreman

Campbell C. Johnson
Martha A. McAdoo

Committee on Ushers

Eva D. Bowles, Chairman

Margaret P. Mead

The Conference is indebted to the Federal Council of Churches, Commission on Race Relations, for contributing the time of Dr. George E. Haynes as Executive Secretary of the Conference, and to the National Urban League for the services of Dr. Charles S. Johnson as Research Secretary. To Fisk University is due the continuance of Dr. Johnson's services for the Conference after his transfer there in September.

Conference Office: Room 947, Woodward Building

NATIONAL INTERRACIAL CONFERENCE

Presiding Officers
Mordecai W. Johnson, President of Howard University
Robert R. Moton, Principal of Tuskegee Institute
Mary van Kleeck, Russell Sage Foundation,
Chairman of Discussion

Morning and afternoon sessions—Auditorium of the Department of the Interior Building, 18th and F Streets, N. W.

Evening sessions, except Sunday—Howard University, Auditorium of the Medical School, 6th and W Streets, N. W.

PROGRAM

Morning and afternoon sessions and the opening session on Sunday evening are limited to delegates. Invited guests, having cards, and reporters are welcome at evening sessions, Monday, Tuesday and Wednesday.

Sunday, December 16 5 p.m.	Reception of delegates at Howard University, 2401—6th Street, N. W., with opportunity to see the University, followed by registration and buffet supper at 6:30 for those desiring it.
Sunday evening 7:30 p.m. Dining Hall Building, Howard University	Music by the Girls' Glee Club of Howard University. Opening Address—The Plan of Research for the Conference: Charles S. Johnson, Fisk University, formerly National Urban League, Research Secretary of the Conference. Report of the Committee on Procedure: E. C. Carter, Chairman. Discussion of Plans for the Conference, by Officers and Delegates.
Monday, December 17 Monday Morning 10 a.m.—12:45 p.m.	TOPIC—HEALTH
10:00—10:30	Presentation of Data, Louis I. Dublin, Chief Statistician, Metropolitan Life Insurance Company, New York.
10:30—10:50	Interpretative Comment, Algernon B. Jackson, M.D., Professor of Public Health, Howard University, Washington, D. C.
10:50—11:05	Questions from the floor.
11:05—11:15	Intermission.
11:15—12:45	Discussion by delegates.
Monday Afternoon 2:30—5 p.m.	TOPIC—EDUCATION
2:30—3:00	Presentation of Data, W. A. Robinson, Principal, Austin High School, Knoxville, Tennessee, formerly Supervisor, Negro High Schools of North Carolina.
3:00—3:30	Interpretative comment, Mabel Carney, Professor of Rural Education, Columbia University, New York.
3:30—3:45	Interpretative Comment, James E. Gregg, Principal, Hampton Institute.
3:45—4:00	Questions from the floor.
4:00—4:10	Intermission.
4:10—5:00	Discussion by delegates.

Monday Evening
8—10 p.m.

8:00— 8:15	Summary of session on Health, Franklin O. Nichols, American Social Hygiene Association, assisted by H. E. Kleinschmidt, National Tuberculosis Association.
8:15— 8:30	Summary of session on Education, Thomas E. Jones, President, Fisk University, assisted by H. M. Bond, Fisk University.
8:30— 9:15	Biological Factors in Negro Mortality, Raymond Pearl, Johns Hopkins University, Baltimore, Md.
9:15—10:00	Educational Achievements and Needs, John Hope, President, Morehouse College, Atlanta, Ga.

Tuesday, December 18
Tuesday Morning
10 a.m.—12:45 p.m.

TOPIC—INDUSTRY AND AGRICULTURE

10:00—10:30	Presentation of Data on Agriculture, Monroe N. Work, Editor, Negro Year Book, Tuskegee Institute, Ala.
10:30—11:00	Presentation of Data on Industry, Niles Carpenter, University of Buffalo, Buffalo, N. Y.
11:00—11:15	Questions from the floor.
11:15—11:25	Intermission.
11:25—12:45	Discussion by delegates.

Tuesday afternoon
2:30—5 p.m.

TOPICS—(1) RECREATION, (2) HOUSING

2:30—2:50	Presentation of Data on Recreation, Forrester B. Washington, Director, Atlanta School of Social Work, Atlanta, Ga.
2:50—3:00	Interpretative comment, Ernest T. Attwell, Playground and Recreation Association of America, New York.
3:00—3:30	Presentation of Data on Housing, T. J. Woofter Jr., University of North Carolina, Chapel Hill, N. C.
3:30—3:40	Questions from the floor.
3:40—3:50	Intermission.
3:50—4:05	A concrete case as yielding scientific data, The Paul Lawrence Dunbar Apartments, New York, Roscoe C. Bruce, Resident Manager, New York.
4:05—5:00	Discussion by delegates.

Tuesday Evening
8—10 p.m.

8:00— 8:15	Summary of session on Industry and Agriculture, Charles H. Wesley, Howard University, assisted by Mary Anderson, Director, Women's Bureau, U. S. Department of Labor.
8:15— 8:30	Summary of session on Recreation and Housing, Mary E. McDowell, University of Chicago Settlement, assisted by George A. Arthur, Julius Rosenwald Fund.
8:30— 9:15	Recreation in Relation to Community Life, Roy Smith Wallace, Playground and Recreation Association of America, and delegate, Harmon Foundation, New York.
9:15—10:00	Race Problems and the Labor Movement, John P. Frey, American Federation of Labor, Washington, D. C.

December 19
Wednesday,
Wednesday Morning
10 a.m.—12:45 p.m.   TOPIC—LAW OBSERVANCE AND ADMINISTRATION

10:00—10:30   Presentation of Data, Thorsten Sellin, University of Pennsylvania, Philadelphia, Pa.

10:30—10:50   Presentation of Data, with special reference to investigation in North Carolina, Lawrence Oxley Director, Bureau of Negro Work, North Carolina Department of Public Welfare, Raleigh, N. C.

10:50—11:05   Questions from the floor.

11:05—11:15   Intermission.

11:15—12:45   Discussion by delegates.

Wednesday Afternoon
2:30—5 p.m.   TOPICS—(1) CITIZENSHIP, (2) RACE RELATIONS

2:30—2:50   Presentation of Data on Citizenship, W. E. B. DuBois, Editor, The Crisis, New York.

2:50—3:05   Interpretative Comment, Charles E. Merriam, University of Chicago, Chicago, Illinois.

3:05—3:35   Presentation of Data on Race Relations, Herbert A. Miller, Ohio State University, Columbus, Ohio.

3:35—3:45   Questions from the floor.

3:45—3:55   Intermission.

3:55—5:00   Discussion by delegates.

Wednesday Evening
8—10 p.m.
8:00— 8:10   Summary of session on Law Observance and Administration, James Weldon Johnson, National Association for the Advancement of Colored People, assisted by Ira D. Reid, National Urban League, New York.

8:10— 8:20   Summary of session on Citizenship, Clark Foreman, Phelps Stokes Fund, assisted by Walter White, National Association for the Advancement of Colored People.

8:20— 8:30   Summary of session on Race Relations, N. C. Newbold, Director of Negro Education, State of North Carolina, assisted by Alain Locke, Howard University.

8:30— 9:15   General summary, with comment on the significance of the Conference for race relations in the United States, Mary van Kleeck, Russell Sage Foundation, New York, Chairman of Discussion in National Interracial Conference.

9:15—10:00   Brief messages from Albert C. Barnes, Barnes Foundation; Edwin R. Embree, Julius Rosenwald Fund; John M. Glenn, Russell Sage Foundation; Mordecai W. Johnson, Howard University; R. R. Moton, Tuskegee Institute; and Anson Phelps Stokes, Phelps Stokes Fund.

Music by the Men's Glee Club of Howard University.

INDEX

For books and for authors not listed in the text discussion
see alphabetical bibliography at the end of the book.

Abell, John B., 76, 84
Abbott, Grace, 176
Abolition, sentiment, 9; propaganda, 10
Absenteeism, in industry, 74-77
Adaptability, in industry, 77-78, 389
Africa, 4, 5; interracial movement in, 371
Africans, the, 6; superstitions of, 132; tuberculosis among, 156-157; hookworm among, 169
Age distribution, urban and rural, 118-119; in school populations, 272, 282-284
Agriculture, Chap. IX; training for, 85; decline of, 97, 388; per cent of Negroes in, 108; disorganization of, 125; scientific methods of, 130
Agriculture Board, 125
Alabama, 18, 248, 346, 348; company towns in, 92, 243; tuberculosis rate in, 158; lynchings in, 358
Alexander, Will W., 367
Allen, Gerald E., 50
American Association for Social Hygiene, 196
American Car and Foundry Company, 75
American Civil Liberties Union, 204
American Conference on Hospital Service, 191
American Federation of Labor, 48, Chap. VIII; Atlantic City Convention, 108
American Fund for Public Service, 105
American Management Association, 78
American Medical Association, 185, 288
American Missionary Association, 293
Amendments, Civil War, and Citizenship, 337; enforcement of, 341
Anderson, Mary, 63
Andrews, E. A., 138

Antagonism, causes of race, 355-356; growth of, 364 (see Race Conflict)
Anthropology, studies of racial immunity, 184
Apartments, 211, 215; model, 223
Apprenticeship, opportunities for, 85, 94, 397; in industrial schools, 295
Archive, The, 372
Arkansas Anti-Tuberculosis Association, 192
Arkwright, Sir Richard, 8
Arlitt, A. H., 273, 274
Army, tuberculosis rates, 157; syphilis in, 166; medical investigators, 180; intelligence tests, 274
Armstrong Association, 174
Arrests, rates of, 311, 445
Art, effect on race attitudes, 371-373
Artisans, 10, 11, 12, 356; in the North before the Civil War, 12; wages of, 56; during slavery, 82; number of white and colored, 83-84
Asbestos Workers Union, 116
Asbury Park, N. J., 268
Atlanta Anti-Tuberculosis Association, 192
Atlanta, Ga., 258, 311; homicides in, 326; riot, 359
Atlantic City, N. J., 96, 348
Attitudes, of employers, Chap. VI; of labor toward industrial training, 86; of Negroes toward jobs and employers, Chap. VII; relation to health, 142; toward Negro education, 224-227; toward segregation, 268; racial, Chap. XXV; studies of, 362-364; of Negroes, 363; influenced by Commission on Interracial Cooperation, 367-371; changing, 371-373; effect on migration, 388; between fellow-workers, 393; effect on crime rates, 447-448 (see Public Opinion)
Atwell, Ernest T., 308

523

Dat